Re-inhabited

Republic for the United States of America

Volume I – America's Truthful History

Jean Hallahan Hertler
with David Carl Hertler

ISBN: 978-0-9972766-0-2 (paperback), ISBN: 978-0-9972766-4-0 (Kindle)
Fourth Edition March 2019

Disclaimer

Please read this disclaimer carefully. Your reading of this book will constitute and be deemed an acceptance of the terms of this disclaimer. If you do not agree with any of the terms below, discontinue reading this book immediately. The information and content provided in this book are the opinions of Jean Hallahan Hertler and David Carl Hertler and is being provided for entertainment purposes only. The information provided herein may not be suitable for your situation. The authors and publisher assume no responsibility for errors, omissions or contrary interpretation of the subject matter herein. Although the authors and publisher have made every effort to ensure the information in this book was correct at press time, the authors and publisher do not assume and hereby disclaim any liability to any party for any loss, damage, or disruption caused by errors or omissions, whether such errors or omissions result from negligence, accident, or any other cause.

For more information visit www.re-inhabited.com
email the authors at: publicinfo@republicoftheunitedstates.org

Fair Use Notice

The material in this book is provided for educational and informational purposes. It may contain copyrighted material, the use of which has not always been specifically authorized by the copyright owner. It is being made available in an effort to advance the understanding of historical issues. It is believed that this constitutes a 'fair use' of any such copyrighted material as provided for in Section 107 of the US Copyright Law. In accordance with Title 17 U.S.C. Section 107. If you wish to use copyrighted material from this book for purposes of your own that go beyond 'fair use', you must obtain permission from the copyright owner. The information in this book does not constitute legal advice.

Re-inhabited: Republic for the United States of America is published in a series of two volumes with Volume II entitled, "The Story of the Re-inhabitation." More information as it develops will be announced at:

www.republicfortheunitedstates.com
www.reinhabited.com

ABOUT THE COVER

The idea was inspired while observing a dejected Mel Gibson on the battlefield in the movie "The Patriot," who had just lost his firstborn son and was so discouraged that he had nothing left to give, until Gibson then saw the flag that his son had been mending. Becoming fully inspired, the Patriot tied the flag to a pole, mounted his horse and caught up to his troop with the flag fully unfurled, causing great encouragement in all of the soldiers. The Patriot then went on to lead his company to victory. The idea for the cover picture expanded by bringing the scene forward in history and including not only Revolutionary War, but also Civil War soldiers, who are following the Patriot carrying the flag of the American Republic, called "Forever Glory." Behind him, in step to the music of the drummer and flutist, are American people from cross sections of life throughout history as they rush to join and follow the Patriot.

The artist, Brian Lee, envisioned a host of American people coming out of the vortex of destruction which represents the Corporate UNITED STATES and gathering forward to safety as they also fulfill the prophetic destiny of the American Republic. When artist, Brian Lee, heard that the book should be included in schools across America, he was inspired to include a little schoolboy in the lower center of the painting who is holding and reading this book that comes alive with visions of the characters and the theme of the painting that are displayed. Where are the American people going?

Genesis 49:10 ~ The sceptre shall not depart from Judah, nor a lawgiver from between his feet, <u>until Shiloh come</u>; and unto him shall <u>the gathering of the people be</u>.

2 Thessalonians 2:1 ~ Now we beseech you, brethren, by <u>the coming of our Lord Jesus Christ</u>, and <u>by our gathering together unto him</u>…

Dr. Benjamin Rush, a signer of the *Declaration of Independence*:

> "The only foundation for…a republic is to be laid in Religion [Christianity]. Without this
> there can be no virtue, and without virtue there can be no liberty, and liberty is the object
> and life of all republican governments."

The American people have been gifted with a heritage that has been reclaimed and provides the opportunity to embrace Life, Liberty, and the Pursuit of Happiness by joining with their American Republic. This legacy may be inherited by becoming a signatory on the *Declaration of Sovereign Intent & Proclamation of Claim and Interest of the Republic for the United States of America* at http://www.republicoftheunitedstates.org/10894-2/

The real man posing as the flag bearer on this cover is a devout Christian who loves his wife and family and loves his country. He is a member of the American Republic, a true patriot that resides in rural Kenosha, Wisconsin.

Original cover painting entitled: "The Gathering" Brian Lee, Michigan

DEDICATION

Above all, to the Father, Son, and Holy Spirit who inspired this oeuvre. Yᵉhovah, may Your Name be praised and remain here forever, along with Your eyes and Your heart. (2 Chronicles 7:16).

To our forefathers and foremothers, who embraced Christianity, the "religion of Liberty," and fulfilled their prophetic calling by birthing a nation in covenant with the *Creator of the universe*.

To the patriots and lovers of Liberty, both seen and unseen, who have given their lives, fortunes, and sacred honor for its cause.

To those of other nations who recognized the prophetic calling and destiny of the American people to be a blessing to all the families of the earth (Genesis 12:3), and who have sacrificed much in obedience to Almighty God in order for America to fulfill that mandate.

To our posterity: our children, our grandchildren, and their grandchildren.

And finally, to the remnant in the Body of Christ that believes they must do their duty to their country as part of their duty to God. Who believe that politics are a part of Christianity in such a country as the American Republic.

ACKNOWLEDGMENTS

The brave Pilgrims, Puritans, early Americans, those who loved the Lord with all their hearts, souls, and minds, guided by the hand of God in the *New World* while fulfilling their prophetic destiny as a unique people that would come to birth forth "one nation under God." A description of their inspiration in this work is beyond words.

Those who shed their blood for the cause of Liberty, known and unknown, both Americans and those of other nations. A description of the inspiration created by the gift of their lives would require a heavenly language to communicate sufficiently.

The honorable of the Military Armed Services, both active and "retired," which set the course that brought forth this story in two volumes, "His-story." We salute you.

Our teachers from both this current time and those of the past, who invested their inspired work as a legacy. It is the work of our teachers that "put the ink in the well" for the Holy Spirit to be able to draw from and compose a panoramic-like picture across the American Republic's timeline.

President James Buchanan Geiger, who has knowledge of the Truth as it relates to both the natural and spiritual realms and when reviewing the very first draft of this work, provided the insight and directive to interface a greater dimension of Truthful world history.

President James Timothy Turner, who months before this oeuvre began, communicated that the Lord told him that a book must be written. How little did we know that Almighty God would profoundly guide its manifestation or that I would be the "glove that held the pen for the Holy Spirit to write" this most unique storyline. Man of God, son of the Republic, faith-full, filled with wisdom, and beloved by many, it has been done with a pen.

Mrs. Karen Turner, First Lady of the re-inhabited American Republic, daughter of Almighty God, who paid a great price for her love of God and country as she recognized the anointing on her husband and released him into his calling of God. "Thank you" with all that is within us.

Acting Secretary of State Jeanine Stewart, who is keenly sharp in discernment, brilliant in studies and executive management, resourceful to no end, assigned this work with wise direction: "write everything you saw, take your time, and make sure it's well documented."

Senator Donald Mack Adams, our (hardworking) and favorite senator, who not only made this publishing possible, but with a standard of excellence. "Semper fi."

Representative David Schmit, an exceptional historian who has contributed a significant and Divine piece for placement in the profound puzzle.

Chaplain Wade Butler (Texas), an inspiring man of God, a true shepherd to the nation of American people, found faithful from the beginning, a builder of people and an encourager, filled with the wisdom of God, our Chaplain and friend.

Rob Krajenke of Michigan, the example of integrity, talented and gifted beyond the "norm."

Brian Horne, who created the extraordinary "gift wrapping on the package" that attracts and invites.

Encouragers and contributors while faithful in the cause of Liberty:

Governor Dean Henning (Wisconsin)
Governor Jim Carpenter (Colorado)
Speaker of the House John Rockwell (Oregon)
Bob Barnet (*Republic News Network*)
Kelby Smith (*His Advocates*)
Justice Roger Waters (Indiana)
Dan and Florence Petersen
David Stephenson
Dep. Sec. of State Robert Bellard (Wisconsin)
State Records Keeper Connie Schulz (Wisconsin)
State Treasurer Cindy Rohan (Wisconsin)
Fred and Virginia Flores
Danny and Apple Flores
Fran Widomski
Ellen Hallahan
Robert Kelly and Nicholas Kelly (*The American's Bulletin*)

CONTENTS

FOREWORD

I encourage the American people to begin to understand their history and heritage. Reading *Re-inhabited: Republic for the United States of America* is a good place to begin your journey. Unless we understand our history and what has been lost then we cannot begin to repair the breach. Jean Hertler has labored tirelessly to provide the American People with an accurate historical account of American History, one that has been hidden in plain sight. The documents have been available, but until now, nobody had put together such a clear easily understood overview. May we all come to a place of understanding our past so that we may act appropriately as we work together to repair the breach in the wall. Thank God for people like Jean and David Hertler who are laying down their lives for the benefit of us all.

James Buchanan Geiger
President
Republic for the United States of America

FOREWORD

The re-inhabitation of the "Republic for the United States of America" is much more than a movement. It is a struggle for the heart and soul of America against satanic forces who are desperate to keep *We the People* from realizing that those evil forces have been defeated. Those evil forces' inability to control this last U.S. presidential election is a tale-tell sign that their power has been broken and their days are numbered. Over many decades the elite have used banks and finance to slowly and methodically transfer the wealth of the American people into their personal coffers. The culprits of this elaborate scheme have been hidden from public view by the American news media and protected from exposure by the "UNITED STATES" Congress for many years. They completely control the U.S. Congress, Administration, agencies and judiciary by bribes, threat, duress, and coercion. It matters not who or how many new members of Congress are elected, the results are always the same, a lower standard of living and less protection for the inherent rights of the American people. Their ultimate goal is to socialize America and take complete control of the resources and workforce of the nation for their own benefit.

After years of research, study, numerous meetings, and discussions, a small group of informed Americans learned that America was in very serious trouble. We realized that unless we acted soon, we, our children, grandchildren, and countless generations of Americans would be little more than slaves in our own country subsisting only on the crumbs allowed us by greedy elite banksters. As a result of our studies and discussions, we realized that the "UNITED STATES" Corporate government Democracy was nothing more than thinly veiled Socialism in disguise. We also discovered that the "UNITED STATES" Congress had never passed any laws to de-commission, void, or annul the ORIGINAL Republic government; neither did they have the lawful authority to do so. *We the People* are the only source of authority that could replace the original Republic form of government with a Democracy. *We the People* were not properly or legally noticed of the change. In the years during and after the Civil War, circa 1860-1882, the Republic was abandoned and replaced by Congress in an unlawful coup d'état without the knowledge, consent, or approval by a vote of "We the People." We understood that the solution is to simply re-inhabit the original offices of the "Republic for the United States of America" by election of the American people. Once the American people have a free and informed choice, the vast majority will clearly choose freedom and prosperity over slavery and poverty.

In 2010 after a monumental effort by thousands of Americans in all 50 states, the Republic was re-inhabited. The first Republic Congress since 1860 was held in November of 2010. Those who experienced the first session of Congress and the meetings surrounding it were greatly moved by the event. It was easy to recognize the stamp of approval given by the Creator on this event. It was truly miraculous and life-changing for most who attended. What the Creator designs and executes by His servants will not fail. He will see to that. Getting started was a great struggle as there was no set of instructions on how to accomplish this great task. By the year 2012, according to reports from the Federal Bureau of Investigation (FBI), we had about 250,000 supporters nationwide. In the fall of 2014, the FBI reported that we had more that 22 million supporters. As I write this it is November, 2017 and I am certain we have reached critical mass. As evidence throughout history, any political change in a country that was supported by ten-percent or more of a population has always been successful, thus ten-percent of the population in support is considered to be critical mass.

Once the informed choice is given to the American people at large, the Republic will become the government of the nation. The will of "We the People" is the law in America. It only takes the People demonstrating their will for the Republic and it will be restored completely. This must be accomplished properly at the ballot box. It cannot be done in the streets by protest. It cannot be accomplished by hate and violence. The members of the Republic do not support hate or violence in any manner. We support and obey the laws of our Creator and heavenly Father, that is, to love Him and our fellowman as we love ourselves. We believe in and practice love and forgiveness even to those who have caused us harm. Love and forgiveness is the most powerful force in the universe. There is no law against the practice of love and forgiveness.

As we show love and forgiveness to those who harm us, we invoke the intervention of our Creator's help in our cause. Who can stand against Him and His servants. We pray for those who hold positions in the U.S. Corporate government that our heavenly Father would open their blinded eyes that they may see the truth. All of us have been misinformed by the U.S. media to a certain extent. Once the truth has been revealed to them, many will become supporters of the Republic and our allies. The Republic is not a religious government. We do follow the principles and practices established by our Creator and heavenly Father. These are the same principles America was established upon and which caused it to prosper until it became one of the greatest nations on the earth. If we return to those principles and practices then America and "We the People" will become great again.

Our time in restoring the Republic is limited. The "UNITED STATES" Corporate Democracy is collapsing even now due to failed fiscal policies. The alleged debt created by the U.S. Congress has reached in excess of $20 trillion and the U.S. Corporation is going to collapse. Meetings are taking place by United Nations about calling the U.S. debt and declaring the "UNITED STATES" Corporate government insolvent. They are planning to place the "UNITED STATES" under the rule of another government as a suzerainty, or subservient nation, because of the insolvency. IF the "Republic for the United States" is in place, we can stop this hostile takeover by the United Nations. The current U.S. Congress will not and cannot stop this.

The Republic has the resources available and the ability to resolve the debt problem. We can and will make America great again by removing the elite banksters' stranglehold on America and returning to an established value standard for our dollar.

The book you are about to read is one of the greatest true history books ever written. The true history needs to be told to the American people. The authors Jean and David Hertler are kindred souls that are dedicated to the Republic. I love them dearly and consider them more than friends; we are family. This book should be mandatory reading in high schools across America. It is well researched and documented by numerous sources. It is a labor of love by two very dedicated Americans who are concerned about the future of America. This book will inform you, but most of all, I hope it inspires you to come to the aid of your country and fellow Americans.

Jean and David realize that the Republic was inspired by the Creator as a gift to the American people. We now have a choice to regain our freedom, prosperity, and integrity. The Republic is more like a family of Americans who take care of each other. Our elected leaders are true servants of "We the People." They hold office for your benefit and the benefit of all Americans. We have built the structure, but we need the American people to step-up and take their rightful places as servant-leaders of our nation. Won't you come and be a part of this awesome family. The lives of you and your future generations depend on it. I am forever in your service.

I pray for the blessings of our heavenly Father on all who are working to restore the Creator's government in America.

James Timothy Turner
Founding Father and Former President
Republic for the United States of America

PREFACE

The god of this world, the prince of the air, blinded the first Adam's race to where even the second Adam's elect have fallen prey. There has been, and there is, a counterfeit king. This "angel of light" has used a "black pope" as a mediator throughout the long list of the papacy in Vatican to an unsuspecting people who thought they were worshipping and obeying the one true God, the *Creator of the universe.*

A counterfeit king, "monarch of monarchs," with two keys of the world's kingdom being spiritual and temporal, the papacy has his own disciples and evangelists to carry out his deeds of darkness through lies and deception. Lucifer has a secret militia that has been in place since shortly after the Light of the Gospel began to shine through a long period of Dark Ages, with Martin Luther's Protestant Reformation in 1517.

Lucifer has built and formed tyrannical governments throughout time. His lust for all-power has strategically pursued a "New World Order." The objective has included a Luciferian one-world global government as he and his sons have ardently sought to continue dominion through the next thousand years, during the Millennial Reign of Christ the King .

Satan has created a matrix of illusion, a Great Deception, by stripping God's absolutes and demoralizing the world. His objective and goals have been to usurp and destroy America, a people in nation who had covenanted with the *Creator of the universe.* The first Christian settlers in America, the Pilgrims and Puritans, arrived on this continent of the western hemisphere in the early 1600s, referring to this yet unknown wilderness as the "New World." *Re-inhabited: Republic for the United States of America* exposes how the kingdom of darkness has been secretly usurping the heritage of those in covenant with Almighty God.

We are now at the end of the Age and, as prophesied in the Word of God, the two kingdoms – the Kingdom of Light/Heaven and the Kingdom of Darkness/Hell, are in the final curtain call in the climax of the Great Drama. The goal of the Kingdom of Darkness, and its *New World Order* Democracy, is to exalt Satan's plan and agenda while at the same time destroying the American Republic and that which gives glory to Yᵉhovah God, the Creator.

Re-inhabited: Republic for the United States of America exposes the only hope for America as well as the world. We find the recipe for hope in looking back in time through America's history and to those who came to the *New World* in order to live the scriptures of the Holy Bible they had learned from the Protestant Reformation. The journey back in time tracing America's heritage reveals a Birthright that projects a unique identity in "No King but King Jesus." With this identity realizes a National Purpose which leads to a Prophetic Destiny which is yet to be fulfilled.

Where Christ came the first time for the Scepter, He will come the second time for the Birthright.

David and Jean Hertler

INTRODUCTION

Re-inhabited: Republic for the United States of America is an unprecedented truthful historical account of America that has been "hidden in plain sight" from the American people. This account is based on historical records and government documents as well as firsthand accounts of events that have been available but never before put together, like pieces of a puzzle, to be clearly seen for the first time ever.

History helps us make sense of the present as well as the future. At this critical juncture in time when America is in great peril and her history is being rewritten by tyrants who despise freedom and liberty, *Re-inhabited* provides answers with evidence of the truth regarding her profound heritage. The key to her restoration is Truth. It is the truth that, when broadcast, will lead to the restoration of America's sacred Liberty, that which made her the mightiest and most blessed nation on earth, looked upon as "a city upon a hill," and a Light to the nations.

Providing this stunning and truthful knowledge to the American people will prompt an earnest seeking of the other Party of the covenantal *Declaration of Independence,* Who in response will then pull back the veil that has contributed to her "spiritual amnesia."

The story is presented in two parts. Part one is entitled, "A Promised Land for a People Covenanted with God and the Great Deception." From America's beginning she was solidified by a foundation of great faith and profound determination to live, without persecution, based on the scriptures learned from the Protestant Reformation. Likewise, there was desire to obey the Great Command of Jesus Christ in the furtherance of the Gospel of His Kingdom throughout the world.

We come to understand that these very unique people experienced a sense of calling by Divine Providence to the "New World" and not only fully relied on Almighty God to cross the expanse of the great Atlantic Ocean in deplorable conditions, but appealed to Him as they explored the wilderness of that *New World.* Not really knowing what to expect, they identified themselves with God's chosen people of the Old Testament, the children of Israel. America's forefathers made the first covenant with Almighty God and with each other that would set the course and destiny for their descendants in this "land flowing with milk and honey."

Ten years later, the Puritans followed in the path of the Pilgrims to the *New World* so that they, too, could have religious freedom to worship the God of the Holy Bible and escape the persecution of the civil authorities of Great Britain who also ruled the Church of England. The Puritans made what we now know as America's second covenant with Almighty God while at the same time declaring the "Divine Rights of Jesus Christ," rejecting the rule of a human monarch. Again, confirmation of destiny was set for America.

There is a very large and critical piece of world history that has not been taught in our schools for many generations that has everything to do with this current world's system as well as the oligarchy who rules it. Just as there was a Protestant Reformation in 1517, there was also a Counter-Reformation that not many are aware of.

The truthful account of history engages a look at the councils held in utmost secrecy between the "kings of the earth," and those with "titles of nobility" who formed a "Holy Alliance" to destroy the Protestant Reformation and any popular government based on it. Their ultimate target of destruction was set as the United States of America and her very unique republican form of governance. A small percentage of the world's populations are aware of who is behind this (un)holy alliance as well as the web and depth of the conspiracy that progressively ushers toward the "New World Order" in this modern day.

Because history books have failed to include America's spiritual heritage, the life and substance of what made her magnificent is lost to her posterity, her offspring. Her descendants have "spiritual amnesia" and have lost not only their heritage, but their identity and national purpose.

The *First Great Awakening* and outpouring of God's Holy Spirit on the colonists one hundred years later would find the thirteen colonies uniting as "one nation under God." The guiding hand of Divine Providence is unmistakable while viewing the timeline of truthful history, "His-story." It was in that era that young George Washington, who was taught by his mother to read from the Holy Bible, formed a deep personal relationship with the Savior of the world. Like his mother, he became a prayer-warrior that groomed him to become the leading Army General in the theatre of the American Revolution, and later to become the American Republic's first President.

Re-inhabited reveals in the truthful pages of history that there was a third covenant made with the "Creator of the universe," and "Supreme Judge of the world," and with firm reliance upon Him; the *Declaration of Independence* was boldly written to proclaim the self-evident truths of the Laws of Nature and Nature's God. In that most profound document was none other than a holy boldness to proclaim Liberty and independence from the mother country. These early Americans signed the document well aware that the cost would be great.

It could only have been with great faith, the substance of things hoped for and the evidence of what is not seen, to have rejected the rule of the world's most powerful monarch, King George III, known to be not only completely blind, increasingly deaf, and substantially evil and cruel, he also had charge over the world's most powerful Navy. Against all natural odds, these "common people" of the eastern seaboard of the North American continent overcame as they "appealed to heaven." The byways of America would resound with "No King but King Jesus!"

While current day revisionists claim that the Founding Fathers who signed the nation's founding document, the *Declaration of Independence,* as well as having framed the operating document, the *Constitution of the United States of America,* were not Christian, at the same time place labels on these men with words that have a different meaning than they did in the founding era. These individuals have rewritten history to arrogantly project that the Founders were Freemasons, while failing to mention that the Luciferian religion was not yet established in the lodges of America.

Re-inhabited presents the Founding Father's intent from the writings of their own words, and by historical government documents demonstrates the depth of character and the virtue that were instilled in these men. Their characters come alive with the Spirit of America, shining forth their legacy for all to see this current day. The blood that was spilled on the Land for the cause of Liberty can still be heard crying out, "Let it not have been spilled in vain."

Part two of *Re-inhabited* exposes the details of the Great Deception that was perpetrated when the American Republic was shoved aside into dormancy and a Corporate Democracy replaced the government as color-of-law by subduing our *Constitution*. From the Founding Father's own words, along with an explanation of precise Biblical scriptures, is revealed America's original sin that not only brought the scourge of a blood bath in civil war but a foothold to the enemy to visit her sins to this now fourth generation. On August 22, 1787, during the debates of the Constitutional Convention, "Father of the Bill of Rights," George Mason (1725-1792) stated:

"Every master of slaves is born a petty tyrant. They bring the judgment of heaven on a Country. As nations cannot be rewarded or punished in the next world they must be in this. By an inevitable chain of causes and effects providence punishes national sins, by national calamities…"

Indeed, there was a door opening to the "Great Deception" that led to her enslavement. "A perfect slave thinks he is free."

The American Republic has amazingly displayed significant parallels to Old Testament Israel. Having experienced a sort of sibling rivalry that divided her children into two sections, North and South, so was it repeated in the "New Israel," as the early Americans thought of themselves.

Exposed from documented evidence is the 1826 scandal that triggered the *Second Great Awakening*. The leader of this *Awakening* admonished the Church in America that they must take right ground with regard to politics or experience a national curse instead of continued blessing. Imagination becomes the storyboard in light of current events of this modern day.

America's story reveals some astounding finds in government documents as regards the secret agenda of the Divine Right enemies of our popular government. With knowledge of who they are comes an understanding of why the Founding Fathers made provision in the American Republic's *Constitution* that those with a "title of nobility" may not hold a government office.

Also revealed is what happened to the <u>original</u> *Thirteenth Amendment* which had been approved by Congress and then ratified by each of the 17 States (at that time) before it disappeared. There are many items of contemplation like how come it was forgotten and why records of this Amendment have since been found in the archives of the British Museum Library in London.

The reader will surmise to satisfaction why so many of the American Republic's presidents have been assassinated and who was behind these assassinations. Revealed from actual government documents is how the American Republic was shoved aside into dormancy and a Corporate Democracy was crafted without the consent of the American people to replace and "act" as the government of the nation.

Presidential Proclamations and Executive Orders are explained bringing to light the understanding how the nation has progressively spiraled into an entity that looks nothing like the original American Republic. It becomes apparent that the god of the Corporate Democracy is not the God of the American Republic which contributes in understanding the moral and spiritual disintegration of America as well as the bigger picture of two kingdoms clashing at this point of climax of the Greatest Drama in all of time. This is not a dry and boring account of history, but one that once entered into, is hard to set down.

Covered is a review of the national curses incurred because of covenant breaking as experienced throughout the past century and progressively manifesting in the current day. Reviewed are social ills, the effect on children, teen pregnancies, illegal drug use, education reform taken over by Big Government and dumb-downed children, an overgrown for-profit Prison Industry filled with yesterday's children, the Church of Satan demanding equal standing in public schools, statuary and monuments, to name just a very few items. Again, the storyboard of imagination is compelled to awakening; denial and bread and circuses will no longer have domain.

Evidence is presented on why and how Federal Government agencies are partnering with so-called nonprofit organizations and together place threatening labels on the American people. The reader will find themselves past the edge of their chair in realizing that they are now named an enemy of the state, a "domestic terrorist" because they are Christian, or support the *Constitution*, or question the Federal Government, or have served in the armed forces. The government they have trusted views them as a greater threat than violent, beheading ISIS.

Finally, there are some amazing stories that include signs in the heavens that bring hope, profound and credible prophetic messages, and a look at a little known monument memorializing America's forefathers who left a message to their descendants of this era in pointing the way back should they have lost their way. The closing of Part Two includes a message from a Revolutionary preacher that inspires hope while it also puts forth a choice and a warning in making the wrong choice.

Where today's Bible scholars claim that America is not found in the Bible, early Americans identified her in the scriptures while the seals of the scrolls opened for their revelation. Having learned to read from scriptures, the Holy Bible being their main textbook throughout life, we cannot dismiss what they saw and believed.

In the midst of great peril America faces today, there is an answer. The answer lies in awakening the American people to her identity, which will lead to the uncovering of the real national treasure, the key to her prophetic destiny. That destiny will impact the whole world.

This author began researching and writing this work in March, 2014 when asked to write a press release pertaining to the support of the Family Research Council's (FRC) letter to the Director of the Federal Bureau of Investigation and Attorney General of the United States in exhortation to remove the Southern Poverty Law Center (SPLC) as a resource from the FBI Hate Crimes website.

Court testimony of the gunman who had entered the FRC's building on August 15, 2012 with intent to mass kill staff members for the reason that the organization opposes same-sex marriages had revealed his selecting as a target the FRC organization because it was listed on the Southern Poverty Law Center's "hate map." Many organizations have been tagged by the SPLC with a "hate group" label because they are ardent defenders of marriage and sexuality as defined in the Hebrew and Christian Bible.

While investigating the matter in order to write the press release, this author stumbled across and discovered an overwhelming conspiracy of the Federal Government and several of its agencies working as cohorts against the re-inhabited American Republic since the very time the American people in all fifty states had given notice to their State governors to return to the original constitutional law form in early 2010.

Assigned an official task to write precisely what had been observed, overwhelmed and feeling "stuck" in not knowing where to begin, wise counsel was offered the author to "think of it as a legal brief for the Courts of Heaven." Immediately there was witness of remarkable inspiration and enabled writing flow that began in establishing the background history as the story of the American Republic. As history was researched, profound information documented with evidence began to appear and fit like pieces of a puzzle into a panoramic-like picture across the American Republic's timeline.

The co-author is a student of the writings of the Founding Fathers and American history. Amazingly, as the ongoing work was discussed, the co-author would "happen" to be studying a historical individual or subject that fit precisely where the author was working at the time. The result of this inspired work is unprecedented in presentation and undeniable with documented evidence.

Re-inhabited: Republic for the United States of America has published in a series of two volumes with Volume II entitled, "The Story of the Re-inhabitation." For more information on the book series or how to be involved visit:

www.republicfortheunitedstates.com
www.reinhabited.com

Re-inhabited

Republic for the United States of America

Part One

A Promised Land for a People Covenanted with God

and the Great Deception

Chapter One

Protestant Reformation vs. Counter-Reformation

America is a special land with a divine purpose for a covenanted people with the living Creator God, the God of Abraham, Isaac, and Jacob. We are one nation under God. The Christian majority is the largest group in America, as polled at 75 to 77 percent in 2012.[1] [2]

The first colonial settlement from England was the Virginia Colony in 1607. While it was largely Christian, its primary purpose was mainly as business ventures for economic prosperity. This was made evident in its first year when gold was discovered nearby. The Colonists nearly starved that first year, because they neglected their crops in search of gold.[3]

Other colonists, known as the Pilgrims, immigrated in 1620 to have freedom of conscience so they could worship God according to the Biblical principles that they had learned through the Scriptures given to them by the Protestant Reformation.

It is necessary to understand history in this matter in order to understand the flow of history to where we are today. The *Protestant Reformation* is considered the greatest religious movement for Christ since the early church.[4] It was a revival of Biblical and New Testament theology.

Philip Schaff, (1819-1893), a Swiss-born, German-educated Protestant theologian and a Church historian who spent most of his adult life living and teaching in America is known for his many writings, one being the 8-volume, "History of the Christian Church," in which he stated:

Philip Schaff, 1880 [5]

"The Reformation of the sixteenth century is, next to the introduction of Christianity, the greatest event in history. It marks the end of the Middle Ages and the beginning of modern times. Starting from religion, it gave, directly or indirectly, a mighty impulse to every forward movement, and made Protestantism the chief propelling force in the history of modern civilization."[6]

The Reformation officially began in 1517 when Martin Luther, a German monk, Catholic priest, and scholar, penned a document attacking the Catholic Church's corrupt practice of selling "indulgences" to absolve sin. Committed to the idea that salvation could be reached only through faith and by divine grace, Luther strongly objected to the fraudulent custom of selling indulgences. Acting on this belief, he wrote the *"Disputation on the Power and Efficacy of Indulgences,"* also known as the *"95 Theses,"*[7] which advocated two central beliefs:

1) that the Bible is the central religious authority, and

2) that individuals may reach salvation only by their faith and not by their deeds.

Although these ideas had been brought forward before, Martin Luther codified them at a moment in history ripe for religious reformation. The *95 Theses*, which became the foundation that sparked the *Protestant Reformation*, were written in a remarkably humble and academic tone, questioning rather than accusing. The overall thrust of the document was nevertheless considered provocative. The first two of the *Theses* contained Luther's central idea, that God intended believers to seek repentance and that faith alone, and not deeds, would lead to salvation. The other *93 Theses*, a number of them directly criticizing the practice of indulgences, supported these first two.[8]

The Church's reaction resulted in his excommunication by the Pope and condemnation as an outlaw by the Emperor.[9] The Catholic Church was ever after divided, and the Protestantism that soon emerged was shaped by Luther's ideas. His writings changed the course of religious and cultural history in the West.

Luther taught that salvation and subsequently eternity in heaven is not earned by good deeds but is received only as a free gift of God's grace through faith in Jesus Christ as Redeemer from sin and that to reject the free gift of God's grace would subsequently result in eternity in Hell. His theology challenged the authority of the Pope of the Roman Catholic Church by teaching that the Bible is the only source of divinely revealed knowledge from God and opposed sacerdotalism (that a priest is able to mediate between God and man), by considering all baptized Christians to be a holy priesthood.

Those who identified with Luther's teaching, were called "Lutherans" even though Luther insisted that "Christian" was the only acceptable name for individuals who professed Christ.[10]

Martin Luther ultimately put the Bible into the hands of the German people in their own language, which made it more accessible, and had a tremendous impact on the church and German culture. The people could read God's Word for themselves, no longer needing the priests "to interpret."[11] It influenced William Tyndale, the father of the *English Authorized Version*, to do the same, and was enabled by that great invention — the world-changing printing press. Luther's hymns influenced the development of singing in churches. His marriage to Katharina von Bora set a model for the practice of clerical marriage, allowing Protestant priests to marry.[12]

While Luther had no idea of the impact making accessible the Holy Bible, the Word of God, would project on the German society – or to the world – this event changed the course of history. People would now come to know the God of the Bible, the Creator of the universe as well as His Son, Jesus the Christ, who is the Word of God[13] and the great Liberator.

Martin Luther
Painted in 1529 by Lucas Cranach the Elder [14]

With religious liberty came also political liberty called "liberalism." The common man began to enjoy the rights of private property and the freedom to make a profit to the detriment of Rome's monopolies. The free-enterprise system was born, the direct result being the creating of the Protestant middle class and private wealth. The middle class peoples, enjoying freedom of the press, freedom of speech, and freedom of conscience, excelled in all the arts and sciences creating invention after invention. The English and the Dutch became worldwide shippers while the Swiss became the great watchmakers. The Protestants of the *New World* were known as "the inventive Americans."

The benefits of the *Protestant Reformation* were many, and it was clearly understood that any wise and good man would seek to preserve that Reformation along with its accompanying freedoms and liberties. For it was the Reformation and the Protestant victory ending the Jesuits' *Thirty Years' War* in Europe as religious beliefs affected ideas of the legitimacy of the political status of rulers (having ranged from 1618 to 1648 during which one in three Germans perished miserably) that brought the world out of Rome's Dark Ages and into the Protestant Modern Era.[15]

"*. . . where the Spirit of the Lord is, there is liberty.*"[16]

At this point, we go back a bit further in time to interject an important foundation in history. Before the Protestant Reformation of 1517, the Catholic Church was the only Church. For 1,260 years Catholicism reigned as the only Christianity in Europe.

Catholicism believes that the Pope is the "father of kings, Vicar of Christ, and governor of the world"—both spiritual and temporal. These two keys of the world's kingdom are representative of *Spiritual Powers* (Church authority) and *Temporal Powers* (civil authority).[17]

Papal regalia and insignia (from *Wikimedia Commons*)[18]
From Wikipedia: "Papal regalia and insignia are the official items of attire and decoration proper to the Pope in his capacity as the head of the Roman Catholic Church and sovereign of the Vatican City State. …The crossed keys symbolise the keys of Simon Peter [apostle of Jesus Christ]. The keys are gold and silver to represent the power of loosing and binding [inferring Matthew 16:19]. The triple crown (the tiara) symbolizes the triple power of the Pope as "father of kings," "governor of the world" and "Vicar of Christ." The gold cross on a monde (globe) surmounting the tiara symbolizes the sovereignty of Jesus."[19]

In 1207 King John of England refused Pope Innocent III's appointed Archbishop as he had his own man selected for the position. Viewed as an impious act and lacking reverence for God, the Pope decreed an interdict which was a punishment by which the faithful remaining in communion with the church are forbidden certain sacraments and prohibited from participation in certain sacred acts. The interdict was a means to compel the monarch to obey his papal decisions.

When King John still wouldn't submit to the Pope's appointment for Archbishop then, King John was excommunicated from the Church by the Pope for his stubbornness. This excommunication was essentially viewed as being barred from God's grace and forgiveness which by 1213 caused King John to surrender under the pressure and resulted in his writing a royal concession that would come to have a profound effect on the world. So profound was his royal action that it would affect world politics to this very day.[20]

King John's concession was a charter which by certain terms led to England becoming a "fiefdom" of Rome. In other words, the crown of England along with its right to the kingdom became surrendered to the Roman Catholic Church. The tenure of Land and its people became subject to feudal obligation (political, military, and social), held "in fee." We will come to understand the depth of the tenets of the lust for money and control as we go forward on the timeline in history.

If the terms of the charter were not met, England and all its colonies and possessions—consider the expanse of the British Empire—would become surrendered and subject to the Pope forever.

Of course, as one can imagine a "feudal obligation," money and payments were involved. The penalty for breaking the 1213 charter agreement was the loss of the Crown Rights to the kingdom of England by default to the Pope and his Roman Church.

On June 15, 1215 when King John couldn't keep up with the required payments to Rome, he then broke the concession and terms of the charter by signing the *Magna Carta* (Latin for "the Great Charter") also called *Magna Carta Libertatum* (Latin for "the Great Charter of the Liberties").[21] [22]

The *Magna Carta* was written by the feudal barons of England and required King John to proclaim certain liberties and accept that his will as king was not arbitrary or that he had unlimited power. It was the first document imposed onto an English king by his subjects in an attempt to limit his powers by law and protect his subjects' privileges. In other words, the king was bound by law—the law of the land. It was a revolutionary document and one of history's most important. It would lead to the rule of constitutional law in the English-speaking world and later inspire America's Founding Fathers in framing the *Constitution of the United States.*[23]

King John of England Signs the *Magna Carta* [24]

On August 24, 1215, the Pope then made a declaration which formally and lawfully took possession of the Crown from royal monarchs of England and which also annulled the *Magna Carta.* Later that year the Pope placed an interdict on the entire British Empire. From that time forward through today the monarchy of England, as well as the entire British Crown, have been under the legal ruling power of the Pope. The papacy has never surrendered this authority.[25]

In modern times the complexity of the structure of the Roman Catholic Church is referred to as "the Vatican," "Vatican City," and "The Holy See." The Holy See is a monarchical-sacerdotal state, which in simpler terms means that it operates as a monarchy in which the Pope is the "king."

Elected from candidates worldwide by 120 members of the College of Cardinals, the Pope remains in office for life, and has supreme executive, legislative, and judicial power over both the State of the Vatican City and the universal Roman Catholic Church. The Pope appoints the senior members of the church hierarchy, as the governing body (of priests; sacerdotal).

The Holy See is recognized under international law and enters into certain international agreements as an absolute monarchy ruling according to the *Apostolic Constitution of 1967.*[26]

We now proceed forward on the timeline of history to 1534 when England broke ties with the Roman Catholic Church due mainly to King Henry VIII's political and marital issues.

King Henry VIII then started the independent Church of England, also known as the Anglican or Episcopal Church. Most of the countries surrounding England did not agree with the King's decision; nor did many of the people in England. Some wanted the Anglican Church to be more like the old Catholic church. The *Protestant Reformers* wanted it to be even simpler and to rely more on Bible teachings than on traditions and ceremony.[27]

The *Protestant Reformers* saw this as an opportunity to bring true reform to the church in England. In time, these reformers came to be called "Puritans," mainly because they wanted to "purify" the Church of England of Catholic traditions that they did not believe to be Biblical.[28] After many years of struggling for change to true Biblical worship, some of the Puritans believed that little progress had been made toward true reform.

One of their beliefs was that they should be allowed to select their own church leaders and ministers. As different kings and queens, "monarchs," took over ruling England throughout this era, they had different ideas about religious practices.[29] We will expand on this topic before continuing with the history of the Puritans.

We must understand history, the hard truth, supported by authoritative and documented evidence, which includes the strategic setting-up, as well as the taking down, of the Monarchs throughout the ages — as well as world events that may truly not be as they appear, or are told. The "by whom" and "for what purpose" is revealed to truth-seekers who have sought a solid foundation in knowledge of the prophetic Word of God, the Holy Bible. They are not taken by surprise as, "Surely the Lord GOD will do nothing, but he reveals his secret unto his servants the prophets,"(Amos 3:7).

He who knows the end from the beginning and from ancient time things which have not been done, saying His plan will be established and He will accomplish His will (Isaiah 46:10). "But there is a God in heaven that reveals secrets, and makes known …what shall be in the latter days (Dan. 2:28)." The Word of God guides His people unto all truth (John 16:13), and as His people seek, they will find (Matt. 7:7). The Word of God is the *Greatest Story Ever Told* and the Living Word (Heb. 4:12) is unfolding before our eyes as we watch the scenes that are recorded on the pages of the Holy Bible manifest in world events.

St. Ignatius of Loyola (1491-1556) [30]
Founder of the "Society of Jesus," also known as "the Jesuits"

The Prince of Darkness (Eph. 6:12), the Devil, would not allow the *Protestant Reformation* to continue without resistance. Satan, the great deceiver (Rev. 12:9) and father of lies (John 8:44)s has a people (John 8: 38-44) just as the *God of heaven* has a people. Therefore, the Devil raised up Ignatius Loyola who founded the "Society of Jesus," commonly called "the Jesuit Order." It was officially recognized as a Roman Catholic religious order by Pope Paul III in 1540.[31] The Jesuits are the "militia of the Pope,"[32] [33] and their purpose was to destroy the Reformation, along with its popular liberties:

† freedom of speech   † freedom of conscience   † freedom of the press
† freedom to keep and bear arms, etc.

…and return the world to the Dark Ages (during which it was illegal to own a crossbow), reestablishing the "Holy Roman Empire."

It initiated the "Counter-Reformation,"[34] beginning at the *Council of Trent*[35] where written and adopted was the <u>antithesis</u> to Luther's Protestant Reformation. The plan, which incorporates the participation of ancient aristocratic family lines of the "Black Nobility" (called "Black" because of their ruthless lack of scruple)[36] [37] is for the Pope to receive universal worship, ruling from Solomon's rebuilt

Temple in Jerusalem.[38]   This means that when their plan is permitted to succeed there will be a future "infallible" Pope[39] who will be "that man of sin" (II Thess. 2:3-12); "antichrist"(I John 2:8); "the beast" (Rev. 13:4-18); "king of fierce countenance"(Dan. 8:23); also called by the Lord Jesus Christ, "the abomination of desolation"(Matt. 24:15 in referring to Dan. 9:27, 12:11); ruling the world from Jerusalem.[40]

Martin Luther in 1520, as quoted in Edward Beecher's, *The Papal Conspiracy Exposed,* (1855):

"If you do not contend with your whole heart against the impious government of the pope, you cannot be saved. Whoever takes delight in the religion and worship of Popery will be eternally lost in the world to come . . . So long as I live I will denounce to my brethren the sore and the plague of Babylon, for fear that many who are with us should fall back like the rest into the bottomless pit."[41]

Pope Clement XIV (1705-1774) as quoted in (27th U.S. Secretary of the Navy) R.W. Thompson's, *The Footprints of the Jesuits,* (1894):[42]

"It was very difficult, not to say impossible, that the Church could recover a firm or durable peace so long as the said society existed."[43] *

(*Noteworthy is an interesting current-day news report entitled, "Pope Francis resisted revenge over 18th century Clement XIV"—available for viewing by endnote reference link.[44])

Pope Clement XIV, portrait 1773 [45]

Because they had become too politically powerful throughout Europe while also gaining economic control of countries, by a Papal Brief, *Dominus ac Redemptor* (July 21, 1773), Pope Clement XIV suppressed the *Society of Jesus*. The Jesuits took refuge in non-Catholic nations, particularly in Prussia (Germany) and Russia, where the Order was either ignored or formally rejected.[46]   King George of England secretly preserved the political and financial power of the Jesuit Order during the years of its suppression until the *Jesuit Company* was formally restored by Pope Pius VII in 1814.[47]   That particular timing is of great significance to our truthful American history—and that of the world.
Historian, Giuseppe Nicolini of Rome (1788-1855) as quoted in Dr. C. A. Yarbrough's 1920 book, *The Roman Catholic Church Challenged in the Discussion of Thirty-Two Questions with the Catholic Laymen's Association of Georgia*:[48]

"The Jesuits, by their very calling, by the very essence of their institution, are bound to seek, by every means, right or wrong, the destruction of Protestantism. This is the condition of their existence, the duty they must fulfill, or cease to be Jesuits."[49]

The Devil and his Jesuit General known as the "Black Pope,"[50] control the *Society of Jesus*, the Papacy and its Vatican Hierarchy, the Sovereign Military Order of Malta, Islamic Shriner Freemasonry, Opus Dei, the Knights of Columbus, Rothschild's Illuminati, the Papal Caesar's International Intelligence Community and the Mafia.[51]

6

Members of these organizations are presented, or "knighted"[52] with "titles of nobility,"[53] with greater titles earned by achievements in rank and deed. These are foreign titles that violate the *Constitution of the United States*, specifically, Article I, Section 9, Clause 8:

"No title of nobility shall be granted by the United States: and no person holding any office of profit or trust under them, shall, without the consent of the Congress, accept of any present, emolument, office, or title, of any kind whatever, from any king, prince, or foreign state."

It is unconscionable that those who hold or have held government offices that have received these *titles of nobility* of the various secret societies have never been censured by the American people.

President John F. Kennedy, 1961 [54]

One of our nation's greatest of heroes, President John F. Kennedy, who was also Catholic, was well aware of the active existence of the Black Nobility and the organized Jesuit-controlled secret societies and openly warned of the dangers and threat they posed to our liberties in his address before the American Newspapers Publishers Association on April 27, 1961 at the Waldorf-Astoria Hotel, New York City (excerpt):

"...The very word "secrecy" is repugnant in a free and open society; and we are as a people inherently and historically opposed to secret societies, to secret oaths and to secret proceedings. We decided long ago that the dangers of excessive and unwarranted concealment of pertinent facts far outweighed the dangers which are cited to justify it. Even today, there is little value in opposing the threat of a closed society by imitating its arbitrary restrictions. Even today, there is little value in insuring the survival of our nation if our traditions do not survive with it. And there is very grave danger that an announced need for increased security will be seized upon by those anxious to expand its meaning to the very limits of official censorship and concealment. ..."[55]

May we honor the memory and service of President Kennedy who gave his life for the American people by exposing the dark forces and implementing measures to restore our country to a republican form of governance in line with our original *Constitution of the United States.* May we not project blame or hate on the Catholic lay people, but instead hold accountable those in the hierarchy of the Roman Catholic Church that are factually a monarchical-sacerdotal[56] **foreign government operating in disguise as a religion.** Along with their Jesuit militia, they have betrayed even their own members, one being President Kennedy. Likewise, we will not remain silent in our truthful American history that includes shocking and even hurtful issues for fear of offending any citizen.

Those, particularly of the Baby Boomer[57] generation, may have some knowledge or at least recall a general sense of societal offense by Catholicism and may not have completely understood why or where it came from. Much has been quieted and hidden through the generations. If a brave soul would speak out they would be scorned as a "conspiracy theorist" with an objective to intimidate them to silence.

There, too, have been some who would speak out and mistakenly misplace blame onto the whole Catholic people that included innocents that truly love the Creator and their fellow man. We will begin to understand the motive behind the gentlemen's etiquette in not going too far in discussing religion or politics.

Where previous generations were not apt to speak openly on matters, it is the opposite in our current society. Let us open our hearts and minds as we carefully consider this quote by Christian apologist and author Dave Hunt (1926-2013):[58]

"We are told to love one another as Christ has loved us. Pop psychology trivializes that command by equating it with a 'positive' attitude. Forgotten is the first duty of love: to speak the truth (Ephesians 4:15). Real love does not flatter or soothe when correction is needed but [rather] points out the error which is blinding and harming the loved one. Christ said, 'As many as I love, I rebuke and chasten; be zealous therefore, and repent' (Revelation 3:19). Instead, the idea is now current that love excludes rebuke, ignores the truth, and seeks unity at any price. Only disaster can result."[59]

It is not our intention to bring a message of paranoia or fear. We seek only to "speak the truth in love" and report our truthful history as a nation which includes segments of history that have been withheld by design throughout the generations.

An investigative researcher and author who lived throughout much of the 19th century and published in the early 20th century, Burke McCarty, had said "You cannot defeat an enemy which you do not understand."[60] Likewise, as a nation, we cannot correct the direction we are headed if we are not willing to be honest in examining the course we and our ancestors have taken – or have been led – to get where we are today.

Unfortunately, there are people who take things to the extreme. "Conspiracy theory" is a label being thrown around at anything that sounds like it might elicit fear or may be perceived as uncomfortable to a point of possibly interrupting the sensed safety in the routine in life. Granted, there are outlandish conspiracy theories in the world today, however, when presented with **evidence documented in fact**, we are confronted with truth that requires putting aside denial and establishes the responsive call to action. It is truth that sets one free.[61]

For those who have already seen and believed this conspiracy that is not theory but have not known a remedy or had hope that there could be one, we bring a message that includes God's timing and intervention. The Creator of heaven and earth remains Faithful and True.[62] America, indeed, was birthed through covenant with the *Creator of the universe*, and whose birth certificate is the *Declaration of Independence* that also declares the Almighty Creator as "the Supreme Judge of the world." The heavenly Father now calls to His people and assures that He has heard their cries; judgment has been executed in the Courts of Heaven with an executable Plan that was written long ago. That very covenant with His people is engrossed in script on parchment[63] "as apples in gold and framed in pictures of silver."[64] [65]

At the founding of America, it is well documented that there were innumerable concerns regarding Jesuit infiltration. As recorded in history, there were many that believed that a conspiracy was raging against the freedoms of the United States.

There is authoritative and documented evidence that establishes in fact that their concerns were not unfounded. The Jesuits, with supreme loyalty only to the Pope and who exist for the sole purpose of countering all that the Reformation accomplished, are indeed deeply involved in end-time affairs. Through their ongoing deceptive efforts, Rome has steadily been working to destroy Protestantism.

The Roman papacy has showed its aggressive nature throughout history which includes recent and bold statements.[66] [67] Anyone who opposes the Pope's authority is counted as a heretic and considered as worthy of extermination. It has been the story throughout history and Rome has not changed. Clearly, the reality in evidence is stacked that Rome is aggressive in expanding its dominion with an objective in giving rise to the Antichrist power. This correlates to fulfillment of Biblical prophecy.

Likewise, Almighty God has a remnant as well as a prophetic destiny for America in this unfolding Drama. A nation that was birthed by covenant with the "Creator of the universe," in obedience she has been exceedingly prosperous, manifesting tremendous fruit, "the head and not the tail,"[68] a super power in the world as she blessed others in her abundance and shared the Light of the glorious Gospel.

It is time to reveal the story behind the effect of the curses of sin and covenant-breaking that has made America spiral to the tail and be no longer the head. As the pages of the Word of God, the Holy Bible, tell story after story of how Almighty God would correct His people using other nations as His rod,[69] our nation's story includes an extensive tale of a dark and deceptive people who have always been lurking around and waiting for America to break covenant with God.

We must be thankful that there are appointed times as projected in Biblical prophecy and that America is now at the juncture in time that our Founding Fathers and Mothers knew would manifest.[70] The storyline includes the danger of secret societies along with the work of the Roman Catholic Jesuit Order. To not bring this story to light and reveal the truth is to omit the truth of our history and avoid knowing our future. What these organizations do is wrong, especially because they cloak their activities with good works, thereby deceiving the innocent.

We have been warned throughout time to stay away from all unions and confederacies, and yet still we fraternize with them, and neglect to see the greatest secret society of all working behind the scenes through deception to set up the final end-time conglomerate of Babylon.[71] Shall we leave people ignorant to the fraudulences working to bind their souls to Satan? Will we not receive an awakening nudge with the call to arise as it is time?[72]

We present a sobering message of truth and urgency for all people. This message is intended to address our identity as a nation, our national calling, purpose, and destiny as the *Republic for the United States of America.* It does include and point to the Great Deception at the end of time for this current Age.

"Knighthood" is not a spiritual acquisition, nor has it been bestowed as such. It is a foreign title given in recognition of one's service to the Pope of Rome who claims temporal sovereignty and allegiance from his subjects in every country. One of the goals of the Knights over the various secret societies is to restore the Temporal Power of the Pope.[73] As the Devil performs his sorcery and manipulates his deception in darkness, so too do his agents operate in secret, or "secret societies." [74] [75]

The Emperor Napoleon in His Study, 1812 [76]

Napoleon Bonaparte (1769-1821), emperor of the French:

"The Jesuits are a **military organization,** not a religious order. Their chief is a general of an army, not the mere father abbot of a monastery. And the aim of this organization is: POWER. Power in its most despotic exercise. Absolute power, universal power, power to control the world by the volition of a single man [i.e., the Superior General of the Jesuits]. Jesuitism is the most absolute of despotisms; and at the same time the greatest and most enormous of abuses."[77] [emphasis added]

Historian, Giulio Cesare Cordara (1704-1785), a Jesuit, as quoted in E. Boyd Barrett's, *The Jesuit Enigma*, (1927):

"...nearly all the Kings and Sovereigns of Europe had only Jesuits as directors of their consciences, so that the whole of Europe appeared to be governed by Jesuits only."[78]

Quote from *The Jesuit Catechism* (1685), by various Jesuit contributors in warning England's King Charles II:

"By reason, the Pope is the head, and Kings are but as arms or hands of the same Body; therefore if they do not their duty being careful to preserve the Body, the Head as Lord and Master may cut them off."[79]

Many writers warned of this Great Conspiracy of the Jesuits. Samuel Morse, the father of Morse Code (1835):

Samuel Morse, 1840 [80]

"They are Jesuits. This society of men, after exerting their tyranny for upwards of two hundred years, at length became so formidable to the world, threatening the entire subversion of all social order, that even the Pope, whose devoted subjects they are, and must be, by the vow of their society, was compelled to dissolve them [Pope Clement had temporarily suppressed the Jesuit Order in 1773 for nearly fifty years].

They had not been suppressed, however, for fifty years, before the waning influence of Popery and Despotism required their useful labors, to resist the light of Democratic liberty, and the Pope [Pius VII] simultaneously with the formation of the Holy Alliance [1815], revived the order of the Jesuits in all their power... they are a secret society, a sort of Masonic order, with super added features of revolting odiousness, and a thousand times more dangerous.

They are not merely priests, or of one religious creed; they are merchants, and lawyers, and editors, and men of any profession, having no outward badge by which to be recognized; they are about in all your society. They can assume any character, that of angels of light, or ministers of darkness, to accomplish their one great end...

They are all educated men, prepared and sworn to start at any moment, and in any direction, and for any service, commanded by the general of their order, bound to no family, community, or country, by the ordinary ties which bind men; and sold for life to the cause of the Roman Pontiff."[81]

James Parton, 1870 [82]

James Parton (1822-1891), English-born, American biographer:[83]

"...if you trace up Masonry, through all its Orders, till you come to the grand, tip-top, Head Mason of the world, you will discover that that dread individual and the Chief of the Society of Jesus are one and the same Person!"[84]

In light of this revelation we can understand the flow of history for the past five centuries. The interaction of the Protestant Christians and the *Reformation* <u>versus</u> the Jesuits and their *Counter-Reformation* enables us to understand events that have occurred as well as the correlating vast system of deception, slavery and murder. This system, religious and political Romanism,[85] is falsely called

"Christianity,"[86] and when revealed to the Apostle John as recorded in the book of Revelation, caused him to wonder "…with great admiration."[87]

We must distinguish between the Jesuit Order, the Roman Catholic hierarchy, and the Roman Catholic people themselves. Most Roman Catholic people have no idea of the power of the hierarchy in the Jesuit Order. They have never been taught the "Doctrine of Temporal Power,"[88] [89] by which the Pope rules, or seeks to rule, ALL civil and political authority of the world. **Temporal Power** is a separate and second power from that of the **Spiritual Power**. *Most Catholic people are not aware of the spiritual wickedness that controls the men ruling the Devil's world system,*[90] as is the case for most Protestant people.

Daniel: 12:9b, 10b ~

> *"…for the words are closed up, and sealed, till the end of the time. …but the wicked shall do wickedly, and none of the wicked shall have understanding: but the wise shall understand."*

Edward Beecher[91] (1803-1895), American Protestant historian, *The Papal Conspiracy Exposed* (1855):

> "Viewing this <u>corporation</u> [the Pope's theocratic Vatican Empire] as a government, the aspect of things is no less impressive. The head of the corporation is both a spiritual and a temporal ruler. He claims to be monarch of all monarchs. His senate of cardinals and electors are princes. His bishops also are lords each in his diocese, but are still his vassals, bound to him by a feudal oath. To him also are bound the rulers of the Jesuits and of the various orders of monks and nuns, who are an all-pervading soldiery, sworn to do his will. To the bishops also are subjected the secular priests, and to them are subjected the people. Thus the whole system is one compact and all-pervading government, the rule of which is absolute obedience to the central power and its agents in regular subordination. It is an immense army under military discipline.
>
> …The pope, the cardinals, the patriarchs, the metropolitans, the bishops, the priests, the deacons are all organized in a vast system, extending itself over the globe, and aiming at universal conquest. In it are the various orders of monks, nuns, Jesuits, bound to it by oaths and sworn to extend its sway.

…He [the Pope] is the acting god of this world. His word is law: the Bible is nothing. The system is in theory and practice an annihilation of God and the Bible, and an enthronement of the pope or the Papal corporation in place of God. …to reign as the only god on earth…"[92] [emphasis added]

Edward Beecher [93]

E. G. White, 1864 [94]
Courtesy of the Ellen G. White Estate, Inc.
Author E. G. White (1827-1915) wrote more than 5,000 periodical articles and 40 books in her lifetime and is considered the most translated American author in the entire history of literature. Her writings cover a broad range of subjects, including her life-changing masterpiece on successful Christian living, "Steps to Christ," has been published in more than 140 languages.[95] Ms. White is quoted in her book, *The Great Controversy* (originally published in 1858):

"Throughout Christendom, Protestantism was menaced by formidable foes. The first triumphs of the Reformation past, Rome summoned new forces, hoping to accomplish its destruction. At this time the order of the Jesuits was created, the most cruel, unscrupulous, and powerful of all the champions of popery. Cut off from earthly ties and human interests, dead to the claims of natural affection, reason and conscience wholly silenced, they knew no rule, no tie, but that of their order, and no duty but to extend its power. The gospel of Christ had enabled its adherents to meet danger and endure suffering, undismayed by cold, hunger, toil, and poverty, to uphold the banner of truth in face of the rack, the dungeon, and the stake. To combat these forces, Jesuitism inspired its followers with a fanaticism that enabled them to endure like dangers, and to oppose to the power of truth all the weapons of deception. There was no crime too great for them to commit, no deception too base for them to practice, no disguise too difficult for them to assume. Vowed to perpetual poverty and humility, it was their studied aim to secure wealth and power, to be devoted to the overthrow of Protestantism, and the re-establishment of the papal supremacy.

When appearing as members of their order, they wore a garb of sanctity, visiting prisons and hospitals, ministering to the sick and the poor, professing to have renounced the world, and bearing the sacred name of Jesus, who went about doing good. But under this blameless exterior the most criminal and deadly purposes were often concealed. It was a fundamental principle of the order that the end justifies the means. By this code, lying, theft, perjury, assassination, were not only pardonable but commendable, when they served the interests of the church. Under various disguises the Jesuits worked their way into offices of state, climbing up to be the counselors of kings, and shaping the policy of nations. They became servants to act as spies upon their masters. They established colleges for the sons of princes and nobles, and schools for the common people; and the children of Protestant parents were drawn into an observance of popish rites. All the outward pomp and display of the Romish worship was brought to bear to confuse the mind and dazzle and captivate the imagination, and thus the liberty for which the fathers had toiled and bled was betrayed by the sons. The Jesuits rapidly spread themselves over Europe, and wherever they went, there followed a revival of popery."[96]

Count Paul von Hoensbroech (1852-1923), German Nobleman and ex-Jesuit, *Fourteen Years a Jesuit*, (1911):

"The Jesuit Order, therefore, stands before us as the embodiment of a system which aims at temporal political dominion through temporal political means, embellished by religion, which assigns to the head of the Catholic religion – the Roman Pope – the role of a temporal overlord, and under shelter of the Pope-King, and using him as an instrument, desires itself the domination over the whole world."[97]

Count Paul von Hoensbroech, around 1900 [98]

As we have come to the end of this Age, and before the return of the Lord Jesus, "Yeshua" in the Hebrew language, the people will need the power of God to overcome.[99] That power is a Person of the Godhead known as the Holy Spirit. He was sent of the Lord Jesus to come and live within those that are born again by faith in Him.[100] Those that blaspheme the Holy Spirit and reject the Lord Jesus will not have forgiveness and are in danger of eternal damnation.[101]

As the mother of a very wise man had told him, "It is possible to be so heavenly minded that we are of no earthly good."[102] May all true patriotic Americans, no matter your spiritual beliefs, open your hearts while examining this story which is based in truth and verified as fact documented in evidence. This is your story.

Chapter Two
A New Covenant for the New World

The National Calling, National Purpose and Prophetic Destiny

In returning to history as it relates to the Puritans, this group of believers decided it was necessary to separate from the Church of England to enable them to live according to the Biblical principles that they had learned through the Scriptures given to them by the *Protestant Reformation*. This began the distinction between the *Puritans* and the *Separatists*. Though the groups shared Biblical beliefs and values, the Puritans chose to remain part of the Church of England, while the Separatists wanted to become completely separate from the official Church of England.[103]

When King James came along, the Separatists thought they might finally be able to gain permission to set-up their own church, but the King denied the request. Because the Church and State were intimately joined, the *Separatists* were considered treasonous, and therefore lived in danger of persecution and imprisonment.

In 1609, the Separatists found it necessary to relocate so they sailed to Holland where freedom of religion was accepted. These Separatists came to be known as "Pilgrims." For more than a decade, they enjoyed religious freedom in Holland and gathered openly for church under the leadership of Pastor John Robinson.

Life in Holland had been difficult as the only work available to immigrants was poorly paid, despite their hard labor, and so poverty was a constant struggle. The hard work had negative effects on both parents and children. They became deeply concerned for the well-being of their children. Furthermore, some of the children were adapting into Dutch culture and abandoning their parents' Biblical values. Another of their leaders, William Bradford, explained:

William Bradford (1590-1657), a conjectural image of Bradford, produced as a postcard in 1904 by A.S. Burbank of Plymouth [104]

"…of all the sorrows most heavy to be borne [in Holland], was that many of the children, influenced by these conditions, and the great licentiousness [immorality] of the young people of the country, and the many temptations of the city, were led by evil example into dangerous courses, getting the reins off their necks and leaving their parents. Some became soldiers, others embarked upon voyages by sea and others upon worse courses tending to dissoluteness and the danger of their souls, to the great grief of the parents and the dishonour of God. So they saw their posterity would be in danger to degenerate and become corrupt."[105] [emphasis added]

The Pilgrims had also desired to bring the Gospel to people who had not yet heard the message of Jesus Christ:

"They cherished a great hope and inward zeal of laying good foundations, or at least of making some way towards it, for the propagation and advance of the gospel of the kingdom of Christ in the remote parts of the world, even though they should be but stepping stones to others in the performance of so great a work."[106]

For the sake of raising their children with a Biblical foundation as well as to participate in the Lord's command of the "Great Commission"[107] in spreading the Gospel, the Pilgrims made the historic decision to immigrate again – this time to the "New World," America.

William Bradford requested permission of the Virginia Company, a royal charter granted by King James I as a colonial business pursuit, to establish a new colony in Virginia, which was agreed upon. The trip was difficult to organize and it was necessary to include about fifty other English people in order to pay for the ship and supplies. The original Pilgrims called themselves "saints" and the others "strangers."

After many setbacks, the *Mayflower* finally left for America on September 6, 1620. The trip across the ocean was rough and uncomfortable.[108] **But they sensed that what they were doing was important and believed they were led of God in the transition.**

On November 11, 1620, the Pilgrims got their first look at the *New World*, a land first inhabited by Indian natives, when they saw Cape Cod. The Pilgrim group had permission to settle in the northern part of Virginia (which today would encompass present day New York). When the *Mayflower* turned south, however, it ran into rough, shallow waters and became in danger of tipping over and sinking. The decision was made to head back to the deeper, safer waters off the tip of Cape Cod. Since Cape Cod was outside the area they were granted to settle in, the group agreed to write a "compact" or "self-governing" agreement.

The <u>*Mayflower Compact*, signed on November 11, 1620, was the first governing document of these people as a new **covenant** for the *New World*</u>.[109] It called for the election of a governor from among the members of their group, something they were already familiar with from their church practices. This was the first act of European **self-government** in the *New World*. <u>At the heart of the *Mayflower Compact* lay an undisputed conviction that God must be at the center of all law and order and that law without a moral base is really no law at all</u>.[110]

Less than half of their 102 members survived the first few months in the *New World* due to poor nutrition and insufficient housing through a New England winter. With the help of the Wampanoag native Indians as their teachers in farming and their friends who aided in survival, Governor William Bradford called for the first Thanksgiving in early autumn 1621 as a three-day feast to celebrate a successful corn harvest.[111] Governor Bradford had chronicled:

> "And thus they found the Lord to be with them in all their ways, and to bless their outgoings and incomings, for which let His holy name have the praise forever, to all posterity."[112]

The general sickness had ceased. Their food was hot, their faith intact. It was hard for him to fathom what more they could possibly want. It was, to him, "all things in abundance and plenty."[113]

Tisquantum ("Squanto") teaching the Plymouth colonists to plant corn with fish Illustration from 1911. [114]

The native "First Americans" Indians of this new land came to them as friends and teachers. One in particular, *Squanto*, was viewed by the Pilgrims as, "a special instrument sent of God for their good beyond their expectation."[115] They formed a successful treaty with Massasoit, chief of the Wampanoag natives in equality, fairness, and tolerance that would be idealized and reflectively remembered of the overall colonial experience.[116]

The pilgrims signing the compact, on board the May Flower, Nov. 11th, 1620 [117]
painted by T.H. Matteson (1813-1884) / engraved by Gauthier 1859

Back in the motherland of England in the 1620s, the economy suffered, many people lost their jobs, and King Charles I made the situation worse by raising taxes which created a political crisis. The Church of England began to punish the Puritans because they were dissenters of official opinions. Where the Puritans had remained in the Church of England and sought to reform it, life was becoming increasingly hard for them.

Because the king of England was head of both Church and State, the Puritans' opposition to religious authority meant they also defied the civil authority of the State.[118]

As Christian believers the Puritans held conviction on the "Crown Rights" of Jesus Christ. They willingly resolved to give total allegiance to their Savior in spite of the disfavor of the English. The theology of the Puritan Fathers on the declaration of the *Crown Rights of Jesus Christ* is clearly seen as follows:

> "Basic in Puritan political thought is the doctrine of divine sovereignty. It was the sovereign God who created the state and gave to it its powers and functions. The earthly magistrate held his position and exercised his power by a divine decree. He was a minister of God under common grace for the execution of the laws of God among the people at large, for the main tenancy of law and order, and for so ruling the state that it would provide an atmosphere favorable for the preaching of the Gospel. He was to so rule that the people of God, the elect, could live individually and collectively a life that was truly Christian."[119]

Following the Biblical admonition of obedience to the Sovereign God instead of an earthly king made the Covenanters rebels to the State. These economic, political, and religious problems in England led to the *Great Migration*. In 1629, King Charles granted a group of Puritans and merchants a charter to settle in New England. Between 1629 and 1640 approximately forty thousand men, women, and children left England and settled in English colonies in New England.

15

The Puritans founded the *Massachusetts Bay Colony* in a town they named Boston. John Winthrop served as its governor, with a few exceptions, for the rest of his life.

Seeking comfort and reassurance in the Bible, they imagined themselves reenacting the story of the Exodus. Like the ancient Israelites, they were liberated by God from oppression and bound to Him by a covenant; like the Israelites, they were chosen by God to fulfill a special role in human history: to establish a new, pure Christian commonwealth.

Onboard the flagship *Arbella*, their leader, John Winthrop, reminded them of their duties and obligations under the covenant. If they honored their obligations to God, they would be blessed; if they failed, they would be punished.[120]

In honor of the birthday of Governor John Winthrop, born June 12, 1587/8:
Gov. John Winthrop, flanked by statues of a Native American (left) and a pilgrim (right). [121]

John Winthrop (1588-1649) aboard the flagship *Arabella*:

"**We are entered into covenant with [God] for this work.** We have taken out a commission. The Lord has given us leave to draw our own articles; we have promised to base our actions on these ends, and we have asked Him for favor and blessing. Now if the Lord shall please to hear us, and bring us in peace to the place we desire, then He has ratified this covenant and sealed our commission, and will expect strict performance of the articles contained in it. But if we neglect to observe these articles, which are the ends we have propounded, and – dissembling with our God – shall embrace this present world and prosecute our carnal intentions, seeking great things for ourselves and our posterity, the Lord will surely break out in wrath against us and be revenged of such a perjured people, and He will make us know the price of the breach of such a covenant."[122]

The Puritans believed they were led to the *New World*, "for the glory of God and the advancement of the Christian faith"[123] [124] where they could freely worship the God of the Bible and would become a beacon of religious light, a model of spiritual promise, a "city upon a hill."[125] Jubilant because they would be removed from the suspicious eyes of Church and Crown, the *Bay Company* could become a <u>self-governing</u> commonwealth where they would be <u>governed by the laws of God</u>, not merely the laws of men.[126]

Puritans give thanks and reverence to Almighty God [127]

Religions with a civil sword can force people to join their church organization, but they cannot force them to join the true Church, whose names are written in the Lamb's book of Life. They can physically force men to have a relationship with the Church, but they cannot force men to have a personal relationship with Jesus Christ. The tragedy comes when Christians assume that the religious organization is the Church and that one must become members of the organization to have a relationship with Jesus Christ.[128]

America's Godly heritage was laid in its foundation. Along with its heritage is a national calling and a prophetic destiny.

By faith, the Pilgrims and Puritans endured and overcame hardships. They also celebrated victories as recorded in preserved volumes of history. They believed the Word of God, the Holy Bible and understood that, just as the Israelites, their survival and their success depended on their covenanted relationship and obedience to the God of their fathers.[129] Blessings came with obedience and, likewise, curses with disobedience.[130] Free to worship as they chose, the Bible was central to their worship.

A summary of the Biblical covenanted blessings of obedience[131] sanctioned for a nation in keeping and obeying God's Law, include:

- Becoming the greatest nation on earth.
- Being blessed with an abundance of food, clothing, and comfortable homes.
- Being blessed with good health and strong children.
- Being blessed with great military strength so that no nation would dare attack them, and in case of war they would be blessed with victory.
- Being blessed with abundant rains and flourishing crops.
- Being blessed with so much wealth that other nations would come to borrow, but they would never have need to borrow from others.

A more narrowed summary of the blessings for obedient performance are: national independence, individual life, liberty, and the pursuit of happiness.

17

A summary of the Biblical covenanted curses of disobedience[132] sanctioned for a nation in not keeping and obeying God's Law, include:

- Becoming a wandering, scattered, homeless, poverty-stricken people.
- Being cursed, despised, and abused wherever they went.
- Suffering terrible diseases, plagues, pestilences, famine, thirst, and, in time of siege, they would eat their own dead.
- Being weak, vulnerable, and continually conquered by their enemies. Their land would be confiscated, their crops devoured, their wives ravished, and their daughters carried away into slavery.
- Among the nations of the world, they would never be the head but always the tail.
- In the end, there would be pitifully few of them left compared to the vast multitude they might have been.

A more narrowed summary of the curses for disobedience in non-performance are: tyranny, oppression, and even death.

The colonies, formed and governed under charters granted by the king of England, continued to grow in number and expand in territory. **Christianity was the American religion** and the general way of life for most in many various sects (denominations) among the Colonies.

In the mid-1700s, between the end of the Puritan era and the first stirrings of independence, Jonathan Edwards, the third president of Princeton University and a Puritan preacher was used mightily of God in a revival known as the "First Great Awakening."[133] This *Great Awakening* was actually a reawakening of a deep national desire for the Covenant Way of life. This longing did not die with the passing of the Puritan era, but only went dormant.

Jonathan Edwards (1703-1758) [134]
Reverend Edwards believed that America was the "isle" prophetically referenced in the Old Testament, Isaiah 60:9, that would be the land in the latter days where God would <u>re-gather the descendants of the ancient Israelites</u> and the plan and "disposition of Providence" for these people to play a significant part in "communicating the blessings of the kingdom of God" to the Jewish people as well as the rest of the world. He also preached about a parallel of ancient Israel and the American people. Edwards stated,

"…a deliverance out of the hand of the king of Assyria, is often used by the prophet Isaiah, as a type of the glorious deliverance of the church from her enemies **in the latter-days**."[135]

Many sermons were preached at that period of time about **America's national purpose and destiny. Most of them projected the belief that this new nation was the fifth Kingdom, the "stone" Kingdom, prophesied by the Old Testament prophet Daniel. America was destined to complete the work that the Reformation had begun and smash the feet of the Babylonian image and bring "liberty and justice for all" to the whole world.**[136]

This was the original "American Dream," our national purpose. It was not secular, but neither did it establish a "religion." It established God and His Word as King and put all men and religions under His authority.[137] Europe was hopelessly rooted in monarchies and feudalism, but America had shed those tyrannical ideas. This spiritual stir would burst forth an unquenchable desire that would produce a new generation of clergymen who would help to prepare America to fight for her life in the coming war for independence.[138] When God pours out His Spirit in a major way, He seldom concentrates on just one area. The fires of revival were also fanned to flame throughout England by a young preacher, George Whitefield. As the pulpits of Bristol, England were closed to him by pastors who strongly disapproved of his nontraditional confrontation of church establishment, Whitefield began to preach in the open.

Burdened for those in less fortunate and perhaps loathsome lifestyles, he would draw crowds by the thousands in open-air preaching, resolved to bring them the Gospel of Jesus Christ. Tens of thousands are reported to have experienced new life in their conversions all throughout England. Whitefield believed that he was called of God to General James Oglethorpe's new colony in America, Georgia. He was anxious to join his Christian friends in America, because "he dared to trust that his preaching might help create one nation under God – thirteen scattered colonies united with each other…"[139]

James Edward Oglethorpe (1696-1785), Governor of the Georgia colony [140]

Under Whitefield's anointed preaching, Americans throughout the colonies were beginning to discover a basic truth which would be a significant foundation stone of God's new nation, and which by 1776 would be declared as self-evident, that in the eyes of their Creator, all men were created of equal value. By the sovereign act of Almighty God, and through the obedience of a few dedicated men, the Body of Christ was indeed forming in America.

George Whitefield preaching on the Word and the Spirit, 1749 [141]

Through this almost universal and simultaneous experience of the *Great Awakening* by an outpouring of God's Holy Spirit, Americans began to become aware of themselves as a nation, a body of believers which had a **national identity** as a people chosen by God for a specific purpose. They were to be not only "a city upon a hill," but a genuine citadel of Light in a darkened world.

As the Pilgrims and Puritans had seen and experienced it, but had now all passed-on and gone home to Glory, it seemed as though the vision of the covenant relationship had died with them. Now, through the shared experience of coming together in large groups to hear the Gospel of Jesus Christ, Americans were rediscovering God's plan to join them together by His Spirit in the common cause of advancing His Kingdom.[142]

In further, they were returning to another aspect of His plan. They were to function in a covenanted nation, not as isolated, individual colonies.[143] The land had been awakened again; now the land was a giant and a growing one at that. It is a matter of God's timing in all things, and always according to His unfolding prophetic Word.[144] [145] The Lord, through the preaching of this covenanted man, George Whitefield, was uniting the thirteen colonies in such a profound and deep way that few people even realized at first what was happening. Wherever Whitefield traveled, he was preaching the same Gospel and the same Holy Spirit was quickening his message in peoples' hearts regardless of their denomination. All were accepting the same Christ in the same way. He was the first man to cut across denominational barriers.

At the same time, geographical barriers became no more significant than denominational ones. They were beginning to discover a basic truth which would be a chief foundation stone of God's new nation, and which by 1776 this phenomenal movement of faith swept the American Colonies, helping to unite them prior to the Revolutionary War.[146] This revival, which lasted about 25 years, left a permanent impact on American Protestant church members resulting from powerful preaching that gave listeners a sense of deep personal revelation of their need of salvation by faith in Jesus Christ. This monumental social event brought with it a move away from ritual and traditionalism in religion and made it more intensely personal by stressing a relationship with the living Lord. For the average church member this "awakening" fostered a deep sense of spiritual conviction and redemption, and by encouraging self-examination along with a commitment to a new standard of personal morality.[147]

It appears as the design of Heaven in orchestrating the people of God to be drawn into covenant renewal with Him on this rich Promised Land flowing with milk and honey and which would soon produce the fruit of expansion across the continent as He shed His grace "from sea to shining sea."[148] Ahead would unfold His Plan to create His government on the earth for a people in nation belonging to Him. He requires His people to participate in His plans. Although the *Author of the Universe* will work through whomever or whatever He chooses in His Divine Plan, there is a special part for those fully surrendered and filled with His Spirit. His devoted sons and daughters are compelled by His Spirit enabling them to move Heaven on earth or, "on earth as it is in heaven,"[149] in participating in the unfolding of His prophetic Word and the Dominion Mandate to be a blessing to all the families of the earth.[150]

The parallel between ancient Israel and the United States was so striking that virtually every preacher and theologian in early America recognized it and made mention of it in some way in their

sermons. They called this nation the "American Israel," the "New Israel," "God's Vineyard," and even "The Kingdom of God."[151]
Rev. Abiel Abbot [152]

Reverend Abiel Abbot[153] (1770-1828) in his *Thanksgiving Sermon*, 1799: "It has been often remarked that the people of the United States come nearer to a parallel with Ancient Israel, than any other nation upon the globe. Hence 'Our American Israel' is a term frequently used; and common consent allows it apt and proper."[154]

20

Chapter Three
An Appeal to Heaven
The First Fragrance of Liberty

Going forward a couple of decades, the British colonies experienced adversities because of Jesuit-controlled King George of England, the monarch with ruling oversight, who was viewed as a tyrant.

King George III in 1765 [155]

An apostate Protestant Anglican King who ruled Great Britain from 1760 to 1820, King George III was completely blind with cataracts, increasingly deaf, and mad with mental illness.[156]   History tells that he was the most evil of English kings whose Prime Minister was the Jesuit Lord Shelburne and whose Parliament established Roman Catholicism as the State religion of Quebec, Canada. King George secretly preserved the political and financial power of the Jesuit Order during the years of its suppression until the *Jesuit Company* was formally restored by Pope Pius VII in 1814.[157]

When the tribulations experienced by the colonists became intolerable and the pleas to the king for relief were left unanswered, it came to a point of despotism where action was needed. These early Americans sent delegates as their representatives from their colonies to a *Continental Congress* to discuss, and at times heatedly debate, their recourse.

Rev. Jacob Duche (1737-1798) [158]

By request of the Continental Congress, Jacob Duche', an Anglican clergyman, opened the first session of Congress at Carpenter's Hall in Philadelphia, with prayer.[159] Reverend Duche' became the first chaplain of the Continental Congress.

The outcome was the birthing, by divine inspiration, the *Declaration of Independence.*[160] This founding document includes an invocation of a divine witness, namely, "the Supreme Judge of the world," and "Divine Providence." The document also invokes God as both a witness and a guarantor.

The *Declaration* follows the classical covenant template by stating who is doing the covenanting, namely, "the Representatives of the United States of America, in General Congress assembled," July 4, 1776.

There is a prologue and historical section detailing the prior relationships of England and the American colonies. These items establish the setting for the *Declaration* and reasons for its creation. [161]

Next, there is a set of stipulations and obligations containing the basic agreements of the American people. These begin as a statement of self-evident truths. There are indirect statements of blessings and curses. The blessings for performance are national independence and individual life, liberty, and pursuit of happiness.   The curses for non-performance are tyranny, oppression, and even death.

There is a provision for its public proclamation to mankind, and copies were to be sent to Parliament and distributed throughout the newly independent States.

These Founders of the American Republic had at an early age learned to read from the Word of God, the Holy Bible. Most were educated in universities and trained as ministers of the Gospel while they also studied law. The Bible was a general requirement and basis of their education. They studied the Old Testament in Latin and sometimes in the original Hebrew language; and the New Testament in Greek.[162] They were scholars in the Word of God. They were equally familiar with secular world history and studied the writings of historians, philosophers and political thinkers such as Baron Charles de Montesquieu,[163] Sir William Blackstone,[164] John Locke,[165] Edward Coke,[166] Marcus Tullius Cicero.[167]

de Montesqieu [168] William Blackstone [169] John Locke [170] Sir Edward Coke [171] Marcus Tullius Cicero [172]
1689-1755 (France) 1723-1780 (England) 1632-1704 (England) 1552-1634 (England) 106 BC – 43 BC (Rome)

It was from studying and analyzing the writings of these great men, along with the Bible, that the Founders' beliefs and convictions had formed.[173] They concluded in agreement with some of those scholars of old that the most reliable textbook[174] for the study of the "divine science of politics" [175] is the Bible. Today, any word that sounds like "politics" tends a reaction of nose-wrinkling similar to that of post-skunk emission. In John Adams' day it was a term of enlightenment referred to in the "politics of liberty" of which made good government.[176] The language of liberty was the language of an enlightened America.[177]

Some of the Founding Fathers were fulltime church ministers while at the same time working in government as delegates, or representatives, of their Colonies. As a people continuing to covenant with God since the Pilgrims first set foot at Plymouth Rock[178] some 150 years earlier, the Founders held the conviction that the welfare of "the American Israel" depended on their maintaining virtue, religion (Christianity), and observance of the holy covenant which they entered into with God just as the Old Testament Israelites.

They also understood that their heritage of the Lord in the blessings of liberty would be extended to all the other nations of the world as they, too, would be attracted to the hope and blessings of liberty. The Founders' vision and quest reached beyond America in their desire of becoming a budding example of a righteous people fulfilling God's Word in being "above all the nations that are upon the earth."[179]

John Quincy Adams (1767-1848), son of Founding Father John Adams and 6th President of the United States:

> "[T]he Declaration of Independence first organized the social compact on the foundation of the Redeemer's mission upon earth … [and] laid the cornerstone of human government upon the first precepts of Christianity." [180]

They knew the price for liberty would be great, but the price to not take a stand for what was given by God would be greater.   As the men of Marlborough, Massachusetts had said at the time of the *Boston Tea Party* not long before,

"Death is more eligible than slavery. A free-born people are not required by the religion of Jesus Christ to submit to tyranny, but may make use of such power as God has given them to recover and support their laws and liberties...[We] implore the Ruler above the skies, that He would make bare His arm in defense of His Church and people, and let Israel go." [181]

The Provincial Congress of Massachusetts 1774 resolved,

"Resistance to tyranny becomes the Christian and social duty of each individual...Continue steadfast, and with a proper sense of your dependence on God, nobly defend those rights which heaven gave, and no man ought to take from us." [182]

Most Crown-appointed governors remained submitted to their king, and one wrote to the Board of Trade in England:

"If you ask an American, who is his master? he will tell you he has none, nor any governor but Jesus Christ." [183]

This may have given rise to the cry which was soon passed up and down the length of America by the *Committees of Correspondence:*

"No king but King Jesus!" [184]

On July 8, 1776 Continental Congress for the first time read the *Declaration of Independence* publicly, as the famous "Liberty Bell" was rung. Congress then established a three-man committee, consisting of Thomas Jefferson, John Adams and Benjamin Franklin, for the purpose of designing a great seal for the United States.[185]

Benjamin Franklin's suggestions for a seal and motto, characterizing the spirit of this new nation, were:

"Moses standing on the Shore, and extending his Hand over the Sea, thereby causing the same to overwhelm Pharaoh who is sitting in an open Chariot, a Crown on his Head and a Sword in his Hand. Rays from a Pillar of Fire in the Clouds reaching to Moses, to express that he acts by Command of the Deity. Motto, Rebellion to Tyrants is Obedience to God."[186]

Benjamin Franklin, 1785 [187]   Benjamin Franklin's Great Seal Design in 1776 [188]

Thomas Jefferson proposed:

"The children of Israel in the wilderness, led by a cloud by day, and a pillar of fire by night."[189]

For the reverse side of the seal, Mr. Jefferson proposed, "Hengist and Horsa, the two brothers who were the legendary leaders of the first Anglo-Saxon settlers in Britain."[190] Thomas Jefferson and John Adams both believed that they (and the British colonists) were descendants of the Anglo-Saxons, who were descendants of the Lost Tribes of Israel.[191] [192] [193]

Samuel Adams, 1772 [194]

As the *Declaration of Independence* was being signed, Samuel Adams declared:

"We have this day restored the Sovereign to Whom all men ought to be obedient. He reigns in heaven and from the rising to the setting of the sun, let His kingdom come." [195]

The eighteenth century was an Age of Reason and in America it was equally an Age of Faith. The marriage of reason and faith (science and religion) gave birth to a conviction that led to an Age of Revolution characterized in the defense of rational self-evident truths by faithful patriots who waved battle flags bearing the motto, "Rebellion to Tyrants is Obedience to God."[196]

Continental Congress' proclamation of independence resulted in war with Great Britain. Known as the *American Revolution* or the *American War for Independence*, the "Patriots," as they called themselves, knew that they had divine favor with Providence to achieve victory after engaging in war with Jesuit-controlled Great Britain, the world's largest empire with the most powerful military force in the world.

Patrick Henry [197]

As Patrick Henry had stated in his famous speech given before the Virginia House of Burgesses:

"…we shall not fight our battle alone. There is a just God who presides over the destinies of nations…" [198]

The position of the Church is evidenced in the sermons of the Patriot Preachers of the day who asserted that they did not hesitate to attack the great political and social evils of their day. For example,

"…the Fathers of the Republic, enforced by their example. They invoked God in their civil assemblies, called upon their chosen teachers of religion for counsel from the Bible, and recognized its precepts as the law of their public conduct. **The Fathers did not divorce politics and religion, but they denounced the separation as ungodly.** They prepared for the struggle, and went into battle, not as soldiers of fortune, but, like Cromwell and the soldiers of the Commonwealth, with the Word of God in their hearts, and trusting in him. This was the secret of that moral energy which sustained the Republic in its material weakness against superior numbers, and discipline, and all the power of England." [199] [emphasis added]

… England sent her armies to compel submission, and the colonists **appealed to Heaven.**"[200] [emphasis added]

The *Declaration of Independence* was eventually enshrined and elevated to a hallowed position. During the 19th century, the *Declaration of Independence* was given annual public readings on the ***Fourth of July*** in many communities, events which had echoes of covenant renewal ceremonies which often are a feature of covenantal communities. John Adams, signer of the *Declaration* is stated in a most significant visionary and prophetic way:

"The Second Day of July 1776, will be the most memorable Epocha, in the History of America. I am apt to believe that it will be celebrated, by succeeding Generations, as the great anniversary Festival. It ought to be commemorated, as the Day of Deliverance by solemn Acts of Devotion to God Almighty. It ought to be solemnized with Pomp and Parade, with Shews, Games, Sports, Guns, Bells, Bonfires and Illuminations from one End of this Continent to the other from this Time forward forever more. **You will think me transported with Enthusiasm but I am not. I am well aware of the Toil and Blood and Treasure, that it will cost Us to maintain this Declaration, and support and defend these States. Yet through all the Gloom I can see the Rays of ravishing Light and Glory. I can see that the End is more than worth all the Means. And that Posterity** [descendants of the early Americans – this current generation] **will tryumph in that Days Transaction** [End Times of the Biblical Last Days], **even altho We should rue** [regret] **it, which I trust in God We shall not.**"[201] [emphasis added]

Since early Americans felt that they were called by God to pick up where Moses left off, there was an incredible sense of compelling as a nation to identify with ancient Israel. This inclination was exhibited in the rapidly growing popularity of university courses in the Hebrew language. People wanted to read and comprehend the Old Testament in the original tongue. Many colleges made the study of Hebrew a requirement. There was even a suggestion that Hebrew be adopted as the national language in place of English.[202] One writer states:

"During the American Revolution, a movement was launched to replace English with Hebrew as the official language of the new nation.

In 1776, anything associated with the British monarchy had a bad taste to the American rebels. Hebrew, on the other hand, was held in high regard by the former British colonists, who viewed it as the mother of all languages, the key to the scriptures and the cornerstone of liberal education.

They named their towns after those cited in the Bible such as Salem and Bethlehem, and their children were named after Biblical figures.

Until 1817, annual commencement addresses at Harvard were delivered in Hebrew, and at Yale the language [Hebrew] was required for freshmen. Many lower schools also stressed Hebrew.

Several members of the new Congress reportedly urged that English be banned altogether and replaced by Hebrew. Though the idea never caught on, Hebrew remained a required course at many major American universities well into the 19th century." [203]

Dr. Stephen Jones in an excerpt from his (2006) book, "The Prophetic History of the United States:"

"Where historians would have us believe that the term 'America' was probably derived from an obscure and not well known Italian explorer named Amerigo Vespucci, this is indeed unlikely. Many of the English settlers were highly educated, well acquainted with many languages, and so it is very likely that they would know the origin of the term, *America*. *America* is an old Saxon and Danish compound word. _Amer_ means 'heavenly,' and _ric_ means 'kingdom.' It literally means 'the Heavenly Kingdom,' or the Kingdom of Heaven. A deeper study of the etymology of the entire name of this nation, 'The United States of America,' results in a profound and insightful meaning. _The_ means 'God's,' that is, owned by God. This is why THEology is the study of God. In Greek, _theos_ means God. And another connection is this: the Spanish word for 'the' is *EL*, which is also the Hebrew word for *God*. The word _United_ means 'greater.' The word _State_ means 'estate.' So, all together, it means **'God's Greater Estate of the Heavenly Kingdom.'**"[204] [emphasis added]

On November 15, 1777, Continental Congress passed the *Articles of Confederation,* "Articles of Confederation and Perpetual Union..." to create *"The United States of America."*[205] An important operational document, it provided that "each State retains its sovereignty, freedom and independence" while entering into "a firm league of friendship with each other for their common defense the security of their liberties, and their mutual and general welfare."[206]

Under the *Articles of Confederation*, the central, or national, government was weak, and had no executive to lead it. It's only political body was Congress, which could not collect taxes or tariffs but only ask the States for donations for the common good. It did have power to oversee foreign relations but could not create an army or navy to enforce foreign treaties. Further, it was not ratified by all the States until 1781.

Having just gained independence from what they experienced as a despotic, powerful central government that was too distant from its citizens, Americans were skeptical about giving much power to any government other than that of their own States, where they could exercise more direct control. However, seeds of nationalism had been sown because of the war as it required a united effort. Most men would probably have lived out their lives without venturing from their own State but for this cause did travel to other States in order to participate in the Continental Army.

The weaknesses of the *Articles of Confederation* were obvious from the beginning. Foreign nations, ruled mostly by Jesuit-controlled monarchies, were inherently contemptuous of the "American experiment" of entrusting rule to common, ordinary people. A government without an army or navy and little real power was considered by them to be rather a joke as well as an opportunity for their own benefit whenever the opportunity would arise.

Without a uniform code meant that each State must establish its own form of government, a chaotic system marked at times by mob rule that burned courthouses and terrorized State and local officials. State laws were passed and almost immediately repealed; sometimes *ex post facto* laws (having retroactive force) made new codes retroactive. Collecting debts was virtually impossible.

In 1786, George Washington wrote to John Jay regarding the deficiencies of the Confederation:

"We have errors to correct; we have probably had too good an opinion of human nature in forming our confederation." [207]

26

George Washington [208]
General and Commander in Chief
of the Continental Army

John Jay, 1794 [209]
First Chief Justice of the United States Supreme Court
from 1789 to 1795

John Jay held conviction that the people of America must become one nation in every respect.[210]

Alexander Hamilton expressed:

"…something noble and magnificent in the perspective of a great Federal Republic, closely linked in the pursuit of common interest, tranquil and prosperous at home, respectable abroad; but there is something proportionally diminutive and contemptible in the prospect of a number of petty States, with appearance only of union…" [211]

Portrait of Alexander Hamilton, 1806 [212]

In May of 1787, a Constitutional Convention was held at Philadelphia to address the weaknesses of the *Articles of Confederation* and discuss the need "to form a more perfect Union." As a covenanted people with Almighty God as well as with each other, they drafted and ratified a document like no other, the *Constitution of the United States*.

The Old Testament book of Deuteronomy is the *Book of God's Law* and where the Founders gleaned near 34 percent of the principles of law that are framed in the *Constitution*, the country's operating document.[213] With the Bible being their main textbook throughout life, they were intimately acquainted with the book of Deuteronomy.

The Founders were acquainted with the main character in the book of Deuteronomy, Moses, the prophet and lawgiver, who was given a divine revelation regarding the future generations of the Israelites. Moses' revelation pertained to Israel breaking covenant with God by participating in idolatry. The resulting prophecy is recorded in Deuteronomy 28:64:

"And the Lord shall scatter thee among all people, from the one end of the earth even unto the other; and there thou shalt serve other gods—gods of wood and stone, which neither you nor your ancestors have known."

For the sake of understanding, we provide some background in what the early Americans came to realize and believe from the prophetic scriptures.

The Old Testament Israelites, sectioned in "tribes" of families, experienced a sort of "sibling rivalry" that resulted in becoming split in two sections.[214] One of the two sections consisted of ten of the tribes known as the northern "House of Israel." The House of Israel suffered judgment of the Almighty for "whoring after other gods" (another way of stating "idolatry"), and were taken captive by the Assyrians, a foreign nation, and hauled away from their Promised Land.[215] In not returning to their land after their captivity ended many years later, the prophecy for the House of Israel had been fulfilled. Those "lost ten tribes" indeed had been scattered.

The other section of the Hebrew people, the southern "House of Judah" consisted of primarily two tribes. Because of the sin of idolatry, the House of Judah also ended in captivity to a foreign nation, Babylon. The House of Judah, however, returned to their portion of the Promised Land after 70 years.

Early Americans identified in the prophetic scriptures that "ancient Israel" was the same as "the lost ten tribes." The Founders discovered an astounding passage of scripture that excited them with a joy and hope for their future as well as for their posterity, their future generations.[216]

Moses prophesied that <u>after</u> the Israelites had been scattered across the world, had suffered and endured the curses of disobedience, they (their descendants) would begin to recall God's generous promises made to them if they would return and obey His divine law. Moses' prophecy included that **He would gather them into a land of their own.**

Deuteronomy 30:1-9 ~

> *"And it shall come to pass, when all these things are come upon thee, the blessing and the curse, which I have set before thee, and **thou shalt call them to mind among all the nations, whither the Lord thy God hath driven thee,***
>
> *And shalt **return unto the Lord thy God, and shalt obey his voice according to all that I command** thee this day, thou and thy children, with all thine heart, and with all thy soul;*
>
> ***That then the Lord thy God will turn thy captivity,** and have compassion upon thee, **and will return and gather thee from all the nations, whither the Lord thy God hath scattered thee.***
>
> *If any of thine be driven out unto the outmost parts of heaven, from thence will **the Lord thy God gather thee, and from thence will he fetch thee:***
>
> ***And the Lord thy God will bring thee into the land which thy fathers possessed, and thou shalt possess it;** and he will do thee good, and multiply thee above thy fathers.*
>
> *And the Lord thy God will circumcise thine heart, and the heart of thy seed, to love the Lord thy God with all thine heart, and with all thy soul, that thou mayest live.*
>
> *And the Lord thy God will put all these curses upon thine enemies, and on them that hate thee, which persecuted thee.*
>
> ***And thou shalt return and obey** the voice of the Lord, and do all his commandments which I command thee this day.*

And the Lord thy God will make thee plenteous in every work of thine hand, in the fruit of thy body, and in the fruit of thy cattle, and in the fruit of thy land, for good: for the Lord will again rejoice over thee for good, as he rejoiced over thy fathers:"

The Founders understood that the prophecy pertained to the descendants and remnants of God's people Israel who had been disbursed throughout the world. They understood that the descendants of Israel would begin to remember the promises of God made to their ancestors, return to the Lord, and be gathered into a land of their own. <u>No other land seemed to fit the characteristics in description as portrayed throughout various scriptures, but Protestant America</u>.

Later prophets spoke of a gathering that would take place in the latter days. The Word of God was given to them after they were already in the Promised Land. Some of them include:

2 Samuel 7:10 ~

> *Moreover I will appoint a place for my people Israel, and will plant them, that they may dwell in a place of their own and move no more.*

Isaiah 2:2-3 ~

> *And it shall come to pass **in the last days**, that the mountain of the Lord's house shall be established in the top of the mountains, and shall be exalted above the hills; and all nations shall flow unto it. And many people shall go and say, Come ye, and let us go up to the mountain of the Lord, to the house of the God of Jacob; and he will teach us of his ways, and we will walk in his paths: **for out of <u>Zion</u> shall go forth <u>the law</u>,** and the word of the Lord from Jerusalem.*

Micah 4:1-2 ~

> *But **in the last days it shall come to pass**, that the mountain of the house of the Lord shall be established in the top of the mountains, and it shall be exalted above the hills; and people shall flow unto it. And many nations shall come, and say, Come, and let us go up to the mountain of the Lord, and to the house of the God of Jacob; and he will teach us of his ways, and we will walk in his paths: **for <u>the law</u> shall go forth <u>of Zion</u>,** and the word of the Lord from Jerusalem.*

Isaiah 18:1-2 ~

> *Woe to the land <u>shadowing with wings</u>, which is beyond the rivers of Ethiopia: That sendeth ambassadors by the sea, even in vessels of bulrushes upon the waters, saying, Go, ye swift messengers, to **a nation scattered and peeled**, to a people terrible from their beginning hitherto; **a nation meted out and trodden down**, whose land the rivers have spoiled!*

It is remarkable in understanding that Bible scholars had claimed great significance to this verse. They point out that those primitive people on the "isle" of the sea (native Indians) are actually remnants of ancient Israel.[217]

Zephaniah 3:10-13 ~

> *From beyond the rivers of Ethiopia my suppliants, even <u>the daughter of my dispersed</u>, shall bring mine offering. **In that day** shalt thou not be ashamed for all thy doings, wherein thou hast transgressed against me:*

29

*for then I will take away out of the midst of thee them that rejoice in thy pride, and thou shalt no more be haughty because of my holy mountain. <u>I will also leave in the midst of thee an afflicted and poor people, and they shall trust in the name of the Lord</u>. The **remnant of Israel** shall not do iniquity, nor speak lies; neither shall a deceitful tongue be found in their mouth: for they shall feed and lie down, and none shall make them afraid.*

The prophet Zephaniah is saying that these native inhabitants of America, the afflicted and poor people, are "remnants of Israel."

Bishop George Berkeley, approx. 1727 [218]
George Berkeley[219] (1685-1753) of Ireland, was an ordained bishop of the Episcopal Church and was a famous philosopher of his day. He is known for his belief that the Old Testament prophet Daniel had prophesied of four great empires that would destroy one another in historic sequence ending with God's kingdom arising and enduring forever.[220] Bishop Berkeley relayed from his studies that all of Daniel's prophecy had been fulfilled except the rise of God's kingdom.

<u>He believed that this final epoch of this profound prophecy would be fulfilled in the new Zion of America</u>. He also concluded that it would not be only the hosts of the scattered Israelites who would come to America to set-up the kingdom of God, but the natives of America—who had been down trodden as prophesied by Isaiah[221]—would also arise and bring an offering to the Lord as the Old Testament prophet Zephaniah had prophesied. Berkeley came to America with an earnest interest to work toward educating the native Indians to fulfill their manifest destiny as related in the prophetic scriptures.[222]

There are many sermons recorded in history that speak of the various prophetic scriptures for "God's New Israel" in the latter days. With early America's churches being central in their communities and lifestyle, those sermons were inspiring to the American people of that day.[223] [224] When brought forward to this day, one has much to ponder in the wonder of it all. Particularly as we see the unfolding of the prophetic scriptures as they relate to the signs of the end times.[225]

The Founders were impressed with the possibility that the prophecy could be fulfilled in their lifetimes. They viewed America as the land where the remnants from various countries would begin to gather. They were stirred with conviction that they were called of God and divinely appointed by Him in restoring His law as had been given to Moses.[226] [227] They envisioned being the first free people of the modern world, "a city upon a hill"[228] with blessings that would result in the other nations of the world eventually coming to the same liberties.

Their heritage of the Lord included the promises of blessing by abiding according to the principles of law as set forth in the covenant with God—just as ancient Old Testament Israel—secured by righteous living. They were convinced and verbalized their convictions in speeches and sermons that living the covenant lifestyle was attainable only by a moral and religious (Christian) people. If they failed God, they understood they would also fail the other nations in their hope to also be free.

We continue on to the time of the Constitutional Convention. In writing, or framing, the *Constitution of the United States*, the authors acknowledged the operating document as the "supreme law of the land." The *Constitution's* Preamble reads:

"We the People of the United States, in Order to form a more perfect Union, establish Justice, insure domestic Tranquility provide for the common defence, promote the general Welfare, and secure the Blessings of Liberty to ourselves and our Posterity, do ordain and establish this Constitution for the United States of America."[229]

This operational document established the three branches of the Federal Government: the executive, legislative, and judicial, and provided for two houses within the legislature. The idea for the three branches of government was derived from the Word of God at Isaiah 33:22:

"For the Lord is our <u>Judge</u> [judicial branch], the Lord is our <u>lawgiver</u> [legislative branch]: the Lord is our <u>King</u> [executive branch], he will save us."

The "Great American Experiment" of liberty was underway.[230]

John Quincy Adams, portrait as 6th President of the United States (1825-1829) [231]
A quote from John Quincy Adams on "The Jubilee of the Constitution," in a discourse delivered at the request of the New York Historical Society, in the City of New York, on April 30, 1839, the 50th anniversary of the inauguration of George Washington as President of the United States, on April 30, 1789:

"Now the *virtue* which had been infused into the Constitution of the United States, and was to give to its vital existence, the stability and duration to which it was destined, was no other than the concretion of those abstract principles which had been first proclaimed in the Declaration of Independence... This was the platform upon which the Constitution of the United States had been erected. <u>Its VIRTUES, its republican character, consisted in its conformity to the principles proclaimed in the Declaration of Independence</u>, and as its administration...<u>was to depend upon the...virtue, or in other words, of those principles proclaimed in the Declaration of Independence and embodied in the Constitution of the United States</u>. . ...Fellow-citizens, the ark of *your* covenant is the Declaration of Independence." [232] [emphasis added]

Both documents, the *Declaration of Independence* and the *Constitution of the United States*, were written by Divine inspiration. Based on that position, they must be considered as the Word of God as applied to the Nation. While the Bible provides moral guidance to individuals, the "supreme law of the land" (Article VI, Section 2), is the moral guide for the Union.[233]

The Nation's founders, delegates, and representatives of the People knew they had a special treasure, a gift from heaven in those sacred, foundational governing documents — their Covenant with Almighty God and with each other. <u>They also knew they must guard its preservation from the Jesuit intrigue directed at this new Christian Republic</u>. They were well acquainted with the Jesuit Order, their secret societies and *Black Nobility* who were vowed to the obedience of the Papacy and his Jesuit General in their apostate mission.

Marquis de Lafayette, French Lt. General [234]
Marquis de Lafayette (1757-1834); French Nobleman and Hero of the American Revolutionary War; served in the Continental Army under General George Washington:

"If the liberties of the United States of America are destroyed it will be by the subtlety of the Roman Catholic Jesuit priests, for they are the most crafty, dangerous enemies to civil and religious liberty."[235]

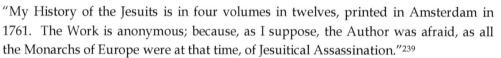

John Adams, former President in 1816 [236]

In 1816 John Adams, former second President of the United States (1797-1801), wrote to former third President Thomas Jefferson (1801-1809):

"Shall we not have regular swarms of them here, in as many disguises as only a king of the gypsies can assume, dressed as painters, publishers, writers and schoolmasters? If ever there was a body of men who merited eternal damnation on earth and in hell it is this Society of Loyola's . . . we are compelled by our system . . . to offer them asylum."[237]

Thomas Jefferson, former President in 1821 [238]

John Adams to Thomas Jefferson (both now aged and retired), November 4, 1816:

"My History of the Jesuits is in four volumes in twelves, printed in Amsterdam in 1761. The Work is anonymous; because, as I suppose, the Author was afraid, as all the Monarchs of Europe were at that time, of Jesuitical Assassination."[239]

The Founders understood the prophetic Word of God and knew that a day would come in future generations when the Great Drama as told in the written Word, the Holy Bible, would climax and by means of a great conspiracy, with a great delusion, by a Great Deceiver.[240]   So closely would the counterfeit resemble the true, it would be near impossible to distinguish between them except by the Holy Scriptures. It would be the people of God knowing Him through covenantal relationship by His Word and through His Spirit that would enable them to discern Satan's counterfeit while pretending to be the work of Almighty God.[241]

The Founding Fathers had firsthand experiential knowledge of the Word of God with "the devil who roamed the earth seeking to destroy"[242] and a time would come when the Great Deceiver and Counterfeit, "Ye Old Deluder Satan,"[243] would seek to usurp all that was good and called blessed.[244] They were well acquainted with the stories of the Old Testament and how God's chosen people revealed the blessings of an obedient people in following God's Word and His Law as well as the contrary—the curses of disobedience. They were acquainted with the scripture story of Moses giving careful instruction to regularly keep the history of their journey and covenant with God before the people and generations to come, their posterity. For this reason they held education of great importance.

The Founding Fathers also knew their God-breathed governance system would only work for a Christian people and so set guards as best they could to prevent the State from interfering with the Church as well as to preserve religious freedom in order to worship the one true God.[245] [246]

Following are just a few of hundreds of chronicled quotes of the Founding Fathers that portray their beliefs, as well as their intent, on the importance of a religious and moral society:

John Adams in a speech to the military in 1798 warned his fellow countrymen:

"We have no government armed with power capable of contending with human passions unbridled by morality and religion . . . Our Constitution was made only for a moral and religious people. It is wholly inadequate to the government of any other." John Adams was a signer of the *Declaration of Independence,* the *Bill of Rights*, and second President of the United States.[247]

Benjamin Rush, Signer of the *Declaration of Independence*:

"[T]he only foundation for a useful education in a republic is to be aid in religion. Without this, there can be no virtue, and without virtue there can be no liberty, and liberty is the object and life of all republican governments... But the religion I mean to recommend in this place is the religion of Jesus Christ." [248]

Noah Webster, author of the first American Speller and the first Dictionary:

"In my view, the Christian religion is the most important and one of the few things in which all children, under a free government, ought to be instructed. No truth is more evident to my mind than that the Christian religion must be the basis of any government intended to secure the rights and privileges of a free people." [249]

Gouverneur Morris, Penman and Signer of the *Constitution:*

"[F]or avoiding the extremes of despotism or anarchy . . . the only ground of hope must be on the morals of the people. I believe that religion is the only solid base of morals and that morals are the only possible support of free governments. [T]herefore education should teach the precepts of religion and the duties of man towards God." [250]

Fisher Ames author of the final wording for the *First Amendment*:

"[Why] should not the Bible regain the place it once held as a school book? Its morals are pure, its examples captivating and noble. The reverence for the sacred Book, that is thus early impressed, lasts long; and probably, if not impressed in infancy, never takes firm hold of the mind." [251]

John Jay, Original Chief Justice of the U. S. Supreme Court:

"The Bible is the best of all books, for it is the word of God and teaches us the way to be happy in this world and in the next. Continue therefore to read it and to regulate your life by its precepts." [252]

James Wilson, Signer of the *Constitution*; U. S. Supreme Court Justice:

"Human law must rest its authority ultimately upon the authority of that law which is divine. . . . Far from being rivals or enemies, religion and law are twin sisters, friends, and mutual assistants. Indeed, these two sciences run into each other." [253]

Noah Webster, author of the first American Speller and the first Dictionary:

"The moral principles and precepts contained in the scriptures ought to form the basis of all our civil constitutions and laws. . . All the miseries and evils which men suffer from vice, crime, ambition, injustice, oppression, slavery, and war, proceed from their despising or neglecting the precepts contained in the Bible."[254]

Robert Winthrop, a legislator, author and orator, on May 28, 1849:

"Men, in a word, must necessarily be controlled by either a power within them or by a power without them; either by the Word of God or by the strong arm of man; either by the Bible or by the bayonet." [255]

George Washington, General of the Revolutionary Army, president of the *Constitutional Convention*, first President of the United States of America, Father of our nation:

"Religion and Morality are the essential pillars of Civil society." [256]

Benjamin Franklin, one of America's most instrumental statesmen, author, scientist, and printer, he also served as a diplomat to France and England, was the President (Governor) of Pennsylvania, founded the University of Pennsylvania, signed the *Declaration of Independence*, the *Articles of Confederation* and the *Constitution*:

"[O]nly a virtuous people are capable of freedom. As nations become corrupt and vicious, they have more need of masters." [257]

Continental Congress, 1778:

"Whereas true religion and good morals are the only solid foundations of public liberty and happiness: Resolved, That it be, hereby earnestly recommended to the several states, to take the most effectual measures for the encouragement thereof..." [258]

An impression is left in the foundation of this country in considering that 106 of the first 108 colleges had begun based on Christianity and a Biblical worldview in education. By the close of 1860 there were 246 colleges in America. Remarkably, seventeen of them were state institutions; almost every other one was founded by Christian sects (denominations) or by individuals who avowed a religious purpose.[259]

In continuing the story of the *Constitutional Convention,* the Founders set guards of accountability in the form of checks and balances in their governance system operating document, the *Constitution,* particularly in areas that would affect that of money and power. The Founders knew money and power are areas that their spiritual enemy, through "cunning, ambitious, and unprincipled men,"[260] would seek entrance in effort to usurp their divine establishment. The natural laws written by James Madison and the other Founding Fathers laid down the separation of powers of the legislative, executive and judicial branches of the government and the *nexus imperium,* the law of checks and balances, as safeguards.[261]

James Madison [262]

James Madison, who wrote the Fifth Amendment to the *Constitution,* stated that power must come from the people:

"The government has only such powers as the people delegate to it through a <u>social covenant, the Constitution which is derived from God's Covenant with man</u> <u>[the Declaration of Independence]</u>.

This derivation limits the power of the process of law and the powers of government. This underline{covenant} cannot be contravened as it is 'the law of nature and of nature's God.'" [263] [emphasis added]

As the *Declaration of Independence* had proclaimed the God-given right of all men being created equal, there was the necessary issue of the institution of slavery and the Slave Trade that was addressed in the framing of the *Constitution*. For the sake of understanding the complexity of the issue we review the history.

Martin Luther King, Jr., 1964 [264]

Martin Luther King, Jr. (1929-1968), a Baptist minister and prominent social activist who led the *Civil Rights Movement,* in his address at Montgomery, Alabama, December 31, 1955, declared:

"If we are to go forward, we must go back and rediscover those precious values - that all reality hinges on moral foundations and that all reality has spiritual control."[265]

In November, 1782 when independence of the *united States of America* was at last conceded by Great Britain, the population was about 2,500,000 free whites and some 500,000 black slaves. Nearly all of the half-million slaves were in the Southern Colonies.

African Slavery had already been implanted on the soil of Virginia before the Pilgrim Fathers set foot at Plymouth Rock in 1620. The institution of slavery and "nobility" of the *Southern Aristocracy* had spread from the Virginia Colony throughout the Southern States. Slavery had spread rapidly prior to the Revolution to every one of the thirteen Colonies. It was recognized and acquiesced by all as an existing and established institution, yet there were many, both in the South and North, who looked upon it as an inherited evil and they were anxious to prevent the increase of that evil. As time passed, it became more firmly established.

Controversy arose as far back as 1699 between the Colonies and the Home Government and it continued up to the time of the *Declaration of Independence* itself.[266] The Northern Colonies were compelled to compromise their Kingdom ideals in order to have an independent nation at all.[267] Independence from the Mother Country had been gained but the curse of slavery was left fastened upon America.[268]

It was this conviction that it was not only an evil — but a dangerous evil — that induced Thomas Jefferson to embody in his original draft of the *Declaration* a clause that strongly condemned the African Slave Trade:

"He [King George III] has waged cruel War against human Nature itself, violating its most sacred Rights of Life and Liberty in the Persons of a distant People [Africans] who never offended him, captivating and carrying them into Slavery in another Hemisphere [the New World, America], or to incur miserable Death, in their Transportation thither. This piratical Warfare, the opprobrium [the disgrace incurred by shameful conduct] of infidel Powers, is the Warfare of the Christian King of Great Britain." [269] [emphasis added]

The clause was afterward omitted to comply with the South Carolina and Georgia delegates in order to get them to agree to sign the document.[270] They refused to ratify it unless it protected their "right" to hold slaves.

Amazing is that slavery had been outlawed in Georgia until 1752 when it was legalized by royal decree and the colonists were then forced to recognize the institution of slavery. Even by 1776 there were many Georgians who still disavowed slavery.

They recognized that all rights come from God alone, who has not given any man the right to force any man into servitude except as payment for sin. And certainly no one had a right to kidnap people from Africa and bring them to America as slaves – or to buy slaves from the kidnappers.[271]

Since the clause was omitted for only the reason of compromise, it is a fair conclusion that where the Fathers included the term "men," in "all men are created equal" to mean black as well as white, bond as well as free. There were more clauses that were deleted from the first draft of the *Declaration*[272] in order to secure the votes of South Carolina and Georgia, and specifically in defining men as being irrespective of race:

"...he has prostituted his negative for suppressing every legislative attempt to prohibit or to restrain this execrable [detestable] commerce determined to keep open a market where MEN should be bought & sold: and that this assemblage of horrors might want no fact of distinguished die, he is now exciting those very people to rise in arms among us, and to purchase that liberty of which *he* has deprived them, by murdering the people upon whom *he* also obtruded them: thus paying off former crimes committed against the *liberties* of one people, with crimes which he urges them to commit against the *lives* of another. In every stage of these oppressions we have petitioned for redress [relief], in the most humble Terms; our repeated petitions have been answered by repeated Injury. A prince whose character is thus marked by every act which may define a tyrant, is unfit to be the ruler of a people who mean to be free. Future ages will scarce believe that the hardiness of one man, adventured within the short compass of twelve years only, on so many acts of tyranny without a mask, over a people, fostered & fixed in principles of liberty." [273] [emphasis added]

The Fathers understood that they would need to address the horror of this inherited institution at a later time.

Declaration of Independence, July 4th, 1776 [274]
painted by John Trumbull (1756-1843) / engraved by W.L. Ormsby (1834-1908)

Chapter Four
America's Original Sin and the Foothold of Satan

After the *American War of Independence* there was a widely held belief that Amrican settlers were destined to expand across the North American continent. The thirteen original States held the territory on the eastern seaboard west of Pennsylvaina to the Ohio River. Territory further west was held by both the French and Spanish Crowns.

United States, March-August, 1789 (eastern)[275]

In 1784 Virginia ceded her claim to her western territory northwest of the Ohio River, presuming that these territories would soon form States that would join the Union. Thomas Jefferson, as chairman of a Select Committee appointed to consider a plan of government for the territory, drafted an Ordinance to govern the territory of which would be divided to create States. Jefferson wrote, **"they shall forever remain a part of the United States of America,"** and **"after the year 1800 of the Christian era, there shall be neither Slavery nor involuntary servitude in any of the said States."**

Thomas Jefferson, 1786 [276]

Also stated in the *Ordinance of 1784* was that those fundamental conditions were *"unalterable but by the joint consent of the United States in Congress assembled, and of the particular State within which such alteration is proposed to be made."*[277]

It seemed that the institution of slavery would be determinedly restricted to a few Southern States with no new States being allowed to enslave others. <u>Misfortune would have it that the necessary votes needed to pass the *Ordinance of 1784* did not happen due to one delegate being absent and therefore the retention of the clause prohibiting Slavery was also lost</u>. Lost was the great opportunity of restricting slavery to the then existing slave States and of settling the question peaceably for all time.[278]

Three years later a similar Ordinance was passed; the *"Ordinance of '87,"* also known as the *Northwest Ordinance*, outlawed slavery in the new Northwest Territories (Ohio, Indiana, Illinois, Michigan, and Wisconsin). Very unfortunately, this did not lawfully apply to any new Southern territories as the new Ordinance excluded the territory south of the Ohio River. The earlier un-passed Ordinance would have included all new southern territories as well.

Map of the Northwest Territory (1787)[279]

As a direct consequence of this failure to include that territory, the States of Tennessee, Alabama and Mississippi were subsequently admitted to the Union as slave States. More slave States added to the Union greatly increased the political power of the Southern States because they now had more members in Congress.

An increase of political power also secured the admission of more slave-holding States such as Florida, Louisiana, and Texas which further enabled the Slave Power to hold the congressional balance of power. The balance of power was in opposition to the original States which had become free, as well as the new free States of the Northwest Territory.[280]

And so, while the *Ordinance of '87* restricted slavery in the North, **it also established a legislative crack between North and South** that only grew until the Civil War settled the issue by the clash of arms that shook the Union from its center to its circumference.

Though the *Northwest Ordinance* of 1787 was passed under the authority of the *Articles of Confederation* just prior to the passage of the *Constitution*, it still carried weight and proved to be the first of a long string of compromises over the slavery issue that at the time seemed to be essential in holding the Union together. <u>The majority had to yield to the minority in order to keep from losing everything</u>. And yet it was understood and believed from an economic point of view that the institution of slavery would fall of its own accord because it could not compete with the labor of free men in the North.

General John A. Logan's (1886) book, *The Great Conspiracy*, is well-known by historians as one of the great resource books for background history on the progression of the Civil War. General Logan (1826-1886) lived a life in public and military service. He was in the United States Army in the Mexican-American War and as a General in the Union Army of the Civil War. When not serving in the Army, he held a political career filling terms in both houses of the Illinois legislature, and then filling office terms in both houses of Congress. General Logan stated,

> "Thus it was, that instead of an immediate interdiction of the African Slave Trade, Congress was empowered to prohibit it after the lapse of twenty years."

The *Constitution of the United States,* Article 1 Section 9:

The Migration or Importation of such Persons as any of the States now existing shall think proper to admit, <u>shall not be prohibited by the Congress prior to the Year one thousand eight hundred and eight</u>, but a tax or duty may be imposed on such Importation, not exceeding ten dollars for each Person.[281] [underline added]

Staff of Gen. William T. Sherman (seated, middle). General John A. Logan is seated on the left. Date: between 1862-1865.[282]

It is recorded in history that the debate among the delegates of the Continental Congress in 1789 concluded with the Founding Fathers having agreed that the Slave Trade would end in twenty years after the adoption of the *Constitution*. That timeframe would allow current slave owners, including some of the Southern delegates to the *Constitutional Convention*, to make adjustments in how they did business, while, at the same time, essentially prohibiting the impairment of current slave contracts. The delegates all planned that slavery would end in a generation.[283]

Rufus King (1755-1827)[284]   Gouverneur Morris (1752–1816) [285]

Rufus King of Massachusetts and Gouverneur Morris of Pennsylvania bitterly opposed slavery.   But because the institution of slavery was dying out and because the South was so economically depressed compared to the North, they agreed with the majority of delegates that the slavery issue could be avoided until after ratification (confirmation) of the new *Constitution*.[286] The Founding Fathers' hopeful predictions that slavery would simply disappear were astoundingly all made wrong because of a revolution in technology.[287]

Eli Whitney, 1794 [288]

In 1793, Eli Whitney invented the cotton gin; a new industry, dependent upon slave labor, was spawned. The South expanded as far west as New Orleans. Alabama and Mississippi entered the Union as slave States.[289] The tactical decision to postpone the confrontation with the slavery issue because it would die a natural death had proven to be disastrous to the North; the avoidance strategy had failed. An unforeseen technological invention created a whole new generation of slave owners. The South had passed a point from which it could not retreat.[290]

The slavery issues festered for the next half century through compromise after compromise. The North argued from the standpoint of morality and Natural Law referencing the *Declaration of Independence*, while the South argued from the standpoint of constitutionality claiming that the *Constitution* gave them the freedom and right to possess slaves as property.

"The First Cotton Gin" [291]
An engraving from Harper's Magazine, 1869
This carving depicts a roller gin,
which preceded Eli Whitney's invention.

In the annals of American history is found a most profound occurrence not taught in our schools today. On June 28, 1787 Benjamin Franklin delivered a powerful speech at the *Constitutional Convention*, which was embroiled in a bitter debate over how each State was to be represented in the new government. The hostility ran so deep that some delegates actually left the Convention. Franklin, being the President (Governor) of Pennsylvania, hosted the rest of the 55 delegates attending the Convention at Philadelphia. Being the senior member of the convention at 81 years of age, he commanded the respect of all present, and as recorded in James Madison's detailed records, he rose to speak in this moment of crisis:

"Mr. President: The small progress we have made after four or five weeks close attendance & continual reasonings with each other-our different sentiments on almost every question, several of the last producing as many noes as ayes, is me-thinks a melancholy proof of the imperfection of the Human Understanding.

We indeed seem to feel our own want of political wisdom, since we have been running about in search of it. We have gone back to ancient history for models of government, and examined the different forms of those Republics which, having been formed with the seeds of their own dissolution, now no longer exist. And we have viewed Modern States all around Europe, but find none of their Constitutions suitable to our circumstances.

In this situation of this Assembly, groping as it were in the dark to find political truth, and scarce able to distinguish it when presented to us, how has it happened, Sir, that we have not hitherto once thought of **humbly applying to the Father of lights to illuminate our understanding**?

In the beginning of the Contest with G. Britain, when we were sensible of danger, we had daily prayer in this room for Divine protection.--Our prayers, Sir, were heard, & they were graciously answered. All of us who were engaged in the struggle must have observed frequent instances of a superintending Providence in our favor.

To that kind Providence we owe this happy opportunity of consulting in peace on the means of establishing our future national felicity. And have we now forgotten that powerful Friend? Or do we imagine we no longer need His assistance?

I have lived, Sir, a long time, and the longer I live, the more convincing proofs I see of this truth-that **God Governs in the affairs of men**. And if a sparrow cannot fall to the ground without His notice, is it probable that an empire can rise without His aid?

We have been assured, Sir, in the Sacred Writings, that '**except the Lord build the House, they labor in vain that build it.**' I firmly believe this; and I also believe that without his concurring aid we shall succeed in this political building no better than the Builders of Babel: We shall be divided by our partial local interests; our projects will be confounded, and we ourselves shall become a reproach and bye word down to future ages.

And what is worse, mankind may hereafter from this unfortunate instance, despair of establishing Governments by Human wisdom and leave it to chance, war and conquest.

I therefore beg leave to move-that henceforth **prayers imploring the assistance of Heaven, and its blessing on our deliberations, be held in this Assembly every morning before we proceed to business,** and that one or more of the clergy of this city be requested to officiate in that service."[292]

Benjamin Franklin (1706-1790) [293]

George Washington, presiding over the *Constitutional Convention*, called for a recess as Dr. Franklin had exhorted. In reconvening, the work of the *Convention* went forward more smoothly. Because of this profound wisdom, its impact as well as its positive effect, after the *Convention*, and nine days after the first Constitutional Congress convened with a quorum (April 9, 1789), they implemented Franklin's recommendation. Two chaplains of different denominations were appointed, one to the House and one to the Senate, with a salary. This practice continued through the years.[294]

Franklin's remarkable motion sheds the light of truth as we consider the modern day accusations and claims of his alleged "deism," which is markedly different from what some today in Christendom describe it to be. Franklin, by his own words, believed that God governs in the affairs of men, which is not comparable to the general understanding of today's definition of deism. <u>There is a mistaken attempt to misplace in time out of historical order the definition of deism which results in implying that Franklin, Jefferson, and others, were not Christian, or "of the faith."</u>[295]

Scene at the Signing of the Constitution of the United States
George Washington presiding the Philadelphia Convention [296]

W. Cleon Skousen[297] was a world-renowned teacher, author, lecturer, and scholar. Holding a Juris Doctorate from George Washington University, Skousen is considered a leader in research of American history which includes a Biblical prophetic view.

Skousen accumulated a wealth of knowledge in Natural Law, also known as the "Laws of Nature," "God's law," on which the Founding Fathers based the governmental structure of the American Republic. Skousen well understood the focus of interest that was concentrated in the minds of the nation's Founders and articulated the importance of the principles that were instilled in the nation's founding and governmental documents. Skousen meticulously gleaned into the pages of his writings the inspiration of the Founders in the "eternal principles of hope" while providing their backgrounds, historical as well as personal writings, accomplishments, and thinking.

Mr. Skousen points out in his book, *The Majesty of God's Law, It's Coming to America*, that most of the Founding Fathers had read the New Testament in Greek and the Old Testament in Latin as well as in the original language of Hebrew. The Founding Fathers were very capable of drawing their own conclusions from the Word of God as related to Church doctrine.

Augustine of Hippo, also known as Saint Augustine [298]

At that period of time, Church doctrine included that of early Church theologian, Augustine, who held various dogmas or beliefs, some of which include that the original sin of Adam and Eve resulted in all of humanity being doomed forever,[299] that God decided to demonstrate his supremacy over Satan by electing a few to be saved no matter what they did (the doctrine of "election"), and that baptism and the prayer of the saints will release the dead who are tortured in purgatory or hell.[300]

Skousen points out that most of the Founders were revolted by Augustine's dogmas on "election" as well as "predestination." From his research, Skousen affirms from the Founders' writings that they describe their conviction in continuing to attend church because they believed in the teachings of Jesus even though they discreetly rejected these dogmas which remained prominent in most of the Christian churches and had often been enforced "at the point of the sword."

Skousen reports that Benjamin Franklin said that he doubted the Augustinian dogmas as early as age fifteen; John Adams said that he never did believe them, and Thomas Jefferson held the same opinion but that "he kept his religious convictions hidden in his heart." Nonetheless, all of these men continued to attend a Christian church of their choice (Franklin on occasion, but regular in financial contribution[301]), "looked beyond the creeds of the day," and went to church to search out the golden nuggets of Bible-based Christianity on which they hoped to build the American civilization.[302]

Benjamin Franklin wrote a personal creed and devotional for private worship at the age of 22. To unite the American people, the Founders undertook to find those basic beliefs set forth in the Bible on which people of all religious faiths, or denominations, could agree. It was Franklin's personal creed that presented five points of fundamental religious belief which are either expressed or implied and have been guideposts for Americans for over two hundred years. They would summarize as:

1. There exists a Creator who made all things, and mankind should recognize and worship him.
2. The Creator has revealed a moral code of behavior for happy living which distinguishes right from wrong.
3. The Creator holds mankind responsible for the way they treat one another.
4. All mankind live beyond this life.
5. In the next life mankind are judged for their conduct in this one.

All five of these tenets are very evident throughout the writings of the Founding Fathers.[303]

Thomas Jefferson, 1791 [304]

Thomas Jefferson, author of the *Declaration of Independence*, was well-studied in the Bible as his principal source for the discovery of the ancient principles of divine law as revealed by God in His Holy Word.[305] He spent two years in the legislature of his home State of Virginia attempting to get the members of the Virginia legislature to adopt as many elements of the "perfect law" that had been revealed to Moses. In fact, to facilitate the adoption of statutes from the pattern of the Bible, he rewrote the entire criminal and civil code of Virginia in terms of principles as described in the Bible. He wanted the members of the legislature to see what a tremendous advantage God's law would be over English common law.[306]

John Adams wanted to structure America according to the Bible. He was studied in the Old Testament in Latin and the New Testament in Greek. Adams was inspired with the hope that someday there would be a society where their only law book would be the Bible.[307] On February 22, 1756 John Adams wrote in his diary:

"Suppose a nation in some distant region should take the Bible for their only law book, and every member should regulate his conduct by the precepts there exhibited! Every member would be obliged in conscience, to temperance, frugality, and industry; to justice, kindness, and charity towards his fellow men; and to piety, love, and reverence toward Almighty God....What a Eutopia, what a Paradise would this region be."[308]

John Adams, 1766 portrait [309]

Can the "deistic" scorn and misrepresentation of the Fathers of this nation be subject to a discrediting toward religion and government along with an agenda to separate the two? By these men's own words and deeds, the answer is reflected in the recorded annals of history as they created America's governance system in this developing nation.[310]

Statue of the Rev. George Whitefield at the University of Pennsylvania [311]

Recorded in history, as well as in the books of Heaven, is that Benjamin Franklin was so impressed by the preaching of George Whitefield, that Franklin built an auditorium in Philadelphia for Whitefield to preach in. That auditorium became the first building of the University of Pennsylvania, and has a bronze statue of George Whitefield placed in his honor.[312] Franklin also printed Whitefield's *Journal*, which grew to be exceedingly popular.

Franklin, as well as all of the Framers of the *Constitution*, realized the value as well as the necessity of Divine guidance in the affairs of men. They also had experiential knowledge of the positive effect of prayer in the weightier matters of politics.

Truly unmistakable was the prompting of the Holy Spirit in which Dr. Franklin exhorted his peers to recall God's intervention and guidance at a very critical time in the past, <u>in that very room where the *Declaration of Independence* was birthed forth, and to strongly consider seeking Him once again at another critical time, in the very unique framing of our American republican form of governance system.</u>[313]

The *Constitutional Convention* was taking place at that very same juncture in time that Thomas Jefferson worked with Congress on a plan of government for the western territory northwest of the Ohio River, the *Ordinance of 1787.* The *Northwest Ordinance* of July 13, 1787, which had become codified into law by the First Congress as *1 Statute 50* on August 7, 1789, declared the *Articles of Confederation* which were adopted on April 23, 1784 as null and void. The *Constitution of the United States* replaced the *Articles of Confederation.*

In 1803, Jefferson was successful in negotiating with France on the land transfer of the vast and rich *Territory of Louisiana* west of the Mississippi River. A concern arose in 1802 when Spain closed the Mississippi and ceded all of the *Louisiana Territory* to France which violated an agreement with the United States to allow the use of New Orleans as a port on the Mississippi. Jefferson realized the danger of having such a power as France holding the natural outlet for a large proportion of the produce of the county.[314]

One can't help wonder whether it was the excitement in being allured to territorial expansion, a sense of impending danger to the continued dominance of the political party which had also supported his views and beliefs for America, or whether he felt the vision for the United States on the North American continent was threatened by the chance that republican France may likely grow her Colony in that proximity that could have blinded his eyes to the fact that its acquisition would inevitably spread that very evil of slavery. A later contemplation of it wrung from his lips the prophetic words: [315]

"Can the liberties of a nation be thought secure when we have removed their only firm basis, a conviction in the minds of the people that **these liberties are of the gift of God? That they are not to be violated but with his wrath? Indeed, I tremble for my country when I reflect that God is just; that his justice cannot sleep forever;** that considering numbers, nature and natural means only, a revolution of the wheel of fortune, an exchange of situation is among possible events; that it may become probable by supernatural interference! The Almighty has no attribute which can take side with us in such a contest." [316] [emphasis added]

In contemplating the words of reflection and insightful understanding of one of this nation's Fathers and specifically the Father that penned the glorious *Declaration of Independence*, it is understood that Jefferson clearly knew history as recorded in the Holy Bible and specifically as it pertained to God's dealings with His people, the Israelites. He knew Almighty God to be a God of justice, and he knew there was consequence for this modern nation, the "New Israel," for breaking covenant in its mistreatment of humanity.

President George Washington, in his *Farewell Address* to the People of the United States, 1796:

"…**cunning, ambitious, and unprincipled men** will be enabled to subvert the power of the people, and to usurp for themselves the reins of government; destroying afterwards the very engines which have lifted them to unjust dominion… The spirit of encroachment tends to consolidate the powers of all the departments in one, and thus to create, whatever the form of government, a real despotism…"[317] [emphasis added]

America's Founding Father and first President, George Washington, spoke words of prophecy to the People as he left office. He was no stranger to the "cunning, ambitious, and unprincipled men," the Jesuits, who sought world domination in temporal power for their Jesuit General.

As a career military man as well as a colonial American, he well understood with experience the tyrannical history of the European monarchs in their claim to the "Divine Right of Kings."[318] He knew the threat of the Roman papacy with its pursuit of ruling by divine right, believing that their civil "temporal power" had come directly from God; that all men were to bow to their authority and control—that if a ruler would not submit his position and the country he ruled into the hands of the Pope, then the individual had no "divine" right to rule.[319]

President Washington in his *Presidential Farewell Address* called morality "a necessary spring of popular government," the belief that every human being is sovereign. In this belief, rather than having a monarch or single ruling individual, the common people could unite and each delegate a small portion of their sovereign powers and duties to those who wished to temporarily serve as officers and employees of the governing body. This system of law form then serves the rest of the people according to the will of the people expressed via the *Constitution*, "the supreme law of the land," in its guaranteed republican form of governance. The central idea of Popular Government is "consent of the governed,"[320] where the government is structured to allow its subjects to enjoy certain un-a-lien-able rights.

Michael Shea in his (2012) book, *In God We Trust: George Washington and the Spiritual Destiny of the United States of America,* "*As Daniel of old was shown the destiny of the planet Earth, so was Washington shown the destiny of our country.*"[321]

As a praying man of God, well acquainted with the Word of God and in personal relationship with the Savior of mankind, Washington was born and raised by his Godly mother in the era of the *First Great Awakening*. His *Farewell Address* reflects this devoted Christian and Patriot as filled with wisdom from above.[322] The "Father of our Country"[323] is also quoted in saying:

> "You do well to wish to learn our arts and ways of life, and above all, the religion of Jesus Christ.
> These will make you a greater and happier people than you are."[324]

We do well to recount the Father of our Country's words of wisdom which warn, as well as exhort. As for the "cunning, ambitious, unprincipled men," let us review part of their *Jesuit Oath*:

> "I do further promise and declare, that **I will have no opinion or will of my own, or any mental reservation whatever**, even as a corpse or cadaver, **but will unhesitatingly obey each and every command that I may receive from my superiors in the Militia of the Pope**… I furthermore promise and declare that I will, when opportunity presents, **make and wage relentless war, secretly or openly, against all heretics, Protestants and Liberals**, as I am directed to do, **to extirpate [completely destroy] and exterminate them from the face of the whole earth**; and that I will spare neither age, sex or condition; and that I will hang, burn, waste, boil, flay, strangle and bury alive these infamous **heretics**, rip up the stomachs and the wombs of their women and crush their infants heads against the walls, in order to **annihilate forever their execrable [utterly detestable] race. That when the same cannot be done openly, I will secretly use the poisoned cup**, the strangulating cord, the steel of the poniard or the leaden bullet, regardless of the honor, rank, dignity, or authority of the person or persons, whatever may be their condition in life, either public or private, **as I at any time may be directed so to do by any agent of the Pope or Superior of the Brotherhood of the Holy Faith, of the Society of Jesus.**[325] [emphasis added]

As the scenes progressed forward through time in the *Great Drama of Life*, there would unfold the script played-out by this faction of evil-doers as they usurped the reins of government, have been bent on destroying the American Republic in its covenant with the *God of Heaven* along with its precious, blood-bought Liberties while seeking to award their "Pope or Superior of the Brotherhood" global dominion.

The God of the Bible judged His Old Testament people, "Israel," for their sins of idolatry and turning away from Him by sending other nations to take them captive in bondage and slavery until their sentence was served and their repentant cry heard in Heaven. As history tends to repeat, God Almighty would prescribe judgment again but this time on His New Testament people, "New Israel," in kind.

The early Americans and their posterity would experience judgment because of their covenant-breaking by the mistreatment of mankind as well as not **yet** fulfilling the Dominion Mandate to be a blessing to all the families of the earth.[326] The discipline of the loving Lord[327] would come through an evil group of people who do not fear God,[328] operate in secret, while at the same time seeking to beat the prophetic clock of their prophesied ending destruction[329] because of their dastardly deeds done to the people of Almighty God.

As the prophetic time table has drawn forward to the latter days of the end of the Age, here unfolds the lawlessness, rebellion, deception, counterfeit, and powerful delusion[330] that the Church has been watching for with blinded eyes.

Indeed, the **spirit of encroachment** that President Washington warned of has consolidated the powers which were framed in the divinely inspired operating document and social covenant, the *Constitution*, into one department—the Executive. Ever so cunning and patient through the generations has the **doctrine of Balaam**[331] been followed even murdering anyone who was in their way, stealing everything, working destruction into despotism.

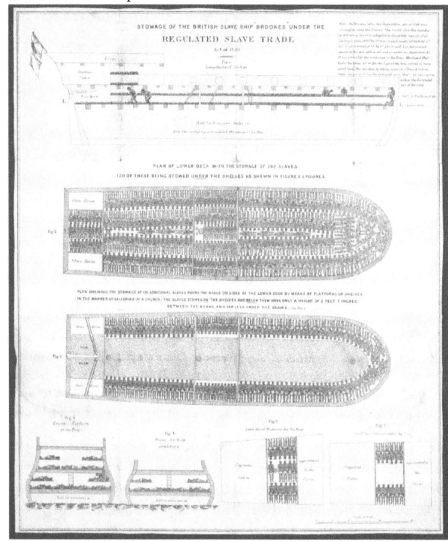

Stowage of the British Slave Ship "Brookes" under the Regulated Slave Trade [332]

The plan of the lower deck of the slave ship, "Brookes," graphically depicts the deplorable stowage of more than 400 slaves, with a third of them stowed on closely fitting shelves.

Library of Congress Description: Act of 1788. Note. The "Brookes," after the Regulation Act of 1788, was allowed to carry 454 Slaves, She could stow this number by following the rule adopted in this plate, namely of allowing a space of 6 ft. by 1 ft. 4 In to each man; 5 ft. 10 In by 1 ft. 4 In to each women, & 5 ft. by 1 ft. 2 In to each boy, but so much space as this was seldom allowed even after the Regulation Act

It was proved by the confession of the Slave Merchant that before the above Act the Brookes had at one time carried as many as 609 Slaves, This was done by taking some out of Irons & locking them spoonwise (to use the technical term) that is by stowing one within the distended legs of the other.

Chapter Five
The Church Must Take Right Ground

We go forward in time to 1814 when Europe was finally at rest after the Napoleonic Wars which had lasted nearly 20 years. The brilliant and crafty Napoleon had covered Europe with the blood of her noblest sons. Finally, there was peace.

Congress of Vienna, 1814-1815 [333]

In the aftermath, European sovereigns, or monarchs, convened a general council in Vienna, Austria in 1814. This council has come to be known as the *Congress of Vienna*. The Congress conducted its proceedings for one year, ending in 1815. The *Congress of Vienna* was a Black Nobility conspiracy against Popular Governments at which the "high contracting parties" announced at its close that they had formed a "holy alliance." <u>This was a religious cloak under which they concealed their deception.</u>

In follow-up business at the *Congress of Verona (1822)*, was the ratification of Article Six of the *Congress of Vienna*, which was a promise to prevent or destroy Popular Governments wherever found, and to reestablish absolute monarchies where they had been set aside. The "high contracting parties" of this compact, which were Russia, Prussia (Germany), France, Austria, <u>and</u> Pope Pius VII, king of the Papal States, entered into a secret treaty to do so.[334] [335]

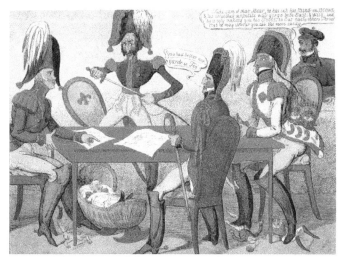

Satirical depiction of the Congress of Verona [336]
The Quintuple Alliance was represented by:
Russia, Austria, Prussia, Kingdom of France, United Kingdom

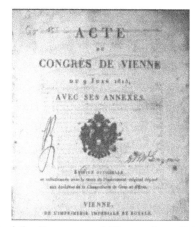

Act of the Congress of Vienna June 9, 1815 [337]

In 1894, Richard Wigginton "R.W." Thompson, U.S. Secretary of the Navy, was aware of this conspiracy against American freedom and the *Constitution* and wrote:

R. W. Thompson, Secretary of the Navy [338]

"The sovereigns of the 'Holy Alliance' had massed large armies, and soon entered into a pledge to devote them to the suppression of all uprisings of the people in favor of free government; and he [Pope Pius VII] desired to devote the Jesuits [the militia of the Pope], supported by his pontifical power, to the accomplishment of that end. He knew how faithfully they would apply themselves to that work, and hence he counseled them, in his decree of restoration, to strictly observe the 'useful advices and salutary counsels' whereby Loyola had made absolution the cornerstone of the society."[339] [emphasis added]

Thompson identified exactly who would be the agents used by the monarchs of Europe to destroy the American Republic, specifically, the Jesuits of Rome. Ever since 1815 there has been a continual assault on America by the Jesuits seeking to destroy the constitutional liberties of this great nation.[340]

On April 25, 1916, U.S. Senator Robert L. Owen (Oklahoma) placed the secret *Treaty of Verona* of November 22, 1822 in the Congressional Record along with the following statement which clearly reflects his conviction that the primary target of the "Holy Alliance" was the United States:

"The Holy Alliance having destroyed popular government in Spain, and in Italy, had well-laid plans also to destroy popular government in the American Colonies which had revolted from Spain and Portugal in Central and South America under the influence of the successful example of the United States. It was because of this conspiracy against the American Republics by the European monarchies that the great English statesman, Canning, called the attention of our government to it."[341] [emphasis added]

Senator Owen understood the purpose of the *Congress of Verona* to be the united monarchies of Europe in "Holy Alliance," seeking to destroy the great American Republic and its blood-bought Liberty. While calling the attention of his fellow members of the Senate to the threat, he wanted to show them *"what this ancient conflict is between the rule of the few and the rule of the many."* (*American Diplomatic Code, 1778-1884*, vol. 2; Elliott, P. 179.)[342]

As if the *Congress of Vienna* was not clear enough as to the objectives of the European monarchs and the Jesuit Order, there were two additional Congresses that were convened. The first of these was held at Verona in 1822. **During this Congress, it was decided that the American Republic would be the specific target of Jesuit emissaries and that Protestant America was to be destroyed at all costs. Every principle of the *Constitution* was to be dissolved and new Jesuitical principles were to be put into place in order to exalt the Papacy to dominion in America.**

The other follow-up Congress was convened at Chieri, Italy in 1825 in which it was concluded:

"In 1825, some eleven years after the revival of the Jesuit Order, a secret meeting of leading Jesuits was held at their College of Chieri near Turin, in Northern Italy. At that gathering, plans were discussed for the advancement of Papal power, world-wide, for the destabilizing of governments who stood in the way and for the crushing of all opposition to Jesuit schemes and ambitions… 'What we aim at, is the Empire of the World…We must give them [the great men, or "kings of the earth"] to understand that the cause of evil, the bad leaven, will remain as long as Protestantism shall exist, that Protestantism must therefore be utterly abolished… Heretics are the enemies that we are bound to exterminate…Then the Bible that serpent which with head erect and eyes flashing threatens us with its venom while it trails along the ground, shall be changed into a rod as soon as we are able to seize it.'"[343] [emphasis added]

The goal of the *Congress of Chieri* was clearly set to destroy Protestantism (the "Christian religion of liberty") at any cost, and restore the temporal power of the Papacy, **globally**.

George Canning, British Secretary of State for Foreign Affairs 1822-1827 [344]

These three "Congressional" meetings, at Vienna, Verona, and Chieri were held with as much **secrecy** as possible. British foreign minister George Canning attended the first two meetings and then contacted the United States government to provide warning that the monarchs of Europe had planned a conspiracy to destroy the free institutions of America.

Thomas Jefferson, who was still living at that time, took an active part to bring about the declaration by President James Monroe in his next annual message to the Congress on December 2, 1823, that the United States would consider it as an unfriendly act as well as an act of hostility to the government of the United States, if this coalition, or any power of Europe ever undertook to establish upon the American continent any control of any American republic (State), or to acquire any territorial rights.

This secret treaty clearly sets forth the conflict between monarchial government and popular government, and the government of the few as against the government of the many. The threat under the secret treaty of Verona to suppress popular government in the American Republic is the basis of the *Monroe Doctrine,* and was America's response to the Jesuit's Congress of Vienna and Verona.[345] [346]

America would consider it an act of war if any European nation (Old World) sought colonial expansion in the western hemisphere (New World). The foreign government cloaked as religion that the Jesuits' serve has been successful in secretly attacking and infiltrating America to accomplish exactly what the *Monroe Doctrine* was declared to protect against because it was done under the facade of being a church.

In a letter to President Monroe in 1823, Thomas Jefferson made the following observations:

"The question presented by the letters you have sent to me, is the most momentous which has ever been offered to my contemplation since that of Independence. That made us a nation, this sets our compass and points the course which we are to steer through the ocean of time opening on us. And never could we embark on it under circumstances more auspicious [favorable]. Our first and fundamental maxim should be, never to entangle ourselves in the broils of Europe. Our second, never to suffer Europe to intermeddles with cis-Atlantic [on this side of the Atlantic Ocean] affairs. America, North and South, has a set of interests distinct from those of Europe, and peculiarly her own. She should, therefore have a system of her own, separate and apart from that of Europe. While the last is laboring to become the domicile of despotism [tyranny], our endeavor should surely be, to make our hemisphere that of freedom.…[We must be] declaring our protest against the atrocious violations of the rights of nations, by the interference of any one in the internal affairs of

49

another, so flagitiously [shameful crime] begun by Bonaparte, and now continued by the equally lawless Alliance, calling itself Holy. … but we will oppose, with all of our means, the forcible interposition of any other power… But the question now proposed involves consequences so lasting, and effects so decisive of our future destinies, as to rekindle all the interest I have heretofore felt on such occasions, and to induce me to the hazard of opinions, which will prove only my wish to contribute still my mite towards anything which may be useful to our country."[347] [emphasis added]

President James Monroe, 1819 [348]   1821 Portrait of Thomas Jefferson [349]

Jefferson was convinced this was a great crisis in America's young history because the vile and sinister Jesuits had been given orders to destroy America. The *Monroe Doctrine* challenged any advance on America by Europe. However, Monroe did not fully comprehend that the crafty Jesuits would not initially use the force of arms to gain their objectives. They would infiltrate within and use cunning, craftiness, and utmost secrecy. They would appeal to and tempt men in their basest tendencies. **They would plant their agents in positions of wealth and power and then manipulate their influence to gain their great prize — the subversion and destruction of every Protestant principle (absolute) as outlined in the *Constitution of the United States*.**[350]

Leaders discuss the Monroe Doctrine, which declared the Western Hemisphere to be free of further European expansion or ideology [351]

50

At this same juncture of time in America were the flames of revival fanned into a *Second Great Awakening* beginning in the first decade of the 1800s in northern towns and cities and continuing through the 1830s. This move of God by His Holy Spirit fostered the greatest reform movement during that period.[352]

The religion of the new American Republic was evangelicalism which, between 1800 and the *Civil War*, was the "grand absorbing theme" of American religious (Christian) life. During some years in the first half of the 19th century, revivals through which evangelicalism had found an expression occurred with such frequency that religious publications that specialized in tracking them lost count. In 1827, one journal exclaimed:

> "…revivals, we rejoice to say, are becoming too numerous in our country to admit of being generally mentioned in our Record."[353]

Timothy Dwight IV by John Trumbull 1817 [354]

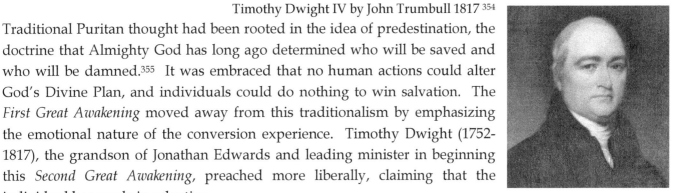

Traditional Puritan thought had been rooted in the idea of predestination, the doctrine that Almighty God has long ago determined who will be saved and who will be damned.[355] It was embraced that no human actions could alter God's Divine Plan, and individuals could do nothing to win salvation. The *First Great Awakening* moved away from this traditionalism by emphasizing the emotional nature of the conversion experience. Timothy Dwight (1752-1817), the grandson of Jonathan Edwards and leading minister in beginning this *Second Great Awakening*, preached more liberally, claiming that the individual has a role in salvation.

Lyman Beecher[356] (1775-1863) was a prominent Christian minister who also fathered a large family that became famous ministers, authors, speakers, and educators. Beecher was a student of Timothy

Dwight at Yale Divinity School. In early 1835, Reverend Beecher had stated "the Millennium would commence in America."[357] He believed, along with many others, that this date would mark the beginning of the seventh and final millennium of world history.

Beecher preached that until the second advent of Christ's return, much had to occur: the fall of Satan's kingdoms (referring to the papacy and the Ottoman-Turkish Empire), the conversion of the Jews, and the spread of true Christianity "through the vast regions of the earth."[358]

Lyman Beecher [359]

About 1825, Charles Finney then emerged as the leader of the campaign for awakening America in this movement of *Great Awakening*. Demands were widespread in calling for his preaching in the major cities of the Eastern seaboard. Charles Finney rejected the traditional Puritan, or Calvinist, theology; a dogma where only a few were chosen by God for salvation.[360] Finney believed that revival was not something sent down by God, but that it could be brought about if the right means were used. He preached that man was free to choose his spiritual destiny and he pressed his audience to make an immediate decision. Having studied to be a lawyer, he was skilled in turning the legal logic that he had developed along with his courtroom skills acquired, to the use of the pulpit.

Reverend Finney was the first preacher to have an "invitation," which called for the people to come forward to make a public witness of their conversion.[361] He also instituted a number of "new measures" which later evangelists would continue. These included the inquiry room for counseling seekers, the anxious or mourners' bench for those responding to the public invitation to Christ, preaching for an immediate decision, emotional prayers which addressed God in a very familiar, informal language, organized choirs and music, advertising and advanced preparation for the revival meeting.[362]

Finney offered new hope to the masses by declaring that one could become saved through a "free will" acceptance of God's grace. After acceptance would come a living faith experience of the outpouring of God's love and a change of heart and mind. The *Second Great Awakening* brought a sense of salvation being available to all peoples, not just a chosen few. Finney believed the Gospel not only brought individuals to salvation but the effect of the conversion of the individual was also a means of cleaning-up society.[363]

Charles Finney and those that followed in his work sought to make America a Christian nation. Finney was a strong abolitionist (in favor of abolishing slavery) and encouraged Christians to become involved in the antislavery movement. Charles Finney declared:

Charles Finney [364]

"The church must take right ground in regards to politics…The time has come for Christians to vote for honest men, and take consistent ground in politics or the Lord will curse them.

God cannot sustain this free and blessed country, which we love and pray for, unless the Church will take right ground. Politics are a part of a religion in such a country as this, and Christians must do their duty to their country as a part of their duty to God…

God will bless or curse this nation according to the course Christians take in politics."[365] [emphasis added]

Christians became the leaders in many other social concerns such as education, prison reform, temperance (abstinence from alcohol), Sabbath observance, and women's rights. The large numbers of Christian workers for social reform became so influential they and the organizations they founded became known as the "Benevolent Empire." The *Second Great Awakening* had a greater effect on society than any other revival in America. The length of time the *Second Great Awakening* had endured to that point was remarkable. For over a quarter-century it had blessed America, including the sending of missionaries abroad, the founding of schools and colleges, and the conversion of tens of thousands.[366]

Finney shared the widespread hope and expectation that the Millennium was just around the corner.[367] The revivals he led enrolled millions of new members in existing evangelical denominations and also led to the formation of new denominations. Many converts believed that the *Awakening* was an indication of a new millennial age. The *Second Great Awakening* also stimulated the establishment of many reform movements designed to remedy the evils of society before the anticipated Second Coming of Jesus Christ.[368]

Finney was greatly encouraged at the number of conversions that took place in another great revival just before the outbreak of the Civil War, that some refer to as the *Third Great Awakening*. He reported that as many as 50,000 conversions had occurred in a single week, but added on a more somber note that the revival lost steam as it headed South.[369] During the years between the presidential inaugurations of Thomas Jefferson and Abraham Lincoln, historians view "evangelicalism emerging as a kind of national church or national religion." The leaders and average members of the "evangelical empire" of the 19th century were American patriots who subscribed to the views of the Founding Fathers that religion was a "necessary spring" for a republican form of government. They believed, as a preacher in 1826 proclaimed, that there was "an association between Religion and Patriotism." They esteemed that converting their fellow citizens to Christianity was an act that simultaneously saved souls and saved the Republic.

The *American Home Missionary Society* assured its supporters in 1826 that "we are doing the work of patriotism no less than Christianity." With the disappearance of efforts by government to create morality in the body politic, signified by the termination in 1833 of Massachusetts's tax support for churches, evangelical, benevolent societies assumed that role, bringing about what today might be called the privatization of the responsibility for forming a virtuous citizenry.[370] In scope and sequence of the story of the American Republic, unique in the entire world because of her covenant with Almighty God and with each other, the presence of Divine Providence is unmistakable.

As we look back to gain an understanding and in seeking answers, in the Light of Truth in the whole story as revealed, we must put the pieces of the history together in proper perspective. In reflection, the *Great Governor of the universe* is a God of justice. His government requires judgment for broken law and in a timeframe ruled according to His perfect will, which is inclusive of His prophetic Word. His Law was violated by a nation of His people who had broken covenant in the mistreatment of mankind. The national sins that our ancestors were not successful in preventing, and by the sin of omission[371] which resulted in America's inability to obey the Creator's command in the Dominion Mandate that ALL men are created equal[372] and that His people should be a blessing to ALL of the families of the earth,[373] therefore result in the national curses of disobedience and judgment by a just God. In the eyes of God, the North was equally responsible for the perpetuation of slavery, and for that reason a blood atonement of equal measure would be required; hence a house divided and civil war.[374] And so again, just like the Old Testament covenanted people of God—the Israelites—experienced "a house divided" into two regional Sections—the *Northern House of Israel* and the *Southern House of Judah*,[375] history repeats itself.

Eventually, because of the sin of idolatry, both Old Testament houses were taken captive by foreigners and enslaved for a period of judgment time.[376] So, too, the American people and their posterity—those who had covenanted with the Creator and viewed themselves as the New Covenant "New Israel," were indeed bound for similar judgment.

No less important is the matter pertaining to the abuse and egregious acts of this nation toward the native Indians, the "First Americans" of this Promised Land. The implementation of God's Plan requires our adhering to Christ's two Great Commandments: to love God with all our heart, mind, soul, and being, and to love our neighbors as ourselves.[377] If we would do that, He would bless our endeavors. That was His covenant made with the American people and that was understood by the Pilgrims, Puritans, and for most of the Founding Fathers.

The double mindedness[378] of this nation, those that kept covenant with the *Great Governor of the Universe* and those corrupted by lusting after mammon[379] in the form of gold, money and all that it can purchase—or steal—indeed brought instability.

The Divine oracle of the *Declaration of Independence* was considered to be inspired by Heaven and declared to the world that the Creator intended for all men to be equal. Instead of obeying the mandate to be a blessing to all the families of the earth, the native inhabitants of this land, the Indians, "First Americans" were driven from their land in ways that would shock the conscience in those that have one.

Instead of using "the sword of the Spirit" and emanating the love of Christ to win their souls to the Kingdom of God, a carnal and physical sword had been used to a level of malice and oppression in an American holocaust.

A man's word is to be his bond; a nation's treaties are to be kept in honor. Instead, over 400 treaties with the native people were violated and broken by United States government.[380] The native Indians "First Americans" were violated, annihilated, and disrespected at the same time their land and resources were stolen from them. The judgment on America was in effect magnified in the prescribed curses of disobedience within the great time table of the prophetic Word of God.

We are not to be discouraged or without hope, as God is a good God[381] and disciplines those He loves.[382] Almighty God, as a loving and forgiving Father teaches, trains, and disciplines His children until they come into full agreement with Him. This is how the Spirit of God works in His people to fulfill God's vow, causing us to "walk in His ways" in compliance with His laws, statutes, and judgments.[383]

We are not to forget that there is a Devil, the "god of this Age (Greek = *aeon*),"[384] whose goal is to set himself above the Creator in the abomination of desolation,[385] working through the craft[386] of deception and a reprobate people[387] to gain the prize of humanity who will worship him. Through "cunning, ambitious and unprincipled men" those who do not fear Almighty God,[388] along with their posterity, intoxicated with lust for money and power, vowed in oath to their god, the Jesuit Superior General "Black Pope" and camouflaged, front-man white-robed Pope.

Their plan was crafted[389] in deception and illusion in the building of their secret Babylonian kingdom, "Mystery Babylon."[390] If it were possible, even the very elect would be deceived.[391]

The love of money and power and the lust created by it presents two evil tools of the Devil that oppose the sacred, inherent un-a-lien-able rights bestowed by the Creator. The lust then enticing self-serving men, blinded by the "god of this age,"[392] becoming vain in their imaginations, their foolish hearts darkened, having turned the truth of God unto a lie, who worship and serve the creature, forsaking the Creator, given to a reprobate mind, are damned.[393]

Romans 1:18-32 ~

> *For the wrath of God is revealed from heaven against all ungodliness and unrighteousness of men, who hold the truth in unrighteousness; Because that which may be known of God is manifest in them; for God hath shewed it unto them. For the invisible things of him from the creation of the world are clearly seen, being understood by the things that are made, even his eternal power and Godhead; so that they are without excuse: Because that, when they knew God, they glorified him not as God, neither were thankful; but became vain in their imaginations, and their foolish heart was darkened. Professing themselves to be wise, they became fools, And changed the glory of the uncorruptible God into an image made like to corruptible man, and to birds, and fourfooted beasts,*

and creeping things.   Wherefore God also gave them up to uncleanness through the lusts of their own hearts, to dishonour their own bodies between themselves: Who changed the truth of God into a lie, and worshipped and served the creature more than the Creator, who is blessed forever. Amen.

For this cause God gave them up unto vile affections: for even their women did change the natural use into that which is against nature: And likewise also the men, leaving the natural use of the woman, burned in their lust one toward another; men with men working that which is unseemly, and receiving in themselves that recompence of their error which was meet.   And even as they did not like to retain God in their knowledge, God gave them over to a reprobate mind, to do those things which are not convenient; Being filled with all unrighteousness, fornication, wickedness, covetousness, maliciousness; full of envy, murder, debate, deceit, malignity; whisperers, backbiters, haters of God, despiteful, proud, boasters, inventors of evil things, disobedient to parents, Without understanding, covenantbreakers, without natural affection, implacable, unmerciful: Who knowing the judgment of God, that they which commit such things are worthy of death, not only do the same, but have pleasure in them that do them.”[394] [emphasis added]

As there is nothing new under the sun,[395] just as Balaak sought Balaam to curse the Old Testament chosen people of God though not permitted by God to curse His beloved people, instead Balaam counseled Balaak a means to cause God's people to enter into sin and idolatry and bring destruction on themselves.[396] **The New Testament people of God in a nation with a Divine calling and destiny** have been infiltrated by a "Judas Goat,"[397] those who follow what Jesus refers to as recorded in the book of Revelation, the "doctrine of Balaam"[398] and have enticed God's people into national sin.

The consequence resulting from the curses of disobedience include enslavement by these fierce men who do not fear Almighty God.[399] The American people, who were to be a citadel of Light, "a city upon a hill," to the rest of the world are instead blinded in sin, largely unaware, deceived, ensnared, and entered into idolatry—worshipping other gods and bringing a curse upon themselves and their posterity, which has increased through the generations.[400]

Each generation has increasingly been as the proverbial frog in the pot of heated water by the Great Deceiver who has enticed the American people to forget their covenant with the Creator God, forfeiting their blessings and their identity.   Each generation that has gone forward through time has endured loss of their God-given liberties in exchange for government-granted privileges that have more deeply ensnared the People.

Unbeknownst to the People, an (**un**)Holy Alliance of *Black Nobility* under vow to the Vatican's Jesuit General brought among them a foreign international aristocracy of elite "Money Changers" through which they operate as the oligarch to the United States Congressional "board of directors" with a well thought-out plan to control and enslave this nation of people whose Light once burned bright throughout the world as a "city upon a hill."

Unbeknownst to the American people are the details of Rome and her Jesuits, Satan's military, who have used them toward their ultimate goal of one-world government under their "infallible" Pope,[401] **ruling from Solomon's rebuilt Temple in Jerusalem**.

Slowly and carefully have the sons of Satan[402] perverted all that was good until by deceit and without the Peoples' knowledge, a **counterfeit document** with an identical name replaced the sacred *Constitution* with the constitution of a municipal Corporation, the all-capital-letter THE UNITED STATES OF AMERICA, INC., (Incorp Delaware Stock Co.).[403] Masquerading as the original government of the

American Republic, their *Progressive*, relentless agenda throughout the generations has wrought slavery as a means of conquest in order to steal the Birthright, Promised Land, and Dominion from God's covenanted people. As we are now in the final scene of this Great Drama right at the close of this Millennial Age (Greek = *aeon*), awaiting the soon return of the King of kings, "No king but King Jesus,"[404] there is a race and a struggle for Americans to **awaken**, realize their national identity as a people chosen by God, once again join together by His Holy Spirit in the common cause of advancing His Kingdom, function as a covenanted nation, with a righteous government "Of the People, By the People, For the People," one nation under God.

Our Founding Fathers understood the Holy Scriptures—they learned to read from them and the Bible was their main text book throughout life.[405] They knew that this covenanted nation with Almighty God was prophesied in the Word of God and their posterity would carry the torch of Liberty through the Latter Days.[406] They knew they were part of the establishing of the Kingdom that the God of heaven had set-up, would never be destroyed, would see the destruction of the enemies of God, and would stand forever.[407]

> *And in the [latter end-time] days of these kings, shall the God of heaven set up a kingdom, which shall never be destroyed: and this kingdom shall not be given to another people, but it shall break, and destroy all these kingdoms, and it shall stand forever. ~ Daniel 2:44* [emphasis added]

And so it is time. As spiritual things are veiled,[408] Mystery Babylon[409] has been a mystery, or hidden, secret. The veil is now pulled away, night is now day. Children of the Light, it is time to arise and shine.[410]

Keep off! The Monroe Doctrine must be respected [411]

Published in 1896, this lithograph depicts Uncle Sam, as armed soldier, standing between European powers (Britain, France, Germany, Spain, and Portugal) and Nicaragua and Venezuela.

Chapter Six

The Divine Right enemies of our Popular Government

In effort to understand that which has been veiled[412] and hidden, we continue forward in the unfolding Drama. As the popular catchphrase, "Just follow the money," suggests a money trail or corruption scheme within high office (certainly consider it political), the trail will reveal the true nature and source of things as America has always been lustfully pursued by those with "titles of nobility."

The Black Nobility secret societies, "the kings of the earth"[413] that include International Bankers, continue on in (**un**)Holy Alliance with the Jesuit's plot to create a totalitarian One-World government.[414] As "the kings of the earth take counsel together and prostitute themselves in fornication to a point of intoxication at their thought and plans, dominion of the *Old World* was not enough; they wanted the *New World,* too.

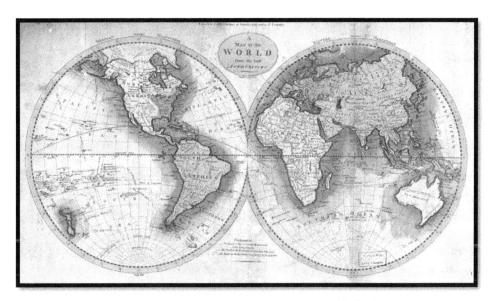

Map of the World from the best Authorities, published in 1795 [415]
Map consists of 2 hemispheres: the *Western New World* and the *Eastern Old World*
Engraved for Carey's Edition of Gunther's new System of Geography; Mathew Carey (1760-1839)

The Founding Fathers and following generations of Americans in covenant with the *Great Governor of the universe* have not known a time where the wealthy elite Jesuit-controlled Freemason Illuminati Rothschild[416] banking family and their privately-owned *Bank of England,* along with their cohorts, have covetously and aggressively sought to institute a central bank in the United States in order to become the oligarchy of controlling power.

The Rothschild's are a renowned International Banking family that claims to be Jewish.[417] In considering the depth of controversies—as well as myths and disinformation—related to the topics of bloodline, religion, and politics, there also exists confusion in presumption that those of Jewish descent— as well as those who have converted to Judaism, the Jewish religion—are related to political Zionism,[418] and then conclude that the entire Jewish people are responsible for the actions of Zionism and its globalist agenda to rule the earth and all of mankind from Jerusalem and surrounding Holy Lands. Clearly the two, Judaism and Zionism, are distinct and separate.[419]

For the sake of important clarification, one is religion and the other is political. Where it becomes confusing is where the two, religion and politics, can unite with a zealous passion in achieving their own goal.[420] "World Zionists" are not the Jewish people, descendants of the Tribe of Judah, one of the children of (Old Testament) Jacob/Israel. The International Bankers, (the Rothschild's, et al) are partnered with the Jesuits in their political Zionist global agenda to achieve a one-world government, the "New World Order."[421]

It boils down to the fact that the Jesuits have infiltrated all aspects of society — religious, government, science and all institutions of higher learning, including seminaries. In summary, there does exist an evil people who fast track in their agenda toward a Luciferian *New World Order* while awaiting entrance of their (false) Christ, the Son of Perdition.[422]

Having "painted the landscape," let it be clear that whatever their religion, the political creed of the Rothschild's includes Zionism. They also bear the title, "Guardians of the Vatican Treasury." The Vatican Treasury holds the imperial wealth of Rome. This guardianship[423] appointment of the House of Rothschild has given the papacy absolute financial privacy and secrecy, as who would ever consider searching a family of orthodox Jews for the key to the wealth of the Roman Catholic Church.[424]

The *Hazard Circular* was a private letter (c1862) by European "creditors" of the United States sent to every bank in New York and New England. In 1865, an article pertaining to Lincoln's Greenbacks appeared in the Rothschild-affiliated newspaper, *Times of London*, including a quote by banking spokesman Lord Goschen as stated in the *Hazard Circular*:

> "If that mischievous <u>financial policy which had its origin in the North American Republic</u> [i.e. constitutionally directed and authorized substance-backed no-debt money] should become indurated [established] down to a fixture, <u>then that government will furnish its own money without cost. It will pay off debts and be without a debt [to the dishonest International Bankers]</u>. It will become <u>prosperous beyond precedent</u> in the history of the civilized governments of the world. The brains and wealth of all countries will go to North America. <u>That government must be destroyed or it will destroy every monarchy on the globe</u>."[425] [emphasis added]

Nicholas Biddle, 1830s [426]

The Rothschild's and their elite comrades sent agents to destroy the American Republic because it was becoming "prosperous beyond precedent." It had the blessing of Almighty God and potential to "destroy every [Jesuit-controlled] monarch [kings of the earth] on the globe." The first documentable evidence of Rothschild involvement in the financial affairs of the United States came in the late 1820s and early 1830s when, through their agent Nicholas Biddle, fought to defeat President Andrew Jackson's move to curtail the International Bankers.

Andrew Jackson (1767-1845) was elected to the Presidency in 1828. He was well known and respected for his bravery and military skill in defeating the British in the *War of 1812*. He fought many open combat battles, but now faced an entirely different kind of enemy. This enemy was surreal in that it presented to be American just like him, purported to be patriotic toward America just like him, and held high positions of responsibility just like him.

Andrew Jackson [427]

The Jesuits were duty-bound to destroy America as determined by the sinister Councils at Vienna, Verona, and Chieri, and it was during the Presidency of Andrew Jackson that they became aggressive in sedition, full force. These Jesuits infiltrated among the American people and appeared to be one of the American people. In fact, they were American citizens, but their loyalty and purpose was to the Pope of Rome. These people were traitors and a serious threat to the continued existence of America.[428]

A committee of bankers was sent to the White House to plead with President Jackson to not take the charter from the Bank of the United States and to restore its governmental deposits. President Jackson's response:

"Gentlemen! I too have been a close observer of the doings of the Bank of the United States. I have had men watching you for a long time, and am convinced that you have used the funds of the bank to speculate in the breadstuffs of the country. When you won, you divided the profits amongst you, and when you lost, you charged it to the bank. You tell me that if I take the deposits from the bank and annul its charter I shall ruin ten thousand families. That may be true, gentlemen, but that is your sin! Should I let you go on, you will ruin fifty thousand families, and that would be my sin! You are a den of vipers and thieves. I have determined to rout you out, and by the Eternal, (bringing his fist down on the table) I will rout you out!" [429]

The Rothschild's lost in their first attempt at maintaining control of the nation's money system when in 1832, President Jackson vetoed the legislation to renew the charter of the "Bank of the United States," a central bank controlled by the International Bankers also known as "kings of the earth." In 1836 the bank went out of business.[430]

John C. Calhoun, 1834 [431]

Jackson's Vice-President was John C. Calhoun of South Carolina. (Jackson had not selected Calhoun for a Vice Presidential "running mate" as done today. Constitutionally, and at that time, an election was run by Electoral College with the most votes electing a President and the second most votes electing a Vice President.) Calhoun fully realized that the love of liberty was very strong in the hearts of the American people. He knew that the institution of slavery was rapidly being constrained because most of the territories on the North American continent purchased from Spain and France were made free, or non-slave holding.

59

Without a continual expansion of slavery, it would eventually be abolished. The slave issue was a means to the Jesuit agenda.

In order to derail the existing anti-slavery movement in America, Calhoun began a newspaper in Washington, the *United States Telegraph*[432] (1826), in which he began to advocate the idea called "States Rights." <u>The *Doctrine of States Rights* would inevitably lead to the great peril of the United States.</u> It suggested that a state had an inherent right to do whatever it wanted. <u>Under the principles of *States Rights*, a State could secede from the Union if it so desired and eventually, the Union of States would cease to exist.</u>[433] [434] Calhoun was bold and brazen in pronouncing that there did not exist a consolidated "perpetual" Union but rather a voluntary confederation of States.[435]

The secret society, *Knights of the Golden Circle* or "KGC," had its beginnings in the organizing of *Southern Rights Clubs* in various southern cities in the mid-1830s. These clubs were inspired by the

philosophies of John C. Calhoun (1782–1850).[436] Calhoun had a distinguished political career serving as a congressman from his home State of South Carolina, as well as a State legislator, Vice President under the administrations of both John Quincy Adams and Andrew Jackson, and as a U. S. Senator.

In addition to the *Southern Rights Clubs*, which advocated the re-establishment of the African slave-trade, some of the inspiration for the *Knights* may have come from a little-known secret organization called the *Order of the Lone Star*, founded in 1834, which helped orchestrate the successful Texas Revolution resulting in Texas independence from Mexico in 1836. Secret societies have been alive and well throughout our nation's history.

Book cover: *An authentic exposition of the K.G.C. Knights of the Golden Circle: Or A history of secession from 1834 to 1861 By a Member of the Order* (1861) [437]

William Wilberforce, 1794 [438]

An interesting item and certainly worthy of strong consideration in overview is that the legislative power of Great Britain, known as Parliament, abolished the Slave Trade in Great Britain in 1807 and then the institution of slavery in 1833 by the dedicated work of Parliament member, William Wilberforce,[439] who spent his life in the cause of abolition.

Certainly, the Cotton Lords of the American South in relationship with their "cousins," the Banking Lords of Great Britain, knew that the institution of slavery was soon to expire in America, as well. With the British Banking Lords losing their central banking charter in 1832 (and like hand-in-glove, the Jesuit's losing their ruling control over these "kings of the earth") by the veto of renewal by then President Andrew Jackson, there was a new plan in the dark works to feed their lust for money while at the same time working toward the ultimate goal of enslaving mankind in pursuit of satisfying their lust for power.

John C. Calhoun manipulated the already festering issue of import tariff to a point of embitterment while he also substantiated the reason <u>for the Southern States to desire to secede from the Union.</u>

John Smith Dye, *The Adder's Den; or Secrets of the Great Conspiracy to Overthrow Liberty in America (1864):*

"The South, being an agricultural region, was easily convinced that a high tariff on foreign imports was injurious to them. He [John C. Calhoun] next undertook to explain to the South that these high duties were placed on specific articles, and was done, as special favor, to protect local interests. Thus he said to the people of the South, You are being taxed to support Northern manufacturers. And it was on this popular issue he planted his nullification flag, and gathered around it his friends and dupes. …This new bastard democracy meant the right to destroy, peaceably or by force (when ready), the [American Republic] Federal Union."[440] [emphasis added]

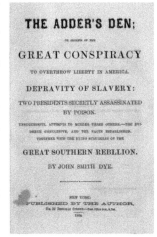

The Adder's Den; or Secrets of the Great Conspiracy to Overthrow Liberty in America
Title page, (1864) by John Smith Dye [441]

In April, 1832, not long after Calhoun started publishing his newspaper, a birthday celebration was held in honor of the memory of Thomas Jefferson who died six years earlier on July 4, 1826. Calhoun and the other *States Rights* party members sought to entrap Jackson in a pro-*States Rights* public endorsement. Some of the guests gave toasts which sought to establish a connection between a *States Rights* view of government and nullification. When it was Jackson's turn to give a toast, he rose and magnificently challenged those present, "Our Federal Union. It must be preserved."[442]

Jackson was "wise as a serpent and meek as a dove,"[443] in his toast that had humiliated Calhoun in public. Jackson stood out as a "stud" in the herd as he stood his ground of his challengers unafraid no matter who they were or what position they might hold. Calhoun then stood up and declared,

"The Union next to our liberties the most dear. May we all remember that it can only be preserved by respecting the rights of the States, and distributing equally the benefits and burdens of the Union."[444]

Calhoun placed the Union second to the sanctity of Liberty. The Union formed because of the *Declaration of Independence* and together with the *Constitution*, are what established Liberty. If the Union were dissolved, the States would be in jeopardy of controversial relations just as the European countries had fought throughout history. The ramification was unthinkable—except to Calhoun and the Jesuits in their objective of destroying America. The nullification crisis that would follow served as the last straw.

Calhoun used the issue of the tariff as propaganda to create friction and strife between the North and the South. Congress could have easily changed the tariff, and in fact was offered as serious gesture in effort to preserve the Union. Obviously the tariff not the real reason for secession. Many spoke out against Calhoun's dishonest and devious efforts.

Daniel Webster (1782-1852), was considered one of the greatest orators in American history, served as a U.S. Representative, a U.S. Senator, and as the Secretary of State for three different Presidents.[445] Webster said:

"Sir, the world will scarcely believe that this whole controversy, and all the desperate means which its support requires, has no other foundation than a difference of opinion between a majority of the people of South Carolina on the one side, and a vast majority of the people of the United States on the other. The world will not credit the fact. We who hear and see it can ourselves hardly yet believe it."[446]

Daniel Webster, 1835 [447]

Webster clearly understood that the real issue went far deeper than a tariff. Calhoun was the Jesuit plant being used to divide America. The scripture is clear in giving account of the strategized result of what this enemy of the Republic sought:

"...if a house be divided against itself, that house cannot stand."[448]

John Quincy Adams in the House of Representatives declared:

"In opposition to the compromise of Mr. Clay, no victim is necessary, and yet you propose to bind us hand and foot, to pour out our blood upon the altar, to appease the unnatural discontent of the South — <u>a discontent having deeper root than the Tariff, and will continue when that is forgotten.</u>"[449]

Adams was keen in discernment as he was accurate in his observation. The tariff issue died, but the agitation and sense of division continued to grow.

Charles Chinquy, 1860s [450]

Charles Chiniquy (1809-1899), a former Catholic priest had stated:

"Rome saw at once that the very existence of the United States was a formal menace to her own life. ...From the very beginning she perfidiously [deliberately] sowed the germs of division and hatred between the two great sections of this country and she felt an unspeakable joy when she saw that she had succeeded in dividing its South from the North on the burning question of slavery. She looked upon that division as her golden opportunity. To crush one party by the other, and reign over the bloody ruins of both, has invariably been her policy. She hoped that the hour of her supreme triumph over this continent was come."[451] [emphasis added]

Calhoun was not a loyal American. He was a loyal Jesuit who vowed to advance the Pope's agenda of world domination in seeking Temporal Powers—which included destroying the American Republic. An extract from a sermon by Roman Catholic priest and editor, D. S. Phelan of St. Louis, Missouri, and printed in his paper, the *Western Watchman, June 27, 1912*:

"Why, if the Government of the United States were at war with the church, we would say tomorrow, To Hell with the Government of the United States; and if the church and all the governments of the world were at war, we would say: -- To Hell with all the governments of the world. Why is it, that in this country, where we have only seven per cent of the population, the Catholic Church is so much feared: She is loved by all her children and feared by everybody. <u>Why is it the Pope has such tremendous power?</u> <u>Why the Pope is the ruler of the World.</u> <u>All the emperors, all the kings, all the princes, all the presidents of the world are as these altar boys of mine</u>..."[452]

John C. Calhoun would fit in the category of the papal altar boys, serving his master in following orders.

Papal Tiara in silver with gems and pearls [453]
in the Treasury of the Basilica of St. Peter at the Vatican

The papal tiara is a crown that was worn by popes of the Roman Catholic Church from as early as the 8th century to the mid-20th. It was last used by Pope Paul VI in 1963 and only at the beginning of his reign. From 1143 to 1963, the papal tiara was placed on the pope's head during a **papal coronation**.

The Triregnum is the Papal Tiara formed by three crowns, symbolizes the triple power of the Pope: **father of kings, governor of the world**, and **Vicar of Christ**.[454] A representation of the triregnum combined with two crossed keys (spiritual/religion and temporal/civil) of Saint Peter continues to be used as a symbol of the papacy and appears on papal documents, buildings, and insignia.[455]

Portrait of Andrew Jackson[456]

Andrew Jackson, in his message to Congress in 1832 stated this:

"The right of the people of a single State to absolve [pardon] themselves at will, and without the consent of the other states, from their most solemn obligations, and hazard the liberties and happiness of millions comprising this nation, cannot be acknowledged. Such authority is believed to be wholly repugnant [averse or contrary], both to the principles upon which the General Government is constituted, and the objects which it is expressly formed to obtain." [457] [emphasis added]

Jackson knew that Calhoun was a Jesuit on a mission to destroy the United States and its constitutional liberties.[458] Jackson had the tenacity and courage to confront and stop the conspiracy even in light of the fact that his life would be endangered... and it was.

Portrait of John C. Calhoun, c1845 [459]

Back home in South Carolina, Calhoun was busy in maturing his plan of attack by seeking to convince the people of the South that it was in their best interest to secede from the Union as they were being taken advantage of by the North through taxation. Though the tariff issue was negated by President Jackson, the seed of nullification (refusal of a U.S. State to aid in enforcement of federal laws within its limits on constitutional grounds) was planted by Calhoun.

The throne of the Slave Power which was located in South Carolina, and the slaveholders throughout the South, who loved slavery better than they did the Union, were his friends that backed Calhoun on the issue. Included in this mix were his duped friends of the Democrats of the free States that had become alarmed for the safety of their party, had made a close alliance and agreed to drop the good-ole democratic doctrine of the rights of man founded in human nature and written in our nation's birth certificate, the *Declaration of Independence.*

All such precious rights were tossed aside while greed and Luciferian agenda seized the great instrument of the Slave Power, *States Rights.* This new bastard democracy meant the right to destroy, whether peaceably or by force, the Federal Union.[460]

Title page of *The Report, Ordinance, and Addresses of the Convention of the People of South Carolina: Adopted, November 24, 1832* [461]

To push Hell's plan forward, a Convention was held on November 24, 1832 at Columbia, South Carolina. This was the first open renouncement that had been made in any State against the Federal Government. Providence is not without warning. About a month earlier, with treason in his heart and treachery in his soul, all alone Mr. Calhoun sat down at his table and penned a document that would be instrumental in dividing the Union of the States.[462] Calhoun had a significant vision, or a dream, as he would sometimes call it, which explains the origin of the black spot on the back of his hand.[463]

The following story of John C. Calhoun's dream of General George Washington comes from the book, *The Civil War in Song and Story* published in 1865, by Frank Moore. It is a unique collection of almost 550 pages with two columns in small type of Civil War stories and songs collected from newspapers and personal accounts by Moore who was editor of the "The Rebellion Record" and "Diary of the American Revolution." The title of the story in relation to John C. Calhoun is called *The Spotted Hand, An anecdote of John C. Calhoun:*

One morning, at the breakfast table, when I, an unobserved spectator, happened to be present, Calhoun was observed to gaze frequently at his right hand, and brush it with his left in a hurried and nervous manner. He did this so often that it excited attention. At length one of the persons comprising the breakfast party – his name I, think, is [Robert] Toombs, and he is a member of Congress from Georgian – took upon himself to ask the occasion of Mr. Calhoun's disquietude.

"Does your hand pain you?" he asked Mr. Calhoun. To this Mr. Calhoun replied, in rather a hurried manner, -- "Pshaw! It is nothing but a dream I had last night, and which makes me see perpetually a large black spot, like an ink blotch, upon the back of my right hand; an optical illusion, I suppose."

Of course these words excited the curiosity of the company, but no one ventured to beg the details of this singular dream until Toombs asked quietly, -- "What was your dream like? I am not very superstition about dreams; but sometimes they have a great deal of truth in them."

"But this was such a peculiarly absurd dream," said Mr. Calhoun, again brushing the back of his right hand; "however, if it does not intrude too much on the time of our friends, I will relate it to you." Of course the company were profuse in their expressions of anxiety to know all about the dream and Mr. Calhoun related it.

John C. Calhoun[464]

"At a late hour last night, as I was sitting in my room writing, engaged in writing, I was astonished by the entrance of a visitor, who, without a word, took a seat opposite me at my table. This surprised me, as I had given particular orders to the servant that I should on no account be disturbed. The manner in which the intruder entered, so perfectly self-possessed, taking his seat opposite me without a word, as though my room and all within it belonged to him, excited in me as much surprise as indignation. As I raised my head to look into his features, over the top of my shaded lamp, I discovered that he was wrapped in a thin cloak which effectively concealed his face and features from my view; and as I raised by head, he spoke –

"What are you writing, senator from South Carolina?" "I did not think of his impertinence at first, but answered him voluntarily," – "I am writing a plan for the dissolution of the American Union." (You know, gentlemen, that I am expected to produce a plan in the event of certain contingencies.) To this the intruder replied, in the coolest manner possible, -- "Senator from South Carolina, will you allow me to look at your hand, your right hand?"

"He rose, the cloak fell and I beheld his face. Gentleman, the sight of that face struck me like a thunderclap. It was the face of a dead man whom extraordinary events had called back to life. The features were those of Gen. George Washington. He was dressed in the Revolutionary costume, such as you see on the Patent Office."

Here Mr. Calhoun paused, apparently agitated. His agitation, I need not tell you, was shared by the company. Toombs at length broke the embarrassing pause. "Well, what was the issue of this scene?" Mr. Calhoun resumed:--

"The intruder, as I have said, rose and asked to look at my right hand. As though I had not the power to refuse, I extended it. The truth is, I felt a strange thrill pervade me at his touch; he grasped it, and held it near the light, thus affording full time to examine every feature. It was the face of Washington. After holding my hand for a moment, he looked at me steadily, and said in a quiet way," – "And with this right hand, senator from South Carolina, you would sign your name to a paper declaring the Union dissolved?

"I answered in the affirmative." "'Yes,' I said, if certain contingency arises, I will sign my name to the Declaration of Dissolution." "But at that moment a black blotch appeared on the back of my hand, which I seem to see now." "'What is that?' said I, alarmed, I know not why, at the blotch on my hand." "That," said he, dropping my hand, "is the mark by which Benedict Arnold is known in the next world."

"He said no more gentlemen, but drew from beneath his cloak an object which he laid upon the table – laid upon the very paper on which I was writing. This object, gentlemen, was a skeleton." "'There' said he, 'there are the bones of Isaac Hayne, who was hung at Charleston by the British. He gave his life in order to establish the Union. When you put your name to the Declaration of Dissolution, why you may as well have the bones of Isaac Hayne before you – he was a South Carolinian, and so are you. But there is no blotch on his right hand.'

"With these words the intruder left the room. I started back from the contact with the dead man's bones, and – awoke. Overcome by labor, I had fallen asleep, and had been dreaming. Was it not a singular dream?" All the company answered in the affirmative, and Toombs muttered, "Singular, very singular," at the same time looking curiously at the back of his right hand, while Mr. Calhoun placed his head between his hands and seemed buried in thought."[465]

We continue with the story of "The Divine Right enemies of our Popular Government." Nicholas Biddle (1786-1844), another Jesuit agent, was a brilliant financier, having graduated from the University of Pennsylvania at the age of thirteen. He was a master of the science of money. By the time Jackson began his Presidency in 1828, Biddle was in full control of the Federal Government's central bank.

This was not the first time that a central bank had been established. Twice before, first under Robert Morris (1734-1806), and then under Alexander Hamilton (1755-1804), had a central bank been attempted, but both had failed because of fraudulent activities by the bankers who were in control. After the *War of 1812*, a central bank was attempted again, and it was in this third attempt that we find Mr. Biddle.[466]

Portrait of Robert Morris, c1785 [467]

Who was behind Nicholas Biddle and the attempt to have a central bank in the United States? G. Edward Griffin, is an American author, documentary film producer, political lecturer and writer, well known as a credible authority on the inner workings of the *Federal Reserve Banking System* and international banking. He is quoted in his best-selling book, *The Creature from Jekyll Island*, now in its 5th edition:

"The blunt reality is that the Rothschild banking dynasty in Europe was the dominant force, both financially and politically, in the formation of the Bank of the United States." [468]

G. Edward Griffin[469]

Derek Wilson, a British journalist who has traced the Rothschilds' rise from their roots as enterprising coin dealers to wealth and power throughout 19th-century Europe, states in his book, *Rothschild: The Wealth and Power of a Dynasty* (1988):

"Over the years since N.M. [Nathan Mayer Rothschild], the Manchester textile manufacturer, had bought cotton from the Southern states, The Rothschilds had developed heavy American commitments. Nathan… had made loans to various states of the Union, had been, for a time, the official European banker for the U.S. government and was a pledged supporter of the Bank of the United States." [470]

Gustavus Myers, 1909 [471]

Journalist and historian Gustavus Myers,[472] (1872-1942) in his book *History of the Great American Fortunes* (1911):

"The Rothschilds long had a powerful influence in dictating American financial laws. The law records show that they were the power in the old Bank of the United States."[473]

The Jesuits used Biddle and Rothschild to gain power through control in American banking because they could then **control the people and effectively re-write the *Constitution* according to papal law.**[474] Jackson courageously met every challenge in effort to stop them.

In retaliation to Jackson's vetoing the renewal of the bank charter and removing federal deposits from the Bank, then placing them into private, regional banks, Biddle vehemently shrank the nation's money supply. He accomplished it by refusing to make loans, which upset the economy and caused money to disappear, caused a high increase in unemployment, companies to become bankrupt because they could not pay their loans, and the nation to go into a panic depression.

Biddle actually believed that he could force Jackson to keep the central bank. He was so filled with pride and arrogance that he was audacious enough to publicly boast that he had caused the economic woes in America. Because of his appalling and foolish braggadocio, others stepped forward in support of Jackson and the central bank failed...

...that is until its re-establishment in 1913. It was re-established then by the same people, the Jesuits and those under their influence, for the same purpose of bringing America to her knees and planting the Temporal Power of the Pope in America.

The Jesuits' conspiracy to initiate and control a central bank in America was temporarily halted during Andrew Jackson's presidency. He had opposed Calhoun's *Doctrine of States Rights*, and had stopped Biddle's attempt to continue the central bank.

The dark powers that reside at Rome compel their militia by means of the Jesuit Oath which declares that it is commendable to murder someone who stands in their way. President Jackson had gained vile enemies in monetary scientists who seethed with hatred, both in America and internationally. On January 30, 1835, an assassination attempt was made against President Jackson. Heaven orchestrated a divine hedge of protection about him as miraculously, both pistols of the assailant misfired, and Jackson was unharmed.

Scene at the Capitol from
Shooting at the President!: The Remarkable Trial of Richard Lawrence,
for an Attempt to Assassinate the President of the United States [475]

It was the first such attempt to be made against the life of a President of the United States of America. The would-be assassin was Richard Lawrence who pled insanity and was found not guilty due to insanity. Lawrence later boasted to friends that he had been in touch with powerful people in Europe who had promised to protect him from punishment should he be caught.[476]

The Jesuit Order was absolute in their determination of taking over America. They infiltrated into government at the highest levels, and used their agents in controlling the American banking system. They would also murder whenever necessary to eliminate any opposition. Andrew Jackson was almost assassinated by a Jesuit plant, who bragged of powerful Europeans, (the Jesuits) that would set him free should he be caught. Other Presidents have incurred the fatal wrath of Rome, while a few escaped or survived certain death.

William Henry Harrison, 1841 [477]

In 1841, William Henry Harrison (Ohio), the son of Founding Father Benjamin Harrison, a signer of the *Declaration of Independence*, was elected by a large majority as the ninth President. His loyalty to the Union was without question, and it was not within the power of the "cunning, ambitious, unprincipled men" to defeat him. At 68-years old he was still strong and in very good health. There was no question that he could complete his four-year term in office.[478]

Strikingly, just thirty-five days after taking the oath of office, on April 4th President Harrison died. He was the first President to die while in office. Although most encyclopedia or reference material will state that he died of pneumonia due to exposure to inclement winter weather while delivering his inaugural address in Washington, D.C., his symptoms match those of arsenic poisoning.[479]

When Harrison entered office, the country was experiencing a brewing aggression between the North and South "sections" over the slave question which was steadily becoming more acute. Only the Jesuit-dominated and controlled government leaders were aware of the "rule or ruin" plan to cause division. The Southern people had no real knowledge of it; they were manipulated by their leaders into believing their lies.[480]

At the same time there was also contention over the annexation of Texas, and whether it would be admitted as a free State — or — as a market for slavery. An assassination attempt had been made on President Jackson just six years earlier. This juncture in time was just twenty years before the Civil War. The influence of the "enemy from within," the Jesuits, was creating tension and a burden upon America.

Statesmen knew about the resulting agenda of the Congresses at Vienna, Verona, and Chieri to destroy Popular Government wherever it was found, with the prime target being the United States Republic along with the destruction of every Protestant principle (absolute). They understood that the Pope's militia, the Jesuits, masqueraded as angels of light[481] and were ordered to carry out this mission. Andrew Jackson faced the ambush of these imperialistic conspirators via the political mine fields of John C. Calhoun and the financial science-craft of Nicholas Biddle.

William Henry Harrison also refused to go along with the Jesuits' goals for America. It was with his election that the "Big Stick" of intimidation was first raised when political intrigue had failed. In his inaugural address, which was a masterpiece, President Harrison clearly, definitely, and finally cut any ground for hope from under them, which these enemies to the Union of States might have had when he stated:

> "We admit of no government by divine right [kings of the earth], believing that so far as power is concerned, the beneficent Creator has made no distinction among men; that all are upon an equality, and that the only legitimate right to govern, is upon the expressed grant of power from the governed."[482] [emphasis added]

With these unmistakable words President Harrison made his position clear; he hurled defiance at the *Divine Right* enemies of our Popular Government. As "we wrestle not against flesh and blood, but against principalities, against powers, against the rulers of the darkness of this world, against spiritual wickedness in high places,"[483] hell moved the sons of Satan to sign President Harrison's death warrant.

Just one month and five days from that day, the honorable President lay as a corpse in the White House. He died from arsenic poisoning, administered by the tools of Rome. The Jesuit oath had been swiftly carried out.[484]

> "I do further promise and declare that I will, when opportunity presents, make and wage, relentless war, secretly or openly, against all heretics, Protestants and Liberals, as I am directed to do, to extirpate them and exterminate them from the face of the earth.... That when the same cannot be done openly, I will secretly use the poison cup regardless of the honor, rank, dignity or authority of the person or persons... whatsoever may be their condition in life, either public or private, as I at any time may be directed so to do by an agent of the Pope or Superior of the Brotherhood of the Holy Faith of the Society of Jesus." [485] [emphasis added]

President Harrison upheld his oath to the *Constitution of the United States,* as well as verbalized an affirmation of the *Declaration of Independence.* The American Republic stood contrary to the Temporal Power that the Pope and the Jesuits were hell-bent to obtain.

John Smith Dye, *The Adder's Den; or Secrets of the Great Conspiracy to Overthrow Liberty in America* (1864):

"General Harrison did not die of natural disease — no failure of health or strength existed — but something sudden and fatal. He did not die of Apoplexy; that is a disease. But <u>arsenic</u> would produce a sudden effect, and it would also be fatal from the commencement. <u>This is the chief weapon of the medical assassin.</u> Oxalic acid, prucic acid, or salts of strychnine, would be almost instant death, and would give but little advantage for escape to the murderer. Therefore his was not a case of acute poisoning, when death takes place almost instantaneously, but of chronic, where the patient dies slowly. He lived about six days after he received the drug."[486]
[emphasis added]

United States Senator Thomas Benton (1782-1858, Missouri) concurred:

"There was no failure of health or strength to indicate such an event, or to excite apprehension that he [President Harrison] would not go through his term with the same vigor with which he commenced it. His attack was sudden and evidently fatal from the commencement."[487] [emphasis added]

Thomas Hart Benton, 1861 [488]

As these plotters against the Union had used the topic of the annexation of Texas to try President Harrison, they used the invasion of Cuba as the test for President Zachary Taylor (1784-1850) who entered office in 1848. Their plans were to launch their nefarious scheme in the early part of his administration. But from the very beginning President Taylor snuffed out all hope of its fulfillment during his term.

If Zachary Taylor had invaded Cuba, the American Republic would engage with Catholic Austria, Catholic Spain, Catholic France and England, who were all waiting and ready to do battle with the *United States of America.* This young republic would not have had any advantage to battle against the united powers of Catholic Europe at that time. That is why the papacy pushed hard on Taylor to invade Cuba.[489]

Taylor committed another "crime" against Rome in that he spoke passionately about the preservation of the Union. The Jesuits were striving to divide the nation, and the President was resolved to keep it together. Jesuit agent, John C. Calhoun, visited the Department of State and requested the President refrain from mentioning the Union in his forthcoming message. Taylor held sound conviction before God concerning what the Founding Fathers had instituted in the principles of Liberty sustained from the Word of God, the Holy Bible[490] and was not influenced by Calhoun.

In his first message to Congress, he said:

"But attachment to the UNION of States should be fostered in every American heart. For more than half a century, during which kingdoms and empires have fallen, this Union has stood unshaken. … In my judgment <u>its dissolution would be the greatest of calamities, and to avert that should be the steady aim of every American.</u> Upon its preservation must depend our own happiness and that of generations to come. Whatever dangers may threaten it, I shall stand by it and maintain it in its integrity to the full extent of the obligations imposed, and power conferred on me by the Constitution." [491] [emphasis added]

Zachary Taylor, 1848 [492]

There was no hedging-in or restricting Taylor; the pro-slavery leaders had nothing to count on in him, therefore, they decided on his assassination. While these Jesuit-controlled politicians were not influential enough to name the would-be President, they were cunning enough to be able to control the nomination of the Vice President. They always chose a "yes" man who was in full sympathy with their plans. They strategized the Vice Presidency as the next best thing.

It had become practically a "trade" between the two groups of politicians. John Tyler (1790-1862), a staunch pro-slavery man, strong for the things his party wanted, was selected as Vice President for Taylor. The President, knowing the character of this running mate, had as little to do with him as possible.

The arch-plotters, fearing that suspicion might be aroused by the death of the President early in his administration, as in the case of President Harrison, "permitted" him to serve sixteen months, when on the *Fourth of July*, arsenic was administered to him during a celebration in Washington at which he was invited to deliver the address. He went in perfect health in the morning, was taken ill around five o'clock, and died five days later on July 9th. He was sick the same number of days and with precisely the same symptoms as was his predecessor, President Harrison.

John Tyler, tenth President of the United States[493]

U.S. Senator Thomas Benton (Missouri), stated in his book (1858, c1854) *Thirty Years' View: A History of the Working of the American Government 1820 to 1850:*

"He sat out all the speeches and omitted no attention which he believed the decorum of his station required. The violent attack began soon after his return to the Presidential mansion."[494]

Vice President John Tyler was immediately sworn-in as President, after the death of "Old Rough and Ready" as Zachary Taylor's friends affectionately called him. Tyler, who had been approached by these assassins previous to the death of President Taylor, had replied to their interrogations on the annexation of Texas question:

"If I should ever become president, I would exert the entire influence of that office to accomplish it."[495]

GENERAL JACKSON SLAYING THE MANY HEADED MONSTER.

1836 - General Jackson Slaying the Many Headed Monster [496]
An American political Cartoon

A satire on Andrew Jackson's campaign to destroy the Bank of the United States and its support among state banks. Jackson, Martin Van Buren, and Jack Downing struggle against a snake with heads representing the states. Jackson (on the left) raises a cane marked "Veto" and says, "Biddle thou Monster Avaunt!! avaunt [away] I say! or by the Great Eternal I'll cleave thee to the earth, aye thee and thy four and twenty satellites. Matty [Martin Van Buren] if thou art true...come on. if thou art false, may the venomous monster turn his dire fang upon thee..."

Van Buren: "Well done General, Major Jack Downing, Adams, Clay, well done all. I dislike dissentions beyond every thing, for it often compels a man to play a double part, were it only for his own safety. Policy, policy is my motto, but intrigues I cannot countenance."

Downing (dropping his axe): "Now now you nasty varmint, be you imperishable? I swan Gineral that are beats all I reckon, that's the horrible wiper wot wommits wenemous heads I guess..." The largest of the heads is president of the Bank Nicholas Biddle's, which wears a top hat labeled "Penn" (i.e. Pennsylvania) and "$35,000,000." This refers to the rechartering of the Bank by the Pennsylvania legislature in defiance of the adminstration's efforts to destroy it.

Chapter Seven

Christianity: the Foundation on which the Whole Structure Rests

President John Tyler indeed made good his promise and the annexation of Texas which was hoodwinked through, prompted the resignation of every member of President Zachary Taylor's Cabinet, with the exception of Daniel Webster. Tyler appointed a new Cabinet with his first selection bringing in, as Henry Clay referred to them as the "secret cabal," Abel P. Upshur and Thomas W. Gilmore. These two Virginians had visited Tyler at his house in Virginia just before General Harrison was poisoned and thus their appointments were Tyler's part in fulfilling his "contract with fidelity."[497]

President John Tyler, 1841 [498]

U.S. Senator Thomas Benton (Missouri) quote from his book (1858, c1854), *Thirty Years' View: A History of the Working of the American Government 1820 to 1850*:

"He [Daniel Webster] had remained with Mr. Tyler until the Spring of 1843, when the progress of the Texas annexation <u>scheme carried on privately</u>, not to say clandestinely, had reached a point to take an official form, and to become the subject of government negotiation, though still secret. Mr. Webster, Secretary of State, was an obstacle to that negotiation. He could not be trusted with the secret, much less conduct the negotiations. How to get rid of him was a question of some delicacy. Abrupt dismissal would have revolted his friends. Voluntary resignation was not to be expected .... A middle course was fallen upon—that of compelling a resignation. Mr. Tyler became reserved and indifferent to him. Mr. <u>Gilmore</u> and Mr. <u>Upshur</u>, with whom he had few affinities, took but little pains to conceal their distaste to him. Mr. Webster felt it and told some of his friends. They said "resign." He did and his resignation was accepted with an alacrity which showed it was waited for. Mr. Upshur took his place and quickly the Texas negotiations became official, still secretly.[499] [emphasis added]

Abel P. Upshur, Secretary of State[500]

Circumstances pointed to Thomas W. <u>Gilmore</u> and Abel P. <u>Upshur</u>, as being the actual assassins of Zachary Taylor. After years of effort, at last, they accomplished one of their daring schemes—the annexation of Texas.

The object of the conspiracy, which ended in the murder of President Harrison, was to secure the annexation of Texas as a market for slavery. The crime they committed was so horrific one must pause and consider what must have been occurring parallel in the unseen spiritual realm.

On February 28, 1844 a very large gun on board of the *USS Princeton* was to be fired as an experiment on a Potomac River pleasure cruise. Many people were on board to witness the demonstration, among whom were the two newest Cabinet officers, Secretary of the Navy Gilmore and Secretary of State Upshur.

The vessel had sailed down the Potomac below the tomb of President Washington, and upon returning late that afternoon, it was decided to fire the gun once more. President Tyler's presence was requested by someone in another area of the ship while Gilmore and Upshur walked, as it were, right into the jaws of death. The long gun, which was named "Peacemaker," exploded, killing a handful of dignitaries among who were Gilmore and Upshur.[501] Tyler was saved from the same fate by being called back to the other end of the vessel, however, his future father-in-law David Gardiner of New York, was not as fortunate.[502]

Awful explosion of the "peace-maker" on board the U.S. Steam Frigate Princeton
on Wednesday, 28th Feb. 1844 [503]

Six years later, the Presidential election of 1856 was a hotly contested one as there was a newly awakened social conscience, in what some refer to as the *Third Great Awakening* in the North that had become quite stirring in the realm of abolitionism. The pro-slavery forces realized that they would never again be able to dominate or control the presidency and obtain their goal of dividing the country. The Jesuit schemers decided their only hope was to take a desperate chance in nominating James Buchanan, a Pennsylvania Democrat, as their only presidential possibility.

James Buchanan had wined and dined with the Southerners giving appearance as though he would go along with their desires. Uncertain of how dependable he would be to their cause, they nominated John C. Breckenridge (1821-1875)[504] of Kentucky as a safety backup. In the Kentucky House of Representatives, Breckenridge had supported *States Rights*.

John C. Breckenridge[505]

At this time an important case had been appealed to the United States Supreme Court. Dred Scott was a Missouri slave who was taken by his slave master to Illinois, a free-State, and then to Minnesota, a free-territory, for an extended period of time and then back to the slave-holding State of Missouri. After his original master died, he sued for his freedom. After the Missouri Supreme Court ruled against him, he appealed to the U.S. Supreme Court in December, 1856, which upheld the decision of the Missouri court, but also used the case to fundamentally change the legal balance of power in favor of slaveholders.

Dred Scott, 1857 [506]   Chief Justice Roger B. Taney [507]

In order that the Dred Scott Decision should not in any way hazard the chances of Buchanan's election, these Jesuit schemers compelled U.S. Supreme Court Chief Justice Roger E. Taney to withhold his decision until after the election.[508] It was not published until two days after the Inauguration, March 6th, 1857. Providence oversees its own irony and sense of humor in that after reading his inaugural address on March 4, 1861, Mr. Lincoln was sworn-in by Chief Justice Taney.[509]

James Buchanan had wined and dined with the Southerners giving appearance as though he would go along with their desires. The new president proved himself a decided "Trimmer,"[510] or one who keeps even the ship of state …to accommodate prevailing political winds.   Although he was a Northern man, he had strongly courted the Southern leaders, leading them to believe that he was with them heart and soul, when in reality he was not.[511]

He was invited to deliver an address on Washington's birthday, and so made a reservation at the National Hotel (which, by the way, was the headquarters for the Jesuit traitors) for himself and friends. The Southern leaders were promptly in touch with him to learn of his intentions as to whether he intended to keep his pre-election promises, or not.[512]

View of Washington City looking down Pennsylvania Ave. toward unfinished Capitol.
National Hotel on left [513]

Buchanan was aware of the northern stir of abolitionists and when the committee asked for a conference, he coolly informed them that **he was President of the North, as well as of the South**. This change of attitude was obvious by his very decided stand against Jefferson Davis and his party. Buchanan made known his intention of settling the question of slavery in the free-States to the satisfaction of the people in those States.[514]

President James Buchanan [515]

James Buchanan didn't have to wait long to find out what the Jesuits would do to him for double-crossing them. The following quotations[516] from the *New York Herald* and the *New York Post* at the time chronicled what followed:

"The appointments favoring the North by the Jeff Davis faction will doubtless be accepted, and treated as a declaration of war, and a war of extermination on one side or the other." (Feb. 25, 1857.)

"On Washington's birthday, Buchanan's stand became known and the next day he was poisoned. The plot was deep and planned with skill. Mr. Buchanan, as was customary with men in his station, had a table and chairs reserved for himself and friends in the dining room at the National Hotel. The President was known to be an inveterate tea drinker; in fact, Northern people rarely drink anything else in the evening. Southern men prefer coffee. Thus, to make sure of Buchanan and his Northern friends, arsenic was sprinkled in the bowls containing the tea and lump sugar and set on the table where he was to sit. The pulverized sugar in the bowls used for coffee on the other tables was kept free from the poison. Not a single Southern man was affected or harmed. Fifty or sixty persons dined at the table that evening, and as nearly as can be learned, about thirty-eight died from the effects of the poison."

"President Buchanan was poisoned, and with great difficulty his life was saved. His physicians treated him understandingly from instructions given by himself as to the cause of the illness, for he understood well what was the matter."

"Since the appearance of the epidemic, the tables at the National Hotel have been almost empty. But more remarkable than the appearance of the epidemic itself, is the supineness [indifference] of the authorities of Washington, in regard to it. Have the proprietors of the Hotel, or clerks, or servants, suffered from it? If not, in what respect did their diet and accommodations differ from those of the guests (Northern)? There is more in this calamity than meets the eye. It's a matter that should not be trifled with." (*New York Post*, March 18, 1857.) [emphasis added]

James Buchanan was poisoned and almost died. He lived because he knew that he had been given arsenic poisoning and so informed his doctors. He knew that the Jesuits poisoned Harrison and Taylor. The Jesuit Order fulfilled their oath again that they would poison, kill, or do whatever was necessary to remove those who opposed their plans. From 1841 to 1857, we saw that three Presidents were attacked by the Jesuits as outlined in the Congresses of Vienna, Verona, and Chieri. Two died and one barely escaped. They allow nothing to stand in their way of total domination of America, and the destruction of the *Constitution*. As they look at America the priests of Rome have stated:

76

"We are determined, like you, to take possession of the United States and rule them; but we cannot do that without acting secretly and with the utmost wisdom.

"…Silently and patiently, we must mass our Roman Catholics in the great cities of the United States, remembering that the vote of a poor journeyman, though he be covered with rags, has as much weight in the scale of power as the millionaire Astor, and that if we have two votes against his one, he will become as powerless as an oyster. Let us, then, multiply our votes; let us call our poor but faithful Irish Catholics from every corner of the world, and gather them into the very hearts of those proud citadels which the Yankees are so rapidly building under the names of Washington, New York, Boston, Chicago, Buffalo, Albany, Troy, Cincinnati, etc.

Under the shadows of those great cities, the Americans consider themselves a giant and unconquerable race. They look upon the poor Irish Catholic people with supreme contempt, as only fit to dig their canals, sweep their streets and work in their kitchens. <u>Let no one awake those sleeping lions, to-day. Let us pray God that they may sleep and dream their sweet dreams, a few years more. How sad will their awakening be when with our outnumbering votes we will turn them, forever, from every position of honor, power and profit! What will those so-called giants think of their matchless shrewdness and ability, when not a single Senator or member of Congress will be chosen, if he be not submitted to our holy father, the Pope? What a sad figure those Protestant Yankees will cut when we will not only elect the President, but fill and command the armies, man the navies, and hold the keys of the public treasury?</u>...

"<u>Then, yes! then, we will rule the United States, and lay them at the feet of the Vicar of Jesus Christ,* that he may put an end to their godless system of education, and sweep away those impious laws of liberty of conscience, which are an insult to God and man!</u>[517] [emphasis added]

* "Vicar of Jesus Christ," is a term used by these priests of Rome in referring to the Pope.

Rep. James Meacham [518]
At the opening of the Thirty-third Congress in 1854, a debate arose as to whether or not to elect chaplains, as had been customary from the beginning of the First Federal Congress in 1789. The so-called "memorialists" who verbally opposed having chaplains did so under the pretext of claiming the practice was unconstitutional. Realistically, they opposed the fact that so many northern pastors were abolitionists, and the slavery question was dividing the Congress and the nation. On March 27, 1854, Representative James Meacham (1810-1856), Vermont), who served as spokesman of the U.S. House Committee on the Judiciary, spoke in favor of continuing the practice of appointing chaplains:[519]

"What is an establishment of religion? It must have a creed, defining what a man must believe; it must have rites and ordinances, which believers must observe; it must have ministers of defined qualifications, to teach the doctrines and administer the rites; it must have tests for the submissive and penalties for the non-conformist. There never was as established religion without all these….

At the adoption of the Constitution…every State…provided as regularly for the support of the Church as for the support of the Government….

Down to the Revolution, every colony did sustain religion in some form. It was deemed peculiarly proper that the <u>religion of liberty</u> should be upheld by a free people.

Had the people, during the Revolution, had a suspicion of any attempt to war against Christianity, that Revolution would have been strangled in its cradle.

At the time of the adoption of the Constitution and the amendments, the universal sentiment was that Christianity should be encouraged, not any one sect [denomination]. Any attempt to level and discard all religion would have been viewed with universal indignation. The object was not to substitute Judaism or Mohammedanism, or infidelity, but to prevent rivalry among the sects [Christian denominations] to the exclusion of others.

It [Christianity] must be considered as the foundation on which the whole structure rests. Laws will not have permanence or power without the sanction of religious sentiment, -- without a firm belief that there is a Power above us that will reward our virtues and punish our vices.

In this age there can be no substitute for Christianity: that, in its general principles, is the great conservative element on which we must rely for the purity and permanence of free institutions. That was the religion of the founders of the republic, and they expected it to remain the religion of their descendants. There is a great and very prevalent error on this subject in the opinion that those who organized this Government did not legislate on religion."[520]

Congress of the United States of America, May, 1854, passed a resolution in the House which declared:

"The great vital and conservative element in our system is the belief of our people in the pure doctrines and divine truths of the gospel of Jesus Christ."[521]

The Word of God shows us that the people of God go through periods of spiritual renewal, and periods of spiritual decline. We could think of these times like waves and troughs, or like mountains and valleys. The period of time for the working of God's Spirit may last many years, as did the *Second Great Awakening* in America, or be brief, as some historians refer to as the *Third Great Awakening* of the late 1850s.[522]

During a renewal, or "awakening," there will be not only a great reviving of Christians, but a very apparent positive impact on the problems of society. Awakenings are not just times of enhanced personal spiritual experience; awakenings have significant social impact to a level of moral restoration. Corrupt, immoral, unjust, and ungodly people and societies often return to honesty, purity, justice, and holiness. It is possible for a culture to be transformed; but first there must be a transformed people.[523]

In New Testament times, awakening came upon the people of God at Pentecost (Acts chapter 2). This pouring out of the Holy Spirit set a pattern that can be seen in later awakenings. Again, as recorded in Acts 4:23-37, is the historical account of a renewal that prepared the infant Church for the fierce persecutions to come.[524] The majority of awakenings in America, and elsewhere, have been accompanied by great orderliness and a profound, majestic sincerity. America has a rich heritage of testimony to the working of God's Spirit through spiritual awakenings.[525]

From the 1830s onward while the Jesuit faction were seeking to sew division between the North and the South through agitation over the slavery issue, Christians worked to free the slaves. Gilbert H. Barnes in his (1933) book, *The Anti-slavery Impulse 1830–1844*, has accurately presented how Christians worked to free the slaves:

"The conjunction of so many elements of the Great Revival [1831] in the anti-slavery agitation was more than coincidence.… In leadership, in method, and in objective, the Great Revival and the American AntiSlavery Society now were one. It is not too much to say that for the moment the antislavery agitation as a whole was what it had long been in larger part, an aspect of the Great Revival in benevolent reform."[526] [emphasis added]

Charles Finney's vision of a truly Christian America, and heralding-in the new millennial age, which he fervently promoted until his death in 1875, actually seemed attainable in 1835. It would be a nation ruled by the moral government of God.

Without fail Finney would promote the obligation of each child of God to "aim at being useful in the highest degree possible,"[527] preferring the interest of God's Kingdom above all other interests. The Holy Spirit continued a work in America with that divine and prophetic vision. America, the "Benevolent Empire" achieved its goals in the first half of the 19th century, making lasting contributions to national life, eliminating much evil, and bringing Christian values into the mainstream of American society.

Methodist revival in 1839 during the Second Great Awakening [528]

In an 1859 sermon, Finney reflected that there had been a continuing spirit of revival in many parts of the United States from the *Second Great Awakening* leading up to the then current *Third Great Awakening*. He claimed that the people of God "saw the tide rising and the cloud gathering, and they said to each other they should soon see a general movement."[529]

Around 1855 in Rochester, New York, Christians of all denominations united in the work, and daily prayer meetings and preaching were held in the different churches in succession; the meetings moving round from church to church in a circle. The secular press had largely ignored this occurrence until there was so much interest in these meetings that the public was demanding that the secular press no longer ignore or withhold publishing stories.

The published news, which included sermons, aroused the masses in every town of New York. From that the revival spread in every direction. Daily prayer-meetings were commenced, which resulted in a great many others. The revival spread to Boston, and became powerful, increasing the next couple of years.[530] In 1856, in connection with the revival in Rochester, a small devotional book had been published on daily public worship as an appointment with God. As the book circulated, churches in many places were stirred to hold daily meetings for prayer and conference. Evangelists, throughout New York, were assisting faithful pastors in preaching and holding daily prayer meetings with constant and growing success. This prompted a businessmen's prayer meeting to form.

Attendance of the prayer meeting increased until October, 1857, when the banking system of America collapsed. The panic and consequent run on the banks caused hundreds of businesses to close, resulting in the loss of jobs for hundreds of thousands. Many people went into bankruptcy and panic swept through New York. Protests, civil unrest, and hunger meetings followed the bank collapse. Prayer meetings grew. Charles Finney had previously stated in a sermon that New York "seemed to be on such a wave of prosperity as to be the death of revival effort." There was a drastic change in this attitude. Business men were bewildered, and rich families were being reduced to poverty.[531]

Business men continued to grow prayer meetings in a business part of the city, particularly near the Stock Exchange. It was professionally managed in providing public notice of the meetings as well as insight and discussion on matters of business and politics. It was believed that God was answering prayer and the business crisis would bring about a greater revival. The commercial crisis and financial panic was the catalyst that triggered this *Third Great Awakening*.

Within six months 10,000 people were gathering daily for prayer in numerous places throughout New York. Statistics were gathered from week to week from different parts of the country. It was estimated that the conversions numbered at least 50,000 per week with the number of national converts being no less than 500,000.[532]

On March 20, 1858, the *New York Times* reported thousands saved:

"In this City, we have beheld a sight which not the most enthusiastic fanatic for church observances could ever have hoped to look upon. We have seen in a business quarter of the City, in the busiest hours, assemblies of merchants, clerks and working men, to the number of 5,000 gathered day after day for simple and solemn worship. Similar assemblies we find in other portions of the City; a theatre is turned into a chapel; churches of all sects are opened and crowded by day and night."[533]

The *New York Times* reported that the nationally known pastor, Dr. Henry Ward Beecher, was leading 3,000 people in devotions at Burton's Theater. Once while he was reading Scripture, Beecher was interrupted by singing from an overflow prayer meeting crowd in an adjoining barroom. He then led the group in thanksgiving that such a thing could happen.[534]

Henry Ward Beecher [535]

Other major cities also developed prayer meetings. The form of worship was always the same in that any person might pray, give a testimony, an exhortation, or lead in singing as they would feel led or be inspired. Although pastors such as Beecher often attended and lent their enthusiastic support, it was the laypeople who provided the leadership.[536]

Little planning was done for the meetings; the chief rules were that a meeting should begin and end punctually, and that no one should speak or pray for very long. In Chicago, the Metropolitan Theater was filled every day with 2,000 people. In Louisville, Kentucky, several thousand met each morning, and overflow meetings were held around the city. In Cleveland, the attendance was about 2,000 each day, and in St. Louis all the churches were filled for months on end.[537]

What impressed observers, and the press, was that there was no fanaticism, hysteria, or objectionable behavior, only a moving impulse to pray. Finney commented, *"The general impression seemed to be, 'We have had instruction until we are hardened; it is now time for us to pray.' Little preaching was done. As the people gathered they were largely silent; there was a great overarching attitude of glorifying God."*[538]

There is an interesting account told of a European cargo ship that sailed into the New York harbor during the awakening and was boarded by the harbor pilot, who was a Christian. As he guided the ship into port, he told the captain and crew what was going on in the city, and a great hush fell over them all, which seemed to him the power of the Spirit. By the time they reached the dock, most of the crew had committed their lives to Christ.[539]

In February, 1858 James Gordon Bennett began to give extensive space in reporting the awakening in his paper, the *New York Herald*. *New York Tribune* editor Horace Greeley gave still greater coverage to the meetings, until in April, 1858 he devoted an entire edition of the *Tribune* to a special revival issue. Other papers quickly followed suit in reporting stories on the great numbers of people all throughout the nation attending the prayer gatherings and professing faith in Christ.[540]

James Gordon Bennett, Sr.[541]
Founder, editor and publisher of the *New York Herald*

Horace Greeley, 1872 [542]
Founder and editor of the *New-York Tribune*

The recently founded Y.M.C.A. began to play a large part in the *Third Great Awakening* in cities such as Philadelphia and Chicago. The years following, the Y.M.C.A. organization was primarily for evangelical Christian ministry intended to provide Christian training and a wholesome atmosphere for underprivileged young men who lived and worked in the big cities. Timothy L. Smith had written in his book, *Revivalism and Social Reform: American Protestantism on the Eve of the Civil War*, of the *"fervently religious orientation of the mid-century Y.M.C.A. [and] ...its intimate bond with the churches... leading ministers participated in the 'Y' affairs at all levels."*[543]

The Philadelphia Y.M.C.A. sponsored a prayer meeting that drew 300 people daily. It began at noon, but people started arriving an hour early so they would be assured of a seat. The "Y" also held evangelistic tent campaigns that could accommodate 1,200 people.

The Chicago Y.M.C.A. served as a sound training school for laypersons. Dwight L. Moody,[544] also known as D.L. Moody (1837-1899), was an American evangelist and publisher, who founded the Moody Church, Northfield School and Mount Hermon School in Massachusetts, the Moody Bible Institute, and Moody Publishers.

Dwight Lyman Moody, c. 1900 [545]

Moody received his first opportunities for Christian service at the Chicago Y.M.C.A. As president of the Chicago Y.M.C.A. for four years, he championed evangelistic causes such as distributing tracts all over the city, and held daily noon prayer meetings. During the Civil War, he refused to fight, saying, "In this respect I am a Quaker," but he worked through the Y.M.C.A. and the United States Christian Commission to evangelize the Union troops.[546]

The colleges of America were heavily influenced by the *Awakening of 1858*. Beyond the many conversions that took place, large numbers of enthusiastic students volunteered for service in foreign missions, or in the ministry.

Baptist Christian minister, hymn-writer, professor, author, historian, and promoter of Church revival and renewal, J. Edwin Orr (1912-1987)[547] wrote:

"… The influence of the awakening was felt everywhere in the nation. It first captured great cities, but it also spread through every town and village and country hamlet. It swamped schools and colleges. It affected all classes without respect to condition…. It seemed to many that the fruits of Pentecost had been repeated a thousandfold…. the number of conversions reported soon reached the total of fifty thousand weekly…."[548]

Coming on the eve of the Civil War with the land torn apart by bitterness, the *Awakening of 1858* was astounding and its effects immeasurable. Amazingly, the awakening did not end with the coming of the opening shots of the Civil War in 1861. During the agonies of war, both the Northern and Southern armies experienced awakenings in the camps. Early in the war a large awakening occurred in the Army of Northern Virginia, and spread throughout the Confederate forces. Even in the tragic atmosphere of death and suffering, the awakening continued.[549]

Overall the *Third Great Awakening* resulted in the addition of approximately one-million converts to the churches of America. God seemed to be strengthening his people for the great trial to come in the *War Between the States*. The revival gave new importance to the work of laymen in churches. It encouraged good interdenominational relationships in ways that had never been encouraged before. It added a large number of young men to the ranks of gospel preachers and filled theological seminaries with those who had committed themselves to preach Christ. It also resulted in the formation of some new seminaries.

The awakening gave the nation a badly needed moral lift. It tied the gospel with social work in a manner that had not been seen in this country before. It gave a boost to missionary giving and resulted in unusual missionary efforts during the *War Between the States*. It prepared the nation for the blood bath it would soon experience in the Civil War years of 1861-1865. It gave birth to the great revivals which swept the armies of the South during the days of the War. It softened the hardship of the period of *Reconstruction* after the War for the South. It continued in the work of later evangelists who labored until the end of the 19th century.[550]

In summarizing America's first century as a people and a nation covenanted with Almighty God, America had broken covenant which resulted in being under Divine judgment as recorded in the prophetic Word of God, the Holy Bible, described as "Mystery Babylon."[551] For about 150 years has this mystery been hidden from the people because of its egregious mistreatment of men. The American people have been blinded by "bread and circus," years of plenty, rocking and rolling covenant-breakers unaware until the bread is now dwindling and the circus is full of perversity.

It is time for the judgment period of Mystery Babylon to end, the veil of hidden things to be pulled back, the Light of the glorious Gospel to shine through, for the manifestation of the sons of God to rise up as creation groans.[552] Currently under the dictates of an executive "pharaoh" who brings legislative "change you can believe in"[553] by just "a pen and a cell phone,"[554] sits on an iron throne that identifies with murder and prostitution,[555] [556] and manipulates the cursed money system that is not constitutionally coined by Congress but created by debt and "out of thin air."

The American people are enslaved in bondage by the Jesuit oligarch "shadow government" who rule the country behind the proud (puppet) pharaoh while at the same time ruling most of the world—the International Banking families and their privately held *Federal Reserve Banking System*[557]—a cursed system where the debt can never decrease and guaranteed to enslave the people of God, bringing demise to future generations.[558] These "cunning, ambitious, unprincipled" individuals have created a judicial system not run by the Judicial branch of a republican form of government but by a **democracy**, an established Socialist/Communist/Illuminati order with Executive branch administrative Admiralty/Maritime law courts that are for-profit, for "law merchants" on behalf of the bankers, most of which are of foreign interests.[559]

The authority of constitutional law has been steadily eroded in the United States by the planned growing dependence upon the law merchant, and the consequent violation of individual rights of Americans.[560] Extracting the wealth of the American people and stealing their land flowing with milk and honey, enslaving them as they've been dumbed-down, spiritually blinded, and **renamed as "U.S. Citizens."** President George Washington in his farewell address to the people, September 17, 1796, item 10:

> "**The name of american, which belongs to you**, in your national capacity, must always exalt the just pride of Patriotism."[561]

The Great Conspiracy of the Civil War years extends to our current times as planned by the Jesuit Superior General "Black Pope" and his faithful soldier agents. In 1862, the Rothschild's privately-owned Bank of England (be not deceived by its name in thinking it as part of the government of England) issued and distributed among the banking fraternity of America, a document entitled "The Hazard Circular," which contained the following language:

"Slavery is likely to be abolished by the war power, and chattel slavery abolished. This, I and my European friends are in favor of, for slavery is but the owning of labor, and carries with it the care of the laborers, while the European plan, LED ON BY ENGLAND, is that capital shall control labor by controlling wages.

The great debt that capitalists will see to it is made out of the war (our own Civil War) must be used to control the value of money. To accomplish this, the Government bonds must be used as a banking basis.

We are now waiting for the Secretary of the Treasury of the United States to make this recommendation. **It will not do to allow the greenbacks, as they are called, to circulate as money any length of time, as we cannot control that, but we can control the bonds and through them the bank issues.**"[562] [emphasis added]

A "new, improved system" of slavery was being born. "...chattel slavery could not compete in efficiency with white labor... more money could be made from the white laborer, for whom no responsibility of shelter, clothing, food and attendance had to be assumed than from the Negro slave, whose sickness, disability or death entailed direct financial loss."[563]

"The perfect slave thinks he's free." A well thought-out plan of an "elite" reprobate people who devised a ways and means based on lies and counterfeits. Studied in human behavior, controlling the masses through its sorcery of bought-out, privately-owned media who broadcast lies as truth, are nothing short of propagating as "Satan's evangelists." Enabled by the Federal Communications Commission (FCC) deregulation and a decades-long orgy of mergers and acquisitions, six major corporations—giants—dominate our media landscape and control 90 percent of everything Americans see, hear and consider important.[564] As Nazi Party leader appointed by Adolf Hitler, Joseph Goebbels stated,

"If you tell a lie big enough and keep repeating it, people will eventually come to believe it. The lie can be maintained only for such time as the State can shield the people from the political, economic and/or military consequences of the lie. It thus becomes vitally important for the State to use all of its powers to repress dissent, for the truth is the mortal enemy of the lie, and thus by extension, the truth is the greatest enemy of the State."[565]

So successful has this dark elite force been that their pride and arrogance causes them to become sloppy and lacking the carefully guarded discretion of their forefathers. Almighty God Yehovah has always had a remnant,[566] a people who know, love, and serve Him, obeying His Word the Holy Bible.[567] As boundaries of loving protection for His beloved children does He command strict obedience to His Word, which is His Law. He leaves free-will choices to His children to respond in love by their obedience.[568]

This remnant has called out in prayer to the *Supreme Judge of the world*, the God of their fathers, in repentance.[569] The Courts of Heaven have undoubtedly heard the saints in declaration of the Word of God[570] that angels respond to,[571] will not return void,[572] and the Father watches over to perform[573] along with petitions, complaints, and restraining orders all under the blood of Jesus, the Advocate[574] of these citizens of Heaven.[575] No longer defendants, but by counterclaim and recognizing the Court-ordered judgment period to have expired for Mystery Babylon,[576] herein presents evidence on behalf of the people of Almighty God, joint heirs with Christ, for the *Republic **for** the United States of America*, one nation under God.

Re-inhabited

Republic for the United States of America

Part Two

The Corporate UNITED STATES Posing as Government

and it's Counterfeit Constitution

George Washington, 1795-1796 [577]　　　　Broadside of George Washington's Farewell Address Part 1 [578]

"George Washington's Farewell Address is one of the most important documents in American history. Recommendations made in it by the first president, particularly in the field of foreign affairs, have exerted a strong and continuing influence on American statesmen and politicians.

The address, in which Washington informed the American people that he would not seek a third term and offered advice on the country's future policies, was published on September 19, 1796, in David Claypoole's *American Daily Advertiser*. It was immediately reprinted in newspapers and as a pamphlet throughout the United States. The address was drafted in July, 1796 by Alexander Hamilton and revised for publication by the president himself. Washington also had at his disposal an earlier draft by James Madison.

The "religion section" of the address was for many years as familiar to Americans as was Washington's warning that the United States should avoid entangling alliances with foreign nations. Washington's observations on the relation of religion to government were commonplace, and similar statements abound in documents from the founding period. Washington's prestige, however, gave his views a special authority with his fellow citizens and caused them to be repeated in political discourse well into the nineteenth century."[579]

Chapter Eight

The Post of Honor and Duty

President George Washington in his farewell address to the people, September 17, 1796:

> "…However combinations or <u>associations</u> of the above description [<u>disguised in order to appear</u> <u>credible with a real purpose to direct, control, counteract, or awe the regular deliberation and action</u> <u>of the constituted authorities in order to cause obstruction</u>] may now and then answer popular ends, they are likely, in the course of time and things, to become potent engines, by which <u>cunning,</u> <u>ambitious, and unprincipled men will be enabled to subvert the power of the people, and to usurp</u> <u>for themselves the reins of government; destroying afterwards the very engines, which have lifted</u> <u>them to unjust dominion.</u>"[580]

Abraham Lincoln was born in a one-room log cabin in Kentucky in 1809, a second child to Thomas and Nancy Lincoln.[581] The family attended a "Separate Baptists"[582] church, which most directly connected to George Whitefield's influence during the *First Great Awakening*. The church had restrictive moral standards and young Abe was trained-up in the way a child should go[583] with a solid Biblical upbringing and a clean, pure, upright life both in public and private.[584]

Lincoln the Rail Splitter [585]

Lincoln's father enjoyed considerable status in Kentucky where he sat on juries, appraised estates, served on country slave patrols, and guarded prisoners. By the time Abe was born, his father owned two 600-acre farms, several town lots, livestock, and horses. He was among the richest men in the county until he had lost all of his land in court cases because of faulty property titles.

The family moved across the Ohio River to Indiana while Abe was yet a small child. His mother died when he was 9 years old and his older sister, Sarah, took charge of caring for him until their father remarried in 1819. Abe became close with his stepmother. Adversity and heartache was not unfamiliar to Abe having then lost his sister while giving birth to a stillborn son.

Abe did not care for the hard labor of frontier life; however, as a teen he worked hard and willingly took responsibility for all chores expected of him as one of the boys in the household. Abe became a skillful axe-man in his work building rail fences. He also attained a reputation for strength and bravery after a very competitive wrestling match to which he was challenged by the renowned leader of a group of ruffians. Young Abe also agreed with the customary obligation of a son to give his father all earnings from work done outside the home until age 21.

While young Lincoln's formal education consisted of approximately a year's worth of classes from several traveling teachers, he was mostly self-educated, an avid reader, and hungrily sought access to any new books that would arrive in the village. He read and reread the *King James Bible*, *Aesop's* Fables, Bunyan's *Pilgrim's Progress*, Defoe's *Robinson Crusoe*, and Benjamin Franklin's Autobiography.

In 1830, the Lincoln family moved west to Illinois, another free, non-slave State. In 1831, as an ambitious 22-year-old now old enough to make his own decisions, Lincoln struck out on his own. Canoeing down the Sangamon River, Lincoln ended up in the village of New Salem in Sangamon County and he was hired by a businessman to take goods by flatboat, accompanied by friends, from New Salem to New Orleans via the Sangamon, Illinois, and Mississippi rivers.

After arriving in New Orleans and witnessing slavery firsthand, he walked back home. Observing the auction of a young "Negro" about his age was deeply affecting to Abe. Particularly as the slave was ordered to display his teeth, the fitness of his muscles and then listened to the auctioneer call for bids. Hearing a shrill cry followed by the stifled sobs of a beautiful mulatto girl, Abe learned that she was the bride of the young man who had just been auctioned and that she was to be auctioned the next day. There was indifference in the crowd to the humanity of this young slave couple.

Abe told his friend that if he were ever given an opportunity to do something about the injustice of slavery, "by God," he would.[586] It was Heaven's design that had written on the table of this young man's heart that he would one day sign the *Emancipation Proclamation*[587] of 3 million slaves.

Lincoln was a self-educated lawyer in Illinois, a Whig Party[588] leader, State legislator during the 1830s, and a one-term member of the Congress during the 1840s. He promoted rapid modernization of the economy through banks, canals, railroads and tariffs to encourage manufacturing; he opposed the war with Mexico in 1846.

Abraham Lincoln as a member of the U.S. House of Representatives [589]
Photo taken around 1846 by one of Lincoln's law students

Lincoln returned to practicing law in Springfield, handling "every kind of business that could come before a prairie lawyer." After a series of highly publicized debates in 1858, during which Lincoln spoke out against the expansion of slavery, he lost the U.S. Senate race to his archrival, Democrat[590] Stephen Douglas.[591] He had been drawn into the political arena by the infamous Dred Scott Decision in which fanatical Romanist Chief Justice Roger Taney brought forth the U.S. Supreme Court decision that the "Negro had no rights which the white man had to respect."[592]

Understanding this unconstitutional ruling to essentially place the Federal Government endorsement in favor of black slavery, aroused "Honest Abe"[593] to action.[594] Lincoln, a moderate from a swing State,[595] secured the Republican Party[596] presidential nomination in 1860. With virtually no support in the slave States, Lincoln swept the North and was elected president in 1860.

Mr. Lincoln was well known while working in law for being impeccably honest and full of integrity. Even his political opponent Stephen Douglas had said of Lincoln that he was a very honest and very able man.[597] Lincoln's reputation of being honest and one of the best lawyers in Illinois brought him a client who was a Catholic priest of Kankakee, Illinois.

Stephen A. Douglas [598]

Charles Chiniquy (1809-1899) was a famous Catholic priest in Canada who had become known as the "Apostle of Temperance of Canada." In 1851, he brought a large number of French Canadians into Illinois to found the French Colony of St. Anne.[599] Chiniquy stated in one of his many testimony pamphlets, *The Finished Wonder,*[600] "In 1851, I went to Illinois and found a French colony. I took with me about 75,000 French Canadians, and settled on the magnificent prairies of Illinois, to take possession in the name of the Church of Rome."[601]

Chiniquy, who had been engaged in a continuing lawsuit with a prominent Catholic layman, Peter Spink, told Abraham Lincoln that Spink was an agent of Bishop O' Regan of the Chicago diocese who instigated the suit as retaliation with an objective to destroy him because of confronting the Bishop for wrongful behaviors.[602]

Though Chiniquy was successful in having the suit closed in the Kankakee court, Spink was successful in getting a change of venue to Urbana, Illinois which included an attempt at having Chiniquy held in jail for several months until the next hearing.[603] Chiniquy's case had been so publicized in the Illinois press that few lawyers were interested in defending him. They realized that they would not simply be fighting for a priest in Chicago; they would be fighting against the Roman Catholic Church.[604]

By advice of a stranger who had sat in the hearing, Chiniquy sent Abraham Lincoln a wire asking for his services. Within twenty minutes while still in the telegraph office, he received a reply, "Yes, I will defend your honor and your life at the next May term of [the court at] Urbana. Signed A. Lincoln."[605]

Charles Chiniquy, 1860s [606]

Mr. Chiniquy relayed a visit he made to the Archbishop at St. Louis who had counseled him to write to the Pope and what transpired afterward. Chiniquy relates:

"I was ... forced to postpone my writing to the pope. For, a few days after my return from St. Louis to my colony, I had to deliver myself again into the hands of the sheriff of Kankakee county, who was obliged by Spink [the plaintiff] to take me prisoner, and deliver me as a criminal in to the hands of the sheriff of Champaign county, on the 19th of May, 1856."[607]

It was then that Chiniquy had first met Abraham Lincoln and describes him:

"He was a giant in stature; but I found him still more a giant in the noble qualities of his mind and heart. It was impossible to converse five minutes with him without loving him. There was such an expression of kindness and honesty in that face, and such an attractive magnetism in the man; that, after a few moments' conversation, one felt as tied to him by all the noblest affections of the heart."[608]

In Charles Chiniquy's defense, Abraham Lincoln depicted the career of Father Chiniquy, how he had been unjustly persecuted and in conclusion said,[609]

"As long as God gives me a heart to feel, a brain to think, or a hand to execute my will, I shall devote it against that power which has attempted to use the machinery of the courts to destroy the rights and character of an American citizen."[610]

Abraham Lincoln kept his word throughout his life and by greater measure in his faithfulness to God and his country. That same year when he reentered the political arena, he gave great historical voice to the conspiracy behind fanatical Romanist U.S. Supreme Court Justice Roger Taney's Dred Scott Decision.[611] Because of ruling in favor of black slavery, Abraham Lincoln fully understood the motive power behind this unholy decision was Rome.[612]

Abraham Lincoln made a lot of enemies as a result of the Chiniquy trial. Before leaving the courtroom, as Mr. Lincoln had finished writing the due bill of a mere $50 for his services of which Chiniquy expected to pay at least $2,000. Lincoln turned to him and said,

"Father Chiniquy, what are you crying for? Ought you not to be the most happy man alive? You have beaten your enemies and gained the most glorious victory, and you will come out of all your troubles in triumph."[613]

Chiniquy answered,

"'Dear Mr. Lincoln ...allow me to tell you that the joy I should naturally feel for such a victory is destroyed in my mind by the fear of what it may cost you. There were, then, in the crowd, not less than ten or twelve Jesuits from Chicago and St. Louis, who came to hear my sentence of condemnation to the penitentiary. But it was on their heads that you have brought the thunders of heaven and earth! Nothing can be compared to the expression of their rage against you, when you not only wrenched me from their cruel hands, but you were making the walls of the court-house tremble under the awful and superhumanly eloquent denunciation of their infamy, diabolical malice, and total want of Christian and human principle, in the plot they had formed for my destruction. What troubles my soul, just now, and draws my tears, is that it seems to me that I have read your sentence of death in their bloody eyes. How many other noble victims have already fallen at their feet!"[614]

Lincoln tried to divert Chiniquy's mind with a joke, "Sign this," he said (pertaining to his mere pittance of a due bill), "It will be my warrant of death." But after Chiniquy had signed it, Lincoln became more solemn, and said,

"I know that Jesuits never forget nor forsake. But man must not care how and where he dies, provided he dies at the post of honor and duty," and he left.[615]

Abraham Lincoln, as far back as 1855 was already a marked man that Rome sought to destroy. Five years later, in 1860, Abraham Lincoln was elected President of the United States of America.

As he traveled from Illinois to Washington City, he passed through the city of Baltimore. He later said to Charles Chiniquy,

"I am so glad to meet you again…you see that your friends, the Jesuits, have not yet killed me. But they would have surely done it when I passed through their most devoted city, Baltimore, had I not defeated their plans, by passing incognito a few hours before they expected me. We have the proof that the company which has been selected and organized to murder me was led by a rabid Roman Catholic, called Byrne; it was almost entirely composed of Roman Catholics; more than that, there were two disguised priests among them, to lead and encourage them. I am sorry to have so little time to see you: but I will not let you go before telling you that, a few days ago, I saw Mr. Morse, the learned inventor of electric telegraphy: he told me that when he was in Rome, not long ago, he found out the proofs of a most formidable conspiracy against this country and all its institutions. It is evident that it is to the intrigues and emissaries of the Pope that we owe, in great part, the horrible evil war which is threatening to cover the country with blood and ruins.

I am sorry that Professor Morse had to leave Rome before he could know more about the secret plans of the Jesuits against the liberties and the very existence of this country."[616]

John Smith Dye, in his 1864 book, *The Adder's Den; or Secrets of the Great Conspiracy to Overthrow Liberty in America* provides further details of the plot:

"Twenty men had been hired in Baltimore to assassinate the President elect on his way to Washington. The leader of this band was an Italian refugee, a barber well known in Baltimore. Their plan was as follows: When Mr. Lincoln arrived in that city, the assassins were to mix with the crowd, and get as near his person as possible, and shoot at him with their pistols. If he was in a carriage, hand grenades had been prepared, filled with detonating powder, such as Orsini used in attempting to assassinate Louis Napoleon. These were to be thrown into the carriage, and to make the work of death doubly sure, pistols were to be discharged into the vehicle at the same moment. The assassins had a vessel lying ready to receive them in the harbour. From thence they were to be carried to Mobile, in the seceded State of Alabama."[617]

Seventy-nine year old Burke McCarty had spent seven years in the late 1800s traveling to various cities gathering facts from books, magazines, newspapers, and court records in order to compile and condense them into salient points of presentation in her book that published in 1922 and in what she describes as a conspiracy not only in Abraham Lincoln's assassination but also in silence on his death. McCarty points out:

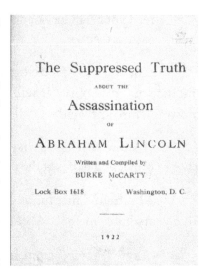

"An Italian barber well known in Baltimore, a Romanist, was to have stabbed him [Lincoln] while seated in his carriage, when he started from the depot."[618]

The Suppressed Truth About the Assassination of Abraham Lincoln [619]
Facts in evidence investigated,
written and compiled by Burke McCarty in the late 1800s.

Fortunately, the first plot of the Jesuits to kill Lincoln failed, as they sought to take Lincoln's life before he ever reached the White House. Senator William Seward and General Winfield Scott learned of the plot and sent Seward's son, Frederick, with a message to President-elect Lincoln at Philadelphia with an exhortation to abandon his public appearances and promptly come to Washington by "an underground route."[620] Lincoln's response was that he intended to fulfill his commitments in Philadelphia and Harrisburg even if he should lose his life.

William H. Seward, 1859 [621]   Winfield Scott, 1862 [622]   Frederick Seward, mid-1800s [623]

Mr. Lincoln had promised to speak and raise the American flag at Independence Hall in Philadelphia the next day, in honor of the birthday of President George Washington. He had also made commitment in accepting an invitation to address the Pennsylvania legislature at Harrisburg in the afternoon.[624]

At Independence Hall he stated that the country must be saved on the basis of "that sentiment in the *Declaration of Independence*, which gave liberty, not alone to the people of this country, but, I hope, to the world, for all future time. …If it cannot be saved upon that principle, it will be truly awful. …

But, if this country cannot be saved without giving up that principle---I was about to say I would rather be assassinated on this spot than to surrender it."[625]

After keeping his engagements and his word, President-elect Lincoln agreed to discreetly take an earlier train to Washington than originally planned, traveling quietly without attracting any publicity. Upon arrival at Washington, he was taken in safekeeping by the largest military and secret service escort a president had been previously been surrounded with.[626]

John Wilkes Booth [627]

Conspiracy appeared to become lifestyle to a rogue group on hell's mission. While riding on a train John Wilkes Booth[628] (eventual assassinator of President Lincoln), dropped a letter written to him by Charles Selby.[629] Shortly after, the letter was found and delivered to President Lincoln, who after having read it wrote the word "Assassination" across it, and filed it in his office where it was found after his death and was placed in evidence as a court exhibit.[630]

An excerpt from the letter:

"Abe must die, and now. You can choose your weapons, the cup, the knife, the bullet. The cup failed us once and might again…. You know where to find your friends. Your disguises are so perfect and complete, that without one knew your face, no police telegraphic dispatch, would catch you. … Strike for your home; strike for your country; bide your time, but strike sure."[631]

It is necessary to recall the Council of Vienna, the Pope, and the Pope's militia – the Jesuits' – in their plans to destroy this country which was founded on the principles of the Word of God, the Holy Bible, and a covenanted people with Almighty God. In consideration of the character of a people that would seek to destroy its freedom, its Bible-believing Protestantism and to assassinate presidents, we see a fierce people, sons of Satan that are evil, vicious, and malicious.

We cannot discount our history in the attempts made on President Andrew Jackson's life, the assassination of President William Henry Harrison, the assassination of President Zachary Taylor, the attempted assassination of President James Buchanan, the attempted assassination of newly elected, not yet inaugurated President-elect Abraham Lincoln; and then finally his assassination.

What does this all project regarding the hierarchy of the Catholic Church? What is clearly seen is that **a foreign government has invaded our country and under the guise of a church**.

Just as our country was infiltrated by this rogue foreign government and in process of being hijacked and usurped, a church had been infiltrated, hijacked, and usurped while its members were largely unaware and being used in the name of our Lord Jesus.

These usurpers have hidden behind a religious mask so that they will not be suspected of the many abominations they continually perpetrate in this country and around the world.

Their time has come to end their exploits in America. Biblical prophecy is yet to complete through fulfillment while we close out this Age and prepare for the next Millennium (Rev. 20) and the return of the King of kings (Rev. 19:16) and Lord of lords (Rev. 19:16), Jesus Christ, Yeshuah haMaschiah,[632] to rule and reign for a thousand years with those who overcome (Rev. 20:4-6, Phil. 3:10-14).

"One of the People's Saints for the Calendar of Liberty 1852" [633]

The artist registers the widespread American sympathy with certain revolutionary movements in Europe. More specifically, the print extols Louis Kossuth, the Hungarian patriot who led an 1848 revolt against the Austrian imperial domination of Hungary.

Kossuth (center) comes to the aid of Liberty (fallen, at left) against Austria, which is shown as a three-headed monster. The monster represents an alliance of "Throne and Altar," i.e., the monarchy and the papacy. Its three heads are those of a dragon with clerical hat and papal tiara (the Vatican), a wolf with a crown (Austria?), and a bear with an eastern crown (possibly Russia, Austria's ally). Around the monster's neck is a pendant with the Jesuit insignia. Kossuth steps from a railing into the ring, wielding the sword of "Eloquence" and confronting the monster with the shield of "Truth," which reflects the face of a prelate (possibly Pope Pius IX).

Kossuth also carries a flag with a liberty cap surrounded by stars, the liberty cap being just above his head. The hero is cheered on by representatives of various nations, waving their respective flags and watching from behind the railing. These include (left to right) an American, an Italian, and a Frenchman who carries a flag of the revolution of 1793. Liberty meanwhile has fallen. Her sword lay broken on the ground while her left foot still presses on the monster's tail. She raises her hand toward Kossuth in an imploring gesture. The Library of Congress's impression of the print is inscribed with a note (probably contemporary) in pencil saying, "Fight for us."

Chapter Nine

The Real Motive Power is Not Seen

President James Buchanan (1857-1861) was the 15th and last *de jure*, lawful, full-term, non-martial law president of the Republic. As President, he was often called a "doughface," a Northerner from Pennsylvania, with Southern sympathies.[634] Buchanan's efforts to maintain peace between the North and the South alienated both sides and contributed to seven of the Southern States seceding from the Union just before he completed his term in office as President and in the prologue to the Civil War.[635] Buchanan viewed that secession was illegal but that going to war to stop it was also illegal.

James Buchanan, mid-1800s [636]

The Ultra-Pro-Slavery men of the South had determined to control or kill President Buchanan.[637] The brush with death from being poisoned and then living with the mournful thoughts of the death of his nephew and friends that night at the National Hotel frightened James Buchanan and made him a most subservient tool of the Jesuits. An old friend of Buchanan's, who had visited him in Washington a few months after, said he had "aged twenty-five years." He had been the picture of health, robust and straight as an arrow when he arrived in Washington for his Inauguration. After he was poisoned with arsenic he was emaciated and bent.[638]

By the time Buchanan left office, popular opinion was against him. His inability to impose peace on sharply divided partisans on the brink of civil war has led to his consistent ranking by historians as one of the worst presidents in American history with his failure to deal with secession the worst presidential mistake ever made.[639]

During the Buchanan administration seven States seceded, headed by South Carolina, taking seven forts, four arsenals and one Navy Yard, and the United States Mint at New Orleans, with $511,000. The total value of the government property stolen at this time was $27 million and $8 million in Indian Trust Bonds.[640]

Buchanan and his Cabinet proved industrious in maneuvering and coordinating in executive management with an obvious objective to destroy and disable the Federal Government. Secretary of the Navy Isaac Toucey,[641] under various pretenses, had dispersed the naval fleet to cruise the coasts of China and Japan while some sailed the Mediterranean and yet others to the West Indies where the elements in the tropical seas would rot the ships. Other fleets were sent to the coast of Africa under the pretense of capturing slaves. There were virtually no U.S. war vessels to be seen in Federal waters.[642]

Secretary of War John Floyd[643] was indeed conniving in transferring all available war material from the free States to the arsenals and forts located in the slave States. He also directed the portion of the Federal army which was stationed on the seaboard, where it was of easy access, to relocate to the western territories and frontier where it would require a year to bring them back.[644]

President Buchanan and his Cabinet (c. 1859) [645]
From left to right: Jacob Thompson, Lewis Cass, John B. Floyd, James Buchanan,
Howell Cobb, Isaac Toucey, Joseph Holt and Jeremiah S. Black

Before the end of Buchanan's administration, nearly all of President Buchanan's Cabinet had fled to escape punishment for their treasonous crimes. Buchanan remained longest and remarked in his final days as President, "As George Washington was the first, James Buchanan will be the last President of the United States."[646] Providence has shown to have the last say in that regard which will be revealed in glorious display as we further the telltale of the Republic.

Mr. Buchanan left his post without honor and the Federal Government in a very unsettled condition. He kept his secret pledge to the South that the Kansas struggle in becoming a State should not be settled during his administration. Gross atrocities were committed by pro-slavery men against the free State people who lived there. Buchanan commenced his administration in Kansas affairs as though the entire territories of the United States belonged exclusively to the Slave Power.[647]

Secret Societies were everywhere organized in Missouri and Kansas. There are affidavits of record in the *Kansas Committee Report* to the testimony that these societies were organized specifically to drive free State people out of the Territory and to make Kansas a slave State.[648]

The Democratic Party had become demoralized from the exalted position of defending human freedom and Popular Government to becoming a reviler of liberty and deadly enemy of free institutions. It set aside the sanctity of the God-given rights of man to make room for Calhoun's rights of the States. Bribery and fraud was the popular means of control in the day — and as long as it served to preserve the institution of slavery and placed Democrats in office. Pro-slavery, disunion, anti-abolition, and a death grip on the spoils were the offers of the day that replaced the Democratic principles established by Jefferson and Jackson.[649]

Abraham Lincoln won the 1860 presidential election without even being on the ballot in ten of the Southern States. It was his victory that triggered the declarations of secession by the seven slave States of the South along with their formation of the *Confederate States of America*, also known as *"the Confederacy,"* even before Lincoln was inaugurated in office.[650]   They seceded, not because they were being oppressed, but because they saw that it was very likely that anti-slavery legislation would now be passed which was disagreeable to them.[651]

The government of the United States (the Union) regarded secession as unlawful and contrary to the *Constitution*; the Federal Government refused to recognize the Confederacy[652] and referred to its attempt at disunion and formation of the Confederate government as *The Great Rebellion*.[653]   The passionate vocalized opinion of the South was that the rapidly populating North and the Federal Government were not preserving or acknowledging the State's rights particularly in their property, namely their slaves, and referred to the dilemma as "the War of the Northern Aggression."[654]

Noteworthy is an article that was published on December 4, 1861 in the *London Index*, a journal established in London by agents of Jefferson Davis to support the cause of the rebellious States. (Bear in mind that Jefferson Davis was a cotton plantation owner and slave-holder of over 100 slaves[655] as well as a U.S. Senator from Mississippi until his State seceded from the United States. A member of the secret organization *Knights of the Golden Circle*,[656] he was then elected interim president of the *Confederate States of America*.)

Jefferson Davis, 1861 [657]

The article stated that Southern leader Calhoun had urged an English gentleman to make known the Southern States' intention to secede from the Union "in order to invite the attention of the British Government to the coming event." It was stated that the Southern States had resolved to secede from the Union previous to 1839 because of claimed violations of the *Constitution* related to tariff "spoliation," or a plundering of their revenues to a point of harm by the Northern States.

Included in the published article was the fact that Southern leader Calhoun had sent an emissary, Mr. Mason[658] of Virginia, on his behalf in secret communication with the Jesuit-controlled British Government as far back as 1841, with a view to securing its powerful aid in unalterable resolve to secede from the Union; and then Mr. Mason pleads...for the armed intervention of England.[659]

James Murray Mason [660]

It is an important consideration that the South produced more than half of the entire world's supply of cotton, a fact that held foreign nations dependent upon the South. As the world's leading industrial power, Great Britain's single most important manufacture at that period of time was cotton cloth, from which about one-fifth of its population, whether directly or indirectly, found employment. About 75 percent of their cotton fiber was imported from the American South.[661]

The "Cotton Lords" of the South had established relationships with the British Lords of business and banking, who had an interest in the affairs of the South. There indeed was a close business relationship between the cotton growing aristocracy in the South and the cotton cloth manufacturers in England. The International Bankers decided that this business connection was America's "Achilles Heel," the door through which the young American Republic could be successfully attacked and overcome.[662]

It had been stated in a "disunion" meeting during the South Carolina legislature, "We must secede… If we can get but one State to unite with us, we must act. Once being independent, we would have a strong ally in England; but we must prepare for secession."[663] The corrupting influence of the moneyed power of the privately-owned United States Bank had already joined hands with the Slave Power back in the Jackson administration.[664] "Relationship banking" has been around for a long time…

The Southern States were swarming with Jesuit-controlled British agents.[665] These agents conspired with local politicians, who were also wealthy plantation owners and slave holders who had control of the Federal Government through its southern Congress members and for the most part, together, worked against the best interests of the United States.

President Lincoln fully realized it was not a Protestant South with which he was contending as is evident in what he had confided in his friend Rev. Charles Chiniquy, the ex-Catholic priest of Illinois whom Lincoln had defended in a court dispute just a few years earlier:

"It is with the Southern leaders of this civil war as with the big and small wheels of our railroad cars. Those who ignore the laws of mechanics are apt to think that the large, strong, and noisy wheels they see are the motive power, but they are mistaken. **The real motive power is not seen; <u>it is noiseless and well concealed in the dark, behind its iron walls.</u>** The motive power are the few well-concealed pails of water heated into steam, which is itself directed by the noiseless, small but unerring engineer's finger.

The common people see and hear the big, noisy wheels of the Southern Confederacy's cars; they call them Jeff Davis, Lee, Toombs, Beauregard, Semmes, etc., and they honestly think that they are the motive power, the first cause of our troubles. But this is a mistake. <u>The true motive power is secreted behind the thick walls of the Vatican, the colleges and schools of the Jesuits, the convents of the nuns, and the confessional boxes of Rome</u>.

There is a fact which is too much ignored by the American people, and with which I am acquainted only since I became President; it is that the best, <u>the leading families of the South have received their education in great part, if not in whole, from the Jesuits</u> and the nuns. Hence those degrading principles of slavery, pride, cruelty, which are as a second nature among so many of those people. <u>Hence that strange want of fair play, humanity; that implacable hatred against the ideas of equality and liberty as we find them in the Gospel of Christ</u>. You do not ignore that the first settlers of Louisiana, Florida, New Mexico, Texas, South California and Missouri were Roman Catholics, and that their first teachers were Jesuits. It is true that those states have been conquered or bought by us since. But Rome had put the deadly virus of her antisocial and anti-Christian maxims into the veins of the people before they became American citizens. Unfortunately, the Jesuits and the nuns have in great part remained the teachers of those people since. <u>They have continued in a silent, but most efficacious way, to spread their hatred against our institutions, our laws, our schools, our rights and our liberties in such a way that this terrible conflict became unavoidable between the North and the South.</u> <u>As I told you before, it is to Popery that we owe this terrible civil war.</u>"[666]

The conspiracy of the British agents and the Slave Power in carefully sown and nurtured propaganda developed into open rebellion which resulted in the secession of South Carolina on December 29, 1860. Within weeks another six States joined the conspiracy against the Union, and broke away to form the *Confederate States of America,* with Jefferson Davis as president.[667]

The conspirators raided armies, seized forts, arsenals, mints and other Union property. Even members of President Buchanan's Cabinet conspired to destroy the Union by damaging the public credit and working to bankrupt the nation.[668] Buchanan claimed to deplore secession but took no steps to check it, even when a U.S. naval ship was fired upon by South Carolinian rebel batteries.

"South Carolina's 'Ultimatum'"
Published in: American political prints, around 1861 [669]

Summary: In late December 1860 three commissioners from the newly seceded state of South Carolina met with lame-duck President Buchanan to negotiate for possession of Fort Sumter, a federal installation in Charleston Harbor. Buchanan's attempts to stay the situation and South Carolina governor Francis Pickens's insistence on Union evacuation of the fort are ridiculed here. Pickens (left) holds a lit fuse to a giant Union cannon "Peacemaker," which is pointed at his own abdomen. He threatens, "Mr. President, if you don't surrender that fort at once, I'll be "blowed" if I don't fire." Buchanan (right) throws up his hands in alarm and cries, "Oh don't! Governor Pickens, don't fire! till I get out of office." In the background a steamer makes its way across Charleston Harbor toward Fort Sumter. The print probably appeared early in 1861, amid mounting tensions over the fate of the fort and uneasy relations between Washington and South Carolina.

The United States government under Buchanan refused to abandon its forts that were in territory claimed by the *Confederacy*. According to the *Constitution* (1787/1789), as well as the previous *Articles of Confederation* (1778), *Declaration of Independence* (1776), and *Articles of Association* (1774), the Union was to be perpetual.[670] Secession was not a lawful option.

Once war with the United States began, the Confederacy fastened its hopes for survival on military intervention by Britain and France. Jefferson's widow, Varina H. Davis, compiled his memoirs in two volumes entitled, "Jefferson Davis: A Memoir by His Wife," in which establishes that <u>the main hope of the Confederate States was in military intervention by foreign countries</u>.[671]

The Confederates relied on European interest in southern cotton exports, believing that "cotton is king." Great Britain had much to lose by (officially) recognizing the Confederacy. Even before the Confederacy fired the first shots and annihilated Fort Sumter in Charleston, South Carolina, U.S. Secretary of State William H. Seward had made clear the Union's intention to declare war on nations recognizing the Confederacy.

The cost to Britain to war with the United States would be high: the immediate loss of American grain shipments, the end of exports to the United States, the seizure of billions of pounds invested in American securities. War would have meant higher taxes, another invasion of Canada, and full-scale worldwide attacks on the British merchant fleet.[672]

General P.G.T. Beauregard [673]

The opening shot of the rebellion was fired on Fort Sumter in South Carolina on April 12, 1861 by Confederate General and Scottish Rite Freemason P.G.T. Beauregard,[674] Jesuit leader of the Southern military operations. Beauregard was a professed Romanist who was raised in a distinguished family of Jesuits.[675]

Although the Confederate States sought the recognition and support of Great Britain, France, and even the Vatican, no European or other foreign nation <u>officially</u> recognized the Confederate States as an independent country.[676] However, a letter exchange[677] between Pope Pius IX[678] and Jefferson Davis reveals something different:

"Richmond, Va., Sept. 25, 1863.

Very Venerable Sovereign Pontiff:

The letters which you have written to the clergy of New Orleans and New York have been communicated to me, and I have read with emotion the deep grief therein expressed for the ruin and devastation caused by the war which is now being waged against the States and people who have selected me as their president, and your orders to your clergy to exhort the people to peace and charity. I am deeply sensible of the christian charity which has impelled you to this reiterated appeal to the clergy. It is for this reason that I feel it my duty to express personally and in the name of the Confederate States our gratitude for such sentiments of christian good feeling and love, and to assure Your Holiness, that the people threatened even on their own hearths, with the most cruel oppression and terrible carnage is desirous as it always has been, to see the end of this impious war; that we have ever addressed prayers to heaven for that issue which Your Holiness now desires; that we desire none of our enemies possessions, that we merely fight to resist the devastation <u>of our country</u> and the shedding of our best blood, and to force them to let us live in peace under the protection of our own institutions, and under our laws, which not only insure to everyone the enjoyment of his temporal rights, but also the free exercise of his religion.

I pray Your Holiness to accept on the part of myself and the people of the Confederate States our sincere thanks for your efforts in favor of peace.

May the Lord preserve the days of Your Holiness and keep you under His divine protection.

(Signed) Jefferson Davis."

An 1870 German drawing shows Pius IX as "Papst und König," Pope and King[679]

Pius IX was not only pope, but until 1870, also the Sovereign Ruler of the Papal States. His rule was considered secular, and as such, he was occasionally accorded the title "king."[680]

The Pope's reply on December 3, 1863:

"Illustrious and honorable President,

Salutation.

We have just received with all suitable welcome the persons sent by you to place in our hands your letter, dated 25th of Sept. last. Not slight was the pleasure we experienced when we learned, from those persons and the letter, with what feelings of joy and gratitude, illustrious and honorable President, as soon as you were informed of our letters to our venerable brother, John, Archbishop of New York, and John, Archbishop of New Orleans, dated the 18th of October of last year, and in which we have with all our strength exerted and exhorted those venerable brothers that in their episcopal piety and solicitude, they should endeavor with the most ardent zeal and in our name, to bring about the end of the fatal Civil War which has broken out in those countries in order that the American people may obtain peace and concord and dwell charitably together.

It is particularly agreeable to us to see that you, illustrious and honorable President, and your people, were animated with the same desires of peace and tranquility which we have in our letters inculcated upon our venerable brothers. May it please God at the same time to make other people of America and their rulers reflecting seriously how terrible is civil war and what calamities it engenders, listen to the inspirations of a calmer spirit and adopt resolutely the part of peace.

As for us, we shall not cease to offer up the most fervent prayers to God Almighty that He may pour out upon all the people of America the spirit of peace and charity, and that He will stop the great evils which afflict them. We at the same time beseech the God of Pity to shed abroad upon you, the light of His Grace and attach you to us by a perfect friendship.

Given at Rome, at St. Peters the 3rd of December, 1863 of our Pontificate Eighteen.

(Signed) Pius IX."   [emphasis added]

For there is nothing covered, that shall not be revealed; neither hid, that shall not be known. Therefore whatsoever ye have spoken in darkness shall be heard in the light; and that which ye have spoken in the ear in closets shall be proclaimed upon the housetops.

The Pope's letter gave *de facto* (concerning fact; in practice or actuality, but not officially established)[681] recognition to the rebellious *Confederate States of America*. He also used his influence with Catholic Church leaders in New York (North) and New Orleans (South) to assist the Confederacy. In reading Pope Pius IX's letter of response, President Lincoln exclaimed, "This letter of the Pope has entirely changed the nature and ground of the war."[682]

It is important realization that Pius IX made significant changes to Catholic Church doctrine when he convened the First Vatican Council (1869-1870) and decreed **papal infallibility**,[683] a dogma of the Catholic Church that states that, in virtue of the promise of Jesus to Peter, **the Pope is preserved from the possibility of error**, "When, in the exercise of his office as shepherd and teacher of all Christians, in virtue of his supreme apostolic authority, he defines a doctrine concerning faith or morals to be held by the whole Church."

Pius IX also defined the dogma of the Immaculate Conception of the Blessed Virgin Mary, meaning that Mary was conceived without original sin. Pius IX also granted the Marian title of *Our Mother of Perpetual Help*, a famous idol in the Byzantine Empire (Crete) that was entrusted to the *Redemptorist Order* of missionary priests.[684]

Brevet Major General Thomas Maley Harris [685]

Thomas Maley Harris[686] (1817–1906) was a physician and Union General during the Civil War. Following the Confederate surrender, Harris served on the military commission which tried the Lincoln Conspirators related to his assassination. Following the trial General Harris authored two books about the trial evidences and proceedings and then later he penned: *Rome's Responsibility for the Assassination of Abraham Lincoln*, which published in 1897 and was recorded in the Library of Congress. From the latter book General Harris writes:

"Our civil and religious institutions had their origin in the protest of Luther and his coadjutors against the despotism and corruptions of the Roman Catholic Church, that brought about the Reformation of the 16th century. Against this Reformation she has never ceased to fight, and never will, until her power shall have been overthrown. She has always been the sworn enemy of our Protestant institutions; and is to-day, as she ever has been bent on their destruction. She has never lost an opportunity to give them a stab in the dark. **In our dissensions over the question of slavery, she thought she saw a chance to destroy our government; and taking the side of slavery, used her whole influence, in the South, to stimulate and encourage secession and rebellion, and in the North to discredit and weaken the cause of the Union.** It was G. T. Beauregard, a rabid Roman Catholic, who first fired on the flag of our country at Fort Sumter; and let loose the dogs of war.

It was the Pope of Rome, and he alone, of all the European potentates, that gave his recognition and his blessing to the Confederate government; and by the very terms of his kind letter to its president, made it manifest that he expected, through his kind offices, to secure its recognition of his claims; and win it for the church. It was the Pope of Rome, and his faithful lieutenant, Louis Napoleon, who, taking advantage of our civil war, undertook to establish a Roman Catholic empire in Mexico, and for this purpose sent Maximilian, a Roman Catholic prince, under the protection of a French army, to usurp dominion, and take possession of the country. All of this was done in the hope that the Union cause would be lost; and that through the strife that she had fomented, two Roman Catholic empires would be established on the American continent, viz. that of Mexico under Maximilian and that of the Confederacy under Jefferson Davis; thus making it possible to make a conquest of the entire continent. This letter of the Pope to Jefferson Davis, couched in such courteous and loving terms, and showing so clearly that his sympathy was with the Southern cause, was well understood by his loyal and faithful subjects all over the North. Roman Catholic officers began to resign and the rank and file began to desert, from the time of the publication of that letter in 1863 to the close of the war. In reply to the boast so freely made by Roman Catholic editors and orators that the Irish fought the battles of the civil war and saved the nation, the following document, received from the Pension department at Washington, is here given…

In other words; of the 144,000 Irishmen that enlisted, 104,000 deserted. And it is reliably stated that most of these desertions occurred after the recognition of the Confederacy by the Pope. It is also a fact that of the five per cent of native Americans rated as deserters, 45 per cent of the 5 per cent were Catholics.

…It is true that there were some able and brave Roman Catholic officers in the Union army, who were truly loyal to the cause; as also many in the ranks who were nominally members of the Roman Catholic Church; but these were they who had been educated in our free schools, and had thus become so imbued with the American spirit, that they were no longer good Catholics. All honor to these!"

At the height of the Civil War, French and British troops had encircled the United States. Great Britain sent eleven thousand additional troops to Crown-controlled Canada, where Confederate agents were provided safe harbor. French troops were in Mexico and stationed on the Texas border where they were able to bypass the Union blockade and deliver supplies to the Confederacy.[687]

In consideration of the concluding decision by Britain and France and why they chose to refrain from formal recognition of the *Confederacy,* the facts in history point to it being that of threat of war by Russia.[688] The following account, written by American banker Wharton Barker and published in 1904 in *The Independent Vol. 56*, recounts Barker's conversation with Russian Czar Alexander II, the celebrated Liberator of the Russian serfs in 1879, a few years before his assassination at the hands of anarchists.

Wharton recounts his meeting with the Czar who confirms that, at the height of the *American Civil War* in 1862-1863, the Imperial Russian government had issued an ultimatum to Britain and France specifying that, if these powers should intervene on the side of the *Confederate States of America*, they would immediately find themselves at war with the Russian Empire. The Czar explained that the Russian battle fleets which arrived in great visual acclaim at New York and San Francisco in September-October of 1863 were visible proof of his policy.

Wharton provides account of Alexander II explaining the Russian approach to the *American Civil War* in the context of other cases in which Russia had acted to preserve a European and world balance of power designed to check the <u>inordinate</u> geopolitical and economic <u>ambitions</u> of Great Britain.

<u>"In the autumn of 1862,"</u> observed the Emperor, <u>"the Governments of France and Great Britain proposed to Russia, in a formal, but not in an official way, the joint recognition by European Powers of the independence of the Confederate States of America.</u> My immediate answer was: 'I will not co-operate in such action; and I will not acquiesce. On the contrary, I shall accept the recognition of the independence of the Confederate States by France and Great Britain as a <u>casus belli [an act or event that provokes or is used to justify war] for Russia.</u> And, in order that the Governments of France and Great Britain may understand that this is no idle threat, I will send a Pacific fleet to San Francisco and an Atlantic fleet to New York.' Sealed orders to both Admirals were given. After a pause, he proceeded: "My fleets arrived at the American ports; there was no recognition of the independence of the Confederate States by Great Britain and France. The American rebellion was put down, and the great American Republic continues.

All this I did because of love for my own dear Russia, rather than for love of the American Republic. <u>I acted thus because I understood that Russia would have a more serious task to perform if the American Republic, with advanced industrial development, were broken up and Great Britain should be left in control of most branches of modern industrial development.</u>" [689] [emphasis added]

There is fragrance of Heaven in an impression that Alexander II's strategy and policy may be compared to today's war-avoidance doctrine of Russian President Vladimir Putin and Russian Foreign Minister Sergey Lavrov. The entire article, as referenced by endnote link, is an extraordinary account of the events of 150 years ago that is like aromatherapy for the serious student of history and eschatology alike, as well as for statesmen.

"And today, before they can understand, they will have to remember," stated Webster Griffin Tarpley, Ph.D., in his article, "American Banker Wharton Barker's First-Person Account Confirms: Russian Tsar Alexander II Was Ready for War with Britain and France in 1862-1863 to Defend Lincoln and the Union – Americans 'Will Understand.'"[690]

Alexander II of Russia [691]

Wharton Barker, c.1911 [692]

Czar Alexander II of Russia was assassinated in 1881 by agents of the Jesuits, who threw hand-made bombs at him as he rode through the city of St. Petersburg, Russia. <u>His proclamation in 1861 had</u>

resulted in the emancipation of 23 million serfs. Because the Jesuits had fomented the Polish rebellion, Russian Czar Alexander II revoked Papal Rome's Concordat with Russia. He also twice broke diplomatic relations with the Papacy — in 1866 and in 1877. For these "crimes" against the Papacy and the Jesuits, as well as for his other "liberal reforms," Russian Czar Alexander II was hated by the Jesuits. They succeeded in murdering him in 1881.[693]

Since the commencement of Mr. Lincoln's presidential term in March, 1861, Russia had emancipated her slaves, and at a significant meeting held in mid-1864, at Geneva, Switzerland, patriotic resolutions were passed, **applauding his emancipation policy**. The good and wise of all countries, from the confines of Russia to the then half-civilized Japan, endorsed and sustained it.[694]

President Lincoln issued the *Emancipation Proclamation* on January 1, 1863, as the nation approached its third year of bloody civil war. The Proclamation declared "that all persons held as slaves" within the rebellious States "are, and henceforward shall be free." Although the *Emancipation Proclamation* did not end racial conflict and ideology in the nation, it captured the hearts and imagination of millions of Americans and fundamentally transformed the character of the war.

From the first days of the Civil War, slaves acted to secure their own liberty. The *Emancipation Proclamation* confirmed their insistence that the war for the Union must become a war for freedom. It added moral force to the Union cause and strengthened the Union both militarily and politically. As a milestone along the road to slavery's final destruction, the *Emancipation Proclamation* has assumed a place among the great documents of human freedom.[695]

The first reading of the Emancipation Proclamation before the cabinet [696]

Summary: Print shows a reenactment of Abraham Lincoln signing the Emancipation Proclamation on July 22, 1862, painted by Francis B. Carpenter at the White House in 1864. Depicted, from left to right are: Edwin M. Stanton, Secretary of War, Salmon P. Chase, Secretary of the Treasury, President Lincoln, Gideon Welles, Secretary of the Navy, Caleb B. Smith, Secretary of the Interior, William H. Seward, Secretary of State, Montgomery Blair, Postmaster General, and Edward Bates, Attorney General. Simon Cameron and Andrew Jackson are featured as paintings.

John Smith Dye, in his 1864 book, *The Adder's Den; or Secrets of the Great Conspiracy to Overthrow Liberty in America* which was "entered according to Act of Congress… in the year 1864 in the Clerk's Office of the District Court of the United States for the Southern District of New York" offers tremendous insight at that period of time in President Lincoln completing his first term of office and the tail end of the Civil War:

"Mr. Lincoln was unanimously re-nominated by the Union Convention that assembled at Baltimore on the 7th of June, for a second term of office. No Convention ever yet assembled in the United States, that so completely represented the will and wants of the American people. We predict that he will carry almost every State, entitled to an electoral vote for President, in November, 1864. To change the policy of the General Government, every man of reflection sees disaster, disgrace, and ruin to the cause of the Union. With the reelection of Abraham Lincoln of Illinois, and Andrew Johnson of Tennessee, the Union will virtually be restored. These are the only Union candidates, and they will receive the undivided support of every Union man.

The embarrassing circumstances which surrounded Mr. Lincoln during the commencement of his present term, the energy by which he overcame all obstacles, and his undying devotion to the cause of his country, entitles him, like our first Presidents, to a second term. With this will come a restoration of our glorious Union, and an honorable and lasting peace. Having finished the great work so ably commenced by the early Fathers, his well earned fame will enter immortality in company with Washington."

Abraham Lincoln giving his second Inaugural Address March 4, 1865 [697]

This photograph of Lincoln delivering his second inaugural address is a famous photograph of the event. President Lincoln stands in the center, with papers in his hand. According to Ronald C. White's *The Eloquent President: A Portrait of Lincoln Through His Words* (2005), John Wilkes Booth is visible in the photograph, in the top row right of center.

In his Second Inaugural Address,[698] March 4, 1865, just a few weeks before his assassination, President Lincoln gave his historic speech reflecting on the War between the North and the South. Understanding America's sin in breaking covenant with Almighty God by violating the liberty of all men proclaimed in her birth certificate the *Declaration of Independence*, clearly he understood the requirement of blood in Divine judgment.

"Fellow-Countrymen:

At this second appearing to take the oath of the Presidential office there is less occasion for an extended address than there was at the first. Then a statement somewhat in detail of a course to be pursued seemed fitting and proper. Now, at the expiration of four years, during which public declarations have been constantly called forth on every point and phase of the great contest which still absorbs the attention and engrosses the energies of the nation, little that is new could be presented. The progress of our arms, upon which all else chiefly depends, is as well known to the public as to myself, and it is, I trust, reasonably satisfactory and encouraging to all. With high hope for the future, no prediction in regard to it is ventured.

On the occasion corresponding to this four years ago all thoughts were anxiously directed to an impending civil war. All dreaded it, all sought to avert it. While the inaugural address was being delivered from this place, devoted altogether to saving the Union without war, insurgent agents were in the city seeking to destroy it without war--seeking to dissolve the Union and divide effects by negotiation. Both parties deprecated war, but one of them would make war rather than let the nation survive, and the other would accept war rather than let it perish, and the war came.

One-eighth of the whole population were colored slaves, not distributed generally over the Union, but localized in the southern part of it. These slaves constituted a peculiar and powerful interest. All knew that this interest was somehow the cause of the war. To strengthen, perpetuate, and extend this interest was the object for which the insurgents would rend the Union even by war, while the Government claimed no right to do more than to restrict the territorial enlargement of it. Neither party expected for the war the magnitude or the duration which it has already attained. Neither anticipated that the cause of the conflict might cease with or even before the conflict itself should cease. Each looked for an easier triumph, and a result less fundamental and astounding. Both read the same Bible and pray to the same God, and each invokes His aid against the other. It may seem strange that any men should dare to ask a just God's assistance in wringing their bread from the sweat of other men's faces, but let us judge not, that we be not judged. The prayers of both could not be answered. That of neither has been answered fully. The Almighty has His own purposes. 'Woe unto the world because of offenses; for it must needs be that offenses come, but woe to that man by whom the offense cometh.' **If we shall suppose that American slavery is one of those offenses which, in the providence of God, must needs come, but which, having continued through His appointed time, He now wills to remove, and that He gives to both North and South this terrible war as the woe due to those by whom the offense came, shall we discern therein any departure from those divine attributes which the believers in a living God always ascribe to Him? Fondly do we hope, fervently do we pray, that this mighty scourge of war may speedily pass away. Yet, if God wills that it continue until all the wealth piled by the bondsman's two hundred and fifty years of unrequited toil shall be sunk, and until every drop of blood drawn with the lash shall be paid by another drawn with the sword, as was said three thousand years ago, so still it must be said "the judgments of the Lord are true and righteous altogether."**

With malice toward none, with charity for all, with firmness in the right as God gives us to see the right, let us strive on to finish the work we are in, to bind up the nation's wounds, to care for him who shall have borne the battle and for his widow and his orphan, to do all which may achieve and cherish a just and lasting peace among ourselves and with all nations." [emphasis added]

Psalm 19:7-9 ~

The law of the Lord is perfect, converting the soul: the testimony of the Lord is sure, making wise the simple. The statutes of the Lord are right, rejoicing the heart: the commandment of the Lord is pure, enlightening the eyes. The fear of the Lord is clean, enduring for ever: the judgments of the Lord are true and righteous altogether.

The outbreak of the rebellion in the United States 1861 [699]
A lithograph designed by Charles Kimmel and published by Kimmel & Forster

Summary: A grand allegory of the Civil War in America, harshly critical of the Buchanan administration, Jefferson Davis, and the Confederacy. In the center stands Liberty, wearing a Phrygian cap and a laurel wreath. She is flanked by the figures of Justice (unblind folded, holding a sword and scales) and Abraham Lincoln. Principal figures (from left to right) are: Confederate president Jefferson Davis (beneath a palm tree about whose trunk winds a poisonous snake), James Buchanan (asleep), his secretary of war John B. Floyd, who was accused of misappropriation of government funds (raking coins into a bag), Justice, Columbia, Lincoln, Gen. Winfield Scott (in military uniform), and various figures exemplifying the generosity and suffering of the Northern citizenry. The left foreground is filled with Confederate soldiers, some of them engaged in tearing the Union flag from the hands of other soldiers. In the background are scenes of war. In contrast, on the right, the sun rises over mountains in the distance beyond a prosperous countryside. The print is evidently a companion piece to "The End of the Rebellion in the United States, 1865," (no.1866-1), a lithograph designed by Charles Kimmel and published by Kimmel & Forster in 1866. The same New York firm issued hundreds of illustrated patriotic envelopes during the Civil War.

108

Chapter Ten

Deeply Divided

Historians have emphasized that "While slavery and its various and multifaceted discontents were the primary cause of disunion, it was disunion itself that sparked the war."[700] The South's insistence of States' rights, "Popular Sovereignty," being the critical issue was entirely with regard to the protection of slavery.

There was resentment toward the issue of the import tariff which was legislated in earlier years to protect the manufacture of goods at home, as the South greatly desired Free Trade, though the Southern States rejected any compromise in preventing the disunion, including any compromise related to the tariff subject.[701] Other important factors of discontent included party politics, abolitionism, Southern nationalism, Northern nationalism, expansionism, economics, and modernization in the Antebellum period, the period before the Civil War.

The *United States of America* had become a nation of two distinct regions, or "Sections." The free States of the Northeast and Midwest[702] had a rapidly growing economy based on family farms, industry, mining, commerce, and transportation, with a large and rapidly growing urban population. Their growth was contributed to high birth rate and large numbers of European immigrants, primarily from Ireland and Germany.

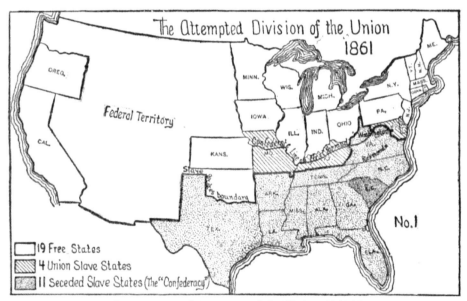

The Attempted Division of the Union 1861 [703]

The South was dominated by a settled plantation system based on slavery. There was some rapid growth taking place in the Southwest, for example Texas, contributed to high birth rates and high migration from the Southeast, but it had a much lower immigration rate from Europe. The South also had fewer large cities, and little manufacturing except in border areas.

Noteworthy and of significant consideration is that slave owners controlled politics and economics though about 70 percent of Southern whites owned no slaves and usually were engaged in subsistence agriculture.[704]

This small group of rich slave owners had seized political control of their own States and were trying to take over the national government in an illegitimate means in order to expand and protect slavery.

19th century engraving depicting a Slave Auction in South Carolina [705]
Published in "Slavery in South Carolina and the ex-slaves," in 1862

Before the Civil War, the South displayed traits of an oligarchy, or a government by the few; in this case significantly influenced by a planter aristocracy.[706] In 1850 only 1,733 families owned more than 100 slaves each, and this elite group provided the cream of the political and social leadership of the Section and nation.[707] The Slave Trade now illegal since 1808, there was some smuggling of African slaves into the country, however, the slave population primarily grew by birth, and breeding was encouraged by slave masters who even made promise to mothers that they would be set free if they would birth 10 babies.

Instead of compunctions of conscience on the subject of African slavery in America, the Southern leaders ultimately persuaded themselves to believe that it was not only moral and sanctioned by Divine Law, but that to perpetuate it was a philanthropic duty, beneficial to both races. In fact it was even declared to be "the highest type of civilization."[708]

Overall, the Northern population was increasing much more quickly than the Southern population, which made it increasingly difficult for the South to continue to influence the national government. By the time of the 1860 election, the heavily agricultural Southern States had fewer Electoral College votes than the rapidly industrializing northern states. Southerners felt a loss of federal concern for Southern pro-slavery political demands, and their continued domination of the Federal Government was threatened. This political calculus contributed to the Southerners' worry about the relative political decline of their region due to the North growing much faster in terms of population and industrial output.

The first crisis between the North and the South took place in 1820 and is referred to as "the Missouri crisis," which led to the *Missouri Compromise*. Thomas Jefferson, yet living, saw the significance and wrote a letter which was meant to be read by his fellow citizens.

Excerpt from a letter by Thomas Jefferson to John Holmes, April 22, 1820:

"…But this momentous question, like a fire bell in the night, awakened and filled me with terror. I considered it at once as the knell of the Union. It is hushed, indeed, for the moment. But this is a reprieve only, not a final sentence. A geographical line, coinciding with a marked principle, moral and political, once conceived and held up to the angry passions of men, will never be obliterated; and every new irritation will mark it deeper and deeper. …"[709] [emphasis added]

Already in 1820 Jefferson was predicting a civil war, forty years before it actually happened. He predicted that this geographical line coincided with a marked principal of **moral** and **political**. There was one set of morals and one set of politics in the South as well as one set of morals and one set of politics in the North, of which could not be obliterated. What this meant was there was one kind of philosophical or cultural ideal accepting information from the civil affairs or ruling order of their region in the North and another differing kind in the South. Inevitably they were going to find each other contemptible.[710]

In the interest of maintaining unity, Congressmen had mostly moderated opposition to slavery, resulting in numerous compromises such as the *Missouri Compromise of 1820* which held that a free State and a slave State would be admitted to the Union together so as not to upset the balance in Congress between the two ideologies.

After the *Mexican-American War* (1846-1848), the issue of slavery in the new territories led to the *Compromise of 1850*. While the compromise averted an immediate political crisis, it did not permanently resolve the issue of the Slave Power, the power of slaveholders to control the national government on the slavery issue.

Part of the 1850 Compromise was the *Fugitive Slave Law of 1850*, requiring that Northerners assist Southerners in reclaiming fugitive slaves, which many Northerners found to be extremely offensive.

As the North and South "Sections" developed bitter and hostile differences in ideologies in national politics, the collapse of the old "Second Party System"[711] in the 1850s hindered efforts of the politicians to reach yet one more compromise. The compromise that was reached, the 1854 *Kansas-Nebraska Act*, outraged many Northerners, and led to the formation of the "Republican Party,"[712] at Ripon, Wisconsin; the first major party with no appeal in the South.

Alexander Stephens [713]

It is worthy to take a look at the ideology of the Southern leaders. Alexander Stephens[714] (1812-1883) from Georgia, served in the House of Representatives both **before** the Civil War and **after** Reconstruction. Stephens was Vice President of the *Confederate States of America* during the Civil War and as the 50th Governor of Georgia from 1882 until his death in 1883. Stephens stated in a speech at Savannah, Georgia, March 12, 1861:

"That African slavery was the immediate cause of the late rupture and present revolution. Jefferson, in his forecast, had anticipated this as the rock on which the old Union would split. The prevailing opinion entertained by him, and most of the leading statesmen at the time of the formation of the old Constitution, was, that the enslavement of the African was in violation of the law of nature – that it was wrong in principle, social, moral and political.

Our new Government is founded on directly the opposite idea and is the first in the history of the world based on the great truth that the negro is not equal to the white man; that slavery is his natural and normal condition. **Thus the stone rejected by the first builders is become the chief stone in the corner of our new edifice.** Negro slavery is but in its infancy; we must increase and expand it. Central America and Mexico are all open to us." [715] [emphasis added]

Howell Cobb, 1844 [716]

Howell Cobb, 1860s [717]

Howell Cobb[718] (1815-1868) from Georgia, was a Southern Democrat, a five-term member of the United States House of Representatives and Speaker of the House from 1849 to 1851. He also served as Secretary of Treasury under President James Buchanan (1857–1860) and was the 40th Governor of Georgia (1851-1853). He is probably best known as one of the founders of the *Confederate States of America*, having served as the president of the provisional Confederate Congress, when delegates of the secessionist states issued creation of the Confederacy.

Cobb was a ruler of the Georgia Masonic mafia as well as a 33rd Degree Scottish Rite Freemason.[719] Cobb also joined Albert Pike's[720] Scottish Rite Supreme Council (of 33)[721] in March, 1860 while serving as Buchanan's Secretary of the Treasury.[722] Cobb stated:

"There is, perhaps, no solution of the great problem of reconciling the interests of labor and capital, so as to protect each from the encroachments and oppressions of the other, so simple as slavery. By making the laborer himself capital, the conflict ceases and the interests become identical."[723] [emphasis added]

Where some held the perspective that the conflict was only between free (employed) and slave (owned) labor, Cobb went beyond and placed it between capital (assets) and labor (workforce). Cobb was inferring that the only way to solve the irrepressible conflict between what he identified as capital and labor was to make slaves of all laborers everywhere and then, he projected, the conflict will cease.

De Bow's Review,[724] was a widely circulated magazine of "agricultural, commercial, and industrial progress and resource" in the South from 1846 until 1884. It bore the name of its first editor, James Dunwoody Brownson DeBow, who wrote much in the early issues. Published at New Orleans, Vol. XXV, for December, 1858, page 663, advocates the enslaving of the white race.[725] De Bow says:

"To say the white race is not the true and best slave race is to contradict all history. Too much liberty is the great evil of our age, and the vindication of slavery the best corrective."[726]

[emphasis added]

Rev. Dr. Benjamin Palmer [727]

The Reverend Dr. Benjamin Palmer[728] (1818-1902), an orator and Presbyterian theologian, was the first moderator of the Presbyterian Church in the *Confederate States of America*.

As pastor of the First Presbyterian Church of New Orleans, his Thanksgiving sermon in 1860 had great influence in leading Louisiana to join the *Confederate States of America*. The moral mouthpiece of the Slaveholders, preaching at New Orleans, said:

> "The providential trust of the South is to perpetuate the institution of domestic slavery as now existing, with freest scope for its natural development. …We must lift ourselves to the highest moral ground, and proclaim to all the world that we hold this trust from God, and in its occupancy are prepared to stand or fall."[729]

On January 27, 1861, before a standing room only audience Ebenezer W. Warren, pastor of the First Baptist Church of Macon, Georgia, delivered a <u>sermon defending black slavery as Biblical</u>. Entitled "Scriptural Vindication of Slavery," following is an excerpt of the sermon:

> "Slavery forms a vital element of the Divine Revelation to man. Its institution, regulation, and perpetuity, constitute a part of many of the books of the Bible …. The public mind needs enlightening from the sacred teachings of inspiration on this subject …. We of the South have been passive, hoping the storm would subside …. Our passiveness has been our sin. We have not come to the vindication of God and of truth, as duty demanded …. it is necessary for ministers of the gospel … to teach slavery from the pulpit, as it was taught by the holy men of old, who spake as moved by the holy Spirit …. Both Christianity and Slavery are from heaven; both are blessings to humanity; both are to be perpetuated to the end of time …. Because Slavery is right; and because the condition of the slaves affords them all those privileges which would prove substantial blessings to them; and, too, because their Maker has decreed their bondage, and has given them, as a race, capacities and aspirations suited alone to this condition of life …."[730]

To grasp a sense of how far this crisis went, in the 1850s, the Baptists split. The Baptists in the South and the Baptists in the North could not stand one another.[731] **Christians of both regions found contempt for one another because of a question of fundamental justice**. The Presbyterians split. The Methodists split. The Whig Party split. Eventually the Democratic Party split into three parts and there was the emergence of the Republican Party which was not even on the ballot in most of the Southern States in 1860. This was something that Jefferson had foreseen and its first revelation was in the *Nullification Crisis of 1832*.

On the surface the issues were about a tariff -- the *Tariff of Abominations* passed in 1828 under the direction of Henry Clay with the support of John Quincy Adams. They wanted a tightened-up Federal Government with oversight in public works, the building of roads, etc. and the ability to fund it. There was a rebellion of farmers who would have to pay these tariffs because a lot of the goods they purchased were imported from Europe.

Henry Clay [732]

The South Carolinians who viewed that slavery was a positive good, seized upon this as an opportunity to challenge the authority of the Federal Government. So they seized on the language used by Thomas Jefferson in his draft for the *Kentucky and Virginia Resolutions* of 1798, <u>although not the actual language</u>. Jefferson had died, his papers had been published, and they found the word "<u>nullification</u>." Where Madison used the word "interposition" in the Virginia Resolution, Jefferson had used the word, "nullification." The South Carolinians claimed that every State had the right to nullify any Federal law including opting-out anytime the State pleased. They lost on this particular issue in 1832. Behind the scene, of course, was their concern of preserving slavery and the ability to do their own thing on all issues concerning slavery.[733] It is important to keep in mind that the Federal Government has the power to control and regulate trade between the States. That meant it legally had the power to control the Slave Trade if it was an interstate Slave Trade. The Southerners, <u>meaning specifically the Slave Power</u>, were deeply concerned because the population in the North was growing faster than the population in the South and therefore the House of Representatives had representation that brought favor from the North and the West. So right there was brewing the making of secession and it was no accident that the first State to secede in 1860 was South Carolina.

John Quincy Adams, 1818 [734]

John Quincy Adams also foresaw this problem. In 1819, while as the U.S. Secretary of State, he kept a diary that is thought of by historians to be a wonderful and insightful document. Following is an entry that Adams made on December 27, 1819 in the middle of the Missouri crisis:

"Jefferson is one of the great men whom this country has produced, one of the men who has contributed largely to the formation of our national character – to much that is good and to not a little that is evil in our sentiments and manners. His Declaration of Independence is an abridged Alcoran of political doctrine, laying open the first foundations of civil society; but he does not appear to have been aware that it also laid open a precipice into which the slave-holding planters of his country sooner or later must fall. With the Declaration of Independence on their lips, and the merciless scourge of slavery in their hands, a more flagrant image of human <u>inconsistency</u> can scarcely be conceived than one of our Southern slave-holding republicans. <u>Jefferson has been himself all his life a slave-holder, but he has published opinions so blasting to the very existence of slavery, that, however creditable they may be to his candor and humanity, they speak not much for his prudence or his forecast as a Virginian planter.</u> The seeds of the Declaration of Independence are yet maturing. <u>The harvest</u> will be what West, the painter, calls <u>the terrible sublime</u>." [735] [emphasis added]

As we move forward in time, in 1857 came the infamous *Dred Scott v. Sanford* case which involved a slave who had been brought by his owner to Minnesota, where slavery was prohibited.

The first Roman Catholic to serve as Chief Justice of the United States Supreme Court,[736] Roger B. Taney, was a staunch supporter of slavery who was intent on protecting Southerners from "northern aggression." Taney was the son of a wealthy slave-owning family, who raised tobacco.[737]

<u>In order that the Dred Scott Decision should not in any way hazard the election of the Jesuit's presidential candidate, James Buchanan, the Jesuit schemers perverted justice by compelling Justice Taney to join their unholy pro-slavery crusade by withholding and keeping secret his unrighteous decision for over six months, until after the election.</u> It was not published until two days after the Inauguration, March 6th, 1857.[738] Justice Taney went beyond the question before him, writing in the Court's majority opinion that, because Scott was a "Negro," he was not a citizen and therefore had no right to sue. He also stated that the framers of the *Constitution* believed that Negroes "had no rights which the white man was bound to respect; and that the Negro might justly and lawfully be reduced to slavery for his benefit.

114

He was bought and sold and treated as an ordinary article of merchandise and traffic, whenever profit could be made by it."[739]

Roger B. Taney [740]   Portrait of Dred Scott, 1888 [741]

Referencing language in the *Declaration of Independence* that includes the phrase, "all men are created equal," Taney reasoned that "it is too clear for dispute, that the enslaved African race were not intended to be included, and formed no part of the people who framed and adopted this declaration..."[742] The Court also declared the *Missouri Compromise as* unconstitutional, thus permitting slavery in all of the country's territories.[743]   The ruling had the immediate effect of enflaming bitter and even violent opposition in the North.

The effect of this Supreme Court ruling permanently incorporated slavery into the *Constitution*. It did so by misinterpreting the reason that the drafters of the *Constitution* delayed the abolition of slavery. The opinion of the Court misconstrued Congress' intent to permit the Slave Trade for a period of years as an unreserved right to own another person (institution of slavery). The Court was incorrect to claim that this clause had created a constitutionally protected right to own a person as property.   The **misinterpretation** of the drafters' intent is found in the following passage of the Supreme Court's opinion:

> "The right of property in a slave is distinctly and expressly affirmed in the Constitution. The right to traffic in it, like an ordinary article of merchandise and property, was guaranteed to the citizens of the United States, and every State that might desire it, for twenty years.   And the Government, in express terms is pledged to protect it in all future time, if the slave escapes his owner..."[744]
>
> [emphasis added]

Drawing a parallel to Proverbs 25:11,

"A word fitly spoken is like apples of gold in pictures of silver,"

Lincoln described the *Declaration of Independence* as an "apple of gold," and the *Constitution* as the "frame of silver" around it when he said,

> "The assertion of that principle, at that time, was the word, 'fitly spoken' which has proved an 'apple of gold' to us. The Union, and the Constitution, are the picture of silver, subsequently framed

around it. The picture was made, not to conceal, or destroy the apple; but to adorn, and preserve it. The picture was made for the apple—not the apple for the picture."[745]

The North held conviction that the *Constitution* was not to be considered independently of the purpose which it was designed to serve. The *Constitution* acts to guard the principles enshrined in the *Declaration of Independence*. As the embodiment of the *Declaration's* principles, the *Constitution* created a frame of government with a clear objective. The *Constitution* is not a collection of compromises, or an empty vessel whose meaning can be redefined to fit the needs of the time; it is the embodiment of an eternal, undisputable truth.

Abraham Lincoln defended the Union and sought to defeat the Confederate insurrection because he held that the principles of the *Declaration* and *Constitution* were inviolable. In his speeches and in his statecraft, Lincoln desired to demonstrate that self-government is not doomed to either be so strong that it overwhelms the rights of the people or so weak that it is incapable of surviving.[746]

The industrializing North and agricultural Midwest became committed to the economic character of free-labor industrial capitalism. Arguments that slavery was undesirable for the nation had long existed, and early in American history were made even by some prominent Southerners. After 1840, abolitionists denounced slavery as not only a social evil but a moral wrong.

Many Northerners, especially leaders of the new Republican Party, considered slavery a great national evil and believed that a small number of Southern owners of large plantations controlled the national government with the goal of spreading that evil. Southern defenders of slavery, for their part, increasingly came to contend that "Negroes" actually benefited from slavery, an assertion that alienated Northerners even further.

Jeremiah 22:13 ~

> *Woe unto him that buildeth his house by unrighteousness, and his chambers by wrong; that useth his neighbour's service without wages, and giveth him not for his work;*

Micah 6:8 ~

> *He hath shewed thee, O man, what is good; and what doth the Lord require of thee, but to do justly, and to love mercy, and to walk humbly with thy God?*

Gordon, or "Whipped Peter"[747]

Gordon, also known as "Whipped Peter," had been a slave, who escaped from a Louisiana plantation in March, 1863. Gordon fled over 40 miles in 10 days while being chased by bloodhounds. Gordon became known as the subject of photographs that documented the extensive scarring of his back from whippings received as a slave.

Abolitionists distributed this photograph of Gordon throughout the United States to provide visual evidence of the brutal mistreatment of slaves. The photo also inspired many free blacks to enlist in the Union Army. Gordon joined the United States Colored Troops soon after their founding, and served as a soldier in the war. In July, 1863, this image appeared in an article about Gordon that published in *Harper's Weekly,* the most widely read journal during the Civil War.

Historian David W. Blight PhD.[748] is a Professor of American History at Yale University and Director of the Gilder-Lehrman Center for the Study of Slavery, Resistance and Abolition. Professor Blight is quoted in the PBS *American Experience* history series documentary, "The Abolitionists:"

> "So many abolitionists had said after [the] Dred Scott [Decision] '…You see, we've been telling you for decades there's a Slave Power conspiracy out there of presidents, Supreme Court, members of Congress, people [amongst the] bankers, of ship owners, to not only preserve but expand the system of slavery until it dominates every aspect of American society and economy. And now there's the Supreme Court saying slavery has an eternal future in the United States.'"[749]   [emphasis added]

Throughout the 1850s as the controversy between the North and South grew in tension particularly with the issue of expansion and whether the new States coming into the Union carved out of the western Territory should be free or slave, the drama heightened over the settling of Kansas.

Newcomers who ventured into Kansas were of an assortment of backgrounds. Most of the Northerners were just ordinary westward-moving pioneers in search of richer lands beyond the sunset.[750] There was a small part of the inflow that was financed by a group of Northern abolitionists or "free-soilers," known as "The Secret Six."[751] *The Secret Six* were a group of wealthy and/or influential northern men who held strong conviction toward abolition.[752]

The Secret Six

| Thomas Wentworth Higginson [753] | Samuel Gridley Howe [754] | Theordore Parker [755] | Franklin Benjamin Sanborn [756] | Gerrit Smith[757] | George Luther Stearns [758] |

In search for money and guns to help continue his free State battles in Kansas, John Brown (1800-1859) became acquainted with these Bostonian/New York gentlemen who were desperate in the cause and believed that violent measure was necessary to end the poison of slavery.[759]

John Brown, 1856 [760]

Brown was born in Connecticut and raised in Ohio by parents who instilled in him a strong belief in the Bible and a strong hatred of slavery. He later moved to Pennsylvania with his large family and continued his family's business of tanning animal skins. Eventually Brown became a conductor in the *Underground Railroad* (a network of antislavery activists and safe houses) and organized a self-protection league for freemen of color and fugitive slaves. Brown held conviction that God had called him as the advocate to lead slaves into freedom, no matter what it may take.[761]

After the *Kansas-Nebraska Act of 1854* gave citizens of those two territories the lawful right to choose for themselves whether their new State entering the Union would permit or prohibit slavery, many abolitionists moved to Kansas in their effort to prevent "the peculiar institution." Brown along with five of his sons was among them. Fervent Northern abolitionists were determined that when the territory was ready to enter the Union as a State, it would do so as a free State. Fervent Southern pro-slavery defenders were also pouring into Kansas, in order to secure it for the benefit of pro-slavery.[762]

On May 21, 1856, "Missouri Pukes," (more politely known as "Border Ruffians")[763] attacked the anti-slavery town of Lawrence, Kansas, with pillaging and burning. A couple of days later, U.S. Senator Charles Sumner from Massachusetts was severely beaten with a cane on the Senate floor by Senator Preston Brooks of South Carolina because of hostile verbal attacks the anti-slavery Sumner had made on another South Carolinian.[764]

An 1856 lithograph cartoon depicting
Sen. Preston Brooks' caning of Rep. Charles Sumner in the U.S. Senate chamber [765]

We will recall Senator Sumner and his significant Congressional participation post-Civil War further on in the American Republic's story which will also provide insight as to his radical belligerence and outspokenness.

As previously stated, Missouri pro-slavery men committed gross atrocities too gory in detail[766] to retell against the free State people who lived in Kansas. Secret Societies were everywhere organized in Missouri and Kansas. There are affidavits of record in the *Kansas Committee Report* to the testimony that these societies were organized specifically to drive free State people out of the Territory and to make Kansas a slave State.[767] There was a passionate mix of many things going on at the same time.

We move forward to 1858, with *The Secret Six* along with other friends and family providing funds and arms to John Brown in the ongoing fight against slavery. Earlier, Brown focused his activities on Kansas. Now he had a more ambitious plan of invading Virginia and inciting a slave insurrection. Whether the members of *The Secret Six* were initially against it or not, they became excited by the prospect of action and set about raising money for Brown.[768]

John Brown had originally asked Harriet Tubman[769] (a fugitive slave, abolitionist and conductor of the Underground Railroad) and Frederick Douglass,[770] (former slave, abolitionist leader and orator) both of whom he had met in his formative years as an abolitionist in Massachusetts to join him in his raid, but Tubman was prevented by illness, and Douglass declined because he believed that Brown's plan would fail.

Harriet Tubman, 1885 [771]　　　　　　　　Frederick Douglass [772]

In October, 1859, accompanied by a group of 20 men, John Brown moved forward in his plan to start an armed slave insurrection by seizing a United States arsenal at Harpers Ferry, Virginia (now West Virginia).　Brown's raiders captured a number of prisoners, including George Washington's great-grand-nephew, Lewis Washington.　Local militia trapped Brown and his men inside the arsenal.

During the short siege, three citizens of Harpers Ferry were killed.　Ironically, the first person to die in John Brown's raid was a black railroad baggage handler who confronted the raiders on the night they attacked the town. A couple of days later, a company of U.S. Marines, under the command of Army Lt. Col. Robert E. Lee, broke into the building killing ten raiders and capturing seven others, including Brown.

In December, 1859, after being tried and convicted of murder, insurrection, and treason against the Commonwealth of Virginia, Brown was hanged.[773]　Brown was viewed as a martyr among abolitionists and his hanging brought inspiration to abolitionists in striving even harder in the cause.

The Southern newspapers reported the raid on Harpers Ferry as an isolated incident; the work of a mad fanatic and his followers.　When information began to surface that Brown had discussed his plans with prominent Northern abolitionists who provided him support by means of finances and arms, Southern attitudes became sour.　Because many in the abolition movement projected Brown as a martyr, many Southerners became convinced that abolitionists intended to commit genocide on white slave owners. The North and South drew even farther apart from each other.[774]

The Harpers Ferry raid is considered one of the major events that ultimately led to the Civil War. Many historians view John Brown and his Harpers Ferry raid as "the match that lit the fuse on the powder keg of secession and civil war."[775]

Harriet Tubman, whom Brown referred to as "General Tubman,"[776] had told a friend on the day of Brown's execution:

"I've been studying, and studying upon it, and it's clear to me, it wasn't John Brown that died on that gallows. When I think how he gave up his life for our people, and how he never flinched, but was so brave to the end, it's clear to me it wasn't mortal man, it was God in him. When I think of all the groans and tears and prayers I've heard on the plantations, and remember that God is a prayer-hearing God, I feel that his time is drawing near."[777]

A few months later on February 27, 1860 then Presidential candidate Abraham Lincoln delivered a speech at Cooper Institute that states an opposite perspective of the incident:

"…That affair, [John Brown and his Harper's Ferry raid] in its philosophy, corresponds with the many attempts, related in history, at the assassination of kings and emperors. An enthusiast broods over the oppression of a people till he fancies himself commissioned by Heaven to liberate them. He ventures the attempt, which ends in little else than his own execution."[778] [emphasis added]

Interior of the engine house during John Brown's raid on Harpers Ferry [779]

Chapter Eleven

House Divided, Liberty Restrained, and a Rump Congress

Abraham Lincoln, the 16th President of the United States, served from March 4, 1861 until his assassination on April 14, 1865, and subsequent death on April 15th, just six days after the Civil War ended.[780]   At the same time Lincoln received a bullet to his head on the eve of "Good Friday," U.S. Secretary of State William H. Seward was stabbed multiple times by *Knights of the Golden Circle* ally[781] to Lincoln-assassin John Wilkes Booth, as he lay in bed recovering from a fractured jaw, the result of a carriage accident.[782]

Lithograph of the Assassination of Abraham Lincoln [783]

Ford's Theatre, 1865 [784]
Site of the assassination of President Lincoln

Seward survived, and after a summer convalescing, returned to the State Department.[785]   Included in the plan of assassinations by *Knights of the Golden Circle* cohorts[786] were Vice President Andrew Johnson and Union General Ulysses S. Grant which both were averted due to a change of plans.[787]

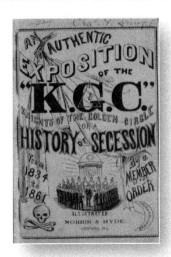

An Authentic Exposition of the "K.G.C." "Knights of the Golden Circle;" or, A History of Secession 1834 to 1861, Illustrated.
Published in 1861 by a Member of the Order [788]

The evidence is unmistakable in the conspiracy to overthrow the government of the American Republic.[789] In the June, 1867 trial of co-conspirator to Lincoln's assassination, John H. Surratt, Assistant District Attorney Nathaniel Nelson made the opening address. An excerpt from the address:

"You are to turn back the leaves of history, to that red page, on which is recorded in letters of blood the awful incidents of that April night on which the assassins' work was done on the body of the chief Magistrate of the American Republic,--a night, on which for the first time in our existence as a nation, **a blow was struck with the fell purpose, not only to destroy a human life, but the life of the nation, the life of LIBERTY itself.**"[790] [emphasis added]

Noteworthy is that after the murder, Mr. Surratt fled America to Canada, then Britain, ending in Rome where he joined the Vatican army, known as the Zouaves.[791]

John Surratt in Zouave uniform [792]

The Jesuit-controlled "front group," the *Knights of the Golden Circle* (KGC)[793] were a militant oath-bound secret society dedicated to promoting Southern rights which included slavery and extending American hegemony over the *Golden Circle* region that encompassed the Caribbean islands, Central America, and Mexico. KGC recruiters told membership candidates, like John Wilkes Booth, that the society was dedicated to expansion southward and protecting constitutional liberties from the ravages of abolitionists and "Black Republicans." But the higher degrees of the society were pledged to a further secret proslavery and empire-building agenda that was not fully shared with the lower degrees.[794]

When President Lincoln had entered office, he not only inherited a national dilemma, he also incurred a unique set of circumstances when seven Southern States seceded from the Union before his inauguration, with four more Southern States following just afterwards.

The secession of States also caused their members of Congress to vacate their Congressional seats as confirmed in the third session of the 36th Congress, House of Representatives[795] (Dec. 3, 1860 to March 3, 1861) as well as the Special Session of the Senate (March 4, 1861 to March 28, 1861,[796] and registered under the 37th Congress in *The Library of Congress,* "House Journal for the First Forty-three Sessions of Congress,") called by proclamation[797] of President Buchanan.

Although both houses of Congress continued to meet with only one-fifth of their members, the quorum to conduct business under the *Constitution* had been lost, therefore resulting in Congress ceasing to exist as a lawful deliberative body. This is known as a "rump," legislature having only a small part of its original membership and therefore being unrepresentative or lacking in authority.[798]

Several Southern Senators and Representatives resigned their seats with the secession of their States; others were expelled. Other Southern Congressmen remained and for the most part contributed to an embittered, hostile situation where conducting business, much more seeking remedy, was futile.

Both the Senate[799] and the House[800] had adjourned their sessions "without day." Adjourning without day, or *sine die*[801] (pronounced "sie-na die-ee,"[802] meaning without a day fixed), is a parliamentary practice that formally ends the duties for the current session of that legislative body. When members of the Senate and the House of Representatives walked out of Congress because their States had seceded, it did in fact create vacancies. Suggestion or thought that the adjournment of Congress without day, or *sine die,* while not having a quorum to do business was what created a suspension of the *Constitution* as well as its law form is <u>not</u> correct.

The foundational government of the United States had established precedence in the universal and fundamental *Law of Perpetuity*. The *Constitution of the United States* will always be "the law of the land" and was very thoughtfully written to sufficiently provide for managing such situations.

Having seceded from the Union, the seven Southern States held their own elections and established a government <u>foreign</u> to the *Constitution*, the *"Confederate States of America,"* also known as *"the Confederacy."* This was an unlawful act as pointed out in President Buchanan's address before the Senate in Special Session on March 4, 1861:[803]

> "…I hold that, in contemplation of universal law, and of the Constitution, **the Union of these States is perpetual.** Perpetuity is implied, if not expressed, in the fundamental law of all national governments. <u>It is safe to assert that no government proper ever had a provision in its organic law for its own termination.</u> Continue to execute all the express provisions of our national Constitution, and the Union will endure forever — <u>it being impossible to destroy it except by some action not provided for in the instrument itself.</u>

> <u>"Again, **if** the United States be not a government proper, but an association of States in the nature of contract merely, can it, as a contract, be peaceably unmade by less than all the parties who made it? One party to a contract may violate it — break it, so to speak; but does it not require **all** to lawfully rescind it?</u>

> "Descending from these general principles, we find the proposition that, **in legal contemplation, the Union is perpetual, confirmed by the history of the Union itself**. The Union is much older than the Constitution. It was formed, in fact, by the <u>Articles of Association</u> in 1774. It was matured and continued by the <u>Declaration of Independence</u> in 1776. It was further matured, and the faith of all the then thirteen States expressly plighted and engaged that it should be perpetual, by the <u>Articles of Confederation</u> in 1778. And finally, in 1787, one of the declared objects for ordaining and establishing the <u>Constitution</u> in 1787 was "to form a more perfect union."

> "But if destruction of the Union by one, or by a part only, of the States, be lawfully possible, the Union is less perfect than before the Constitution, having lost the vital element of perpetuity.

It follows, from these views, that no State, upon its own mere motion, can lawfully get out of the Union; that resolves and ordinances to that effect are legally void; and that acts of violence, within any State or States, against the authority of the United States, are insurrectionary or revolutionary, according to circumstances...."

By violation of the *Constitution* it became a matter of National issue in that the property of the United States was taken outside of due process of law.

The people of the Southern States were enflamed with Slaveholder/politician propaganda while manipulated to support the efforts of the Confederacy in seeking to destroy the Union. Treason was Northern vocabulary to describe the Confederacy's secession. Though exhaustive effort was made to preserve the Union in offering every compromise conceivable, the Southern congressmen who had remained seated in Congress refused **any** offer or effort made to preserve the Union.[804]

On April 12, 1861, after the Confederacy initiated "war," or which more appropriately should be referred to as "insurrection," there was no alternative for the North but to impede the insurrection and reclaim Federal Government property, as well as the lands of the South. As President Buchanan stated in his Presidential Proclamation, no State on its own action can lawfully leave the Union because of the universal and fundamental law of perpetuity. Any attempt to secede would be legally void. The Southern States could not by law make themselves a sovereign nation or create their own sovereign government. President Buchanan went on to proclaim that any acts of violence within any State or States against the authority of the United States, would be insurrectionary or revolutionary. The only solution was for President Lincoln, who was now the Executive in office, to call forth the militia and federalize them, and suppress the insurrection. President Lincoln also had the responsibility to act against domestic violence as directed by Article IV, Section 4 of the *Constitution*:

"The United States shall guarantee to every State in this Union a Republican Form of Government, and shall protect each of them against Invasion; and on Application of the Legislature, or of the Executive (when the Legislature cannot be convened) against domestic Violence."[805]

President James Buchanan, 1859 [806]   President Abraham Lincoln, 1861 [807]

Congress was not in session at that time. Both houses had just previously closed session with no quorum to function as a deliberative body under the *Constitution*, and closed "without day," or *sine die*. President Lincoln responded to the crisis by Presidential Proclamation in which he summoned both houses of Congress to assemble on the 4th of July. The proclamation to convene Congress was made in the same Presidential Proclamation that he called forth the militia.

On April 15, 1861, President Lincoln issued Presidential Proclamation 80, "Calling Forth the Militia and Convening an Extra Session of Congress."[808]

By the President of the United States of America

A Proclamation

Whereas the laws of the United States have been for some time past and now are opposed and the execution thereof obstructed in the states of South Carolina, Georgia, Alabama, Florida, Mississippi, Louisiana, and Texas by combinations too powerful to be suppressed by the ordinary course of judicial proceedings or by the powers vested in the marshals by law:

Now, therefore, I, Abraham Lincoln, President of the United States, in virtue of the power in me vested by the Constitution and the laws, have thought fit to call forth, and hereby do call forth, the militia of the several states of the Union to the aggregate number of 75,000 in order to suppress said combinations and to cause the laws to be duly executed.

The details for this object will be immediately communicated to the state authorities through the War Department.

I appeal to all loyal citizens to favor, facilitate, and aid this effort to maintain the honor, the integrity, and the existence of our National Union and the perpetuity of popular government and to redress wrongs already long enough endured.

I deem it proper to say that the first service assigned to the forces hereby called forth will probably be to repossess the forts, places, and property which have been seized from the Union; and in every event the utmost care will be observed, consistently with the objects aforesaid, to avoid any devastation, any destruction of or interference with property, or any disturbance of peaceful citizens in any part of the country.

And I hereby command the persons composing the combinations aforesaid to disperse and retire peaceably to their respective abodes within twenty days from this date.

Deeming that the present condition of public affairs presents an extraordinary occasion, I do hereby, in virtue of the power in me vested by the Constitution, convene both Houses of Congress. Senators and Representatives are therefore summoned to assemble at their respective chambers at 12 o'clock noon on Thursday, the 4th day of July next, then and there to consider and determine such measures as, in their wisdom, the public safety and interest may seem to demand.

In witness whereof I have hereunto set my hand and caused the seal of the United States to be affixed.

Done at the city of Washington, this 15th day of April, A.D. 1861, and of the Independence of the United States the eighty-fifth.

ABRAHAM LINCOLN.

By the President:

WILLIAM H. SEWARD,

Secretary of State.

Where any thought, suggestion, or "patriot myth" may arise pertaining to President Lincoln having violated or usurped Congress' powers in Article I, Section 8, Clause 11, "the War Powers Clause," of the *Constitution*, (*The Congress shall have the power… To declare War, grant Letters of Marque and Reprisal, and make Rules concerning Captures on Land and Water;)*[809] we must clarify and understand that war was not declared in this matter of insurrection and domestic violence.

Congressional provision had indeed been made in law by the "Calling Forth" Act of 1792[810] (and in 1795[811] by authorizing the President to federalize the militia) by delegating authority to the President to call out the militia and issue it orders when invasion appeared imminent, or to suppress insurrections.

While the Act gave the President some lawful ability to promptly respond in case of invasion, it constrained his authority in the case of insurrections by requiring that a federal judge certify that the civil authority and the militia were powerless to meet the urgent situation. The President was also required to order the insurrectionaries to disband before he could mobilize the militia.[812]

Under Article II, Section 3 of the *Constitution*, the President has the power to convene and adjourn Congress. President Lincoln had responded and acted within the law.

The "so-called" seceded States were determined to control the Federal Government property within its borders. Seven forts, four arsenals, one Navy Yard, and the United States Mint at New Orleans stolen at this time held value at $27 million.[813]

It was when Lincoln made the decision to send provisions to Fort Sumter in South Carolina so the garrison would not starve, first notifying the South Carolina governor of the situation and his simple intention, that prompted the attack by Confederate forces and led to the secession of four more States.

At this same time it was necessary for Lincoln to confront the threat of disloyal citizens in Union States. The greatest threat was that of the border States of Missouri, Kentucky, and especially Maryland because of being located precisely north of Washington. The nation's capital already faced a Confederate Virginia just across the Potomac River. Securing the nation's capital was critical to the fate of the United States and dependent on holding Maryland in the Union.[814]

In mid-April, 1861, by authorizing the suspension of the *Writ of Habeas Corpus* via Executive Orders, Lincoln was able to manage the threat posed by disloyal citizens while also strategizing to secure Maryland for the Union.[815] [816]

In America's early days, Executive Orders were simple tools of communication in the Executive branch, primarily for death announcements and war department information similar to an interoffice memorandum in the days before computers and the World Wide Web. There were very few issued prior to the Civil War. Since that time it is astounding to see how Executive Orders have taken on a whole new meaning.[817]

It will become apparent how operations in law form changed and progressed into another body politic during this period of the House divided. This was the plan of Rome and its militia, the Jesuits, operating through their secret societies as they have sought to create a new "government" in accordance with their *New World Order* agenda.

Habeas Corpus in Latin means "you have the body." A *writ* is a judicial action such as a court order. A *Writ of Habeas Corpus* is an order that commands an individual or a government official who has restrained another to produce the prisoner before a civil court of justice in order to justify the prisoner's detention so that the court can determine the legality of custody and decide whether to order the prisoner's release.[818]

The Founding Fathers believed the *Writ of Habeas Corpus* was so essential to preserving liberty, justice, and republican form of government that they included in the very first article of the *Constitution* a limitation of its suspension for times only in cases of rebellion or invasion and when the public safety may require it.[819]

Article 1, Section 9, Clause 2 ~

The Privilege of the Writ of Habeas Corpus shall not be suspended, unless when in Cases of Rebellion or Invasion the public Safety may require it.[820]

Thomas Jefferson, 1791 [821]

James Madison, 1783 [822]
Madison was a member of the
Continental Congress in his 30s

In a July 31, 1788 letter from Thomas Jefferson to James Madison just after the initial framing of the *Constitution*, he stressed the importance of preserving the right of *habeas corpus*, supporting his stance by recalling history on the subject. Jefferson was firm in his position that the appropriate means in handling relative issues would be by a *trial by jury* as being the more just of the two.[823]

In effort to establish the critical importance of the *Writ of Habeas Corpus*, as well as an example of what the ramifications could be like in an uncareful suspension of this most precious liberty, we will review some history to gain insight. In 1804, during the last full year of his single term as Vice President to then President Thomas Jefferson, Aaron Burr (1756-1836),[824] engaged in the famous duel with his political rival Alexander Hamilton. Burr was never tried for the unlawful duel of which conviction and sentencing was death. Any charges against him were eventually dropped, however, Hamilton's death ended Burr's political career. Burr left Washington and traveled west seeking new opportunities, both economic and political.

Portrait of Aaron Burr, 1802 [825]   Portrait of Alexander Hamilton, 1806, 2 years after death[826]

In the autumn of 1806 the Jefferson Administration was perturbed with the mysterious behavior of the former vice president, Aaron Burr, in that his display of actions pointed to involvement in a conspiracy with a group of his associates who were planters, politicians, and army officers.[827]

There was evidence that Burr was making plans to precipitate a war with Spain and then set-up a separate government in the Western states (at that time would have included the Midwestern territory) of which were already irritated with Spain because of restrictions it had posed on commerce on the Mississippi prior to the Louisiana Purchase.)

The Louisiana Purchase [828]

Having reason to believe that Burr intended to seize New Orleans then attack Mexico and create an independent nation in the center of North America (inclusive of part of what we know today as the Southwest) as well as parts of Mexico, Jefferson was convinced that Burr was planning treason and took radical measures accordingly.[829]

Burr claimed that he intended to take possession of and farm 40,000 acres in the Texas Territory leased to him by the Spanish Crown. Although some historians are not clear regarding Burr's true intentions, others claim that he intended to take parts of Texas as well as a good portion of the Louisiana Purchase for personal gain.[830]

General James Wilkinson, 1797 [831]

General James Wilkinson[832] was a key partner of Burr's.[833] Commanding General of the Army during the 1780s, Wilkinson was known for his attempt to separate Kentucky and Tennessee from the Union. Burr had persuaded President Thomas Jefferson to appoint Wilkinson to the position of Governor of the Louisiana Territory in 1805. Of interest in this period of time is that General Wilkinson had declared Martial Law in New Orleans and arrested two alleged accomplices of Burr. He would later send a letter to Jefferson claiming that he had evidence of Burr's treason.[834]

In continuing, General Wilkinson disregarded the *Writ of Habeas Corpus* as issued by the Supreme Court of the New Orleans Territory and sent his prisoners under military guard to Charleston and then on to Washington while violating another *Writ of Habeas Corpus* issued by the United States District Court. Steps were taken to charge them with treason while they were detained at Washington under military arrest. Before charges could be established and before the prisoners could secure a release by *Writ of Habeas Corpus*, Jefferson asked Congress on January 23, 1807 to authorize him to suspend the privilege of the *Writ of Habeas Corpus*.

On that same day the Senate actually passed a Bill suspending the *writ* for three months "in all cases of treason, misprision of treason, or other high crimes or misdemeanor endangering the peace, safety or neutrality of the United States, in case of arrest by virtue of warrant or authority from the President or Governor of any State or Territory, or person acting under direction or authority of the President."[835]

This measure was considered very radical and prompted a stern outcry throughout the country. After hot opposition by the Federalists, the Bill was defeated in the House of Representatives on January 26, 1807 with a majority vote of 113 to 19.[836]

Representatives discussed the Bill before voting, determining that the communication from the President did not provide evidence of any danger to the United States that would warrant an extreme measure such as suspension of this *writ*. To bring forward an understanding of the seriousness of the suspension of the *Writ of Habeas Corpus*, following are a few statements by members of the House made during their discussion:[837]

Mr. Smilie: "A suspension of the privilege of the writ of habeas corpus is, in all respects, equivalent to repealing that essential part of the Constitution which secures that principle which has been called, in the country where it originated, the "palladium of personal liberty."

Mr. Burwell: "...He would ask gentlemen, if they seriously believed the danger sufficiently great to justify the suspension of this most important right of the citizen, to proclaim the country in peril, and to adopt a measure so pregnant with mischief, by which the innocent and guilty will be involved in one common destruction? ...What, then, will be said of us, if now, when the danger is over, firm in the attachment of the people to the Union, with ample resources to encounter any difficulties which may occur, we resort to a measure so harsh in its nature, oppressive in its operation, and ruinous as a precedent? While, in former times, it was thought unsafe to suspend this most important and valuable part of the Constitution, he would ask, whether the necessity at the present time could be considered greater? With regard to those persons who may be implicated in the conspiracy, if the writ of habeas corpus be not suspended, what will be the consequence? When apprehended, they will be brought before a court of justice, who will decide whether there is any evidence that will justify their commitment for farther prosecution."

Mr. Elliot: "...we can only act, in this case, with a view to national self-preservation. We can suspend the writ of habeas corpus only in a case of extreme emergency; that alone is salus populi which will justify this lex suprema [Latin, "The health of the people should be the supreme law"[838]]. And is this a crisis of such awful moment? Is it necessary, at this time, to constitute a dictatorship, to save the people from themselves, and to take care that the Republic shall receive no detriment? What is the proposition? To create a single Dictator, as in ancient Rome, in whom all power shall be vested for a time? No; to create one great Dictator, and a multitude, an army of subaltern and petty despots; to invest, not only the President of the United States, but the Governors of States and Territories, and, indeed, all persons deriving civil or military authority from the supreme Executive, with unlimited and irresponsible power over the personal liberty of your citizens. Is this one of those great crises that require a suspension, a temporary prostration of the Constitution itself? Does the stately superstructure of our Republic thus tremble to its centre, and totter towards its fall? Common sense must give a negative answer to these questions."

"...We contend that the framers of the Constitution never contemplated the exercise of such a power, under circumstances like the present; and that the Constitution itself, instead of authorizing, has prohibited such discretion, unless in an extreme case. And can any member lay his hand upon his heart and say, that the present is a case of that description? He who cannot do this must, with us, consider the proposed measure as unconstitutional. ...By the provisions of the famous statute of Charles II, which has even been called a second magna charta, its privileges are guarantied to all British subjects at all times. An eminent English author, and the most popular writer upon subjects of legal science, considers its suspension as the suspension of liberty itself; declares that the measure ought never to be resorted to but in cases of extreme emergency; and says that the nation then parts with its freedom for a short and limited time, only to resume and secure it forever. Hence, he compares the suspension of the habeas corpus act in Great Britain to the dictatorship of the Roman Republic."

Mr. Eppes: "...By this bill, we are called upon to exercise one of the most important powers vested in Congress by the Constitution of the United States. A power which suspends the personal rights of your citizens, which places their liberty wholly under the will, not of the Executive Magistrate only, but of his inferior officers. Of the importance of this power, of the caution which ought to be employed in its exercise, the words of the Constitution afford irresistible evidence. The words of the Constitution are: "The privilege of the writ of habeas corpus shall not be suspended, unless when, in cases of rebellion or invasion, the public safety may require it." The wording of this clause of the Constitution deserves peculiar attention. It is not in every case of invasion, nor in every case of rebellion, that the exercise of this power by Congress can be justified under the words of the Constitution. The words of the Constitution confine the exercise of this power exclusively to cases of rebellion or invasion, where the public safety requires it. In carrying into effect most of the important powers of Congress, something is left for the exercise of its discretion. We raise armies when, in our opinion, armies are necessary. We may call forth the militia to suppress insurrection or repel invasion, when we consider this measure necessary. But we can only suspend the privilege of the habeas corpus, "when, in cases of rebellion or invasion, the public safety requires it." Well, indeed, may this caution have been used as to the exercise of this important power. It is in a free country the most tremendous power which can be placed in the hands of a legislative body. It suspends, at once, the chartered rights of the community, and places even those who pass the act under military despotism.

The Constitution, however, having vested this power in Congress, and a branch of the Legislature having thought its exercise necessary, it remains for us to inquire whether the present situation of our country authorizes, on our part, a resort to this extraordinary measure.

...I consider the provision in the Constitution for suspending the habeas corpus as designed only for occasions of great national danger. Like the power of creating a Dictator in ancient Rome, it prostrates the rights of your citizens and endangers public liberty."

Mr. R. Nelson: "…What is a writ of habeas corpus? It is a writ directing a certain person in custody to be brought before a tribunal of justice, to inquire into the legality of his confinement. If the judge is of opinion that the confinement is illegal, the person will of course be discharged; if, on the contrary, from the evidence, he shall be of opinion that there is sufficient grounds to suspect that he is guilty of offence, he will not be discharged. Now, to me, it appears that this is a proper and necessary power to be vested in our judges, and that a suspension of the writ of habeas corpus is, in all cases, improper. If a man is taken up, and is denied an examination before a judge or a court, he may, although innocent, in this case, continue to suffer confinement. This, in my opinion, is dangerous to the liberty of the citizen. He may be taken up on vague suspicion, and may not have his case examined for months, or even for years. Would not this bear hard upon the rights of the citizen?

…This precedent, let me tell gentlemen, may be a ruinous, may be a most damnable precedent--a precedent which, hereafter, may be most flagrantly abused. The Executive may wish to make use of more energetic measures than the established laws of the land enable him to do; he will resort to this as a precedent, and this important privilege will be suspended at the smallest appearance of danger. The effect will be, that whenever a man is at the head of our affairs, who wishes to oppress or wreak his vengeance on those who are opposed to him, he will fly to this as a precedent; it will truly be a precedent fraught with the greatest danger; a precedent which ought not to be set, except in a case of the greatest necessity; indeed, I can hardly contemplate a case in which, in my opinion, it can be necessary.

…In my opinion, this is a measure which ought never to be proposed, unless when the country is so corrupt that we cannot even trust the judges themselves. This, I consider the cause of the frequent suspension of this privilege in England. Whenever the whole mass of society becomes contaminated, and the officers of the judicial court are so far corrupted as to countenance rebellion, and release rebels from their confinement, it may be then time to say, they shall no longer remain in your hands; we will take them from you. But I apprehend there is no such danger here, and I repeat it, we are at once creating one of the most dangerous precedents, and passing one of the most unjust acts that was ever proposed."

Mr. Sloan: "…I, therefore, consider it of great magnitude, and it is certainly excited against the best Government on earth, under which the people enjoy the greatest happiness."

Mr. Smilie: "…I consider this one of the most important subjects upon which we have been called to act. It is a question which is neither more nor less than, whether we shall exercise the only power with which we are clothed, to repeal an important part of the Constitution? It is in this case only, that we have power to repeal that instrument. A suspension of the privilege of the writ of habeas corpus is, in all respects, equivalent to repealing that essential part of the Constitution which secures that principle which has been called, in the country where it originated, the "palladium [safeguard] of personal liberty.

…We have taken from the statute book of this country, this most valuable part of our Constitution. The convention who framed that instrument, believing that there might be cases when it would be necessary to vest a discretionary power in the Executive, have constituted the Legislature the judges of this necessity, and the only question now to be determined is, Does this necessity exist? There must either be in the country a rebellion or an invasion, before such an act can be passed.

...to suspend one of the most valuable privileges that is secured to the citizen. ...Are gentlemen aware of the danger of this precedent? This is the first attempt ever made under the Government to suspend this law. If we suspend it when the Executive tells us there is no danger, on what occasion may it not be suspended? Let us suppose that it shall be suspended on this occasion, what will be its effect? Parties will probably forever continue to exist in this country. Let us suppose a predominant party to conjure up a plot to avenge themselves. Do not gentlemen see that the personal liberty of all their enemies would be endangered? I mention this to forewarn gentlemen of the dangerous ground before them. ...If foreign nations see that we are obliged, under such circumstances, to suspend the writ of habeas corpus, will it not show that the Constitution is incapable of supporting itself, without the application of the most dangerous and extraordinary remedies?"

Mr. Dana: "...I have been accustomed to view the privilege of the writ of habeas corpus as the most glorious invention of man. ...There is another principle, which appears to me highly objectionable. It authorizes the arrest of persons, not merely by the President, or other high officers, but by any person acting under him. I imagine this to be wholly without precedent. If treason was marching to force us from our seats, I would not agree to do this. I would not agree thus to destroy the fundamental principles of the Constitution, or to commit such an act, either of despotism or pusillanimity [cowardliness]."

Congress not having approved a suspension of the *Writ of Habeas Corpus*, President Jefferson next ordered Burr arrested and indicted for treason, although firm evidence was not provided. Given the force of the presidency, as Thomas Jefferson was determined to have Burr convicted, the trial was a major test of the *Constitution* and separation of powers. Burr was acquitted (declared not guilty) of treason.

President Thomas Jefferson, 1800 [839]   Chief Justice John Marshall, 1832 [840]

Jefferson also challenged the authority of the Supreme Court and its Chief Justice John Marshall.[841] It appears as though the checks and balances as provided by the *Constitution* were wisdom sufficient in the situation. After the death of General Wilkinson, it was discovered that he was a paid agent of the Catholic monarch of the Spanish Crown as well as a co-conspirator of Aaron Burr turned sour.[842]

What we point out at this time is the view of the Founding Fathers and early statesmen as to the sacred preservation of American liberty, their conviction that a suspension of the privilege of the *Writ of Habeas Corpus* is one of the most important powers, in all respects, equivalent to repealing that essential part of the *Constitution*. We see that they considered it as dangerous ground in suspending the *writ* by both setting precedence for future incidents of the Executive power as well as opening the door to a possible dictatorship by inferior officers. Liberty is the key and liberty would be lost. In losing liberty, life and the pursuit of happiness would be jeopardized as well. We hold this thought in mind as we continue.

Although the Maryland legislature did not vote to secede from the Union, there were mob attacks on Union troops in Baltimore and the sabotage of railroad and communication lines.[843] It was under these conditions that Lincoln authorized the suspension of the *Writ of Habeas Corpus* along the route traveled by Union troops from Philadelphia to Washington.[844]

On May 25, 1861, Maryland legislator John Merryman was arrested for attempting to hinder Union troops at Baltimore headed to Washington. Merryman was held at Fort McHenry by Union military officers when his attorney sought a *Writ of Habeas Corpus* so that a federal court could examine the charges. Because Lincoln had suspended the *Writ of Habeas Corpus* in this locale, the commanding officer of Fort McHenry refused to release Merryman to the civil authorities.[845]

John Merryman [846]

Supreme Court Chief Justice Roger Taney, author of the infamous Dred Scott decision, was a native of Maryland. He also sat as a judge on the U.S. Circuit Court for Maryland. Merryman's lawyers made petition addressed to Taney.[847] Because of Taney's siding with the Slave Power in the Dred Scott decision and sympathizing with the Southern States, he issued a ruling that President Lincoln did not have the authority to suspend the *Writ of Habeas Corpus*.[848]

President Lincoln never directly responded to Chief Justice Taney's challenge to "respect" and "enforce" the civil process of the courts. He did, however, in several public messages including his address at the opening of Congress on July 4, 1861, explain that in the midst of a rebellion, defending the viability of a constitutional government based on the consent of the governed was a more important executive responsibility than scrupulously observing specific protections of civil liberties.

Lincoln pointed out that the *Constitution* provided for suspension of the *Writ of Habeas Corpus* during invasions and insurrections and <u>also authorized different kinds of governmental power during a rebellion then it would permit during times of peace and domestic security</u>.

In President Lincoln's July 4, 1861 address, he asked Congress to validate his actions by authorizing them after the fact. His message also details his first full explanation of the purpose of the "contest" or "giant insurrection." It will well serve the reader to take the time to read the message which provides firsthand details and perspectives while also gaining a glimpse of the character of the honorable President Lincoln (available by endnote reference link).[849]

<u>With the convening of the 37th United States Congress because of the "so-called" secession of States there was a loss of Congressional members in representation of these States (in perpetuity) leaving a "rump;" there was not a quorum for either of the houses of Congress to conduct business under the *Constitution* and therefore lawfully ceased to exist as a deliberative body under the *Constitution*.</u>

On September 22, 1862, President Lincoln issued Presidential Proclamation 93, "Declaring the <u>Objectives of the War</u> Including Emancipation of Slaves in Rebellious States on January 1, 1863." The objective of the War was clearly understood in his opening statement:

"I, Abraham Lincoln, President of the United States of America and Commander in Chief of the Army and Navy thereof, do hereby proclaim and declare that hereafter, as heretofore, the war will be prosecuted for the object of practically restoring the constitutional relation between the United States and each of the States and the people thereof in which States that relation is or may be suspended or disturbed."[850]

Two days later on September 24, 1862, President Lincoln issued Presidential Proclamation 94, "Suspending the Writ of Habeas Corpus,"[851] which also included the directive of enforcing Martial Law under circumstances presented by those guilty of committing disloyal practices.

By the President of the United States of America

A Proclamation

Whereas it has become necessary to call into service not only volunteers, but also portions of the militia of the States by draft in order to suppress the insurrection existing in the United States, and disloyal persons are not adequately restrained by the ordinary processes of law from hindering this measure and from giving aid and comfort in various ways to the insurrection: Now, therefore, be it ordered, first, that during the existing insurrection, and as a necessary measure for suppressing the same, all rebels and insurgents, their aiders and abettors, within the United States, and all persons discouraging volunteer enlistments, resisting militia draft or guilty of any disloyal practice affording aid and comfort to rebels against the authority of the United States, shall be subject to martial law and liable to trial and punishment by courts-martial or military commissions; second, that the writ of habeas corpus is suspended in respect to all persons arrested, or who are now or hereafter during the rebellion shall be imprisoned in any fort, camp, arsenal, military prison, or other place of confinement by any military authority or by the sentence of any court-martial or military commission.

In witness whereof I have hereunto set my hand and caused the seal of the United States to be affixed.

Done at the city of Washington, this 24th day of September, A.D. 1862, and of the Independence of the United States the eighty-seventh.

ABRAHAM LINCOLN

By the President:

WILLIAM H. SEWARD,

Secretary of State

It was when the Southern States' governments refused to comply with the *Constitution* that President Lincoln was forced to respond as constitutional law had provided.

It was when President Lincoln convened Congress under the authority of the Executive branch while Congress was lacking a quorum (rump) and unable to lawfully operate in representative government under the *Constitution,* and directing Martial Law specifying the terms to be under circumstances presented by those guilty of committing disloyal practices, as well as the suspension of the *Writ of Habeas Corpus* that the law form was temporarily set aside.

During a time of rebellion and insurrection, without a lawful and convened Congress to seek authorization from, it was necessary for the President to promptly respond as the *Constitution* had provided in securing the public safety by these means.

Proclaiming Martial Law under his prescribed terms and suspending the *Writ of Habeas Corpus* was essential and necessary in order to preserve the Union and maintain governance under the spirit of the *Constitution*. Otherwise known as "color of law," or giving appearance of law while the republican form of governance was temporarily set aside and an interim governance or law form functioned in its place.

By perpetuity, the *Constitution* still remained as "the law of the land." However, the legislative body was lacking and could not lawfully function under the *Constitution*.

The Executive branch still had the lawful authority to function, and did so in order to fulfill the obligation of the government to do the business of the People.

Color of law **was to have been used in the interim -- ONLY until the insurrection was impeded and the People of the Southern States could reestablish LOYAL State governments in Union and then elect Congressional officers that would represent them and who would operate lawfully under the** ***Constitution.*** This obligation fell squarely on the Executive branch.

Lincoln's mandate to the rump "interim Executive Congress" was very strict and limited and could not be binding on the American people or the *de jure* government. **In order for laws to be binding they must have the consent of the American People through their representatives as Article IV, Section 4 of the** ***Constitution*** **guarantees to EVERY State in the Union a representative form of governance.**[852]

Lincoln acted unilaterally based solely on his duty to preserve the Union. He did not have a lawful constitutional Congress to appeal to, to get the consent of the American people for these changes. The only mandate he could give this temporary administrative body (a rump Congress) was to maintain the business of the government so the Union would not collapse. Administration and enforcement is the only authority that the Executive branch has. The rump "interim Executive Congress" was not a Congress of the People <u>and</u> the States. By constitutional law, the Federal Government had to be returned to the American people as soon as the insurrection was put down. President Lincoln was fully aware of constitutional law, operating within the law, and making provision to see that constitutional law was followed and accomplished. As he had espoused in his message before the opening of the 37th Congress on July 4, 1861, the rebellion of the Southern States presented the question: "Must a government, of necessity be too strong for the liberties of its own people, or too weak to maintain its own existence?"[853]

President Lincoln had a tremendous task and continual struggle to uphold the dictates of his oath to support the *Constitution*, stay within the bounds of the law while seeking to restore the House divided, and preserve the Union under these extreme circumstances.

There is no doubt that honest Abe would call on Almighty God to pour out heaven's wisdom liberally upon him. In light of the American Republic's truthful history, there can be no doubt in comprehending that restoring the Republic with the States in Union was a major contributing factor to the "Great Conspiracy" of Lincoln's assassination. Hell, and its sons, could not stand Liberty or those who support it.

Continuing to this present day is an administrative Congress of the Executive branch acting in *color of law*.

Abraham Lincoln, with his son Tad, 1865 [854]

We continue to demonstrate how the Corporate UNITED STATES was secretly and deceptively formed during this timeframe of *color of law* in order to pervert the system and direct it toward a *New World Order* global agenda. What standing in law could the UNITED STATES CORPORATION actually have? None, as it is a counterfeit government that usurped Lincoln's *color of law* "interim Executive government" while secretly shoving aside and leaving dormant the American Republic. Nothing the *de facto* counterfeit "government" has done since has been done in actual law.

Because the *Constitution* is preserved as the operating document and "the law of the land" in perpetuity, it has always been the right of the People to elect a government to fully function under the original *Constitution*. When the majority of the American people awaken and standup, a permanent *de jure* government election will be accomplished, the property, including the military and lawful civil authority of the *Republic for the United States of America* will be restored and the *de facto* counterfeit government will be forced to cease and desist.

James Buchanan had remarked in his final days as President, "As George Washington was the first, James Buchanan will be the last President of the United States."[855] So it was for a season. However, Providence has had the last say in that regard and which will be revealed in glorious display further along in the story of the American Republic.

On April 24, 1863, President Lincoln commissioned *General Orders No. 100* [856] as <u>a special field code under Martial Law rule and which justified the seizure of power while extending the laws of the District of Columbia. It also contributed to fictionally implementing the provisions of Article I, Section 8, Clauses 17-18 of the *Constitution* beyond the ten-miles-square boundary of Washington, D.C. and into the several States.</u>

General Orders No. 100, later became also known as the *Lieber Instructions/Lieber Code,*[857] **which extended the *Laws of War* and *International Law* onto American soil. ***This is how the United States Federal Government became a military ruler of the American People of the several once independent American States, and their land.*****

136

President Abraham Lincoln, 1863 [858]

The story continues… While issuing Lieber's Code is most often viewed as the founding of the *law of war*, it is in fact more correct in viewing it in this situation of insurrection during the latter half of the *"War Between the States"* as the Martial Law regulation governing all of the non-Confederate States, the Northern States.

Previously existing humanitarian customary *law of war* principles were put into the form of a Military Order, which was not the Lieber Code's primary purpose.[859] *General Orders No. 100* was the authority under Martial Law for the military arrests and military commission trials of "disloyal" civilians in the North, and the enemy-citizens of the South. Along with the declaration of Martial Law to be enforced under circumstances presented by those guilty of committing disloyal practices, it was necessary to give notice of what acts would subject one to military arrest and military trial. The first section of *General Orders No. 100, Section I,* is entitled "Martial Law – Military jurisdiction – Military necessity."[860]

This definition was pertinent to the Code's *Article 90,*[861] which provided: "A traitor under the *law of war*, or a war-traitor, is a person in a place or district under Martial Law who, unauthorized by the military commander, gives information of any kind to the enemy, or holds intercourse with him." Thought-provoking is that an "enemy" in a Civil War could be friends, family, neighbors, and others in close association. An extreme consequence in one case was that a father was found guilty of having communicated with the "enemy" by sending a letter to his own son.

Where "patriot myth" holds that President Lincoln was assassinated just a few days after the *Civil War* ended and before he was able to repeal Martial Law, that Martial Law never ended and continues to this day — that is <u>not</u> correct. Recorded history documents the fact that the American Republic had been shoved aside and left dormant while a *de facto* corporation run by "cunning, ambitious, and unprincipled men" deceptively usurped government controls.

That Corporation is a completely different entity with its own constitution and law form known as a Democracy. That entity has run its operation in states of national emergency in order to manipulate its agenda upon the American people.

An unmistakably accurate summarization of the situation is the 1973 Introduction to *Senate Report 93-549* (93rd Congress, 1st Session):

"<u>A majority of the people of the United States have lived all of their lives under emergency rule. For 40 years, freedoms and governmental procedures guaranteed by the Constitution have, in varying degrees, been abridged by laws brought into force by states of national emergency</u>. The problem of how a constitutional <u>democracy</u> reacts to great crises, however, far antedates the Great Depression. As a philosophical issue, its origins reach back to the Greek city-states and the Roman Republic. And, in the United States, actions taken by the Government in times of great crises have – <u>from, at least, the Civil War in important ways shaped the present phenomenon of a permanent state of national emergency</u>."[862] [emphasis added]

Every opportunity manifested toward "progress" in the *New World Order* agenda has been seized by the sons of Satan. "You never want a serious crisis to go to waste [because] it's an opportunity to do things you could not do before."[863] Such a statement is an example of testimony and evidence of opportunistic "cunning, ambitious, and unprincipled" politicians who never miss a chance to convert crises and "national emergencies" into "political pork for special interests."[864]

It was understood by Presidential Proclamation that a directive of being subject to Martial Law was <u>specific with terms of circumstances</u> named in the Proclamation[865] or with wording as a directive for the military commander "if he shall find it necessary."[866]

With regard to the suspension of the *Writ of Habeas Corpus,* wording is specific that it would continue throughout the duration of the said rebellion or as a directive to the military commander "if he shall find it necessary."[867] Specifically, "this suspension will continue throughout the duration of the said rebellion or until this proclamation shall, by a subsequent one to be issued by the President of the United States, be modified or revoked," and refer to terms of circumstances that specifically pertain along with an admonishment requiring "all magistrates, attorneys, and other civil officers within the United States and all officers and others in the military and naval services of the United States to take distinct notice of this suspension and to give it full effect, and all citizens of the United States to conduct and govern themselves accordingly and in conformity with the Constitution of the United States and the laws of Congress in such case made and provided."[868]

In the case of declaring Martial Law and a further suspension of the *Writ of Habeas Corpus* Lincoln had proclaimed for Kentucky on July 5, 1864, he specifically directed, "…the said suspension and establishment of Martial Law to continue until this proclamation shall be revoked or modified, but not beyond the period when the said rebellion shall have been suppressed or come to an end."[869]

High-level Freemason Andrew Johnson,[870] who succeeded President Lincoln, issued a Presidential Proclamation which did revoke Lincoln's proclamation of the suspension of the *Writ of Habeas Corpus,* except in the Southern States, the District of Columbia, and territory of the southwest.

President Andrew Johnson [871]

Proclamation 148 - Revoking the Suspension of the Writ of Habeas Corpus, Except in Certain States and Territories, December 1, 1865:[872]

By the President of the United States of America

A Proclamation

Whereas by the proclamation of the President of the United States of the 15th day of September, 1863, the privilege of the writ of habeas corpus was, in certain cases therein set forth, suspended throughout the United States; and

Whereas the reasons for that suspension may be regarded as having ceased in some of the States and Territories:

Now, therefore, be it known that I, Andrew Johnson, President of the United States, do hereby proclaim and declare that the suspension aforesaid and all other proclamations and orders suspending the privilege of the writ of habeas corpus in the States and Territories of the United States are revoked and annulled, <u>excepting as to the States of Virginia, Kentucky, Tennessee, North Carolina, South Carolina, Georgia, Florida, Alabama, Mississippi, Louisiana, Arkansas, and Texas, the District of Columbia, and the Territories of New Mexico and Arizona</u>.

In witness whereof I have hereunto set my hand and caused the seal of the United States to be affixed.

Done at the city of Washington, this 1st day of December, A.D. 1865, and of the Independence of the United States of America the ninetieth.

ANDREW JOHNSON.

By the President:

WILLIAM H. SEWARD,

Secretary of State.

But then in 1866 he twice made Presidential Proclamation declaring "that the insurrection which heretofore existed in the States of Georgia, South Carolina, Virginia, North Carolina, Tennessee, Alabama, Louisiana, Arkansas, Mississippi, and Florida <u>is at an end</u> and <u>is henceforth to be so regarded</u>."[873]

And then, "do hereby proclaim and declare that the insurrection which heretofore existed in the State of Texas <u>is at an end</u> and <u>is to be henceforth so regarded</u> in that State as in the other States before named in which the said insurrection was proclaimed <u>to be at an end</u> by the aforesaid proclamation of the 2d day of April, 1866. <u>And I do further proclaim that the said insurrection is at an end and that peace, order, tranquility, and civil authority now exist in and throughout the whole of the United States of America</u>."[874]

Factually, Johnson's proclamation was far from the truth and the civil unrest disgracefully continued when he as the Executive had the constitutional duty to protect the States and the People from domestic violence and insurrection. So we see it was <u>not</u> a matter of those lawful actions of limited Martial Law and the suspension of the *Writ of Habeas Corpus* in <u>not</u> having been repealed or revoked.

In that period of time the organic American Republic was left dormant and shoved aside while a foreign entity usurped government controls deceiving the American People and the rest of the world while taking progressive action as an imposter in their counterfeit corporation and while moving forward in their agenda of a *New World Order*.

Lincoln wanted the Southern States to re-enter the Union with the same status with which they had left the Union.[875] Had he lived and completed his second Presidential term, he would never have allowed the long duration of "Reconstruction" which was like hell on earth for the blacks as well as the Southern whites.

Near the end of the Civil War Lincoln met with three commanding Union officers on the *River Queen* steamboat. President Lincoln expressed his desire for a **prompt** and complete **reconciliation** with the South and its citizens. Lincoln articulated to Generals Grant and Sherman what would become known as the *River Queen Doctrine,* offering the South the most generous terms:

"…to get the deluded men of the rebel armies disarmed and back to their homes… Let them once surrender and reach their homes, [and] they won't take up arms again…Let them all go, officers and all, I want submission and no more bloodshed…I want no one punished; treat them liberally all around. **We want those people to return to their allegiance to the Union and submit to the laws.**"[876]

The *River Queen* [877]

"The Peacemakers"
Sherman, Grant, Lincoln, and
Porter [878] aboard the River Queen
on March 27th & March 28th, 1865

Instead of following Lincoln's plan of wisdom for **reconciliation and restoration** with the South, this high-level Freemason, President Johnson, kept the House divided so the Republic would not stand, abandoned the blacks in his racial prejudice and held open wide the door that had been left open in the curses of disobedience in breaking covenant with Almighty God and His *Laws of Nature* where ALL men are created equal.

Mark 3:25 ~

And if a house be divided against itself, that house cannot stand.

From 1862 until 1871 the nation had been under a different law form than that in times of peace. President Lincoln referred to this *color of law* interim government as **"the Executive Government"** in his September 22, 1862 Presidential Proclamation described as "Declaring the Objectives of the War Including Emancipation of Slaves in Rebellious States on January 1, 1863."[879] He also twice made reference to **"the Executive Government"** in his January 1, 1863 President Proclamation known as *"The Emancipation Proclamation."*[880]

By the President of the United States of America:

A Proclamation.

Whereas, on the twenty-second day of September, in the year of our Lord one thousand eight hundred and sixty-two, a proclamation was issued by the President of the United States, containing, among other things, the following, to wit:

"That on the first day of January, in the year of our Lord one thousand eight hundred and sixty-three, all persons held as slaves within any State or designated part of a State, the people whereof shall then be in rebellion against the United States, shall be then, thenceforward, and forever free; and the Executive Government of the United States, including the military and naval authority thereof, will recognize and maintain the freedom of such persons, and will do no act or acts to repress such persons, or any of them, in any efforts they may make for their actual freedom.

"That the Executive will, on the first day of January aforesaid, by proclamation, designate the States and parts of States, if any, in which the people thereof, respectively, shall then be in rebellion against the United States; and the fact that any State, or the people thereof, shall on that day be, in good faith, represented in the Congress of the United States by members chosen thereto at elections wherein a majority of the qualified voters of such State shall have participated, shall, in the absence of strong countervailing testimony, be deemed conclusive evidence that such State, and the people thereof, are not then in rebellion against the United States."

Now, therefore I, Abraham Lincoln, President of the United States, by virtue of the power in me vested as Commander-in-Chief, of the Army and Navy of the United States in time of actual armed rebellion against the authority and government of the United States, and as a fit and necessary war measure for suppressing said rebellion, do, on this first day of January, in the year of our Lord one thousand eight hundred and sixty-three, and in accordance with my purpose so to do publicly proclaimed for the full period of one hundred days, from the day first above mentioned, order and designate as the States and parts of States wherein the people thereof respectively, are this day in rebellion against the United States, the following, to wit:

Arkansas, Texas, Louisiana, (except the Parishes of St. Bernard, Plaquemines, Jefferson, St. John, St. Charles, St. James Ascension, Assumption, Terrebonne, Lafourche, St. Mary, St. Martin, and Orleans, including the City of New Orleans) Mississippi, Alabama, Florida, Georgia, South Carolina, North Carolina, and Virginia, (except the forty-eight counties designated as West Virginia, and also the counties of Berkley, Accomac, Northampton, Elizabeth City, York, Princess Ann, and Norfolk, including the cities of Norfolk and Portsmouth), and which excepted parts, are for the present, left precisely as if this proclamation were not issued.

And by virtue of the power, and for the purpose aforesaid, I do order and declare that all persons held as slaves within said designated States, and parts of States, are, and henceforward shall be free; and that the <u>Executive government</u> of the United States, including the military and naval authorities thereof, will recognize and maintain the freedom of said persons.

And I hereby enjoin upon the people so declared to be free to abstain from all violence, unless in necessary self-defence; and I recommend to them that, in all cases when allowed, they labor faithfully for reasonable wages.

And I further declare and make known, that such persons of suitable condition, will be received into the armed service of the United States to garrison forts, positions, stations, and other places, and to man vessels of all sorts in said service.

And upon this act, sincerely believed to be an act of justice, warranted by the Constitution, upon military necessity, I invoke the considerate judgment of mankind, and the gracious favor of Almighty God.

In witness whereof, I have hereunto set my hand and caused the seal of the United States to be affixed.

Done at the City of Washington, this first day of January, in the year of our Lord one thousand eight hundred and sixty three, and of the Independence of the United States of America the eighty-seventh.

By the President:

ABRAHAM LINCOLN

WILLIAM H. SEWARD,

Secretary of State.

We will come to see in the American Republic's story that "cunning, ambitious, and unprincipled men" maneuvered their way inside this "Executive Government" to strategic positions of control while the House was divided and yet operating under this different law form. These sons of Satan, despisers of Liberty, would put President Lincoln out of the way and cleverly continue his executive government while masquerading as the American Republic.

George Washington, 1795-1796 [881]

Just as President Washington warned in his *Farewell Address*, these "artful associations" would progressively subvert the power of the people and usurp for themselves the reins of government while destroying the very mechanisms used to promote them to unjust dominion. They would operate by a spirit of encroachment while consolidating the powers of the three branches of government into one. All of this was crafted in secret without the knowledge of, or full disclosure provided to, the American People.[882]

When they saw that the time was ripe, within the next decade, the artful associations of "cunning, ambitious, and unprincipled men" would proceed with their shrewdly devised plan to re-incorporate this executive government and counterfeit the original *Constitution* using a similar name (THE UNITED STATES OF AMERICA, INC.[883]). They would then trick the American People into this ensnaring and fraudulent jurisdiction.

High-level Freemason Howell Cobb[884] would see the manifestation of his satanic-inspired solution of "reconciling the interests of labor and capital."[885] Indeed, the American People as a whole would be made into merchandise (Rev. 18:11-13) and Cobb's Luciferian brethren would glean the spoils of the American Peoples' assets and labor. They would progress forward toward their goal of a Luciferian one-world global government.

The door had been opened that led to the "Great Deception" and enslavement — "A perfect slave thinks he is free." This Great Deception includes an illusion of operating under constitutional law. It was "radical" congressmen who inadvertently converted the law form from a Republic to a Democracy out of desperation, knowing they were up against a world system controlled by Satan's sons. That counterfeit constitution was snuck into operation by the sons of Satan just a few years after the (unlawful) legislation was put forth...

Abraham Lincoln and his Emancipation Proclamation 1888, The Strobridge Lith. Co., Cincinnati. [886]
Text of Emancipation Proclamation with two U.S. flags and eagle over head-and-shoulders portrait of Abraham Lincoln and flanked by allegorical figures of Justice and Liberty.

With the *Emancipation Proclamation* signed by President Lincoln in 1863, slavery was now ended in the Southern States. There were nearly 4 million freedmen of African descent who had been brought to America by force and enslaved — or their ancestors were. By this time, a large percentage of these newly freedmen were born on American soil. The next step after emancipation would be contending on behalf of their citizenship, and the rights that go with being a citizen.

In order to comprehend the effect of the radical legislation enacted by desperate Congressmen in their strategy to provide freedom to the black race, as well as rights of citizenship, we bear in mind that these desperate Congressmen at the same time actively strategized a means to preserve the Union from determined "cunning, ambitious, and unprincipled men" associated in occult secret societies — all under the direction of the Jesuit Order in their Counter-Reformation agenda. We must understand citizenship as it was created in 1776 as a result of the *Declaration of Independence* and winning the *War for Independence*.

The *Declaration of Independence* resulted in a change of government. The sovereignty in government was transferred from one man (King George III) to the collective body of the American People. Where British Colonists had been "subjects of the king," they had now become "citizens of the State," no longer subjects of King George III, but foreign to him.

"Citizen" is a better suited description for one living under a republican form of government where the individual participates in the government. The term "citizen," in referring to an individual in any government, implies that they enjoy a greater degree of participation in the affairs of their government than would be implied if they were referred to as a "subject."

In the new government of the free and independent States who were united in the cause, there would be no sovereign (king) and there would be no subject (ruled by that tyrant king). The individuals composing the political body were properly designated as "citizens" because they would participate in their government.

While the *Revolutionary War* lasted, the Colonies, calling themselves "States," joined together in a league where they were strengthened in cooperation and thereby referred to themselves as the "United States." They formed a Continental Congress that represented their State legislatures. The independence demanded by the Colonies, and the citizenship that came to be recognized by Great Britain, were the independence and citizenship of thirteen sovereign and independent States—not of any one national political body.

They were States united and the compact they agreed upon as a league of States was not entered into to create a new political body reaching or operating upon the unit of the citizen. All powers possessed by the confederated government (association of States) were derived from, and to be exercised upon, the State legislatures which created it—representing States, not individuals.

And so the inhabitants of the thirteen States ceased to be colonial subjects of Great Britain and became citizens of their respective States. The *Declaration of Independence* affirmed that the united Colonies ought to be free and independent States.

Articles of Confederation and Perpetual Union Between the States
Title Page; Williamsburg, Virginia, 1777 [887]

The *Articles of Confederation* were written and adopted on November 15, 1777 by delegates of the States as their governing document. Article 2 states, *"Each state retains its sovereignty, freedom, and independence, and every power, jurisdiction, and right, which is not by this Confederation expressly delegated to the United States, in Congress assembled."*[888]

Under the *Articles of Confederation*, State citizens were not also citizens of the political body of the United States. No citizenship of the United States was recognized or even existed.

At that time, a few of the Founding Fathers publicized their thoughts and political beliefs in the *Federalist Papers*. The *Federalist Papers* are a collection of 85 letters written by statesmen Alexander Hamilton, James Madison, and John Jay. They were published anonymously in newspapers in an effort to urge going forward with the new Constitution. They expressed that the failure of the *Articles of Confederation* was related to the principle of legislation for States or governments rather than on behalf of individual State citizens. Their discussions in their papers included the need of giving the Union energy and duration by extending laws of the federal government (of the States as a collective body) to the individual citizens of America.[889]

The *Constitution of the United States* was proposed on September 17, 1787 and the operations of the new government began under it on March 4, 1789. The people were State citizens until the *Constitution of the United States* was passed and then they also became citizens of the United States.

There was only State citizenship until the *Constitution of the United States* was ratified. Then there was State citizenship and citizenship of the United States. So first was State citizenship and then was citizenship of the United States in the origin and character of citizenship under the "peculiar organization" of the United States as it came to be formed by the *Constitution of the United States.*[890]

The *Constitution* was the object in forming a new government and altered the status of the people who were subject to its jurisdiction. Beforehand the people had been only citizens of their States; they now became also citizens of the United States. The government created by the *Constitution* became a government with citizens of its own and was no longer a mere government over the States.

The original *Constitution* remained unchanged concerning citizenship from 1789 until July 28, 1868 when the (unlawful) 14th Amendment was adopted. The 14th Amendment declared a new law of citizenship that had a radical effect by reversing the origin and character of citizenship—both State and National.[891]

The 14th Amendment would "broaden" citizenship by reversing its origin and character thereby substantially affecting the nature and direction of the nation.[892] [893] "Cunning, ambitious, and unprincipled men" would patiently await a ripened and clandestine opportunity to further transition citizenship into something that shocks the conscience. In the next sixty years, a "citizen of the United States" would be transitioned into a commercial utility known as a "U.S. citizen." Think "love of money" and "economic enslavement."[894]

The *Naturalization Act of 1790* provided the first rules to be followed in the granting of national citizenship (to immigrants not born on American soil), though it limited naturalization and citizenship to "free white persons," ruling out the black race.[895] The 1857 Dred Scott Decision stipulated that African slaves and their descendants could never be citizens and had no citizenship rights. While the *Emancipation Proclamation* signed by President Lincoln in 1863 did free the slaves in the Southern States, it was the (non-original) 13th Amendment passed in 1865 that outlawed slavery throughout the United States.[896] The 13th Amendment, Section 1 states:

> Neither slavery nor involuntary servitude, except as a punishment for crime whereof the party shall have been duly convicted, shall exist within the United States, or any place subject to their jurisdiction.

Having been ratified by the required three-fourths of the several State legislatures (27 of the 36 States at that time—the Southern States under Martial Law), on December 18, 1865, Secretary of State William Seward certified that the (non-original) 13th Amendment had been ratified.[897] We point out the fact that in the mayhem the nation endured, along with the continued strife and turmoil in Congress, this amendment was ratified under Lincoln's Executive government. That law form, separate and distinct from the law form of the American Republic, had not been repealed in order to return to the law form of the American Republic.

The (non-original) 13th Amendment did not make a provision for or grant rights of citizenship to the freedmen. In 1868, the 14th Amendment would be the next effort to grant citizenship to people born or naturalized in the United States. But, to be qualified for citizenship, they must first be subject to its jurisdiction. Finally acknowledged as "people," human beings with a body and soul opposed to being "property" or a "thing," there would need to be a provision in law to address the matter of jurisdiction for these people.

Complicating the matter is that these freedmen left their countries by force, involuntarily — or their ancestors did — and they did not expatriate from their native mother country and voluntarily take residence in the United States. Those who were natural born on American soil were not considered American citizens.

The *Expatriation Act of 1868* provided in "law" an acknowledgement that all people have a natural or God-given right to expatriate, or renounce their citizenship and allegiance to their native country, and to take residence and become a citizen in another country.

The day before Secretary of State William Seward issued an unconditional certificate of ratification of the 14th Amendment,[898] the (once again rump) Congress (unlawfully) passed "*An Act concerning the Rights of American Citizens in foreign States*," also known as "The Expatriation Act." [899] [900] Included in this legislation was a means, as a matter of necessity, in "keeping the public peace" evidenced in the Preamble of the *Expatriation Act of 1868.*

The Expatriation Act Preamble

An Act concerning the Rights of American Citizens in foreign States, Approved, July 27, 1868

"WHEREAS the right of expatriation is a natural and inherent right of all people, indispensable to the enjoyment of the rights of life, liberty, and the pursuit of happiness; and whereas in the recognition of this principle this government has freely received emigrants from all nations, and invested them with the rights of citizenship; and whereas it is claimed that such American citizens, with their descendants, are subjects of foreign states, owing allegiance to the governments thereof; and whereas it is necessary to the maintenance of public peace that this claim of foreign allegiance should be promptly and finally disavowed:…"

The Preamble of this Act, which has no effect of law, is carefully worded in expressing recognition that people from countries around the world had left their native country to come to America and who still owe an allegiance to their "mother" country's government. Specified is an exhortation, not a legal demand, for those people to promptly and formally renounce their allegiance to that foreign government (i.e. in Africa).

The Preamble is stating that because the United States government gave such people the right of citizenship, the people that were not natural born Americans (kidnapped Africans and their offspring who were born in America, however, not acknowledged in law as citizens) "should" (not a mandated word like "must") give up their political allegiance to their country of origin.

From the perspective of the freedmen of African descent, it is lawful notice as well as an offer to the freedmen to voluntarily expatriate and abandon their country of origin (or of their ancestor's), renouncing it, and then becoming a citizen of the (new government democracy of the) United States which would be offered to them through the 14th Amendment.

Bearing in mind that the 14th Amendment was officially announced the day after this Act was passed; there was a reason in seeking to keep "peace" under this (unlawful, unannounced) governmental system of Democracy which was going forward. At the same time, the American Republic was shoved aside and this new federal Democracy, with a "broadened" citizenship, was going forward.

There had to be a provision in law to allow for a change in jurisdiction. Section One of the *Expatriation Act* declares as a matter of law that one can remove himself from any body politic, political system, country and/or nation because it is a natural right of all people.[901]

With the white supremacy Freemason aristocracy still in control of the Southern States and preventing the emancipated blacks from their God-given rights, the Radical Republicans inadvertently thought their plan of passing "law" regarding citizenship and "civil <u>rights</u>" by federal powers would guarantee the freedmen what should have been theirs as God-given and preserved by the *Constitution* as "civil <u>liberties</u>." With the (unlawful) ratification of the 14th Amendment, <u>all</u> white citizens <u>also</u> came under the jurisdiction of this "broadened" federal citizenship.[902]

We will soon see and comprehend the tactics of encroachment that "cunning, ambitious, and unprincipled men" would craft shortly thereafter in their plans of transitioning American citizens and their posterity—unknowingly and without full disclosure—into another type of citizenship. "Citizens of the United States" would be transitioned into fictional "U.S. citizens." President Washington warned that this end would be "a real despotism."[903]

The Lincoln Family [904]
Mrs. Mary Lincoln with sons Robert and Tad, and President Abraham Lincoln
Produced by Currier & Ives, New York, 1867

The End of the Rebellion in the United States, 1865 [905]

A sequel to Kimmel's grand image "The Outbreak of the Rebellion in the United States" (no. 1865-19), issued the year before.

The artist depicts in symbolic terms the downfall of the Confederacy. Columbia, crowned with stars, and Liberty, wearing a Phrygian cap and holding an American flag, stand on a pedestal in the center. On the pedestal are carved the likenesses of George Washington and Abraham Lincoln. In front of the pedestal Justice, armed with sword and scales, leads a charge of Union troops toward the right. Immediately behind Justice stands President Andrew Johnson, and behind him Union generals Butler, Grant, and Sherman are visible. A black soldier stands in the foreground and a freed slave kneels before Liberty's pedestal.

An eagle bearing thunderbolts flies overhead, also toward the right, where the vanquished Confederates are gathered. Jefferson Davis (holding a sack of money), Robert E. Lee (offering his sword in surrender), and John Wilkes Booth (with a pistol and knife) are prominent among them. In the distance are a leaning palmetto tree with a dead serpent hanging limp from it and (beyond) Fort Sumter flying an American flag.

Chapter Twelve

The Secret Agenda of the Kings of the Earth

Having previously pointed out the importance of money as a key element in control and power of a nation, let's take a look at the financial situation of the Union and Federal Government during the *Civil War.*

In his State of the Union Address before Congress on December 3, 1861, Abraham Lincoln responded to the bankers argument that the people could not be trusted with their constitutional power and the political, monetary system of free enterprise our Founding Fathers conceived by saying:

> "No men living are more worthy to be trusted than those who toil up from poverty – none less inclined to take or touch aught which they have not honestly earned. Let them beware of surrendering the political power which they already possess which if surrendered will surely be used to close the door of advancement against such as they and fix new disabilities upon them till all liberty shall be lost."[906]

Lincoln and his Secretary of the Treasury, Salmon P. Chase, went to the New York bankers and applied for loans in order for the Government to fund the war. The bankers were willing to lend it but only under terms of a staggering 24 to 36 percent interest, an amount that is equivalent to extortion and would bankrupt the North.

Salmon P. Chase [907]
Secretary of the Treasury

Lincoln consulted a trusted friend, Colonel Dick Taylor of Chicago and asked for advice. In what may indeed be the best piece of advice ever given to a President, Colonel Taylor responded that the solution was easy; the Union had the power under the *Constitution* to solve its financing problem by printing its money as a sovereign government. Colonel Taylor advised President Lincoln to "just get Congress to pass a bill authorizing the printing of full legal tender treasury notes or greenbacks, and pay your soldiers with them and go ahead and win your war with them also."[908]

Colonel Edmund Dick Taylor [909]

Lincoln followed Colonel Taylor's advice and funded the war by printing paper notes backed by the credit of the government. These legal-tender U.S. Notes or "Greenbacks" represented receipts for labor and goods delivered to the United States. They were paid to soldiers and suppliers and were exchangeable for goods and services of a value equivalent to their service to the community. The Greenbacks aided the Union not only in winning the war but in funding a period of unprecedented economic expansion.

A $1 Legal Tender Note from the Series 1862-1863 greenback issue [910]
Engraved signatures of Chittenden (Register of the Treasury)
and Spinner (Treasurer of the United States)

Lincoln's government was blessed in creating the greatest industrial giant the world had yet seen. The steel industry was launched, a continental railroad system was created, a new era of farm machinery and inexpensive tools were promoted, free higher education was established, government support was provided to all branches of science, the Bureau of Mines was organized, and labor productivity was increased by 50 to 75 percent.

The Greenback was not the only currency used to fund these achievements; but they could not have been accomplished without it, and they could not have been accomplished on money borrowed at the outrageous rates the bankers were attempting to extort from the North.[911]

President Lincoln later wrote Colonel Taylor to express gratitude and stated that following through on his advice resulted in giving "the people of this Republic the greatest blessing they every had—their own paper money to pay their own debts."[912]

He explained his monetary policy just before the close of the Civil War in 1865:

"…The government should create, issue, and circulate all the currency and credit needed to satisfy the spending power of the government and the buying power of the consumers. The privilege of creating and issuing money is not only the supreme prerogative of government, but it is the government's greatest creative opportunity.   By the adoption of these principles the long felt want for a uniform medium will be satisfied. The taxpayers will be saved immense sums of interest, discounts, and exchanges.   The financing of all public enterprise, the maintenance of stable government and ordered progress, and the conduct of the Treasury will become matters of practical administration.   The people can and will be furnished with a currency as safe as their own government. Money will cease to be master and become the servant of humanity…."[913]

Lincoln succeeded in restoring the government's power to issue the national currency, but his revolutionary monetary policy was vehemently opposed by powerful forces. The threat to "established interests" stimulated an editorial in *The London Times* explaining the (Jesuit-controlled Rothschild's privately owned) Bank of England's attitude towards it:

"If this mischievous financial policy, which has its origin in North America, shall become indurated down to a fixture, then the Government will furnish its own money without cost. It will pay off debts and be without debt. It will have all the money necessary to carry on its commerce. It will become prosperous without precedent in the history of the world. The brains, and wealth of all countries will go to North America. That country must be destroyed or it will destroy every monarchy on the globe."[914]

Had Lincoln's monetary policy been implemented, it would have ushered in a worldwide economic renewal. Because he "defied" the bankers in proposing to print constitutional interest-free money to pay for the war debt, Lincoln was assassinated a few weeks after his monetary policy was introduced and before he could complete his Reconstruction Plan to reestablish constitutional government in a restored Republic, in a reconciled Union of States.

There were no further issues of Greenbacks and they were eventually removed from circulation. Unbeknownst to the American People, the "government" continued to operate but under the private authority dictate of an "oligarch" of creditor financiers… also known as "cunning, ambitious, and unprincipled men."[915] The institution that became established instead was the Federal Reserve, a privately-owned central bank given the power in 1913 to print Federal Reserve Notes (dollar bills) and lend to the government (of which the American People are responsible for payment) WITH INTEREST. The government has been submerged in debt that has grown exponentially ever since, until it is now reported an un-repayable $18 trillion.[916]

According to a 2013 study conducted by a university economics professor, the (*de facto*) Federal Government has accumulated over $70 trillion in unreported debt, an amount nearly six times the declared figure.[917] The miscalculation of what it owes was derived by leaving out certain unfunded liabilities that include government loan guarantees, deposit insurance, and actions taken by the Federal Reserve as well as the cost of other government trust funds. Factoring in those figures brings the total amount the government owes to a staggering $70 trillion.[918]

"For nearly a century, Lincoln's statue at the Lincoln Memorial has gazed out pensively across the reflecting pool toward the Federal Reserve building, as if pondering what the bankers had wrought since his death and how to remedy it."[919]

Proverbs 22:7 ~

> *The borrower is servant to the lender.*

Abraham Lincoln's funeral, a very public affair conducted in numerous American cities, enabled millions of Americans to share moments of profound grief following his shocking assassination at Ford's Theater in April, 1865. Lincoln's body was carried back to Illinois by train, and along the way funeral observances were held in various cities. The funeral procession of President Lincoln visited 11 cities and over 1 million people filed past his coffin. He was mourned by millions throughout the world.[920]

President Lincoln's funeral procession in New York City [921]
11,000 military men and 75,000 civilians marched in Lincoln's funeral procession
in New York City

In the very large collection of official condolences received by the United States government upon the death of Abraham Lincoln, coming from every civilized country in the world, there was not one word from the Pope of Rome.[922] Most significant is that the Pope had more "subjects" in the United States than any other ruler in Europe.[923]

The people of Italy, the revolutionists who were struggling for a free and united Italy separate from the Papal States, when they learned of the assassination of President Lincoln, had sent beautiful messages of condolences along with their intimate knowledge of the life of Lincoln. It is reported that the messages of condolences were frank in placing the blame on the Jesuits.[924]

Edwin M. Stanton, Secretary of War [925]

About six months before the Civil War ended, Secretary of War Edwin Stanton asked Judge Advocate General Joseph Holt, the highest-ranking officer in the military justice system at that time, to investigate and report on a conspiracy to undermine the Federal Government and to dissolve the Union.[926]

Holt referenced evidence and reports provided by two high-ranking politically conscious Union officers, Brigadier General Henry B. Carrington[927] and Colonel John P. Sanderson,[928] both educated men as lawyers and published authors. Having studied the stack of evidence, Holt composed and completed a 14,000-word report which was organized into eight sections, making several incisive points, and describing the *Knights of the Golden Circle*, or *KGC*, as the "echo and faithful ally" of the Confederacy."[929]

Joseph Holt [930]
Judge Advocate General

Henry B. Carrington [931]
Brigadier General

John P. Sanderson [932]
Colonel

The Holt Report, published 1864 [933]

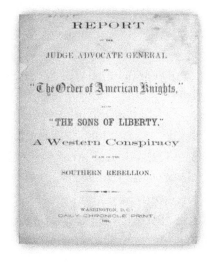

After receiving the *"Report of the Judge Advocate General on 'The Order of American Knights,' alias 'The Sons of Liberty' : a western conspiracy in aid of the Southern Rebellion (1864),"*[934] Secretary of War Stanton promptly turned the report over to the Union Congressional Committee who had several thousands of copies made for distribution and also released it to the newspapers who published summaries or extracts of the report.[935] Commonly known as "the *Holt Report*," this important historical document, published in October, 1864, is an official Federal Government report on the presence and conspiracy of secret societies, specifically the *Knights of the Golden Circle* under its various aliases.[936]

The report is by far the most trenchant analysis in the government's files of the prewar and wartime *KGC*.

The response of the Southern Slave Power and Democrats was outrage and political finger-pointing with claims of "secret society myth." It cannot be disregarded, as reported in the Library of Congress *"Scope and Content: Note of the Joseph Holt Papers, 1817-1895,"* that Mr. Holt was also "a Southerner and Democrat." Interesting is that Holt supported the Union by upholding his sworn oath of office to the *Constitution of the United States* and understood the intent of the Founding Fathers in the *Declaration of Independence*. [937]

Let us go a bit deeper into the secret societies, who and what were behind them? What did these Federal Government officials know or understand and seek to expose?

Albert Pike[938] (1809-1891) was born in Boston, passed entrance exams at Harvard University, though due to financial limitations chose not to attend and was mostly self-educated. Having moved to Arkansas as a young man, Pike was a schoolteacher, newspaper editor, and then became a lawyer, admitted to the bar in 1837. Albert Pike was a Captain in the Mexican-American War and a Brigadier General in the Confederate Army. He was also a 33rd degree Freemason and strong evidence indicates that Pike was the genius behind the influence and power of the Masonic-influenced *Knights of the Golden Circle* (KGC).[939] [940] He's been called a genius, a villain, and an occultist.[941]

Having long been captivated by Native American culture, Pike learned to communicate with several tribes in their native language. Before settling in Arkansas in 1832, Pike traveled as a member in a trading party throughout the Southwest meeting various tribes like the Choctaw, Cherokee, Creeks, and Seminole. Once settled in Arkansas, he would regularly embark on hunting and camping excursions with various tribes and then began to provide his law services in advocating Indian rights before Congress.[942] In particular, Pike pressed for federal payment of claims due for Indian lands that had been confiscated in the early 19th century.

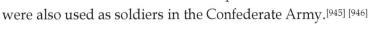

Pierre Jean De Smet (1801-1873) [943]

In the mid-1800s, Jesuit priest Pierre-Jean de Smet, (1801-1873) one of the most influential American Jesuits of the 19th century, began a lifetime relationship with native Indians of the Mid and North West.[944]

Jesuit priest de Smet, along with his Jesuit coadjutor Albert Pike, took full advantage of the trust and enduring respect they had established with the native Indians in accomplishing Rome's agenda. Not only were the native Indians inducted as soldiers to repel the movement of Protestant settlers to the Oregon Territory, they were also used as soldiers in the Confederate Army.[945] [946]

c1899 print of the U.S. cavalry pursuing American Indians[947]

Later, the plan was to use the reunited (post-Civil War) 14th Amendment Corporate UNITED STATES Federal Army to massacre the natives during the *American Indian Wars*,[948] the most famous of which were fought on the great Western plains between 1860 and 1890. It would not be the last time their plan would include "ethnic cleansing."[949]

Pike was a founding father and head of the *Ancient Accepted Scottish Rite of Freemasonry*, being the *Sovereign Grand Commander of the Southern Supreme Council* and head of *Illuminized Freemasonry* in the United States from 1859[950] and retained that position until his death in 1891. Pike had a strong role in the secessionist movement in the South as well as the convention which organized the Confederacy in Montgomery, Alabama.[951]

1874 illustration in *Harper's Weekly*, an American political magazine [952]

"The Union as it Was
This is a White Man's Government
The Lost Cause
Worse that Slavery"

Description: Man, "White League" shaking hands with a Ku Klux Klan member over a shield illustrated with an African American couple holding their dead baby. In the background is a man hanging from a tree.

Where authors of the early 20th century, not long after Pike's death, claim that Pike was the chief judicial officer and the Grand Dragon of the *White Knights of the Ku Klux Klan*, footnote references and quotes of Pike that verify these authors' claims appear to be lacking. Apparently, records, newspaper clippings, and rare books of the *Ku Klux Klan* are reported to have mysteriously disappeared all over the nation including from the Library of Congress.[953] [954]

Pike was said to be a Satanist, who indulged in the occult. Apparently he possessed a bracelet which he used to summon Lucifer and with whom he had constant communication. [955]

Pike was the Grand Master of a Luciferian group known as the "Order of the Palladium," or "Sovereign Council of Wisdom," which had been founded in Paris in 1737. Having originated in Egypt, Palladism was a Satanic cult that was introduced to the inner circle of the Masonic lodges.[956] It was aligned with the "Palladium of the Templars."

Pike succeeded the highest officer, Isaac Long, who in 1801 brought a statue of Baphomet (Satan) and the skull of the Templar Grand Master Jacques de Molay from Paris to Charleston, South Carolina,[957] when at that time he helped establish the *Ancient and Accepted Scottish Rite*.[958] Charleston had been selected because it was geographically located on the 33rd parallel of latitude, which is of significance to Satanists.

This particular council is considered to be the "Mother Supreme Council of all Masonic Lodges of the World,"[959] and all regular Supreme Councils of the world today descend from the Mother Supreme Council of Charleston.[960] The *Holy See of the Dogma* for the whole Masonic world was set-up at Charleston, the "sacred city of the Palladium."[961] There is no small wonder that South Carolina had been the first

State to secede from the Union in "The Great Rebellion,"[962] or that the first shot of the Civil War was fired at Charleston.

Also the "Sovereign Pontiff of Lucifer," Albert Pike, was the president of the *Supreme Dogmatic Directory*, which was composed of 10 brothers of the highest grades who formed Pike's *Supreme Grand College of Emeritus Masons* with the *Sovereign Executive Directory of High Masonry* **established at Rome** under Pike's partner and co-founder of ***Illuminized Freemasonry***, Giuseppe Mazzini (1805-1872).[963]

Mazzini was the Italian revolutionary leader and worldwide director of *Illuminized Freemasonry* from 1834 to 1872, having divided worldwide management powers with Pike in 1859 according to a plan that incorporated *The Palladium Rite* as a super-secret, very powerful group which would govern all other Freemasonry and groups.[964]

In 1871, Pike published the 861-page Masonic handbook[965] known as the "Morals and Dogma of the Ancient and Accepted Scottish Rite of Freemasonry."[966] On page 321 is written:

> "LUCIFER, the *Light-bearer*! Strange and mysterious name to give to the Spirit of Darkness! Lucifer, the Son of the Morning! Is it *he* who bears the *Light*, and with its splendors intolerable blinds feeble, sensual, or selfish Souls? Doubt it not!"[967]

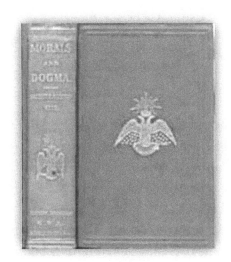 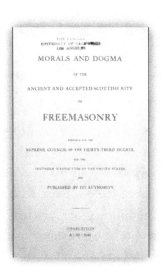

Spine, cover, and title page of Albert Pike's
Morals and dogma of the ancient and accepted Scottish Rite of Freemasonry [968]

Between 1859 and 1871, Pike strategized a military blueprint for three world wars and various revolutions throughout the world which he calculated would bring the Luciferian conspiracy into its final stage upon this earth.[969] Pike presented his plan in a letter written in 1871 to Giuseppe Mazzini,[970] a political activist and head of the Mafia and Freemasons in Italy.

> "**The First World War** must be brought about in order to permit the Illuminati to overthrow the power of the Czars in Russia and of making that country a fortress of atheistic Communism. The divergences caused by the "agentur" (agents) of the Illuminati between the British and Germanic Empires will be used to foment this war. At the end of the war, Communism will be built and used in order to destroy the other governments and in order to weaken the religions."

"**The Second World War** must be fomented by taking advantage of the differences between the Fascists and the political Zionists. This war must be brought about so that Nazism is destroyed and that the political Zionism be strong enough to institute a sovereign state of Israel in Palestine. During the Second World War, International Communism must become strong enough in order to balance Christendom, which would be then restrained and held in check until the time when we would need it for the final social cataclysm."

"**The Third World War** must be fomented by taking advantage of the differences caused by the "agentur" of the "Illuminati" between the political Zionists and the leaders of Islamic World. The war must be conducted in such a way that Islam (the Moslem Arabic World) and political Zionism (the State of Israel) mutually destroy each other. Meanwhile the other nations, once more divided on this issue will be constrained to fight to the point of complete physical, moral, spiritual and economical exhaustion… We shall unleash the Nihilists and the atheists, and we shall provoke a formidable social cataclysm which in all its horror will show clearly to the nations the effect of absolute atheism, origin of savagery and of the most bloody turmoil. Then everywhere, the citizens, obliged to defend themselves against the world minority of revolutionaries, will exterminate those destroyers of civilization, and the multitude, disillusioned with Christianity, whose deistic spirits will from that moment be without compass or direction, anxious for an ideal, but without knowing where to render its adoration, will receive the true light through the universal manifestation of the pure doctrine of Lucifer, brought finally out in the public view. This manifestation will result from the general reactionary movement which will follow the destruction of Christianity and atheism, both conquered and exterminated at the same time."

Strikingly, there appears to have been a fulfillment in plans for the first two World Wars and the characteristics portrayed in Pike's plan for a *Third World War* is unfolding before our eyes.

Albert Pike [971]
Pike's Freemason regalia depicts the number "33"

Giuseppe Mazzine [972]

Even though Pike was a Confederate Brigadier General who committed the most heinous atrocities of the Civil War, his tomb is within the *House of the Temple* located just 13 blocks from the Capitol Building in Washington, DC.[973] [974]

In 1944 and 1953 special Acts of Congress allowed Albert Pike to be entombed within the building, behind his sculpture. The *House of the Temple* also features a museum in Pike's honor.[975] Albert Pike was a high-ranking member of the Illuminati who is yet today revered in the *New World Order* circles. **The god of the Illuminati and the *New World Order* is Lucifer.** The Word of God, the Holy Bible, refers to Lucifer as Satan.[976]

Albert Pike, 33rd degree Freemason and author of *Morals and Dogma* is quoted:[977]

"The Masonic religion should be, by all of us initiates of the high degrees, maintained in the purity of the Luciferian doctrine. . . Yes, Lucifer is God, and unfortunately Adonay (Jesus) is also God. For the eternal law is that there is no light without shade, no beauty without ugliness, no white without black, for the absolute can only exist as two Gods: darkness being necessary to light to serve as its foil as the pedestal is necessary to the statue, and the brake to the locomotive. . ." The doctrine of Satanism is a heresy; and the true and pure philosophic religion is the belief in Lucifer, the equal of Adonay (Jesus); but Lucifer, God of Light and God of Good, is struggling for humanity against Adonay, the God of darkness and evil."[978] [emphasis added]

After the Civil War, Pike was found guilty of treason and jailed, only to be pardoned by fellow Freemason President Andrew Johnson on April 22, 1866, who met with him the next day at the White House. On June 20, 1867, Scottish Rite officials conferred upon President Johnson the 4th to 32nd Freemasonry degrees, and Johnson later went to Boston to dedicate a Masonic Temple.[979]

Albert Pike made no significant mark as a Confederate Brigadier General, besides treason against the *United States of America*, yet Pike's statue is the **only** Confederate officer represented among the outdoor Civil War statuary of Washington City, not far from Capitol Hill.

In this eleven-foot bronze statue, Pike is presented in civilian attire as a Masonic leader, not as a Confederate General. He carries a copy of his famous *Morals and Dogma* in his left hand. The large granite pedestal below Pike contains a bronze lady in Greek dress who sits on one level of the pedestal and holds the banner of the Scottish Rite. The statue was listed on the *National Register of Historic Places* on September 20, 1978, in a National Register nomination of the Civil War Monuments in Washington, D.C.[980]

Albert Pike Statuary Washington, DC [981]

Photo created/published between 1909 and 1919

In the latter decades of the 19th century, in the period of time that the Republic had been secreted into dormancy and the Corporate UNITED STATES counterfeited its control over America, British-centered finance gained supremacy over American industry and U.S. policy-making. ***Under British sponsorship, Pike's Scottish Rite, Southern Jurisdiction, came to rule over much of the world's Freemasonry.***

Pike is proudly "credited" on the website of *The Scottish Rite of Freemasonry Supreme Council 33° Southern Jurisdiction's* world headquarters at Washington, D.C. with a revival of the organization during the Reconstruction period after the Civil War.[982] During the Reconstruction Era, its headquarters moved from South Carolina to Washington, D.C.[983] into a newly constructed Temple strategically located[984] in the

158

District of Columbia. More striking information will be revealed on this subject further in the American Republic's story.

Theodore Roosevelt, the Master Mason [985]

Vice President Theodore Roosevelt, a passionate Freemason, became U.S. President on September 14, 1901, upon the Jesuit assassination of President William McKinley.[986] Teddy Roosevelt's reign was the Lost Cause[987] triumphant as his revered exiled uncle, James Bulloch,[988] the Confederacy's chief foreign agent in Great Britain during the Civil War, had ghostwritten young Teddy's book on naval history; and Teddy's elitist masters had finally achieved their plan to conquer Cuba in the 1898 *Spanish-American War.*[989] Let it be known that the Washington, D.C. statue honoring the treasonous Luciferian, Albert Pike, was dedicated just 39 days after Teddy Roosevelt's inauguration.[990]

William McKinley [991]
25th President of the United States
1897-1901

James Dunwoody Bulloch and Irvine Bulloch.[992]

The Bulloch brothers were uncles to President Theodore Roosevelt. Both were Confederate naval officers during the Civil War.

"Uncle Jimmy" was a Confederate secret agent and their "most dangerous man" in Europe, according to Union State Department officers. James Bulloch provided revenue for the *Confederate States of America* from sales and shipping of Confederate cotton to Britain. It is thought very possible that he was connected to the Lincoln assassination plot as well as a kidnapping plot with covert connections in Canada. [993] This photo was taken after the Civil War.

Where Almighty God had been pouring Light on the Western hemisphere which birthed the "city upon a hill,"[994] the American Republic, Satan was working darkness to counter it in the Eastern hemisphere.

Freemasonry is closely linked with the Illuminati. <u>The Order of Illuminati[995] was formed in Bavaria on May 1, 1776 by Adam Weishaupt[996] (1748-1830) on the principles he learned from his training as a Jesuit.</u> The Illuminati, meaning "enlightened," is a name given to several groups that form an organization which masterminds events and controls world affairs through governments and corporations by conspiracy with secret plans to change society.

Johann Adam Weishaupt, 1799 [997]

Illuminati members take a vow of secrecy and pledge obedience to their superiors or "masters." Secret Societies have existed throughout history. Each of them has been propelled by different aims and with different roles in society. They operate in "secret" because of their subversive and conspiratorial goals. Most secret societies throughout the centuries have catered to those of wealthy affluence who were fascinated with occultism.

There are two realms of influence concerning Secret Societies, the **spiritual** and **political** machinations. The political relates to the *"Doctrine of Temporal Power,"*[998] [999] by which the Pope rules, or seeks to rule, **ALL** civil and political authority of the world. *Temporal Power* is a separate and second power from that of the **Spiritual Power**. Most people are not aware of the spiritual wickedness that controls the men and women who operate in the Devil's world system.[1000] The Illuminati actively operates in both realms.[1001]

Banned in 1777 by a new Bavarian ruler who saw the despotism, another reorganization of the Bavarian Illuminati group occurred in 1780. By 1788 it was thought destroyed through aggressive legislation and criminal charges but it actually went underground and infiltrated Masonic lodges across Europe.[1002] Many members were recruited from Freemason lodges and infiltrated entire lodges.

Although the several secret society groups that form the Illuminati organization are not unified on the surface they are deeply interconnected through their worship of Lucifer. It is by this Satanic religion that they have a common goal.

Their ultimate collaborated goal is establishment of a global *New World Order* with one government and one religion with their world leader who will receive universal worship, ruling from Solomon's rebuilt Temple in Jerusalem.[1003] This means that when their plan is permitted to succeed there will be a future "infallible" Pope[1004] who will be "that man of sin,"[1005] "antichrist,"[1006] "the beast,"[1007] "king of fierce countenance;"[1008] also called by the Lord Jesus Christ, "the abomination of desolation,"[1009] ruling the world from Jerusalem.[1010]

The Illuminati organization has evolved through the years, however, their goal remains. A point must be made with regard to the claims of the Scottish Rite Freemasons with regard to America's Founding Fathers having belonged to their establishment and depicting pictures of President Washington wearing Freemason regalia. Their world headquarters at Washington, D.C. has dedicated a banquet Hall as a memorial to him.

One must ponder the extent of their motive and what President Washington would think of their memorial.[1011] Records in history give evidence by President Washington's own words that he believed that the American Freemason lodges of his day were not "contaminated" with the principles ascribed to the Jesuits' Illuminati. Washington also stated that he had not been in a lodge more than twice.

George Washington had become the most respected man of the age in early America. According to renowned American historian, John Clark Ridpath (1840-1900),[1012] in his *Universal History*, General Washington had funded the Revolution with $74,485 from his own purse.[1013]

Although Washington had been initiated into English Freemasonry in 1752 as a young man, he was largely inactive. Aware of the history and presence of the Jesuits at Georgetown University, Washington warned the whole country to beware of secret societies.[1014] On September 25, 1798, one year before Washington's death, he wrote a letter to Pastor G. W. Snyder in which he stated:

> "I have heard much of the nefarious, & dangerous plan, & doctrines of the Illuminati… [I have little more to add than] thanks for your kind wishes, and favourable sentiments, except to correct an error you have run into, of my Presiding over the English lodges in this Country. The fact is, I preside over none, nor have I been in one more than once or twice, within the last thirty years. I believe, notwithstandings, that none of the Lodges in this Country [unlike the British, French and German lodges] are contaminated with the principles ascribed to the [Jesuits'] Society of the Illuminati."[1015][1016]   [Emphasis added]

We end the brief behind-the-scenes view of secret societies and move forward.

Just before the end of the Civil War and before Abraham Lincoln began his second term as President, he visited with New Jersey State Senator James Scovel and shared:

> "Young man, if God gives me four years more to rule this country, I believe it will become what it ought to be--what its Divine Author intended it to be--no longer one vast plantation for breeding human beings for the purpose of lust and bondage. But it will become a new Valley of Jehoshaphat, where all the nations of the earth will assemble together under one flag, worshipping a common God, and they will celebrate the resurrection of human freedom."[1017]   [emphasis added]

Black slavery was forcibly eradicated, but the law was weak in that it was unable to change men's hearts. The bitter experience of war changed the dominant attitude toward black people from racial inferiority to racial hatred. Encountered would be another century along with Civil Rights legislation as another attempt to fix what was not done in the 1860s.[1018] The struggle that was to rid the country of human slavery of the black race, would result in fastening upon the whole nation an economic or money slavery, which has endured to the present time…

In order to grasp a greater scope of the extent of deception and usurpation in what had been done in enslaving America, it is of significance to ponder and acknowledge the original 13th Article of Amendment of the *Constitution*, which had been ratified on March 12, 1819:

> "If any citizen of the United States shall accept, claim, receive, or retain any title of nobility or honour, or shall without the consent of Congress accept and retain any present, pension, office, or emolument of any kind whatever, from any Emperor, King, Prince, or foreign Power, such person shall cease to be a citizen of the United States, and shall be incapable of holding any office of trust or profit under them, or either of them."   [emphasis added]

This original 13th Amendment was replaced by an unlawful amendment thereby displacing the "*titles of nobility*"[1019] clause. The (non-original) 13th Amendment (freeing the slaves) was enacted by

Lincoln's executive government on December 18, 1865, eight months after President Lincoln was assassinated. The original and lawful 13th Amendment, as presented, had been ratified on March 12, 1819 with the vote of the Virginia General Assembly and that published the *Revised Code of the Laws of Virginia* with the original 13th Article of Amendment included in the *Constitution of the United States.*

1819 Laws of Virginia [1020]
Shown are the title page and page 30
which displays the publishing of the
13th "Titles of Nobility"
Article of Amendment in place

Courtesy of Barefoot Bob Hardison,
and "Barefoot's World"

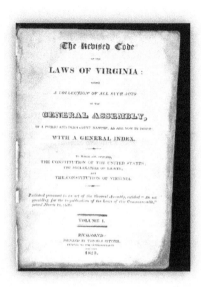
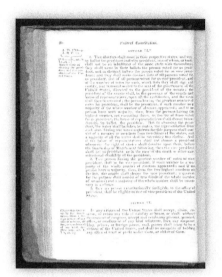

The original and ratified Article of Amendment added a heavy and serious penalty in losing one's citizenship for receiving a title of nobility that is not included in the unlawful replacement Amendment that pertains to freeing the slaves. The original contained the "titles of nobility" clause as provided for in Article I, Section 9, Clause 8 of the *Constitution:*

"No Title of Nobility shall be granted by the United States: And no Person holding any Office of Profit or Trust under them, shall, without the Consent of the Congress, accept of any present, Emolument, Office, or Title, of any kind whatever, from any King, Prince, or foreign State."

Any person holding or accepting a title of nobility or honor, or receiving any emolument, other than their legitimate earnings, under any guise from external sources, would cause that person to "cease to be a citizen of the United States" and be "incapable of holding any office of trust or profit under them or either of them."

The original 13th Article of Amendment was proposed, properly ratified, and was a matter of record in the several States' archives until 1876, during the period of Reconstruction after the Civil War, at which time it had quietly and fraudulently "disappeared," never repealed. The presently acknowledged 13th Amendment pertaining to freeing the slaves had been substituted in its place.

The records of the original and lawful 13th Article of Amendment were thought to be destroyed by invading British troops during the time of the burning of the new capitol building at Washington City the *War of 1812.*

The Capitol Building, which then housed the small *Library of Congress,* was burned and pillaged in August, 1814.[1021] Providence saw to it that records have since been found in the archives of the British Museum Library in London and in the archives of several of the States and Territories.

Capture and burning of Washington by the British, in 1814 [1022]

The fact of its existence had been lost to memory until researchers "accidentally" discovered in the public library at Belfast, Maine a copy of the 1825 Maine constitution and that of the *Constitution of the United States* which included this original Article of Amendment. Subsequent research shows that it was in the records of the ratifying States, and subsequently admitted States and Territories until 1876.

The last to drop it from record was the Territory of Wyoming after 1876. The most intriguing discovery was the 1867 Colorado Territory edition which includes both the original "missing" 13th Article of Amendment and the current unlawful 13th Amendment, on the same page.

The 1876 Laws of Wyoming similarly show the original and lawful "missing" 13th Article of Amendment, the current 13th Amendment (freeing the slaves), and the current 15th Amendment on the same page. The current 13th Amendment is listed as the 14th and the current 15th Amendment is listed as the 15th, the current 14th Amendment being omitted in the 1876 Wyoming edition.

Because of a long history of abuses and excesses against the rights of man during Colonial times, the Founding Fathers held an intense disdain and distrust regarding a privileged "Black Nobility." For that reason they established as law in the *Constitution of the United States* two injunctions against the use of recognition of "titles of nobility or honor" and acceptance of any emoluments whatever from external sources. The first pertains to the Federal Government, Article I, Section 9, and the second pertains to the individual States, Article I, Section 10.

The *Revolutionary War* for independence was primarily waged to eliminate these abuses and excesses of the "Nobility" from the life of the nation, recognizing the equality of all men. Because there was no penalty attached to accepting, claiming, receiving or retaining a title of nobility, honor, or emoluments in the *Constitution* as originally ratified, the 13th Article of Amendment was proposed in December of 1809.

The intent of amending the *Constitution* was to institute a penalty for accepting or using a "title of nobility or honour" to set oneself apart from, or superior to, or possessing of any special privileges or immunities not available to any other citizen of the *United States of America*. It also instituted the same penalty for accepting and retaining any present, pension, office, or emolument of any kind whatever, from any Emperor, King, Prince, or foreign Power, <u>which includes the Vatican</u>.   An emolument is payment in any form for services rendered or to be rendered, or as understood today, as a graft or a bribe.

Senator Philip Reed (Maryland) [1023]

On January 18, 1810, Senators led by Philip Reed of Maryland issued their first version of a proposed Article of Amendment to the *Constitution*, (known now as the *Titles of Nobility Amendment*, or *T.O.N.A.* or more properly -- the original Thirteenth Article of Amendment to the *Constitution of the United States*).   Records show that the vote to send the final version of the Article of Amendment to the States for ratification was taken on Thursday, April 26th.

First, a motion to delay voting on the proposed Article of Amendment was defeated 8-20, then the proposal was approved by the margin of 26 to 1, with seven Senators either absent or not voting. History projects them as very able and worthy men, some of the most extraordinary and illustrious Americans of that day.

The House of Representatives voted to approve the Article of Amendment on May 1, 1810. With considerable support both from Federalists in New York and Massachusetts, and "Democratic-Republicans"[1024] in the South, <u>the Article of Amendment was approved by a vote of 87-3</u>. Eighteen of the 21 members from Virginia voted for it.   Seventeen of the 18 members from Pennsylvania voted for it, while those from New York numbered 7 for, 1 against, with 6 absent or not voting. Rhode Island's Richard Jackson, Jr. was absent, but Revolutionary War veteran Elisha R. Potter voted for it.

Rep. Elisha Reynolds Potter (Rhode Island) [1025]

In its final form, as sent to the legislatures of the 17 States for ratification, it reads as follows:

"If any citizen of the United States shall accept, claim, receive, or retain any title of nobility or honour, or shall without the consent of Congress, accept and retain any present, pension, office, or emolument of any kind whatever, from any Emperor, King, Prince, or foreign Power, such person shall cease to be a citizen of the United States, and shall be incapable of holding any office of trust or profit under them, or either of them."

The first State to ratify the Article of Amendment was Maryland, which did so on Christmas Day, December 25, 1810. (A Table showing the dates on which the remaining States voted to ratify or reject the amendment is available for viewing by reference in this subject's endnote. Also shown are the official publications which researchers have uncovered in the various archives.)[1026]

The researchers are now in physical possession of other existing volumes of the same after years of searching old bookstores and auctions. The researchers' collection also includes many private printings and newspapers that contain the lawful 13th Amendment in its proper place.

The ratification of the Article of Amendment by Maryland was followed closely by Delaware, Pennsylvania, New Jersey, Georgia, North Carolina, Vermont, Kentucky, and Tennessee, all of which occurred in 1811. Massachusetts and New Hampshire had ratified it in 1812, by which time the *War of*

1812 had commenced. New York and Connecticut rejected the Article of Amendment in 1813 and Rhode Island did so in 1814.

Having learned that the *Mother Supreme Council of all Masonic Lodges of the World* sits on the 33rd parallel of latitude at Charleston, it is not a wonder that South Carolina tabled the proposal on December 21, 1814. This left the proposed Article of Amendment one vote shy of final ratification; the vote of Virginia was either lost or not taken in the chaos and confusion of the *War of 1812*.

Authorized by an Act of the *Virginia General Assembly* (February 15, 1817), the complete revision of the State's laws were entrusted to five of Virginia's most prominent lawyers and legal scholars: William Brockenbrough, Benjamin Watkins Leigh, Robert White, and judges of the Supreme Court of Appeals, Spencer Roane and John Coalter.

When their work was concluded, the Virginia General Assembly voted on March 12, 1819 to publish the *Revised Code of the Laws of Virginia* with both the Constitution of Virginia <u>and</u> the *Constitution of the United States* <u>including the original 13th Article of Amendment intact and in its proper place. Thus, the vote of Virginia was indeed accomplished and the Article of Amendment had been ratified.</u>

The General Assembly of Virginia authorized the distribution of the *Revised Code of 1819* with 10 copies designated for the executive branch of Virginia, five copies for the Clerk of the General Assembly, and four copies for the Secretary of State of the United States; one copy each for Thomas Jefferson, James Madison, and President James Monroe; one copy each for the federal Senate, House, and Library of Congress, and one copy for every judge in the courts of the United States of America in Virginia. Thus was the Federal Government notified of the actions of the Virginia General Assembly ratifying the 13th Article of Amendment.

By February of 1820, sufficient copies of the *Revised Code* had been printed to make it available for public sale, and it was advertised as such in a Richmond newspaper. Research conducted on this subject indicates that at least six or seven other Virginia newspapers also carried advertisements for the new Code.

A point to be made regarding an apparent effort to remove law without the consent of the American people was for a secret agenda that served the purpose of the *Society of Jesus* also known as "the Jesuits," along with those of "Black Nobility," also known as the "kings of the earth," a wealthy aristocracy of "cunning, ambitious, and unprincipled men."

Those disloyal citizens should have been held accountable in violating constitutional law, prosecuted in the courts of Justice and then exiled from America as a penalty in losing their citizenship. Again, we purport a devious plan by devious men, those with "titles of nobility," misguided by lust for power and wealth. The masters they serve whether by being "knighted," or by oath, provide their rewards as they work toward the goal of <u>*Temporal Powers*</u> in "entitlement" for the <u>papacy</u> and the Jesuit General, also known as the Black Pope.

Psalm 2:1-4 ~

> *Why do the heathen rage, and the people imagine a vain thing? The kings of the earth set themselves, and the rulers take counsel together, against the Lord, and against his anointed, saying, Let us break their bands asunder, and cast away their cords from us. He that sitteth in the heavens shall laugh: the Lord shall have them in derision.*

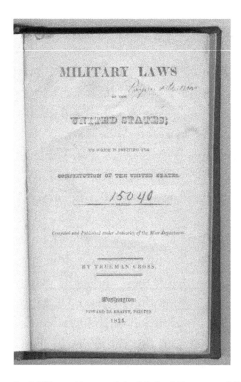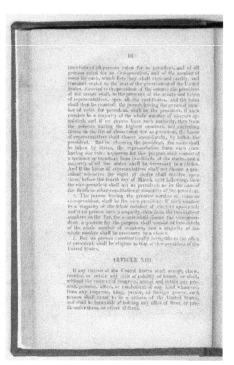

1825 book, *Military Laws of the United States; to Which is Prefixed the Constitution of the United States Compiled and Published under Authority of the War Department* [1027]
By Major Trueman Cross (Deputy Quarter-Master-General of the Army)
Left: Title page;   Right: page displaying the original Thirteenth Article of Amendment in its proper place.

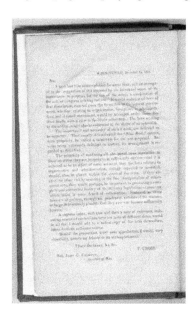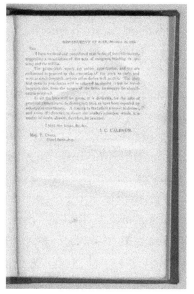

Left: Page displaying Major T. Cross' letter of request to the Secretary of War for authorization
Right: Page displaying authorization by Secretary of War John C. Calhoun

Courtesy of the *TONA Research Committee,* a group that describes themselves as "ordinary, concerned American citizens who happened to stumble on a bit of interesting historical data, and as time has gone on, have banded together with an indefatigable sense of curiosity and duty, have expended a very great amount of time and no little amount of personal funds to ferret out the history of the 13th Titles of Nobility and Honour Article of Amendment to the Constitution For The United States."[1028]

Chapter Thirteen

Reconstruction – "The Second Civil War"

We now continue forward to the period after the Civil War known as the *Reconstruction Era.*[1029] The Civil War prevailed from April 12, 1861 to that precise date four years later, April 12, 1865. In considering the profound opening and close of the *War Between the States* as well as the length of time being precisely four years, it is equally profound in considering the Hebrew meaning of the number "four," which relates to the word "door."[1030] A door had been left open to the curses of disobedience in breaking covenant with the *God of the universe* and His *Laws of Nature* where all men are created equal. The nation's birth certificate, the *Declaration of Independence* had been violated.

The American peoples' social covenant with each other as well as its operating document, the *Constitution of the United States*, which was derived from the *Declaration of Independence*, the Nation's covenant with Almighty God, had been "misinterpreted" and manipulated in the cause of the "Great Rebellion." The Land of Liberty was stained with the blood of the black slaves and bathed in blood resulting from war of "the House divided" while struggling to end that original sin of America.[1031] All of that blood shed on the land cries out to the Creator.[1032]

James Madison, known as the Father of the *Constitution*,[1033] had emphasized that the American peoples' social covenant with each other, the *Constitution*, was derived from the *Declaration of Independence*, the Nation's covenant with Almighty God:

"The government has only such powers as the people delegate to it through a social covenant, the Constitution which is derived from God's Covenant with man. This derivation [origin] limits the power of the process of law and the powers of government. This covenant cannot be contravened [broken] as it is 'the law of nature and of nature's God.'" [1034] [emphasis added]

President James Madison, 1816 [1035]

Drawing a parallel to Proverbs 25:11, "A word fitly spoken is like apples of gold in pictures of silver," President Lincoln described the *Declaration of Independence* as an "apple of gold," and the *Constitution* as the "frame of silver" around it when he said:

"The assertion of that principle, at that time, was the word, 'fitly spoken' which has proved an 'apple of gold' to us. The Union, and the Constitution, are the picture of silver, subsequently framed around it. The picture was made, not to conceal, or destroy the apple; but to adorn, and preserve it. The picture was made for the apple—not the apple for the picture."[1036]

The *Constitution* acts to guard the principles enshrined in the *Declaration of Independence*. As the embodiment of the *Declaration's* principles, the *Constitution* created a frame of government with a clear objective. The *Constitution* is not a collection of compromises, or an empty vessel whose meaning can be redefined to fit the needs of the time; it is the embodiment of an eternal, undisputable truth.

Abraham Lincoln defended the Union and sought to defeat the Confederate insurrection because he held that the principles of the *Declaration* and *Constitution* were inviolable. In his speeches and in his statecraft, Lincoln aimed to demonstrate[1037] that self-government is not doomed to either be so strong that it overwhelms the rights of the people or so weak that it is incapable of surviving.[1038]

Having put President Lincoln out of the way, Great Deception was then crafted in darkness through secrets in the *Reconstruction Era* which brought about an illusion where the American people, along with their posterity through the generations, were deceived into bondage of a new type of citizenship by means of a central (growing-out-of-control) Federal Government which became an oligarchic (government by the few) Democracy where citizens became "subjects"—and slavery became manifest to ALL.

There was an appearance of patriotic American pride, flag-waving, and patriotic song-singing on the surface, however, things were not as they appeared to be… or were told.

Isaiah 29:15 ~

> *Woe unto them that seek deep to hide their counsel [plans] from the Lord, and their works are in the dark, and they say, Who seeth us? and who knoweth us?*

Psalms 44:21 ~ Would not God discover this? For he knows the secrets of the heart.

Luke 8:17 ~

> *For nothing is hidden that will not be made manifest, nor is anything secret that will not be known and come to light.*

Ecclesiastes 12:14 ~

> *For God will bring every deed into judgment, with every secret thing, whether good or evil.*

Howell Cobb, 1860s [1039]

We will recall that Howell Cobb of Georgia, a member of Albert Pike's[1040] Scottish Rite Supreme Council (of 33)[1041] in March, 1860 while serving as Buchanan's Secretary of the Treasury[1042] stated:

> "There is, perhaps, no solution of the great problem of reconciling the interests of labor and capital, so as to protect each from the encroachments and oppressions of the other, so

simple as slavery. By making the laborer himself capital, the conflict ceases and the interests become identical."[1043]

Where on the surface it was thought that there was a conflict going on only between free (employed) and slave (owned) labor, Cobb went beyond and further defined the issue from a financial and ownership standpoint of being between capital (assets) and labor (workforce). Cobb inferred that the only way to overpower the conflict being experienced on the issue of slavery was narrowed to actually being one between money and workforce, with the solution in making slaves of all laborers everywhere.

A "new, improved system" of slavery was being born. "…chattel slavery could not compete in efficiency with white labor… more money could be made from the white laborer, for whom no responsibility of shelter, clothing, food and attendance had to be assumed than from the Negro slave, whose sickness, disability or death entailed direct financial loss."[1044]

As the love of money is the root of all evil (1 Tim. 6:10), there is also the lust for power and the ultimate plan of the Jesuits and their Freemasons in their "Counter-Reformation."[1045] The plan incorporates the secret societies working in unison so their master, the Pope of Rome, will receive universal worship, ruling from Solomon's rebuilt Temple in Jerusalem.[1046]

The *Reconstruction Era* covers the transformation of the Southern States with the reconstruction of State and society from 1863 to 1877, **as well as the reconstruction of the whole country as citizenship was federalized[1047] through the unlawful 14th Amendment to the *Constitution*.** This is also the Era in which the American Republic was shoved aside and left dormant while Lincoln's interim executive government was usurped and a Democracy was formed. The American people were tricked into the jurisdiction of this **foreign** Corporate Democracy.

It is of utmost importance to comprehend what had transpired in this Great Conspiracy as well as what the difference is between a Republic and a Democracy. With understanding we will see how the nation shifted from being a Republic in covenant with the *God of the universe* to being a Democracy ruled by Satan and his sons. One represents the Kingdom of Light, the other the Kingdom of Darkness.

Prior to the Civil War, the United States was referred to as a plural noun: "These United States," which was an association of state governments in alliance for their common good under a federal branch that supervised their interactions but rarely, if ever, interfered in their laws or social practices.

Ever since the American Revolution and its uprising against the English monarchy, King George III, a suspicion of centralized "shadow" authority had existed in America. Yet the attempted secession of the Southern States remarkably prompted a reevaluation of the balance of power in government and suddenly the Federal authorities were viewed by many as the best refuge for the most oppressed and impoverished citizens. These United States became the United States.[1048]

During Reconstruction, the Federal Government determined the conditions that would return the surrendered Southern States back into the Union. In this era, "the Union was preserved; however, the Republic was not."[1049]   It is imperative that we hold this very fact in mind as we proceed forward in viewing the American Republic's story in the Light of truth.

We will recall that it was when the Southern States' governments refused to comply with the *Constitution* that President Lincoln was forced to respond as constitutional law had provided. It was when President Lincoln convened Congress under the authority of the Executive branch while Congress was lacking a lawful quorum (rump) and unable to lawfully operate in representative government under

Article IV, Section 4 of the *Constitution*, along with instituting Martial Law and the suspension of the *Writ of Habeas Corpus*, that the law form was temporarily set aside.

During a time of insurrection and domestic violence, President Lincoln had no other recourse but to give a directive enforcing Martial Law under circumstances presented by those guilty of committing disloyal practices, as well as suspension of the *Writ of Habeas Corpus*. Proclaiming these directives was essential and necessary in order to preserve the Union and maintain governance under the spirit of the *Constitution*.

Otherwise known as "color of law," or giving appearance of law while the republican form of governance was temporarily set aside and an interim governance or law form functioned in its place. By the Law of Perpetuity, the *Constitution* still remained as "the law of the land." However, the legislative body was lacking and could not lawfully function under the *Constitution*.

The Executive branch still had the lawful authority to function, and did so in order to fulfill the obligation of the government to do the business of the People. **Color of law was to have been used in the interim ONLY until the People of the Southern States could reestablish LOYAL State governments in Union and then elect Congressional officers that would represent them and who would operate lawfully under the *Constitution*.** This oversight and obligation fell squarely on the Executive branch.

Lincoln's mandate to the "interim Executive Congress" was very strict and limited and could not be binding on the People or the *de jure* (lawful) government. In the American Republic the whole sovereignty rests with the People and is exercised through their Representatives in Congress assembled. In order for laws to be binding they must have the consent of the American people through their representatives as Article IV, Section 4 of the *Constitution* guarantees to EVERY State in the Union a representative form of governance.[1050] Anything contrary would be "repugnant" to the *Constitution*.[1051]

Lincoln acted unilaterally based solely on his duty to preserve the Union. He did not have a lawful Congress to appeal to in order to get the consent of the People for these changes, so the only mandate he could give this temporary administrative body (rump Congress) was to maintain the business of the government so the Union would not collapse. Administration and enforcement is the ONLY authority that the Executive branch has. The rump "interim Executive Congress" was NOT a Congress of the People and the States.

By constitutional law, the Federal Government had to be returned to the People as soon as the insurrection and domestic violence was put down.

President Lincoln was fully aware of constitutional law, operated within the law, and made provision to see that constitutional law was followed and accomplished. He understood that *color of law* was to have been used in the interim ONLY until the People could elect a Congress that would operate lawfully under the *Constitution*. He referred to this *color of law* interim government as "the Executive Government" in his September 22, 1862 Presidential Proclamation described as "Declaring the Objectives of the War Including Emancipation of Slaves in Rebellious States on January 1, 1863."[1052]

President Lincoln also twice made reference to "the Executive Government" in his January 1, 1863 President Proclamation known as "*The Emancipation Proclamation*."[1053]

We have previously demonstrated by historical fact documented with evidence that it was President Lincoln's intention for the Southern States to be restored in the Union with the same status with which they had "so-called"[1054] seceded or left the Union.[1055] His Presidential Proclamation, known as his "10 Percent Plan," was his Reconstruction Plan.

It was proclaimed by executive authority that ex-Confederates and disloyal citizens were disqualified from voting or from holding office. This was a logical and wise precedent for reestablishing loyal State governments.

Near the end of the Civil War, as Commander-in-Chief, President Lincoln had articulated his commanding order to the leading Union Military Generals to carry out a complete reconciliation with the South and its citizens offering the South the most generous terms in what would come to be known as the "River Queen Doctrine."[1056] President Lincoln displayed diplomacy while at the same time taking steps of compliance in constitutional law.

In the light of the American Republic's truthful history, there can be no doubt in comprehending that the goals of restoring the Republic with the reconciled States in Union was a major contributing factor to the "Great Conspiracy" of Lincoln's assassination by nefarious "cunning, ambitious, and unprincipled men.

Understanding the love of money as the root of all evil (1 Tim. 6:20) as well as the means to control and enslave, we understand that Lincoln's money policy[1057] and constitutional-issued Greenbacks by the U.S. Treasury resulted in giving "the people of this Republic the greatest blessing they ever had—their own paper money to pay their own debts."[1058] Indeed, this was another major contributing factor in his assassination.[1059]

President Lincoln was assassinated just a few days after the Civil War ended and before he was able to follow through with his Reconstruction Plan. The Southern States would have reestablished their loyal State governments in Union, elections would have been held in the Southern States to fill the vacant Congressional seats so they would have Federal representation, and which would also return Congress to being a lawful deliberative body under the *Constitution*.

There was a serious change made in Lincoln's honorable and constitutional Reconstruction Plan after he was put away. Coming into compliance with Article IV, Section 4 of the *Constitution* was diverted and instead, in 1866, one year after the war, elections for members of the 40th United States Congress went forth in the North only. High-level Freemason former Vice President and now succeeding President, Andrew Johnson, revoked and annulled the suspension of the *Writ of Habeas Corpus* in the North, however, continued the suspension of the *Writ of Habeas Corpus* in the Southern States, the District of Columbia, and the southwest Territory.[1060]

In this chapter as well as the next, we will cover some key points of this Era in an effort to project a picture of the Great Struggle that occurred while seeking to finally achieve Liberty for ALL as proclaimed in America's founding document, the *Declaration of Independence,* which is also a covenant with the Creator.

In further, life, liberty, and the pursuit of happiness was to be guarded for ALL in that sacred covenant with "Nature's God," which was later outlined and enumerated in the government's operating document, the *Constitution of the United States,* which was carefully written under Divine inspiration significantly based on God's law and Biblical principles. This is what was intended for this covenant-nation with a republican form of government and in finally ending slavery, as the Founding Fathers presumed would eventually come to fruition.

With various pieces like that of a puzzle put together to form a picture, visible for this period of time will be depicted shades of darkness representing what "cunning, ambitious, and unprincipled men" had done in darkness through secrets and lies of deception to usurp dominion and secretly enslave all of the American people. The picture will also depict what some well-intentioned statesmen had inadvertently[1061] done in desperation while seeking to outmaneuver the "cunning, ambitious, and unprincipled men" in great effort to secure Liberty for all.

In the end, we will step back with chin-in-hand while studying a glimpse of the greater picture and recognize the counterfeit with a better understanding of how "the Union was preserved; however, the Republic was not."[1062]

The Union victory created some of the most far-reaching transformations as reflected by the amendments then made to the *Constitution*. The first twelve amendments, which had been ratified <u>before the war</u>, all served to <u>limit government power</u>. Those <u>after</u> the Civil War, in particular the (non-original and unlawful) 13th Amendment which abolished slavery, and the revolutionary (unlawful) 14th Amendment which granted citizenship and guaranteed civil rights to all those born in the United States instead of recognizing our God-given un-a-lien-able rights, <u>marked unprecedented expansions of federal power</u>.[1063]

In review of Reconstruction up to this point, starting in March 1862, in an effort to prevent reconstruction by the "Radicals" in Congress, President Lincoln appointed provisional Military Governors to reestablish <u>loyal</u> Union governments in Southern States that were captured by the Union Army. Although those States would not be recognized by the "Radicals" until a much later period of time and with prescribed conditions to the Radicals' satisfaction, appointing Military Governors kept the administration of Reconstruction under Presidential control in his executive duties under the *Constitution*, rather than that of the increasingly unsympathetic Radical Congress.[1064]

On March 3, 1862, Lincoln appointed staunch Democrat then Senator Andrew Johnson,[1065] as Military Governor with the rank of Brigadier General in his home State of Tennessee.

Senator Andrew Johnson, 1860 [1066]

On May 26, 1862, Lincoln appointed Edward Stanly[1067] as Military Governor of the coastal region of North Carolina with the rank of Brigadier General. Stanly resigned almost a year later after angering Lincoln by closing two schools for black children in New Bern. It is also reported that Stanly was in a dispute with President Lincoln over the *Emancipation Proclamation*.

Brig. General Edward Stanly [1068]

Gen. George Shepley [1069]

After Brigadier General George F. Shepley[1070] was appointed as Military Governor of Louisiana in May, 1862, Shepley sent two anti-slavery representatives, Benjamin Flanders[1071] and Michael Hahn,[1072] elected in December, 1862, to the House of Representatives which had come to accept them and then voted in favor to seat them.

In July, 1862, Lincoln appointed Colonel John S. Phelps[1073] as Military Governor of Arkansas, though he resigned not long after due to poor health.

Rep. Benjamin Flanders [1074]   Rep. Michael Hahn [1075]   Colonel John S. Phelps[1076]

This selection of men from a variety of backgrounds represents both Northerners and Southerners, as well as both Republicans and Democrats. The picture entails the Chief Executive thoughtfully selecting representation from among a mix as he sought harmony and prudence in the overwhelmingly difficult task of putting the Union back together.

In late 1863, President Lincoln issued a Presidential Proclamation toward amnesty (pardon/forgiveness) and reconstruction on behalf of the rebellious States, which came to be known as his "10 Percent Plan." Union forces were advancing into the South after a couple of critical victories in battle and the Federal Government turned its attention to a plan that would resurrect the Union and ensure the loyalty of the former Confederacy.

Any rebel State would be enabled to form a loyal State Union government if a number equal to ten percent of its white males who had voted in 1860 took an oath of allegiance to the *Constitution* and the Union and had received a presidential pardon. Participants were required to swear their support for laws and proclamations that addressed emancipation of slaves. Excluded from the pardon were high-ranking members of the Confederacy.[1077]

On December 8, 1863, President Lincoln issued Presidential Proclamation 108 - Amnesty and Reconstruction:[1078]

By the President of the United States of America

A Proclamation

Whereas in and by the Constitution of the United States it is provided that the President "shall have power to grant reprieves and pardons for offenses against the United States, except in cases of impeachment;" and

Whereas a rebellion now exists whereby the loyal State governments of several States have for a long time been subverted, and many persons have committed and are now guilty Of treason against the United States; and

Whereas, with reference to said rebellion and treason, laws have been enacted by Congress declaring forfeitures and confiscation of property and liberation of slaves, all upon terms and conditions therein stated, and also declaring that the President was thereby authorized at any time thereafter, by proclamation, to extend to persons who may have participated in the existing rebellion in any State or part thereof pardon and amnesty, with such exceptions and at such times and on such conditions as he may deem expedient for the public welfare; and

Whereas the Congressional declaration for limited and conditional pardon accords with well-established judicial exposition of the pardoning power; and

Whereas, with reference to said rebellion, the President of the United States has issued several proclamations with provisions in regard to the liberation of slaves; and

Whereas it is now desired by some persons heretofore engaged in said rebellion to resume their allegiance to the United States and to re-inaugurate loyal State governments within and for their respective States:

Therefore, I, Abraham Lincoln, President of the United States, do proclaim, declare, and make known to all persons who have, directly or by implication participated in the existing rebellion, except as hereinafter excepted, that a full pardon is hereby granted to them and each of them, with restoration of all rights of property, except as to slaves and in property cases where rights of third parties shall have intervened, and upon the condition that every such person shall take and subscribe an oath and thenceforward keep and maintain said oath inviolate, and which oath shall be registered for permanent preservation and shall be of the tenor and effect following, to wit:

I,_____, do solemnly swear, in presence of Almighty God, that I will henceforth faithfully support, protect, and defend the Constitution of the United States and the Union of the States thereunder; and that I will in like manner abide by and faithfully support all acts of Congress passed during the existing rebellion with reference to slaves, so long and so far as not repealed, modified, or held void by Congress or by decision of the Supreme Court: and that I will in like manner abide by and faithfully support all proclamations of the President made during the existing rebellion having reference to slaves, so long and so far as not modified or declared void by decision of the Supreme Court. So help me God.

The persons excepted from the benefits of the foregoing provisions are all who are or shall have been civil or diplomatic officers or agents of the so-called Government; all who have left judicial stations under the United States to aid the rebellion; all who are or shall have been military or naval officers of said so-called Confederate Government above the rank of colonel in the army or of lieutenant in the navy; all who left seats in the United States Congress to aid the rebellion; all who resigned commissions in the Army or Navy of the United States and afterwards aided the rebellion; and all who have engaged in any way in treating colored persons, or white persons in charge of such, otherwise than lawfully as prisoners of war, and which persons may have been found in the United States service as soldiers, seamen, or in any other capacity. And I do further proclaim, declare, and make known that whenever, in any of the States of Arkansas, Texas, Louisiana, Mississippi, Tennessee, Alabama, Georgia, Florida, South Carolina, and North Carolina, a number of persons, not less than one-tenth in number of the votes cast in such State at the Presidential election of the year A. D. 1860, each having taken the oath aforesaid, and not having since violated it, and being a qualified voter by the election law of the State existing immediately before the so-called act of secession, and excluding all others, shall reestablish a State government which shall be republican and in nowise contravening [breaking or violating] said oath, such shall be recognized as the true government of the State, and the State shall receive thereunder the benefits of the constitutional provision which declares that "the United States shall guarantee to every State in this Union a republican form of government and shall protect each of them against invasion, and on application of the legislature, or the executive (when the legislature can not be convened), against domestic violence."

And I do further proclaim, declare. and make known that any provision which may be adopted by such State government in relation to the freed people of such State which shall recognize and declare their permanent freedom, provide for their education, and which may yet be consistent as a temporary arrangement with their present condition as a laboring, landless, and homeless class, will not be objected to by the National Executive.

And it is suggested as not improper that in constructing a loyal State government in any State the name of the State, the boundary, the subdivisions, the constitution, and the general code of laws as before the rebellion be maintained, subject only to the modifications made necessary. by the conditions hereinbefore stated, and such others, if any, not contravening said conditions and which may be deemed expedient by those framing the new State government.

To avoid misunderstanding, it may be proper to say that this proclamation, so far as it relates to State governments, has no reference to States wherein loyal State governments have all the while been maintained. And for the same reason it may be proper to further say that whether members sent to Congress from any State shall be admitted to seats constitutionally rests exclusively with the respective Houses, and not to any extent with the Executive. And, still further, that this proclamation is intended to present the people of the States wherein the national authority has been suspended and loyal State governments have been subverted a mode in and by which the national authority and loyal State governments may be reestablished within said States or in any of them; and while the mode presented is the best the Executive can suggest, with his present impressions, it must not be understood that no other possible mode would be acceptable.

Given under my hand at the city of Washington, the 8th day of December, A. D. 1863, and of the Independence of the United States of America the eighty-eighth.

ABRAHAM LINCOLN.

By the President:

WILLIAM H. SEWARD, Secretary, of State.

President Abraham Lincoln, Feb. 9, 1864[1079]

It is noteworthy that President Lincoln used the words, "so-called act of secession." He understood the *Law of Perpetuity* and that once a State entered the Union with their State constitution approved and accepted by Congress, the State could not lawfully leave, or secede, from the Union.

Also noteworthy is Lincoln's effort to be in compliance with Article IV Section 4 of the *Constitution* by working toward reestablishing loyal State governments for the Southern States and bringing them back into the Union of States as well as providing protection to the people of those States from invasion or domestic violence. He sincerely sought constitutional protection and benefits for the people of the South as well as the North.

Lincoln's effort was reasonable in directing loyal, qualified citizens of those States by appropriate oath to reestablish their State governments in a manner loyal to the *Constitution* as well as swear allegiance to be law-abiding inclusive of any Congressional legislation pertaining to the liberation of slaves.

President Lincoln displayed diplomacy while also following constitutional law (specifically Article 1, Section 5, Clause 1) by acknowledging that it was up to the respective Houses of Congress in validating the qualifications of and in admitting members sent to Congress from any State and not to him as the Executive.

Lincoln was adamant in carrying out a complete reconciliation with the South and its citizens in very generous terms. The Nation had been devastated and war-torn for four very long and hard years. The number of sons and husbands killed in war were 360,000 Union soldiers and 260,000 Confederate soldiers. The wounds and scars of the souls of their loved ones left behind was exponentially greater in number amidst the Nation's population of about 35 million at that time.[1080]

President Lincoln understood the need to move quickly—and wisely—in directing the nation toward healing and reconciliation. His *Ten Percent Plan* was a foundational start toward resolving large issues. Major challenges that had to be addressed included:[1081]

- How the South, physically devastated by war and socially revolutionized by emancipation, would be rebuilt.
- How the liberated slaves would fare as free men and women.
- How the Southern States would be reintegrated into the Union.
- Who would direct the process of Reconstruction: the President, the (interim Executive) Congress, or the Southern States themselves.

There were other questions that clamored for answers like what should be done with the captured Confederate ringleaders, all of whom were liable to charges of treason. Jefferson Davis[1082] who was the President of the Confederate States (and formerly had a several year service as a U.S. Senator, U.S. Representative, had previously been a U.S. Secretary of War) was imprisoned in 1865 for two years, never brought to trial, (a violation of the Sixth Amendment of the *Constitution* which guarantees the right to a speedy and public trial[1083]) and then pardoned by President Johnson in December, 1868.

President of the Confederacy Jefferson Davis [1084]

The factors that play into understanding the whole scenario is nothing short of tremendous. In this man's situation, it is reported that after two years of imprisonment he was released on $100,000 bond of which a contributor was Gerrit Smith,[1085] a member of "The Secret Six." *The Secret Six* were a group of wealthy and/or influential northern men who held strong conviction toward abolition.[1086] So we see emotions, convictions, and opinions were wide and varied at this tremendous time of upheaval.

Hon. Gerrit Smith of New York [1087]

One issue up and coming was the struggle that the four million slaves that had been suddenly emancipated were faced with: the question, "How free is free?" It was a question that turned out to be an extremely difficult and complex one. Was freedom simply the absence of bondage, or did it mean the right to obtain an education, receive healthcare, negotiate wages, to vote, and to own land? [1088]

The "interim Executive Congress" was not in agreement with Lincoln's Reconstruction policies as they felt Lincoln was too lenient with the Southern rebels and feared the restoration of the planter aristocracy to power along with possible re-enslavement of the black people.[1089] During the war, the Radical Republicans often opposed Lincoln in his selection of Generals as well as his efforts to bring States back into the Union. The radicals of Lincoln's party—Charles Sumner,[1090] Benjamin Wade,[1091] George Julian,[1092] and Thaddeus Stevens[1093] held disdain for Lincoln from the beginning and had attempted to usurp his power wherever and whenever possible.[1094] The Radicals were men of principles. Before the war they had been the strongest Republicans opposing the expansion of slavery. During the war they were the first to call for arming of black troops and for issuing emancipation. They were supporting the rights of black people long before there was any conceivable political benefit to be gained.[1095]

Sen. Charles Sumner [1096]

Sen. Benjamin Wade [1097]

Rep. George Washington Julian [1098]

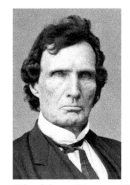

Rep. Thaddeus Stevens [1099]

The Radical Republicans proposed an alternative to Lincoln's *Ten Percent Plan*. The *Wade-Davis Bill*[1100] of 1864 was a Bill proposed for the reconstruction of the South written by two Radical Republicans, the aforementioned Senator Benjamin Wade of Ohio and Representative Henry Winter Davis[1101] of Maryland. In contrast to President Lincoln's more lenient *Ten Percent Plan*, the *Wade-Davis Bill* made re-admittance to the Union for former Confederate States contingent on a majority in each Southern State to take the "Ironclad oath"[1102] to the effect they had never supported the Confederacy.

Rep. Henry Winter Davis [1103]

The *Wade-Davis Bill* passed both houses of Congress on July 2, 1864, and was handed to President Lincoln less than an hour before the adjournment of the session *sine die*. Lincoln responded with a "pocket veto"[1104] and therefore the Bill never took effect. It was Lincoln's objective to mend the Union by carrying out his *Ten Percent Plan.*

As eloquently expressed in his Presidential Proclamation of July 8, 1864, Lincoln believed it would be too difficult to repair all the ties within the Union if the *Wade-Davis Bill* was implemented.[1105] The Radical Republicans retaliated and refused to seat delegates from Louisiana after that State had reorganized its government in accordance with Lincoln's *Ten Percent Plan.*[1106]

The Radicals criticized Lincoln's leniency. Their goal of reconstruction was to readmit the Southern States into the Union on terms that were acceptable to the North. That meant full political and civil equality for black Americans and denying political rights to white proslavery leaders of the Secession movement. The Radicals wanted to insure that the newly freed black men and women were protected and given their rights as Americans.[1107]

Just five days after the surrender of the Confederate forces President Lincoln was assassinated on April 14, 1865 and died the next day. Succeeding Abraham Lincoln as President was then Freemason Vice President Andrew Johnson.[1108] Johnson continued the part of Commander-in-Chief of Military Rule as he moved forward with his own Reconstruction policy.

Andrew Johnson taking the oath of office in the small parlor of the Kirkwood House (Hotel)[1109]
Washington, April 15, 1865.

Southerners anxiously waited for the first seven weeks of Johnson's presidency to hear what he would mandate before allowing them back into the Union. At the time many white Southerners, including the leadership of the Confederacy, expected and would have accepted relatively harsh policies. It soon became clear that Andrew Johnson wanted a speedy, lenient restoration of the Union with as little change made to the *Constitution* as possible.

The rebel States were encouraged to quickly form new governments with no interference from the Federal Government. The President's leniency surprised many in the North while Southerners responded with relief.[1110]

Johnson laid out only minimal requirements. The Southerners were required to admit that they lost the war, the war was over, and slavery and secession were dead. Johnson was harder on the planter aristocracy in that he insisted that wealthy plantation owners and Confederate leaders personally approach him and beg for clemency. That set the tone in eliminating the planter class from leadership of Southern politics as a pardon was necessary in order to vote, hold office, as well as to get their property back if it's been seized by the Federal Government.

Johnson had been raised in poverty and held no sympathy for the wealthy plantation owners. He identified with poor white Southerners. Before the war, they had far outnumbered the slave owners. Now, Johnson was anxious to protect poor whites from what they perceived as a new threat.

With freedom of the black people, it meant that they would have to compete with this new element for livelihood, for social position, and political power. Johnson's aim was to bring the white South and the white North back together. The black people were not a consideration in Johnson's vision of the postwar South. He felt their place was in the labor force without rights to land or much of anything else.[1111]

Johnson's disrespect for the freedmen infuriated many in Washington, and none more than U.S. Representative Thaddeus Stevens of Pennsylvania. Stevens had been an aggressive abolitionist long before the war. With the Republican Party, he led that small, vocal faction known as the Radicals.[1112]

Let it be emphasized again that Congress remained a rump "interim Executive Congress," not a lawful deliberative body under the *Constitution* as there remained vacant seats for States and the people of those States who were not represented. The only business this temporary administrative body (rump Congress) could perform was to maintain the business of the government so the Union would not collapse.

The Federal Government was under *color of law* in this interim period <u>until</u> the People of the Southern States could reestablish <u>loyal</u> State governments in Union and then elect Congressional officers that would represent them and who would operate lawfully under the *Constitution*.

In regards to any legislation, in order for laws to be binding they must have the consent of the American people through their representatives as Article IV, Section 4 of the *Constitution* guarantees to EVERY State in the Union a representative form of governance.[1113] Anything else, or contrary, would be repugnant to the *Constitution*.[1114] By constitutional law, the Federal Government had to be returned to the People as soon as the insurrection was put down.

The "interim Executive Congress" ran on high-adrenaline in this juncture of time. Having come through the devastation of war in which many of the statesmen had served in active military duty as officers, they also were in upheaval because of the assassination of the Commander-in-Chief, still dealt with Southern hostilities as some Southern States attempted to return rebel Confederate treasonous officers to Congress, and had a new President they felt was too lenient with the Southern States.

An extreme add-to in the mix was that President Johnson began showing a change in heart where he actually aided the unrepentant former Confederate "traitors." Where historians have marked Johnson's change of heart as "mysterious,"[1115] in light of the knowledge of Johnson's involvement in Freemasonry as well as being quickly installed in the high-level Scottish degrees[1116] and acclaimed by Masons to be the first President to become a Scottish Rite Mason,[1117] Johnson's change of heart is no longer a mystery.   Aiding the unrepentant treasonous Freemason Confederate ringleaders would not achieve loyal State governments in returning to the Union.

President Andrew Johnson in Masonic Regalia, 1869 [1118]

The Union was yet in disrepair, there were the issues of civil rights for the newly freedmen in which the new President didn't care about. Then consider Congress' serious concern in being limited in Congressional powers while they were yet a temporary administrative body, not a lawful deliberative body under the *Constitution.*

Likewise, hanging over their heads was the dreaded thought that the Southern men who would fill those vacant seats in the Halls of Congress and also hold in their hands the balance of legislative power[1119] that could very well be the tipping of a second insurrection and fate of the Republic… We can sense their frustration while discerning their fears. They were desperate.

The story becomes more dramatic as we continue to piece together documented facts displayed as evidence and thought-provokingly not fully told in history textbooks… Let's look at a few items on the history timeline.

In January, 1865, General William Sherman issued *Special Field Order 15* which set aside confiscated plantation land along the coast of South Carolina and Georgia for black families to settle in 40-acre plots. By June that year, 40,000 freedmen and women were living on the land given to them with seed and farming necessities provided by the *Freedmen's Bureau.*

Gen. William T. Sherman [1120]

In March, 1865, the *Freedmen's Bureau* had been established within the War Department as an agency to smooth the transition from slavery to freedom. The *Bureau* built schools for the former slaves and fed and clothed war refugees, black and white. The *Bureau's* agents had military authority to settle labor disputes and conflicts between former slaves and masters.

The Freedmen's Union Industrial School, Richmond, Virginia [1121]

Glimpses at the Freedmen's Bureau: Issuing rations to the old and sick [1122]

Congress had chartered the *Freedmen's Savings Bank.* In April, 1865, the Confederate Army surrendered and a few days later President Lincoln was shot and mortally wounded. Andrew Johnson became the seventeenth President.

On May 29, 1865 Johnson announced <u>his own plan</u> of Presidential Reconstruction in a <u>Presidential Proclamation "Granting Amnesty to Participants in Rebellion, with Certain exceptions."</u>[1123]

By the President of the United States of America

A Proclamation

Whereas the President of the United States, on the 8th day of December, A. D. 1863, and on the 26th day of March, A. D. 1864, did, with the object to suppress the existing rebellion, to induce all persons to return to their loyalty, and to restore the authority of the United States, issue proclamations offering amnesty and pardon to certain persons who had, directly or by implication, participated in the said rebellion; and

Whereas many persons who had so engaged in said rebellion have, since the issuance of said proclamations, failed or neglected to take the benefits offered thereby; and

Whereas many persons who have been justly deprived of all claim to amnesty and pardon thereunder by reason of their participation, directly or by implication, in said rebellion and continued hostility to the Government of the United States since the date of said proclamations now desire to apply for and obtain amnesty and pardon.

To the end, therefore, that the authority of the Government of the United States may be restored and that peace, order, and freedom may be established, I, Andrew Johnson, President of the United States, do proclaim and declare that I hereby grant to all persons who have, directly or indirectly, participated in the existing rebellion, except as hereinafter excepted, amnesty and pardon, **with restoration of all rights of property**, except as to slaves and except in cases where legal proceedings under the laws of the United States providing for the confiscation of property of persons engaged in rebellion have been instituted; but upon the condition, nevertheless, that every such person shall take and subscribe the following oath (or affirmation) and thenceforward keep and maintain said oath inviolate, and which oath shall be registered for permanent preservation and shall be of the tenor and effect following, to wit:

I,_____ ,do solemnly swear (or affirm, in presence of Almighty God, that I will henceforth faithfully support, protect, and defend the Constitution of the United States and the Union of the States thereunder, and that I will in like manner abide by and faithfully support all laws and proclamations which have been made during the existing rebellion with reference to the emancipation of slaves. So help me God.

The following classes of persons are excepted from the benefits of this proclamation:

First. All who are or shall have been pretended civil or diplomatic officers or otherwise domestic or foreign agents of the pretended Confederate government.

Second. All who left judicial stations under the United States to aid the rebellion.

Third. All who shall have been military or naval officers of said pretended Confederate government above the rank of colonel in the army or lieutenant in the navy.

Fourth. All who left seats in the Congress of the United States to aid the rebellion.

Fifth. All who resigned or tendered resignations of their commissions in the Army or Navy of the United States to evade duty in resisting the rebellion.

Sixth. All who have engaged in any way in treating otherwise than lawfully as prisoners of war persons found in the United States service as officers, soldiers, seamen, or in other capacities.

Seventh. All persons who have been or are absentees from the United States for the purpose of aiding the rebellion.

Eighth. All military and naval officers in the rebel service who were educated by the Government in the Military Academy at West Point or the United States Naval Academy.

Ninth. All persons who held the pretended offices of governors of States in insurrection against the United States.

Tenth. All persons who left their homes within the jurisdiction and protection of the United States and passed beyond the Federal military lines into the pretended Confederate States for the purpose of aiding the rebellion.

Eleventh. All persons who have been engaged in the destruction of the commerce of the United States upon the high seas and all persons who have made raids into the United States from Canada or been engaged in destroying the commerce of the United States upon the lakes and rivers that separate the British Provinces from the United States.

Twelfth. All persons who, at the time when they seek to obtain the benefits hereof by taking the oath herein prescribed, are in military, naval, or civil confinement or custody, or under bonds of the civil, military, or naval authorities or agents of the United States as prisoners of war, or persons detained for offenses of any kind, either before or after conviction.

Thirteenth. All persons who have voluntarily participated in said rebellion and the estimated value of whose taxable property is over $20,000. [emphasis added]

Fourteenth. All persons who have taken the oath of amnesty as prescribed in the President's proclamation of December 8, A. D. 1863, or an oath of allegiance to the Government of the United States since the date of said proclamation and who have not thenceforward kept and maintained the same inviolate.

Provided, That special application may be made to the President for pardon by any person belonging to the excepted classes, and such clemency will be liberally extended as may be consistent with the facts of the case and the peace and dignity of the United States.

The Secretary of State will establish rules and regulations for administering and recording the said amnesty oath, so as to insure its benefit to the people and guard the Government against fraud.

In testimony whereof I have hereunto set my hand and caused the seal of the United States to be affixed.

Done at the city of Washington, the 29th day of May, A. D. 1865, and of the Independence of the United States the eighty-ninth.

ANDREW JOHNSON.
By the President:
WILLIAM H. SEWARD,
Secretary of State.

The "interim Executive Congress," as well as citizenry, was furious with Johnson in his Reconstruction plan. The land that had been confiscated from Confederate plantation owners and given to the former slaves, "freedmen" which had been worked and planted by these people—the land, a means to take care of themselves—who were never paid wages for their labor throughout their tenure as slaves and had nowhere to go when emancipated was now returned to the treasonous, unrepentant Confederate plantation aristocracy by this Presidential Proclamation of amnesty.

Johnson took full advantage while Congress was in recess and passed out pardons by the thousands.[1124] By September of 1865, hundreds of Presidential pardons were being issued in a single day to where special clerks had to be hired to keep up with the paperwork.[1125]

Soon after there was scandal and outrage when President Johnson's limited pardon policy had been violated and abandoned as evidenced and displayed in Southern States electing former Confederate officers to both State Legislatures and Congressional seats.

On the first day of the congressional season, December 4, 1865, the Republicans in Congress banged shut the door in the face of the newly elected Southern delegations. More than sixty former Confederates arrived to take their seats in Congress, including four generals, four colonels and six Confederate cabinet officers.[1126] To add insult to injury there was Alexander Stephens, the former vice president of the Confederacy and who was still under indictment for treason.[1127]

The original Confederate Cabinet [1128]
L–R: Judah P. Benjamin, Stephen Mallory, Christopher Memminger, Alexander Stephens,
LeRoy Pope Walker, Jefferson Davis, John H. Reagan and Robert Toombs

Public offices were overrun with the wealthy plantation owners, the former Slave Power who reestablished white supremacy and refused to extend the vote to black men. Perhaps one way of looking at it is that in seeking able representatives, the voters of the Southern States had turned instinctively to their experienced statesmen. It was a natural but costly blunder in that most of the Southern leaders were tainted by active association with the "Lost Cause."[1129] Another viewpoint is that there was a nestled control of power among a select (oligarchic) group who manipulated precisely who would be sent to Congress.

Congress had the delegated right to refuse the Southern delegates per Article 1, Section 5, Clause 1 of the *Constitution*:

"Each House shall be the Judge of the Elections, Returns and Qualifications of its own Members, and a Majority of each shall constitute a Quorum to do Business; but a smaller Number may adjourn from day to day, and may be authorized to compel the Attendance of absent Members, in such Manner, and under such Penalties as each House may provide."[1130]

Shmoop University, Inc., is a credible academic resource written by educators and experts from America's top universities, including Stanford, Harvard, and UC Berkeley.[1131] The Shmoop Editorial Team explains Article 1, Section 5, Clause 1:

"This clause has two separate and seemingly unrelated parts. <u>First, the House and the Senate are given the power to judge the qualifications of their own members</u>. In the case of a disputed Senate election, for example, in which both candidates claim to have won the vote, it is ultimately up to the Senate itself to decide which candidate gets the seat. Second, a majority of either chamber's membership is required to be present to constitute a quorum. Congress can continue to conduct business with less than a quorum present, but any member can then issue a "quorum call," requiring either that a majority of the members actually show up or that the house takes a temporary adjournment."[1132]

The second point is also very important to bear in mind with regard to the subject of "quorum" in the houses of Congress.

It was very clear that high-level Freemason President Johnson experienced a change of heart when he began showing support for white supremacy in the South and favored pro-Union Southern political leaders who had aided the Confederacy once war had been declared.[1133] Johnson's change of heart also alienated Congress.[1134]

Let us be reminded as stated in the previous chapter that on April 22, 1866 President Johnson pardoned fellow Freemason and Grand Master Mason Albert Pike who had been found guilty of treason and imprisoned. Quite interesting is that President Johnson met with Pike the very next day at the White House.[1135] Johnson received the (high-level) Scottish Rite degrees of Freemasonry at the White House in 1867.[1136]

Albert Pike in Freemason regalia [1137]

By November, 1865, Southern legislatures began drafting "Black Codes" in attempt to restore slavery in a more subtle form while also reestablishing white supremacy.   These laws had the intent and the effect of restricting the freedom of the black American "freedmen" by compelling them to work in a labor economy based on low wages or debt. President Johnson was supportive of the Southerners in this endeavor.

On December 1, 1865, President Johnson had issued a Presidential Proclamation[1138] that revoked and annulled the suspension of the *Writ of Habeas Corpus*,"[1139] in the Northern States as had previously been proclaimed by President Lincoln in ALL of the States; however, President Johnson "excepted" (excluded or omitted) the Southern States, the District of Columbia, and Southwest Territory. The suspension of the *Writ of Habeas Corpus* continued in those areas of the country.

Throughout the *Reconstruction Era* the law form moved further away from returning to a republican form of government and steadily toward a Democracy. The Southern States were <u>not able</u> to reestablish State governments in republican form, nor did they have representation in Congress as "laws" were being passed by a rump Congress, a <u>violation</u> of Article IV Section 4 of the *Constitution*.

On December 6, 1865, President Johnson then announced that the rebellious States had satisfied his conditions and that in his view the Union was now restored.[1140] He declared the reconstruction process complete. Infuriated at his ignorance in many regards, Radical Republicans in Congress refused to recognize new governments in Southern States.

Johnson continued the suspension of the *Writ of Habeas Corpus* in the Southern States and yet began pulling Union Army troops in the South from the one million Union soldiers the previous May down to where there were only 152,000. Southern towns and cities began to experience a large influx of freedmen. The black populations of the ten largest cities in the South doubled over the next five years.[1141]

Bearing in mind Johnson's support of white supremacy in the South and favoring pro-Union Southern political leaders who had aided the Confederacy once war had been declared,[1142] it adds to the intrigue in learning that certain high-level Freemasons were used to stifle the capture of John H. Surratt, co-conspirator to the assassination of President Lincoln. One of them was President Andrew Johnson, and another avid Freemason, Secretary of War Edwin M. Stanton.[1143]

With the knowledge that Surratt was in Liverpool, England, Stanton's War Department refused to make the least attempt to arrest him. A few weeks later President Johnson revoked the reward for the arrest of Surratt, greatly increasing the assassin's chances to escape.[1144] Secretly, Johnson served the Jesuits by working with his Masonic brethren who protected Lincoln's assassin in obedience to their master, Grand Master Mason Albert Pike.[1145]

U.S. War Department, Washington, April 20, 1865. 100,000 reward! [1146]

"The murderer of our late beloved president, Abraham Lincoln is still at large. $50,000 reward! will be paid by this department for his apprehension, in addition to any reward offered by municipal authorities or state executives. $25,000 reward! will be paid for the apprehension of John R. Surrat, one of Booth's accomplices. $25,000 reward! will be paid for the apprehension of Daniel C. Harrold, another of Booth's accomplices. Liberal rewards will be paid for any information that shall conduce to the arrest of either of the above-named criminals, or their accomplices ... Edwin M. Stanton, Secretary of War"

As previously stated, Pike is "credited" on the website of the Scottish Rite of Freemasonry world headquarters at Washington, D.C. with a revival of the organization during the Reconstruction period after the Civil War.[1147]

On December 13, 1865, the *Joint Committee on Reconstruction* was established after both houses of Congress agreed to establish a joint committee of 15 members—nine from the House of Representatives and six from the Senate.[1148] It was created "to inquire into the condition of the States which formed the so-called *Confederate States of America*, and report whether they or any of them are entitled to be represented in either house of Congress…"[1149] This committee divided into four subcommittees to hear testimony and gather evidence pertaining to the situation and status in each of the four Military Districts in the South.

On December 18, 1865 the (non-original) 13th Amendment (freeing the slaves),[1150] was certified by Secretary of State William Seward as ratified. At this same time, a terrorist group was formed primarily composed of Confederate Army veterans organized to intimidate blacks and other ethnic and religious minorities. They were referred to as the *Ku Klux Klan* (KKK).

The group first met in Pulaski, Tennessee. The KKK is the first of many secret terrorist organizations who were organized in the South for the purpose of reestablishing white authority.[1151] There is no question that Masonry was an influence in the Klan's structure after the Civil War.[1152]

In February, 1866 a black delegation led by Frederick Douglass met with President Johnson at the White House to advocate black suffrage. The President expressed his opposition and the meeting ended in controversy.[1153] This same month Johnson <u>vetoed</u> a Bill (later re-passed) extending the life of the *Freedmen's Bureau.*

On April 9, 1866 the "interim Executive Congress" passed the *Civil Rights Bill* over President Johnson's veto the previous month.[1154] Johnson objected to the Bill stating that black people did not deserve to become citizens, and if they were given citizenship it would discriminate against the white race. Johnson also expressed <u>concern that both the *Civil Rights Bill* and the *Freedmen's Bureau Bill* would centralize power at the Federal level, thus depriving States of the authority to govern their own affairs. Where this is viewed as a typical prewar *States' Rights* philosophy, we now understand another aspect of concern of the centralized Federal powers (big government) created in this Era.</u>[1155]

Illustration in *Harper's Weekly* of the Memphis Riot of 1866 [1156]
Caption: "Scenese in Memphis, Tennessee, during the riot—
shooting down Negroes on the morning of May 2, 1866"

In May, 1866, there were three days of racial violence in Memphis, Tennessee where white mobs destroyed hundreds of homes, churches, and schools in the black community. Five black women were raped, at least 46 black people most of whom were Union veterans were killed and more than 70 were wounded. Two whites also died in the riots.[1157]

On June 20, 1866, the *Joint Committee on Reconstruction* issued a Report which was signed by twelve of its Republican members. The Report was widely circulated and the American people were provided the means to view the facts which placed a serious challenge on the integrity of President Johnson and his views, as well as surmise the investigated conclusions arrived at by the Congressional Committee.[1158]

Also in June, 1866, Republicans in Congress proposed the 14th Amendment to rivet the principles of the *Civil Rights Bill* into the *Constitution*. They feared that the Southerners might one day gain control of Congress and repeal the Civil Rights law that the Southerners hated. The (interim Executive) Congress sent the Amendment to the State legislatures who gave a positive response, meeting the required three-fourths of the several States (27 of the 36 at that time) to go forward. The Republicans agreed that no State should be welcomed back into the Union without first ratifying the (unlawful) 14th Amendment. President Johnson advised the Southern States to reject it.[1159]

In July, 1866, Tennessee was the first former Confederate State to be readmitted to the Union. Around that same time the *New Orleans Massacre*, also known as the *New Orleans Race Riot*, occurred. While the riot was typical of numerous racial conflicts in this Era, this incident had special significance. It spurred national opposition to the more than moderate Reconstruction policies of President Johnson and propelled a far more reaching Congressional Reconstruction in 1867.[1160]

The riot took place as black and white delegates attended the *Louisiana Constitutional Convention*. The Convention had reconvened because the Louisiana State legislature had recently passed the Black Codes and refused to extend voting rights to black men. The mayor, who headed city government before the Civil War and had been an active supporter of the Confederacy, was reinstated as acting mayor.

As a delegation of 130 black New Orleans residents marched behind the U.S. flag toward the Convention, the mayor led an organized mob of ex-Confederates, white supremacists, and members of the New Orleans police to block their way. With intention to prevent the delegates from meeting, the mayor claimed their intent was to put down any unrest that may come from the Convention.

Having reached the Convention, the police and white mob members attacked the delegates. It was an enflamed mess to where by the end of the massacre; at least 200 black Union war veterans were killed including 40 delegates at the Convention. Altogether 238 people were killed and 46 were wounded.[1161]

Illustration in *Harper's Weekly* of the New Orleans Riot of 1866

Caption: "The riot in New Orleans — [left] murdering negroes in the rear of Mechanics' Institute ;

[right] Platform in Mechanics' Institute after the riot." [1162]

Because of the riots and violence, angry Northerners were compelled to help the *Republican Party* take control of both houses of Congress in the elections held (in the North only) in 1866. In that same month, July, 1866, both houses of (the interim Executive) Congress passed a Bill to extend the *Freedmen's Bureau* in response to the Southern *Black Codes*, the terrorism of the KKK, as well as other groups who were taking guns away from freedmen. President Johnson vetoed the Bill which increased hostility between him and the Radical Republicans; Congress overrode the veto.

The *Freedmen's Bureau Bill* provided many additional rights to ex-slaves, including the distribution of land, schools for their children, and military courts to ensure these rights. The *Freedmen's Bureau Act* made provision for ex-slaves to be entitled to "any of the civil rights or immunities belonging to white persons, including the right to...inherit, purchase, lease, sell, hold and convey real and personal property, and to have full and equal benefit of all laws and proceedings for the security of person and estate, including the constitutional right of bearing arms."[1163]

A *United States Colored Troops* recruiting poster, May 22, 1863 – Oct 1865

Caption beneath poster: "Come and Join Us Brothers, Published by the Supervisory Committee For Recruiting Colored Regiments"

During this time of severe upheaval in the South, President Johnson further demobilized Union army troops to where there were only 38,000 by autumn. More than half of the troops stationed in areas such as Louisiana were black.[1164] President Johnson ignored constitutional law and specifically Article IV Section 4 in guaranteeing every State in the Union protection against domestic violence.

The battle between President Johnson and the (interim executive) Congress grew until the Congressional elections of 1866 (held in the North only), when the Radicals gained House majority and took control of policy, removed former Confederates from power, and began to liberate the freedmen. We again point out that this was not a constitutional Congress, or a lawful deliberative body under the *Constitution*.

Likewise, we see desperate Congressional members who were well aware of a high-level Freemason as President and Commander-in-Chief, were intimately apprised of the evils of Freemasonry as well as their agenda in infiltrating the government at all levels. They were also well aware of a new and substantially ornate Freemason Temple being built in the Nation's capital, like an in-your-face statement of intentions. They also fully understood that if the Freemason Confederate rebels were to fill Congressional vacant seats, they would lose the legislative balance of power "to the Devil."

The Radicals were still opposed to rapid restoration of the Southern States and wanted to keep them out as long as possible while applying federal power to bring about a drastic social and economic transformation in the South. Moderate Republicans in Congress were more in-tune with the time-honored principles of *States' Rights* and self-government. They preferred policies that restrained the States from abridging citizens' rights rather than those that directly involved Federal Government in individual lives. Both schools of thought influenced actual policies adopted. By 1867, both groups came to agree on the necessity to enfranchise black voters even if it took federal troops to do it.[1165]

The result of the 1866 elections was significant in the early Reconstruction Era as high-level Freemason President Andrew Johnson battled in bitter dispute over the conditions of Reconstruction with the hardliner anti-slavery (and former Anti-Masonic Party[1166]) Congressmen within the "Radicals" of the Republican Party. Because Johnson was the only Southern Senator that stayed seated in Congress and supported the Union during the Civil War, it was thought that Andrew Johnson was a Radical when he became president in 1865.

Johnson displayed a very apparent change of heart and he soon became their leading opponent. He held partiality toward his Freemason brethren also known as Confederate plantation owners/white aristocracy in the South, while Radical Republicans wanted to continue the military occupation of the South in order to force the Southern States to give the newly freed slaves civil rights along with the right to vote. Because Republicans attained the House majority (assuming themselves to be a lawful Congress or deliberative body in the midst of the desperate struggle to save the Union), enough seats were captured to override Johnson's vetoes.

Understanding that the Congressional elections of 1866 (in the North only) enabled the Radical Republicans to dominate the Congress, let's take a look at who some of them were as well as some intriguing background information.

Sen. Charles Sumner [1167]

U.S. Senator Charles Sumner (1811-1874) of Massachusetts[1168] was an academic lawyer and a powerful orator. Sumner was the leader of the antislavery forces in Massachusetts and one of the most influential leaders of the Radical Republicans in the United States Senate during the Civil War while working to destroy the Confederacy, abolish slavery, and at the same time keep on good terms with Europe. During *Reconstruction*, he worked to minimize the power of the ex-Confederates while he sought to guarantee equal rights to the freedmen. Earlier in Sumner's political career he had been a Whig, Free Soiler, and a Democrat, and finally had gained fame as a Republican. He devoted immense effort toward the destruction of the Slave Power, the efforts of slave owners to take control of the Federal Government which would ensure the continuation and expansion of slavery. In 1856, (Democratic) South Carolina U.S. Representative Preston Brooks nearly killed Sumner on the Senate floor while beating Sumner with his cane two days after Sumner delivered an intense anti-slavery speech called "The Crime Against Kansas." In the speech, Sumner described Brooks' cousin, U.S. Senator Andrew Butler of South Carolina, as "a pimp for slavery."

During the war, Sumner was a leader of the Radical Republican faction that criticized President Lincoln for being too lenient on the Southern States. An accomplished statesman, he specialized in foreign affairs and worked closely with President Lincoln to prevent the British and the French from intervening on the side of the Confederacy during the Civil War. Sumner's expertise and energy made him a powerful chairman of the Senate Committee on Foreign Relations. As the chief Radical leader in the Senate during Reconstruction, Sumner worked hard to provide equal civil and voting rights for the freedmen on the grounds that "consent of the governed" was a basic principle of American republicanism, and to block ex-Confederates from power so they would not reverse the North's victory in the Civil War. Sumner teamed with the House of Representatives leader Thaddeus Stevens and battled President Andrew Johnson's reconstruction plans while seeking to impose a Radical program on the South.

Rep. Thaddeus Stevens [1169]

U.S. Representative Thaddeus Stevens (1792-1868) of Pennsylvania[1170] was one of the most influential leaders of the Radical Republican faction of the Republican Party during the 1860s. A fierce opponent of slavery and discrimination against black people, Stevens sought to secure their rights during Reconstruction, in opposition to President Andrew Johnson. As chairman of the House Ways and Means Committee during the Civil War, he was instrumental in making provision for the war's financing. Stevens was born in poverty in rural Vermont, with one leg crippled by a clubfoot. On top of these challenges, his alcoholic father had abandoned his family. As a young man he moved to Pennsylvania and quickly became a successful lawyer. Finding an interest in municipal affairs, Stevens then entered politics. He became a strong advocate of free public education while serving in the Pennsylvania House of Representatives. He joined the Whig Party, and was elected to Congress in 1848. He was not popular because of his activities in opposition to slavery; therefore he did not seek reelection in 1852. After a brief alliance with the Know-Nothing Party, Stevens joined the newly formed Republican Party, and was elected to Congress again in 1858. Along with fellow Radicals such as Senator Charles Sumner, he opposed the expansion of slavery and other Southern States' views. Stevens pushed for emancipation throughout the war and vocalized frustration related to President Lincoln's lenience toward Southern States. He guided the government's financial legislation as chairman of the House Ways and Means committee. As the war progressed towards a Union victory, Stevens held that the freedmen should be provided for through the confiscation of plantation owners' land. Moderate Republicans were not always supportive of Stevens' views. Stevens held conflict with President Johnson, who sought rapid restoration of the seceded states without guarantees for freedmen. The difference in views caused an ongoing battle between Johnson and Congress, with Stevens leading the Radical Republicans. The result of the 1866 election (held in the North only) empowered Republicans in the (interim executive) Congress and the Radicals took control of Reconstruction away from Johnson. Stevens' last great battle was to secure articles of impeachment in the House against Johnson, though the Senate's decision was one vote short of convicting the President.

Stevens's first political cause was Anti-Masonry, which became widespread in 1826 after the disappearance and murder of William Morgan, a former Freemason in Upstate New York; former fellow Freemasons assassinated Morgan because of his publishing a book revealing the order's secret rites.

Stevens had been told by fellow attorney (and future president) James Buchanan that he could advance politically if he joined Freemasonry. Some historians may speculate that a reason Stevens may have opposed Freemasonry as well as politicians who were Masons, was because Freemasonry barred "cripples" from joining and Stevens was born with a club foot. Stevens took to Anti-Masonry with enthusiasm, and remained loyal to it even after most others had dropped the cause.

By 1829, Anti-Masonry had evolved into a political party that proved popular. Stevens quickly became prominent in the movement, attending the party's first two national conventions in 1830 and 1831.

In September, 1833, Stevens was elected to a one-year term in the Pennsylvania House of Representatives as an Anti-Mason, and once in Harrisburg sought to have the body establish a committee to investigate Freemasonry. Stevens gained attention far beyond Pennsylvania for his oratory against Masonry, and also quickly became expert in legislative maneuvers. In 1835, a split among the Democrats put the Anti-Masons in control of the legislature. Granted subpoena powers, Stevens summoned leading State politicians who were Freemasons, including Governor George Wolf. The witnesses invoked their Fifth Amendment right against self-incrimination, and when Stevens verbally abused one of them, it created a backlash that caused his own party to end the investigation. The quarrel cost Stevens reelection in 1836, and the issue of Anti-Masonry died in Pennsylvania. Nevertheless, Stevens remained an opponent of Freemasonry for the rest of his life.

The subject of the **Anti-Masonic Party** and how it came into being, as well as a wonderful revelation into the spiritual heartbeat of America that brought about the **Second Great Awakening** will be presented in the Light of truth and come together like pieces of a puzzle. We will see a physical manifestation of two spiritual kingdoms clash on earth—the Kingdom of Heaven and the Kingdom of Darkness. We will recall that just as Almighty God has a people, Lucifer/Satan has a people. While all that pertains to Heaven operates in the Light, all that pertains to Hell operates in darkness and deception while crafting its evil deeds.

John 8:44 ESV ~

> *You are of your father the devil, and your will is to do your father's desires. He was a murderer from the beginning, and has nothing to do with the truth, because there is no truth in him. When he lies, he speaks out of his own character, for he is a liar and the father of lies.*

John 3:20 ~

> *For everyone who does evil hates the Light, and does not come to the Light for fear that his deeds will be exposed.*

When the people of Almighty God proclaim the sovereignty of God and expose the people of Lucifer/Satan as well as their deeds done in darkness, the principalities and powers, the rulers of the darkness of this world and spiritual wickedness in high places are brought into the Light and pulled down from power.

Ephesians 6:12 ~

> *For we wrestle not against flesh and blood, but against principalities, against powers, against the rulers of the darkness of this world, against spiritual wickedness in high places.*

Ephesians 5:11 (AMP) ~

> *Take no part in and have no fellowship with the fruitless deeds and enterprises of darkness, but instead [let your lives be so in contrast as to] expose and reprove and convict them.*
>
> [emphasis added]

Then a move of God's Holy Spirit is released on the earth, the veil (2 Cor. 3:16) to the spiritual is pulled back allowing men to have eyes to see. What is seen is enough to cause them to repent, return to Almighty God, and Heaven moves on earth while the *Supreme Judge of the world* destroys His peoples' enemies.

2 Corinthians 3: 14-18 ~

> *But their minds were blinded: for until this day remaineth the same vail untaken away in the reading of the old testament; which vail is done away in Christ. But even unto this day, when Moses is read, the vail is upon their heart. Nevertheless when it shall turn to the Lord, the vail shall be taken away.*

2 Corinthians 3:17-18 ~

> *Now the Lord is that Spirit: and where the Spirit of the Lord is, there is liberty. But we all, with open face beholding as in a glass the glory of the Lord, are changed into the same image from glory to glory, even as by the Spirit of the Lord.*

John 8:32 ESV ~

> *And ye shall know the truth, and the truth shall make you free.*

Romans 2:16 ~

> *On that day when, according to my gospel, God judges the secrets of men by Christ Jesus.*

Just as the early Americans proclaimed "No king but King Jesus,"[1171] when declaration is made and voice given to the Word of God, who is the son of God, Jesus, (John 1:14) the angels respond (Ps. 103:20) in all places of His dominion. When the Name of the Lord is sanctified among a repentant people who acknowledge and call upon Him (Ezek. 43:7-9), He will respond and do great and mighty things (Jer. 33:3).[1172]

As we consider the facts of this chapter along with the next, let us view the pieces of the puzzle in the Light of truth, see how they fit together, and understand the picture. We will be amazed as our minds are enlightened with a greater picture that pertains to the Truth in where we are today. Where truth seems stranger than fiction,[1173] it is reality as well as the key to Liberty (John 8:32) and America's prophetic destiny. We continue...

The *Anti-Masonic Party*,[1174] also known as the *Anti-Masonic Movement*, was started in 1826 to protest the official cover-up of the murder of William Morgan,[1175] a defecting Freemason in western New York. Anti-masonry became the nation's first powerful "third party."

Anti-masons held that Freemasonry was a dangerous and powerful secret society that privileged its members legally, politically, and economically over all non-members by controlling government at all levels. Anti-masons called on constituents to restore constitutional self-government by being resolved in voting-out Freemasons from elected office and seeking to have State laws passed that would declare the fraternity to be illegal.

The movement spread like wild-fire as *Anti-masons* provided a credible explanation why government seemed unresponsive to popular demands. Freemasonry was exposed as having infiltrated the republican form of governance at all levels and sought control acting like an "oligarchic shadow government." It expanded by means of rewarding its members with government positions and other (unconstitutional) benefits. The *Anti-Masonic Party* was founded on the fundamental principle that no man, or group of men, is above the law.[1176]

As negative views of Freemasonry among the public began to diminish in the late 1830s, most members of the *Anti-Masonic Party* joined the <u>Whigs</u>, the party most in-line with its views on other issues. Although lasting only a decade, the *Anti-Masonic Party* introduced important innovations to American politics, such as nominating conventions and the adoption of party platforms.[1177]

Just a few more of some of the leading members of the Radical Republicans:[1178]

<u>U.S. Senate president pro tempore Benjamin Wade (1800-1878) of Ohio</u> [1179] was a U.S. Senator during Civil War reconstruction known for his leading role among the Radical Republicans. Senator Wade was a <u>Whig</u> before the Republican Party had been formed. Had the impeachment of Andrew Johnson in 1868 led to a conviction at trial in the Senate, Senate president pro tempore Wade would have become the 18th President of the United States.

Sen. Benjamin Wade [1180]

<u>U.S. Representative George Julian (1817-1899) of Indiana</u>[1181] was a 19th century politician, lawyer and writer who served in Congress. He was one of the leading opponents of slavery in politics before the war, had been a <u>Whig</u> before becoming the Free Soil Party's candidate for vice president in 1852, and a noted Radical Republican during the Civil War and Reconstruction.

Rep. George Washington Julian [1182]

<u>U.S. Representative John Armor Bingham (1815- 1900) of Ohio</u>[1183] had been judge advocate in the trial of the President Lincoln's assassinators and a prosecutor in the impeachment trials of Andrew Johnson. He was also the principal framer of the *Fourteenth Amendment* to the United States Constitution. He was the main author of Section 1 of this Amendment which, in time, would come to be critical in interpreting its intent. Rep. Bingham was a member of the *Opposition Party*[1184] which was made-up of former <u>Whigs</u> and *Know-Nothing Party* members, before he became a member of the Republican Party.

Rep. John Armor Bingham [1185]

<u>U.S. Representative Henry Winter Davis (1817-1865) of Maryland</u>[1186] Early held strong anti-slavery views, though by inheritance he was himself a slave holder. He began political life as a <u>Whig</u>. After the Whig Party disintegrated, he became a member of the Know Nothing Party, and

served as a member of the House of Representatives from 1855 to 1861. By his independent course in Congress he won the respect and esteem of all political groups. Davis was a Radical Republican and bitter opponent of Lincoln's plan for the Reconstruction of the Southern States, which he thought too lenient.

Rep. Henry Winter Davis [1187]

In viewing the birth year of the individuals, one could reason that Rep. Thaddeus Stevens was the only one of age and in politics in the era of the *Anti-Masonic Party*. By the time the others came along the *Anti-Masonic Party* had dissolved and its members were absorbed into the *Whig Party*.

It serves us well to also mention that Secretary of State William H. Seward under President Abraham Lincoln and then succeeding President Andrew Johnson was part of the *Anti-Masonic Party* before becoming a Whig and then a Republican. We will remember the traumatic assassination attempt on his life at the same time as the assassination of President Lincoln.

Luke 6:43-45 ~ "A Tree is Known By Its Fruit"

> *For a good tree bringeth not forth corrupt fruit; neither doth a corrupt tree bring forth good fruit. For every tree is known by his own fruit. For of thorns men do not gather figs, nor of a bramble bush gather they grapes.* A good man out of the good treasure of his heart bringeth forth that which is good; and an evil man out of the evil treasure of his heart bringeth forth that which is evil: for of the abundance of the heart his mouth speaketh.

Capt. William Morgan [1188]
Whose stand for righteousness led to his murder
that led to the formation of the Anti-Masonic Party
and *Second Great Awakening*

1865 engraving made after Lincoln's assassination, showing Lincoln as equal to Washington.
Washington holds "Constitution," while Lincoln holds "Emancipation."
Both are supporting the shield (coat of arms) of the United States that is above a sword and cannon.
Main text in the drawing: "Under Providence, Washington made, and Lincoln saved, our country." [1189]

Chapter Fourteen

American Republic v. Corporate Democracy

The Counterfeit Begins

In 1869 Reverend Charles Finney (1792-1875)[1190] published his book, *The Character, Claims and Practical Workings of Freemasonry.*[1191] Charles Finney was the minister and leader of the *Second Great Awakening* in America. Finney has been called "The Father of Modern Revivalism," in that he led spiritual revival and renewal in the Church throughout America.

 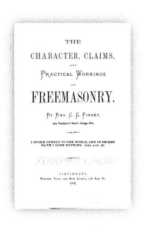

Rev. Charles Finney[1192] and the title page of his 1869 book,
The Character, Claims and Practical Workings of Freemasonry [1193]

There is significant enlightenment in understanding the revival and renewal that occurred during the period 1825-1835, particularly in upstate New York and Manhattan.   It occurred after the murder of William Morgan, a former Freemason who had announced his intentions of publishing a book that included the oaths taken for the first few degrees of Freemasonry.

As Finney concludes the story in exposing Freemasonry, he reminisces on the public reaction, specifically the various denominations of the Church in the northern states at the time, in renouncing and denouncing the institution which he relays had resulted in,

> "God set[ting] the seal of His approbation upon the action taken by those churches at that time, by pouring out His Spirit upon them. Great revivals immediately followed over that whole region. The discussion of the subject and the action of the churches took place in 1827-'8 and '9, and in 1830 the greatest revival spread over this region that had ever been known in this or any other country."[1194]

What Finney was speaking of is what we know today as the *Second Great Awakening*.

In Finney's aforementioned book, he introduces his own experience with Freemasonry.   Finney explains that his uncle persuaded him to become a Freemason at the age of 21 while away from home and among strangers as it would be a means where he "should find friends everywhere."

Finney took three degrees while at that Masonic lodge before then moving to New York where he studied law. Finney again joined a Masonic lodge where he "soon became secretary of the lodge, and met regularly with the lodge." He mentions that the lodge was composed mostly of professed Christians as well as "profane men" that he "never would have associated [with] had they not been Freemasons."

Having "been brought up with very few religious privileges," Finney stated that he "had but slight knowledge on moral subjects" and so at the time "was not, therefore, greatly shocked ...with the immorality of anything through which I passed."[1195]

Matthew 6:22-24 ~

> *The light of the body is the eye: if therefore thine eye be single, thy whole body shall be full of light. But if thine eye be evil, thy whole body shall be full of darkness. If therefore the light that is in thee be darkness, how great is that darkness! No man can serve two masters: for either he will hate the one, and love the other; or else he will hold to the one, and despise the other. Ye cannot serve God and mammon.*

1 John 1:6-7 ~

> *If we say we have fellowship with him while we walk in darkness, we lie and do not practice the truth. But if we walk in the light, as he is in the light, we have fellowship with one another, and the blood of Jesus his Son cleanses us from all sin.*

Finney said that it was after taking the first three degrees and especially "the Master's degree" that he was "struck with one part of the obligation, or oath, as not being sound either in a political or moral point of view."

It was nearly four years after joining the New York lodge when he experienced a conversion to Christ. Finney states, "I soon found that I was completely converted from Freemasonry to Christ, and that I could have no fellowship with any of the proceedings of the lodge. Its oaths appeared to me to be monstrously profane and barbarous." He then requested his discharge from the lodge.[1196]

Finney relayed that it was a few years later after William Morgan's murder and then his book was published that publicly exposed the first three Masonic oaths, that Finney felt he would no longer have to keep secret the truth of the "oaths, principles, and proceedings." Finney stated that he felt a freedom of mind to speak about it and to "renounce the horrid oaths that I had taken."

Finney went into more detail of how he found that he had been grossly deceived and imposed upon.

> "Indeed, I came to the deliberate conclusion, and could not avoid doing so, that my oaths had been procured by fraud and misrepresentation, and that the institution was in no respect what I had been previously informed that it was... the institution is highly dangerous to the State, and in every way injurious to the Church of Christ."[1197]

Telling the story as published in his book forty years later, Finney explains that at the time of William Morgan's murder in 1826, the facts were well-known to the public. Through the years, Finney relays, "...much pains have been taken by Freemasons to rid the world of the books and pamphlets, and every vestige of writing relating to that subject, by far the larger number of young people seem to be entirely ignorant that such facts ever occurred."[1198]

Because of the very critical nature of Finney's exposure of Freemasonry and in consideration of how it relates to understanding the persona, convictions, and stance of the Radical Republicans, let's take a look at "Chapter II, Scrap of History" and view Finney's story directly:

> IN number I must remind readers of some facts that occurred about forty years ago; which, as matters of history, though then well-known to thousands, are probably now unknown to the great majority of our citizens. Elderly men and women, <u>especially in the Northern States</u>, will almost universally remember the murder of William Morgan by Freemasons, and many facts connected with that terrible tragedy. <u>But, as much pains have been taken by Freemasons to rid the world of the books and pamphlets, and every vestige of writing relating to that subject, by far the larger number of young people seem to be entirely ignorant that such facts ever occurred.</u> I will state them as briefly as possible.
>
> About forty years ago, an estimable man by the name of William Morgan, then residing in Batavia, N.Y., being a Freemason, after much reflection, made up his mind that it was his duty to publish Freemasonry to the world. <u>He regarded it as highly injurious to the cause of Christ, and as eminently dangerous to the government of our country, and I suppose was aware, as Masons generally were at that time, that nearly all the civil offices in the country were in the hands of Freemasons; and that the press was completely under their control, and almost altogether in their hands. Masons at that time boasted that all the civil offices in the country were in their hands. I believe that all the civil offices in the county where I resided while I belonged to them, were in their hands. I do not recollect a magistrate, or a constable, or sheriff in that county that was not at that time a Freemason.</u>
>
> A publisher by the name of [David C.] Miller, also residing in Batavia, agreed to publish what Mr. Morgan would write. This, coming to be known to Freemasons, led them to conspire for his destruction. This, as we shall see, was only in accordance with their oaths. <u>By their oaths they were bound to seek his destruction, and to execute upon him the penalty of those oaths.</u>
>
> They kidnapped Morgan and for a time concealed him in the magazine of the United States Fort-- Fort Niagara, at the mouth of Niagara River, where it empties into Lake Ontario. They kept him there until they could arrange to dispatch him. In the meantime, the greatest efforts were made to discover his whereabouts, and what the Masons had done with him. Strong suspicions came finally to be entertained that he was confined in that fort; and the Masons, finding that those suspicions were abroad, hastened his death. <u>Two or three have since, upon their death-bed, confessed their part in the transaction.</u> They drowned him in the Niagara River. The account of the manner in which this was will be found in a book published by Elder [John G.] Stearns, a Baptist elder. The book is entitled *Stearns on Masonry*.[1199] It contains the deathbed confession of one of the murderers of William Morgan. On page 311, of that work, you will find that confession. But as many of my readers have not access to that work, I take the liberty to quote it entire, as follows:

"CONFESSION.

"THE MURDER OF WILLIAM MORGAN, CONFESSED BY THE MAN WHO, WITH HIS OWN HANDS, PUSHED HIM OUT OF THE BOAT INTO NIAGARA RIVER!

"The following account of that tragical scene is taken from a pamphlet entitled, 'Confession of the murder of William Morgan, as taken down by Dr. John L. Emery, of Racine County, Wisconsin, in the summer of 1848, and now (1849) first given to the public:'

"This 'Confession' was taken down as related by Henry L. Valance, who acknowledges himself to have been one of the three who were selected to make a final disposition of the ill-fated victim of masonic vengeance. This confession it seems was made to his physicians, and in view of his approaching dissolution, and published after his decease.

"After committing that horrid deed he was as might well be expected, an unhappy man, by day and by night. He was much like Cain--'a fugitive and a vagabond.' To use his own words, 'Go where I would, or do what I would, it was impossible for me to throw off the consciousness of crime. If the mark of Cain was not upon me, the curse of the first murderer was--the blood-stain was upon my hands and could not be washed out.

'He therefore commences his confession thus:--'My last hour is approaching; and as the things of this world fade from my mental sight, I feel the necessity of making, as far as in my power lies, that atonement which every violator of the great law of right owes to his fellow men' In this violation of law, he says, 'I allude to the abduction and murder of the ill-fated William Morgan.'

"He proceeds with an interesting narrative of the proceedings of the fraternity in reference to Morgan, while he was incarcerated in the magazine of Fort Niagara. I have room for a few extracts only, showing the final disposition of their alleged criminal. Many consultations were held, 'many plans proposed and discussed, and rejected.' At length being driven to the necessity of doing something immediately for fear of being exposed, it was resolved in a council of eight, that he must die: must be consigned to a 'confinement from which there is no possibility of escape--THE GRAVE.' Three of their number were to be selected by ballot to execute the deed. 'Eight pieces of paper were procured, five of which were to remain blank, while the letter D was written on the others. These pieces of paper were placed in a large box, from which each man was to draw one at the same moment. After drawing we were all to separate, without looking at the paper that each held in his hand. So soon as we had arrived at certain distances from the place of rendezvous, the tickets were to be examined, and those who held blanks were to return instantly to their homes; and those who should hold marked tickets were to proceed to the fort at midnight, and there put Morgan to death, in such a manner as should seem to themselves most fitting.' Mr. Valance was one of the three who drew the ballots on which was the signal letter. He returned to the fort, where he was joined by his two companions, who had drawn the death tickets. Arrangements were made immediately for executing the sentence passed upon their prisoner, which was to sink him in the river with weights; in hope, says Mr. Valance, 'that he and our crime alike would thus be buried beneath the waves.' His part was to proceed to the magazine where Morgan was confined, and announce to him his fate--theirs was to procure a boat and weights with which to sink him. Morgan, on being informed of their proceedings against him, demanded by what authority they had condemned him, and who were his judges. 'He commenced wringing his hands, and talking of his wife and children, the recollections of whom, in that awful hour, terribly affected him. His wife, he said, was young and inexperienced, and his children were but infants; what would become of them were he cut off; and

200

they even ignorant of his fate?' What husband and father would not be 'terribly affected' under such circumstances--to be cut off from among the living in this inhuman manner?

"Mr. V.'s comrades returned and informed him that they had procured the boat and weights, and that all things were in readiness on their part. Morgan was told that all his remonstrances were idle, that die he must, and that soon, even before the morning light. The feelings of the husband and father were still strong within him, and he continued to plead on behalf of his family. They gave him one half hour to prepare for his 'inevitable fate.' They retired from the magazine and left him. "How Morgan passed that time,' says Mr. Valance, 'I cannot tell, but everything was quiet as the tomb within.' At the expiration of the allotted time, they entered the magazine, laid hold of their victim, 'bound his hands behind him, and placed a gag in his mouth.' They then led him forth to execution. 'A short time,' says this murderer, 'brought us to the boat, and we all entered it--Morgan being placed in the bow with myself, along side of him. My comrades took the oars, and the boat was rapidly forced out into the river. The night was pitch dark, we could scarcely see a yard before us and therefore was the time admirably adapted to our hellish purpose.' Having reached a proper distance from the shore, the oarsmen ceased their labors. The weights were all secured together by a strong cord, and another cord of equal strength, and of several yards in length, proceeded from that. 'This cord,' says Mr. V., 'I took in my hand [did not that hand tremble?] and fastened it around the body of Morgan, just above his hips, using all my skill to make it fast, so that it would hold. Then, in a whisper, I bade the unhappy man to stand up, and after a momentary hesitation he complied with my order. He stood close to the head of the boat, and there was just length enough of rope from his person to the weights to prevent any strain, while he was standing. I then requested one of my associates to assist me in lifting the weights from the bottom to the side of the boat, while the others steadied her from the stern. This was done, and, as Morgan was standing with his back toward me, I approached him, and gave him a strong push with both my hands, which were placed on the middle of his back. He fell forward, carrying the weights with him, and the waters closed over the mass. We remained quiet for two or three minutes, when my companions, without saying a word, resumed their places, and rowed the boat to the place from which they had taken it.'"

They also kidnapped Mr. Miller, the publisher; but the citizens of Batavia, finding it out, pursued the kidnappers, and finally rescued him.

<u>The courts of justice found themselves entirely unable to make any headway against the wide-spread conspiracy that was formed among Masons in respect to this matter.</u>

<u>These are matters of record. It was found that they could do nothing with the courts, with the sheriffs, with the witnesses, or with the jurors; and all their efforts were for a time entirely impotent. Indeed, they never were able to prove the murder of Morgan, and bring it home to the individuals who perpetrated it. But Mr. Morgan had published Freemasonry to the world. The greatest pains were taken by Masons to cover up the transaction, and as far as possible to deceive the public in regard to the fact that Mr. Morgan had published Masonry as it really is.</u>

Masons themselves, as is affirmed by the very best authority, published two spurious editions of Morgan's book, and circulated them as the true edition which Morgan had published. These editions were designed to deceive Masons who had never seen Morgan's edition, and thus to enable them to say that it was not a true revelation of Masonry.

In consequence of the publication of Morgan's book, and the revelations that were made in regard to the kidnapping and murdering of Mr. Morgan, great numbers of Masons were led to consider the subject more fully than they had done; and the conscientious among them almost universally renounced Masonry altogether. **I believe that about two thousand lodges, as a consequence of these revelations, were suspended.**

The ex-president of a Western college, who is himself a Freemason, has recently published some very important information on the subject though he justifies Masonry. **He says that, out of a little more than fifty thousand Masons in the United States at that time, forty-five thousand turned their backs upon the lodge to enter the lodge no more. Conventions were called of Masons that were disposed to renounce it.** One was held at Leroy, another at Philadelphia, and others at other places, I do not now remember where. **The men composing these conventions made public confession of their relation to the institution, and publicly renounced it.** At one of these large conventions they appointed a committee to superintend the publication of Masonry in all its degrees. This committee was composed of men of first-rate character, and men quite generally known to the public. Elder Bernard, a Baptist elder in good standing, was one of this committee; and he, with the assistance of his brethren who had been appointed to this work, obtained an accurate version of some forty eight degrees. He published also the proceedings of those conventions, and much concerning the efforts that were made by the courts to search the matter to the bottom, and also several speeches that were made by prominent men in the State of New York. This work was entitled "Light on Masonry."[1200] In this work any person who is disposed may get a very correct view of what Freemasonry really is. This and sundry other reliable works on Freemasonry may be had at Godrich's, and Fitch & Fairchild's bookstores, in Oberlin. In saying this, it is proper to add that I have no direct or indirect pecuniary interest in the sale of those or of any book on Freemasonry whatever, nor shall I have in the sale of this which I am now preparing for the press. Freemasons shall not with truth accuse me of self-interest in exposing their institution.

Before the publication of "Bernard's Light on Masonry," great pains were taken to secure the most accurate knowledge of the degrees published by the committee, as the reader of that work will see, if he reads the book through. An account of all these matters will be found in "Light on Masonry," to which I have referred. In the Northern or non-slaveholding States Masonry was almost universally renounced at that time. But it was found that it had taken so deep a root that in all New England there was scarcely a newspaper in which the death of William Morgan, and the circumstances connected therewith, could be published. This was so generally true throughout all the North that newspapers had to be everywhere established for the purpose of making the disclosures that were necessary in regard to its true character and tendency. The same game is being played over again at the present day. The "Cynosure," the new anti-masonic paper published at Chicago, is constantly intercepted on its way to subscribers. Four of its first six numbers failed to reach me, and now in December, 1868, I have received no number later than the sixth. The editor informs me that the numbers are constantly intercepted. The public will be forced to learn what a lawless and hideous institution Freemasonry is. But at present I refrain from saying more on this point.

It was found that Masonry so completely baffled the courts of law, and obstructed the course of justice, that it was forced into politics; and for a time the anti-masonic sentiment of the Northern States carried all before it. Almost all Masons became ashamed of it, felt themselves disgraced by having any connection with it, and publicly renounced it. If they did not publish any renunciation, they suspended their lodges, had no more to do with it, and did not pretend to deny that Masonry had been published.

Now these facts were so notorious, so universally known and confessed, that those of us who were acquainted with them at the time had no idea that Masonry would have the impudence ever again to claim any public respect. I should just as soon expect slavery to be re-established in this country, and become more popular than ever before--to take possession of the Government and of all the civil offices, and to grow bold, impudent, and defiant--as I should have expected that Masonry would achieve what it has. When the subject of Freemasonry was first forced upon our churches in Oberlin, for discussion and action, I cannot express the astonishment, grief and indignation that I felt on hearing professed Christian Freemasons deny either expressly or by irresistible implication that Morgan and others had truly revealed the secrets of Freemasonry. But a few years ago such denial would have ruined the character of any intelligent man, not to say of a professed Christian. But I must say, also, that Masonry itself has its literature. Many bombastic and spread-eagle books have been published in its favor.   They never attempt to justify it as it is revealed in "Light on Masonry," nor reply by argument to the attacks that have been so successfully made upon it; neither have they pretended to reveal its secret. <u>But they have eulogized it in a manner that is utterly nauseating to those that understand what it really is.</u> <u>But these books have been circulated among the young, and have no doubt led thousands and scores of thousands of young men into the Masonic ranks, who, but for these miserable productions, would never have thought of taking such a step.</u>

[emphasis added]

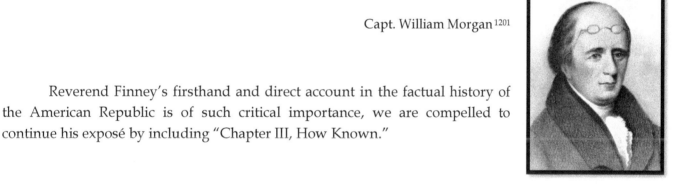

Capt. William Morgan [1201]

Reverend Finney's firsthand and direct account in the factual history of the American Republic is of such critical importance, we are compelled to continue his exposé by including "Chapter III, How Known."

WE are prepared in this number to take up the question, How are the public to know what Freemasonry really is? This we may answer.

1. Negatively. (1.) Masonry cannot be known from a perusal of the eulogistic books which adhering Masons have written. **Of course they are under oath in no way whatever to reveal the secrets of Masonry. But it is their secrets that the public are concerned to know.** Now their eulogistic books, as any one may know who will examine them, are silly, and for the most part little better than twaddle. If we read their orations and sermons that have been published in support of Masonry, and the books that they have written, we shall find much that is silly, much that is false, and a great deal more that is mere bombast [long-windedness] and rhodomontade [pretentious boasting]. I do not say this rashly. Any person who will examine the subject for himself must admit that this language is strictly true. But I shall have occasion hereafter when we come to examine the character of the institution, to show more clearly the utter ignorance or dishonesty of the men who have eulogized it. Let it be understood, then, that adhering Masons do not profess to publish their secrets. And that which the country and the church are particularly interested to understand they never publish--their oaths, for example; and, therefore, we cannot tell from what they write what they are under oath to do.

(2.) We cannot learn what Masonry is from the oral testimony of adhering Masons.

Let it be pondered well that every one of them is under oath to conceal and in no way whatever to reveal the secrets of the order. This Freemasons do not deny. Hence, if they are asked if the books in which Masonry has been published are true, they will either evade the question or else **they will lie; and they are under oath to do so.**

Observe, adhering Masons are the men who still acknowledge the binding obligation of their oaths. Now, if they are asked if those books truly reveal Masonry, they consider themselves under an obligation to deny it, if they say anything about it. And, as they are well aware that to refuse to say anything about it is a virtual acknowledgment that the books are true, and would therefore be an indirect revelation of Masonry; they will almost universally deny that the books are true. Some of them are ashamed to say anything more than that there is some truth and a great deal of falsehood in them.

(3.) As they are under oath to conceal the secrets of Masonry, and in no way whatever to reveal any part of them, their testimony in regard to the truthfulness or untruthfulness of those books is of no value whatever. It is mere madness to receive the testimony of men who are under oath, and **under the most horrid oaths that can be taken--oaths sustained by the most terrific penalties that can be named to conceal their secrets** and to deny that they have been published, and that those books contain them--I say it is downright madness to receive the testimony of such men, it matters not who they are. Masons have no right to expect an intelligent person to believe their denials that these books have truly revealed Masonry. Nor have they a right to complain if we reject their testimony. What would they have us do? **Shall we believe the testimony of men who admit that they are under oath to conceal and never in any way reveal the secrets of their order, when they deny that their secrets are revealed in certain books, and shall we ignore the testimony of thousands who have conscientiously renounced those horrid oaths, at the hazard of their lives, and declared with one accord, and many of them under the sanction of judicial oaths lawfully administered, that Morgan, Bernard and others have truly revealed the secrets of Freemasonry?** <u>There are at this day thousands of most conscientious men who are ready to testify on oath that those books contain a substantially correct exposition of Freemasonry as it was and is.</u> I say again that Freemasons have no right to expect us to believe their denials; for while they adhere to Masonry they are under oath to "conceal and never reveal" any part of its secrets and of course they must expressly or impliedly deny every revelation of its secrets that can be made. Would they have us stultify ourselves by receiving their testimony ?

2. Positively. **How, then, are we to know what Masonry is? I answer:**

(1.) From the published and oral testimony of those who have taken the degrees; and afterward, from conscientious motives, have confessed their error, and have publicly renounced Masonry. But it has been said that these are perjured men, and therefore not at all to be believed. But let it be remarked that this very accusation is an admission that they have published the truth; for, unless they have published the secrets of Masonry truly, they have violated no Masonic oath. Therefore, when Masons accuse them of being perjured, the very objection which they make to the testimony of these witnesses is an acknowledgment on the part of Masons themselves that they have truly published their secrets. But again. If to reveal the secrets of Masonry be perjury, it follows that to accuse the revealers of Masonry of perjury, is itself perjury; because by their accusation they tacitly admit that that which has been published is truly a revelation of Masonry, and therefore their accusation is a violation of their oath of secrecy. Let it then be understood that the very objection to

204

these witnesses, that they have committed perjury, is itself an acknowledgment that the witnesses are entirely credible, and have revealed Masonry as it is.   And not only so--but in bringing forward the objection, they commit perjury themselves, if it be perjury to reveal their secrets, because, as I have said, in accusing the witnesses of perjury, they add their testimony to the fact that these witnesses have published Masonry as it is. So that by their own testimony, in bringing this charge of perjury, they themselves swell the number of witnesses to the truthfulness of these revelations.

(2.) Renouncing Masons are the best possible witnesses by whom to prove what Masonry really is.   They are competent witnesses. They testify from their own personal knowledge of what it is. They are in the highest degree credible witnesses. First, because they testify against themselves. They confess their own wrong in having taken those terrible oaths, and in having had any part in sustaining the institution. Secondly, their testimony is given with the certainty of incurring a most unrelenting persecution.

Adhering Freemasons are under oath to persecute them, to destroy their characters, and to seek to bring them to condign punishment. This we shall see when we come to examine the books.

Adhering Masons have persecuted, and still persecute, those that reveal their secrets, just as far as they dare. They are in the highest degree intolerant, and this every Mason knows. In a recent number of their great Masonic organ, published in New York, they advise the Masons in Oberlin in no way to patronize those who oppose them.   Those who renounce Masonry are well aware of their danger**.   But, notwithstanding, they are constrained by their consciences, by the fear and love of God, and by regard to the interests of their country, to renounce and expose it**. Now, surely, witnesses that testify under such circumstances are entitled to credit; especially as they could have had no conceivable motive for deceiving the public. Their testimony was wrung from them by conscience. And the authors of the books that I have named, together with several others--such as Richardson, Stearns, and Mr. Allyn,[1202] and I know not how many others — **are sustained by the testimony of forty-five thousand who publicly renounced Masonry, out of a little more than fifty thousand that composed the whole number of Freemasons then in the United States. Now, it should be well remembered that** the five thousand who still adhered belonged almost altogether to the slaveholding States, and had peculiar reasons for still adhering to the institution of Masonry.   And, further, let it be distinctly observed that, as they adhered to Masonry, their testimony is null, because they still regarded themselves as under oath in no wise to reveal their secrets; consequently, they would, of course, deny that these books had truly revealed Masonry. I say again, it is mere madness to receive their testimony. [emphasis added]

In 1912, Martin L. Wagner, Pastor of St. Johns English Evangelical Lutheran Church in Dayton, Ohio published *Freemasonry: An Interpretation*.[1203] Mr. Wagner includes in his published work that John Quincy Adams, who was President of the United States at the time of the William Morgan murder, spoke against Freemasonry because of the excitement produced by the murder of Morgan.

Because of the facts that surfaced in court testimony of witnesses, the investigative action taken by the New York Legislature that brought exposure, and then the opposing stand of defense for Freemasonry by the Grand Lodge of Rhode Island, President John Quincy Adams was led to make an impartial examination and investigation of Freemasonry of which Wagner states had been done by purely patriotic motives. Wagner provides in his book President Adams' views as they were expressed in letters and in his "Address to the People of Massachusetts."[1204]

"I saw a code of Masonic legislation adapted to prostrate every principle of equal justice and to corrupt every sentiment of virtuous feeling in the soul of him who bound his allegiance to it. I saw the practice of common honesty, the kindness of Christian benevolence, even the abstinence of atrocious crimes, limited exclusively by lawless oaths and barbarous penalties, to the social relations between the brotherhood and the craft. I saw slander organize into a secret, widespread and affiliated agency, fixing its invisible fangs into the hearts of its victims, sheltered by the darkness of the lodge room, and armed with the never ceasing penalties of death.

I saw self-invoked imprecations of throats cut from ear to ear, of hearts and vitals torn out and cast off and hung on spires. I saw wine drank from a human skull with solemn invocation of all the sins of its owner upon the head of him who drank it. I saw a wretched mortal man dooming himself to eternal punishment, when the last trump shall sound, as a guarantee for idle and ridiculous promises. Such are the laws of Masonry; such are their indelible character, and with that character perfectly corresponds the history of Masonic lodges, chapters, encampments, and consistories, from that day to the present. <u>A conspiracy of the few against the equal rights of the many; anti-republican in its sap from the first blushing of the summit of the plant to the deepest fiber of its root. Notwithstanding these horrid oaths and penalties of which a common cannibal would be ashamed, the General Grand Royal Arch Chapter of the U. S. forbade their abandonment. That Masonry sanctions these barbarities, is therefore proven beyond a question.</u>"

President John Quincy Adams [1205]

Jude 4 ~

For there are certain men crept in unawares, who were before of old ordained to this condemnation, ungodly men, turning the grace of our God into lasciviousness, and denying the only Lord God, and our Lord Jesus Christ.

Jude 11 ~

Woe unto them! for they have gone in the way of Cain, and ran greedily after the error of Balaam for reward, and perished in the gainsaying of Core.

According to former "Worshipful Master" Mason Jack Harris in his (1986) book, *Freemasonry Invisible Cult*, <u>Freemasonry is an anti-Christian cult with damnable heresies in its teachings and doctrines.</u>[1206]

A Worshipful Master is the senior officer of a Masonic Lodge who chairs all of the business of his lodge. He is vested with considerable powers without referring to the lodge members and also presides over rituals and ceremonies. The office of Worshipful Master is the highest honor to which a lodge may appoint any of its members.[1207]

A cult is defined as any group that embraces, teaches, or practices religious doctrine contrary to the accepted and established truth of Biblical Christianity. Harris states his belief that the humanistic teachings of Freemasonry in all of its branches will be a primary catalyst allowing the antichrist and one-world apostate church to come to power in the Latter Days.[1208]

In his book that provides insight to the basics of Freemasonry, Mr. Harris quotes the most well-known and important of Masonic authorities such as Albert Mackey, Albert Pike, J.S.M. Ward, and Frank C. Higgins who by their own words and doctrine agree that Masonry is indeed a religion.[1209] Harris goes on to point out that Masonry would categorize as a false religion.

A few of the vital practices and duties as a member of Freemasonry include:

- Never to mention God's name.[1210]
- Prayers may not be closed in the name of the Lord Jesus Christ because it would offend lodge brothers of other religions.[1211]
- Any book of law, not the Bible, must be on their altar. This practice allows Freemasonry to initiate men from nearly all religions because every religion has a book of "law."[1212]
- The Bible as spoken of in Freemasonry is not the same as the Christian New Testament theology as based on Jesus Christ, the son of Almighty God. In Freemasonry, holy writ refers to whichever religion is being discussed. Where many Christian Masons (an oxymoron-type phrase) believe they are worshipping Almighty God in the lodge because of Biblical terminology being used, they are in fact worshipping the god of Masonry. It is the god of Naturalism.[1213] (Albert Pike, Freemasonry's revered leader whose bones are entombed at their world headquarters in Washington, DC, declared Lucifer (Satan) as the god of their religion.)
- The men meet together in the lodge on one common level. In the Church of Christ members are gathered together in the name of the Lord Jesus Christ.[1214] It is not possible to meet in Jesus' name in the Masonic Lodge.[1215]
- Although there are Bible verses and Christian symbols displayed in the lodge room, most Christian symbols are limited as in relation to the Knights Templar. In the third degree, many Bible verses are presented to point out the fact of and in explaining eternal life and immortality, however, not once is Jesus Christ projected as the person of eternal life[1216] or as the Resurrection and the Life.[1217]
- Each degree of Masonry uses Bible verses to support the ritual, however, is not used in a manner or for the purpose that the Author of the Bible gave it. For instance, Hosea 11:4a states, *"I drew them with cords of a man, with bands of love..."* The Masonic bible references this scripture as a cable tow, a six-foot blue cord wrapped around the candidate's neck as he is led blindfolded into the lodge room. The length of the cable tow relates to the measurement of distance that Freemasonry will bury the mutilated body of someone who reveals its secrets.[1218]

2 John 7 ~

For many deceivers are entered into the world, who confess not that Jesus Christ is come in the flesh. This is a deceiver and an antichrist.

2 John 9-10 ~

Whosoever transgresseth, and abideth not in the doctrine of Christ, hath not God. He that abideth in the doctrine of Christ, he hath both the Father and the Son. If there come any unto you, and bring not this doctrine, receive him not into your house, neither bid him God speed:

Harmon R. Taylor is a former Grand Chaplain of a Freemason Lodge. He has shared a letter in public that brings insightful detail and exhortation.[1219]

A Grand Chaplain Speaks Out

By Harmon R. Taylor

GRAND LODGE FREE AND ACCEPTED MASONS OF THE STATE OF NEW YORK GRAND CHAPLAIN 1983-1984 REV. HARMON R. TAYLOR

Dear Servant of God, Knowing that you desire to serve the Lord with all your heart, I share this letter with you. Perhaps you have been struggling with the same situation. On November 22nd, I sent the facts contained in this letter to all Masonic bodies of which I am a member. I invite you to prayerfully read it. It will explain why I as a Grand Chaplain of the Grand Lodge of Free and Accepted Masons of the State of New York am requesting a demit from all bodies of the Masonic fraternity. There is much more that I could share. I would be happy to share more if it will help you in the Lord's service.

Many have asked me if Freemasonry is a religion. I have always responded "No." Others have told me that it is a religion. Study has revealed the fact that learned writers in the fraternity say MASONRY IS A RELIGION. The Lord Jesus Christ said, "In the mouth of two or three witnesses, every word is established" (Matthew 18:16). In order to be brief, I will quote only four Masonic authorities that masonry is a religion.

Albert Mackey, one of the most well known Masonic authorities, wrote in A LEXICON OF FREEMASONRY (Pg. 402): "The religion, then, masonry, is pure theism...".

Albert Pike, the most important of all American Masonic authorities wrote in MORALS AND DOGMA (Pg. 213-214): "Every Masonic lodge is a temple of religion, and its teachings are instructions in religion...this is true religion revealed to the ancient patriarchs; which masonry has taught for many centuries, and which it will continue to teach as long as time endures."

J.S.M. Ward, a Masonic authority who has written several important books on masonry, wrote in his book FREEMASONRY: ITS AIMS & IDEALS (Pg.185): "I consider freemasonry is a significantly organized school of mysticism to be entitled to be called a religion." Ward continues on page 187, "Freemasonry...taught that each man can by himself, work out his own conception of god and thereby achieve salvation." It holds that there are many paths that lead to the throne of the all-loving father which all start from a common source. Freemasonry believes, according to Ward, "that though these paths appear to branch off in various directions, yet they all reach the same ultimate goal, and that to some men, one path is better and to other, another."

"Frank C. Higgins, a high mason, wrote in ANCIENT FREE MASONRY (Pg.10), "It is true that Freemasonry is the parent of all religion."

These Masonic witnesses all agree in their doctrine that masonry is, indeed, a religion. It is necessary now to ascertain whether masonry is a true religion or a false religion. In an article entitled, "HOW TO RECOGNIZE A FALSE RELIGION" (Faith for the Family Nov/Dec 1974), a prominent Christian leader wrote:

 "All false religions, have some things in common. Here are three simple tests by which any religion should be judged:

FIRST: What is its attitude toward the Bible?

SECOND: Any religious teaching should be tested by this question; What is its attitude toward Jesus Christ?

THIRD: In judging a religious system, we should ask, What is its attitude toward the blood of Jesus Christ!"

According to these three tests, masonry is a false religion manifesting a satanic attitude toward the Bible, the Deity of Jesus Christ, and the blood atonement of Jesus Christ. In order to establish this charge, keep in mind the Word our Lord Jesus Christ who said, "In the mouth of two or three witnesses every word shall be established." Please consider now the testimony of Masonic authorities which reveal Masonry's satanic attitude toward the Bible, the Deity of Jesus Christ and the vicarious atonement for the sins of mankind by the shedding of Christ's blood on the cross. Joseph Ford Newton, a famous authority and writer, in an article entitled "The Bible and Masonry" wrote "The bible so rich in symbolism is itself a symbol...thus, by the very honor which masonry pays the Bible, it teaches us to revere every book of faith in which men find help for today and hope for tomorrow, joining hands with the man of Islam as he takes his oath on the Koran, with the Hindu as he makes covenant with God upon the book that he loves best."

Albert Pike, in *Morals & Dogma*, wrote (Pg.718) "Masonry propagates no creed except it's own most simple sublime one; that universal religion, taught by nature and reason."

One who is truly born-again can see from the above statement that masonry totally rejects the doctrine of an infallible, God-breathed, inerrant Bible.

According to the Second Test, masonry is a false religion because it totally rejects the crucial doctrine of the Deity of the Lord Jesus Christ.

J.D. Buck, M.D., another Masonic writer of importance, in his book *Symbolism of Mystic Masonry* wrote (Pg.57) "In the early Church as in the secret doctrine, there was not one Christ for the world but a potential Christ in every man. Theologians first made a fetish of the impersonal, Omnipresent divinity; and then tore the Christos from the hearts of all humanity in order to Deify Jesus; that they might have a God-Man particularly their own."

One would have to look far and wide in the writings of false teachers to find statements more blasphemous than this about the person of Jesus Christ, my Lord.

According to the Third Test, masonry is a false religion because masonry dogmatically rejects the doctrine of salvation from the penalty of sin by faith in the vicarious atonement of Christ's shed blood on the cross.

Thomas Milton Steward, another Masonic author, in his book *Symbolic Teaching on Masonry and Its Message,* to support his doctrine quoted favorable an apostate Episcopal minister who wrote (Pg.177), "Did Jesus count Himself, conceive of Himself as a proprietary sacrifice and of His work as an expiation? The only answer possible is, clearly, He did not...He does not call Himself the world's priest, or the world's victim."

Salvation by Faith in the vicarious atonement are not "ignorant perversions of the original doctrines" as masonry teaches, but they are vital ingredients of the Glorious Gospel of Christ, which is the power of God unto Salvation to everyone who believes. THEREFORE, masonry fails all three tests. It manifests a satanic attitude toward the Bible, the Deity of Christ, and the vicarious atonement. In addition to failing these tests, there is much more proof that masonry is a false religion.

For instance, Henry C. Clausen, 33 degree, Sovereign Grand Commander of the Supreme Council 33 Degree mother council of the world, in the NEW AGE, November, 1970, (Pg.4) wrote regarding masonry, "It is dedicated to bringing about the Fatherhood of God, the Brotherhood of Man, and making better men in a better world."

The doctrine of the Fatherhood of God and the Brotherhood of Man is not found in the Bible. It is a doctrine taught consistently by apostates. Also, the Bible makes it crystal clear that no organization, masonry included, can make better men. Only God can make better men!

According to a Masonic creed, found in the Masonic Bible, masonry teaches that "character determines destiny."

The teaching that character determines destiny is a false doctrine of the Arch Deceiver of Souls. The Bible says, "There is none that doeth good," and "For by Grace are you saved through faith, and that not of yourselves; it is a gift of God, not of works, lest any man should boast."

Masonry is anti-Christian in its teachings. For example, J.M. Ward in FREEMASONRY - ITS AIMS AND IDEALS wrote (Pg.187), "I boldly aver that freemasonry is a religion, yet it no way conflicts with any other religion, unless that religion holds that no one outside its portals can be saved." Ward, in his statement, reveals the fact that masonry has no conflict with any apostate religion on the face of the earth, but he also reveals that **masonry is in conflict with Christianity**. The Bible says, "Neither is there salvation in any other, for there is none other name under heaven given among men whereby we MUST be saved" (Acts 4:12). Jesus said, "No man cometh unto the Father but by Me." (Jn. 14:6). The Bible is plainly teaching that there is only one way to heaven and that is Christ.

A prominent college president said of masonry, "**It is a luciferian religion**. We are fully aware of its diabolical origin and purpose. I believe that any born-again Christian, when the facts from the lips of Masonic writers themselves are presented showing that masonry is a religion and is *the worship of Satan,* will immediately withdraw." To this I must add my hearty agreement!

210

The God and Father of the Lord Jesus Christ, the only True and Living God, has clearly commanded Christians, "Be ye not unequally yoked together with unbelievers, and swear not at all, and have no fellowship with the unfruitful works of darkness, but rather reprove them."

Charles Finney, the famed evangelist who God used to bring a revival in America in the 1830's, in his book, FREEMASONRY wrote (Pg.115), "Surely, if masons really understood what Masonry is, as it is delineated in these books, no Christian Mason would think himself to remain at liberty to remain another day a member of the fraternity. It is as plain as possible that a man knowing what it is, and embracing it in his heart, cannot be a Christian man. To say he can is to belie the very nature of Christianity."

For me, the signs of the time compared with prophetic Scripture, make it apparent that we are living in the last days prior to the Rapture of the Church. Satan is hard at work trying to hinder believers' spiritual growth, as well as trying to keep the unsaved from entering God's Family. **Freemasonry, I have come to believe, is one of Satan's master deceptions**. Many ministers, elders, deacons, trustees, and Sunday School teachers belong to this cult. Today, my membership ends! Today, a new ministry begins. There is a tremendous need to scrutinize the cultic nature of Freemasonry in view of the massive infiltration of its effects on the working body of the Church. It should be exposed to the True Light - Jesus Christ!

Love in Christ, Harmon R. Taylor   [emphasis added]

3 John 11 ~

Beloved, follow not that which is evil, but that which is good. He that doeth good is of God: but he that doeth evil hath not seen [known] God. [emphasis added]

And so we see for ourselves some of the background or "backdrop" that magnified the conflict experienced by the Radical Republicans of the "interim Executive Congress." They fully understood that Congress was lacking the representatives of the vacant seats for the Southern States but to fill them, and the Halls of Congress, would very likely be filling them with the ex-Confederate/Slave Power/Freemasons who would forever seek to gain the legislative balance of power and institute slavery again. What the men of principles (Radical Republicans) did not realize is that the "cunning, ambitious, and unprincipled men," as George Washington warned us about, were working towards making slaves of ALL Americans—black and white—in spite of any legislation or constitutional amendments the desperate Congressmen would enact.

The sons of Satan would then craft an illusion once they had fully infiltrated the Federal Government (and state and local governments just like a cancer), and trick the American people into their jurisdiction of Mystery Babylon—the Corporate UNITED STATES, also known as UNITED STATES OF AMERICA, INC. It was an easier task now that the Union was no longer a Republic, but had become a Democracy beginning with the 14th Amendment.

We continue on the timeline of historical events a little further in abbreviated fashion through the Congressional Reconstruction Plan, point out some items not in our current day school textbooks, and then differentiate between the American Republic and the Corporate Democracy.

In early to mid-1867, Republicans passed three laws of Congressional Reconstruction over Johnson's vetoes. The Acts stipulated the new terms in which Southern State governments were required

211

to apply for readmission to the Union, essentially starting all over again after President Johnson had tried to proclaim the Reconstruction process complete (Presidential Proclamations dated June 13, 1865,[1220] April 2, 1866,[1221] and August 20, 1866[1222]).[1223] They bitterly fought President Andrew Johnson while weakening his powers. The Radicals were vigorously opposed by the Democratic Party and were often opposed by Moderate and Liberal Republicans as well.

Radical Republican leaders Rep. Thaddeus Stevens and Senator Charles Sumner led the campaign for full voting rights for all black Americans. In a speech Stevens gave before the House of Representatives on January 3, 1867 in support of the Reconstruction bill then being debated, he issued a response to those who said his stance was radical and inflammatory:

"I am for negro suffrage in every rebel State. If it be just, it should not be denied; if it be necessary, it should be adopted; if it be a punishment to traitors, they deserve it."[1224]

Rep. Thaddeus Stevens [1225]

Sen. Charles Sumner [1226]

Senator Charles Sumner's position on slavery had been clear since becoming a Senator in 1851. As one of the founders of the Republic Party, Senator Sumner declared:

"Familiarity with that great story of redemption, when God raised up the slave-born Moses to deliver His chosen people from bondage, and with that sublimer story where our Saviour died a cruel death that all men, without distinction of race, might be saved, makes slavery impossible.

Because Christians are in the minority there is no reason for renouncing Christianity, or for surrendering to the false religions; nor do I doubt that Christianity will yet prevail over the earth as the waters cover the sea."

On February 5, 1867 with the passing of the *Habeas Corpus Act of 1867*,[1227] the Radicals ensured that their Reconstruction program would prevail by removing the power of the U.S. Supreme Court to review such cases. The Judicial branch of government through the U.S. Supreme Court accepted this restriction while affirming the inviolability of the Union (secession from the Union is illegal) in *Texas v. White*.[1228] [1229]

It is appropriate and most important at this time to call to attention the new construction that took place in this era of what is known as "the old Masonic Temple" in Washington City. As recorded at the U.S. Department of the Interior National Park Service in the National Register of Historic Places,[1230] ground was broken in the fall of 1867 and the cornerstone laid on May 20, 1868 in a public ceremony.

National Register of Historic Places Inventory – Nomination Form [1231]
For the "Old Masonic Temple" in Washington, District of Columbia
Prepared by an architectural historian October, 1973

It is stated on the aforementioned recorded government document that President Johnson had issued an Executive Order for Masons employed by the government to be released from work to participate in the ceremonies. It is also stated,

"President Andrew Johnson, in his character as a Master Mason, marched the entire length of the route, as did the architects and master-builders."

It was shortly thereafter in 1870 that Albert Pike and the Supreme Council moved from Charleston, South Carolina to the new Temple in Washington, DC.

On the recorded National Register of Historic Places nomination form it is stated:[1232]

"...On December 17, 1868, the Grand Lodge first met in the completed Temple. The building was dedicated and permanently occupied on May 20, 1870. Even before the dedication the Masonic Hall, located in one of the most fashionable areas of the city, was becoming a popular place for concerts and balls. By 1876 it was known as 'the scene of some of the most brilliant balls and State socialables given at the capital.' Some of the more notable occasions included a banquet given by the British Minister for the Prince of Wales, a memorable ball and supper given by the Illinois Association and attended by President Grant, and a debutante party given by silver magnate Sen. Wm. Stewart. At the latter, attended by 500 persons, 'the dressing was the most gorgeous and extravagant ever seen in this city. . . A magnificent supper was spread; the music was the best that could be afforded; so much nakedness was probably never revealed in Washington.'"

One who contemplates could almost imagine behind-the-scenes plans for strategizing this secret society organization's world headquarters the *"Mother Supreme Council of all Masonic Lodges of the World,"*[1233] moved in the Nations' capital city in the midst of the *Reconstruction Era* while the country was war-torn!!!

In our current era, one might also be triggered in reflection and draw parallel of an insensitive plan publicized in 2010 for the construction of a Muslim community center and mosque to be built three blocks from Ground Zero in New York, the site of the September 11th attacks in which the Corporate UNITED STATES Federal Government claims was done by Islamic terrorists.[1234]

Was the new construction of the soon-to-be world headquarters of *The Scottish Rite of Freemasonry Supreme Council, 33° Southern Jurisdiction, U.S.A.,* moved from Charleston, South Carolina to the Nation's capital right after the Civil War somewhat of an announcement of a type of victory?

Unmistakably revealing is the strategic location of this secret society organization's world headquarters the *"Mother Supreme Council of all Masonic Lodges of the World."*[1235] At the initiation of Washington City, Freemason architects designed the layout of the streets of the city to be an inverted Pentagram.[1236]

The Pentagram is the sign of Baphomet, the god of Freemasonry. It was to signify that Baphomet is the ruler of Washington D.C., with the White House as positioned at the "mouth" of Baphomet at the bottom point of the Pentagram. It was to make the President the mouthpiece of Baphomet.

The Temple in symbolism (located between the two upper points of the Pentagram) equates to the flame of a candle, or enlightenment or Intellect (the related position is the brains of Baphomet in the inverted Pentagram).

There is considerable detail involved in the architecture, of which is available for additional studies by the referenced endnotes.[1237]

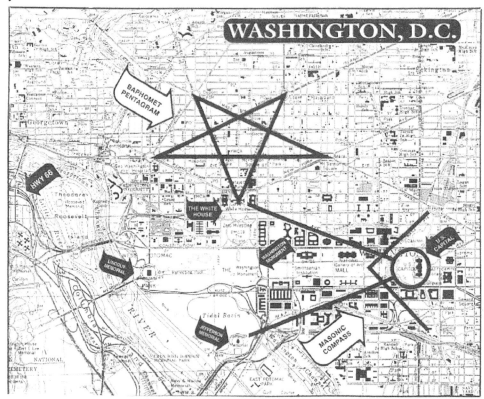

Layout of the streets of Washington, DC[1238]

Baphomet Pentagram and Masonic Compass

There is a great deal of symbolism in positioning location of buildings as well as meaning in particular memorials that is not commonly known.

Baphomet[1239]

Head of Baphomet in an inverted pentagram[1240]

Continuing on in an abbreviated timeline of some of the significant historical events, on February 24, 1868, Congress sought to restrain presidential opposition by commencing an impeachment trial against President Johnson.

Congress claimed that Johnson violated the provisions of the recently passed *Tenure of Office Act*[1241] which required the consent of the Senate in the firing of any officials who had required Senate confirmation in the first place.[1242] Before this time, no president had before been impeached and the House held debates for two months before they voted to charge Johnson with "high crimes and misdemeanors."[1243]

Johnson Impeachment Committee [1244]
Seated left to right: Benjamin F. Butler, Thaddeus Stevens, Thomas Williams,
John A. Bingham. Standing: James F. Wilson, George S. Boutwell, John A. Logan.

On May 16, 1868, the Senate held impeachment hearings and the final result was 35 to 19, exactly one vote short of the required two-thirds needed for conviction. Aides carried a very ill Rep. Thaddeus Stevens in an armchair to attend the impeachment hearing. As he was being carried out, Stevens was furious in the failure to impeach President Johnson and responded to an inquiry in the crowd of what the result was. **"The country is going to the Devil!"**[1245]

He obviously well understood the Freemason agenda, their man Johnson, and that his remaining in office was a victory for the sons of Satan and the Kingdom of Darkness.

Stevens had only a few weeks to live and used them to write legislation and work on plans for free schools. After death, his body lay in state in the Capitol building. Only Abraham Lincoln had ever received more tribute.[1246] Rep. Stevens had directed that he be buried in a cemetery that was not restrictive based on race, as were other cemeteries at the time.[1247] He composed his own tombstone epitaph, which reads:

"I repose in this quiet and secluded spot, not for any natural preference for solitude. But finding other cemeteries limited as to race by charter rules, I have chosen this that I might illustrate in my death the principles which I advocated through a long life, equality of man before his creator."[1248]

We understand the desperation of this Congressional body; however, **we review the American Republic's history in light of constitutional law**. Technically and lawfully, the rump (interim Executive) Congress was not a lawful deliberative body under the *Constitution* and passed laws while the Southern States did not have representation in Congress as guaranteed by Article IV, Section 4 of the *Constitution*. The Southern States did not cease to be states because secession is not lawful or possible. Therefore, the citizens of those States did not cease to be citizens of the Union.

The (interim Executive) Congress passed the *Reconstruction Acts of 1867*[1249] that divided the Confederate States (except for Tennessee, which had been readmitted to the Union[1250]) into five military districts.

The (interim executive) *Congressional Reconstruction Plan* included the appointment of Military Generals over each military district who were then responsible for appointing state officers such as Governor and other various officials. Each of those Southern States was forced to accept the (unlawful) 13th and (unlawful) 14th Amendments to the *Constitution*,[1251] which was thought to have achieved freedom and political rights for black Americans.

Democratic Platform—

"This is a white man's government—We regard the Reconstruction Acts (so called) of Congress as usurpations, and unconstitutional, revolutionary, and void."[1252]

Summary
1868 cartoon showing man with a "CSA" *Confederate States of America* belt buckle and holding a knife engraved with "the lost cause." Also pictured is a stereotyped Irishman holding a club and on it written, "a vote;" and another man wearing a "5 Avenue" button, holding a wallet that has written on it "capital for votes." All three men have their feet on an African American soldier sprawled on the ground.

In the background, a "colored orphan asylum" and a "southern school" are in flames; African American children have been lynched near the burning buildings.

Thomas Nast, artist; Library of Congress

We will recall that this 13th Amendment (freeing the slaves), unconstitutionally replaced the original 13th Article of Amendment (titles of nobility), of which had been ratified on March 12, 1819. We will understand that the 14th Amendment declared a new law of citizenship that had a radical effect by reversing the origin and character of citizenship—both State and National.

The original Constitution remained unchanged concerning citizenship from 1789 until July 28, 1868 when the 14th Amendment was adopted. The 14th Amendment would broaden citizenship by reversing its origin and character thereby substantially affecting the nature and direction of the nation.[1253]

"Cunning, ambitious, and unprincipled men" would patiently await a ripened and clandestine opportunity to further transition citizenship into something that shocks the conscience. "Citizens of the United States" would be transformed into a commercial utility known as a "U.S. citizen."

Where these Radical Republicans sought to preserve the Union and exterminate the Luciferian agenda of the Freemasons, by reflecting we see that operating outside of the *Constitution* and President Lincoln's intention of quickly restoring the <u>loyal</u> (by excluding ex-Confederates from holding office) Southern States into the Union ended in forcing these (unlawful) Amendments to the *Constitution* and initiated the beginnings of a Democracy.

The *Constitution* contains an oath of office only for the President. For other members, including members of Congress, the *Constitution* specifies only that they "shall be bound by Oath or Affirmation to support this constitution." In 1789, the First Congress reworked this requirement into a simple fourteen-word oath:

"I do solemnly swear (or affirm) that I will support the Constitution of the United States."[1254]

In July, 1862 the (interim executive) Congress passed a resolution adopting a new oath — the "Ironclad Test Oath." It was originally devised by Congress at that time for ALL federal employees, lawyers, and federal elected officials.[1255] It reads:

I, _____, do solemnly swear (or affirm) that I have never voluntarily borne arms against the United States since I have been a citizen thereof; that I have voluntarily given no aid, countenance, counsel, or encouragement to persons engaged in armed hostility thereto; that I have neither sought nor accepted nor attempted to exercise the functions of any office whatever, under any authority or pretended authority in hostility to the United States; that I have not yielded a voluntary support to any pretended government, authority, power or constitution within the United States, hostile or inimical thereto. And I do further swear (or affirm) that, to the best of my knowledge and ability, I will support and defend the Constitution of the United States, against all enemies, foreign and domestic; that I will bear true faith and allegiance to the same; that I take this obligation freely, without any mental reservation or purpose of evasion, and that I will well and faithfully <u>discharge the duties of the office</u> on which I am about to enter, so help me God.[1256] [emphasis added]

In comparing the original oath as specified in the *Constitution* to the *Ironclad Test Oath*, we find that a significant positional change had been made. By this resolution, the (interim executive) Congress made members of Congress to now be classified as civil officers/officials rather than representatives of the People as originally designed. This new oath also contributed to a <u>change of law form</u>.

Members of Congress and legislators of the free States were by constitutional design to be the direct representation of the People, sent in their place to "support the Constitution." They were intended to be members and to hold seats in Congress and the State legislatures, not to be civil officers. <u>This Act is repugnant to the *Constitution* and contributed to the transition from a Republic to a Democracy</u>. It deprived the American people of suffrage (the right to vote) and representation as guaranteed and specified in the *Constitution*.[1257]

The (unlawful) 14th Amendment affirmed the *Ironclad Oath* while it also gave all pardoning power to Congress rather than to the President.[1258] The *Constitution* specifies in Article II, Section 2 that the President "shall have Power to grant Reprieves and Pardons for Offences against the United States, except in Cases of Impeachment." Amendment XIV, Section 3:

No person shall be a Senator or Representative in Congress, or elector of President and Vice President, or hold any office, civil or military, under the United States, or under any state, who, having previously taken an oath, as a member of Congress, or as an officer of the United States, or as a member of any state legislature, or as an executive or judicial officer of any state, to support the Constitution of the United States, shall have engaged in insurrection or rebellion against the same, or given aid or comfort to the enemies thereof. But Congress may by a vote of two-thirds of each House, remove such disability. [emphasis added]

The sons of Satan would come to take advantage of this legislated change in law form by infiltrating the "interim Executive" government and secretly crafting a jurisdiction for ALL of their intended chattel "slaves" as they manipulated money and workforce under their control, and creating an illusion where the American people would think they were free.

The logic of the Radical Republican Congress was steeped in their desperation to ensure that once the Southern States were reconciled in the Union with Congressional representation, rebels in the Southern State legislatures would not have the ability to amend their State constitutions to reinstall slavery. They also calculated that by giving black males the right to vote, it would disable the white supremacist Democratic Party and prevent losing Republican congressional control.

Although the (interim executive) Congress made way for black American suffrage (the right to vote in public elections), they failed to secure land for black Americans, which resulted in white Americans economically controlling black Americans. The *Freedmen's Bureau*[1259] was authorized to administer the new laws and help black Americans attain their economic, civil, educational, and political rights.

The newly created (loyal) State governments were generally republican in character and were governed by political coalitions of black Americans, Northerners who had migrated to the South (called "carpetbaggers" by Southern Democrats), and Southerners who allied with the black Americans and carpetbaggers (referred to as "scalawags" by their opponents).

1872 cartoon depiction of a Carpetbagger[1260]
A Northerner who moved to the South during the *Reconstruction Era* was called a Carpetbagger. Many white Southerners denounced them, fearing they would loot and plunder the defeated South and form political alliance with the Radical Republicans.

This uneasy coalition of black and white Republicans passed significant civil rights legislation in many States. Courts were reorganized, judicial procedures improved, and public school systems established.

Segregation existed but was somewhat flexible. As black Americans slowly progressed, white Southerners resented their achievements and their empowerment, even though they were in a political minority in every State but South Carolina.[1261]

A greater number of the white populace rallied around the Democratic Party which sought to maintain the preexisting social order of white supremacy in the South[1262] and regain control of their State governments.[1263] They were very much related to the *White Knights of the Ku Klux Klan* which was, if not founded by, it was at least certainly influenced by, Luciferian Albert Pike.[1264] When bribery failed, their members which were led by merchants, Democratic politicians, and plantation owners, used violent coercion to eliminate their competitors, white and black.[1265]

Two members of the Ku-Klux Klan in their disguises [1266]
Illustration in *Harper's Weekly,* 1868

Between 1868 and 1871 terrorist organizations, especially the *Ku Klux Klan*, murdered blacks (as well as whites) who tried to exercise their right to vote or receive an education.[1267]   Their objective was to undermine Reconstruction so that the "Great American Experiment"[1268] would fail and blacks would never again receive such an opportunity.

Ironically, (or perhaps not really), the *Klan* contributed to prolonging the *Reconstruction Era* when it was actually formed with the objective of defeating reconstruction. In response to the plea for assistance by the Southern States who were working toward reconstruction, the (interim executive) Congress passed three *Enforcement Acts[1269]* in 1870 and 1871.

Visit of the Ku-Klux [1270]
African American woman cooking, man seated alongside, and three children, with man from Ku Klux Klan aiming rifle in doorway.

By early 1871, <u>if States failed</u> to prosecute anyone who conspired to deprive citizens of the right to serve on juries, hold office, enjoy equal protection under the law, or vote, the federal district attorneys could now prosecute them.   In passing this legislation, the Federal Government furthered its path in "unchartered territory" of a Democracy and began to resemble a Democracy as well.[1271]

The white South did not hold a monopoly on widespread racist sentiments. The North was the birthplace of segregation, particularly in its urban areas.   Blacks were separated from whites in Northern modes of public transportation like horse-drawn buses, stagecoaches, railway cars, and steamboats—or they were excluded altogether. They were not permitted to sit next to whites in theaters or lecture halls, and they could only enter restaurants or hotels as servants. The North rather emulated the South during Reconstruction and yet demanded that the white South recognize the fact of emancipation.[1272]

Reconstruction ended for various reasons. Although the Federal Government's refusal to redistribute the treasonous Confederate plantation owners' land to the freedmen was long remembered as a betrayal with gloomy repercussions, this was not the reason for ending Reconstruction. It was the Southern white terrorism and violence, with intentions of destroying black leadership and coercing black labor that was primarily the cause of the collapse and subsequent takeover by the so-called "Redeemers." By the early 1870s most Southern States had been "redeemed," as referred to by many white Southerners, from Republican Radical rule.

This counterrevolution was permitted through the lack of federal presence in the South, from the continual demobilization of troops, to the understaffed *Freedmen's Bureau*. Northerners lost interest in the cause of the freedmen as the *Reconstruction Era* extended for over a decade.

As whites regained power over the South by 1877 and throughout the century that followed, whites from both North and South branded the *Reconstruction Era* as a disaster because they claimed that blacks were in charge, and also claimed that blacks were unfit to rule, unprepared for the rights, responsibilities, and freedoms granted to them.[1273]

In the century that followed, there was gross exaggeration among historians about the Era—including some of the nation's considered foremost scholars having written exaggerated, irate histories that portray the period of supposed deplorable treatment of white Southerners along with twisted blatant racist tales concerning the "ignorance and savage lust" of black officeholders.

The two sides of the Civil War reunited during the late 19th century by ignoring the fate of the black population and basing their reunited culture on the concept of white supremacy in other aspects such as education and society. It was actually black success in ambition, confidence, and aptitude that appeared to threaten the society of the former Confederacy in their power structure, institutions, labor system, and society more than black corruption or ignorance ever could.

But by discrediting the era in which blacks were most active politically, it is reported that historians, filmmakers, politicians, and writers from across the country astoundingly, yet effectively, acquitted (cleared as guiltless) the white South of depriving blacks of their legal rights. They permitted racial segregation and discrimination, even endorsing it for over a century.[1274]

Example of Racial Segregation:
Separate water fountains
for "White Men" and "Colored Men" [1275]

Radical Reconstruction ended at different times in different States throughout the next decade. Ultimately, all three branches of the Federal Government had turned away when blacks most needed them. In retrospect, the Radicals in Congress had certainly tested the limits of federal commitment and power. In the end, the country was simply unprepared to commit itself to a vision of racial equality that most white citizens did not believe in—not even the Northerners who preached abolition.

By the time the last federal troops had been withdrawn in 1877, Reconstruction was all but over and the Freemason white supremacist Democratic Party controlled the destiny of the South—as well as the North.[1276] This next era is known as the "Gilded Age" and was an era "overlaid in gold," as it was an era of rapid economic growth, especially in the North and West.[1277] Few Radicals were still alive and the Republican Party had assumed the role of ally to the big business interests who were rapidly accumulating power and capital while turning the country into the world's leading industrial power by the turn of the century.[1278]

Again, we emphasize that any legislation passed by the "interim executive Congress" was not lawful in that it violated Article IV Section 4 of the *Constitution*. In the American Republic the whole sovereignty rests with the People and is exercised through their representatives in Congress assembled. In order for laws to be binding they must have the consent of the American people through their representatives as Article IV, Section 4 of the *Constitution* guarantees to EVERY State in the Union a representative form of governance.[1279]

Additionally, the *Ironclad Oath* taken by ALL federal employees and elected officials contributed to a change of law form that is contrary to a republican form of governance. Any legislation passed in this period of time and thereafter is by law repugnant to the *Constitution of the United States* and therefore null and void. The re-inhabited American Republic has correctly established re-inhabitation in its pick-up point through 1860, preceding the loss of Congressional quorum in both houses, as well as the period of executive authority under Martial Law and suspension of the *Writ of Habeas Corpus*.

President Lincoln referred to this *color of law* interim government as "the Executive Government" in his September 22, 1862 Presidential Proclamation described as "Declaring the Objectives of the War Including Emancipation of Slaves in Rebellious States on January 1, 1863."[1280] He also twice made reference to "the Executive Government" in his January 1, 1863 Presidential Proclamation known as "The Emancipation Proclamation."[1281] For this reason we will now refer to the Congressional body with the Southern seats refilled as "the *de facto* (in practice but not necessarily ordained by law) Congress." [1282]

We point out that on December 1, 1865 President Andrew Johnson made his last Presidential Proclamation before leaving office and proclaimed that December 25, 1868 would be a day of "Granting Full Pardon and Amnesty for the Offense of Treason Against the United States During the Late Civil War."[1283] It appears to be quite the Christmas gift in looking out for his Freemason brethren and in-line with his Freemason oath.

Accelerating forward, we point out that the *de facto* Congress passed the **District of Columbia Organic Act of 1871**,[1284] which created a <u>private corporation</u> with a Trademark name of the-all-capital-letter, **THE UNITED STATES OF AMERICA, INC.**, (hereinafter "Corporate UNITED STATES") for the ten-miles-square region that includes the City of Washington, in the District of Columbia.[1285]

CHAP. LXII. — *An Act to provide a Government for the District of Columbia.*   Feb. 21, 1871.

Be it enacted by the Senate and House of Representatives of the United States of America in Congress assembled, That all that part of the territory of the United States included within the limits of the District of Columbia be, and the same is hereby, created into a government by the name of the District of Columbia, by which name it is hereby constituted a body corporate for municipal purposes, and may contract and be contracted with, sue and be sued, plead and be impleaded, have a seal, and exercise all other powers of a municipal corporation not inconsistent with the Constitution and laws of the United States and the provisions of this act.

The Statutes at Large and Proclamations of the United States of America,
from December 1869 to March 1871, Vol. XVI , page 419
CHAP. LXII – An Act to provide a Government for the District of Columbia — Feb. 21, 1871

This regional area which had constitutionally been designated for carrying out the business needs of the Federal Government had now experienced a <u>private</u> incorporation and given a business name which was unlawfully and strategically manipulated at every opportunity under the circumstances of change in law form.

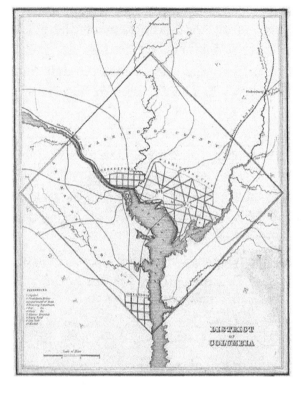

1835 Map of the District of Columbia [1286]

On July 9, 1790, Congress passed the *Residence Act*, which approved the creation of a national capital along the Potomac River and encompass an area of no more than "ten miles square."

The exact location was to be selected by President George Washington, who signed the bill into law a week later. Formed from land donated by the states of Maryland and Virginia, the initial shape of the federal district was a square measuring 10 miles on each side, totaling 100 square miles.

In 1846, based on a petition to Congress by the residents of the Virginia portion of the District (Alexandria County) and the City of Alexandria, the area of 31 square miles which was ceded by Virginia was returned, leaving 69 square miles of territory originally ceded by Maryland as the current area of the District in its entirety (north and east of the Potomac River).

Next, all of the States in the Union were re-formed as franchises, or political subdivisions, so that a NEW Union of the United States could be created. **This new Union, the Corporate UNITED STATES, was under the private rule of those private banking interests who privatized the District of Columbia through incorporation.** These new laws for the District of Columbia supplanted those established on February 27, 1801[1287] and May 3, 1802.[1288]

The key to when the States became federal franchisees is related to the date when such States enacted the Field Code in law. The Field Code was a codification of the common law that was adopted first by New York and then by California in 1872, and shortly afterwards <u>the *Lieber Code* was used to bring the Corporate UNITED STATES into the 1874 Brussels Conference, and into the Hague Conventions of 1899 and 1907</u>.

The *Code of Laws of the United States*, also known as *U.S. Code*, is the official compilation and codification of the general and permanent federal laws of the United States. United States Title Code 28, "Judicial Code and Judiciary" was revised, codified and enacted into law on June 25, 1948 as HR3214 and Public Law 773.[1289] United States Title Code 28 Section 3002 (15) describes the definition of "United States" to mean[1290] —

(A) a Federal **corporation**;
(B) an agency, department, commission, board, or other entity of the United States; or
(C) an instrumentality of the United States.

The *District of Columbia Act of 1871* also provided for adopting its own constitution which was IDENTICAL to the original *Constitution* except that it was missing the original *Constitution's* 13th Article of Amendment (titles of nobility) and the Corporate UNITED STATES' constitution's 14th, 15th and 16th Amendments are then respectively numbered as the 13th, 14th and 15th Amendments.

When the *Confederate States of America* formed, it too had used the original *Constitution of the United States* in creating its constitution. The document is largely a word-for-word copy of the original United States *Constitution*, but with several key changes which designate how the Confederacy intended to be different from the Union, and why.[1291] It was not a new idea for these sons of Satan to counterfeit America's sacred operating document, or to continue to masquerade in deception.

The first attempt by the (interim Executive) Congress to define citizenship was on April 9, 1866 with the passage of the *Civil Rights Act.*[1292] This Act provides that:

"All persons born in the United States and not subject to any foreign power are declared to be citizens of the United States."

The intent behind this enactment was to make discrimination against any class of citizen unlawful. It would provide a means in law for citizens who were denied these equal accommodations (obtaining services and accommodations of innkeepers, public transportation, places of public entertainment, etc.) the right of action and damages for such denial.[1293]

Just two months later Republicans in Congress proposed the 14th Amendment as a means to rivet the principles of the *Civil Rights Act* into the *Constitution.* They feared that the Southern white aristocracy Freemasons would one day regain control of Congress and repeal the Civil Rights law that they loathed. The language of Section one of the 14th Amendment is very similar:

"All persons born or naturalized in the United States, and subject to the jurisdiction thereof, are citizens of the United States and of the State wherein they reside."

When the Reconstruction Amendments to the (*de facto*) Constitution, the 13th, 14th, and 15th, first came up for interpretation before the (*de facto*) U.S. Supreme Court in the famous *Slaughter-House Cases,* Associate Justice Noah Swayne stated:

"Fairly construed, they may be said to rise to the dignity of a new Magna Charta."

It was understood by those in the Judiciary that subsequent Supreme Court decisions would require reviewing cases with a much narrower scope. Attorney John Wise in his 1906 book, *A Treatise on American Citizenship,* points out that the 14th Amendment is broader in language than the 13th, yet no broader than the 13th in granting any power upon the Federal Government to legislate upon its own initiative. It declared a new law of citizenship, but the only power of legislation conferred by it upon Congress was power to enact restrictive legislation against any State action which might be taken contrary to the amendment itself.[1294]

As the new Democracy of the Corporate UNITED STATES proceeded forward, *de facto* Congress would attempt to pass many acts enforcing the provisions of the Reconstruction Amendments. The enactments would give rise to an amount of litigation unprecedented in the history of the Constitution.[1295]

"Cunning, ambitious, and unprincipled men" would continually plot their course in fully usurping controls of America as they progressed forward in their global agenda. Now that the American Republic was shoved aside and a Democracy put in place, it would be easier to rule in secret and evolve the New World to look more like the Old. As we unfold documented evidence recorded in history of what they did and how it was done, even unbelievers will recognize the overriding evil that has kept this evil-run system going for decades and centuries. Man doesn't live for centuries so for evil to perpetuate there has to be an overriding evil that oversees it.

We can put ourselves in the shoes of the Radical Republicans who inadvertently thought their plan of passing "law" regarding citizenship and "civil <u>rights</u>" by federal powers would guarantee the freedmen what should have been theirs as God-given and preserved by the *Constitution* as "civil <u>liberties</u>." They understood the real enemy and did their best to outmaneuver the situation. We can almost hear Rep. Thaddeus Stevens in the halls of Congress shouting in the midst of a failed impeachment, **"The country is going to the Devil!"**[1296] Beloved Mr. Stevens is in the cloud of witnesses (Heb. 12:1) now watching as the sons and daughters of Liberty carry forth the torch of sacred fires. He knows the sons of Satan will not prevail.

It is understood in law that any contract entered under duress, or by nondisclosure, is null and void.* Full disclosure was not provided to the American people regarding the secret agenda to permanently and deceitfully change the law form, not returning to functioning with the original *Constitution of the United States*, the operating document established in perpetuity. There was no full disclosure provided to the American people in the usurping of the Peoples' social covenant and sacred operating document — the *Constitution* — with a counterfeit constitution, or the plan to develop a corporate Democracy.

> *NOTE: *Marbury v. Madison, 1803,* "A law repugnant to the Constitution is void." With these words, Chief Justice John Marshall established the Supreme Court's role in the new government. Hereafter, the Court was recognized as having the power to review all acts of Congress where constitutionality was at issue, and judge whether they abide by the Constitution.

In just a few decades one of hell's sons would technically designate the American People to be "enemies" of the (Corporate) UNITED STATES. This is thought-provoking insight as to why the American people have ever since experienced adversity with the counterfeit government, and also projects meaningful consideration of the *Trading with the Enemies Act* which was introduced later in 1917.

Citizens with <u>*sovereign authority*</u> as granted them by "Nature's God" by inherent right had created a constitutional Republic to guarantee those rights. In stark contrast, desperate Congressmen inadvertently created a Democracy that ended up being manipulated by "cunning, ambitious, and unprincipled men" to fortify its power over its citizens. It pretends to be taking citizens under its protection, but the cost of protection is servitude. American citizens would be tricked into "volunteering" to become subjects; free men and women to become vassal slaves.

Hosea 4:6 ~   *"My people perish for lack of knowledge…"*

The 14th Amendment has always been a subject of controversy. Over the years many people have questioned the amount of power it vests in the Federal Government. Some have questioned its validity. On one occasion Judge Walter Ellett of the Utah Supreme Court remarked:

> "I cannot believe that any court in full possession of its faculties could honestly hold that the amendment was properly approved and adopted." [1297]

Utah Chief Justice Walter Ellett [1298]

NOTE: Based on conclusive fact-in-law research, early America virtually followed no uniform standard for spelling or for punctuation. Though some may disagree with this conclusion, for practical purposes of this writing we will not differentiate the capitalization of the word "citizen" to depict the two types of citizen, one spelled with a capital "C" and the other spelled with a lower case "c."[1299]

It is important to understand the difference between a Republic and a Democracy.

Republic v. Democracy

by David Barton of WallBuilders.[1300] Reprinted with general permission. Author's endnotes are included in the endnotes of this chapter.

> We have grown accustomed to hearing that we are a democracy; such was never the intent. The form of government entrusted to us by our Founders was a republic, not a democracy.[1301] Our Founders had an opportunity to establish a democracy in America and chose not to. In fact, the Founders made clear that we were not, and were never to become, a democracy:
>
> **James Madison:** "[D]emocracies have ever been spectacles of turbulence and contention; have ever been found incompatible with personal security, or the rights of property; and have, in general, been as short in their lives as they have been violent in their deaths."[1302]
>
> **John Adams:** "Remember, democracy never lasts long. It soon wastes, exhausts, and murders itself. There never was a democracy yet that did not commit suicide."[1303]
>
> **Fisher Ames** (Author of the House Language for the First Amendment): "A democracy is a volcano which conceals the fiery materials of its own destruction. These will produce an eruption and carry desolation in their way.[1304] The known propensity of a democracy is to licentiousness [excessive license] which the ambitious call, and ignorant believe to be liberty."[1305]
>
> **Gouverneur Morris** (Signer and Penman of the Constitution): "We have seen the tumult of democracy terminate . . . as [it has] everywhere terminated, in despotism. . . . Democracy! savage and wild. Thou who wouldst bring down the virtuous and wise to thy level of folly and guilt."[1306]
>
> **John Quincy Adams:** "[T]he experience of all former ages had shown that of all human governments, democracy was the most unstable, fluctuating and short-lived."[1307]

Benjamin Rush (Signer of the Declaration): "A simple democracy . . . is one of the greatest of evils."[1308]

Noah Webster: "In democracy . . . there are commonly tumults and disorders.... Therefore a pure democracy is generally a very bad government. It is often the most tyrannical government on earth."[1309]

John Witherspoon, (Signer of the Declaration): "Pure democracy cannot subsist long nor be carried far into the departments of state, it is very subject to caprice and the madness of popular rage."[1310]

Zephaniah Swift (Author of America's First Legal Text): "It may generally be remarked that the more a government resembles a pure democracy the more they abound with disorder and confusion."[1311]

Many Americans today seem to be unable to define the difference between the two, but there is a difference, a big difference. That difference rests in the source of authority.

A pure democracy operates by direct majority vote of the people. When an issue is to be decided, the entire population votes on it; the majority wins and rules. A republic differs in that the general population elects representatives who then pass laws to govern the nation. A democracy is the rule by majority feeling (what the Founders described as a "mobocracy"[1312]); a republic is rule by law. If the source of law for a democracy is the popular feeling of the people, then what is the source of law for the American republic? According to Founder Noah Webster:

"[O]ur citizens should early understand that the genuine source of correct republican principles is the Bible, particularly the New Testament, or the Christian religion."[1313]

The transcendent values of Biblical natural law were the foundation of the American republic. Consider the stability this provides: in our republic, murder will always be a crime, for it is always a crime according to the Word of God. However, in a democracy, if majority of the people decide that murder is no longer a crime, murder will no longer be a crime.

America's immutable principles of right and wrong were not based on the rapidly fluctuating feelings and emotions of the people but rather on what Montesquieu identified as the "principles that do not change."[1314] Benjamin Rush similarly observed:

"[W]here there is no law, there is no liberty; and nothing deserves the name of law but that which is certain and universal in its operation upon all the members of the community."[1315]

In the American republic, the "principles which did not change" and which were "certain and universal in their operation upon all the members of the community" were the principles of Biblical natural law. In fact, so firmly were these principles ensconced in the American republic that early law books taught that government was free to set its own policy only if God had not ruled in an area. For example, Blackstone's Commentaries explained:

"To instance in the case of murder: this is expressly forbidden by the Divine. . . . If any human law should allow or enjoin us to commit it we are bound to transgress that human law. . . . But, with regard to matters that are . . . not commanded or forbidden by those superior laws such, for instance, as exporting of wool into foreign countries; here the . . . legislature has scope and opportunity to interpose."[1316]

The Founders echoed that theme:

"All [laws], however, may be arranged in two different classes. 1) Divine. 2) Human. . . But it should always be remembered that this law, natural or revealed, made for men or for nations, flows from the same Divine source: it is the law of God. . . . Human law must rest its authority ultimately upon the authority of that law which is Divine."[1317] **James Wilson, Signer of the Constitution; U. S. Supreme Court Justice**

"[T]he law . . . dictated by God Himself is, of course, superior in obligation to any other. It is binding over all the globe, in all countries, and at all times. No human laws are of any validity if contrary to this."[1318] **Alexander Hamilton, Signer of the Constitution**

"[T]he . . . law established by the Creator . . . extends over the whole globe, is everywhere and at all times binding upon mankind. . . . [This] is the law of God by *which he makes his way known to man and is paramount to all human control.*"[1319] **Rufus King, Signer of the Constitution**

The Founders understood that Biblical values formed the basis of the republic and that the republic would be destroyed if the people's knowledge of those values should ever be lost.

A republic is the highest form of government devised by man, but it also requires the greatest amount of human care and maintenance.   If neglected, it can deteriorate into a variety of lesser forms, including a democracy (a government conducted by popular feeling); anarchy (a system in which each person determines his own rules and standards); oligarchy (a government run by a small council or a group of elite individuals): or dictatorship (a government run by a single individual). As John Adams explained:

"[D]emocracy will soon degenerate into an anarchy; such an anarchy that every man will do what is right in his own eyes and no man's life or property or reputation or liberty will be secure, and every one of these will soon mould itself into a system of subordination of all the moral virtues and intellectual abilities, all the powers of wealth, beauty, wit, and science, to the wanton pleasures, the capricious will, and the execrable [abominable] cruelty of one or a very few."[1320]

Understanding the foundation of the American republic is a vital key toward protecting it.

[emphasis added]

With a greater view of the historical panoramic picture after having put factual pieces together in the Light of truth,[1321] we now have "eyes to see" that the sons of Satan, by deceit and counterfeit, created a corporate Democracy to replace the American Republic. The *God of the universe*, the Creator, the God of Abraham, Isaac, and Jacob,[1322] Yᵉhovah is His Name,[1323] [1324] is God of the American Republic.

Almighty God is Party to the covenantal *Declaration of Independence,* an everlasting covenant. The blessings of the covenant secured to the other party, the American people, are conditional. The blessings had been compromised because of violating the declared absolute that ALL men are created as equal. ALL means ALL. Covenant-breaking resulted in curses, of which the god of the Corporate Democracy, who is Lucifer/Satan, along with his reprobate[1325] sons have operated and ruled the world system, also known as Mystery Babylon.[1326]

Satan is a liar and the father of lies.

John 8:44 ~

> *Ye are of your father the devil, and the lusts of your father ye will do. He was a murderer from the beginning, and abode not in the truth, because there is no truth in him. When he speaketh a lie, he speaketh of his own: for he is a liar, and the father of it.*

Satan and his kingdom (world system) have a counterfeit parallel plan for nearly everything Almighty God does in His perfect plan. It is a crafty imitation of the real, or a **"fiction."** His copy is a perversion of all that Almighty God the Creator has made. Satan is exceedingly clever. When he fell in rebellion, he didn't lose the gifts and genius God created in him. He is a master deceiver.[1327] Operating in deception and as a counterfeiter, Satan has never created anything himself, but only copies and perverts all God has made. He masquerades and pretends.

2 Corinthians 11:14 ~ *And no marvel: for Satan himself is transformed into an Angel of light.*

It is not surprising that his servants also masquerade, pretend, and "act" as servants of righteousness…

2 Corinthians 11:15 ~

> *Therefore it is no great thing, though his ministers transform themselves, as though they were the ministers of righteousness, whose end shall be according to their works.*

Satan's counterfeits, or fictions, are in fact the opposite of God's realities of which they mimic. Calling a counterfeit a reality, or vice versa, is the same as calling evil good or good evil, darkness light or light darkness, or bitter sweet or sweet bitter.[1328]

Isaiah 5:20 ~

> *Woe unto them that speak good of evil, and evil of good, which put darkness for light, and light for darkness, that put bitter for sweet, and sweet for sour.*

There are two Kingdoms—the Kingdom of Light, or Heaven where the Creator of the universe YHWH resides and rules; and the Kingdom of Darkness, or Hell, the place of eternal separation from YHWH in everlasting torment[1329] which is associated with the "god of this world (age),"[1330] Satan.

These two kingdoms are engaged in active warfare with the war coming to its climax as this current Millennial Age comes to a close. The goal of the Kingdom of Darkness, and its Corporate Democracy, is to exalt Satan's plan and agenda while at the same time destroying the American Republic and that which gives glory to Yᵉhovah God, the Creator.

In the perspective of realities versus counterfeits,[1331] delusory counterfeits and **"fictions"** eventually will lead to destruction. It is like building a house upon sand which inevitably will give way and collapse.

Matthew 7:26-27 ~

> *And every one that heareth these sayings of mine, and doeth them not, shall be likened unto a foolish man, which built his house upon the sand: And the rain descended, and the floods came, and the winds blew, and beat upon that house; and it fell: and great was the fall of it.*

At the same time the *Act of 1871* came into "law," the **Federal Dictionary Act**[1332] was passed which defined the word, "person" to extend and be applied to "bodies politic" as well as "corporate" (corporations or corporate fictions). Placing creation on equal status as the creature defies the Word of God, the Holy Bible, as God Almighty had appointed man to take dominion, or have *sovereign authority*, of creation.[1333]

The Statutes at Large and Proclamations of the United States of America,
from December 1869 to March 1871, Vol. XVI , page 431
CHAP. LXXI – An Act prescribing the Form of the enacting and resolving Clauses of Acts and
Resolutions of Congress, and Rules for the Construction thereof. Feb. 25, 1871

There was no full disclosure given to the American people that their "government" had created corporate fictions to have equal status in law as that of a living man or woman. This is a violation of the *Laws of Nature* and *Nature's God*.

A remarkable and most noteworthy statement of an 1855 account in former Catholic priest Charles Chiniquy's book, *Fifty Years in the Church of Rome*, published in 1886 and archived at Columbia University Libraries,[1334] advises his firsthand knowledge of laws that had been passed for Catholic bishops making their person a corporation with the right of personally possessing church properties:

> "I had, many times, considered the infamy and injustice of the law which the bishops have had passed all over the United States, making every one of them a corporation, with the right of possessing personally all the church properties of the Roman Catholics. But I had never understood the infamy and tyranny of that law so clearly as in that hour."[1335]

It takes "eyes to see" and the wisdom from above[1336] to enable us to discern or to tell the difference between realities and toxic counterfeits, or "fictions." The historical facts documented in evidence are before us. We have been given free will to decide what we will do with the knowledge we have been given.[1337]

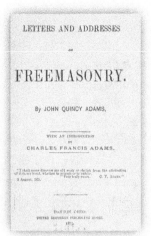

Left: title page of *Letters on the Masonic Institution,* by John Quincy Adams [1338]
Published in 1847 (originally published in 1833)

Right: title page of
Letters and Addresses on Freemasonry,
Published in 1875 [1339] with an Introduction by his son, Charles Frances Adams

Because there was a "revival" of Freemasonry after the Civil War, Charles Adams brought his father's book back into print.

John Quincy Adams was the sixth President of the United States of America. He was also a former U.S. Ambassador, U.S. Secretary of State, U. S. Representative, and the son of Founding Father, John Adams. As Secretary of State he helped formulate the *Monroe Doctrine.* In 1830, he was elected to the U.S. House of Representatives on the *Anti-Mason Party* ticket of which he was instrumental in establishing.

He was President in 1826 when the Freemason scandal pertaining to the murder of William Morgan occurred. Because of the tremendous excitement that occurred in the country, along with phenomenal obstruction of justice at every level of government, Adams conducted his own investigation. John Quincy Adams was so convinced of the unethical, unscriptural, and unholy secret society, that he carried on an active and heated literary and speaking campaign against Freemasonry. His book, *Letters on Freemasonry,* contains critically important correspondence written by Mr. Adams on the controversial subject. Originally published in 1833, copies amazingly (or maybe not so amazingly) disappeared, until recent years.

Included in Adams' writings is an important fact. Where effort was made in defending the society during public outrage, a Mason made public claim that Adams, as well as his illustrious father, were Masons; the matter was clearly established that neither had ever been initiated in the Order or had knowledge of the Masonic secrets, oaths and penalties. The book makes reference to Thomas Jefferson's writings pertaining to George Washington that make it clear that they, too, were vehemently opposed to the society of Freemasonry.[1340]

Adams was known to be a devout Christian. There is no doubt that it was his sense of duty as a Christian which compelled him to fiercely battle against injustice and prejudice, and to support freedom, liberty, and human rights. He never quit fighting for the abolition of slavery.[1341] He held an intense desire to expose the Masonic Lodge and left a legacy to the American people through his writings while directing that "they must ever remain as a standing testimony."

President John Quincy Adams, 1826 [1342]

Chapter Fifteen

Progressively One Nation Without God

Celebration of completion of the First Transcontinental Railroad May 10, 1869 [1343]
At what is now Golden Spike National Historic Site, Promontory Summit, Utah

The era after Reconstruction spans the last quarter of the 19th century from 1878 to the early 1900s. Known as the "Gilded Age," the name for this era was derived in the 1920s stemming from author Mark Twain's 1873 novel, *The Gilded Age: A Tale of Today*, satirizing this period of serious social problems masked by a thin gold gilding. It was an era of rapid economic growth, especially in the North and West. Railroads were the major growth industry.[1344]

After years of war and long, sobering preoccupation with reconstruction of the South that seemed as though it would never end, interest was lost toward assisting the Freedmen in adjusting to a new way of life, intervening on their behalf in the midst of domestic terrorizing by secret societies, as well as guiding one nation under God toward healing.

The Federal Government, along with the North and West, became focused on big business and industrialization. It was an era where railroads expanded across the country allowing travel by rail to cut travel time, making travel safer than horse and wagons. Transcontinental railway made supplies more readily available to both East and West. Those who invested in the railroads and various industries like steel and oil, most financed by Rothschild's of London, became extremely wealthy. [1345]

The love of money blinded any sense of integrity as these men would cheat each other while monopolizing control of their industries and charging the American People dearly for products and services. "Cunning, ambitious, and unprincipled men," would use unscrupulous methods to get rich in the last quarter of the 19th-century. They would come to be known as "Robber barons"[1346] though the American people were not aware that their deeds were orchestrated in darkness through secret societies.[1347]

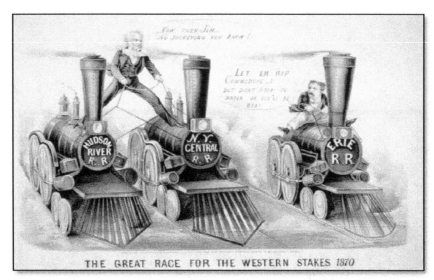

The great race for the Western stakes 1870 [1348]

Summary: Print shows Cornelius Vanderbilt and James Fisk in a race for control of New York's rails. Throughout 1868 and 1869, the two men had fought for control of the Erie Railroad. Here, Vanderbilt straddles his two railroads, the "Hudson River R.R." and the "New York Central R.R.," admonishing his competitor, "Now then Jim--No Jockeying You Know!" The dwarflike Fisk, sitting astride the "Erie R.R.," replies, "Let em rip Commodore!--But Don't Stop to Water or You'll be Beat."

The corruption in politics was outrageous as Congress became "the best Congress that money could buy." In this Corporate Democracy, the American People were pushed aside while big business took front, center, and control. Amendments to the Corporate constitution continued. The first twelve amendments, which had been ratified before the war, all served to limit government power. Those amendments (unlawfully) ratified after the Civil War, marked unprecedented expansions of federal power.[1349] Federal power with lobbied interests—corporation-lobbied interests.

In the Gilded Age, about three-hundred lawsuits were heard before the (*de facto*) Supreme Court seeking equal protection and due process of law based on the Equal Protection Clause of the 14th Amendment, though amazingly only 30 served the black Freedmen—the object of the Amendment.

Plessy v. Ferguson was an 1896 (*de facto*) U.S. Supreme Court landmark case that upheld State racial segregation laws for public facilities under the doctrine of "separate but equal." The Supreme Court ruling in this case legitimized the State laws establishing racial segregation in the South and provided a basis for further segregation laws. It also legitimized laws in the North requiring racial segregation such as in the Boston school segregation.[1350]

In 1938, the ruling pertaining to this case prompted U.S. Supreme Court Justice Hugo Black to note:

"Of the cases in this court in which the Fourteenth Amendment was applied during its first fifty years after its adoption, less than one half of one percent invoked it in protection of the Negro race, and more than fifty percent asked that its benefits be extended to corporations."[1351]
U.S. Supreme Court Justice Hugo LaFayette Black (1886-1971)[1352]

232

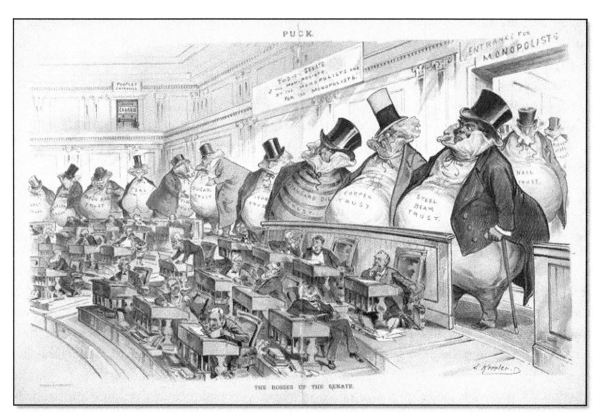

The Bosses of the Senate, a cartoon by Joseph Keppler[1353]
First published in *Puck* Magazine, 1889

"This frequently reproduced cartoon, long a staple of textbooks and studies of Congress, depicts corporate interests—from steel, copper, oil, iron, sugar, tin, and coal to paper bags, envelopes, and salt—as giant money bags looming over the tiny senators at their desks in the Chamber. Joseph Keppler drew the cartoon, which appeared in *Puck* [magazine] on January 23, 1889, showing a door to the gallery, the "people's entrance," bolted and barred. The galleries stand empty while the special interests have floor privileges, operating below the motto: **"This is the Senate of the Monopolists by the Monopolists and for the Monopolists!"**

Keppler's cartoon reflected the phenomenal growth of American industry in the 1880s, but also the disturbing trend toward concentration of industry to the point of monopoly, and its undue influence on politics. This popular perception contributed to Congress's passage of the Sherman Anti-Trust Act in 1890."

There was an unusual move by corporate interests to claim the rights of "personhood"—as in "artificial person" (corporation)—seeking the same rights of the "natural person," living men and women such as the American people. Some historians describe what happened in this era as a corporate takeover, or "coup," as well as a conspiracy because it occurred based solely by a very peculiar legal precedent with no Supreme Court decision ever made on the subject.[1354] Nor was there legislation enacted by Congress that specifically gave equal status of rights and protection of the American people to corporations.

An American history textbook, *The Rise of American Civilization,* first published in 1927 by Columbia University history professor Charles Beard and women's suffragist Mary Beard, included the topic of a particular 1882 Supreme Court railroad case. The Beard's attributed conspiracy in this case that related to the intent of the language of the 14th Amendment because of suspicious circumstances around the paid testimony of a Congressman who served on the Joint Committee of Reconstruction. Former New York U.S. Representative Roscoe Conkling was now claiming that the Committee's intent of the word "person" that was included in the language of the Equal Protection clause of the 14th Amendment was intended not just for "natural persons" (i.e. black Americans) but for the benefit of "artificial persons" (corporations). [1355] Adding to the intrigue is that this former Congressman had become a railroad lawyer.[1356]

New York Congressman Roscoe Conkling (1829-1888)[1357]

It was 1937 when another historian and law librarian, Howard Jay Graham, considered the pre-eminent scholar on the Fourteenth Amendment, wrote a law review on the topic after conducting deep research through Congressional journals and other original source materials. The name of the review itself is thought-provoking, *The "Conspiracy Theory" of the Fourteenth Amendment,* as well as the fact that it shot holes in Conkling's testimony pertaining to the original intent of the Joint Committee of Reconstruction. The review ends with Graham's personal conclusion that Conkling probably perjured himself for the benefit of his railroad friends.[1358]

The point we wish to convey is that corporations became very powerful in the Gilded Age. Corporations went from being a legal fiction used to establish colleges and businesses for trade purposes to being positioned as the most powerful force in American politics.[1359] The Supreme Court and Congress allowed corporations overreach and powers that the American People, "We the People," no longer experience. Scandals, corruption, bribes, graft, appointments to lucrative government offices and increased government salaries, would become the norm in the Corporate UNITED STATES.[1360] [1361]

Critical in our understanding of America's Truthful history is the fact that secret societies would also evolve with a modern presence in American government while working in the shadows and monopolizing industries steering the *New World* toward globalism. Particularly, the Trilateral Commission as well as "the granddaddy of modern secret societies"—the Council on Foreign Relations. These organizations, filled with secret society members of other various occult organizations, continued forward into the "Progressive Era" selecting in place politicians who loved Darwin more than Almighty Creator God, Party to the covenant of the *Declaration of Independence.*[1362]

Caption: "THAT SALARY GRAB. 'You took it.'"

Cartoon showing politicians pointing fingers at each other.
December 27, 1873
Frank Leslie's Illustrated Newspaper

The Salary Grab Act was passed by the (*de facto*) U.S. Congress on March 3, 1873. The effect of the Act was to double the salary of the President (at the time would equate to $50,000) the day before the second-term inauguration of President Ulysses S. Grant. Doubled salaries were also in place for Supreme Court Justices. Hidden in the salary increases was also a fifty-percent increase for members of Congress, conveniently retroactive to the beginning of their just-ending term.

Public outcry led Congress to rescind the congressional salary increase.[1363]

The *Progressive* movement in America dawned with the 20th century. Animated by a common dedication to statism (the practice or doctrine of giving a centralized government control over economic planning and policy),[1364] and influenced by the (evolution) ideas of Darwin, self-identified Progressives believed that the problems associated with the urban and industrial revolutions required government to assume a more active and powerful role in the lives of citizens. The Progressive movement was espoused with those who did not acknowledge or desire to live in covenant with the *Supreme Judge of the World*, or the *Great Governor of the Universe*.

de facto Corporate UNITED STATES Presidents
Theodore Roosevelt,[1365] 1901–1909 (left), William Howard Taft,[1366] 1909–1913 (center), and Woodrow Wilson,[1367] 1913–1921 (right)

The *Progressive Era* was a period of widespread social activism and political reform across America, from the 1890s to the 1920s. These men were the main *Progressive Era* presidents; their administrations saw intense social and political change in American society.[1368]

As the Northern churches lost their Biblical basis and began to absorb Transcendentalist principles of Emerson, Thoreau, and others, Christianity became leavened with a philosophy based upon morality without God. It was based on an optimistic view that man could become good without a personal relationship with God and emanated nothing more than religious hypocrisy.[1369]

In this era of "ear tickling,"[1370] certain religious-type words were cleverly used in political speeches to give appearance of acknowledging Almighty God, however, lacked spiritual "substance." An intimacy with the Word of God, discernment by His Spirit, and hindsight will reveal a shift in spiritual climate.

In the early 1900s America, via the Corporate UNITED STATES, became a secular nation that disclaimed the Creator as the Originator of all human rights, as declared in the *Declaration of Independence*.

This brought about a secularized religion in the North and Providence saw that the South obtained its desire for prosperity which came about through the *Federal Reserve Act* passed in 1913.[1371]

Professor Paul Moreno, Hillsdale College, the William and Berniece Grewcock Chair in Constitutional history and director of academic programs at the College's Kirby Center, on "Progressivism:"

"Animated by the ideas of historicism and relativism, which dominated the intellectual climate of the 19th century, Progressives argued that truths are contingent on a specific time and context – rather than permanent and enduring for all people and all ages. <u>The principles and institutions of government must change and evolve over time in tandem with social and scientific changes.</u>

"Woodrow Wilson echoed these sentiments, declaring, 'All that Progressives ask or desire is […] to **interpret the Constitution according to the Darwinian principle**; all they ask is recognition of the fact that a nation is a living thing and not a machine.' <u>Rejecting the timeless principles of the Declaration of Independence</u>, Progressives such as Wilson, Teddy Roosevelt, and Supreme Court Justices Louis Brandeis and Oliver Wendell Holmes <u>believed that the Constitution's arrangement of government, based upon the separation of powers, checks and balances, and federalism, only impeded effective government.</u>

"Progressives argued that for a truly just and democratic government, the business of politics – namely, elections – should be separated from the administration of government. Government would be overseen by nonpartisan and therefore politically neutral experts. The president, as the only nationally elected public official, best embodies the will of the whole people. Therefore, he has a legislative mandate to create administrative agencies and government aid programs to improve the lives of citizens."[1372] [emphasis added]

Proverbs 14:34 ~ "Righteousness exalteth a nation: but sin is a reproach to any people."

James Wilson, U.S. Supreme Court Justice [1373]

We must consider the words of wisdom of James Wilson (1742-1798), Signer of the *Constitution*; U. S. Supreme Court Justice,

"Human law must rest its authority ultimately upon the authority of that law which is divine. . . . Far from being rivals or enemies, <u>religion and law are twin sisters, friends, and mutual assistants</u>. Indeed, these two sciences run into each other."[1374] [emphasis added]

Just before the Progressive era manifested, U.S. Supreme Court Justice David Josiah Brewer (1837-1910), had given the court's opinion in the 1892 case of *Church of the Holy Trinity v. United States*. In opening he stated:

"<u>Our laws and our institutions must necessarily be based upon and embody the teachings of the Redeemer of mankind. It is impossible that it should be otherwise; and in this sense and to this extent our civilization and our institutions are emphatically Christian.</u> …This is historically true. From the discovery of this continent to the present hour, there is a single voice making this affirmation."[1375] [emphasis added]

Justice David Josiah Brewer [1376]

Justice Brewer continued in the court's opinion by citing several facts in historical government beginning with reciting the commission of Christopher Columbus through (then) current times, claiming that the Christian religion is "… part of the common law…not Christianity with an established church…but Christianity with **liberty of conscience** to all men."[1377]

1 Timothy 1:6-11 ~

> *…From which some having swerved have turned aside unto vain jangling; Desiring to be teachers of the law; understanding neither what they say, nor whereof they affirm. <u>But we know that the law is good, if a man use it lawfully; Knowing this, that the law is not made for a righteous man, but for the lawless and disobedient, for the ungodly and for sinners</u>, for unholy and profane, for murderers of fathers and murderers of mothers, for manslayers, For whoremongers, for them that defile themselves with mankind, for menstealers, for liars, for perjured persons, and if there be any other thing that is contrary to sound doctrine; According to the glorious gospel of the blessed God, which was committed to my trust.* [emphasis added]

Justice John Marshall Harlan [1378]

In their Progressive quest, the "cunning, ambitious, and unprincipled men" managed to secret their luciferian Counter-Reformation *New World Order* agenda into the nation by means of disguising the *de facto* Corporate UNITED STATES while masquerading as the American Republic. The undeniable fact that two governments exist in America is made clear by Supreme Court Justice Marshall Harlan in his dissenting opinion *Downes v. Bidwell*, 182 U.S. 244 (1901):

"The idea prevails with some-indeed, it found expression in arguments at the bar-that <u>we have in this country substantially or practically two national governments; one to be maintained under the Constitution [*de jure*], with all its restrictions; the other to be maintained by Congress [*defacto*], outside and independently of that instrument</u> by exercising such powers as other nations of the earth are accustomed to exercise."[1379] [emphasis added]

Cover of McGuffey's First Eclectic Reader, 1841 [1380]

In this Progressive era as the 20th century began, many classrooms started each day with the *Pledge of Allegiance*, a prayer and a reading from the Bible. Many churches turned their schools over to a State-run educational system. State-run schools continued to teach moral values using the *McGuffy Reader*[1381] with its Bible verses. America had one of the best school systems in the world. It began to change with the **Progressive** movement.

In 1925, when the newly formed *American Civil Liberties Union (ACLU)* offered to defend any teacher prosecuted under law for teaching the theory of evolution. A young Tennessee science teacher agreed to stand as a defendant to challenge the Tennessee State law.[1382]

Biblical creation had always been taught throughout America. Teaching the theory of evolution was against the Tennessee State law.

While the ACLU lost the case, it set in motion a re-evaluation in the teaching of science. <u>Within four decades the laws were reversed so that teaching Creation is now outlawed while teaching Evolution is mandatory</u>. By 1947 the ACLU was influential in using the court system to change school policy.

At this same juncture in the Progressive movement, the Corporate UNITED STATES began to generate debts via bonds etc., which came due in 1912. With banking and finance monopolized by a consortium of eight families, only four of which resided in the U.S., these families had bought-up and owned the bonds tied to the U.S. debt. Knowing the Corporate UNITED STATES was unable to make payment on the debt these families, affiliated in the Luciferian Illuminati organization,"[1383] made demands of payment. These families are the Goldman Sachs, Rockefellers, Lehmans and Kuhn Loebs of New York; the Rothschilds of Paris and London; the Warburgs of Hamburg; the Lazards of Paris; and the Israel Moses Seifs of Rome.[1384]

<u>These families settled the debt by receiving payment of ALL of the Corporate UNITED STATES' assets — and — for ALL of the assets of the Treasury of the United States</u>. In 1913, the Corporate UNITED STATES had no funds to carry out the necessary business needs of the government so they went to the same families, asked to borrow money, and were declined. Of particular interest is that the families had foreseen this situation and had, the previous year, finalized the creation of <u>a private corporation by the name "Federal Reserve Bank."</u> The Corporate UNITED STATES then formed a relationship with the *Federal Reserve Bank* whereby they could transact their business via <u>note</u> rather than with <u>money</u>.

On December 23, 1913, the *Federal Reserve Act*[1385] was passed by *de facto* Congress and signed into law by <u>Jesuit Coadjutor</u> President Woodrow Wilson[1386] in February, 1914. Just five senators passed this Act while the rest were home for the Christmas holiday. President Wilson did not even read this "routine banking bill" and later admitted that it was the greatest mistake of his career.

Signing of the Federal Reserve Act[1387]
Courtesy of Woodrow Wilson Presidential Library;
Painting by Wilbur G. Kurtz

PRESIDENT'S SIGNATURE ENACTS CURRENCY LAW

Wilson Declares It the First of Series of Constructive Acts to Aid Business.

Makes Speech to Group of Democratic Leaders.

Conference Report Adopted in Senate by Vote of 43 to 25.

Banks All Over the Country Hasten to Enter Federal Reserve System.

Gov-Elect Walsh Calls Passage of Bill A Fine Christmas Present.

WILSON SEES DAWN OF NEW ERA IN BUSINESS

Aims to Make Prosperity Free to Have Unimpeded Momentum.

HOME VIEWS OF CURRENCY ACT

FOUR PENS USED BY PRESIDENT

U.S. Newspaper, Dec. 24, 1913 [1388]
Woodrow Wilson signs
creation of the Federal Reserve

The following is a quote of *de facto* President Wilson after signing the *Federal Reserve Act* into law and as cited at Moneymasters.org, a well-known organization for its non-fiction, historical video documentary that traces the origins of the political power structure that rules our nation and the world today.[1389]

"I am a most unhappy man. I have unwittingly ruined my country. A great industrial nation is controlled by its system of credit. Our system of credit is concentrated. The growth of the nation, therefore, and all our activities are in the hands of a few men. We have come to be one of the worst ruled, one of the most completely controlled and dominated Governments in the civilized world no longer a Government by free opinion, no longer a Government by conviction and the vote of the majority, but a Government by the opinion and duress of a small group of dominant men."[1390]

The 1913 creation of "the Fed" fused the power of the eight Families to the military and diplomatic might of the *de facto* Corporate UNITED STATES' "government." If their overseas loans went unpaid, the Oligarchs could now deploy U.S. Marines to collect the debts. Morgan, Chase and Citibank formed an international lending syndicate.[1391]

This Act of the *de facto* Congress created and set-up the *Federal Reserve System*, the central banking system of the United States, and granted it the legal authority to issue *Federal Reserve Notes*, now commonly known as the U.S. Dollar, and Federal Reserve Bank Notes as legal tender.

The Act created a neo-Babylonian Empire in the modern world and put the American people into financial bondage to strategic bankers of Europe who controlled political leaders through the power of money.

Because the *de facto* Corporate UNITED STATES "government" gave away the right to create money to private banking interests, allowing them to create money out of nothing and loan it to the so-called "government" at interest, the American people are enslaved in debt that is impossible to satisfy while it continues to grow.

There is no logical reason why Congress should not have created the nation's money itself and spent it into circulation without interest—except for the purpose of another agenda. Instead the nation's trust has been blindly placed in carnally-minded men who represent private financial interests.[1392]

The relationship between the Corporate UNITED STATES and the *Federal Reserve* was one actually made between two private corporations, and did not involve government. The *Clearfield Doctrine* states:

"Governments descend to the level of a mere private corporation, and take on the characteristics of a mere private citizen...where private corporate commercial paper [Federal Reserve Notes] and securities [checks] is concerned. ... For purposes of suit, such corporations and individuals are regarded as entities entirely separate from government."[1393] [emphasis added]

What the *Clearfield Doctrine* is saying is that when private commercial paper is used by corporate government, then Government loses its sovereignty status and becomes no different than a mere private corporation.

As such, government (and their commercial judicial courts) then become bound by the rules and laws that govern private corporations which means that if they intend to compel an individual to some specific performance based upon its corporate statutes or corporation rules, then the government, like any private corporation, must be the "holder in due course" of a contract or other commercial agreement between it and the one upon whom demands for specific performance are made and further, the government must be willing to enter the contract or commercial agreement into evidence before trying to get the court to enforce <u>its demands, called statutes</u>.[1394]

That is where most people err in understanding the *Federal Reserve Banking System...* Again, it is not part of the Corporate UNITED STATES, but is a private corporation doing business with a private corporation. The private contracts that set the whole system up even recognize that if anything therein proposed is found illegal or impossible to perform, it is excluded from the agreements and the remaining elements remain in full force and effect.

The 16th Amendment of the Corporate UNITED STATES' constitution was passed by the *de facto* Congress on July 2, 1909 and ratified on February 3, 1913. It states:

> "The Congress shall have power to lay and collect <u>taxes on incomes</u>, from whatever source derived, without apportionment among the several States, and without regard to any census or enumeration." [emphasis added]

This was the first amendment to gain ratification in more than 40 years. The 16th Amendment in effect altered Article I, Section 9, Clause 4:[1395]

> "No capitation, or other direct, tax shall be laid, unless in proportion to the census or enumeration herein before directed to be taken."

Clearly understand that without providing lawful notice and full disclosure to the American people, the Corporate UNITED STATES adopted a counterfeit of the original *Constitution of the United States* as <u>its</u> operating document and was now "acting" as the operating government in America. With that understanding, we can now comprehend how it became possible for (*de facto*) Congress to amend <u>its</u> (Corporate) constitution and implement the modern income tax system. Americans have held considerable concern about and centered a good deal of focused energy on their income taxes ever since.

Tax protesters have challenged the *Internal Revenue Service* (IRS) tax collection system based on the effect of the 16th Amendment having altered Article I, Section 9 of the *Constitution*. However, in light of the fact that the Corporate UNITED STATES initially created their (counterfeit) constitution by simply drafting and adopting it the same as other corporations, such is the nature of corporate enactments.

Again, for the importance of notation in separating the fraudulent *de facto* Corporate UNITED STATES from the *de jure* American Republic, this Amendment has nothing to do with the original *Constitution of the United States*. The Supreme Court ruled that the 16th Amendment did nothing that was not already done other than to make plain and clear the right of the (Corporate) United States to tax corporations. That is correct considering that the IRS was created under the authority of the *de facto* Corporate UNITED STATES.

Perhaps it is considered as a memorial to President Abraham Lincoln that the date of his death would be set by the Jesuits to correspond with April 15th as the day all "taxpayers" are required to have made their *"annual confessions"* by filing their income tax returns with their Internal Revenue Service (IRS).[1396]

This 16th Amendment appears to work in-hand with the *Federal Reserve Act* that created a Central Bank that consolidated (the unlawful and unconstitutional) banking practices into a single private banking system through which the American economy and government could be controlled and managed from behind the scenes. This is what turned Babylon from a mere "country" into an "empire" in the modern era.[1397]

On May 13, 1913, the Congress of the *de facto* Corporate UNITED STATES passed its 17th Amendment, of which was ratified on April 8, 1913. This Amendment would be a violation of the original *Constitution of the United States* as it forbids Congress from even discussing the matter of where Senators are elected, which is the subject matter of this Amendment.

According to the United States Supreme Court, for Congress to propose such an Amendment they would first have to pass an amendment that gave them the authority to discuss the matter. The *Constitution of the United States* at Article I Section 3, Clause 1 states:

> The Senate of the United States shall be composed of two Senators from each State, <u>chosen by the legislature thereof</u>, for six Years; and each Senator shall have one vote.[1398]

The 17th Amendment to the *de facto* Corporate UNITED STATES constitution:

> The Senate of the United States shall be composed of two Senators from each State, <u>elected by the people thereof,</u> for six years; and each Senator shall have one vote. The electors in each State shall have the qualifications requisite for electors of the most numerous branch of the State legislatures.
>
> When vacancies happen in the representation of any State in the Senate, the executive authority of such State shall issue writs of election to fill such vacancies: Provided, That the legislature of any State may empower the executive thereof to make temporary appointments until the people fill the vacancies by election as the legislature may direct.
>
> This amendment shall not be so construed as to affect the election or term of any Senator chosen before it becomes valid as part of the Constitution.[1399]

Each State, regardless of population, gets two seats in the Senate. Each senator's term lasts six years. In the *de jure* original *Constitution of the United States*, senators were not elected by the people but were instead chosen by their State legislatures. By the turn of the 20th century, many of the reform-minded citizens of the Progressive Era verbalized widespread accusations that this system of "indirect election" led to corruption in political machines manipulating Senate elections.

Some "cunning, ambitious, and unprincipled" individuals sought to literally buy a seat in the Senate by bribing State legislators. The 17th Amendment, a significant *Progressive Era* reform passed in 1913, allowed for the direct election of senators by the people.[1400]

1904 Political cartoon showing a Standard Oil tank as an octopus with many tentacles wrapped around the steel, copper, and shipping industries, as well as a state house, the U.S. Capitol, and one tentacle reaching for the White House. [1401]

Illustrated in *Puck* magazine, v. 56, no. 1436 (Sept. 7, 1904).

The Founding Fathers were Divinely inspired in writing the format and specifics with checks and balances in this sacred (original) government operating document. It is absurd to even suggest that if Senators chosen by their State legislatures could be bought-off, that Senators that are elected (or shall we in actuality say, "selected") in a popular election fueled by money interests and bought and paid-for by campaigns, wouldn't be immorally motivated as well.

Accordingly, in 1914, the freshman class and all Senators that successfully ran for reelection in 1913 by popular vote were seated in the Corporate UNITED STATES Senate Corporate-capacity only. As a matter of point for comparison sake, IF this had been the *de jure* government of the American Republic, their respective seats from their States would be considered to have remained vacant because neither the State Senates nor the State Governors appointed new Senators to replace them as required by the original *de jure Constitution* for placement of a national Senator.

In 1917, the *de facto* Corporate UNITED STATES entered *World War I* and passed the *Trading with the Enemies Act* which defined, regulated, and punished trading with enemies, who were then required by that Act to be licensed by the government to do business.

In 1918, *de facto* President Woodrow Wilson was reelected by the Electoral College, however, we point out again that this event took place within the Corporate UNITED STATES. Had it been the *de jure* (lawful) American Republic, the Electoral College elections would have required vote-confirmation by the original constitutional properly organized/elected Senate in Congress.

With the Corporate UNITED STATES, only Corporate Senators participated in the Electoral College vote-confirmation. Therefore, if this were indeed the legitimate original constitutional government of the American Republic, President Wilson was not constitutionally confirmed into office for his second term as President of the *United States of America.*

For the sake of pointing out the two very distinct and separate entities — the *de jure* American Republic and the *de facto* Corporate UNITED STATES — we make note of the operational "government" error in law if it had indeed had been the American Republic. Having established this point, it's clear that President Wilson was then in fact seated in the *de facto* Corporate UNITED STATES Presidential/CEO-capacity.

The *de jure* (lawful) American Republic's government seats indeed had been vacated and the American people did not seat any *de jure* constitutional government officers in this corporate entity.

In 1933, the *de facto* Corporate UNITED STATES became "bankrupt" as declared by President Franklin D. Roosevelt in various Executive Orders (6073,[1402] 6102,[1403] 6111,[1404] 6260[1405]), also recognized and acknowledged in the 1973 Senate Report 93-549,[1406] and then forced what was called "a banking holiday" in order to exchange money-backed[1407] Federal Reserve Notes (FRNs) with "legal tender"[1408] Federal Reserve Notes.

March 4, 1933, President Franklin D. Roosevelt Orders a 4-Day Bank Holiday [1409]

Accordingly, the *Trading with the Enemies Act* was adjusted to recognize the people of the United States as enemies of the Corporate UNITED STATES.

De facto President Franklin D. Roosevelt,[1410] 32nd U.S. President, 32nd degree Freemason,[1411] and member of the secret society *Skull and Bones*, as well as a member of the *Council on Foreign Relations*, is known as having achieved the greatest <u>progress</u> for socialism in his administration (1933-1945), particularly with his *New Deal* program. Noteworthy is there was a general consensus among Americans that a vast underground horde of communists was working to overthrow the government through subversive means. Following World War II, socialism was equated with communism.

Outside of modern history no president has been so criticized as a socialist, communist, and traitor to the American system than Franklin Delanore Roosevelt. Today these same programs are among the nation's most widely accepted and popular, such as Social Security, mandatory bank-deposit insurance, and regulation of securities sales.

President Franklin D. Roosevelt in
Freemason regalia
at the initiation ceremony for his sons James
and Franklin, Jr.
at the Architect Lodge in Manhattan on
November 7, 1935 [1412]
Published in German Newspapers

Franklin Delano Roosevelt, 1933 [1413]

FDR made two powerful statements when he said, "Presidents are selected, not elected," and "In politics, nothing happens by accident. If it happens, you can bet it was planned that way."[1414]

Of numerous treasonous acts having been committed by FDR, a <u>few</u> include:

- On March 9, 1933, the United States was declared as bankrupt by Executive Orders and the governors of the then 48 States pledged the "full faith and credit" of their States, including the citizenry, as collateral for loans of credit from *the Federal Reserve System.*

- On April 5, 1933 President Franklin D. Roosevelt signed Executive Order 6102,[1415] [1416] "forbidding the hoarding of gold coin, gold bullion, and gold certificates within the continental United States."[1417] Where even the *de facto* Corporate UNITED STATES constitution enumerates that only gold and silver coin may be used as tender in payment of debts, FDR and "the best Congress that money can buy" now confiscated every gold coin, bar, or certificate and required the American people to turn in their gold to the Federal Government or else they would face a fine of $10,000 or 10 years in jail. The amount of the fine would equate in value to approximately $177,900 in today's currency.[1418]

- The people were allowed to keep a small amount or some rare coins; those that did give up their gold received $20/oz. Gold as legal money disappeared in the United States, paving the way for the *de facto* "government" to engage in near-unconstrained debasement of the currency.

- On June 5, 1933, the *de facto* Congress passed House Joint Resolution (HJR) 192.[1419] Upon being passed, HJR 192 was immediately implemented to suspend the gold standard and abrogate the gold clause in the *de facto* Corporate UNITED STATES' constitution. Since that time, Americans have not had the ability to <u>lawfully</u> pay a debt or <u>lawfully</u> own anything. <u>The only provision and ability is to tender in transfer of debts, with the debt being perpetual. The suspension of the gold standard, and prohibition against paying debts, removed the substance for the (*de facto*) constitutional law to operate on, and created a void in law.</u> This substance was replaced with a "public national credit system" where <u>debt is "legal tender" money.</u>

  The day after President Roosevelt signed the resolution, the treasury offered the public new government securities, minus the traditional "payable in gold" clause. HJR 192 stipulates that one cannot demand a certain form of currency that they want to receive if it is dollar-for-dollar. The *Federal Reserve Banking System* workbook on bank reserves and deposit expansion, "Modern Money Mechanics,"[1420] <u>defines all currency as the American peoples' credit, referred to as "monetized debt."</u>

- In 1921, the *de facto* federal *Sheppard-Towner Maternity Act*[1421] was passed creating birth "registration" which led to what we now know as the "birth certificate." It was known as the "Maternity Act" and was sold to the American people as a law that would reduce maternal and infant mortality, protect the health of mothers and infants, as well as for other purposes. One of those "other purposes" provided for the establishment of a federal bureau designed to cooperate with State agencies in the overseeing of its operations and expenditures. This can now be seen as the <u>first attempt</u> of "government by appointment," or cooperation of (*de facto*) <u>State governments to aid the (*de facto*) Federal Government in usurping the legislative process of the several States</u> as exists today through the federal grant in aid to the States programs.[1422]

  Prior to 1921 the records of births and names of children were entered into family Bibles, as were the records of marriages and deaths. These records were readily accepted by both the family and the law as "official" records. <u>Since 1921, the American people have been registering the births and names of their children with the government of the State in which they are born, even though there is no federal law requiring it. The State claims an interest in every child within its jurisdiction,</u> telling the parents that registering their child's birth through the birth certificate serves as proof that the child was born within territories of the United States, thereby making the child a United States citizen. (One who contemplates will consider this a thought-provoking 14th Amendment jurisdiction trick.)

- Since the (*de facto*) Corporate UNITED STATES went bankrupt in 1933, <u>all new money has to be borrowed into existence. All (*de facto*) States started issuing serial-numbered "warehouse receipts"</u>

certificates for births and marriages in order to pledge the people as collateral against those loans and municipal bonds taken out with the Federal Reserve banks. The "full faith and credit" of the American people is said to be that which back the nation's debt. That simply means the American people's ability to labor (work) and pay back that debt.

In order to catalog its laborers, the government needed an efficient, methodical system of tracking its chattel property to that end. Humans today are looked upon merely as resources: "human resources." The people are resources to the government; their birth certificates are a security on the New York Stock Exchange.[1423] All birth certificates in America are printed on full-color security paper. At the bottom, there are a series of red numbers printed on the right hand corner of the birth certificate, that reflect a security stock exchange number on the World Stock Exchange, in which the American people are worth money to the International Bank that bought the "corporate government" in the 1930's.[1424] The American people have become owned property, or "chattel slaves."

For certain, at least in the 1950s, Certificates of Live Birth included a registered number for the newborn child and the mother's name was required under the item of "Informant."

On a 1957 Certificate of Live Birth
the mother is categorized in Item 18 as "Informant."

Jesuit Father also known an "Colonel" Edward Mandell House (1858-1938)[1425] was a powerful American diplomat, politician, and presidential advisor to Woodrow Wilson, commonly known as "Colonel" House, although he had no military experience. He was a highly influential back-stage politician in Texas before becoming a key supporter of the presidential bid of Woodrow Wilson in 1912.

Woodrow Wilson offered Mr. House any Presidential cabinet position he wanted except Secretary of State, however, House declined as he preferred to work in the shadows as the president's most trusted advisor.[1426]

It was a peculiar role that President Wilson had delegated upon his intimate friend, Col. Edward Mandel House. Colonel House was a peculiar individual. The predominant opinion in Wilson's Washington in those days is suggested by the extraordinary influence House wielded.

Never elected to any office, never confirmed by (the *de facto*) Congress, Colonel House nevertheless exercised more power in America than anyone except the President himself. Wilson once went so far as to say, "Mr. House is my second personality. His thoughts and mine are one."[1427]

Edward Mandell House had close contacts with both J.P. Morgan and the old banking families of Europe, including the Rothschild's.[1428] It was House who persuaded President Wilson to sign the Federal Reserve Act.[1429]

Col. Edward Mandel House [1430]

Although House did not hold office, he was Wilson's chief advisor on European politics and diplomacy during World War I (1914-18) and at the Paris Peace Conference of 1919. In early 1919, House along with Wilson, were part of the five-man American delegation to the high-level negotiations of the *League of Nations* (which is now equated to the United Nations[1431]). The Jesuits' goal in these negotiations for the post WWI *League of Nations* was an attempt in setting-up a One-World government from which they could control the world.[1432]

President Wilson had to leave these very important meetings in Paris and in his place entrusted House to close the negotiations. Quite interesting and not long after, Wilson ended his relationship with House and several other top advisors as he believed that they deceived and betrayed him in the negotiated settlement agreements of the *League of Nations*.[1433] After that time, House never again acted as the chief U.S. delegate, and the intimate relationship between House and Wilson quickly dissolved, never recovering.[1434]

Colonel House is accredited in giving a very detailed outline of the plans to be implemented to enslave the American people. In a private meeting with Woodrow Wilson (*de facto* President 1913 – 1921) he is quoted in the following, of which we exhort careful attention to the details:

"Very soon, every American will be required to register their biological property [that's you and your children] in a national system designed to keep track of the people and that will operate under the ancient system of pledging. By such methodology, we can compel people to submit to our agenda, which will affect our security as a charge back for our fiat paper currency.

Every American will be forced to register or suffer being able to work and earn a living. They will be our chattels [properties] and we will hold the security interest over them forever, by operation of the law merchant [judges in the de facto court system] under the scheme of secured transactions. Americans, by unknowingly or unwittingly delivering the bills of lading [Birth Certificates] to us will be rendered bankrupt and insolvent, secured by their pledges.

They will be stripped of their rights and given a commercial value designed to make us a profit and they will be none the wiser, for not one man in a million could ever figure our plans and, if by accident one or two should figure it out, we have in our arsenal plausible deniability. After all, this is the only logical way to fund government, by floating liens and debts to the registrants in the form of benefits and privileges. This will inevitably reap us huge profits beyond our wildest expectations and leave every American a contributor to this fraud, which we will call "Social Insurance." Without realizing it, every American will unknowingly be our servant, however begrudgingly. The people will become helpless and without any hope for their redemption and we will employ the high office [presidency] of our dummy corporation [Corporate UNITED STATES] to foment this plot against America."[1435] [emphasis added]

In 1912, House published what is viewed as a strange novel, "Philip Dru, Administrator: A Story of Tomorrow," which portrays much about the progressive mentality of the period.[1436] In this story, Americans had become virtual serfs of the barons of industry and finance.

Philip Dru, a brilliant young West Point officer turned social worker and writer, decides to fight against the corrupt and selfish cabal oppressing the masses: "He comes panoplied in justice and with the light of reason in his eyes. He comes as the advocate of equal opportunity, and he comes with the power to enforce his will."

Dru leads the people against the selfish capitalists and their minions, and after a brief bloody, cleansing (civil) war—the last war required before justice prevails forever—he sets out to remake America. He appoints himself dictator, writes a new constitution, and creates a welfare state. Then Dru turns to world affairs, and, together with the leaders of the other powers, establishes a permanent order of peace and justice.

This story that was authored by President Wilson's proclaimed "second personality," projects a phenomenon of déjà vu while reviewing the plans of the sons of Satan and their occult agenda.

We continue with the list of a few of the treasonous acts committed by *de facto* President Franklin D. Roosevelt:

- By completing a birth certificate application, "confession" is made by the signer as being a "legal fiction" subject of the Corporate UNITED STATES, 14th Amendment citizen, "U.S. Citizen" that waves their rights in favor of State-issued privileges. The "legal fiction" is also known as a "strawman"[1437] where the living individual is made into a legal "fiction" or corporation using their name in all-capital-letters.[1438]   There is much to be said on this subject that tends to shock the conscience while realizing the sinister evil that has been masterminded by wicked, misguided men —"cunning, ambitious, and unprincipled men."

- The perversion of sourcing the sacred joining of a man and a woman in marriage into a commercial system of State-issued privileges through "marriage licenses" whereby (*de facto*) courts, which are actually private corporations, presume the right to trespass on families and kidnap children.[1439] This perverted deception in the world we live in but haven't known about is basically viewed in legal finance as the merger of two corporations through the (*de facto*) State and by legal license, anything produced out of the merger-marriage becomes property of the State.

Appellate Court of Illinois, NO. 5-97-0108 (1997):

> "Marriage is a civil contract to which there are three parties-the husband, the wife and the state."

Van Koten v. Van Koten. 154 N.E. 146 (1926):

> "…When two people decide to get married, they are required to first procure a license from the State. If they have children of this marriage, <u>they are required by the State to submit their children</u> to certain things, such as school attendance and vaccinations. Furthermore, if at some time in the future the couple decides the marriage is not working, they must petition the State for a divorce. Marriage is a three-party contract between the man, the woman, and the State"

Linneman v. Linneman, 1 Ill. App. 2d 48, 50, 116 N.E.2d 182, 183 (1953), citing Van Koten v. Van Koten, 323 Ill. 323, 326, 154 N.E. 146 (1926)

"The State represents the public interest in the institution of marriage."

Linneman, 1 Ill. App. 2d at 50, 116 N.E.2d at 183 (1953):

"This public interest is what allows the State to intervene in certain situations to protect the interests of members of the family. The State is like a silent partner in the family who is not active in the everyday running of the family but becomes active and exercises its power and authority only when necessary to protect some important interest of family life. Taking all of this into consideration, the question no longer is whether the State has an interest or place in disputes such as the one at bar, but it becomes a question of timing and necessity."

Also, this same case law states...

"The state has a wide range of power for limiting parental freedom and authority in things affecting the child's welfare... In fact, the entire familial relationship involves the State."

The American people, inclusive of those in personal relationship with Almighty God through His Son, Jesus the Christ, are at risk of losing their posterity,[1440] their children, that the Word of God describes as their "inheritance of the Lord." [1441]

- On August 14, 1935, FDR signed into (*de facto*) law the *Social Security Act*,[1442] which was created to provide the Corporate UNITED STATES the "excess capital" needed to at least start paying some of the interest it owed in bankruptcy. Citizens were not given full disclosure when advised that they were required by law to enlist with the Social Security program. "Marketed" by the government to its constituents as a personal benefit of good, in actuality, the individual was used as a means to create a Trust account for the express purpose of generating Beneficiary funds to the (*de facto*) United States General Trust Fund (GTF). The truth is that tremendous funding has gone through this Trust Fund for the benefit of the Corporate UNITED STATES, not that of the individual.[1443]

Signing of the Social Security Act[1444]

248

Deuteronomy 28: 15 ~

> *But it shall come to pass, if thou wilt not hearken unto the voice of the Lord thy God, to observe to do all his commandments and his statutes which I command thee this day; that all these curses shall come upon thee, and overtake thee…*

Chapter Sixteen

The Moral and Spiritual Disintegration of America

Continuing on in the story of the Great Conspiracy and Great Deception... In 1944, under the *Bretton Woods Agreement,* the Corporate UNITED STATES was quit-claimed to the *International Monetary Fund (IMF).* The IMF was granted drawing account access from the United States Treasury in exchange for the *de facto* Corporate UNITED STATES president's acquiring control over the governors and general managers of the IMF, respectively, <u>now making the Corporate UNITED STATES a **foreign-controlled** private corporation.</u>[1445]

Historical marker of the location of the Bretton Woods Monetary Conference, 1944 [1446]

This action was codified into Corporate UNITED STATES' law as United States Code (USC) Title 22 § 286, also known as the "Bretton Woods Agreements Act":

"§ 286. Acceptance of membership by the United States in International Monetary Fund. "The President is hereby authorized to accept membership for the United States in the International Monetary Fund (hereinafter referred to as the "Fund"), and in the International Bank for Reconstruction and Development (hereinafter referred to as the "Bank"), provided for by the Articles of Agreement of the Fund and the Articles of Agreement of the Bank as set forth in the Final Act of the United Nations Monetary and Financial Conference dated July 22, 1944, and deposited in the archives of the Department of State. (July 31, 1945, ch. 339, § 2, 59 Stat. 512.)

"Other provisions:
Par value modification. For the Congressional direction that the Secretary of the Treasury maintain the value in terms of gold of the Inter-American Development Bank's holdings of United States dollars following the establishment of a par value of the dollar at $38 for a fine troy ounce of gold pursuant to the Par Value Modification Act and for the authorization of the appropriations necessary to provide such maintenance of value, see 31 USC § 449a."

Note: As a means to cover-up the *Bretton Woods Agreements* (BWA) quitclaim of the (*de facto*) United States Government and control to the *IMF*, the *de facto* United States Congress abolished the references in the *United States Code* referring to the BWA. Other than removing such references that pertain to abolishment of the United States, the effect of the *Bretton Woods Agreement* (BWA) remained the same.

Lyndon B. Johnson, *de facto* U.S. Senator (Texas) and Majority Leader, 1950s[1447]

Churches in America have been manipulated to think they must avoid payment of taxes to the IRS by organizing as "501c3 tax-exempt religious organizations."[1448] In 1954, *de facto* Congress approved an Amendment proposed by then high-level Freemason Senator Lyndon B. Johnson[1449] to change the U.S. tax code to prohibit tax-exempt organizations from endorsing or opposing political candidates.

Essentially the result was a "gag order" on the pulpit[1450] in not bringing "politics" before the people while preaching on sin and immorality. We contemplate that it was also a means of ensuring that there would be no repeat in history of a "Black Robe Regiment,"[1451] patriot preachers of the Revolutionary era.

James Caldwell (1734-1781), was a Presbyterian minister at Elizabeth, New Jersey and one of many clergymen who actively participated in the patriot cause of the Revolutionary War. On June 23, 1780, at the battle of Springfield, New Jersey, when his company ran out of wadding for loading their muskets, Rev. Caldwell bolted into a nearby church, scooped-up as many Isaac Watts' hymnals as he could carry while distributing them to the troops and shouting "Now, boys, give 'em Watts! Give 'em Watts!" Caldwell and his wife were both killed before the war ended.[1452]

Rev. James Caldwell [1453]

Churches are now set-up as corporations with fiscal reporting responsibilities to the government.[1454] Ministers of the Word of God are required "by law" to become licensed (asking permission of the government) to marry people before God. People used to simply record their nuptials in their family Bible; the *de facto* Corporate UNITED STATES now requires a license (permission or privilege) be granted and obtained in order to be allowed to marry.

When an organization such as a church files an IRS 501c3 application, it is giving its consent to be governed by all applicable statutes and 501c3 rules pertaining to Title 26 of the US Internal Revenue Code. A church which has filed a 501c3 application has agreed to relinquish its constitutional right to practice religion without government interference. So, in effect, the church disestablishes its religious nature (with Jesus Christ as its Head) and instead becomes a secular agency of government policy. One of the implications directs an inability to speak (or preach the counsel of God) while also consenting to government dictates by silence. The 501c3 church can only operate under the "color" of religion—a very serious Biblical matter of Divine condemnation.[1455]

The Word of God already establishes that His ministries are tax exempt:

Ezra 7:24 ~ You are also to know that you have no authority to impose taxes, tribute or duty on any of the priests, Levites, musicians, gatekeepers, temple servants or other workers at this house of God.

In 1962, the *de facto* States were forced to carry out their business dealings in terms of Federal Reserve Notes (foreign notes), which violates the *Constitution* as enumerated in the national (Article I, Section 10, Clause 1), and State constitutions.
The *Constitution of the United States*, Article 1, Section 10, Clause 1:

No State shall enter into any Treaty, Alliance, or Confederation; grant Letters of Marque and Reprisal; coin Money; emit Bills of Credit; <u>make any Thing but gold and silver Coin a Tender in Payment of Debts</u>; pass any Bill of Attainder, ex post facto Law, or Law impairing the Obligation of Contracts, or grant any Title of Nobility.[1456]

Out of that necessity, the *de facto* States began protecting themselves from the people by forming corporations just as the Corporate UNITED STATES. **Accordingly, those newly formed corporate State administrations began adopting the Corporate UNITED STATES' suggested Uniform Codes and licensing structures[1457] that allowed better and more powerful control over the American people.**
The original *de jure* jurisdiction of government of this nation had no constitutional capacity to do such a thing. The States' constitutions were lawfully required to be approved by Congress before they became a State and <u>could not be repugnant to the national *Constitution*</u>.[1458]
The original *de jure Constitution* secures that the government does not govern the people. Rather, <u>the people govern themselves</u> in accordance with the limits of Law as it is derived from the people through the *Constitution*, which the people granted to the *Constitution* as "the supreme law of the land." The people govern themselves. Self-governance is the foundational nature of our constitutional Republic.
By 1972, every *de facto* State government in the union of States formed such private corporations ("Corporation State of _____"), in accordance with the International Monetary Fund's (IMF's) admonition. The American people ceased to have any ability to seat original *de jure* jurisdiction government officials in their *de facto* State government seats.
In 1947 the *de facto* U.S. Supreme Court was asked to interpret the First Amendment's prohibition on laws "respecting an establishment of religion" in *Everson v. Board of Education*. Citing reference to President Thomas Jefferson's responding letter to the Danbury Baptists in 1802 with a <u>misused metaphor</u> of the mythical "wall of separation," the justices famously declared, the First Amendment "was intended to erect 'a wall of separation between church and State'...[that] must be kept high and impregnable. We could not approve the slightest breach."[1459]
<u>This figure of speech</u>, which has since been cited "over, often, and loud enough" as though it were *de jure* constitutional law and as the organizing theme of church-state jurisprudence, <u>is nowhere to be found in the *Constitution*</u>. The original intent of Founding Father Thomas Jefferson's letter to the Danbury Baptist Association of Danbury, Connecticut[1460] was to calm their fears that Congress was not in the process of choosing any one single Christian denomination to be the "state" denomination, as was the case with the Anglican Church in England. In his letter to the Danbury Baptists, who had experienced harsh

persecution for their faith, Jefferson borrowed phraseology from the famous Baptist minister Roger Williams who said, "…the hedge or wall of separation between the garden of the church and the wilderness of the world, God hath ever broke down the wall…"[1461] Jefferson's letter included:

Portrait of Thomas Jefferson, 1800 [1462]

"Believing with you that religion is a matter which lies solely between man and his God, that he owes account to none other for faith or his worship, that <u>the legislative powers of government reach actions only, and not opinions</u>, I contemplate with solemn reverence that act of the whole American people which declared that their legislature should 'make no law respecting an establishment of religion, or prohibiting the free exercise thereof,' thus building a wall of separation between Church and State."[1463]

This personal letter reassured the Baptists that the government's hands were tied from interfering with, or in any way controlling, the affairs or decisions of the churches in America.

Serving as a U.S. Minister in France at the time, Jefferson did not sign the *Constitution* nor was he present at either of the Constitutional Conventions. When the First Amendment and religious freedom were debated in the first session of Congress in 1789, he was not present to hear the discussion of the Fathers regarding the First Amendment; he had to rely on secondhand information to learn what had transpired.

His letter to the Danbury Baptists, written 13 years <u>after</u> the First Amendment, renders these current day *de facto* U.S. Supreme Court rulings and political references to being seriously erroneous in claiming Jefferson's "first-hand" reflection of the intent of the constitutional delegates.

The Old House of Representatives [1464]

"Church services were held from 1807 to 1857 in what is now called 'Statuary Hall.' The first services in the Capitol, held when the government moved to Washington City in the autumn of 1800, were conducted in the 'hall' of the House in the north wing of the building. In 1801 the House moved to temporary quarters in the south wing, called the 'Oven,' which it vacated in 1804, returning to the north wing for three years. Services were conducted in the House until after the Civil War. The Speaker's podium was used as the preacher's pulpit."

It is significant to note that the United States Capitol regularly served as a church building; a practice that began even before Congress officially moved into the building and lasted until well after the Civil War. Thomas Jefferson was a regular attendee at these church services throughout his service as Vice President and then President, as were many other statesmen. In fact, he was in attendance at a church service held at the Capitol building just two days after he penned his letter to the Danbury Baptists.[1465]

School opens with prayer, 1940 [1466]

The misguided and misinterpreted 1947 *de facto* U.S. Supreme Court ruling set the tone for what came next. On June 25, 1962, the *de facto* U.S. Supreme Court struck down voluntary school prayer. Prayer in schools prior to 1962 was common in school districts throughout America. Some teachers led in spontaneous prayer, simply expressing their thoughts and desires while others implemented structured prayers, such as the Lord's Prayer or others approved by local school boards. New York students prayed each day:

"Almighty God, we acknowledge our dependence on Thee and beg Thy blessing over us, our parents, our teachers, and our nation."

It was this simple prayer which came under fire and went to the *de facto* U.S. Supreme Court for the landmark decision in *Engels v. Vitale*.[1467]

Statistical evidence shows what has happened in our country since this landmark *de facto* U.S. Supreme Court ruling began this separation of religious principles from our educational system, government, and public affairs. The downward slide in behavior started about the time of this ruling.

The decision to remove prayer from the school system was an effort to steal the birthright of the American people in their covenant with Almighty God as well as the removing of the pillars of our country's foundation—religion and morality—that our first President, George Washington, had emphasized as part of America's foundation.

There was <u>progressive</u> effort to replace America's founding values and Christian Biblical worldview in the classrooms with <u>Darwinian</u> materials on the "<u>theory</u>" of evolution and the <u>religion</u> of secular humanism which has overtaken the mindset of society through school administrators, teachers, professors, legislators and judges throughout the country.

1871 Editorial Cartoon: "A Venerable Orang-outang,"
a caricature of Charles Darwin as an ape
published in *The Hornet*, a satirical magazine [1468]

As God was expelled from our schools, so was the reverential fear of Almighty God which has resulted in the moral and spiritual disintegration of America while at the same time contributing to the chaotic "everything goes" attitude America experiences today.

The message the *de facto* U.S. Supreme Court sent to the American people that landmark day was that it was okay to remove God from His rightful place and open the door in jeopardizing the people in the curses that come in not teaching our posterity to obey God and keep Him forefront in life.

In removing the Christian heritage of American history and the presuppositional Biblical worldview from schools, "We hold these <u>truths</u> to be self-evident" have become no longer evident. There can be no denying that this was a very dark victory for the principalities and powers, rulers of darkness

(Eph. 6:12) as a spiritually bankrupt group of carnally-minded men that love money more than truth (2 Pet. 2:14-15) in the same way that Balaam counseled Balaak in how to cause the people of God to bring a curse upon themselves (Num. 22-25; Rev. 2:4).

The effect is seen in the deterioration of the cornerstone of society, the very fabric of our nation — the family. With no conscious fear of God, there was no longer any conscious reason to treat marriage vows as sacred, or to bring up God-fearing children.

From there America spiraled quickly into demise in all other immoral circumstances that we find ourselves in today: teen pregnancies, violent crime, suicide, drugs and alcohol abuse which are the very logical fruits of a society that have forgotten the curse that comes with disobedience to the Word of God.

The Holy Bible is the Creator's manual that instructs how to live an abundant life while also warning of the consequences of foolish and sinful choices in not heeding the safety of the loving boundaries set for His creation. The elimination of the fear of God, symbolized by the *de facto* U.S. Supreme Court's action in the matter of school prayer, led to a dramatic increase in crime, sexually transmitted diseases, premarital sex, illiteracy, suicide, chemical dependency, public corruption, and other social ills.

Evidence has been documented through research that has been professionally compiled and tabulated using government data made available by agencies such as the Department of Health and Human Services, the Center for Disease Control, Statistical Abstracts of the United States, Vital Statistics of the United States, the U.S. Department of Commerce, and the Bureau of Labor Statistics.[1469]

An over 100-page report that includes graphs[1470] and statistical analysis, entitled "America, To Pray Or Not To Pray?: A Statistical Look at What Happened When Religious Principles Were Separated From Public Affairs,"[1471] is documented by *Specialty Research Associates* under the direction of David Barton of *WallBuilders*. Following are a few examples of the reported results:

Young People:
- For 15 years before 1963, pregnancies in girls ages 15 through 19 years of age had been no more than 15 per thousand. After 1963, pregnancies increased **187%** in the next 15 years.
- For younger girls, ages 10 to 14 years, pregnancies since 1963 are up **553%**.
- Before 1963, sexually transmitted diseases among students were 400 per 100,000. Since 1963, they were up **226%** in the next 12 years.

The Family:
- Before 1963, divorce rates had been declining for 15 years. After 1963 divorces increased **300%** each year for the next 15 years.
- Since 1963 unmarried people living together is up **353%**.
- Since 1963, single parent families are up **140%**.
- Since 1963, single parent families with children are up **160%**.

Education:
- The educational standard of measure has been the [Scholasatic Aptitude Test] SAT scores. SAT scores had been steady for many years before 1963. From 1963 they rapidly declined for 18 consecutive years, even though the same test has been used since 1941.

- In 1974-75, the rate of decline of the SAT scores decreased, even though the scores continued to decline. That was when there was an explosion of private religious schools. There were only 1,000 Christian schools in 1965. Between 1974 and 1984 Christian schools increased to 32,000.
- That could have an impact if the private schools had higher SAT scores. In checking with the SAT Board it was found that, indeed, the SAT scores for private schools were nearly 100 points higher than public schools.
- In fact, the scores were at the point where the public schools had been before their decline started in 1963 when prayer and Bible reading/instruction was removed from the schools.
- The scores in the public schools were still declining.
- Of the nation's top academic scholars, 3 times as many come from private religious schools, which operate on 1/3 the funds as do the public schools.

The Nation:
- Since 1963 violent crime has increased **544%.**
- Illegal drugs have become an enormous and uncontrollable problem.
- The nation has been deprived of an estimated 30 million citizens through legal abortions just since 1973.

Clearly seen in each study is the negative impact starting around the year 1962 when religious principles were separated from public affairs like school prayer. The divorce rate became so high that many young children didn't really understand the dynamics of what a family is. Violent crimes had risen steadily since the early 1960's, and the overloaded prison system then became a thought-provoking for-profit "Prison Industry" in many facets, one being the creation of bonds related to the convict and then sold on the Stock Exchange.[1472] Another for-profit aspect of the Prison Industry is contracts made with private corporations that gain at taxpayer expense by servicing the numerous and growing prisons. The Corporate sons of Satan have gone so far as to have (unconstitutionally) incarcerated Americans of victimless crimes, "warehousing" them for profit. We will expand on this subject further into this chapter.

Once ranked as having the best education in the developed world, according to *The Learning Curve*,[1473] [1474] developed by the education firm, *Pearson*, the *de facto* United States ranks seventeenth out of forty countries ranked in overall educational performance. The top ten countries in educational performance are Finland, South Korea, Hong Kong SAR, Japan, Singapore, United Kingdom, Netherlands, New Zealand, Switzerland, and Canada.[1475] The *de facto* United States spends more money on education than most countries in the world.[1476] International competition for U.S. industry is in decline with less quality-educated citizens entering the workforce. Most noteworthy is the effort made to move industry and jobs from our country through the *North American Free Trade Agreement* (NAFTA) that further affects the availability of employment for the American people.[1477]

With jobs on decline, the unemployment rates are steadily increasing toward catastrophe although the Federal Government reports that the economy is getting better.[1478] The "cunning, ambitious, and unprincipled men" got their Free Trade demands after all…

The Founding Fathers understood that teaching morals has a very positive impact on education. Our Founding Fathers felt that good moral citizenship was essential for the success of the nation. In our young nation, the Bible was used as a text book for the purpose of teaching children moral principles to live by.

The *New England Primer*, full of moral Bible verses, taught children to spell and was used in schools from 1692 until after 1900. Noah Webster's *American Spelling Book*, first written in the 1780s became the most popular book in American education. The famous *"Blue-Backed Speller"* set a publishing record of a million copies a year for 100 years.

Noah Webster [1479]
The Schoolmaster of the Republic
Library of Congress, Illustration created 1886

Americans from north to south and from east to west learned their letters, morality, and patriotism from Webster's dictionaries, spellers, catechisms, history books, etc. Noah Webster's early *"Blue-Backed Speller"* even contained a "Moral Catechism" with rules from the Scriptures upon which to base moral conduct.[1480] Concerning education, Noah Webster stated:

"Education is useless without the Bible."[1481]

"The Bible was America's basic text book in all fields."[1482]

"God's Word, contained in the Bible, has furnished all necessary rules to direct our conduct."[1483]

Noah Webster, 1833 [1484]   Cover of the New England Primer [1485]

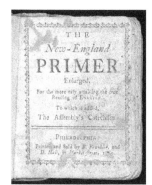

This is the exact opposite of the school curriculum today. The Corporate UNITED STATES' Courts in this country have revised the First Amendment, thus erecting a wall of atheism around every public school in America, where God is not allowed to be mentioned; this is not the same wall that Thomas Jefferson envisioned. The *de facto* States' educational system is now run by *de facto* Federal Government dictates… and money.

In 1963, the *de facto* U.S. Supreme Court ruled that sanctioned and organized Bible reading in public schools in the United States is unconstitutional.[1486] In 1980, the *de facto* U.S. Supreme Court ruled that posting the Ten Commandments in a school classroom violated the *Constitution of the United States*.[1487]

The effect of rejecting our American heritage and covenant with the Creator, Almighty God, is visible by the negative effect on all sectors of our society. History clearly presents that when societies are corrupted, they come to a point of destruction. A nation that refuses to teach its children right from wrong, good from evil; will become a corrupt nation, where sin prevails, evil abounds, and children do as they please.

In a 1985 *de facto* U.S. Supreme Court case that decided whether a law that authorizes a period of silence in public schools for "meditation or voluntary prayer" is a violation of the *First Amendment Establishment Clause*, Associate Justice William Rehnquist pointed out the error of the 1947 *de facto* Supreme Court ruling based on a misleading metaphor of a letter written in 1802 by Thomas Jefferson to the Danbury Baptists:

"It is impossible to build sound constitutional doctrine upon a <u>mistaken understanding of Constitutional history</u>...The establishment clause had been expressly freighted with Jefferson's <u>misleading metaphor</u> for nearly forty years...

"<u>There is simply no historical foundation for the proposition that the framers intended to build a wall of separation [between church and state]</u>... The recent court decisions are in no way based on either the <u>language or intent</u> of the framers."[1488]

The *de facto* U.S. Supreme Court decision was 6-3, in holding that a "moment of silence" law is unconstitutional when the explicit purpose and meaning of such a statute is to promote prayer.

On the topic of education, the American people have been injured because of the *Goals 2000: Educate America Act*[1489] and its "cohort in crime," the *School-to-Work Opportunities Act of 1994*.[1490] The educational reform created by this legislation which supposedly was the solution to the "Nation At Risk" in lagging student achievement levels was very obviously a distorted means to federalize education,[1491] or, in other words, shift control of the education system from parents and local school officials instead to Washington, DC.[1492]

Goals 2000 and its *Outcome-Based Education* (sometimes called *Performance-Based Education*, and formerly called *Mastery Learning*) was recognized by parents[1493] as a process that rejected the basics (the "3Rs" of Reading, 'Riting 'n 'Rithmatic) and substituted material that was subjective, often psychological, and mostly not capable of measurement.[1494] In reality, it provided the framework for a "cradle-to-grave" takeover of American families."[1495] What this educational reform had actually done was plow more tax money into the same dinosaur establishment that had failed our children.[1496]

One example of serious failure was the "whole language" fad that turned out to be a fraud and was unsupported by scientific evidence as reported by Dr. Samuel L. Blumenfeld in his book, *The Whole Language/OBE Fraud: The Shocking Story of How America Is Being Dumbed Down by Its Own Education System.*

While it was proved that "whole language" is a failure, numerous studies confirmed that training in "phonics" is not only vital but the only effective means to teach reading of the English language. Yet many teachers (at least in the 1990s) had not been taught how to teach phonics, if they even understood what phonics was. The responsibility for this debacle lies not with the teachers but with the educational colleges and the highly political public school educators' union, the *National Education Association (NEA)*, who were the source and motivating contributors.[1497]

Phyllis Schlafly was a national leader of the conservative movement since the publication of her best-selling 1964 book, "A Choice Not An Echo." She was a leader of the pro-family movement since 1972, when she started her national volunteer organization called "Eagle Forum."

Mrs. Schlafly was a lawyer and served as a member of the *Commission on the Bicentennial of the U.S. Constitution*, 1985-1991, appointed by then *de facto* President Ronald Reagan. She testified before more than 50 Congressional and State legislative committees on constitutional, national defense, and family issues.

A *Phi Beta Kappa* graduate of Washington University, Mrs. Schlafly received her *Juris Doctorate* from Washington University Law School, and received her *Master's* degree in Political Science from Harvard University. In 2008, Washington University/St. Louis awarded Mrs. Schlafly an honorary *Doctor of Humane Letters*. The mother of six children, she was the *1992 Illinois Mother of the Year*.

In Mrs. Schlafly's May, 1994 *The Phyllis Schlafly Report*, on Big Brother Education, 1994, and *"Outcome-based Education Nonsense,"* it was reported that "Schools Produce Juvenile Delinquents." Let us view an excerpt of this alarming report based on a conclusive study:

> "Study after study of adolescents at correctional institutions has shown that the one thing they have in common is that they cannot read. With a research grant funded by the U.S. Department of Justice, Michael Brunner set out to determine if the latter causes the former.
>
> He spent two years analyzing and integrating the literature on illiteracy and recidivism. In a new book called 'Retarding America: The Imprisonment of Potential,' he comes to the chilling conclusion that reading failure is a major cause, rather than just a correlate, of anti-social behavior.
>
> The measure of literacy expectations in the past has always been what an individual can talk about and comprehend. Studies show that most juvenile delinquents simply cannot read and write what they can talk about and comprehend.
>
> Brunner found that a high percentage of incarcerated juveniles were diagnosed early in school as "learning disabled" even though there was no evidence of specific neurological abnormalities. (It may be just a coincidence, but the more students get labeled "learning disabled," the more state and federal government money flows into the local school system.) These children never received the kind of reading instruction that is successful, namely, intensive, systematic phonics. They never learned how to identify sounds in isolation, to blend individual speech sounds into words, or to segment polysyllabic words into speech sounds.
>
> A number of reading instruction programs have been introduced into juvenile correctional institutions, and Brunner describes the experiences of some of the instructors in these programs. They have discovered that failure to learn to read is a major cause for the frustration and low self-esteem that lead to juvenile delinquency.
>
> Brunner reports a poignant interview with "Joey," who could decipher only four words. His years in the public school system were a time of constant humiliation because he could not read. He said, "I

just liked to fight [so] don't nobody laugh at me." In the correctional institution, Joey was successfully taught to read with remedial intensive phonics.

Another teenager, interviewed at Ironwood Maximum Security Prison after he was successfully taught by the phonics method, almost became a new person as a result of his new accomplishment. "People act like I'm there now that I can read," he said. These teenagers were experiencing success for the first time in their lives.

Brunner challenges the laws that mandate schooling until age 18 and believes that they contribute to juvenile delinquency. Interviews with special education teachers indicate that forcing a child to experience the humiliation of failure over and over again leads to anti-social aggressiveness and juvenile crime.

Brunner relates Pavlov's conditioned reflex experiments: An individual must have a goal, must have sustained pressure to achieve that goal, and must not be denied the means to achieve that goal. If, instead, the child experiences sustained frustration in trying to achieve that goal, anti-social behavior results.

The anti-social aggression that Pavlov created in the laboratory is being created in tens of thousands of classrooms across our nation because the schools use pedagogy that produces failure. All the ingredients to create anti-social aggression through sustained frustration are present in the reading methods used in most public schools today.

The widely-used anti-phonics Whole Language method (which is part and parcel of Outcome- Based Education) makes the goal of reading unattainable for the average child who has not had help from other sources. The student is continually pressured to achieve this unattainable goal by teachers, parents and peers.

The student has no alternative for achieving this goal because elementary schools typically offer no choice in curriculum, and compulsory attendance laws imprison him in a failure-producing environment. For many, this unrelenting frustration explodes into resentment and hostility of a magnitude that is incomprehensible to those who find reading as easy as breathing and typically cannot remember how they learned.

The only immediate solution to widespread illiteracy is for parents to teach their children to read at home by a proven phonics method -- and this effort is especially necessary for those children who may be targets for recruitment into anti-social behavior."

Taking into account that there are well over 2 million prisoners in State, federal and private prisons throughout the country and that no other society in human history has imprisoned so many of its own citizens, we must pause, take note, and give careful attention to what has been happening to our children —and understand a generation of our now adult children as well.[1498] Statistics show that the Corporate UNITED STATES has imprisoned more people than any other country.[1499] One-half million more than China, which has a population that is five-times greater than that of the U.S. Included in statistics is the fact that the United States holds 25-percent of the world's prison population, but only 5-percent of the world's people. An American citizen has a six-times greater chance of being incarcerated than in most other countries.[1500] Over the past 45 years, the U.S. prison population has risen by 700-percent. Incredibly, one in 99 American adults are behind bars in the United States. Mind-blowing is that one in 31 adults are under some form of correctional control (e.g. prison, jail, parole and probation populations).[1501]

From less than **300,000** inmates in **1972**, the jail population has amazingly grown to **2 million** by the year **2000**. In **1990** it was **1 million**. Just **ten years ago** there were only **five** private prisons in the country, with a population of **2,000** inmates; **now**, there are **100** that house (or more correctly stated, "warehouse") **62,000** inmates. According to reports, it is projected that by the coming decade, the number will reach **360,000**.

We cannot discount that these large numbers of living souls also include those of yesterday's school children in the public education school system that was turned over to the management of the privatized *de facto* Corporate UNITED STATES federal "government."[1502]

In the mid-1980s this author worked for an advertising agency with a main client who manufactured door closers. At that time, the client advised that they had been approached by officials of the Prison Industry with a request to manufacture a door closer specifically for prison cells because plans were in place to build many new prison facilities to deal with overcrowding as well as the anticipation of expanding incarcerations. *Goals 2000* and *Outcome-based Education* were passed shortly thereafter in 1994 and obviously were a consideration in that Prison Industry business plan.

Besides a growth of prison population from illegal drug-related incarcerations (of which the *de facto* government has contributed to the importation and distribution of illegal drugs throughout American communities[1503]) most of which were victimless crimes, plans for housing a new workforce were in place to be ready for the soon coming generation of manufactured illiterates in their complex of industries to be marketed on Wall Street. The privatization and plans for prison expansions began in the 1980s with Wall Street stocks feverishly selling. Private prisons are the biggest business in the *Prison Industry Complex*. The American people are largely unaware that the prisons and jails are not municipally owned and/or run. A reported 18 corporations provide employees as guards of 10,000 prisoners in 27 States. Two of the largest that control 75 percent of the market are *Corrections Corporation of America* (CCA)[1504] and *G4S Secure Solutions* (founded as *The Wackenhut Corporation*).[1505]

Private prisons receive a guaranteed sum of money for each prisoner separate from the cost of maintenance for each inmate. There is no doubt that private business with guaranteed per capita along with prisoners given added time for any infraction, as well as prisoners losing "good behavior time," is logically motivated by money.[1506]

1 Timothy 6:10 ~

> *For the love of money is the root of all evil: which while some coveted after, they have erred from the faith, and pierced themselves through with many sorrows.*

If the means of the exponential growth of the prison population as well as prisons in the last 40 years isn't shocking enough, the answer to the question as to why and how such an atrocity would occur we consider a study by the *Progressive Labor Party* which has accused the Prison Industry of being "an imitation of Nazi Germany with respect to forced slave labor and concentration camps."[1507] This organization also states:

"The private contracting of prisoners for work fosters incentives to lock people up. Prisons depend on this income. Corporate stockholders who make money off prisoners' work lobby for longer sentences, in order to expand their workforce. The system feeds itself." [1508]

The Prison Industry Complex is one of the fastest-growing industries in the United States and its investors are on Wall Street.

"This multimillion-dollar industry has its own trade exhibitions, conventions, websites, and mail-order/Internet catalogs. It also has direct advertising campaigns, architecture companies, construction companies, investment houses on Wall Street, plumbing supply companies, food supply companies, armed security, and padded cells in a large variety of colors."[1509]

For the "cunning, ambitious, and unprincipled men," who have created and invested in the Prison Industry, it has been a means of striking it rich while at the same time working toward their occult agenda of a totalitarian society for their *New World Order.*

Consider also that in the manner of big business and large profit margins, Prison Industry executives have no need to be concerned with worker strikes or paying unemployment insurance or vacations and comp time. All of their workers are full-time, and never arrive late or are absent because of family or other problems. If the workers don't like their pay of pennies per hour and refuse to work, then they are locked-up in isolation cells.[1510]

While we are coming to comprehend and understand that "all wars are bankers wars,"[1511] and the fact that those of money interests create war and have been known to financially invest on both sides of a conflict,[1512] an astounding supporting fact is that the *de facto* federal Prison Industry produces 100-percent of ALL military helmets, ammunition belts, bullet-proof vests, ID tags, shirts, pants, tents, bags, and canteens.

In looking at the large percentages of markets owned by the Prison Industry in various manufacturing industries,[1513] one who contemplates might consider this fact as one of the real reasons for the current dilemma of high unemployment in the country and the fact that unemployment supersedes that of the Great Depression.[1514] [1515]

While this subject could easily continue with innumerable facts that would shock the conscience in those that have one, we must point out that there are at least 37 *de facto* States that have legalized the contracting of prison labor by private corporations that base their operations inside of State prisons.[1516] The companies on that list are well-known and nearly every family in America, as well as the world, does business with them. Sometimes daily. The following are some of the corporations that contract with *Correctional Corporation of America* and *The GEO Group, Inc.*[1517] to produce American slave labor goods. They include Intel, Northern Telecom, TWA, Nordstrom's Boeing, Motorola, Microsoft, AT&T, prison for profitWireless, 3Com, Revlon, Macy's, Pierre Cardin, Texas Instrument, Dell, Compaq, Honeywell, Hewlett-Packard, Nortel, Lucent Technologies, Target, and many more.

It is reported that all of these businesses are excited about the economic boom generation by prison slave labor and most actively lobby for mandatory sentencing.[1518]

On the subject of *de facto* States in the prison labor business, the *de facto* State of Wisconsin *Blue Book* includes revealing information. Included in the Executive Branch section under the category of the *Department of Corrections,* is listed the "Prison Industries Board" along with a description of that Agency's responsibilities.[1519]

The Board develops a plan for the manufacturing and marketing of prison industry products, the provision of prison industry services, and research and development activities. No prison industry may be established or permanently closed without this Board's approval and also makes recommendations to the *de facto* State governor for changes.[1520]

It would be an interesting pursuit to investigate precisely who owns or has stock in the private companies that provide services to the prisons. Just as several *de facto* U.S. presidents have invested their money in the Prison Industry,[1521] perhaps there are some vested *de facto* Wisconsin employees or officials who have had a business interest and sought to have a corner on "the market."

The *Blue Book* also provides "Prison Population and Correctional Expenditures By State, 1980-2011" that is well worth review by U.S. tax payers.[1522] The tens of thousands of dollars charged the tax payers annually per inmate is nothing short of immoral, as well as criminal.

In 2012 it was reported that a professional study concluded that it costs the United States taxpayers an average of $30,000 per year to incarcerate an inmate, but the nation spends only an average of $11,665 per public school student.[1523] Perhaps the wrong individuals are behind bars.

It was reported for the year 2011 that nearly 90-percent of all inmates imprisoned in the United States were for victimless crimes.[1524] Human rights organizations have reported that *de facto* federal law is now stipulating long prison sentences with no possibility of parole for victimless crimes. In 13 States, "three strikes" laws condemn an individual to <u>life in prison</u> after being convicted of three felonies. <u>Felonies include possession of illegal drugs, like marijuana</u>.[1525] Had this *de facto* law been in place in the 1970s, a large percentage of America would have been incarcerated, and still be there. There are families who have had no hope of the return of their sons and daughters, brothers and sisters, nephews and nieces, husbands and wives.

Likewise, the unconstitutionally incarcerated individuals have been hopeless in going home. <u>If they are released, they struggle with "getting off paper" and gaining freedom from parole officers with the *de facto* Department of Corrections</u> as there seems to be a motivating drive to re-incarcerate them. In fact, *Human Rights Watch*,[1526] a global nonprofit, nongovernmental human rights organization run by professionals such as lawyers, journalists, and academics scholars have released a specially prepared report entitled "Profiting from Probation,"[1527] that discusses some of the evils of the privatization of the criminal justice system which includes probation.

Judicial Watch,[1528] a conservative non-partisan education foundation, has reportedly found that more than 1,000 courts across several States are seeking to generate revenue by collecting unpaid debts from those convicted of misdemeanors without hiring any municipal staff to administer probation. Most are poor, unable to pay and end-up having their probation rescinded to where they end in prison.

On an increasing basis, the U.S. prison population is made up of nonviolent "offenders" who are unable to pay their court costs. An estimated $40 million in revenue in just the State of Georgia comes from county and city courts who incarcerate convicted individuals who are too poor to pay court-imposed fines and fees. That means that America's prisons are increasingly being turned into debtors prisons.[1529]

We recall from the Reconstruction Era just after the Civil War that the Southern legislatures began drafting "Black Codes" in attempt to restore slavery in a more subtle form while also reestablishing white supremacy. These laws imposed restrictions on black citizens in an attempt to control their labor and by compelling them to work in a labor economy based on low wages or debt.[1530] As newly freed slaves were unable to maintain sharecropping contracts with their former masters, they would forfeit their wages or sometimes be "hired out" to work off their debt.[1531]

The current day Prison Industry has its roots in this "Black Codes" ideology, or shall we rather say, "enslavement and marketing strategy." The *de facto* criminal "justice system" in reality is a fraudulent system of <u>commercial</u> "law merchants." The wrong individuals are behind bars.

Convicts who had violated the Black Codes of the Reconstruction Era [1532]

The historic plan of 33rd degree Freemason Howell Cobb[1533] (1815-1868) in the secret society objective of making all laborers everywhere to be capital[1534] has now epitomized slavery with maximum return on investments as exemplified in what has been done in the *de facto* "Justice System" and Prison Industry of sharecropping our family members. Also, the occult racial prejudice appears to continue with preference in especially targeting Blacks and Latinos as their slaves.[1535]

Howell Cobb, 1868 [1536]

Following is what Almighty God has to say on the subject as recorded in His Word in the book of Revelation and pertaining to the future fall of Mystery Babylon ~

Revelations 18:11-13 ~

> *And the merchants of the earth will weep and mourn over her, for no one buys their merchandise anymore: merchandise of gold and silver, precious stones and pearls, fine linen and purple, silk and scarlet, every kind of citron wood, every kind of object of ivory, every kind of object of most precious wood, bronze, iron, and marble; and cinnamon and incense, fragrant oil and frankincense, wine and oil, fine flour and wheat, cattle and sheep, horses and chariots, and bodies and souls of men.*

Revelations 18:15-17a ~

> *The merchants of these things, who became rich by her, will stand at a distance for fear of her torment, weeping and wailing, and saying, 'Alas, alas, that great city that was clothed in fine linen, purple, and scarlet, and adorned with gold and precious stones and pearls! For in one hour such great riches came to nothing.'*

Pertaining to the curses of disobedience in covenant-breaking:

Deuteronomy 28:32 ~

> *Thy sons and thy daughters shall be given unto another people, and thine eyes shall look, and fail with longing for them all the day long: and there shall be no might in thine hand.*

Deuteronomy 28:41 ~

> *Thou shalt beget sons and daughters, but thou shalt not enjoy them; for they shall go into captivity.*

The *de facto* federal "government's" latest edition of education reform currently being swept across America is the "Common Core" national standards.[1537] While there is considerable controversy among educators and parents alike about these new national standards, the advocates who are promoting *Common Core* offer upbeat propaganda descriptions of utopian educational goals along with guidelines in learning standards of what students should know and be able to achieve in grades kindergarten through high school in English language arts and math.[1538]

Especially in mathematics, promoters of *Common Core* insist that it is the only way to address the problem of lagging educational achievement by American students. But scholars and experts claim that the *Common Core* math standards fall significantly behind in what students need for more advanced work and in some ways amount to a massive experiment with American children.

It is reported that most educators would agree that mathematical education in the country is at crisis level because of the way that math is currently taught, particularly in the basics of adding, subtracting, multiplying, and dividing numbers. These educators also claim that *Common Core* does nothing to address this problem.[1539]

Today, there are deficiencies in the manner of teaching the 'ole 3R's of "Reading, 'Riting, 'n 'Rithmetic" that used to be the basis of America leading the world in education. Why fix something that wasn't broken? Why change what was excellent? Experts point out that hidden in *Common Core* is the real objective: presenting the minimal amount of material that high-school graduates need to be able to enter the work force in an entry-level job, or to enroll in a community college.

Sufficient college preparation is not provided and, therefore, it would be unlikely for the students to become degreed in a technical area such as the hard sciences, engineering, economics, statistics, or mathematics. *Common Core* will put students at least two years behind their peers in high-performing countries, and leave them unprepared for authentic college course work.[1540]

But those goals and standards are only two facets of the hodgepodge of the *de facto* federal funding, preschool-to-workforce invasive student tracking, and "one-size-fits-all computer-based learning" that has become the *Common Core*[1541] in the government indoctrination system referred to as "public education."[1542]

"Government" controls are in place through *Common Core* to affect not only public education but all aspects of education, including private, Christian, and home education.   The effect of this agenda is widely broad-based and will affect all Americans whether they have children or not. Although there are many sources of information available about *Common Core*, few of them address this educational "Standards Initiative" from a Biblical perspective.[1543]

Dr. Marlene McMillan[1544] is an international speaker, author, and business consultant who has spent a lifetime learning the principles of Liberty and sharing them with others.[1545] She is known as the "Nation's Expert on the Principles of Liberty."

Having earned a Master of Divinity from Southwestern Baptist Theological Seminary and a Doctor of Ministry from Tyndale Theological Seminary, Dr. Marlene has written extensively on Liberty and how to make daily application of the Bible in our culture especially in the areas of law, government, history, economics, and education.   Dr. Marlene is the author of several books and also homeschooled her seven children all the way through high school.

Dr. Marlene points out that *Common Core* is part of the *New World Order* planned *Agenda 21*,[1546] a program created by the United Nations which "is a comprehensive plan of action to be taken globally, nationally and locally by organizations of the United Nations System, Governments, and Major Groups in every area in which human impacts on the environment."[1547]

Dr. Marlene explains that it involves a *Dialectic Process* of communication, by which a person is moved from a belief in absolute truth to a belief in relativism. It is also the method by which a child who has not yet established fixed beliefs is turned into a malleable tool to be formed into the perfect citizen of a totalitarian state. *Common Core* is *Dialectic* education for global citizens as well as "an educational tower of Babel." Just as the tower of Babel was rebellion toward God, *Common Core* is unbiblical "to the core."[1548]

Why is there a planned agenda in "educating" a generation of children to think alike, make decisions in the same way or talk in the same *Politically Correct* manner? To raise citizens for the *New World Order,* they have to be processed and conditioned in a particular manner.[1549]

Dr. Marlene teaches that Liberty is won or lost just like a relay race. It depends on "the passing of the baton" to each generation. She explains the definition of Liberty as the opportunity to make a choice to assume responsibility and accept the consequences. Responsibility ensures and maintains Liberty generation after generation. It gives people the opportunity to be all they want to be, and to attain their goals. Dr. Marlene advises that she teaches people to think from principles:

> "Because an issue cannot be passed down from one generation to the next, but you can pass a principle. You don't know what issues the next generation will face.   Issues are always changing. Principles do not change, so when you teach people to think from principles, you end up with people who are empowered. They recognize that some new law may look like it will solve the issue today, but it actually puts our grandchildren in bankruptcy! Or it means that people in other parts of the country will be damaged by this law. And it makes you start thinking about the consequences of the choices you make, and the bills you support."

The magnitude of influence that curriculum writers have over the future of a nation is monumental. *Common Core* contributes to changing the principles of education and a new method of teaching that makes students docile, compliant and unable to understand.[1550]

A trademark statement of Dr. Marlene: "People who live in liberty think differently than people who live in bondage." She teaches that "think" is a distinguishing factor between people who live in bondage. Mindlessness or lack of ability to think or pay attention is all that is necessary in order for tyrants to enslave people. Regardless of what they are called, says Dr. Marlene, a tyrant is still a tyrant when he takes away one's essential liberty and a slave is still a slave no matter what they're called if their conscience is violated. That's one of the key differences between a free man and a slave—a right to exercise their conscience.[1551]

As parental and local control of education diminishes, centralized national control of education increases. Tests, college entrance exams and Advanced Placement curricula have all been changed to conform to the new *Common Core* standards. This circumvents parental control, the teacher's ability to adjust content and methods to their individual student's needs and control by locally-elected school boards in favor of a patented methodology mandated from afar (like "afar" as Washington, DC or the global *New World Order* headquarters).[1552]

Ze'ev Wurman, a former senior policy advisor with the *Office of Planning, Evaluation, Policy Development* at the *de facto* U.S. Department of Education, has written a white paper on *Common Core* for the *Pioneer Institute*, a Massachusetts independent, non-partisan, privately funded research organization in the educational arena. Entitled, "Common Core's Validation, A Weak Foundation for a Crooked House," the white paper is available at the *Pioneer Institute* website with an introduction to the paper as follows:

> "Advocates of Common Core's mathematics standards claim they are rigorous, reflect college-readiness, and are comparable with those of high achieving countries. But five of the 29 members of the Common Core Validation Committee refused to sign a report attesting that the standards are research-based, rigorous and internationally benchmarked. The report was released with 24 signatures and included no mention that five committee members refused to sign it. The two members of the Common Core Validation Committee with college-level mathematics content knowledge refused to sign off on them, finding them significantly lower than those of high-achieving countries."[1553]

The Southern Poverty Law Center (SPLC) is a massively funded liberal nonprofit organization that claims to specialize in civil rights and public interest litigation.[1554] The SPLC has drawn severe criticism, specifically in 2014 for an indirect connection in the shooting of an employee of the Family Research Council, as well as its propagating heavily politicized biased and inaccurate data on "hate groups," not hate crimes.[1555]

The SPLC has been identified for its extremist views, slandering word craft, and unlawful targeting of Christian, conservative, and constitutional groups.[1556] Alarmingly, this organization is associated in partnership with the *de facto* Federal Government *Department of Justice* (DOJ) and agencies, such as the *Federal Bureau of Investigations* (FBI) and the *Department of Homeland Security* (DHS). The SPLC also provides official publications and training in the education and law enforcement fields.

The SPLC website promotes official-sounding propaganda that treacherously labels and stereotypes while also categorizing individuals and groups of American people according to the SPLC's "standard" of ideologies.

The SPLC markets its propaganda with target groups as bogeymen while promoting their publications for free to "Get Informed." On the topic of education and *Common Core*, the SPLC has artfully manipulated strategic word craft in slander-mongering Christian people with extremist hyperbole in their clouded propaganda report entitled, "Public Schools in the Crosshairs: Far-Right Propaganda and the Common Core State Standards."[1557]

Isaiah 5:20 ~

> *Woe unto them that speak good of evil, and evil of good, which put darkness for light, and light for darkness, that put bitter for sweet, and sweet for sour.*

The first sentence of the SPLC website introduction related to their report on *Common Core* is enough to discern, if not, smell this organization's agenda…

> "Across the United States, a fierce wave of resistance is engulfing the Common Core State Standards, threatening to derail this ambitious effort to lift student achievement and, more fundamentally, to undermine the very idea of public education."[1558]

The report also states, "Our nation's founders understood that education is a public responsibility and necessary for self-government," while projecting a sense of patriotism in quoting the *Northwest Ordinance of 1787* in noting that "schools and the means of education shall forever be encouraged."[1559] SPLC authors come dangerously close in aligning their organization to fit the ideology description of their categorized "Patriot Movement" hate group by recklessly citing foundational knowledge. We delight in completing the whole sentence of that *Ordinance*:

Article 3 of the Northwest Ordinance; July 13, 1787, *An Ordinance for the government of the Territory of the United States northwest of the River Ohio*.

> "Religion, morality, and knowledge, being necessary to good government and the happiness of mankind, schools and the means of education shall forever be encouraged. The utmost good faith shall always be observed towards the Indians; their lands and property shall never be taken from them without their consent; and, in their property, rights, and liberty, they shall never be invaded or disturbed, unless in just and lawful wars authorized by Congress; but laws founded in justice and humanity, shall from time to time be made for preventing wrongs being done to them, and for preserving peace and friendship with them."[1560]

NOTE: It has been duly noted that since the public release of this individual chapter in pdf format in March, 2015 and before the end of the year at the time of preparing this book for publishing, the SPLC no longer totes a category of "Patriot Movement" in its "Extremist Files: Ideologies" on its website. The category has been renamed as "ANTIGOVERNMENT MOVEMENT" and the word "Patriot" has been entirely removed. Additionally, a subtitle has been added that asserts their motive for the purported "ANTIGOVERNMENT MOVEMENT" to be the election of the first African-American president.[1561]

Proverbs 22:6 ~

Train up a child in the way he should go: and when he is old, he will not depart from it.

Thomas Jefferson, while President (1801-1809), chaired the school board for the District of Columbia where he authored the first plan of education adopted by the city of Washington. This plan used the Bible and *Isaac Watts' Psalms, Hymns and Spiritual Songs, 1707*, as the principal books for teaching students to read. On March 23, 1891, President Jefferson wrote from Washington, DC to Moses Robinson:

"The Christian Religion, when divested of the rags in which they [the clergy] have enveloped it, and brought to the original purity and simplicity of its benevolent institutor, is a religion of all others most friendly to liberty, science, and the freest expansion of the human mind."[1562]

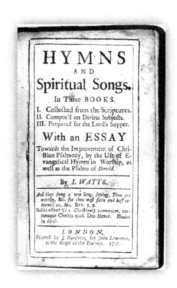

Title page of Isaac Watts' Psalms, *Hymns and Spiritual Songs*, 1707 [1563]

Deuteronomy 28: 15 ~

But it shall come to pass, if thou wilt not hearken unto the voice of the Lord thy God, to observe to do all his commandments and his statutes which I command thee this day; that all these curses shall come upon thee, and overtake thee...

Chapter Seventeen

The Curses of Covenant Breaking
~ Today America is in Apostasy and in Peril

On June 4, 1963, a little known and covered-up attempt was made to strip the privately-owned Federal Reserve Bank of its power to loan money to the "government" at interest. On that day, President John F. Kennedy signed *Executive Order No. 11110* that returned to the *(de facto)* U.S. government the power to issue currency, without going through the Federal Reserve.

President John F. Kennedy, 1961 [1564]

President Kennedy's Order gave the *(de facto)* U.S. Treasury the power "to issue silver certificates against any silver bullion, silver, or standard silver dollars in the Treasury." This meant that for every ounce of silver in the U.S. Treasury's vault, the government could introduce new money into circulation.

In other words, the paper certificates, or currency, had value because they were backed or certified by the value of the silver which was dedicated. In all, Kennedy brought nearly $4.3 billion in U.S. silver certificate Notes into circulation. The ramifications of this bill are enormous.

Pres. John F. Kennedy signs
Executive Order 11110 [1565]

With the stroke of a pen, President Kennedy was on his way to putting the Federal Reserve Bank of New York out-of-business. When enough of these silver certificates were placed into circulation they would have replaced and eliminated the demand for Federal Reserve Notes (FRNs). This is because the silver certificates are backed by silver and the Federal Reserve Notes are not backed by anything of substance (fiat).

The effects of *Executive Order 11110* would have prevented the national debt from growing to an unrealistic and unpayable level. It would have provided the ability to repay the debt, ended the relationship with the privately-owned Federal Reserve Bank that creates money out of thin air to its own (stockholder's) personal wealth, and "rent" the use of their FRNs to the American people. It would have expired use of the FRNs in circulation along with any further "debt" owed to the Federal Reserve Bank. *Executive Order 11110* gave the U.S. the ability to create its own money backed by silver and move away from fiat value-less "cursed" currency.

Silver Certificate, 1957 [1566]

Just five months later, on November 22, 1963, President John Fitzgerald Kennedy was assassinated. No more silver certificates were issued. The Executive Order was not repealed by *de facto* Presidents Lyndon Johnson,[1567] Richard Nixon,[1568] Gerald Ford,[1569] Jimmy Carter[1570] or Ronald Reagan.[1571]

President Ronald Reagan, 1981 [1572]

If one of those presidents had utilized *Executive Order 11110*, the debt would have been eliminated. Perhaps the assassination of JFK was a warning to future presidents who would attempt to eliminate the U.S. debt or by eliminating the Federal Reserve's control over the creation of money and the American people. President Kennedy's *Executive Order 11110* remained on the books until September 9, 1987 when President Ronald Reagan issued *Executive Order 12608*[1573] which specifically revoked the sections added by *Executive Order 11110* and effectively revoked the entire Order.[1574] The "powers" behind the Federal Reserve won and were free to loot and pillage the national wealth of America. Noteworthy is that virtually all of the nation's accumulated debt has been created since 1963.

President Kennedy challenged the "invisible" oligarch banking powers, "Money Changers,"[1575] that truly was the dictating force that ran the government. He challenged the two most successful vehicles ever used to drive up debt: war and creation of money by a privately-owned Central bank. President Kennedy's efforts to have all troops out of Vietnam by 1965 and *Executive Order 11110* would have severely cut into the profits and control of the New York banking establishment.[1576]

The following cartoons were published in the 1912 book, *U.S. Money vs. Corporation Currency, 'Aldrich Plan,'* by Alfred Owen Crozier, a prominent Midwestern attorney. Mr. Crozier had written eight books on topic of the U.S. political, legal, and monetary problems in the early 1900s.

As "a picture tells a thousand words," Crozier created cartoon graphics that powerfully communicate the truthful effect of the planned Federal Reserve central bank takeover that still speaks in this current day. His focus was centered in projecting the threat to the American Republic by corporation currency printed by private firms for their own profit and supplanting constitutional money.

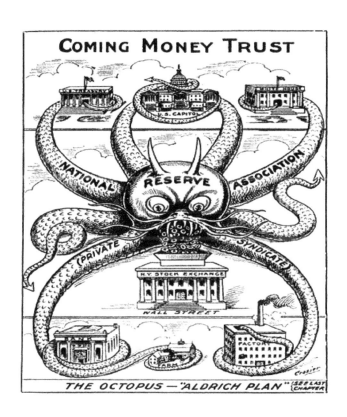

"Frontispiece – The Octopus – 'Aldrich Plan'" [1577]

"White Man's Burden" – Bank Incubus on U.S." [1578]

Published in Alfred Crozier's
U.S. Money vs. Corporation Currency, "Aldrich Plan," 1912

For purpose of careful consideration of the historical accounts that have been presented, following are quotes of notable individuals throughout the past 150 years:

Rothschild Brothers of London, 1863:

"The few who understand the system, will either be so interested from its profits or so dependent on its favors, that here will be no opposition from that class."

Nathan Rothschild[1579]
father

Lionel[1580]
de Rothschild/son

Anthony Nathan[1581]
de Rothschild/son

Nathaniel [1582]
de Rothschild/son

Mayer Amschel [1583]
de Rothschild/son

Mayer Amschel Bauer Rothschild: "Give me control of a nation's money and I care not who makes its laws."

Senators and Congressmen:

"Most Americans have no real understanding of the operation of the international money lenders. The accounts of the Federal Reserve System have never been audited. It operates outside the control of Congress and manipulates the credit of the United States" — **Senator Barry Goldwater (U.S. Senator, Arizona)**

U.S. Senator Barry Goldwater[1584]

"This [Federal Reserve Act] establishes the most gigantic trust on earth. When the President [Woodrow Wilson] signs this bill, the invisible government of the monetary power will be legalized....the worst legislative crime of the ages is perpetrated by this banking and currency bill."
— **Congressman Charles A. Lindbergh, Sr., 1913 (U.S. Representative, Minnesota)**

Congressman Charles A. Lindbergh, Sr. [1585]

"From now on, depressions will be scientifically created." — **U.S. Rep. Charles A. Lindbergh Sr., 1913 (Minnesota)**

"The financial system has been turned over to the Federal Reserve Board. That Board as ministers the finance system by authority of a purely profiteering group. The system is Private, conducted for the sole purpose of obtaining the greatest possible profits from the use of other people's money" – **U.S. Rep. Charles A. Lindbergh Sr., 1923 (Minnesota)**

"The Federal Reserve bank buys government bonds without one penny..."

— **U.S. Rep. Wright Patman (Texas), Congressional Record, Sept 30, 1941**

U.S. Rep. Wright Patman[1586]

"We have, in this country, one of the most corrupt institutions the world has ever known. I refer to the Federal Reserve Board. This evil institution has impoverished the people of the United States and has practically bankrupted our government. It has done this through the corrupt practices of the moneyed vultures who control it." — **U.S. Rep. Louis T. McFadden (Pennsylvania) in 1932**

"The Federal Reserve banks are one of the most corrupt institutions the world has ever seen. There is not a man within the sound of my voice who does not know that this nation is run by the International bankers." — **U.S. Rep. Louis T. McFadden (Pennsylvania)**

"Some people think the Federal Reserve Banks are the United States government's institutions. They are not government institutions. They are private credit monopolies which prey upon the people of the United States for the benefit of themselves and their foreign swindlers." — **Congressional Record 12595-12603 — U.S. Rep. Louis T. McFadden (Pennsylvania), Chairman of the Committee on Banking and Currency (12 years) June 10, 1932**

Congressman Louis Thomas McFadden, 1931 [1587]

John Danforth, former Senator and U.S. Ambassador to the United Nations [1588]

"I have never seen more Senators express discontent with their jobs....I think the major cause is that, deep down in our hearts, we have been accomplices in doing something terrible and unforgivable to our wonderful country. Deep down in our heart, we know that we have given our children a legacy of bankruptcy. We have defrauded our country to get ourselves elected." — **U.S. Senator John Danforth (Missouri)**

"These 12 corporations [12 Federal Reserve Districts and Banks] together cover the whole country and monopolize and use for private gain every dollar of the public currency..." — **Attorney Alfred Owen Crozier, before the Senate Banking and Currency Committee – 1913**

Alfred Owen Crozier, (1863–1939) [1589]

Senator Henry Cabot Lodge, 1901 [1590]

"The [Federal Reserve Act] as it stands seems to me to open the way to a vast inflation of the currency... I do not like to think that any law can be passed that will make it possible to submerge the gold standard in a flood of irredeemable paper currency." — **U.S. Senator Henry Cabot Lodge Sr., 1913 (Massachusetts)**

From the Federal Reserve's Own Admissions:

Putting it simply, Boston Federal Reserve Bank -- "When you or I write a check there must be sufficient funds in our account to cover the check, but when the Federal Reserve writes a check there is no bank deposit on which that check is drawn. When the Federal Reserve writes a check, it is creating money."

Modern Money Mechanics Workbook, Federal Reserve Bank of Chicago, 1975 -- "Neither paper currency nor deposits have value as commodities, intrinsically, a 'dollar' bill is just a piece of paper. Deposits are merely book entries."

Donald J. Winn, Assistant to the Board of Governors of the Federal Reserve System -- "The Federal Reserve system pays the U.S. Treasury 020.60 per thousand notes --a little over 2 cents each-- without regard to the face value of the note. Federal Reserve Notes, incidentally, are the only type of currency now produced for circulation. They are printed exclusively by the Treasury's Bureau of Engraving and Printing, and the $20.60 per thousand price reflects the Bureau's full cost of production. Federal Reserve Notes are printed in 01, 02, 05, 10, 20, 50, and 100 dollar denominations only; notes of 500, 1000, 5000, and 10,000 denominations were last printed in 1945."

Robert H. Hemphill, Atlanta Federal Reserve Bank -- "We are completely dependent on the commercial banks. Someone has to borrow every dollar we have in circulation, cash or credit. If the banks create ample synthetic money we are prosperous; if not, we starve. We are absolutely without a permanent money system.... It is the most important subject intelligent persons can investigate and reflect upon. It is so important that our present civilization may collapse unless it becomes widely understood and the defects remedied very soon."

From General Law:

The Federal Tax Lien Act of 1966 -- "The entire taxing and monetary systems are hereby placed under the U.C.C. (Uniform Commercial Code)."

Stanek vs. White, 172 Minn.390, 215 N.W. 784 -- "There is a distinction between a 'debt discharged' and a debt 'paid.' When discharged, the debt still exists though divested of its charter as a legal obligation during the operation of the discharge, something of the original vitality of the debt continues to exist, which may be transferred, even though the transferee takes it subject to its disability incident to the discharge."

Lewis vs. United States, 680 F. 2d 1239 9th Circuit 1982 -- "The regional Federal Reserve banks are not government agencies. ...but are independent, privately owned and locally controlled corporations."

Past Presidents, not including the Founding Fathers:

President James A. Garfield (March 4, 1881 – September 19, 1881 by assassination) -- "Whoever controls the volume of money in any country is absolute master of all industry and commerce."

President James Garfield, 1870-1880 [1591]

President Woodrow Wilson[1592]

President Woodrow Wilson (1913-1921) -- "A great industrial nation is controlled by its system of credit. Our system of credit is concentrated in the hands of a few men. We have come to be one of the worst ruled, one of the most completely controlled and dominated governments in the world--no longer a government of free opinion, no longer a government by conviction and vote of the majority, but a government by the opinion and duress of small groups of dominant men."

Founding Father's Quotes on Banking:

President Thomas Jefferson -- "I believe that banking institutions are more dangerous to our liberties than standing armies. Already they have raised up a monied aristocracy that has set the government at defiance. The issuing power (of money) should be taken away from the banks and restored to the people to whom it properly belongs."

President Thomas Jefferson, 1800 [1593]

President Andrew Jackson, Vetoed Bank Bill of 1836 -- "If Congress has the right [it doesn't] to issue paper money [currency], it was given to them to be used by...[the government] and not to be delegated to individuals or corporations."

President Andrew Jackson[1594]

James Madison [1595]

President James Madison -- "History records that the <u>money changers</u> have used every form of abuse, intrigue, deceit, and violent means possible to maintain their control over governments by controlling money and it's issuance."

Various Other Sources:

Ralph M. Hawtrey, Secretary of the British Treasury -- "Banks lend by creating credit. They create the means of payment out of nothing"

Buckminster Fuller (1895-1983, American architect, systems theorist, author, designer and inventor) -- "To expose a 15 Trillion dollar rip-off of the American people by the stockholders of the 1,000 largest corporations over the last 100 years will be a tall order of business."

Robert A. Heinlein, *Expanded Universe* -- "Every Congressman, every Senator knows precisely what causes inflation...but can't, [won't] support the drastic reforms to stop it [repeal of the Federal Reserve Act] because it could cost him his job."

Henry Ford (1863-1947, American industrialist, the founder of the Ford Motor Company) -- "It is well that the people of the nation do not understand our banking and monetary system, for if they did, I believe there would be a revolution before tomorrow morning."

Henry Ford, 1919 [1596]"

Eustace Mullins (American writer and biographer. His best-known work is The Secrets of The Federal Reserve) -- "...the increase in the assets of the Federal Reserve banks from 143 million dollars in 1913 to 45 billion dollars in 1949 went directly to the private stockholders of the [Federal Reserve] banks."

Eustace Mullins -- "As soon as Mr. Roosevelt took office, the Federal Reserve began to buy government securities at the rate of ten million dollars a week for 10 weeks, and created one hundred million dollars in new [checkbook] currency, which alleviated the critical famine of money and credit, and the factories started hiring people again."

Eustace Mullins (1923-1910) [1597]

John Maynard Keynes, (the father of 'Keynesian Economics' which our nation now endures) "Consequences of Peace" -- "Should government refrain from regulation (taxation), the worthlessness of the money becomes apparent and the fraud can no longer be concealed."

Sir Josiah Stamp, (President of the Bank of England in the 1920's, the second richest man in Britain) -- "Banking was conceived in iniquity and was born in sin. The Bankers own the earth. Take it away from them, but leave them the power to create deposits, and with the flick of the pen they will create enough deposits to buy it back again. However, take it away from them, and all the great fortunes like mine will disappear and they ought to disappear, for this would be a happier and better world to live in. But, if you wish to remain the **slaves of Bankers and pay the cost of your own slavery**, let them continue to create deposits."

Major L .L. B. Angus -- "The modern Banking system manufactures money out of nothing. The process is perhaps the most astounding piece of sleight of hand that was ever invented. Banks can in fact inflate, mint and unmint the modern ledger-entry currency."

Horace Greeley (1811-1872, Editor of the New-York Tribune, among the great newspapers of its time) -- "While boasting of our noble deeds we're careful to conceal the ugly fact that by an iniquitous money system we have nationalized a system of oppression which, though more refined, is not less cruel than the old system of **chattel slavery**.

Horace Greeley, 1872 [1598]

Asst. Sec. U.S. Treasury Harry Dexter White (left) and John Maynard Keynes, honorary advisor to the U.K. Treasury at the inaugural meeting of the International Monetary Fund's Board of Governors in Savannah, Georgia on March 8, 1946.[1599]

John Maynard Keynes (the father of 'Keynesian Economics' which our nation now endures) in his book, *The Economic Consequences of the Peace* **(1920) --** "By this means government may secretly and unobserved, confiscate the wealth of the people, and not one man in a million will detect the theft."

Quote from the Civil Servants' Year Book, "The Organizer" January 1934 -- "Capital must protect itself in every way...Debts must be collected and loans and mortgages foreclosed as soon as possible. When through a process of law the common people have lost their homes, they will be more tractable and more easily governed by the strong arm of the law applied by the central power of leading financiers. People without homes will not quarrel with their leaders. This is well known among our principal men now engaged in forming an imperialism of capitalism to govern the world. By dividing the people we can get them to expend their energies in fighting over questions of no importance to us except as teachers of the common herd."

Thomas A. Edison (1847-1931, American inventor and businessman) -- "People who will not turn a shovel full of dirt on the project (Muscle Shoals Dam) nor contribute a pound of material, will collect more money from the United States than will the People who supply all the material and do all the work. This is the terrible thing about interest ...But here is the point: If the Nation can issue a dollar bond it can issue a dollar bill. The element that makes the bond good makes the bill good also. The difference between the bond and the bill is that the bond lets the money broker collect twice the amount of the bond and an additional 20%. Whereas the currency, the honest sort provided by the Constitution pays nobody but those who contribute in some useful way.   It is absurd to say our Country can issue bonds and cannot issue currency. Both are promises to pay, but one fattens the usurer and the other helps the People. If the currency issued by the People were no good, then the bonds would be no good, either. It is a terrible situation when the Government, to insure the National Wealth, must go in debt and submit to ruinous interest charges at the hands of men who control the fictitious value of gold. **Interest is the invention of Satan**."

Thomas Edison, 1922 [1600]

United States budget for 1991 and 1992 part 7, page 10 -- "The Federal Reserve banks, while not part of the government..."

Editorial from 1907 edition of *The Brisbane Worker* (Australia) -- "The Money Power! It is the greatest power on earth; and it is arrayed against Labour. No other power that is or ever was can be named with it... it attacks us through the Press - a monster with a thousand lying tongues, a beast surpassing in foulness any conceived by the mythology that invented dragons, werewolves, harpies, ghouls and vampires. It thunders against us from innumerable platforms and, Yes, so far as we are concerned, the headquarters of the Money Power is Britain. But the Money Power is not a British institution; it is cosmopolitan. It is of no nationality, but of all nationalities. It dominates the world. The Money Power has corrupted the faculties of the human soul, and tampered with the sanity of the human intellect..."

Eddie Ward, Labor Minister of Australia, during the inception of the World Bank and Bretton Woods -- "...I am convinced that the agreement [Bretton Woods] will enthrone a world dictatorship

of private finance more complete and terrible than and Hitlerite dream. It offers no solution of world problems, but quite blatantly sets up controls which will reduce the smaller nations to vassal states and make every government the mouthpiece and tool of International Finance. It will undermine and destroy the democratic institutions of this country - in fact as effectively as ever the Fascist forces could have done - pervert and paganise our Christian ideals; and will undoubtedly present a new menace, endangering world peace. World collaboration of private financial interests can only mean mass unemployment, slavery, misery, degradation and financial destruction. Therefore, as freedom loving Australians we should reject this infamous proposal."

Eddie Ward, 1935 [1601]

President Lyndon B. Johnson, 1964 [1602]

In 1965, 33rd degree Freemason, Illuminati, and Council on Foreign Relations member[1603] *de facto* President Lyndon Johnson[1604] [1605] (1908-1973), passed *The Coinage Act of 1965* which superseded the 1792 *An Act Establishing a Mint and Regulating the Coinage of the United States*.[1606] Where dimes, quarters, half dollars and dollars had contained 90 percent silver, the silver (and the value of it) was now removed.

This was a violation of Article I, Section 10, Clause 1 of the *Constitution of the United States* (even of the *de facto* constitution), "No State shall...coin Money; emit Bills of Credit; make any Thing but gold and silver Coin a Tender in Payment of Debts..."

Little by little the wealth of the American people was being extracted from them. The people became the borrower, not the lender. The people became the tail and not the head (Deut. 28:13).

In mid-1965 there was entrance of a militant-type movement to interject a homosexual gay rights agenda in society. In May, 1965 there was a homosexual gay march held in front of Independence Hall in Philadelphia.[1607] This 1965 event marked the beginning of the gay rights movement as it was the first time that activists from various cities openly identified as gay and called for equality.[1608] One participant of this march stated, "We created the mind-set for the expression of dissent."

In 2005 *The Pennsylvania Historical and Museum Commission*, the overseer of Independence Hall, approved the *Gay Pioneers Historical Marker* across from Independence Hall and the Liberty Bell Center that designates the site where the first organized annual gay and lesbian rights demonstrations took place.[1609] Each *Fourth of July* from 1965 to 1969 a protest for equality was held in front of Independence

Hall and the Liberty Bell.[1610] Within that timeframe the movement established homosexual organizations throughout the country.

George Washington in Military Service [1611]
"Washington receiving a salute on the field of Trenton"

Sodomy was viewed as a crime in the days of our Founding Fathers. It is recorded in history that General George Washington, the nation's first Commander-in-Chief, not only was the first to forbid but also punish homosexuals in the military. He ordered that a sodomite in his ranks be "drummed out" of the military in disgrace. Since moral behavior was necessary for society in general, it was even more necessary for military personnel in whose hands rested the security as well as the future of the nation.[1612]

Because of the nature of the crime, the penalties for the act of sodomy were often severe. One example we bring forth is that Thomas Jefferson indicated that in his home State of Virginia, "dismemberment" of the offensive organ was the penalty for sodomy. In fact, Jefferson himself authored a bill penalizing sodomy by castration. The laws of the other States showed similar or even more severe penalties.[1613]

Thomas Jefferson, 1788 [1614]

What transpired that May day in 1965 in front of the historical and sacred place of the signing of the *Declaration of Independence* would not have ended with approval by that document's signers. A historical marker may have made its way in the area, however, contrary to what the demonstrators and their counterparts had in mind.

There has been a media campaign to seek "tolerance" in society by implying that people are "born that way" in order to legitimize and popularize sodomy. The sin of "unnatural affection"[1615] is a violation of the *Laws of Nature* and an abomination before *Nature's God* as acknowledged in the *Declaration of Independence*.[1616]

Homosexuality is currently referred to as "LGBT," (Lesbian, Gay, Bisexual, Transgender). It has also been promoted as a propaganda campaign to promote this lifestyle in same sex marriage as well as in educating children in public schools of this "alternative lifestyle."[1617] Even former *de facto* President/CEO, Mr. Obama, has given speeches in support of this sinful lifestyle, both at home and abroad,[1618] that has offended leaders of other countries that are covenanted with Almighty God.[1619] [1620]

In late 2014, a press conference was held in front of Independence Hall where plans were unveiled for the *50th Anniversary Celebration of the LGBT civil rights movement* at Independence Hall on July 4, 2015. Held on July 2-5, the 50th Anniversary festivities included panels, LGBT history exhibits, parties, a festival, and special events with the highlight of the 50th Anniversary Celebration on a large stage in front of Independence Hall on Saturday, July 4. The *Independence National Historical Park* issued a permit for the activities on *Independence Mall* and joined the celebration on *Independence Square*.[1621]

In June, 2013 the *de facto* U.S. Supreme Court ruled that married same-sex couples were entitled to federal benefits and, by declining to decide a case from California, effectively allowed same-sex marriages there.[1622] The Supreme Court of the Corporate UNITED STATES disregarded what Almighty God says in His Word, the Holy Bible, about the institute of marriage: marriage is ordained by God to be between one man and one woman.[1623]

Same-sex marriage is a perversion of the institution of marriage and an offense to the God of Creation who created and instituted marriage.[1624] This "Supreme Court" is accountable before the *Supreme Judge of the world* in condoning this unnatural and sinful lifestyle in which the sexually immoral will not see the Kingdom of God (1 Cor. 6:9), and further, brings curses on this nation.

A 1969 *de facto* U.S. Supreme Court decision that held that people could view whatever they wished in the privacy of their own homes caused the *de facto* U.S. Congress to fund the *President's Commission on Obscenity and Pornography*, set up by *de facto* then-President Lyndon B. Johnson to study pornography.[1625] The Commission's report was published in 1970. Therein was recommended sex education, funding of research into the effects of pornography and restriction of children's access to pornography, and recommended against any restrictions for adults.

On balance, the report found that obscenity and pornography were not important social problems, that there was no evidence that exposure to such material was harmful to individuals, and that current legal and policy initiatives were more likely to create problems than solve them.

The report was widely criticized and rejected by Congress. The Senate rejected the Commission's findings and recommendations by a 60–5 vote, with 34 abstentions (choosing to abstain, or not vote, is a tendency perhaps of Freemasonry cowardice toward their Oligarchic masters); and in particular:

- There was "no evidence to date that exposure to explicit sexual materials plays a significant role in the causation of delinquent or criminal behavior among youths or adults."
- That "a majority of American adults believe that adults should be allowed to read or see any sexual materials they wish."
- That "there is no reason to suppose that elimination of governmental prohibitions upon the sexual materials which may be made available to adults would adversely affect the availability to the public of other books, magazines, or films."
- That there was no "evidence that exposure to explicit sexual materials adversely affects character or moral attitudes regarding sex and sexual conduct."
- That "Federal, State, and Local legislation prohibiting the sale, exhibition, or distribution of sexual materials to consenting adults should be repealed."

Although 60 Congressional members displayed moral sense in their votes, the truth of America's "essential pillars of Civil society being religion and morality"[1626] is in consideration of what the Word of God has to say –

Psalms 101:3a ~   *I will set no wicked thing before mine eyes…*

Focus on the Family, a global Christian ministry dedicated to helping families thrive, reports on the effects of pornography and makes available the findings of extensive research by behavioral scientists and PhDs.

"Whether legally classified as obscene or indecent, <u>all pornography is harmful</u>. Pornography reduces human beings to sexual commodities that can be bought, sold, used and discarded. No one is immune to the mental, emotional, spiritual and even physical consequences of viewing pornographic material. These effects are not confined to the individuals viewing pornography; they extend to families and culture as well."[1627]

Just before his execution on January 24, 1989, serial killer and rapist of at least 25 women and girls, Ted Bundy, granted an interview to psychologist Dr. James Dobson. In the interview, Bundy explained the progression into his compulsive pornography addiction and how it fueled the monstrous crimes he committed.[1628]

"I've lived in prison a long time now, and I've met a lot of men who were <u>motivated</u> to commit <u>violence</u>. Without exception, <u>every one of them was deeply involved in pornography</u> – deeply consumed by the <u>addiction</u>. The F.B.I.'s own study on serial homicide shows that <u>the most common interest among serial killers is pornography</u>." -- Ted Bundy

Since the inception of the internet and the World Wide Web, parents have found the need to protect their children and themselves from internet filth. An internet filtering company addressed the subject of pornography in an article, "What Serial Killers and Murderers Think About Pornography:"

"Viewing pornography doesn't necessarily cause violent behavior; however... if someone has aggressive or violent tendencies, <u>viewing violent pornography may exacerbate those tendencies by giving the viewer the idea that fantasies might be 'normal'</u>." Included in the article are a list of 13 serial killers and murderers and what they think about pornography."[1629]

In summary, the results reported by 33rd degree Freemason then-Senator Lyndon B. Johnson's Congressional Commission's study on pornography is gross error.

Pornography in magazines, movies, and videos has been available for decades. With the arrival of the internet, access to pornography has been easy with a reported explosion in use. Millions of people, mostly men, are daily purchasing and viewing pornography without having to leave the privacy of their homes. A reported small but yet significant percentage get hooked on the habit as an addiction, sometimes with disastrous results.[1630]

What we wish to point out is the reality of the compulsive sexual addiction to pornography, a progression in the habit-forming potential of viewing pornography, as well as the behavior that produces "feel-good" chemicals in the brain such as endorphins, dopamine, and serotonin. These chemicals create a feeling similar to the high from a drug, like cocaine. Continued participation in the addiction produces an immediate and powerful thrill that highly motivates an individual to repeat the behavior. Studies have concluded that individuals do not become addicted to pornography per se but become hooked on the mood-changing feelings they experience when using pornography.[1631]

Serious consequences can result from compulsive use of pornography. The addiction lives and thrives in fantasy. For some, all of the addiction remains in fantasy. For others, the addiction involves other people. But for all sex addicts, central to the addiction is the "creation of a play." This is where the term "acting out" was derived. The fantasy—the play—produces an illusion which closes with a sense of satisfaction. It has been established that individuals who commit sexual offenses such as molestation, abuse, pedophilia, rape, "peeping," and "flashing," are often heavily involved in pornography long before they act-out sexually.[1632]

In the course of acting-out sexually, a learned behavior in sexual deviancy occurs by "conditioning." When viewing pornographic images of specific items take place, such as child pornography, a conditioning or response takes place in the viewer.[1633]

Reports by State-based *Internet Crimes Against Children (ICAC)* task forces through its law enforcement and fieldwork confirm the positive correlation between the possession of child pornography and the commission of crimes against children. The conclusion by this research institute indicates that the viewing of pornographic depictions of children is correlated to child molestation. Evidence from actual investigations and experience in law enforcement and fieldwork projects that it is a small leap from viewing child pornography to molesting children.[1634]

Former psychologist and expert researcher in sexual addiction, Dr. Victor Cline,[1635] claimed that sexually acting-out can become an addiction in itself. Not all consumers of pornography sexually act-out, and not all rapists are addicted to pornography. Many individuals keep the fantasies inside their heads and never act on them, and many rapists are power-hungry individuals or sociopaths who simply enjoy hurting others. Those who use or are exposed to pornography are at risk for eventually acting-out the deviant behavior they view. The risk may be higher for some than for others, but the possibility of acting-out is always there.[1636]

We lead now to a tender topic related to child pornography and pedophilia (also spelled paedophilia), which is a psychiatric disorder in which an adult or older adolescent experiences a primary or exclusive sexual attraction to prepubescent children, generally age 11 years or younger.

In today's language, "pedophilia" is often referred to in relation to any sexual interest in children, or the act of child sexual abuse.[1637] With thousands of children who have disappeared in the last few decades,[1638] it has remained a mystery for many in what has happened to them. Christian Ministries have made an ever growing attempt to counter this heinous activity, even here in America. [1639] [1640] [1641] [1642] [1643] [1644] [1645]

Beauty from Ashes Ministries, Inc.,[1646] a not-for-profit, faith-based public charity dedicated to reaching and assisting women and children involved in and/or associated with the sex industry; commercialized sexual exploitation, trafficking and adult entertainment has posted on its website some established statistics on Human Trafficking:[1647]

Human Trafficking Quick Facts

1. Slavery has been outlawed in every country but still occurs everywhere. (The Universal Declaration of Human Rights)

2. Human Trafficking is now considered the 2nd largest and fastest growing illegal trafficking activity in the world. (United Nations Office on Drugs and Crime, 2008)

3. The United Nations estimates the total market value of human trafficking at $32+ billion-a-year. (United Nations Office on Drugs and Crime, 2008)

4. 80% of victims are women and 50% are children. (Trafficking in Persons Report 2007 U.S. Department of State)

5. A prostituted child is forced to serve between 100 to 1,500 clients per year, per child. (The United States Dept. of Justice, Child Exploitation and Obscenity Section, 2007)

6. One million children are forced to work in the sex industry every year. Between 100,000 and 300,000 children in America are at risk for sex trafficking each year. (The United States Dept. of Justice, Child Exploitation and Obscenity Section, 2007)

7. Among the millions trafficked each year hundreds of thousands are teenage girls, and others as young as 5, who fall victim to the sex trade. (The United States Dept. of Justice, Child Exploitation and Obscenity Section, 2007)

8. Child pornography is a multi-billion dollar industry and among the fastest growing criminal segments on the Internet. (National Center for Missing and Exploited Children)

9. As many as 2.8 million children live on the streets, a third of whom are lured into prostitution within 48 hours of leaving home. (The United States Dept. of Justice, Child Exploitation and Obscenity Section, 2007)

10. The average age of entry into prostitution in U.S. is 13 years old. (The United States Dept. of Justice, Child Exploitation and Obscenity Section, 2007)

In view of these statistics and the wonder of why justice has not prevailed on behalf of our inheritance from the Lord (Ps. 127:3) and His inheritance from us (Deut. 32:9), our children, we now present a staggering revelation. Pedophilia perpetrators and those involved in child sex trafficking rings that are also associated with *de facto* "government" officials at the highest level are finally beginning to be indicted and prosecuted.[1648] [1649] [1650] [1651] [1652]

There are other heinous scandals that have occurred or are occurring at the highest levels in government as well as among the Global Elite that are not reported by corporate-controlled Mainstream News Media[1653] for these horrific and odious crimes against humanity involving, in particular, children.[1654]

Certainly cover-ups and dropping coverage of scandalous reports has occurred as is evidenced in history as was the appalling and scandalous report by *The Washington Times* in 1989 which amazingly ceased in mainstream news.[1655]

Those who bravely attempt to report or prosecute the scandalous and heinous crimes with associations at the highest of levels tend to disappear or lose their lives.[1656] [1657] We are familiar with names like Andrew Breitbart,[1658] Michael Hastings,[1659] and Tom Clancy.[1660] Or perhaps not unless the reader engages in "alternative news," as corporate-controlled mainstream news tends to refrain from such reports.[1661]

In relation to this very topic of child abduction which occurs by *de facto* government agencies, specifically, "Child Protective Services,"[1662] honorable individuals have lost their lives as they have exposed reports backed by substantial evidence such as former Georgia state Senator Nancy Shaefer.[1663] [1664] Another honorable individual who has lost his life as he took action in prosecuting these perverted and heinous criminals was District Attorney Ray Gricar.[1665]

An award-winning psychology statistics and research professor who teaches college and university classes at both the undergraduate and graduate level, former head men's college basketball coach, former mental health therapist and current author and broadcaster,[1666] Dave Hodges,[1667] has bravely reported on the *de facto* "government" seizing American children from their parents and then sex trafficking them.[1668]

It is an alarming truth that Americans must face and process that their "government" would do such a thing. Denial and turning our heads the other way will not prevent the Satanist global elite sociopaths from kidnapping our children. The *de facto* Federal "Government" agency, *Human, Health and Services (HHS)* in collusion with their 50 *de facto* state-level agencies, *Children Protective Services (CPS)* — all under the oversight of *Obamacare* — are engaged in actively fulfilling the United Nations-formed *Agenda 21,* which is designed to breakdown the family and take control of our children.

The taking control includes sadistic torture of our children in this most horrific atrocity. An accurate account of how this criminal network system "legally" accomplishes their agenda through the *de facto* Corporate United States is covered in Professor Hodges' article, "The Obama Youth Movement & the Seizing of American Children."[1669] The aforementioned article, as well as many others, is available for viewing by the links within the endnote references within this topic.

The threat is real in the United States that children are being stolen from families, put into sex trafficking rings and being trafficked around the world. It has been a wonder since the mid-1980s when the *Missing Children Milk Carton Program* began what has happened to these thousands of children.[1670] The Global Elite around the world are finally being exposed and indicted in spite of their comrades within the judicial system having used their offices to protect these sociopaths. One British High Court Justice is now finally named as a codefendant in a lawsuit with charges for child abduction and sex trafficking.[1671]

One of the functions of child sex trafficking has been pointed out as an avenue to secretly fund Muslim warfare in other countries and indicates a strong link of support by the highest level of *de facto* "government" officials and Federal departments and agencies.

Various accomplished journalists have bravely stood-up in righteous indignation to uncover and expose *de facto* Federal Government involvement in human trafficking.[1672] These journalists have reported evidence that the *de facto* "Department of Justice" works in partnership with the *Federal Bureau of Investigation* (FBI) by concealing and altering reports and thereby neglecting and ignoring their duties in this outrageous criminal activity.[1673] [1674] The *de facto* Congress is not ignorant of what transpires in the world, or perpetrated by their corporate "buddies."[1675]

Moving forward on the timeline of "progression" in America's downward spiral in curses, in 1973 the *de facto* U.S. Supreme Court issued a decision on abortion[1676] that legalized the murder of the unborn. The Court ruled that a right to privacy under the due process clause of the (unlawful) 14th Amendment extended to a woman's decision to have an abortion. Also, in the (unlawful) 14th Amendment the word "born" is used, signifying that the citizenship and protection of the so-called 14th Amendment do not operate until they are "born" (i.e. left the womb).[1677]

With no consideration of the Word of God in allowing this "child sacrifice" by the murder of innocents on this sacred land of a covenanted people, the result has brought a curse on the earth as well as on the land.[1678] A mother's womb should be the safest place in the world.

In the 1960-70s, the "cunning, ambitious, and unprincipled "sons of Satan[1679] that sought to destroy this nation worked to do so by destroying the youth through the drug culture, bringing illegal drugs onto our land, introducing them to our youth which resulted in destroying lives and families. It changed the culture of society and assisted in turning a people away from the worship of Almighty God. Every family in America has been affected by a loved one caught in addiction to drugs whether by death, disability, or by incarceration.

The United States has the largest prison population in the world, with approximately 2.3 million behind bars. More than half a million of those people are incarcerated for a *de facto* government drug law violation.[1680]

Richard Nixon, President, 1971

The "War on Drugs" actually began with *de facto* President Richard Nixon and his attack on marijuana, however, *de facto* President Ronald Reagan is known as the "Just Say No" president because of his campaign against recreational drugs in America as well as a strong policy of international drug eradication.

Under Reagan's policy, during a time when Americans were being presented with strong anti-drug propaganda, the *Central Intelligence Agency* (CIA) was in fact an accomplice to a large narcotics smuggling ring in the United States.[1681] In fact, it was Reagan's policies that led to the cooperation between the CIA and the Contras. The "Contras" is a label given to the various rebel groups that were active from 1979 to the early 1990s in opposition to the *Sandinista Junta of National Reconstruction* government in Nicaragua.[1682]

After years of federal investigation, in 1998 the CIA finally admitted to its involvement in drug trafficking in the United States. The CIA admitted to allowing cocaine trafficking to take place by Contras who were being supported by the CIA and using facilities and resources supplied by the *de facto* United States government, while preventing investigation into these activities by other agencies.

This had been done because funds for the support of militant groups in South America had been withdrawn by *de facto* Congress so therefore the CIA allowed the Contras to engage in the drug trade in the United States in order to make money to fund their military operations. The CIA was forced to publish the information by the Congressional Committee when they were found of wrongdoing.[1683]

This scandal was not given extensive coverage by Mainstream News Media. We will recall that those who would fit in the category of "cunning, ambitious, and unprincipled men" would also fit in the category of those who own the largest shares of market of the Mainstream News Media.[1684] We also call to mind that during the timeframe of the Clinton Administration, Arkansas was one of the major trafficking centers for the drug trade operations. It does not slip from mind that *de facto* President Bill Clinton was governor of Arkansas before he became a *de facto* U.S. President.[1685]

Bill Clinton, 1993 as President [1686]

We continue forward.

The land of America has been stolen from the American people by collateralizing both the public and the private lands for the benefit of *foreign* interests.[1687]

Real estate taxes have ensured that no one truly owns their home and land. Americans who have resisted payment of taxes have also faced being evicted by Sheriff's Sale of their homes.

Repeatedly through the years, when Americans would appear in court to defend themselves, declare their constitutional rights to their land, and point out banking fraud, even citing the *Bill of Rights,* they have been told by the black-robed judges (that in actuality are "law merchants" who receive a kickback percentage from the banks and credit unions on foreclosures[1688] [1689]) that their *Constitution* is "ancient," "no longer any good," "there's a new constitution now, more updated," and then threatened with jail for citing the *Bill of Rights*.[1690]

Since money is an important tool of control in the for-profit Corporate U.S. and its subsidiary Corporation States, you can be certain that court fines are included in jail sentencing.

In 1971, *de facto* President Richard Nixon took the nation off the international gold standard and moved it to a petrodollar system that also influences our country's "foreign policy" efforts in oil-rich nations. Adding to the **lust** for wealth and power is the manipulation through "foreign policy" to create wars and destroy nations of people while stealing their resources as spoil.[1691]

Opposite of God's mandate that His children are to be a blessing to all the families of the earth,[1692] our sons and daughters are used in the United States military (also made into for-profit corporations[1693] [1694] [1695] [1696] [1697]) expending their lives in the exploits of foreign countries and civilian people overseas. The *Constitution* (including the *de facto* constitution) makes no provision for our military to be the "police of the world" or being involved in other nations' business.

The shame in all the bloodshed of innocent civilians that has been done in other countries in the name of "Democracy" and the American people—the contemplation of this evil shocks the conscience in the stench of realization of the lust for wealth, power, and apparently the <u>lust for blood by these sons of Satan</u>.[1698]

George H.W. Bush as President in 1989 [1699]

George H.W. Bush[1700] (1924-), 41st *de facto* U.S. President and self-proclaimed Globalist, has held extensive affiliations with secret societies and multi-nationalists. Mr. Bush is a member of the *Bohemian Club*[1701] as well as a 33rd degree Freemason. Mr. Bush is also a member of the *Skull and Bones* Society,[1702] *Council on Foreign Relations*,[1703] *Trilateral Commission*,[1704] and *Order Of The Garters*.[1705]

On August 2, 1990, *de facto* President George H. W. Bush pronounced the name of the global takeover agenda by those who seek world domination when he announced the "***New World Order***"[1706] in his Gulf War speech.[1707]

It is generally thought that Bush coined the phrase *New World Order* in his famous speech on September 11, 1990 (notice the date—the number "11" has meaning to Satanists and September 11th seems to be a favored date[1708] as it is precisely 11 years later to the day of the 9/11 attacks in 2001), however, it had in actuality been coined by many individuals. *De facto* President Woodrow Wilson coined the phrase in his 14-point *League of Nations* speech. The legacy of the 1900's progressive movement has both matured and engulfed America.

In June, 1992, the United Nations held an "Earth Summit" at Rio de Janerio, Brazil, where presentation was made in a plan for the 21st century entitled, "Sustainable Development Agenda 21." The term *Sustainable Development* was first introduced to the world in a 1987 report, "Our Common Future," which was crafted by the *United Nations World Commission on Environmental and Development*, authored by Gro Harlem Brundtland, Vice President of the *World Socialist Party*.

The term was first offered as official U.N. policy at its *Earth Summit* held in 1992, in a document called *UN Sustainable Development Agenda 21*,[1709] today referred to simply as "Agenda 21."

While in office as *de facto* president, George H.W. Bush signed the document on behalf of the United States with a pledge to adopt the goals. This means that the American people have been brought under the international control and authority of the Illuminati/communist-controlled United Nations.[1710]

De facto President George H. W. Bush, addressing the General Assembly of the United Nations, Feb. 1, 1992:

> "It is the sacred principles enshrined in the United Nations Charter to which the American people <u>will</u> henceforth pledge their allegiance." [1711]

Agenda 21 is a plan by the "elite" of the world toward their global *New World Order* agenda to control the world based entirely on socialist control mechanism.[1712] The objectives as laid out in the document include:

- An end to national sovereignty
- The abolition of private property
- The restructure of the family unit
- Increasing limitations and restrictions on mobility and individual opportunity

The 40-chapter document describes a world where everything Americans as well as all citizens of the world, have cherished and held true will no longer exist. The plans of the sons of Satan include ideas that nature will be elevated above man and the surface of mother earth is not to be scratched, human beings are to be concentrated into "human settlement zones," educational systems are to focus on the environment as the central organizing principle, the <u>deliberate</u> "dumbing down" of America, and education of the children is gearing toward the transfer of children's loyalty from families to the government, which will be a global international government.

All aspects of life are covered. "All rights must take a back seat to the collective."[1713] An element of "Precautionary Principle" infers that an individual is guilty until proven innocent. These items are the exact opposite to the *Bill of Rights* that guarantee a number of personal freedoms as well as limit the government's powers.

In 1993, *de facto* President Bill Clinton,[1714] in compliance with *Agenda 21*, signed *Executive Order 12852*[1715] to create the *President's Council on Sustainable Development*[1716] in order to harmonize U.S. environmental policy with United Nations directives as outlined in *Agenda 21*. The Executive Order directed all agencies of the *de facto* Federal "Government" to work with *de facto* State and *de facto* local community governments in a joint effort to reinvent government using the guidelines outlined in *Agenda 21*.

As a result, with the assistance of groups like *ICLEI - Local Governments for Sustainability*, <u>sustainable development has emerged as government policy in every town, county and State in the nation</u>. In 1997, Mr. Clinton signed *Executive Order 13053*[1717] to add members to and extend the Council's charter. In 1999, Mr. Clinton signed *Executive Order 13114*[1718] to <u>again</u> extend the Council's charter. ALL subsequent presidents have reinforced the aforementioned Executive Orders toward *Agenda 21* and Global Government.

Succeeding *de facto* President George W. Bush,[1719] son of the previous president with similar name, is a member of the *Bohemian Club* and the *Skull and Bones Society*—both Satanic secret societies. This Bush followed fast in his father's footsteps as he did more to advance the Globalist One World order agenda in America than any president prior to his eight years in office.

As a result of the tragedies of September 11, 2001 Mr. Bush announced a Global War on Terror, ordered an invasion of Afghanistan that same year, and then in Iraq in 2003. Hundreds of thousands of innocent civilian men, women, and children were killed in those invasions through the Globalist agenda.

George W. Bush as President in 2003 [1720]

Many were awakened during this Bush administration to the fact that global world government was much further advanced than was thought. Where many in Christendom understood from the prophetic scriptures there would someday in the future be a one-world government, now became a visible reality with an identifiable, unrelenting control on all the nations of the world. What was once blown-off as "conspiracy theories" were no longer concealed because secret societies propaganda and weird-looking handshakes became visibly exposed for the world to see.

Although "government" officials and their globalist cohorts made great effort to conceal in secrecy the evidence of September 11, 2001, a great deal of evidence surfaced over the next decade with hardcore facts.[1721]

CONSPIRACY, YES. THEORY, NO.

Truth has become visible and known to those Americans who've been crudely and rudely awakened to the deception of the controlling factors in our world today.[1722] Many innocent lives were lost because of this deception and still are being sacrificed today for the cause of Globalism.[1723] Barack Hussein Obama's[1724] *de facto* presidency brought to maturity the finalization of the *League of Nations*, which is now the *United Nations*, as a global world government complete with legislative, military (NATO) and judicial (World Court) branches.

Barack Obama As President in 2012 [1725]

Many and more journalists are describing Mr. Obama in their reports as simply the elitist Oligarchies' manipulated puppet[1726] [1727] who does as told toward achieving their plan that was envisioned and designed by Luciferian Satanist Albert Pike.

The sons of Satan operate in chaos to bring "on earth as it is in hell" while awaiting their Prince of Darkness (Eph. 6:12), the antichrist, to rule the world from Jerusalem. As previously stated, the plan incorporates the participation of ancient family lines of the "Black Nobility"[1728] [1729] and their Jesuit-principled Illuminati.[1730] Together with all of the various secret societies, these sons of Satan are deeply interlinked through their core foundation, Lucifer.

From that core their common goal is for the Pope of Rome to receive universal worship, ruling from Solomon's rebuilt Temple in Jerusalem.[1731] This means that when their plan is permitted to succeed there will be a future "infallible" Pope[1732] who will be "that man of sin,"[1733] "antichrist,"[1734] "the beast,"[1735] "king of fierce countenance;"[1736] also called by the Lord Jesus Christ, "the abomination of desolation,"[1737] ruling the world from Jerusalem.[1738]

Mr. Obama signed more Executive Orders to expand on the *Sustainable Development* plan devised by the ranks of hell in pursuit of the destruction of Liberty. "Social justice" is described as the right and opportunity of all people "to benefit equally from the resources afforded us by society and the environment."[1739] Mr. Obama loudly declared over and often enough on his version of social justice as the redistribution of wealth.[1740]

Former *de facto* President/CEO Mr. Obama's version of social justice played out as sharing the wealth of the American workers with the banks, which were "too big to fail," while placing the bailout debt on the American people and their posterity. *Agenda 21* decrees that private property is a social injustice because only those owning property are able to benefit or build wealth from it. From this perspective social injustices would include National sovereignty as well as lack of universal health care.

Clearly, Barack Hussein Obama is a sold-out Globalist. America and the entire world have gone beyond the threshold of Global Governance; it's here. We saw Mr. Obama use his pen and his cell phone[1741] regarding important matters in which he bypasses the *de facto* U.S. Congress and goes straight to the United Nations of which he was appointed Chairman and Head of the Security Council. Treason describes this violation of the *Constitution*—even his constitution of the Corporate UNITED STATES. Both Constitutions state in Article I, Section 9, Clause 8:

> "No title of nobility shall be granted by the United States: and no person holding any office of profit or trust under them, shall, without the consent of the Congress, accept of any present, emolument, office, or title, of any kind whatever, from any king, prince, or foreign state."

The stage is set and the players are in place as the curtain is opened to all the once-hidden backdrops of the Oligarchy Secret Societies used to form and finalize their global *New World Order* takeover. All the conspiracies and hidden secrets are in acceleration and being revealed not only to the American people, but to the entire world.

The tyranny of the Illuminati Communism, Socialism, and Marxism has infiltrated and set controls over all of the earth. The sons of Satan now await the entrance and front stage limelight for their leader who they hope is about to step onto the world stage.[1742]

The list of items and "rabbit holes" is seemingly endless in the atrocities that have come out of and because of the Corporate UNITED STATES. It is all a result of the curses of disobedience and the effect of a nation who turned away in apostasy from Almighty God. A few more atrocities for consideration:

- An escalation of trampling the Amendments of the *Constitution* (even of the Corporate counterfeit constitution) by stealing the American peoples' homes by fraudulent foreclosure granted by law merchant "Kangaroo" courts[1743] to the benefit of banks that have no investment interest in mortgage "loans" in light of the fact that money is created out of thin air.

In 1913 when the power to create money was given to a consortium of private bankers who formed the Federal Reserve Bank, any creation of new money injected into the economy came in the form of debt. Likewise, the principle of fractional reserve banking, done by individual banks, created more money by increasing debt. Every time a mortgage is signed in order to purchase a house, the mortgage banker uses the individual's signature to create new money. They do not lend their own money.

The individual's signature creates it out of thin air, and then the "borrower" is required to pay principle and interest on the "loan" as if the mortgage banker had "loaned" some hard-earned money that another bank customer had deposited into their account.[1744]

The system is fraudulent in that the facts are kept hidden in the "illusion" of banking and are not disclosed. We, therefore, have a debt-based economy, which works only as long as the economy improves. We are now at the place where the debt is so massive that it has reached the point of collapse.

- Converting "peace officers" into militarized police units[1745] with an obvious agenda and coming effort to take away the American peoples' rights including the *Second Amendment* right to keep and bear arms by an all-out gun grab.

- Various "false flag"[1746] attacks on the American people and on our soil.

- A counterfeit "government" in power today that has gone as far as to ask the United States military personnel whether or not they would "fire on" (go to war against) the American People.[1747]

- This "government" has actively removed leadership within the U.S. Military that would refuse such an order.[1748]

- At the highest level of this counterfeit "government," there is espionage and treason taking place in funding terrorist organizations through over 19,000 Swiss bank accounts that contribute to the murdering of our sons and daughters of the United States Military as well as innocent civilians in the purposely created war in the Middle East. Every attempt by honorable Military leaders and citizens to report and expose this treason at every level of "government" as well as mainstream media has been ignored. An honorable Military leader has been falsely imprisoned in a civilian Federal prison while attempting to report the treason.[1749]

- United States Army soldiers, our sons and daughters, are being told that Christians, Tea Party supporters and anti-abortion activists are a radical terror threat, enemies of America, and that any soldier found to be supporting these groups would be subject to discipline under the *Uniform Code of Military Justice*.[1750]

- A *Department of Defense* (DOD) manual that was leaked in August, 2013 revealed how the DOD was teaching that the Founding Fathers were "extremists" and would not have been welcome in today's military.[1751] The manual also makes statement that people who embrace "individual liberties" and honor "States' rights," among other characteristics, as potential "extremists" who are likely to be members of "hate groups." [1752] [1753] [1754]

- A 2012 study funded by the *Department of Homeland Security* (DHS) characterizes Americans who are "suspicious of centralized federal authority," and "reverent of individual liberty" as "Extreme Right-Wing" terrorists.[1755] [1756] The report takes its definitions from a 2011 study entitled, *"Profiles of Perpetrators of Terrorism."*[1757]

- Both studies were produced by the DHS *National Consortium for the Study of Terrorism and Responses to Terrorism* (START) at the University of Maryland. The organization was launched with $12 million in funding by the DHS.[1758]

Following are the characteristics used to identify and categorize "terrorists:"

o Americans who believe their "way of life" is under attack;
o Americans who are "fiercely nationalistic" (as opposed to universal and international in orientation);
o People who consider themselves "anti-global" (presumably those who are wary of the loss of American sovereignty);
o Americans who are "suspicious of centralized federal authority;"
o Americans who are "reverent of individual liberty;"
o People who "believe in conspiracy theories that involve grave threat to national sovereignty and/or personal liberty."

The report also lists people who are opposed to abortion and "groups that seek to smite the purported enemies of God and other evildoers" as terrorists.[1759] [1760]

- The Southern Poverty Law Center (SPLC) is a massively funded liberal nonprofit organization that claims to be "dedicated to fighting hate and bigotry and to seeking justice for the most vulnerable members of our society."[1761] The SPLC reports an over $40 million annual budget[1762] and massive "endowment" of over $300 million[1763] that supports its staff of about 200 that make-up a built-in law firm as well as advertising and news agencies.[1764] The SPLC significantly contributes to *de facto* Federal Government reports, specifically for the *Department of Homeland Security* (DHS), in identifying and naming constitutionalists as terrorists.[1765] The SPLC President and CEO as well as the SPLC Analyst and Instructor for the *Federal Law Enforcement Training Center*, are <u>named as members</u> of the Homeland Security Advisory Council and the "Countering Violent Extremism (CVE) Working Group."[1766]

- The SPLC is listed on the *Federal Bureau of Investigation's* (FBI's) Hate Crimes website as a Public Outreach <u>Partner</u> in <u>sharing information</u> and <u>cooperating in solving problems of "Hate Groups."</u>[1767] Bear in mind that the FBI is the principal investigative arm of the U.S. Department of Justice.[1768]

- The SPLC website has an online list of "hate groups" of which they claim are compiled using hate group publications and websites, citizen and law enforcement reports, field sources and news reports.[1769] [1770] While their rhetoric and word craft ties "hate groups" with actual "hate crimes,"[1771] the SPLC acknowledges alleged "hate group" activities to include constitutionally-protected activities such as "marches, rallies, speeches, meetings, leafleting, or publishing," and that the "hate group" designation "does not imply a group advocates or engages in violence or other criminal activity."[1772] However, they do not distinguish between racist or violent groups and legitimate organizations that participate peacefully in the political process—tarring all with the same label.[1773]

Certainly in a civil society, proven racists, bigots, and hate mongers deserve rejection. The SPLC, while claiming to hold high the banner of tolerance, fails to observe basic standards of responsible judgment, honest reporting, and simple decency.

The SPLC prefers to engage in character assassination.[1774] It is a dangerous and concerning contemplation that this organization is partnered with the "government" as an official and professional non-partisan watchdog while fabricating and distorting evidence and actually working as an enemy to all that is good. Claiming to act in the name of tolerance, the SPLC has displayed activities in pursuit to destroy it.[1775]

- Among the SPLC "Extremist Files"[1776] are lists of organizations that they label as "hate groups,"[1777] individuals they profile and label as prominent extremist individuals of hate,[1778] and purports to "examine the histories and core beliefs – or ideologies – of the most common types of extremist movements" while illustrating connections between individuals, groups and extremist ideologies. "Extremist Ideology"[1779] is a label used for what the SPLC in partnership with the *de facto* Federal Government characterizes as "Sovereign Citizens,"[1780] and "Extreme Right." These two "ideologies" include Christians (believers and followers of the Lord Jesus Christ, the Creator of the Universe)[1781] as well as Patriots (those who uphold the *Constitution*, "the Supreme Law of the Land").[1782]

Included on the SPLC "Extreme Right" hate group lists are churches that support traditional family values.   The SPLC labels and stereotypes those that oppose the homosexual lifestyle as "extremists" and categorizes them as a "hate group."   For the most part, the mainstream media have dutifully accepted the SPLC's self-characterization as a courageous foe of those "hateful" groups and have disregarded the SPLC's own history of making inflated and reckless charges of racism and "hate."[1783]

NOTE: It has been discovered that since March, 2015 when this individual chapter was released to the public in pdf format, the footnote reference link, http://www.splcenter.org/get-informed/intelligence-files/ideology/sovereign-citizens-movement now automatically redirects to https://www.splcenter.org/fighting-hate/extremist-files/ideology/sovereign-citizens-movement. In searching the original footnote reference link through the *"Internet Archive Wayback Machine"*[1784] which is an internet archive digital library that provides a history of internet sites on the World Wide Web the resulting search report with snapshots in history for http://www.splcenter.org/get-informed/intelligence-files/ideology/sovereign-citizens-movement reveals that the webpage was apparently programmed to redirect around September 8, 2015.[1785]

The new webpage link, where the former link is redirected to, https://www.splcenter.org/fighting-hate/extremist-files/ideology/sovereign-citizens-movement, reveals in a snapshot history report that the first snapshot in history of this webpage is September 6, 2015.[1786] **The beginning date for this webpage in recorded history is a date <u>after</u> this chapter was released to the public.**

Though there is no noted change in verbiage, the updated webpage very interestingly now includes in the upper right-hand column of the webpage the subtitle, "Associated Extremist Profiles" with one very interesting individual's photo, name, and hometown.[1787] We will report further telling information on this matter in Volume II of *Re-habited: Republic for the United States of America*, entitled, "The Story of the Re-inhabitation."

- Shocking, is the SPLC has listed names and photographs of honorable American leaders on their hate website.[1788] Some of these honorable leaders and victims of character assassination are:

  - Chuck Baldwin, Pastor, Liberty Fellowship
  - David Barton, Founder and President, WallBuilders
  - Lt. General Jerry Boykin (Ret.), Executive Vice President, Family Research Council
  - Gary DeMar, President, American Vision
  - Tom DeWeese, President, American Policy Center
  - Lou Engle, Visionary & Co-Founder, TheCall solemn assemblies; International House of Prayer
  - Joseph Farah, founder, CEO, editor and nationally syndicated columnist of WorldNet Daily (WND)
  - Colonel Bo Gritz, Vietnam Veteran, POW rescues
  - Tony Perkins, President, Family Research Council
  - Stewart Rhodes, Founder, Oath Keepers

- Alarming is that the *de facto* Federal Government departments and agencies are partnered with the SPLC to counter the so-called "Hate and Extremism."[1789]   The SPLC is the source of training for "Hate and Extremism"[1790] which is made available to the approximately 18,000 Law Enforcement agencies in the U.S.[1791] This is how our local police are trained in the hate group propaganda and rhetoric that points to identifying Americans as "domestic terrorists."

The SPLC's "Hate & Extremism" initiative publishes its findings in the *SPLC Hatewatch blog* and in its quarterly journal, the *Intelligence Report,* which claims to be "the nation's preeminent periodical monitoring the radical right in the U.S.,"[1792] and provide their "comprehensive updates" to the nation's Law Enforcement agencies.[1793] The SPLC states on its website, "Our free law enforcement trainings teach officers how to recognize hate groups, symbols and activity; the threat potential of specific groups; and how to respond to hate group activity. The Intelligence Files contains updated biographical profiles of leading hate groups and extremist leaders, plus background on the various extremist ideologies. And our Hate Map helps officials locate extremist groups within their communities."[1794]

- Alarming is the SPLC's "Teaching Tolerance Project"[1795] which has led teacher trainings, published the *Teaching Tolerance* magazine for educators, developed online lesson plans, and produced documentaries for teachers to discuss controversial topics related to gender identity and purported "prejudice" and "bias" in the classroom. This program markets itself as a program focused on social justice, civil rights, multiculturalism, and anti-bias education.

However, the *Teaching Tolerance* program materials, sample curricula, and resources focus disproportionately on conveying acceptance of homosexuality and endorsement of the Lesbian, Gay, Bi-sexual, and Transgender (LGBT) community. Through lesson plan templates and teacher training programs arranged through local school districts, the SPLC encourages teachers to address controversial issues related to gender and sexual orientation in the classroom with children starting in preschool and kindergarten.[1796]

As we continue, we will keep in mind all of the Federal Government departments and agencies in affiliation with each other while the Department of Homeland Security (DHS), Department of Justice (DOJ), and Federal Bureau of Investigations (FBI) are in unique partnership with the hate-labeling *Southern Poverty Law Center* (SPLC).

- It was in March/April 2010 when the *Internal Revenue Service* (IRS) began targeting and auditing Conservative groups [1797] [1798] [1799] [1800] which happens to be the same time American citizens in all 50 States gave lawful notice and issued warrants and orders to *de facto* Governors, Lieutenant Governors, and Secretary of States of all 50 States to return their States to the original *Constitution of the United States.*[1801]

- In the aforementioned IRS scandal of lost or destroyed pertinent emails of key IRS management staff, the Treasury Inspector General for Tax Administration has confirmed that there are also nearly 2,500 documents relating to investigations of the improper disclosure of confidential <u>taxpayer</u> information by the IRS to the White House. Yes, the (Obama Administration) White House.[1802]

For the last 30 years the *Freedom of Information Act* (FOIA) has been the federal regulation directing that any official requests for private taxpayer information made by the White House be personally signed by the president and that the *Congress's Joint Committee on Taxation (JCT)* be notified of the request. The JCT issues an annual report on all requests for IRS information, of which there are none shown for Mr. Obama in the period of time of his presidential administration. This contradicts Mr. Obama's pledge to make his "the most transparent Administration in history."[1803]

The White House told Congress that it <u>refuses</u> to dig into its computers for emails that could shed light on what kinds of private taxpayer information the IRS shares with President Obama's top aides, and has passed the buck back to the IRS to deal with Congress on the matter— "eventually."[1804] In fact, the White House has removed that federal regulation, making official a policy to reject requests for records to that office. The White House said the cleanup of FOIA regulations is consistent with court rulings that hold that the office is <u>not subject to the Transparency Law</u>.[1805]

The rule change means that there will no longer be a formal process for the public to request that the White House voluntarily disclose records as part of what's known as a "discretionary disclosure."[1806] White House record-keeping duties are being handled like the archiving of e-mails.

- The co-author of this writing retired in 2011 after 30 years of service in a Federal Government position with the *United States Postal Service*. This co-author calls to the attention of American citizens that he received a letter dated December 10, 2014 from the Chief Human Resources Officer and Executive Vice President of the *United States Postal Service* to inform him that the U.S. Postal Service had incurred "a cyber-intrusion" of some of their information systems of which contained information that compromised his personally identifiable information such as his name, date of birth, social security number, and address."[1807] In light of the IRS scandal and reports that the White House has received private citizen's personal information, in light of this *de facto* "government's" labeling of Christians and Patriots to be domestic terrorists and enemies of the State, this co-author contemplates who may have a personal interest in his personal information as well as where his information has gone.

Also, due to miscommunication in his retirement counseling (twice), his annuity was lessened by a significant amount of which he has been unsuccessful in working to correct the situation and unable to receive response from the Federal Government *Office of Personnel Management Retirement Operations Center* since a certified formal request dated June 16, 2014.   In light of the Congressional House Committee on Ways and Means' "Timeline of the IRS's Abuse of Conservatives" stating that IRS personnel have been politically selective, and in light of the fact that there is evidence of affiliation of Federal Government departments and agencies in partnership with the conservative hate-mongering of the SPLC toward Christians and Patriots, this co-author considers the potential of selected oppression toward him within the Federal Government where his retirement annuity is concerned.

At the time of this writing, both houses of the *de facto* Congress are avidly working toward legislation priority "on how to share information when a government agency or private company undergoes a cyber attack." All three of the *de facto* legislative bills being worked on would authorize liability protections for companies so they could exchange cyber threat data with government agencies.[1808]

- It was in 2010 when the SPLC (who is partnered with *de facto* Federal Government departments and agencies) began to include Patriots and Christians in their hate group labels. In 2010, the SPLC created a list entitled "Meet the Patriots," which included people such as Chuck Baldwin, Joseph Farah, Sheriff Richard Mack, Stewart Rhodes, Joel Skousen, Orly Taitz, and Alex Jones as supporters of this "patriot movement."[1809]   A supplement entitled "The Enablers" was also released, which included Judge Napolitano, Michele Bachmann, Glenn Beck, and Ron Paul.[1810]

In 2010, 13 groups were added: American Family Association, Family Research Council, Illinois Family Institute, Americans for Truth About Homosexuality, Heterosexuals Organized for a Moral Environment, Family Research Institute, Abiding Truth Ministries, American Vision, Chalcedon Foundation, Dove World Outreach Center, Faithful Word Baptist Church, Traditional Values Coalition, and MassResistance.[1811] The SPLC states in its "Intelligence Report, *The Year in Hate & Extremism, 2010*: "For the second year in a row, the radical right in America expanded explosively in 2010… by far the most dramatic growth came in the antigovernment "Patriot" movement — conspiracy-minded organizations that see the federal government as their primary enemy…"[1812]

NOTE: It has been discovered that since this individual chapter in pdf format was released to the public in March 2015, the footnote reference link, "SPLC.org, Extremist Files, Ideology, Patriot Movement, http://www.splcenter.org/get-informed/intelligence-files/ideology/patriot-movement

(accessed 3/10/2015)," has been notably changed by the SPLC. At the time of formatting this book for publishing, the aforementioned reference link, when placed in the internet search browser, now automatically redirects to

"https://www.splcenter.org/fighting-hate/extremist-files/ideology/antigovernment," with a page entitled, "ANTIGOVERNMENT MOVEMENT." The verbiage is the same except:

1. The word "Patriot" is now removed in the first sentence which stated, "The antigovernment 'Patriot' movement has experienced a resurgence, growing quickly since 2008."

2. The third paragraph has been edited to replace the world "Patriot" with the word, "antigovernment."

3. A subtitle has been added: "The antigovernment movement has experienced a resurgence, growing quickly since 2008, when President Obama was elected to office. Factors fueling the antigovernment movement in recent years include changing demographics driven by immigration, the struggling economy and the election of the first African-American president."

Further, in searching this link through the *"Internet Archive Wayback Machine"*[1813] which is an internet archive digital library that provides a history of internet sites on the World Wide Web, the resulting search report for https://www.splcenter.org/fighting-hate/extremist-files/ideology/antigovernment was saved 5 times with recorded snapshots between the first recorded history of this webpage as August 6, 2015 and January 14, 2016.[1814] The beginning date for this webpage in recorded history is a date after this chapter was released to the public.

The aforementioned link report: http://www.splcenter.org:80/get-informed/intelligence-files/ideology/patriot-movement was saved 19 times with recorded snapshots from June 12, 2014 to the last snapshot in history on September 18, 2015.[1815] It is duly noted that this link now automatically redirects to the new "ANTIGOVERNMENT MOVEMENT" page determining a significant revision away from the use of the word, "Patriot." Also, for one who contemplates, the added subtitle of "racial blame" may suggest an ideology of "racial game."

- Coincidentally (or perhaps not), it was in 2010 when the *Department of Homeland Security* (DHS) began "investigations" into acts and threats of "Sovereign Citizen Extremists (SCE)."[1816] The DHS "Intelligent Assessment" dated February 5, 2015 and produced in cooperation with the FBI,[1817] was circulated to Law Enforcement on that date, but not to the public.[1818] According to this Assessment, the DHS defines *Sovereign Citizen Extremists* (SCEs) as:

  > "groups or individuals who facilitate or engage in acts of violence directed at public officials, financial institutions, and government facilities in support of their belief that the legitimacy of US citizenship should be rejected; that almost all forms of established government, authority, and institutions are illegitimate; and that they are immune from federal, state and local laws."

This *de facto* Corporate takeover definition brings serious consideration to when the term "acts of violence" will be redefined. We recall America's founding document and birth certificate, the *Declaration of Independence,* as well as what the Founding Fathers held as conviction pertaining to governmental tyranny:

"But when a long train of abuses and usurpations, pursuing invariably the same Object evinces a design to reduce them under absolute Despotism, it is their right, it is their duty, to throw off such Government, and to provide new Guards for their future security."

The SPLC—in partnership with the DHS, DOJ, FBI, IRS, etc.—categorizes any challenge or questioning of their violating constitutional law, "the Supreme law of the land," as an extremist ideology of which Law Enforcement agencies have been trained to profile as domestic terrorists.

Ideologies, a set of ideas or beliefs—down to one's thoughts—are now challenged. The "cunning, ambitious, and unprincipled" individuals have dastardly infiltrated American law enforcement to where training in police science now includes psychologically altered perceptions about what is a serious threat in their communities.[1819]

Police science is now conditioned to make "thought police," trained in knowing how to deal with "thought crimes." It is a battle for the mind, as the liberty of conscience is what births forth one's identity.

As hell on earth comes against *"For as he thinks in his heart, so is he,"* (Proverbs 23:7a), as you are trained in righteousness according to the Word of God, the Holy Bible, in the character of the Lord, in virtues, in the Beatitudes, in being transformed by the renewing of your mind according to the Word of God that ye may be able to prove the perfect will of God—recognize the deception as a dangerous lie.

Bouvier's Law Dictionary 1856 Edition:

> LIBERTY. Freedom from restraint. The power of acting as one THINKS fit, without any restraint or control, except from the laws of nature.

- The Department of Homeland Security (DHS) *National Consortium for the Study of Terrorism and Responses to Terrorism* (START) published a survey in July, 2014 in which it is stated that the state and local police ranked sovereign citizens as America's most serious terrorist threat, with Islamists coming in second.[1820] [1821] [1822] Please re-read that statement while bearing in mind the Federal Government's definition of "Sovereign Citizen Extremists" and "domestic terrorists." Please re-read that statement again.

- "Clergy Response Teams" are being trained by the *de facto* Federal Government to "quell dissent" and pacify citizens to obey the government in the event of a declaration of Martial Law. The first directive is for Pastors to preach to their congregations the New Testament book of Romans chapter 13, the often taken-out-of-context Bible passage that was used by Adolf Hitler to hoodwink

Christians into supporting him, in order to teach them to "obey the government" when Martial Law was declared.[1823] [1824]   The erroneous, misleading interpretation of Romans chapter 13 in the New Testament teaches that Christians are obligated to submit to government regardless of whether the "government" acts within the confines and jurisdiction of God's law or not.[1825]

We are reminded of Reverend Charles Finney, the leader of the campaign for awakening America in what is known as the *Second Great Awakening*, who proclaimed,

> "God cannot sustain this free and blessed country, which we love and pray for, unless the Church will take right ground. Politics are a part of a religion in such a country as this, and Christians must do their duty to their country as a part of their duty to God… God will bless or curse this nation according to the course Christians take in politics."[1826]

- In January, 2014, the Satanic Temple in Oklahoma City announced plans to erect a statue of Baphomet sitting beneath an inverted pentagram and flanked by two children gazing upward in adoration at the Oklahoma State Capitol building.[1827] A symbol of Satanism, Baphomet is an ancient idol with a goat's head and legs, human arms and torso, and angel wings.

- The groups' petition to install their monument on the Oklahoma Capitol lawn is in response to the State's installation of a Ten Commandments monument outside the Capitol in 2012. The Satanic Temple spokesperson said that the purpose of the statue, which will be cast in bronze, is to "celebrate our progress as a pluralistic nation founded on secular law."[1828]

- In Mainstream News Media September, 2014, public school children in Orange County, Florida will be subject to the passing out of Satanic-themed coloring books. Members of *The Satanic Temple* announced that they will be joining a national atheist group in handing out literature during the school year such as "pamphlets related to the Temple's tenets, philosophy and practice of Satanism, as well as information about the legal right to practice Satanism in school." Both the secular activist group, *Freedom From Religion Foundation*, and *The Satanic Temple*, a New York City-based organization that "facilitates the communication and mobilization of politically aware Satanists," disagree with the decision to allow religious materials, both plan to combat Bible distribution by giving out their own ideological literature at public schools in Orange County.[1829]

- Parents of students at a Northern California high school have learned that its freshman sex education teachers are also members of *Planned Parenthood* that participate in conferences with leading members of the porn industry that focus on topics like using explicit instructional media for sex ed, the history of sex toys, and how to effectively share one's sex life "on the stage and on the page." The school district's use of "racy sex checklists, a diagram of the 'Genderbread Person,' and coaching students in asking each other if it's okay to take their clothes off" is among student education.[1830]

- In October, 2014 Houston, Texas city officials subpoenaed sermons given by local pastors who oppose an equal rights ordinance that provides protections to the "Lesbian, Gay, Bisexual and Transgender" (LGBT) community.

- The equal rights ordinance seeks to legally ban anti-gay discrimination (current language that includes or targets those who have Biblical convictions of traditional family values) among businesses that serve the public, private employers, in housing and in city employment and city contracting. One of the hotly contested parts of the ordinance includes transgender people as barred from access to a restroom would be legally enabled in filing a discrimination complaint.[1831]

- An honorable 71-year old American citizen and Vietnam War Veteran was charged and incarcerated with cruel and unusual punishment in his home State of Florida for reporting a serious crime taking place within the Florida State and County "governments." Terry Trussell of Dixie County discovered that the Dixie County School Board accepted a $1 million bribe from the Florida Governor in exchange for implementing *Common Core* in their schools after the people of Dixie County made clear that they did not want the questionable and unproven curriculum taught to their children. Mr. Trussell's story, available by endnote link, is one that reveals corruption at the highest of levels in a surreal scenario that Americans in times past would have thought to only read about in science-fiction novels.[1832]

The perversity of the *de facto* Corporate structure has penetrated virtually every aspect of our lives, including the Church, the schools and institutions of higher education, the courts, law enforcement as well as the military. This world system of counterfeits and frauds, murder and destruction — even a for-profit and perversity child abduction pedophile ring — is propelled by the god of this Age[1833] along with his hell-bound children in what is known in the Bible as "MYSTERY BABYLON."[1834]

The United States thus found itself under Divine judgment for its sin of breaking covenant with the *God of the universe*. It began with not following through in the sacred declaration that "all men are created equal" in the founding document, the *Declaration of Independence*, the Founding Fathers' best attempt at the time and under the circumstances knowing they would have to address it at a future time.

While in convention to adopt the nation's operating document, the *Constitution of the United States*, they managed to agree and provide for an expiration of the Slave Trade twenty years later, however, the institution of slavery itself was left in assumption-mode that it would soon expire as it was distasteful, and almost everybody thought it would go away.

The issue would have been eliminated with the *Ordinance of 1784* as drafted for the Northwest Territory but a legislative crack was left open and did not pass as one statesman did not show up for the vote. Three years later, when making another attempt at the *Northwest Ordinance*, the territory south of the Ohio River had been taken out of the Northwest Territory and was then put under the jurisdiction and control of the Slave Power. God's covenanted people left open the door and the Devil held it open with his foot, so when opportunity came along, his sons could walk in and bring hell along.

Add in the mix of covenant-breaking, the mistreatment and abuse of the native Indian "First Americans." By not fulfilling the Genesis 3:12 mandate in being a blessing to all the families of the earth and winning them to the Kingdom of Heaven by the *sword of the Spirit* (Eph. 6:17) instead, a physical sword was used. The people of God and their posterity were not careful to keep covenant with Almighty God or to ensure those holding positions in government upheld the same character principles (absolutes) the country was founded upon. Thus, wicked and greedy men gained control over our institutions in their agenda of Counter-Reformation.

The Christian people in America have a history of voting by association with a political party, not on Christian character issues. They convinced themselves that carnally-minded men could be entrusted with power as they were promised with the "ear tickling"[1835] of what they wanted to hear.

Our Founding Fathers referenced the Bible and adopted its principles of laws following the Almighty's design for a perfect judicial system and republican form of government. If implemented by men that do not live in reverential fear of the Lord, conducting themselves according to the counsel of His Word, it will never become a reality in the earth. As early Americans identified themselves with Old Testament Israel, a people who were in covenant with Him, there are signs in modern days that parallel America with Ancient Israel.[1836] Judgment has had to occur as "the Supreme Governor of the universe," is a God of justice. His punishment is for His people out of mercy — and to His enemies, it is for justice.[1837] He does not change[1838] and He cannot lie.[1839] The timing of the judgment is progressive and accelerating. America is in apostasy and because of it, in peril.

A GOVERNMENT / OF THE PEOPLE / BY THE PEOPLE / FOR THE PEOPLE
Mural by Elihu Vedder, 1896 [1840]
Mural displayed in the lobby to the Main Reading Room, Library of Congress
Thomas Jefferson Building, Washington, D.C.

Chapter Eighteen

Turn, Repent, Return, and the Re-inhabited Republic

President George Washington, 1797 [1841]

Introduction to George Washington's First Inaugural Address, April 30, 1789, as presented in the National Archives, The Center for Legislative Archives:[1842]

"Presidential inaugurations are important civic rituals in our nation's political life. The Constitution requires that presidential electoral votes be opened and counted by the Senate and House of Representatives meeting together, that the candidate with a majority of electoral votes be declared the victor, and that the president-elect, before taking charge of the office, swear an oath of office to 'preserve, protect and defend the Constitution of the United States.'

In 1788, the Confederation Congress scheduled the first presidential inauguration for the first Wednesday in March of the following year. However, the early months of 1789 proved to be unseasonably cold and snowy and bad weather delayed many members of the First Federal Congress from arriving promptly in New York City, the temporary seat of government. Until a quorum could be established in both the House and the Senate, no official business could be conducted. Finally, on April 6, 1789 - over a month late - enough members had reached New York to tally the electoral ballots. The ballots were counted on April 6 and George Washington won unanimously with 69 electoral votes. Washington was then notified of his victory and traveled to New York City from his home in Virginia.

On April 30, 1789, George Washington took the oath as the first president of the United States. The oath was administered by Robert R. Livingston, the Chancellor of New York, on a second floor balcony of Federal Hall, above a crowd assembled in the streets to witness this historic event. President Washington and the members of Congress then retired to the Senate Chamber, where Washington delivered the first inaugural address to a joint session of Congress. Washington humbly noted the power of the nations' call for him to serve as president and the shared responsibility of the president and Congress to preserve 'the sacred fire of liberty' and a republican form of government.

At that auspicious moment marking the birth of the federal government under the Constitution, Senator William Maclay of Pennsylvania observed that even the great Washington trembled when he faced the assembled representatives and senators. 'This great man was agitated and embarrassed,' Maclay added, 'more than ever he was by the levelled Cannon or pointed Musket.' **After concluding his remarks, the President and Congress proceeded through crowds lined up on Broadway to St. Paul's Church, where a service was conducted.** Social gatherings and festivities closed the nation's first inaugural day. Subsequent presidential inaugurations took place on March 4th (or March 5th when the fourth fell on a Sunday), until the Twentieth Amendment changed the date to January 20th beginning in 1937." U.S. Senator William Maclay (Pennsylvania) [1843]

First President of the *United States of America*, George Washington, known as "Father of our Country,"[1844] excerpts from his Inaugural Address, April 30, 1789 ~

"…it would be peculiarly improper to omit in this first official Act, my fervent supplications to that Almighty Being who rules over the Universe, who presides in the Councils of Nations, and whose providential aids can supply every human defect, that his benediction may consecrate to the liberties and happiness of the People of the United States, a Government instituted by themselves for these essential purposes: and may enable every instrument employed in its administration to execute with success, the functions allotted to his charge. In tendering this homage to the Great Author of every public and private good I assure myself that it expresses your sentiments not less than my own; nor those of my fellow-citizens at large, less than either. No People can be bound to acknowledge and adore the invisible hand, which conducts the Affairs of men more than the People of the United States. Every step, by which they have advanced to the character of an independent nation, seems to have been distinguished by some token of providential agency. And in the important revolution just accomplished in the system of their United Government, the tranquil deliberations and voluntary consent of so many distinct communities, from which the event has resulted, cannot be compared with the means by which most Governments have been established, without some return of pious gratitude along with an humble anticipation of the future blessings which the past seem to presage. These reflections, arising out of the present crisis, have forced themselves too strongly on my mind to be suppressed. You will join with me I trust in thinking, that there are none under the influence of which, the proceedings of a new and free Government can more auspiciously commence.

"…I dwell on this prospect with every satisfaction which an ardent love for my Country can inspire: since there is no truth more thoroughly established, than Since we ought to be no less persuaded that the propitious smiles of Heaven there that exists in the economy and course of nature, an indissoluble union between virtue and happiness, between duty and advantage, between the genuine maxims of an honest and magnanimous policy, and the solid rewards of public prosperity and felicity:, can never be expected on a nation that disregards the eternal rules of order and right, which Heaven itself has ordained: And since the preservation of the sacred fire of liberty, and the destiny of the Republican model of Government, are justly considered as deeply, perhaps as finally staked, on the experiment entrusted to the hands of the American people.

"Having thus imported to you my sentiments, as they have been awakened by the occasion which brings us together, I shall take my present leave; but not without resorting once more to the benign parent of the human race, in humble supplication that since he has been pleased to favour the American people, with opportunities for deliberating in perfect tranquility, and dispositions for deciding with unparalleled unanimity on a form of Government, for the security of their Union, and the advancement of their happiness; so his divine blessing may be equally conspicuous in the enlarged views, the temperate consultations, and the wise measures on which the success of this Government must depend."[1845] And so was the official launching of the *United States of America* at its first temporary capitol in New York City with the inauguration of its first president, a man of God who was known for his humility, battle courage in faithfully serving as Commander of the Continental Army in the *Revolutionary War of Independence*, as a praying man who did not fail to acknowledge Almighty God.

Beloved by his peers and the American people alike, endeared as "Father of our Country," President Washington gave an address at Federal Hall upon his inauguration with an oath to preserve, protect and defend the brand new *Constitution of the United States.* His inaugural address has come to be known as a prophetic word for America. Should America ever turn from her covenant with *"the Almighty Being who presides over the Universe... the Great Author of every public and private good... the propitious smiles of Heaven can never be expected on a nation that disregards the eternal rules of order and right, which Heaven itself has ordained."*

Following through with a "divine service"[1846] at St. Paul's Chapel, just a few blocks from Federal Hall in New York City, the *United States of America* was consecrated to Almighty God.

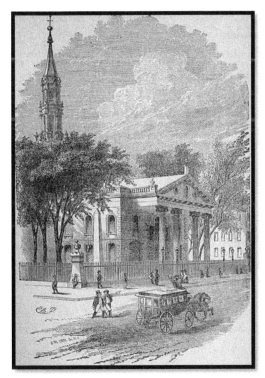

St Paul's Chapel in 1882 [1847]
Nearly 100 years after President George Washington
dedicated the United States of America to Almighty God

St. Paul's Chapel in 2009
New York City, America's first Capital [1848]

We've traced America's history and seen her original sins in the mistreatment of people, not honoring the *Declaration of Independence*, America's "birth certificate," that declares before the *Creator of the universe* and *Supreme Judge of the world* that all men are created equal. At times in America's history, she has used a physical sword in greedy gain of another's resources which is contrary to the "sword of the Spirit"[1849] in fulfilling the mandate in being a blessing to all the families of the earth.[1850]

Because of breaking covenant with Almighty God, the curses of disobedience[1851] included giving foothold to the sons of Satan who are used of Almighty God as His rod of correction to discipline[1852] His beloved people and as a means to compel them to turn back to Him, remain in covenant obedience, and be secure in the blessings of obedience.[1853]

The sons of Satan, a dark and misguided people, have secretly operated through the generations in following the counsel of Balaam[1854] to cause the American people and her posterity to further fall into the curses of disobedience to where a once great nation, a city upon a hill,[1855] a nation that has traditionally sent more missionaries with the Light of the glorious Gospel into the world than any other, to now have need to receive more missionaries than any other country.[1856]

America has been spiraling out of control in immorality while ungodly, apostate leaders[1857] of a counterfeit government have their hell-bound feet on the accelerator. America has been receiving warnings and judgments by her beloved Creator in a passionate calling for her to return[1858] to Him before His justice requires destruction.[1859] There are those who have eyes to see and ears to hear,[1860] understand the call of the Beloved to repent and return and then in response exhort others who think they see and hear[1861] but instead are angered at the message of judgment. "Not in America. God bless America," is proclaimed in pride and denial.[1862]

The "spell" of bread and circus has been comfortable enough. While God's hedge of protection is being removed, America's borders are wide open. The financial system is about to crash and local police are being militarized. We cannot take an eye off of our children in fear of their molestation or kidnap. Our waterways are polluted, and our produce is genetically modified into "frankenfood." Disease is exponentially spreading and the weather patterns have become frightfully destructive. The sons of Satan are moving forward in implementing their *Agenda 21*[1863] [1864] plan for the 21st century[1865] of ultimate takeover and mass destruction, while yet even the Church sleeps.

Those who know the Almighty through His Word, the Holy Bible, and by His Holy Spirit will understand that He has many characteristics. He is a God of love.[1866] He demonstrated His great love for humanity in that He so loved the world that He gave his one and only Son, that whoever believes in him shall not perish but have eternal life.[1867] Even while we were still sinners, Christ died for us.[1868] The Lord is compassionate and gracious, slow to anger, abounding in love.[1869]

We must understand that the Creator is also a God of holiness and justice. Heavenly beings around the throne of God proclaim ceaselessly, "Holy, holy, holy is the Lord Almighty."[1870] The Almighty says in His Word, the Holy Bible, "Be holy, because I am holy."[1871] The Almighty is a God who hates evil and injustice. He has a holy wrath against all ungodliness and wickedness of men.[1872] He has righteous indignation, a holy anger, fury, and jealousy against that which offends his righteousness; it is a vindication of God's truth against every kind of falsehood.[1873]

God's nature is loving,[1874] merciful,[1875] patient,[1876] and kind.[1877] Likewise, as a God of justice, He can be severe in His wrath toward evil, bringing judgment and punishment.[1878] It is necessary to understand both aspects in the character of the Almighty. He says in His Word that He disciplines those

306

He loves[1879] and as a loving Father to those who are reconciled to Him by faith in His Son's finished work on the cross,[1880] we must understand His nature with reverential fear of the Lord which is the beginning of wisdom.[1881] **His punishment is for His people out of mercy and to His enemies it is for justice.**[1882] We do well to know that He does not change[1883] and He cannot lie.[1884]

Revelation 3:19 ~

> *As many as I love, I rebuke and chasten: be zealous therefore, and repent.*

Proverbs 3:12 ~

> *For whom the Lord loveth he correcteth; even as a father the son in whom he delighteth.*

As we are in the latter days of the end of the Age known by the signs of the times,[1885] we near a time where there will be a final judgment when God, through his Son Jesus Christ, Yeshua haMashiach in his original Hebrew language,[1886] will judge all of humanity. Some will receive eternal life in the presence of the Creator while others will receive eternal damnation.[1887] There are yet prophetic events that must transpire throughout the world before that time comes.

Throughout history, God has always had a remnant of people that He has called His own.[1888] In this particular topic, we deal with a nation that has been in covenant with Him since its inception. The terms of the covenant are the blessings of obedience along with the curses of disobedience.[1889] In His loving kindness, He has been calling for His people and the Nation to return to Him. There have been profound occurrences of communication from God Almighty. Let us reason together.[1890]

Hosea 13:9 ~

> *O Israel, thou hast destroyed thyself; but in me is thine help.*

Hosea 14:2 ~

> *Take with you words, and turn to the Lord: say unto him, Take away all iniquity, and receive us graciously: so will we render the calves of our lips.*

Hosea 14:9 ~

> *Who is wise, and he shall understand these things? prudent, and he shall know them? for the ways of the Lord are right, and the just shall walk in them: but the transgressors shall fall therein.*

A Profound Message

David Wilkerson[1891] (1931-2011) was a well-known Christian evangelist and founding pastor of the nondenominational Times Square Church in New York City.[1892] In 1958, Wilkerson believed he was called of God to go to New York to minister to gang members and drug addicts, as told in his best-selling book, "The Cross and the Switchblade."

David Wilkerson, 1931-2011 [1893]

Pastor Wilkerson's burden for the lost in the City increased while at the same time he founded "Teen Challenge," a nationwide ministry that reaches out to people with life-controlling habits, and which has been recognized as one of the most effective of its kind. He distributed powerful Biblical messages that encouraged righteous living and complete reliance on God.

Through the years, Pastor Wilkerson also delivered thought-provoking, heart-pricking prophetic messages regarding America based on lessons in Biblical history that conclusively demonstrated that, in apostasy, the *United States of America* was becoming ripe for divine judgment characterized with one of the judgments being a dramatic economic meltdown. Pastor Wilkerson stated that he was not a prophet, but a "watchman."[1894]

As the Bible reveals an unmistakable pattern of God warning people and nations in ancient times, He continues to warn them in the modern world. Biblical history portrays that before judgment, God warns. Bible stories regarding ancient Israel would tell of Him sending warning of forthcoming national judgment through different means, and why. The warnings would be communicated through audible voices, dreams, prophetic messages or acts, through signs, a written word, supernatural occurrences as well as the outworking of natural events.

God says in His Word that He does not change.[1895] He is the same yesterday, today, and forever.[1896] He is able and does send prophetic warning in the modern world just as He had in ancient times. It is logical to expect that He will communicate warning of danger or calamity in a way that is consistent with those given in ancient Biblical times.

On September 16, 2001, just five days after the 9/11 attack on the twin towers of the World Trade Center as well as at the Pentagon in Washington, and a downed plane in Pennsylvania, Pastor Wilkerson preached a message at Times Square Church that is quite profound.[1897] [1898] A text version of *"The Towers Have Fallen but We Missed the Message"* is available for viewing by endnote link,[1899] however, the wording is a little different. There is also a depth of passion conveyed in the recorded sermon that is not possible in experience via the text version.

In his message, Pastor Wilkerson tells the story in which six weeks prior to the disaster the Holy Spirit had forewarned his pastoral staff that a calamity was coming. All scheduled events for the coming weeks were canceled and his congregation was stirred to intercessory prayer four nights per week.

Pastor Wilkerson tells of experiencing the Lord's presence in the prayer meetings as well as receiving divine revelation pertaining to a coming tragedy along with instructions to intercede in prayer for America.

In his message, Pastor Wilkerson assured his listeners that God was not taken by surprise in the calamity as God knows the thoughts of all human beings,[1900] including every ruler and terrorist. The Lord monitors the movements of every individual and knows when we sit down or stand up.[1901]

He stated that God has everything under control[1902] and nothing takes place on the earth without his knowledge of it, his permission for it, and, at times, his doing behind it.[1903] Wilkerson compels his listeners, as Christians, that they would know that God has delivered a message to America as well as the world through this disaster. Where some ministers and theologians claim that God had nothing to do with these disasters because He wouldn't allow such awful things to happen, Wilkerson advises that nothing could be further from the truth and that this kind of thinking is causing our nation to rapidly miss the message that God wants to speak to us through the tragedy. His warning of turning a deaf ear to what God is loudly proclaiming is an earnest admonition in hopes of preventing what could be much worse for an unrepentant America.[1904]

The audience was reminded that the apostle Paul admonished, as recorded in 1 Corinthians 10:11 and that the scriptures, including the Old Testament, are examples and written for our admonition in how God moves. He referenced the Old Testament prophet Isaiah in speaking directly to what was just experienced in the calamity and **drew a parallel of America to ancient Israel**. He spoke of the Lord sending "light afflictions" upon his people to call them to repentance and wooing them out of idolatry and back into His blessing and favor.

Wilkerson recalled God's chosen nation, ancient Israel, in their response of rejecting God's call to repentance.[1905] "They would not hear, but hardened their necks."[1906] The people of Israel would mock the prophets who called them to humility and continued in their apostasy.[1907] God sent "wake-up calls" to Israel. The first wake-up call to Israel came in an invasion by Assyria.[1908] Though the damage was minimal, God was clearly speaking to His people. The Lord's chosen nation lost their sense of security and missed the message that God was speaking.

A second "wake-up call" came to ancient Israel in the form of an invasion by sudden attack. In the Biblical story told by the prophet Isaiah, he relays that God was faithful to speak to his people: *"The Lord sent a word into Jacob, and it hath lighted upon Israel."*[1909] It was a clear word and sent to the whole nation.

Pastor Wilkerson relayed that God always sends His word and never in history has the Lord left His people clueless in a time of calamity. He never abandons His people or forces them to figure out things on their own. He always provides a word of understanding.[1910] He has watchmen who hear and understand what He is speaking so that they can proclaim the warnings to the people along with the reason for the calamities.[1911]

Pastor Wilkerson exhorted and reasoned with the people that there are those in Christendom who refuse to receive the message of warning that the Lord wants His people to know. He stated that if we don't hear God's truth and face it, our nation is doomed.

He quoted from the book of Isaiah,

"The Lord shall set up the adversaries of Rezin against him, and join his enemies together...for the people turneth not unto him that smiteth them, neither do they seek the Lord of hosts."[1912]

He clarifies through the Word of God that God used enemy nations to chasten His people for their national pride and as a warning and a call to the nation to repent and to return to Him.[1913] The people of Israel did not receive the warning and they watched in horror as their buildings began to collapse and fires raged throughout their cities. God's people began to cry, *"The bricks are fallen down...the sycamores are cut down."[1914]*

Drawing a parallel to the then recent September 11th attacks and the emotions stirred by the disasters in New York and Washington, Wilkerson went on to state that Israel did not repent or receive their attack as a message of warning from God. In fact, God's people proclaimed a floodtide of pride as a nation, *"All the people...say in the pride and stoutness of heart....[1915]*

Once the attack died down and the Israelites regained their confidence they declared, *"The bricks are fallen down, but we will build with hewn stones: the sycamores are cut down, but we will change them into cedars."[1916]* They weren't receiving the calamity as from the Lord and proclaimed that they would rebuild everything back bigger and better. "We're a God-blessed nation and we're going to come through this disaster stronger than ever."

Pastor Wilkerson projected a short-lived parallel to America in people flocking to the churches for about two weeks, national leaders on the steps of the Capitol building singing, "God bless America," sporting events observing a moment of silence at halftime, and all think they're having a spiritual experience. He referred to it as hypocrisy and giving lip service[1917] to God while our nation continues to slide into the mire of immorality. Wilkerson stated that the Lord reminded him that many of the leaders who were singing "God stand beside us," had worked to rule Him out of American society, determined to remove His Name from American history books, and they've allowed the murder of millions of babies through abortion.

Pastor Wilkerson spoke from the depths of his heart in what he believed God was trumpeting to the American people: time is running out. God has sent prophets and watchmen who have warned over and again. Where God has prospered America above all nations, He has endured America's worship of gold and silver, sane-less sensuality, and mockery of Him. He's endured the continuous shedding of innocent blood and murdering of babies, tireless efforts to eradicate His Name even from American history books.

Pastor Wilkerson admonished that God was behind the 9/11 strike on American soil in order to wake America from the path of destruction in hopes of saving her. His desire is that America would repent and turn from her wicked ways so that He can heal her land and destroy her enemies.[1918]

When a nation is under Divine correction, it will react in one of two ways: a nation being chastised will either humble itself and repent as did Old Testament Ninevah, or it will give lip service to God but proudly rely on its own strength to rise above the correction. Wilkerson recalled a similar judgment on the Old Testament House of Judah. He interjected that prayer and remembrance are good, however, there is a true need for prayer and <u>repentance</u>. We are at the same crossroads now. There is a call of God to turn back to Him as our American ancestors knew Him and had covenanted with Him.

Just as God had sent ancient Israel and ancient Judah prophet after prophet to warn them, they would not open their eyes to see. They heard the message but wouldn't listen and respond.

Pastor Wilkerson spoke about God's justice and righteousness and how the Almighty weeps over those calamities that befall innocent people.

He reminded his hearers of the bottle of tears[1919] of the saints and stated that he believes those tears that are shed by Christians are God's own tears as prompted by His Holy Spirit within them. He weeps through those who are His beloved children.

Wilkerson said that every tear that is shed as a believer in Jesus, a lover of Christ, those are the tears of God. Jesus is still man and He weeps. He weeps for His children and the bottled tears are the only evidence He can give. However, there are times that He will restrain His pity because His justice demands that He keep His own Word.

The greatest example of this is the sacrifice of his Son, Jesus. Justice demanded that the sins of the whole world be laid on this innocent man, the Son of God, and that He would be condemned to die for all at the hands of wicked men. God's own Son gave himself as a willing sacrifice to offer deliverance and salvation to all of mankind, to all that would believe in Him and call upon His Name.[1920]

Wilkerson emphasized that God does feel pain and takes no pleasure in it.

"Cast away from you all your transgressions, whereby ye have transgressed; and make you a new heart and a new spirit: for why will ye die, O house of Israel? For I have no pleasure in the death of him that dieth, saith the Lord God: wherefore turn yourselves, and live ye." (Ezekiel 18:31-32)

Wilkerson made mention of a prophetic message he had been given in September, 1992 of what would befall New York City if America would not return to God in repentance. The description is beyond that of 9/11. <u>He stated that if America rejects God's call to turn back to Him, she will face the same judgments that ancient Israel faced and the whole nation is doomed</u>. It will entail the nation's economy, violence, fires, and military vehicles throughout the land. In Wilkerson's 2001 message, he stated that the window of opportunity was very short at that time.

He points to the way of avoidance in this judgment. He speaks of a reprieve if there were a Godly man for a President of the nation who would prove to have a spirit like the Old Testament character Josiah who sought the Almighty, completely trembling at the Word of God in seeking Him with all his heart. God heard him.[1921] Wilkerson exhorts those that would have ears to hear that the word for the people has been, "Turn to Me and I will turn to you, thus saith the Lord."[1922]
Amos 3:7 ~

Surely the Lord God will do nothing, but he revealeth his secret unto his servants the prophets.

We move on now to tell of another profound message of warning by the Almighty through another man of God in northern New Jersey just across the river from Manhattan, a borough (same as a county) of New York City. <u>It is the same exact scripture verse</u>, <u>the same exact word of God</u>, <u>given at the same exact time</u> as was received by David Wilkerson.

Rabbi Jonathan Cahn and his book *The Harbinger*

Jonathan Cahn[1923] is President of *Hope of the World* ministries, Senior Pastor and Messianic Rabbi of the *Jerusalem Center/Beth Israel* in Wayne, New Jersey. He ministers the Gospel on radio and television to Jew and Gentile throughout the world.

Just as David Wilkerson had received a message of warning for America and New York City in 1992, Rabbi Cahn writes that he had been led to give a message about ten years prior to 9/11 which amazingly relates to national judgment beginning in New York City.[1924]

Following is an introduction as wonderfully described by *The 700 Club*,[1925] to the prophetic mystery and message that Rabbi Cahn experienced and reveals in his book, "The Harbinger." **Cahn tells of the supernatural connection between ancient Israel and America.** It is a message of warning concerning the coming calamity and a call of God for the nation to return to Him.

LIGHT TO THE NATIONS

The massive scale of the 9/11 attack on the World Trade Center made for startling images and a new frightening, sober reality for America. But through this devastation Rabbi Cahn was given an understanding of what this meant to America through Isaiah 9:10, and the uncanny parallel this attack has to events in 8th century Israel.

Jonathan says before God judges a nation, He sends warning. He sent warning to ancient Israel. The attacks of 9/11 were a warning, and like ancient Israel, if the nation ignores God's warning there will be dire consequences, Jonathan says. Harbinger means "warning." In his book, The Harbinger, a prophetic mystery and message conveyed in the form of a novel, Jonathan tells of the supernatural connection between ancient Israel and America. An unnamed Prophet speaks. However, the events are real, filled with insights the Lord revealed to Jonathan in the years after 9/11.

There are nine harbingers of what happens after the first attack if the nation refuses to return to God. The judgments are progressive, with periods of normalcy in-between, but continue if there is no national repentance. The economic implosion and other national ills spring from this event. Israel and America are the only two nations that God sovereignly planted as a light to the nations. "Those who laid America's foundations saw it as a new Israel, an Israel of the New World. And as with ancient Israel, they saw it as a covenant with God," the Prophet says. To whom much is given, much is required.

THE HARBINGERS

Based on Isaiah 9:10, - "The bricks have fallen, but we will build with hewn stones: the sycamores are cut down, but we will plant cedars in their place," the northern 10 Tribes of Israel refused to repent after they were struck by the Assyrians - which was a warning from the Lord. Instead of listening to the alarm, of turning back, and humbling themselves in repentance, they boasted of their resolve, that they would rebuild stronger and better than before. They ignored the warning and rejected the call to return. They defied it. Sadly, their defiance led to the nation's total destruction years later. The ancient prophecy forms the key to the nine harbingers of judgment, which are given to a nation in danger of judgment – each of which have reappeared on American soil – marking America as the nation in danger of judgment.

Statue of Liberty and World Trade Towers on fire
September 11, 2001, "9/11" [1926]

The First Harbinger: The Breach. In 732 B.C., the hedge of protection was removed and Israel's enemies invade the land and wreak havoc. The calamity traumatizes the nation but it takes place on a limited scale, as with 9/11. The warning is the removal of the hedge. <u>On September 11, 2001, America's hedge of protection was removed – the breach of America's security, and was a sign that God has lifted His protective hand.</u>

The Second Harbinger: The Terrorist. It was the dark shadow of Assyrian terror that loomed over the kingdom of Israel. The danger against which the prophets had warned. And when, years later, Israel's final judgment came, the Assyrians would again be the means through which it would happen. <u>So, too, the attack on America is carried out by terrorists.</u> <u>The Assyrians were a Semitic people, children of the Middle East.</u> <u>So too were the terrorists of 9/11.</u>

The Third Harbinger: The Fallen Bricks. The most visible signs of the attack on ancient Israel were that of the fallen buildings and the ruin heaps of fallen bricks. The third harbinger is the sign of the fallen bricks of the fallen buildings. <u>On Sept 11, 2001, Americans were confronted with the same sign, fallen bricks of the fallen buildings of the wreckage of Ground Zero.</u> <u>America was not turning back to God.</u> <u>It was a short-lived spiritual revival that never came.</u>

The Fourth Harbinger: The Tower. Israel defiantly began rebuilding on the devastated ground, vowing to rebuild higher and stronger. <u>So, too, in the wake of 9/11, American leaders vowed to rebuild at Ground Zero higher and stronger – the Tower begins to rise at Ground Zero.</u> <u>Those involved act unwittingly.</u>

The Fifth Harbinger: The Gazit Stone. We will rebuild with quarried stone - The Israelites carve out quarried stone from mountain rock and bring it back to the ground of destruction where clay bricks once stood. <u>Three years after 9/11, a stone is quarried out of the mountain rock of New York.</u> <u>This massive stone was brought back to Ground Zero.</u> <u>In ancient Israel this stone became a misplaced embodiment of the nation's confidence in its own power.</u> <u>So too the massive stone at Ground Zero became the symbolic cornerstone of the rebuilding.</u> <u>Public ceremonies accompanied the stone placement.</u> <u>Plans to rebuild Ground Zero would be frustrated for years.</u> <u>Eventually they would remove the stone from Ground Zero altogether.</u>

The Sixth Harbinger: The Sycamore. The Sycamores have been cut down - The attack on ancient Israel resulted in the striking down of the sycamore tree, a biblical sign of national judgment. The fallen sycamore is a sign of uprooting, a warning and, in ignoring the warning, it becomes a prophecy of judgment. <u>On 9/11, as the North Tower fell it sent debris and wreckage which struck and uprooted an object – a sycamore tree growing at Ground Zero.</u>

The tree was made into a symbol and named The Sycamore of Ground Zero. When it fell in ancient Israel it prophesied the nation's downfall and the end of its kingdom. What happens to America depends on if the warning is heeded.

The shockwave of the falling World Trade Towers destroyed a sycamore tree which was standing in front of St. Paul's Chapel for more than a century. Artist Steve Tobin used its roots as the base for a bronze sculpture memorial.[1927]

The Seventh Harbinger: The Erez Tree. But we will plant cedars in their place - In their defiance of God, the Israelites replace the fallen sycamore with a Cedar tree. The cedar, being stronger than the sycamore becomes a symbol of the nation's arrogant hope that it will emerge from the crisis stronger than before. The English name for this tree is "Cedar," but the Hebrew word is "Erez." Erez stands not only for cedar but for a conifer tree of the panacea family. In November of 2003, a tree was lowered at the corner of Ground Zero into the soil where the fallen sycamore once stood. The tree was a conifer, a panacea tree, the biblical Erez. A ceremony was held around the tree and it, too, became a symbol – entitled The Tree of Hope. There is always hope. A nation's true hope is found only in returning to God.

The Eighth Harbinger: The Utterance. The Eighth Harbinger was the public speaking of the ancient vow of defiance. For this harbinger to manifest, the vow would have to be spoken in the nation's capital by a national leader, as it had been in ancient Israel. On Sept 11, 2004, every object mentioned in the prophecy of Isaiah 9:10 had manifested. The public utterance of the prophecy had to take place publicly, which happened on Sept 11, 2004 when VP candidate John Edwards, giving a speech in the capital city, quoted this exact scripture word for word in Wash., DC. Without realizing it, he was joining the two nations together and, without realizing it, pronouncing judgment on America. The ancient and the modern were bound together.

The Ninth Harbinger: The Prophecy. The Ninth Harbinger is the proclaiming of the ancient vow as prophecy, as a matter of public record, and spoken before the words come true. On Sept 12, 2001, the day after 9/11, America issues its official response to the attack. The one in charge of issuing the response was Tom Daschle, Senate Majority Leader. As he closes his speech he makes a declaration – he proclaims the ancient vow of defiance, word for word, to the world. By doing so he prophesies the nation's future course, all of which comes to pass.

The Second Shaking – The mystery of the Harbinger continues – and lies behind everything from the Global War on Terror, the Collapse of the American economy, the crash of Wall Street, the Great Recession, and more.

Amazingly, events happened with an unseen hand, and people acted unwittingly in the unfolding of this prophecy. The Prophet character says that "The Almighty has His own purposes." God, in His mercy, always reaches out in mercy. At Ground Zero, the ground of devastation becomes the ground of restoration. **Incredibly it was at the site of Ground Zero in the miracle church, St Paul's**

Chapel, that this nation was dedicated to God by first president George Washington & other leaders at his inauguration in 1789. The nation's first government was formed in New York City before DC was formed. God is calling the nation back to Himself. "The heart of God wills for salvation," the Prophet says. "Greater than his judgments are His compassions."

THE STORY BEHIND THE MESSAGE: Not long after 9/11 Jonathan sensed that somehow these events were linked to what happened to ancient Israel per Isaiah 9, the first massive divine warning given to that nation. A number of years later, he was standing at the corner of Ground Zero and his attention was drawn to an object that was the first puzzle piece of an ancient mystery and a prophetic warning for America. He first shared the word at his congregation *Beth Israel* in 2005. A few years later he was led to begin committing the message to book form. When the Lord started revealing these things Jonathan had an urgent sense that this word needed to get out.

Rabbi Cahn explains that when 9/11 had happened, he was drawn to Isaiah 9:9-10. He was praying that particular point in Israel's history that was linking-up with the recent catastrophe in America.

Later, when standing on the corner of Ground Zero, he noticed an object that drew his attention and that began the unfolding of a mystery that kept unfolding until it linked an ancient mystery that is behind what is happening in America concerning 9/11, the economic collapse of 2008, the crash of Wall Street. He points out that the mystery is directly related to the actions and actual words of American leaders. He said the mystery goes back 2-1/2 thousand years and is a warning of judgment and a prophetic call of God.[1928]

Cahn explains that the first sign or one of the first signs of a pattern of national judgment is that God removes the hedge of protection after repeatedly calling to a nation to finally wake them up. Israel had known God and Israel had turned away from God so He called them and called them. Finally, He allowed their hedge of protection to be removed. He allowed a strike to come into the land by an enemy. It was temporary and limited. It was to call the nation back to Him.

Then there was a grace period when they somewhat hung in the balance. But instead of repenting and turning back to God they made a vow as in Isaiah 9:10:

> "The bricks are fallen down, but we will build with hewn stones: the sycamores are cut down, but we will change them into cedars."

So the Israelites defied God. They said we're coming back stronger than ever and so what happened is they sealed the course of judgment on their nation and ultimately years later Israel was destroyed.

Cahn points out that America has a history in covenant with God and is turning away from Him. He points out that God is calling her to return to Him without it happening so finally He allows the same thing to happen as had happened to ancient Israel. He allowed the hedge of protection to be removed and enemies to strike. It's limited, it's contained, it's just a warning but it's a grace period.

He points out that the churches were filled for a short time and the people proclaimed, "God bless America, God bless America." But there was no real repentance; there was no real turning and seeking God to learn if there was a problem. Cahn points out that it was the same response, same pattern as that of ancient Israel. It was a response of defiance claiming that America was going to come back stronger than ever.

315

The story goes on to point out that when Israel responded in this manner "harbingers" of judgment or "omens" of warning appeared in Israel. Those same nine harbingers of judgment have now reappeared on American soil with precision that involves American leaders, objects, reenactments, and ceremonies. Some occurred in New York, and some in Washington.

Examples involve a tree and a stone. One of the harbingers was a stone called the "gazzit" stone. It's a stone of judgment. It's a stone that has been quarried and is put in the location the bricks had fallen when their towers had collapsed. They said "We will rebuild with quarried stone" and they make a vow that represents defiance. Cahn points out the same exact thing occurred in America after 9/11 when they took a stone from a nearby quarry, put it down on Ground Zero, had a ceremony around it, American leaders gathered and pronounced vows over that stone.

Another harbinger is that of the sycamore tree which had to have fallen in the catastrophe. When the last tower of the World Trade Center collapsed it sent out a beam which struck down a tree which happened to be a sycamore, the same exact type of tree as in Isaiah.

Remarkably the tree was at the corner of Ground Zero in the courtyard of St. Paul's Chapel. Amazing is this fits as another mystery in that the Chapel is related to the founding of America. This is the Chapel where George Washington had dedicated America to God after he was sworn-in as America's first President. It is where President Washington had prophetically stated would happen to America if she ever turned from God.

Another harbinger is that the sycamore tree would have to be replaced with another particular tree as was done in ancient Israel and recorded in Isaiah 9. That's exactly what is done; an Erez tree of the exact Biblical description is lowered into the same soil where the sycamore had been. They had a ceremony around the replacement tree, they pronounce the exact vow over it, which is another defiance. The vow is another harbinger which seals judgment on the nation. Mind-blowing is that ancient Israel had done this at their capitol city, Samaria. **New York City was America's first capitol.**

The replacement Erez tree at Ground Zero died and was removed in the Spring of 2014. Rabbi Cahn stated, *"The ancient sign of nearing national judgment has been manifested. The erez tree has fallen. The seventh harbinger now speaks of impending judgment. The Tree of Hope, the symbol of America's resurgence ... is dead."*[1929]

Cahn describes another harbinger that happened on September 12th, the day after 9/11 when Congress gathered on Capitol Hill and the Senate majority leader stepped to the podium and pronounces the exact vow of Isaiah 9:10. The leader is unaware of what he is doing by pronouncing that scripture and judgment on the nation. It was another link of America to ancient Israel. Cahn projected a holy boldness as he faithfully delivered this message of warning at the January, 2013 inaugural prayer breakfast.[1930] [1931]

Rabbi Cahn has expanded on the harbinger of the Shemitah in his book, "The Mystery of the Shemitah," published in September, 2014. He explains 'the mystery of the sevens" in years and demonstrates with unmistakable fact that the year 2001 incurred a dreadful attack on American soil which related to a stock market collapse and financial devastation. He also points out an amazing link to seven years later in 2008, which incurred another financial collapse. At the time of this writing, we are looking another seven years forward which points to the year 2015.[1932] We are reminded of God calling to the nation to return to Him and the unmistakable connection of progressive, intense judgments that are imminent if the nation does not return.

In summary, we have presented two men of God who have faithfully and obediently delivered a message to this nation from the "Almighty Being who rules over the Universe."[1933] Will this nation have "ears to hear" and "eyes to see," turn, repent, return, and follow the Almighty's direction?

Amos 5:4 ~

> *For thus saith the Lord unto the house of Israel, Seek ye me, and ye shall live:*

Amos 5:14-15 ~

> *Seek good, and not evil, that ye may live: and so the Lord, the God of hosts, shall be with you, as ye have spoken. Hate the evil, and love the good, and establish judgment in the gate: it may be that the Lord God of hosts will be gracious unto the remnant of Joseph.*

Another Profound Story

Another profound story is that of an American man who has worked at the Hebrew University of Jerusalem as a translator of the Dead Sea Scrolls as well as a researcher deciphering ancient Hebrew manuscripts. He is a man who gives expression of a passionate love for God. Nehemia Gordon[1934] has a captivating testimony[1935] of a personal revelation of the Father heart of God and in placing the Biblical priestly blessing over His children.

Part of The Psalms Scroll, one of the Dead Sea scrolls.[1936]
This scroll fragment was displayed in the exhibit at the Library of Congress in 1993. It was provided courtesy of the Israel Antiquities Authority. [1937]

Numbers 6:22-27 American Standard Version (ASV) [emphasis added]~

> *And [YHWH] Jehovah spake unto Moses, saying, Speak unto Aaron and unto his sons, saying, On this wise ye shall bless the children of Israel: ye shall say unto them,*
> *[YHWH] Jehovah bless thee, and keep thee:*
> *[YHWH] Jehovah make his face to shine upon thee, and be gracious unto thee:*
> *[YHWH] Jehovah lift up his countenance upon thee, and give thee peace.*
> *So shall they put my name upon the children of Israel; and I will bless them.*

Growing up in an orthodox Jewish tradition with a rabbi father, Mr. Gordon explains the Jewish tradition in <u>not</u> verbalizing God's name. He also explains the missing vowels of God's name, "YHWH," as well as why they had been removed and hidden from the Jewish people.

Mr. Gordon relays how he sought the Lord with an earnest desire to know how to pronounce His name, to pray to his Creator in His name, and in correlation to orally prescribing the Biblical priestly blessing.

The Aleppo Codex is a medieval manuscript of the Hebrew Bible (Tanakh), associated with Rabbi Aaron Ben Asher. The Masoretic scholars wrote it in the early 10th century, probably in Tiberias, Israel. It is in book form and contains the vowel points and grammar points (nikkudot) that specify the pronunciation of the ancient Hebrew letters to preserve the chanting tradition. It is perhaps the most historically important Hebrew manuscript in existence. Of its original 487 pages, 193 disappeared between 1947 and 1958.

Gordon also shares that his mentor, an elder in Jerusalem who had taught him from an ancient rabbinical text, told him that God did not answer their prayers because they did not pray using His name.

Gordon's story includes an amazing discovery of the full set of vowels in God's name while working on his masters studies at the Hebrew University. While proofreading and comparing the *Aleppo Codex*, "the most important manuscript of the Bible in the world," to the Bible, he had an extraordinary experience.

At the precise moment of discovering the full set of vowels in God's Name as recorded in the *Aleppo Codex*, he received a telephone call from someone in New York City who advised of a plane implosively entering a World Trade Tower. In the emotion of the moment, Mr. Gordon prayerfully asked God for a second witness to confirm the vowels discovered in His Name and then continued his work.

Again, coming across God's Name with the vowels in the name as recorded in the *Aleppo Codex*, his phone rang at that precise moment to relay the news of another plane implosively entering another World Trade Tower. He was stunned with various emotions of both weeping and joy of all that was occurring at once in that moment of time.

St. Paul's Chapel, New York City [1938]

Mr. Gordon's story continues forward to about ten years later while visiting Ground Zero and **St. Paul's Chapel** where he shares a heart-touching and extraordinary setting in which **he finds God's name in Hebrew at the front of the chapel – twice, which Biblically is a sign of a confirmation in witness.**[1939] A picture taken of one of the names is used on the cover of his book entitled, "Shattering the Conspiracy of Silence" and subtitled, "The Hebrew Power of the Priestly Blessing Unleashed," as he tells of the blessing of speaking forth God's name over His children. Gordon brings emphasis to the final line of blessing in Numbers 6:27:

So shall they put <u>my name</u> upon the children of Israel; and I will bless them.

Relating God's Word in precision of where America must be at this time is described in 2 Chronicles 7:14 and of which Christendom should be very familiar.

If my people, which are called by my name, shall humble themselves, and pray, and seek my face, and turn from their wicked ways; then will I hear from heaven, and will forgive their sin, and will heal their land. ~ 2 Chronicles 7:14

In going a step beyond and reading two verses further, we see that **God desires that His name would remain there.**

Now mine eyes shall be open, and mine ears attent unto the prayer that is made in this place. For now have I chosen and sanctified this house, <u>that my name may be there for ever</u>: and mine eyes and mine heart shall be there perpetually. ~ 2 Chronicles 7:15-16

The nation's original covenant with God was with the American Republic known as the *United States of America*. The Corporate UNITED STATES has a different god whose name is Lucifer, or Satan. Let there be no mistake of God's provision and love in calling forth men and women who have answered His call to re-inhabit that which was left dormant 144 years earlier.

Will the American people turn, repent, return, and complete the restoration of God's Republic? Will the American people wake-up, rise-up, and stand-up God's Republic?

Will the American people bless the Almighty in maintaining His holy name on the land as originally covenanted, and receive His blessing?

Hebrews 13:15 ~

By him therefore let us offer the sacrifice of praise to God continually, that is, the fruit of our lips giving thanks to <u>his Name</u>.

Zephaniah 3:9 ~

For then will I turn to the people a pure language, that they may all call upon the name of the Lord, to serve him with one consent.

Zephaniah 3:20 ~

At that time will I bring you again, even in the time that I gather you: for I will make you a name and a praise among all people of the earth, when I turn back your captivity before your eyes, saith the Lord.

A Well Hidden National Monument Points the Way

Kirk Cameron[1940]

Kirk Cameron[1941] is a well-known actor and producer, well-noted in Christendom for his inspirational documentaries and films. Mr. Cameron has worked with devout fortitude while teaching Americans how to share their faith as well as how to live and raise a Gospel-centered marriage and family.

As a father of six children, Cameron had concerns about society's obvious and rapid moral decline. Coupled with the country's growing out-of-control national debt, Cameron also expressed concern about the serious spiritual downturn as synchronized in the same hellacious down-spiraling vortex as morality. In a quest to figure out what was wrong in our country Cameron began to trace the steps taken by the Pilgrims to discover America's beginnings.

The true story follows this father of six across Europe and the United States as he sought to discover **America's true "national treasure"** – the people, places, and principles that made America the freest, most prosperous and generous nation the world has ever known.

The story is told in his documentary, *"Monumental: In Search of America's National Treasure,"* which was co-produced with Dr. Marshall Foster,[1942] president and founder of the *World History Institute*. Produced in format as venturing on a journey, Cameron takes his audience along for a firsthand view of the sequential, unfolding stories while envisioning being in the shoes of the Pilgrims.[1943]

The National Monument to the Forefathers
Plymouth, Massachusetts; Photo by T.S. Custadio [1946]

The journey includes uncovering the true roots of America which go all the way back to the ancient Hebrew republic. Cameron reports that those roots at Jamestown, Virginia in the very early 1600s are also traceable back to Europe. *"This is the trail of freedom that leads us all the way back to the ancient Hebrews under Moses where he first delivered those laws of liberty — when he told them to elect leaders, men of character that you willingly submit yourself to, to self-govern, rather than have a king. To me, the most inspiring demonstration of those principles was found in the Pilgrims."[1944]*

The trail ended at a bit of surprise: a very well hidden national monument. The *National Monument to the Forefathers*, dedicated to the Pilgrim settlers, was built through the efforts of the *Pilgrim Society*. Founded in 1820, the construction of such a monument was one of the organization's primary goals. The cornerstone was laid in 1859 and the 81-foot tall monument[1945] was completed in 1889.

The monument is thought to be the world's largest solid granite monument, and is the third-tallest statue in the United States.[1947] Yet, it is not well-known, taught to school children, or marketed to Americans as a historical landmark. It is reported that even the residents of the Plymouth, Massachusetts area are unaware that this magnificent historical monument exists.[1948]

Dr. Foster advises that the Pilgrim's way was "the only successful strategy of liberty that has ever been carried out in the history of mankind."

The monument features a central figure, 36 feet tall, weighing 180 tons, representing <u>Faith</u>, who has her right arm raised and finger pointing to heaven, "where God is and because her faith is in the God of the Bible; in Jesus Christ. They knew that the only faith that could bring true liberty was a faith in the one true God and His Bible."

In Faith's left hand is an open Geneva <u>Bible</u> with open pages which portray that the Pilgrims read it, and as they read it they had faith in God. God gave them <u>wisdom </u>which is reflected on the statue of Faith with a star on the top of her forehead. "She's given wisdom to know how to live in this world."[1949]

The monument overlooks Plymouth Harbor with the central statue Faith facing the Harbor almost as if looking back and remembering where the Pilgrims came from, the hardship and sacrifices that it took in order to be free from civil and religious tyranny as well as to arrive in America, along with a conviction in what it takes to never go back.

There are four seated statues surrounding Faith, each weighing almost 20 tons, and are tied to faith. "Because without faith it falls apart…and that's the beginning of it all," stated Dr. Foster. The four surrounding statues represent <u>Education</u>, <u>Law</u>, <u>Morality</u>, and <u>Liberty</u>,[1950] <u>the Biblical principles and values in relationship with Almighty</u>. There are several smaller figures around the base which represent various other <u>virtues</u> as well as depictions of the Pilgrims and their journey.[1951]

Dr. Foster pointed out that the Forefathers had left us a formula for liberty as expressed in the matrix of those principles and values as reflected in this monument that is dedicated to the Pilgrims, who made tremendous sacrifice against all odds in pursuit of civil and religious liberty.

In the film while standing at the monument, Dr. Marshall Foster explained to Mr. Cameron,[1952]

"Hardly anybody in America knows about it and yet the people of America put this together over a 70-year period. [It was] paid for by the Congress, paid for by the state legislature in Massachusetts as a strategy laid-out. We call it the "Matrix of Liberty" that was given to us by the Forefathers, by the Pilgrims. One hundred thirty years ago when they built this, <u>they wanted to leave this behind for us so that if we would ever forget how liberty is built, we would know what to do to regain it</u>."

Could it be the *Protestant Reformation* and then having access to the Holy Bible in their own language that is the fulfilling of Moses' prophecy pertaining to the descendants of Old Testament Israel in the "recalling" of God's promises and His divine law? Could the religious and civil persecution in seeking to follow the Holy scriptures now learned in the *Protestant Reformation* have been the hand of God in leading the Pilgrims, and then the Puritans, to gather in a land of their own—the New World, the "New Israel," where they could have the liberty to worship God and the freedom to live in covenant with Him?

Monument Dedication   Pilgrim Passengers of the Mayflower

The Founders believed that the prophecy pertained to the descendants and remnants of God's people Israel who had been disbursed throughout the world. They believed that they were the descendants of Israel who were now able to remember the promises of God made to their ancestors, return to the Lord in covenant with Him, and be gathered into a land of their own. No other land, or people, seemed to fit the characteristics in description as portrayed throughout the various scriptures, as Protestant America.

As seen in the scriptures, after ancient Israel was already in the Promised Land, the later prophets spoke of <u>a gathering that would take place in the latter days.</u> It is time to remember. It is time to return to the Lord in covenant with Him.

Hosea 5:15 ~

I will go and return to my place, till they acknowledge their offence, and seek my face: in their affliction they will seek me early.

Hosea 6:1-3 ~

Come, and let us return unto the Lord: for he hath torn, and he will heal us; he hath smitten, and he will bind us up. ...he [will] revive us: ... he will raise us up, and we shall live in his sight. Then shall we know, if we follow on to know the Lord: his going forth is prepared as the morning; and he shall come unto us as the rain, as the latter and former rain unto the earth.

322

Signs in the Sun, Moon and Stars

In the story of creation in the beginning book of the Bible, we see the creation of the heavens as in relation to outer space.

Genesis 1:14 ~

> *And God said, Let there be lights in the firmament of the heaven to divide the day from the night; and let them be for **signs**, and for **seasons**, and for days, and years.*

God created the sun, moon, and stars for signs, which are "signals." The word "seasons" is mistranslated and should correctly read as "feasts." An expanded examination of the translation relates to a "Divine appointment." We understand that there are some Divine appointments that are scheduled, like a Feast of the Lord, such as *Passover* or the *Feast of Tabernacles*. In the original Hebrew language it implies a "dress rehearsal."

For example, each year Passover was observed by the Jewish people who went to the "dress rehearsal" of killing the Passover lamb on that particular Feast day. It was representative, or a "rehearsal," leading up to when the ultimate event was going to happen, such as Jesus being the ultimate Passover Lamb of God who was sacrificed for the sins of the world.

Jesus was crucified and died on Passover. He was buried on the *Feast of Unleavened Bread* and rose on the *Feast of First Fruits*. His Holy Spirit was poured out in the Upper Room 50 days later on the *Feast of Pentecost*. The Biblical Feasts in the Spring are "shadows" of every major event in the first coming of the Messiah. The Biblical Feasts in the Fall are also "shadows" of every major event in Jesus the Christ's second coming.

Jesus said there would be signs in the sun, moon and stars[1953] before His second coming, we present evidence of prophetic signs, or "signals," that the *Creator of the universe* is indeed communicating a message to the world and particularly to those who are paying careful attention.

Luke 21:25 ~

> *And there shall be signs in the sun, and in the moon, and in the stars; and upon the earth distress of nations, with perplexity; the sea and the waves roaring...*

The sign or "signal," in this case of the moon, points to a particular Feast Day of the Lord.

A "blood moon" is a total lunar eclipse that appears reddish in color by the effect of the earth coming between the sun and moon. When a rare series of four total lunar eclipses occur precisely on Feasts of the Lord, we understand that the Lord is communicating to mankind that certain very significant events are about to occur in the world.

There is a pattern of a series of four, or "tetrad," of lunar eclipses that have occurred on Feast days of the Lord in history that represented major world occurrences.[1954] This would include:

- Jesus' crucifixion and resurrection in **32 and 33 A.D.**
- The Jewish Diaspora and Great Plague of Europe that paved the way for Jewish settlement in **162-63 A.D.**
- Charlemagne spoils the Muslim attempt at conquering Europe in **795-96 A.D.**
- The Muslims defeat the Holy Roman Empire after years of Jewish and Christian persecution in **842-43 A.D.**
- The Muslims attempt to conquer the world (Europe) a second time; millions of Jewish and Christians are martyred in **860-61 A.D.**
- Spanish Inquisition begins with expulsion of Jews in the name and exploitation of Christianity. God enables Christopher Columbus to discover their new home in the western hemisphere in **1493-94 A.D.**
- Prophecy is fulfilled in Israel being again declared a nation after 2,000 years. The Dead Sea scrolls are discovered and re-authenticate the Hebrew Bible in **1949-50 A.D.**
- Jerusalem is restored as the capital of Israel. The Temple Mount was seized by Israel for the first time in 2,000 years in **1967-68 A.D.**
- The Lord's "perfect" <u>Sign</u> of the Times, unprecedented and unparalleled in scope and statistics in **2014-15 A.D.** with the fourth blood moon being a "super moon."

The National Aeronautical Space Administration (NASA) has on staff some of the most brilliant physicists and astronomers in the world. These scientists have precisely and accurately documented every lunar and solar eclipse from 3,000 BC to 3,000 AD. The recent 2014-2015 Biblical Blood Moon Tetrad, evidenced by NASA, is phenomenal, unprecedented, and unique. Previous Blood Moon Tetrads throughout world history cannot and do not compare to this recent Tetrad.[1955]

The correlation between Biblical prophecy and the confluence of events as if harmonized in concert together are unmistakable and undeniable as arranged by the *Creator of the universe.*

These recent Blood Moons and their accompanying heavenly signs supersede the signs the Creator displayed in the heavens during the crucifixion, death, burial, and resurrection of Jesus Christ.[1956] [1957]

As "a picture is worth a thousand words," the following two graphs created by career Statistician Paul Grevas[1958] demonstrate the mathematical impossibility in the synchronization of particular lunar and solar eclipses in relation to precise Biblical Feast days. In these graphs, Mr. Grevas focuses on the decade of 2010 to 2019 and presents an unprecedented incredible display of perfect symmetry never before communicated in the heavens throughout the 6,000 years since Adam and Eve.

The recent Blood Moon Tetrad of which has just occurred, is an improbable mathematical occurrence of 1.85 x 10 to the 139th power! That's 139 zeroes, way beyond comprehension.

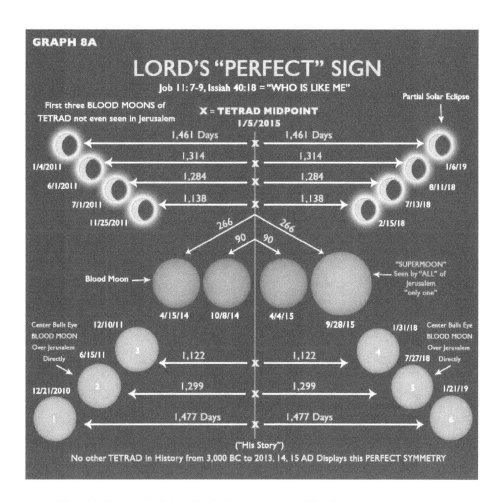

Graphic by Statistician Paul Grevas: www.bloodmoonscoming.com

Statistician Paul Grevas points out in his discovery that none of the seven previous Biblical Blood Moons display the perfection, as reflected in the above graph, at about the Midpoint.

Mr. Grevas specifically points out that the <u>Midpoint</u> of the four Biblical Blood Moons <u>in each Tetrad ties the Creator's entire constellation of each one together</u>.

"It's the nerve center, the heartbeat, the focal point of how prophetically relevant in importance each Tetrad is for God's Heavenly Sign messages He beams to us on earth," states Paul Grevas.

"The Midpoint is the basis… [and] shall convey to you that we are on the Edge of Time." This career statistician points out that the previous seven Biblical Blood Moon charts failed in reflecting charted perfection at least one time as to the number of days of a Solar or Lunar Eclipse occurrence to the Midpoint, from its complement.

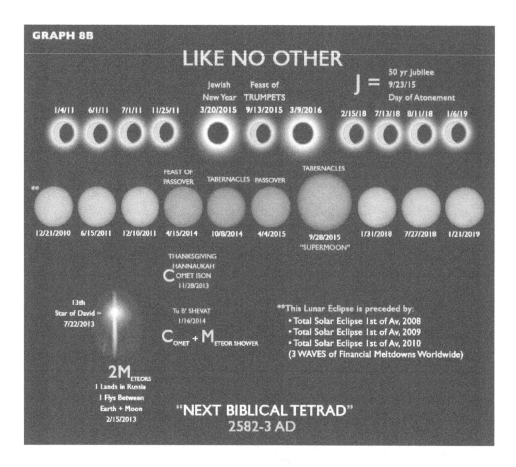

Graphic by Statistician Paul Grevas: www.bloodmoonscoming.com

Another magnificent and truly Divine discovery of Mr. Grevas happened when he charted all 40 solar and lunar eclipses for the decade 2010- 2019.[1959] All 40 of the eclipses "happen" to display January 5, 2015 as the Midpoint on the graph. Mr. Grevas came to the realization that this date "happens" to be the Feast of Epiphany, also known as "Three Kings' Day," which is an annual commemoration of the "Adoration of the Magi" and celebrates the revelation of God the Son, Jesus the Christ, as a human. The Feast also memorializes the visit of the Magi to the Christ child as well as Jesus' physical manifestation to the Gentiles.

Additionally, these 40 eclipses plotted on the graph displays perfect symmetry as well as a visible formation of a menorah. A menorah is described in the New Testament book of Revelation as the seven-lamp (six branches) ancient Hebrew lamp stand. It was made of pure gold and used in the transportable sanctuary set-up by Moses in the wilderness and then 300 years later in the temple in Jerusalem.

According to NASA, the next Biblical Tetrad will not occur for another 600 years, in 2582-83. Statistican Grevas advises that it will be inferior in perfection to the recent Biblical Blood Moon Tetrad.

There is wisdom in acknowledging the "Language of Heaven" in the message being spoken in the heavens through the signs and signals, Divine appointments for something very significant and global about to occur.

Where today's Bible scholars claim that America is not found in the Bible, Americans throughout the 1800s, identified her in the scriptures while the seals of the scrolls popped open for their revelation.

Having learned to read from the scriptures, the Holy Bible being their main textbook throughout life, many of them having learned the original languages of the Old and New Testaments, we cannot dismiss what they saw and believed.

United States Capitol (1857-1872) [1960]
Washington City, District of Columbia

In February, 1857, on the anniversary of President Washington's birthday, two sermons were preached in the Capitol of the United States, at the request of several members of Congress. Entitled, "A Defence of Armageddon, or Our Great Country Foretold in the Holy Scriptures," the subject pertained to the fulfillment of prophecy with reference to the United States.

The daily and dominant newspaper of the Capital, *The National Intelligencer,*[1961] published an account summarizing the sermon(s) of which is an excerpt:

> "...The events which he detailed with reference to our own country, were made to fit with such surprising chronological accuracy to the predictions, that it was by the almost unanimous desire of a large and attentive audience that his lecture was continued in the afternoon. At the appointed time, three o'clock, P.M., it was no easy task to find a seat in the great hall of the Capitol, so deeply interested were the people to hear the sequel of the morning discourse..."[1962]

The sermon was published and circulated to the American public for years afterward. An excerpt from a "Remark" in the front matter pages of the published sermons (1859):

> "For nearly two years it has been before the public and met the favorable notice of many of the ablest journals and reviews in America. Learned theologians, civilians and statesmen have freely accredited its truthfulness, and mathematicians pronounce its chronological argument *demonstration.* Indeed, almost all who examine it believe it."[1963]

Title page of the published sermons by Reverend F. E. Pitts'
A Defence of Armageddon, or Our Great Country Foretold in the Holy Scriptures [1964]
delivered in the Capitol of the United States at the request of
several Members of Congress
on the anniversary of President Washington's birthday, 1857

A main point we wish to make with regard to this documented historical event at our Nation's Capital is that Reverend Pitts amazingly points to the scriptures using precise calculations of mathematics and science in timing as to the birth of the American Republic precisely on July 4, 1776. He explains the scriptures to provide an account of understanding in how only the American Republic fits the description in all regards. In the discourse, Reverend Pitts mentions a "coincidence" of a solar eclipse occurring at the time Cyrus, king of Persia in Old Testament times, made a decree for the emancipation of the Tribes in captivity at Babylon (he refers to as "Israel), as well as the occurring of a lunar eclipse (that we understand today was a "Biblical Blood Moon" and part of a Tetrad) at the time of the crucifixion of Christ.

One with imagination can envision how quiet the room must have been as his audience intently listened to Reverend Pitts explain the details of the Old Testament prophet, Daniel, in his visions that covered the lapse of ages to "the time of the end" and how the American Republic precisely fits the description in the scriptures as the "Stone Kingdom."

The Stone Kingdom is the fifth and final kingdom of all the ages prophesied in the scriptures as having a special part in ending all earthly despotic political governments in unholy alliance that hold the "doctrine of devils" in the "Divine right of kings," while at the same time bringing the principles of popular freedom (also known as "liberty") over the whole world. In other words: "liberty and justice for all." Reverend Pitts ties-in the visions of Isaiah, Ezekiel, Jeremiah and the Apostle John that embrace the same subjects and, measuring the same period, creates a profound and legitimate deduction.

An Open Vision and a Word from the Lord

This story is one that has taken great work in research and discovery through reading out-of-print books from the 1800s, Congressional Journals, Congressional Committee reports, and government documents as recorded through the centuries. It has been reading through encyclopedias and other resources of profound quotes and writings of the Forefathers, Founding Fathers, Presidents, Statesmen, Scientists, Preachers, Constitutions, and Court Decisions. It has been an investigative journey in reading through other's well-documented work published in books and teaching materials as well as posted on the World Wide Web.

It has been a journey of listening to the voice of the Holy Spirit in profound guidance which sometimes came through others that unknowingly contributed or "happened" to be studying an item of interest that "happened" to fit right where we had been working in America's story. All of these various factors in the history of the people as a nation were put in historical sequence and interwoven with the spiritual, that which brought Life to America's covenant with "the God of the universe."

In this current day of the "Church Age," the true Church is not a building made of wood and brick but is made of "living stones," of which Jesus is the Chief Cornerstone,[1965] a sure foundation, who together make a spiritual house of the Lord.[1966]

These living stones are individual believers who are born-again by faith into new life by the incorruptible seed of the Holy Spirit and by the Word of God[1967] who is Jesus the Christ, Yeshuah haMashiach.[1968] The Lord God leads and guides His followers, His sons and daughters, into all Truth by His Holy Spirit.

John 16:13 ~

> *But when He, the Spirit of truth, comes, He will guide you into all the truth; for He will not speak*
> *on His own initiative, but whatever He hears, He will speak; and He will disclose to you what is to*
> *come.*

It is this Holy Spirit that speaks today to bring into remembrance[1969] to His people of the New Covenant, the New Testament believers in Christ Jesus as well as the descendants of His people who covenanted with Him on this land, who are gathered in these latter days in which He has a message to relay to them.

The God of Creation that communicated through dreams and visions to His people in the ancient time of the Old Testament is the same God of Creation[1970] that still speaks to His people. He doesn't change.[1971] He provided His living Word that still speaks to us today and reveals to us His plans that include the latter days of this end of the Age.

Joel 2:28-29 ~

> *And it shall come to pass afterward, that I will pour out my spirit upon all flesh; and your sons and*
> *your daughters shall prophesy, your old men shall dream dreams, your young men shall see visions:*
> *And also upon the servants and upon the handmaids in those days will I pour out my spirit.*

As we come to conclusion in the American Republic's story, the Spirit of the Lord has impressed upon His daughter an open panoramic-type picture of this story as just now told. In stepping back His daughter saw this panoramic picture in full view and she experienced a realization that what she had seen was an open vision.

In viewing the end of the panorama she saw where we are today; the destruction is frightfully overwhelming to describe what the sons of Satan have planned for America as well as all the inhabitants of the world. The nations of the world watch and wait for the American people to awaken as the fate of "the city upon a hill"[1972] will contribute to their own.

The Lord wanted the picture to be written down for the people.[1973] He wants them to see from His perspective. He's calling to us and He wants us to come home. He says that He loves us. He wants to bless us with life, liberty, and the pursuit of happiness. That's the purpose for the "divine science of politics" which is good government. It's His law, His principles of law for the nation. He wants us to <u>know His name, to call upon His name</u>, and to love Him. He wants to walk amongst us.

He says, "Turn. Repent. Return. Run to Me. I will embrace you, I will wipe your tears, wipe your tears. I will destroy your enemies. As covenanted with Me your enemies are My enemies. Come, come, My people. This is the way. Turn. Let the veil be pulled back. See. See. Come. Rise, Shine."

Ephesians 5:14 ~ ...

> *Awake thou that sleepest, and arise from the dead, and Christ shall give thee light.*

Isaiah 60:1 ~

> *Arise, shine; for thy light is come, and the glory of the Lord is risen upon thee.*

Revelations 18:4-5 ~

> *...Come out of her, my people, that ye be not partakers of her sins, and that ye receive not of her plagues. For her sins have reached unto heaven, and God hath remembered her iniquities.*

Now that the veil is pulled away[1974] and the vision is before you with eyes to see, will you be part of the latter day remnant[1975] of God's people? You have the liberty of conscience to choose.[1976] It is a day of decision.[1977]

Malachi 3:16-18 ~

> *Then they that feared the Lord spake often one to another: and the Lord hearkened, and heard it, and a book of remembrance was written before him for them that feared the Lord, and that thought upon his name.*

> *And they shall be mine, saith the Lord of hosts, in that day when I make up my jewels; and I will spare them, as a man spareth his own son that serveth him.*

> *Then shall ye return, and discern between the righteous and the wicked, between him that serveth God and him that serveth him not.*

Chapter Nineteen

TODAY, the Church Must Take Right Ground

Rev. Dr. Nathaniel Whitaker (1708-1795)[1978]

Portions taken from a sermon by Patriot Preacher Nathaniel Whitaker, D.D., "An Antidote against Toryism [or the Curse of Meroz]," delivered at Salem, Massachusetts and printed in 1777.[1979]

Judges 5:23 ~

> *Curse ye Meroz, said the angel of the Lord, curse ye bitterly the inhabitants thereof, because they came not to the help of the Lord to the help of the Lord against the mighty.*

God is love.[1980] For God so loved the world, that he gave his only begotten Son, that whosoever believeth (trusts) in him should not perish, but have everlasting life.[1981] But as many as received Him, to them gave He power to become the sons of God, even to them that believe on His name.[1982]

On February 22, 1756 John Adams wrote in his diary:

"Suppose a nation in some distant region should take the Bible for their only law book, and every member should regulate his conduct by the precepts there exhibited! Every member would be obliged in conscience, to temperance, frugality, and industry; to justice, kindness, and charity towards his fellow men; and to piety, love, and reverence toward Almighty God....What a Eutopia, what a Paradise would this region be." [1983]   John Adams, 1766 portrait [1984]

President Abraham Lincoln, 1863 [1985]

Some 109 years later President Abraham Lincoln stated to State Senator Scovel of New Jersey:

"Young man, if God gives me four years more to rule this country, I believe it will become what it ought to be--what its Divine Author intended it to be--no longer one vast plantation for breeding human beings for the purpose of lust and bondage. But it will become a new Valley of Jehoshaphat, where all the nations of the earth will assemble together under one flag, worshipping a common God, and they will celebrate the resurrection of human freedom." [1986]

A vision expressed by two great patriots. This was a vision that many saw and dreamed about—including the Pilgrims and the Puritans. America was special back then and is very special today. God has made it that way. Knowing God and loving Him is the recipe for the Utopia.

Psalm 16:11 ~

Thou wilt show me the path of life; in thy presence is fullness of joy; at thy right hand there are pleasures for evermore.

God is about life, liberty, and the pursuit of happiness. To live in harmony with one another: harmony in families, in churches, in communities, and cities. This is what is meant when Jesus prayed, "on earth as it is in heaven." The first Adam fell into sin and resulted in a whole race of sinners. That is why government is needed: because of the fall of man. All were born with a sin nature.

James Madison (1751-1836),[1987] known as the "Chief Architect of the Constitution," and was the 4th President of the United States. Author of 29 of the 85 *Federalist Papers*, which argued successfully in favor of the ratification of the *Constitution*, Madison stated:

President James Madison, 1816 [1988]

"If men were angels, no government would be necessary. If angels were to govern men, neither external nor internal controls on government would be necessary. In framing a government which is to be administered by men over men, the great difficulty lies in this: you must first enable the government to control the governed; and in the next place oblige it to control itself."[1989]

A government is needed where men and women are given the opportunity to govern themselves, "self-government." It must entail a structured government with a blueprint; a constitution designed from a Master Plan, by the Creator of man. That, precisely, would be from His manual for man in how to live, the "Word of God," the Holy Bible. James Madison also stated:

"We have staked the whole future of American civilization, not upon the power of government, far from it. We have staked the future of all of our political institutions upon the capacity of mankind for self-government; upon the capacity of each and all of us to govern ourselves, to control ourselves, to sustain ourselves according to the Ten Commandments of God." [1990]

So God has created us as a freeborn people and He desires for us to be happy. He has provided us knowledge of boundaries as a guide to live with for our own welfare, protection, and well-being. He has given us His laws and precepts. By His Holy Spirit and His Holy Word, He inspired men to frame the *Constitution*. It is the operating document provided for the governance of His people as a nation "in order to form a more perfect union." Guided by the wisdom of His written Word, a Divine blueprint was presented which included three branches of government.

Isaiah 33:22 ~

"For the Lord is our <u>judge</u> [judicial], the Lord is our <u>lawgiver</u> [legislative], the Lord is our <u>King</u> [executive] he will save us."

Reader whoever you are, know this: the government instituted for the American Republic is God's government.

Isaiah 9:7 ~

"Of the increase of his government and peace there shall be no end."

This is His Republic—a Republic of laws, not of men.[1991] The "Laws of Nature," are the laws of God for His freeborn people.

So God is love, but God is also just. As recorded in Isaiah 14:12-17, God cast Lucifer (Satan) out of heaven because of Satan's rebellion. God hates sin. As recorded in Proverbs 6:16-19:

These six things doth the Lord hate: yea, seven are an abomination unto him: A proud look, a lying tongue, and hands that shed innocent blood, An heart that deviseth wicked imaginations, feet that be swift in running to mischief, A false witness that speaketh lies, and he that soweth discord among brethren.

Satan, as drawn by Gustave Doré,[1992]
illustrated in John Milton's *Paradise Lost,* 1866

God wants His Church (the Body of Christ) to know who they are, their very true identity, and in that identity exercise a righteous hate. To hate the things that God hates, such as killing the preborn, pornography, and sodomy.

Psalmist David, in Psalm 139:19-22:

Surely thou wilt slay the wicked, O God: depart from me therefore, ye bloody men. For they speak against thee wickedly, and thine enemies take thy name in vain. Do not I hate them, O Lord, that hate thee? and am not I grieved with those that rise up against thee? I hate them with perfect hatred: I count them mine enemies.

So this is the character of God; that He is love, but He is also just. He hates sin, and sin has no place in His Kingdom. He taught us to pray in like manner.

Matthew 6:10 ~

Thy kingdom come, Thy will be done in earth, as it is in heaven.

As God's people, as His sons and daughters, our assignment is to bring His Kingdom to earth. I remind you that when the Church takes their God-given authority to do just that, then <u>nothing</u> is impossible because everything is possible in His Kingdom.

From the sermon, "Antidote Against Toryism,"[1993] by Patriot preacher of the *American Revolution,* Nathaniel Whitaker, D.D.:

"True benevolence is, therefore, exercised in opposing those who seek the hurt of society, and none are to be condemned as acting against the law of love, because they hate and oppose such as are injurious to happiness. Even God's hatred of sin, and the punishment he inflicts on the wicked, arise from his love of happiness, from the benevolence of his nature. But the weakness and corruption of nature, in the best, is such, that God hath not entrusted to men at large the exercise of the resentment due to such characters, nor allowed them to inflict those punishments which their crimes call for, even in this world, except in some special cases. On the contrary, he hath strictly prohibited all his subjects taking vengeance for private or personal injuries in a private and personal manner, and required, that if "one smite us on the one cheek, we turn to him the other also,"[1994] and in the language of love, exhorts us: *'Dearly beloved, avenge not yourselves.'* Yet there are cases in which he requires us, as his servants, to take vengeance on his enemies. And it deserves our particular notice, that all these cases respect crimes which tend to destroy human happiness. ...So God requires us to execute vengeance on the murderer, the thief, the adulterer, reviler, and the like; all which sins strike at the peace and happiness of human society."

The foundation is set as we proceed to take a look at what the *Supreme Judge of the World,* who does not change,[1995] speaks to us even today pertaining to:

"Curse ye Meroz, said the angel of the Lord, curse ye bitterly the inhabitants thereof: because they came not to the help of the Lord, to the help of the Lord against the might."[1996]

After wandering in the wilderness for forty years because of their sin of <u>unbelief</u> God chose Joshua to take his people across the river Jordan. God's perfect justice allowed only the descendants of His people to go into the Promised Land. In order to enter the land, they were required to defeat seven nations much more powerful than themselves, God's people. But God went before them and they victoriously inhabited their new land. The Promised Land; a land with milk, and honey, and grapes the size of grapefruit. Yet they forgot about God and fell into idolatry, the worship of other gods.

Now Moses warned God's people:

"But thou shalt remember the Lord thy God: for it is he that giveth thee power to get wealth, that he may establish his covenant which he sware unto they fathers, as it is this day. And it shall be, if thou do at all forget the Lord thy God, and walk after other gods, and serve them, and worship them, I testify against you this day that ye shall perish." [1997]

Moses Receiving the *Law of the Covenant* [1998]
from the *Creator of the universe*
for the people of Old Testament Israel
Lithograph published in 1877

Declaration of Independence, the *Law of the Covenant*
made with the *Creator of the universe* and the American people
1823 William Stone facsimile [1999]

So God's people, Israel, while living in the land that God gave them, did indeed serve other gods and they fell in great sin.

"And the children of Israel again did evil in the sight of the Lord, when Ehud was dead. And the Lord sold them into the hand of Jabin, king of Canaan, that reigned in Hazor; the captain of whose host was Sisera, which dwelt in Harosheth of the gentiles. And the children of Israel cried unto the Lord: for he had nine hundred chariots of iron; and twenty years he mightily oppressed the children of Israel. After twenty years and God hearing their cries God commanded his people (people now living in captivity) to take vengeance and form an army to fight against Jabin, the king of Cannon and Sisera, the captain of his host."[2000]

God raises up and inspires two: Deborah and Barak. God comes alongside of these two to help. He inspires them with courage and faith in His power and grace to oppose the tyrant and shake off his yoke.

Ten thousand men from the tribes of Zebulon and Naphtali were designed by God to have the honor of conquering this potent king. Where ten other tribes mustered and were ready for the war, it appears that Zebulon and Naphtali only, were the people that put their lives in jeopardy, in the high places in the field.

A little army — raised up from only two tribes out of twelve — of Deborah and Barak, marched out and wage war against their oppressor, for the recovery of their freedom. Not only did God give victory to Israel, but utterly destroyed the whole host of Jabin. Not one escaped, except Sisera the captain-general, and God delivered him to be slain by the hand of a woman.[2001]

> "Women have sometimes been the deliverers of their country, and can, when God inspires them with courage, face the proudest foe. Oh, how easy is it with God to save from the greatest danger, and, by the weakest instruments, conquer the most powerful enemies! [So,] Deborah and Barak deeply impressed with a sense of God's mercy in this deliverance, sang this song [recorded in Judges ch. 5] as an expression of their joy and gratitude, from which, would time allow many instructive lessons might be deduced."[2002]

Reader, do you see the character of our God? Do you see God's mercy? Do you see that God loves to help a remnant?

If we would reflect and compare the situation of the early American Colonies against the fleets and armies of the British during the *American Revolution*, we would see evidence that God raised up patriots with providential inspiration, courage, faith, His power and grace, all to oppose the tyrant-oppressor, King George.

The Almighty raised-up a great General, and that General led a remnant. God is into remnants! Why? So He can get the glory. God loves us and He wants to help us against the oppressor. If we would cry out and return and repent and turn from our wicked ways. Wicked ways? How does America turn from killing the preborn? How does she turn from pornography and all of society's immorality? How does she turn society from sodomy?

Deborah and Barak celebrated, but what about the people of Meroz? No mistake about it, the inhabitants of Meroz were negatively wicked, they only failed in their duty they did not arm to recover their liberties when wrested from them by the hand of tyranny.[2003] This is all the fault charged on them; yet for this they incurred the fearful curse, which is what you must see as the central focus and real wake-up call to the Church. Observe the curse pronounced:

Curse ye Meroz, curse ye bitterly the inhabitants thereof.

> "Their conduct, on that occasion, was such as deserved - a severe punishment from the other states, who are commanded to separate them unto evil, as a just reward of their neglect. ...This curse was to be pronounced and inflicted by all the people, who are here required to be of one heart, and engage seriously, religiously, and determinately in cursing them, and as God ministers to execute his wrath upon them."[2004]

In review, here we have God's people who got caught-up in idolatry and all sorts of sin. God allows Jabin to take them into captivity for some twenty years. The people cry out to God to have mercy on them. God leads them out of bondage and sets them free from the oppressor. But a group of people sitting and embracing a cowardly spirit, never raised a hand and never offered substance of any kind to help the cause. What kind of people were they? Does America have those types of people? Does the Church in America have those types of people?

God created us as a freeborn people. That's right, freeborn people. He gave us boundaries to live within. He gave us laws. He gave us the *Declaration of Independence*. Americans fought the British to win our independence. Then He gave us the *Constitution* to protect our God-given rights and allow us to have what He has always wanted for us. Happiness!

God is very serious about His government. This is His design for a freeborn people. How serious? That the cause of liberty is the cause of God and in truth requires the taking of arms and to repel force by force, when our liberties are invaded. This requirement is also well-pleasing to Him. It is lawful to levy war against those who oppress even when they are not in arms against us.

The lack of taking up arms and exerting ourselves in the service of our country when called thereto by the public voice in order to recover and secure our freedom, is a heinous sin in the sight of God. God requires a people struggling for their liberties to treat those of the community who will not join them as open enemies and to reject them as unworthy to enjoy the privileges which others enjoy. The cause of freedom is the cause of God.

Let us touch on our *Constitution*. "We the People," and the design for a strong county government — the government closest to the body politic.

First, if we look at moral liberty which lies in an ability or opportunity to act or conduct as the agent pleases. He is not hindered by any external force as he chooses or wills to act, is perfectly free in a moral sense; and so far as he possesses this freedom, so far, and no farther, is he a moral, accountable creature, and his actions are worthy of praise or blame.

John Locke [2005] 1632-1704 (England)

Now let us look at natural liberty, which would mean the freedom of action and conduct which all men have a right to, antecedent to their being members of society. The great John Locke (1632-1704) defined it as *"that state or condition in which all men naturally are to order all their actions and dispose of themselves and possessions as they think fit, within the bounds of the law of nature, without asking leave, or depending on the will of any man."*

In this state all men are equal, and no one hath a right to govern or control another. And the law of nature or the eternal reason and fitness of things is to be the only rule of his conduct, of the meaning of which everyone is to be his own judge. But since we live in a world of sin corruption, with all the lust and passions of men that blind their minds and harden their hearts, that perfect law of love is little considered, and less practiced; so that a state of nature, which would have been a state of perfect freedom and happiness had man continued in his first rectitude, in a state of war, rapine and murder.

This is why God gave us His designed government — the American Republic. The absolute necessity that societies should form themselves into politic bodies, in order to enact laws for the public safety, and appoint some to put them in execution, that the good may be encouraged, and the vicious deterred from evil practices; and these laws should always be founded on the law of nature.

It would appear or one might conclude that perfect civil liberty differs from natural only in this, that in self-government in the natural state of our actions, persons and possessions, are under the direction, judgment and control of none but ourselves; but in a civil state, under the direction of others, according to the laws of that state in which we live; which, by the supposition, are perfectly agreeable to the law of nature.

So in the <u>first case</u>, <u>private judgment</u>; in the <u>second</u>, the <u>public judgment</u> of the sense of <u>the law of nature is to be the rule of conduct</u>. When this is the case, civil liberty is perfect, and everyone enjoys all that freedom which God designed for his rational creatures in a social state. All liberty beyond this is mere licentiousness—a liberty to sin, which is the worst of slavery. But when any laws are enacted which cross the law of nature, there civil liberty is invaded, and God and man justly offended.

Therefore, when the oppressors (Luciferian agents) make-up laws and enact or execute laws that are repugnant to the *Constitution*, they invade this liberty, they violate their trust, and oppress their subjects, and their constituents may lawfully depose them by force of arms, if they refuse to reform.

In 1773 the men of Marlborough, Massachusetts understood this when they stated:

"Death is more eligible than slavery. A free-born people are not required by the religion of Jesus Christ to submit to tyranny, but may make use of such power as God has given them to recover and support their laws and liberties..."[2006]

The "Minute-Men" of the Revolution [2007] Published by Currier & Ives, c1876.

In 1774 Provincial Congress of Massachusetts stated:

"Resistance to tyranny becomes the Christian and social duty of each individual...continue steadfast, and with proper sense of your dependence on God, nobly defend those rights which heaven gave, and no man ought to take from us."[2008]

Provincial Congress established militia throughout Massachusetts and declared to their volunteers to have at least one-third of the militia ready for any surprise attack by the British army. This one-third militia regiment was called "Minutemen" because they would be ready to fight at a minutes' notice, would drill as citizen soldiers on the parade ground, and then go to the church to hear exhortation and prayer. Many times the deacon of the church, or <u>even the pastor</u>, would lead the drill. <u>They proclaimed, "Our cause is just" and believed it was their Christian duty to defend it</u>.

The Provincial Congress of Massachusetts charged the minutemen:

"You...are placed by Providence in a post of honor, because it is the post of danger... The eyes not only of North America and the whole British Empire, but of all Europe, are upon you. Let us be, therefore, altogether solicitous that no disorderly behavior, nothing unbecoming our characters as Americans, as citizens and Christians, be justly chargeable to us." [2009]

Therefore the freedom of a society or State consists in acting according to their own choice, within the bounds of the law of nature, in governing themselves independent of all other States. This is the liberty whereby God has made every State free, and which no power on earth may lawfully abridge, but by their own consent; nor can they lawfully consent to have it abridged, but where it appears for the greater good of society in general: and when this end cannot be attained, they have a right to resume their former freedom, if in their power.

Let us proceed to prove that the cause of civil liberty is the cause of God. This follows from what has now been said. For if the law of nature is the law of God, and if God has given every society or State liberty independent of all other States, to act according to their own choice in governing themselves with the bounds of the law of nature, then it follows that this freedom is of God, and he that is an advocate for it espouses the cause of God, and he that opposes it opposes God Himself.

This liberty has God not only given, but entailed on all men, so that they cannot relinquish it to any creature without sin. Therefore, should any State, through fear, relinquish this freedom to any other power, it would be offensive to God.

So way back in time when Israel was a free, independent commonwealth, planted by God in Canaan, it is much the same manner He planted us in America. The nations around Israel had always viewed them with an envious and jealous eye, as well as they might, since they drove out seven nations more powerful than themselves, and possessed their land. But when Israel forgot God and fell into all sorts of grievous sins and provoked God, He often permitted those neighboring nations to invade Israel's rights that they might be brought to a sense of their sin and duty.

Going back to the story in Judges, chapters 4 and 5, we find that Jabin, the king of Canaan, one of those nations, was God's rod to humble the Israelites. Jabin invaded Israel, robbed them of their rights, and held them in slavery for twenty years. Jabin acted the part of a cruel tyrant (oppressor), and ended in provoking God to his own destruction.

Jabin had long ruled over Israel; but this gave him no right to be cruel. His dominion was still mere usurpation, as he robbed them of the liberty God had given them; and with a single view to recover this and punish the invader, God commanded Israel to wage war on the tyrant, and shake-off the yoke. God commanded war on the oppressor! Israel obeyed the divine mandate, assembled their forces, called on the various States to join them in the glorious conflict; and God Himself cursed those who would not assist to punish this oppressor.

So why did the people of Meroz stay home? What kind of people would disobey God and not fight against Jabin, the tyrant? Why were the men of Meroz seeming so lost to all noble and generous feelings that would not choose to die in the field of martial glory? Did these men and women of Meroz just simply want to continue to live a life of submission and enjoy all their privileges at Jabin's sovereign disposal, but carry the heavy conviction to see themselves, their friends, their spouses, their children and country, subjected to the arbitrary will and disposal of a merciless tyrant? Were these the kind of people that simply trembled at the power of Jabin, with his 900 iron chariots, and thought him invincible, and end up opposing God Himself, Whose cause they were called to espouse.

This Biblical story is very applicable to the colonists during the *American Revolution* who were called "rebels" by the king of England. The king's servants offered pardon to all those who would lay themselves at his feet to dispose of as he would see fit, and bind them, their children and estates, at his pleasure, in all cases whatsoever. What gracious terms! What a slap in the face! What a joke!

Since the fall of man and throughout all of time there have always been some that just don't have the courage and guts to fight for their God-given freedom.

During the *Revolution* there were freeborn sons of America so lost to all sense of honor, liberty, and every noble feeling, that they pressed toward submission to the king.

In this very present time and hour we dare say that there are men and women choosing to submit to a tyrant. Be it known that the cowardly spirit of the inhabitants of Meroz was found amongst the colonists and is also found in America today.

According to the book of Judges and the story of Jabin these people of Meroz were rebels against the God of Heaven. They fell under His and His peoples' curse as well as those who oppose or neglect to promote the same glorious cause.

So, we have learned that to take-up arms and repel force-by-force when our liberties are invaded is well pleasing to God.

Going back to the two tribes led by Deborah and Barak, in obeying God they well understood the law of nature was sufficient to justify them. If they then conformed to the <u>law of love in taking up arms</u>, and <u>if God required them to make war</u> on Jabin, then it was undeniably pleasing to God. And if God approved their conduct in this case, He certainly will approve the same conduct in all similar cases.

Therefore, when one country or state invades the liberties of another, it is lawful, and well-pleasing to God for the oppressed to defend their rights by force of arms. <u>Yes, to neglect this, when there is a rational prospect of success, is a sin—a sin against God</u>, and discovers a want of that benevolence, and desire of the happiness of our fellow-creatures, which is the highest glory of the saints.

The British and their king, the oppressor, bound and riveted those chains of slavery on the colonists which caused a very dark cloud of oppression. Their enforcement was fleets and armies. God gave the colonies the right to wage war; <u>it was their lawful duty to levy war against the oppressor</u>. In reality the king who was the oppressor was also the aggressor who had already initiated the *American Revolution* by his acts of oppression.

Oppression is never welcome to people and there is this self-preservation, an instinct by God, implanted in our nature. Therefore, we sin against God and nature, when we tamely resign our rights to tyrants, or quietly submit to public oppressors, when it is in our power to defend ourselves.

Oppressors are enemies to the great law of nature and to the happiness of mankind. For this, God commanded Israel to commence a war against Jabin, that being free from his power, happiness and peace might be restored. And those who are indolent, and backward to take-up arms and exert themselves in the service of their country, in order to recover and secure their freedom, when called upon by the public voice, are highly criminal in the sight of God and man. <u>Resistance to tyranny is obedience to God</u>!!!

The *Declaration of Independence*, July 4, 1776 states:

"We hold these truths to be self-evident: that all men are created equal; that they are endowed by their Creator with certain unalienable rights; that among these are life, liberty, and the pursuit of happiness; that to secure these rights, governments [the American Republic] are instituted among men, deriving their just powers from the consent of the governed; [We the People] that whenever any form of government [Corporate UNITED STATES, which operates by fraud with a counterfeit constitution and is led by CEOs and a Board of Directors, imposters along with "judges" that are actually and in fact "law merchants"] becomes destructive of these ends, it is the right of the people [We the People] to alter or to abolish it and institute new government [the American Republic], laying its foundation on such principles, and organizing its power in such form, as to them shall seem most likely to affect their safety and happiness."

The modern day people of Meroz are the Church! The Church has bought a lie about the *First Amendment* in a misleading metaphor which was started by gross misinterpretation of a letter by Thomas Jefferson to the Danbury Baptists written on January 1, 1802. There is now no separation of church and state. The churches are 501c3 corporations manipulated by a fraudulent excuse of protecting their tax-exempt status when in fact the right to be tax-exempt is from God's Word found in Ezra 7:24.

Ezra 7:24 ~

> *Also we certify you, that touching any of the priests and Levites, singers, porters, Nethinims, or ministers of this house of God, it shall not be lawful to impose toll, tribute, or custom, upon them.*

Most of the Church in America is either hiding behind or ignorant of this misconception of "obey them that have the rule over you," referencing Romans chapter 13. Clergy are telling their congregations to pray for government leaders and even tyrants. To pray that they might get saved and then America will enjoy a great turnaround.

Jonathan Mayhew (1720-1766), was the famous Congregational minister of West Church in Boston. Having graduated with honors from Harvard in 1747, he was given the distinguished position of Dudlein Lecturer at Harvard in 1765. Reflecting the colonists' feelings toward King George III's hated *Stamp Act*, Jonathan Mayhew delivered a powerful patriotic sermon in 1765 stating:

"The king is as much bound by his oath not to infringe the legal rights of the people, as the people are bound to yield subjection to him. From whence it follows that at soon as the prince sets himself above the law, he loses the king in the tyrant. He does, to all intents and purposes, un-king himself." [2010]

Jonathan Mayhew[2011]

So it is that the President of the *United States of America* is as much bound by his oath to the *U. S. Constitution* not to infringe the lawful "Bill of Rights" of the people, as the people are bound to yield subjection to a constitutionally-sound man continually abiding. He is required to be a man of great integrity, with a real desire to serve the American people.

But from whence it follows that as soon as the President sets himself above "the supreme law of the land" and comes out from under God's umbrella of authority and to embrace the so-called "Progressive Agenda" (movement) to take on the role of a deceptive tyrant, he loses the presidency in the tyrant. He does, to all intents and purposes, un-President himself. He is very much subject to impeachment.

So I ask you Church, all clergy that believe or hide behind Romans chapter 13 and 2 Peter 2:13-14, how can you, your congregations, your synods, your denominations have the gall to celebrate the *Declaration of Independence* on the 4th of July? Remember, it was many preachers, deacons, and congregations that shed their blood for our independence.

Charles Finney a great 19th century revivalist said:

"If there is a decay of conscience, the pulpit is responsible for it. If the public press lacks moral discernment, the pulpit is responsible for it. If the church is degenerate and worldly, the pulpit is responsible for it. If the world loses its interest in Christianity, the pulpit is responsible for it. If Satan rules in our halls of legislation, the pulpit is responsible for it. If our politics become so corrupt, that the very foundations of our government are ready to fall away, the pulpit is responsible for it." 2012

Applying Finney's quote to modern day Christianity, the seminaries have greater responsibility for it. A watered-down Gospel is being taught by the professors in most Christian or religious schools. The Patriot Preachers have faded away and this is the underlining problem.

We admonish the clergy and congregations across America to listen and heed. You were all destined to be living at "such a time as this," but not all of you—because of your choice—are destined to work for Jesus Christ to advance His kingdom. Remember this—it is a real honor to be a soldier in His army, to bring Him glory.

Charles Finney also stated:

"**The church must take right ground in regards to politics**...The time has come for Christians to vote for honest men, and **take consistent ground in politics or the Lord will curse them.**

God cannot sustain this free and blessed country, which we love and pray for, unless the CHURCH will take right ground. **Politics are a part of religion in such a country as this, and Christians must do their duty to their country as a part of their duty to God...**

God will bless or curse this nation according to the course Christians take in politics."2013 [emphasis added]   Charles Finney, 1850 2014

It is time for the clergy to mount up and join "the Black Robe Regiment." **This is a present hour call by God.**

First: teach the Church their true identity in Christ. This is a must. Christians need and must know who they are. A study in Romans teaches the "Mystery of the Gospel." A study of Romans chapters 5, 6, 7, 8 is very important. Study to understand Romans 7:1-6. The Church must learn their authority in Christ.

There are many Patriot groups across America. Almost all of the groups think they can fix this socialist Corporation in Washington, DC. The phony impostors are puppets-on-a-string and are controlled by Luciferians. It doesn't matter what party (Democrats or Republican, etc.), and it doesn't matter who the people are running the show. They are controlled by a foreign Oligarchy with the CEO running his Executive Congress using a Corporate constitution. The truth is, in more recent years, the CEO doesn't even follow their own (counterfeit) constitution. Instead, there is "a pen and a cell phone."

Have "ears to hear," Patriots. You need a new way, a fresh way, and an authentic structure to advance your cause to bring America back to Go in His safety, to bring America back for our children and grandchildren, for our posterity. Picture a locomotive. A giant locomotive made of gold. On its side are the words, "The Republic." On the front is written the word, "Constitution." On the top is written, "Declaration of Independence." The locomotive is pulling millions of cars decorated in silver and gold. On the side of the car is written, "We the People." On the caboose is a sign written with ruby and silver stones, "There is no place like home." That train is coming to your town. Get on board.

The American Republic is God's government. It is His provision for His people who are abiding in covenant with Him. In turning toward God, He will remove the veil which will then reveal the things the sons of Satan have done in darkness. We will see how on the brink of utter destruction we are. It will be a fearful thing to see, as we are currently there.

Repentance is the key—and crying out to Him with heart-felt sorrow for our individual sins as well as for our national covenant-breaking as a nation. Return to Him with all of your heart; He promises to hear from Heaven and answer. He will even heal our land. As a covenanted nation we will then be able to fulfill the mandate of Genesis 12:3 to be a blessing to all the families of the earth. Our Forefather's vision for America will manifest in America as "a city upon a hill," a light to the nations where they will come to learn the law of the Lord. Operating in God's government will aid in healing this land. This is the structure where Americans will be able to pray 2 Chronicles 7:14 and really mean it. Why? Because the American Republic will give us constitutional courts in Equity and do away with Admiralty/Maritime courts that are about "summary judgments," where the imposter with the black robe is the prosecutor and inquisitor, and runs the cash register as a law merchant. The *Supreme Judge of the universe*, constitutional courts in Equity, and the American people are the only remedy to return America to what she was birthed to be.

Then God will heal our land!

The Cradle of Liberty [2015]
Currier & Ives lithograph, 1876

"The Gathering," by Brian Lee
Cover painting on Volume I: "America's Truthful History,"
Re-inhabited: Republic for the United States of America

Justice and judgment are the habitation of thy throne:
mercy and truth shall go before thy face.   ~ Psalm 89:14

Now it is in mine heart to make a covenant with the Lord God of Israel,
that his fierce wrath may turn away from us.   ~ *2 Chronicles 29:10*

Ye children of Israel, turn again unto the Lord God of Abraham, Isaac, and Israel,
and he will return to the remnant of you...   ~ *2 Chronicles 30:6b*

Declaration of Independence: A Transcription

Note: The following text is a transcription of the Stone Engraving of the parchment Declaration of Independence (the document on display in the Rotunda at the National Archives Museum.) The spelling and punctuation reflects the original.[2016]

In Congress, July 4, 1776.

The unanimous Declaration of the thirteen united States of America, When in the Course of human events, it becomes necessary for one people to dissolve the political bands which have connected them with another, and to assume among the powers of the earth, the separate and equal station to which the Laws of Nature and of Nature's God entitle them, a decent respect to the opinions of mankind requires that they should declare the causes which impel them to the separation.

We hold these truths to be self-evident, that all men are created equal, that they are endowed by their Creator with certain unalienable Rights, that among these are Life, Liberty and the pursuit of Happiness.-- That to secure these rights, Governments are instituted among Men, deriving their just powers from the consent of the governed, --That whenever any Form of Government becomes destructive of these ends, it is the Right of the People to alter or to abolish it, and to institute new Government, laying its foundation on such principles and organizing its powers in such form, as to them shall seem most likely to effect their Safety and Happiness. Prudence, indeed, will dictate that Governments long established should not be changed for light and transient causes; and accordingly all experience hath shewn, that mankind are more disposed to suffer, while evils are sufferable, than to right themselves by abolishing the forms to which they are accustomed. But when a long train of abuses and usurpations, pursuing invariably the same Object evinces a design to reduce them under absolute Despotism, it is their right, it is their duty, to throw off such Government, and to provide new Guards for their future security.--Such has been the patient sufferance of these Colonies; and such is now the necessity which constrains them to alter their former Systems of Government. The history of the present King of Great Britain is a history of repeated injuries and usurpations, all having in direct object the establishment of an absolute Tyranny over these States. To prove this, let Facts be submitted to a candid world.

He has refused his Assent to Laws, the most wholesome and necessary for the public good.

He has forbidden his Governors to pass Laws of immediate and pressing importance, unless suspended in their operation till his Assent should be obtained; and when so suspended, he has utterly neglected to attend to them.

He has refused to pass other Laws for the accommodation of large districts of people, unless those people would relinquish the right of Representation in the Legislature, a right inestimable to them and formidable to tyrants only.

He has called together legislative bodies at places unusual, uncomfortable, and distant from the depository of their public Records, for the sole purpose of fatiguing them into compliance with his measures.

He has dissolved Representative Houses repeatedly, for opposing with manly firmness his invasions on the rights of the people.

He has refused for a long time, after such dissolutions, to cause others to be elected; whereby the Legislative powers, incapable of Annihilation, have returned to the People at large for their exercise; the State remaining in the mean time exposed to all the dangers of invasion from without, and convulsions within.

He has endeavoured to prevent the population of these States; for that purpose obstructing the Laws for Naturalization of Foreigners; refusing to pass others to encourage their migrations hither, and raising the conditions of new Appropriations of Lands.

He has obstructed the Administration of Justice, by refusing his Assent to Laws for establishing Judiciary powers.

He has made Judges dependent on his Will alone, for the tenure of their offices, and the amount and payment of their salaries.

He has erected a multitude of New Offices, and sent hither swarms of Officers to harrass our people, and eat out their substance.

He has kept among us, in times of peace, Standing Armies without the Consent of our legislatures.

He has affected to render the Military independent of and superior to the Civil power.

He has combined with others to subject us to a jurisdiction foreign to our constitution, and unacknowledged by our laws; giving his Assent to their Acts of pretended Legislation:

For Quartering large bodies of armed troops among us:

For protecting them, by a mock Trial, from punishment for any Murders which they should commit on the Inhabitants of these States:

For cutting off our Trade with all parts of the world:

For imposing Taxes on us without our Consent:

For depriving us in many cases, of the benefits of Trial by Jury:

For transporting us beyond Seas to be tried for pretended offences

For abolishing the free System of English Laws in a neighbouring Province, establishing therein an Arbitrary government, and enlarging its Boundaries so as to render it at once an example and fit instrument for introducing the same absolute rule into these Colonies:

For taking away our Charters, abolishing our most valuable Laws, and altering fundamentally the Forms of our Governments:

For suspending our own Legislatures, and declaring themselves invested with power to legislate for us in all cases whatsoever.

He has abdicated Government here, by declaring us out of his Protection and waging War against us.

He has plundered our seas, ravaged our Coasts, burnt our towns, and destroyed the lives of our people.

He is at this time transporting large Armies of foreign Mercenaries to compleat the works of death, desolation and tyranny, already begun with circumstances of Cruelty & perfidy scarcely paralleled in the most barbarous ages, and totally unworthy the Head of a civilized nation.

He has constrained our fellow Citizens taken Captive on the high Seas to bear Arms against their Country, to become the executioners of their friends and Brethren, or to fall themselves by their Hands.

He has excited domestic insurrections amongst us, and has endeavoured to bring on the inhabitants of our frontiers, the merciless Indian Savages, whose known rule of warfare, is an undistinguished destruction of all ages, sexes and conditions.

In every stage of these Oppressions We have Petitioned for Redress in the most humble terms: Our repeated Petitions have been answered only by repeated injury. A Prince whose character is thus marked by every act which may define a Tyrant, is unfit to be the ruler of a free people.

Nor have We been wanting in attentions to our Brittish brethren. We have warned them from time to time of attempts by their legislature to extend an unwarrantable jurisdiction over us. We have reminded them of the circumstances of our emigration and settlement here. We have appealed to their native justice and magnanimity, and we have conjured them by the ties of our common kindred to disavow these usurpations, which, would inevitably interrupt our connections and correspondence. They too have been deaf to the voice of justice and of consanguinity. We must, therefore, acquiesce in the necessity, which denounces our Separation, and hold them, as we hold the rest of mankind, Enemies in War, in Peace Friends.

We, therefore, the Representatives of the united States of America, in General Congress, Assembled, appealing to the Supreme Judge of the world for the rectitude of our intentions, do, in the Name, and by Authority of the good People of these Colonies, solemnly publish and declare, That these United Colonies are, and of Right ought to be Free and Independent States; that they are Absolved from all Allegiance to the British Crown, and that all political connection between them and the State of Great Britain, is and ought to be totally dissolved; and that as Free and Independent States, they have full Power to levy War, conclude Peace, contract Alliances, establish Commerce, and to do all other Acts and Things which Independent States may of right do. And for the support of this Declaration, with a firm reliance on the protection of divine Providence, we mutually pledge to each other our Lives, our Fortunes and our sacred Honor.

Delaware:
George Read | Caesar Rodney | Thomas McKean |

Pennsylvania:
George Clymer | Benjamin Franklin | Robert Morris | John Morton | Benjamin Rush | George Ross | James Smith | James Wilson | George Taylor |

Massachusetts:
John Adams | Samuel Adams | John Hancock | Robert Treat Paine | Elbridge Gerry

New Hampshire:
Josiah Bartlett | William Whipple | Matthew Thornton |

Rhode Island:
Stephen Hopkins | William Ellery |

New York:
Lewis Morris | Philip Livingston | Francis Lewis | William Floyd | Button Gwinnett | Lyman Hall | George Walton |

Georgia:
Button Gwinnett | Lyman Hall | George Walton |

Virginia:
Richard Henry Lee | Francis Lightfoot Lee | Carter Braxton | Benjamin Harrison | Thomas Jefferson | George Wythe | Thomas Nelson, Jr. |

North Carolina:
William Hooper | John Penn | Joseph Hewes

South Carolina:
Edward Rutledge | Arthur Middleton | Thomas Lynch, Jr. | Thomas Heyward, Jr. |

New Jersey:
Abraham Clark | John Hart | Francis Hopkinson | Richard Stockton | John Witherspoon |

Connecticut:
Samuel Huntington | Roger Sherman | William Williams | Oliver Wolcott |

Maryland:
Charles Carroll | Samuel Chase | Thomas Stone | William Paca |

The Constitution of the United States: A Transcription

Note: The following text is a transcription of the Constitution as it was inscribed by Jacob Shallus on parchment (the document on display in the Rotunda at the National Archives Museum.) *The spelling and punctuation reflect the original.*[2017]

We the People of the United States, in Order to form a more perfect Union, establish Justice, insure domestic Tranquility, provide for the common defence, promote the general Welfare, and secure the Blessings of Liberty to ourselves and our Posterity, do ordain and establish this Constitution for the United States of America.

Article. I.

Section. 1.

All legislative Powers herein granted shall be vested in a Congress of the United States, which shall consist of a Senate and House of Representatives.

Section. 2.

The House of Representatives shall be composed of Members chosen every second Year by the People of the several States, and the Electors in each State shall have the Qualifications requisite for Electors of the most numerous Branch of the State Legislature.

No Person shall be a Representative who shall not have attained to the Age of twenty five Years, and been seven Years a Citizen of the United States, and who shall not, when elected, be an Inhabitant of that State in which he shall be chosen.

Representatives and direct Taxes shall be apportioned among the several States which may be included within this Union, according to their respective Numbers, which shall be determined by adding to the whole Number of free Persons, including those bound to Service for a Term of Years, and excluding Indians not taxed, three fifths of all other Persons. The actual Enumeration shall be made within three Years after the first Meeting of the Congress of the United States, and within every subsequent Term of ten Years, in such Manner as they shall by Law direct. The Number of Representatives shall not exceed one for every thirty Thousand, but each State shall have at Least one Representative; and until such enumeration shall be made, the State of New Hampshire shall be entitled to chuse three, Massachusetts eight, Rhode-Island and Providence Plantations one, Connecticut five, New-York six, New Jersey four, Pennsylvania eight, Delaware one, Maryland six, Virginia ten, North Carolina five, South Carolina five, and Georgia three.

When vacancies happen in the Representation from any State, the Executive Authority thereof shall issue Writs of Election to fill such Vacancies.

The House of Representatives shall chuse their Speaker and other Officers; and shall have the sole Power of Impeachment.

Section. 3.

The Senate of the United States shall be composed of two Senators from each State, chosen by the Legislature thereof, for six Years; and each Senator shall have one Vote.

Immediately after they shall be assembled in Consequence of the first Election, they shall be divided as equally as may be into three Classes. The Seats of the Senators of the first Class shall be vacated at the Expiration of the second Year, of the second Class at the Expiration of the fourth Year, and of the third Class at the Expiration of the sixth Year, so that one third may be chosen every second Year; and if Vacancies happen by Resignation, or otherwise, during the Recess of the Legislature of any State, the Executive thereof may make temporary Appointments until the next Meeting of the Legislature, which shall then fill such Vacancies.

No Person shall be a Senator who shall not have attained to the Age of thirty Years, and been nine Years a Citizen of the United States, and who shall not, when elected, be an Inhabitant of that State for which he shall be chosen.

The Vice President of the United States shall be President of the Senate, but shall have no Vote, unless they be equally divided.

The Senate shall chuse their other Officers, and also a President pro tempore, in the Absence of the Vice President, or when he shall exercise the Office of President of the United States.

The Senate shall have the sole Power to try all Impeachments. When sitting for that Purpose, they shall be on Oath or Affirmation. When the President of the United States is tried, the Chief Justice shall preside: And no Person shall be convicted without the Concurrence of two thirds of the Members present.

Judgment in Cases of Impeachment shall not extend further than to removal from Office, and disqualification to hold and enjoy any Office of honor, Trust or Profit under the United States: but the Party convicted shall nevertheless be liable and subject to Indictment, Trial, Judgment and Punishment, according to Law.

Section. 4.

The Times, Places and Manner of holding Elections for Senators and Representatives, shall be prescribed in each State by the Legislature thereof; but the Congress may at any time by Law make or alter such Regulations, except as to the Places of chusing Senators.

The Congress shall assemble at least once in every Year, and such Meeting shall be on the first Monday in December, unless they shall by Law appoint a different Day.

Section. 5.

Each House shall be the Judge of the Elections, Returns and Qualifications of its own Members, and a Majority of each shall constitute a Quorum to do Business; but a smaller Number may adjourn from day to day, and may be authorized to compel the Attendance of absent Members, in such Manner, and under such Penalties as each House may provide.

Each House may determine the Rules of its Proceedings, punish its Members for disorderly Behaviour, and, with the Concurrence of two thirds, expel a Member.

Each House shall keep a Journal of its Proceedings, and from time to time publish the same, excepting such Parts as may in their Judgment require Secrecy; and the Yeas and Nays of the Members of either House on any question shall, at the Desire of one fifth of those Present, be entered on the Journal.

Neither House, during the Session of Congress, shall, without the Consent of the other, adjourn for more than three days, nor to any other Place than that in which the two Houses shall be sitting.

Section. 6.

The Senators and Representatives shall receive a Compensation for their Services, to be ascertained by Law, and paid out of the Treasury of the United States. They shall in all Cases, except Treason, Felony and Breach of the Peace, be privileged from Arrest during their Attendance at the Session of their respective Houses, and in going to and returning from the same; and for any Speech or Debate in either House, they shall not be questioned in any other Place.

No Senator or Representative shall, during the Time for which he was elected, be appointed to any civil Office under the Authority of the United States, which shall have been created, or the Emoluments whereof shall have been encreased during such time; and no Person holding any Office under the United States, shall be a Member of either House during his Continuance in Office.

Section. 7.

All Bills for raising Revenue shall originate in the House of Representatives; but the Senate may propose or concur with Amendments as on other Bills.

Every Bill which shall have passed the House of Representatives and the Senate, shall, before it become a Law, be presented to the President of the United States; If he approve he shall sign it, but if not he shall return it, with his Objections to that House in which it shall have originated, who shall enter the Objections at large on their Journal, and proceed to reconsider it. If after such Reconsideration two thirds of that House shall agree to pass the Bill, it shall be sent, together with the Objections, to the other House, by which it shall likewise be reconsidered, and if approved by two thirds of that House, it shall become a Law. But in all such Cases the Votes of both Houses shall be determined by yeas and Nays, and the Names of the Persons voting for and against the Bill shall be entered on the Journal of each House respectively. If any Bill shall not be returned by the President within ten Days (Sundays excepted) after it shall have been presented to him, the Same shall be a Law, in like Manner as if he had signed it, unless the Congress by their Adjournment prevent its Return, in which Case it shall not be a Law.

Every Order, Resolution, or Vote to which the Concurrence of the Senate and House of Representatives may be necessary (except on a question of Adjournment) shall be presented to the President of the United States; and before the Same shall take Effect, shall be approved by him, or being disapproved by him, shall be repassed by two thirds of the Senate and House of Representatives, according to the Rules and Limitations prescribed in the Case of a Bill.

Section. 8.

The Congress shall have Power To lay and collect Taxes, Duties, Imposts and Excises, to pay the Debts and provide for the common Defence and general Welfare of the United States; but all Duties, Imposts and Excises shall be uniform throughout the United States;

To borrow Money on the credit of the United States;

To regulate Commerce with foreign Nations, and among the several States, and with the Indian Tribes;

To establish an uniform Rule of Naturalization, and uniform Laws on the subject of Bankruptcies throughout the United States;

To coin Money, regulate the Value thereof, and of foreign Coin, and fix the Standard of Weights and Measures;

To provide for the Punishment of counterfeiting the Securities and current Coin of the United States;

To establish Post Offices and post Roads;

To promote the Progress of Science and useful Arts, by securing for limited Times to Authors and Inventors the exclusive Right to their respective Writings and Discoveries;

To constitute Tribunals inferior to the supreme Court;

To define and punish Piracies and Felonies committed on the high Seas, and Offences against the Law of Nations;

To declare War, grant Letters of Marque and Reprisal, and make Rules concerning Captures on Land and Water;

To raise and support Armies, but no Appropriation of Money to that Use shall be for a longer Term than two Years;

To provide and maintain a Navy;

To make Rules for the Government and Regulation of the land and naval Forces;

To provide for calling forth the Militia to execute the Laws of the Union, suppress Insurrections and repel Invasions;

To provide for organizing, arming, and disciplining, the Militia, and for governing such Part of them as may be employed in the Service of the United States, reserving to the States respectively, the Appointment of the Officers, and the Authority of training the Militia according to the discipline prescribed by Congress;

To exercise exclusive Legislation in all Cases whatsoever, over such District (not exceeding ten Miles square) as may, by Cession of particular States, and the Acceptance of Congress, become the Seat of the Government of the United States, and to exercise like Authority over all Places purchased by the Consent of the Legislature of the State in which the Same shall be, for the Erection of Forts, Magazines, Arsenals, dock-Yards, and other needful Buildings;—And

To make all Laws which shall be necessary and proper for carrying into Execution the foregoing Powers, and all other Powers vested by this Constitution in the Government of the United States, or in any Department or Officer thereof.

Section. 9.

The Migration or Importation of such Persons as any of the States now existing shall think proper to admit, shall not be prohibited by the Congress prior to the Year one thousand eight hundred and eight, but a Tax or duty may be imposed on such Importation, not exceeding ten dollars for each Person.

The Privilege of the Writ of Habeas Corpus shall not be suspended, unless when in Cases of Rebellion or Invasion the public Safety may require it.

No Bill of Attainder or ex post facto Law shall be passed.

No Capitation, or other direct, Tax shall be laid, unless in Proportion to the Census or enumeration herein before directed to be taken.

No Tax or Duty shall be laid on Articles exported from any State.

No Preference shall be given by any Regulation of Commerce or Revenue to the Ports of one State over those of another: nor shall Vessels bound to, or from, one State, be obliged to enter, clear, or pay Duties in another.

No Money shall be drawn from the Treasury, but in Consequence of Appropriations made by Law; and a regular Statement and Account of the Receipts and Expenditures of all public Money shall be published from time to time.

No Title of Nobility shall be granted by the United States: And no Person holding any Office of Profit or Trust under them, shall, without the Consent of the Congress, accept of any present, Emolument, Office, or Title, of any kind whatever, from any King, Prince, or foreign State.

Section. 10.

No State shall enter into any Treaty, Alliance, or Confederation; grant Letters of Marque and Reprisal; coin Money; emit Bills of Credit; make any Thing but gold and silver Coin a Tender in Payment of Debts; pass any Bill of Attainder, ex post facto Law, or Law impairing the Obligation of Contracts, or grant any Title of Nobility.

No State shall, without the Consent of the Congress, lay any Imposts or Duties on Imports or Exports, except what may be absolutely necessary for executing it's inspection Laws: and the net Produce of all Duties and Imposts, laid by any State on Imports or Exports, shall be for the Use of the Treasury of the United States; and all such Laws shall be subject to the Revision and Controul of the Congress.

No State shall, without the Consent of Congress, lay any Duty of Tonnage, keep Troops, or Ships of War in time of Peace, enter into any Agreement or Compact with another State, or with a foreign Power, or engage in War, unless actually invaded, or in such imminent Danger as will not admit of delay.

Article. II.

Section. 1.

The executive Power shall be vested in a President of the United States of America. He shall hold his Office during the Term of four Years, and, together with the Vice President, chosen for the same Term, be elected, as follows

Each State shall appoint, in such Manner as the Legislature thereof may direct, a Number of Electors, equal to the whole Number of Senators and Representatives to which the State may be entitled in the Congress: but no Senator or Representative, or Person holding an Office of Trust or Profit under the United States, shall be appointed an Elector.

The Electors shall meet in their respective States, and vote by Ballot for two Persons, of whom one at least shall not be an Inhabitant of the same State with themselves. And they shall make a List of all the Persons voted for, and of the Number of Votes for each; which List they shall sign and certify, and transmit sealed to the Seat of the Government of the United States, directed to the President of the Senate. The President of the Senate shall, in the Presence of the Senate and House of Representatives, open all the Certificates, and the Votes shall then be counted. The Person having the greatest Number of Votes shall be the President, if such Number be a Majority of the whole Number of Electors appointed; and if there be more than one who have such Majority, and have an equal Number of Votes, then the House of Representatives shall immediately chuse by Ballot one of them for President; and if no Person have a Majority, then from the five highest on the List the said House shall in like Manner chuse the President. But in chusing the President, the Votes shall be taken by States, the Representation from each State having one Vote; A quorum for this Purpose shall consist of a Member or Members from two thirds of the States, and a Majority of all the States shall be necessary to a Choice. In every Case, after the Choice of the President, the Person having the greatest Number of Votes of the Electors shall be the Vice President. But if there should remain two or more who have equal Votes, the Senate shall chuse from them by Ballot the Vice President.

The Congress may determine the Time of chusing the Electors, and the Day on which they shall give their Votes; which Day shall be the same throughout the United States.

No Person except a natural born Citizen, or a Citizen of the United States, at the time of the Adoption of this Constitution, shall be eligible to the Office of President; neither shall any Person be eligible to that Office who shall not have attained to the Age of thirty five Years, and been fourteen Years a Resident within the United States.

In Case of the Removal of the President from Office, or of his Death, Resignation, or Inability to discharge the Powers and Duties of the said Office, the Same shall devolve on the Vice President, and the Congress may by Law provide for the Case of Removal, Death, Resignation or Inability, both of the President and Vice President, declaring what Officer shall then act as President, and such Officer shall act accordingly, until the Disability be removed, or a President shall be elected.

The President shall, at stated Times, receive for his Services, a Compensation, which shall neither be encreased nor diminished during the Period for which he shall have been elected, and he shall not receive within that Period any other Emolument from the United States, or any of them.

Before he enter on the Execution of his Office, he shall take the following Oath or Affirmation:—"I do solemnly swear (or affirm) that I will faithfully execute the Office of President of the United States, and will to the best of my Ability, preserve, protect and defend the Constitution of the United States."

Section. 2.

The President shall be Commander in Chief of the Army and Navy of the United States, and of the Militia of the several States, when called into the actual Service of the United States; he may require the Opinion, in writing, of the principal Officer in each of the executive Departments, upon any Subject relating to the Duties of their respective Offices, and he shall have Power to grant Reprieves and Pardons for Offences against the United States, except in Cases of Impeachment.

He shall have Power, by and with the Advice and Consent of the Senate, to make Treaties, provided two thirds of the Senators present concur; and he shall nominate, and by and with the Advice and Consent of the Senate, shall appoint Ambassadors, other public Ministers and Consuls, Judges of the supreme Court, and all other Officers of the United States, whose Appointments are not herein otherwise provided for, and which shall be established by Law: but the Congress may by Law vest the Appointment of such inferior Officers, as they think proper, in the President alone, in the Courts of Law, or in the Heads of Departments.

The President shall have Power to fill up all Vacancies that may happen during the Recess of the Senate, by granting Commissions which shall expire at the End of their next Session.

Section. 3.

He shall from time to time give to the Congress Information of the State of the Union, and recommend to their Consideration such Measures as he shall judge necessary and expedient; he may, on extraordinary Occasions, convene both Houses, or either of them, and in Case of Disagreement between them, with Respect to the Time of Adjournment, he may adjourn them to such Time as he shall think proper; he shall receive Ambassadors and other public Ministers; he shall take Care that the Laws be faithfully executed, and shall Commission all the Officers of the United States.

Section. 4.

The President, Vice President and all civil Officers of the United States, shall be removed from Office on Impeachment for, and Conviction of, Treason, Bribery, or other high Crimes and Misdemeanors.

Article III.

Section. 1.

The judicial Power of the United States, shall be vested in one supreme Court, and in such inferior Courts as the Congress may from time to time ordain and establish. The Judges, both of the supreme and inferior Courts, shall hold their Offices during good Behaviour, and shall, at stated Times, receive for their Services, a Compensation, which shall not be diminished during their Continuance in Office.

Section. 2.

The judicial Power shall extend to all Cases, in Law and Equity, arising under this Constitution, the Laws of the United States, and Treaties made, or which shall be made, under their Authority;—to all Cases affecting Ambassadors, other public Ministers and Consuls;—to all Cases of admiralty and maritime Jurisdiction;—to Controversies to which the United States shall be a Party;—to Controversies between two or more States;— between a State and Citizens of another State,—between Citizens of different States,— between Citizens of the same State claiming Lands under Grants of different States, and between a State, or the Citizens thereof, and foreign States, Citizens or Subjects.

In all Cases affecting Ambassadors, other public Ministers and Consuls, and those in which a State shall be Party, the supreme Court shall have original Jurisdiction. In all the other Cases before mentioned, the supreme Court shall have appellate Jurisdiction, both as to Law and Fact, with such Exceptions, and under such Regulations as the Congress shall make.

The Trial of all Crimes, except in Cases of Impeachment, shall be by Jury; and such Trial shall be held in the State where the said Crimes shall have been committed; but when not committed within any State, the Trial shall be at such Place or Places as the Congress may by Law have directed.

Section. 3.

Treason against the United States, shall consist only in levying War against them, or in adhering to their Enemies, giving them Aid and Comfort. No Person shall be convicted of Treason unless on the Testimony of two Witnesses to the same overt Act, or on Confession in open Court.

The Congress shall have Power to declare the Punishment of Treason, but no Attainder of Treason shall work Corruption of Blood, or Forfeiture except during the Life of the Person attainted.

Article. IV.

Section. 1.

Full Faith and Credit shall be given in each State to the public Acts, Records, and judicial Proceedings of every other State. And the Congress may by general Laws prescribe the Manner in which such Acts, Records and Proceedings shall be proved, and the Effect thereof.

Section. 2.

The Citizens of each State shall be entitled to all Privileges and Immunities of Citizens in the several States.

A Person charged in any State with Treason, Felony, or other Crime, who shall flee from Justice, and be found in another State, shall on Demand of the executive Authority of the State from which he fled, be delivered up, to be removed to the State having Jurisdiction of the Crime.

No Person held to Service or Labour in one State, under the Laws thereof, escaping into another, shall, in Consequence of any Law or Regulation therein, be discharged from such Service or Labour, but shall be delivered up on Claim of the Party to whom such Service or Labour may be due.

Section. 3.

New States may be admitted by the Congress into this Union; but no new State shall be formed or erected within the Jurisdiction of any other State; nor any State be formed by the Junction of two or more States, or Parts of States, without the Consent of the Legislatures of the States concerned as well as of the Congress.

The Congress shall have Power to dispose of and make all needful Rules and Regulations respecting the Territory or other Property belonging to the United States; and nothing in this Constitution shall be so construed as to Prejudice any Claims of the United States, or of any particular State.

Section. 4.

The United States shall guarantee to every State in this Union a Republican Form of Government, and shall protect each of them against Invasion; and on Application of the Legislature, or of the Executive (when the Legislature cannot be convened), against domestic Violence.

Article. V.

The Congress, whenever two thirds of both Houses shall deem it necessary, shall propose Amendments to this Constitution, or, on the Application of the Legislatures of two thirds of the several States, shall call a Convention for proposing Amendments, which, in either Case, shall be valid to all Intents and Purposes, as Part of this Constitution, when ratified by the Legislatures of three fourths of the several States, or by Conventions in three fourths thereof, as the one or the other Mode of Ratification may be proposed by the Congress; Provided that no Amendment which may be made prior to the Year One thousand eight hundred and eight shall in any Manner affect the first and fourth Clauses in the Ninth Section of the first Article; and that no State, without its Consent, shall be deprived of its equal Suffrage in the Senate.

Article. VI.

All Debts contracted and Engagements entered into, before the Adoption of this Constitution, shall be as valid against the United States under this Constitution, as under the Confederation.

This Constitution, and the Laws of the United States which shall be made in Pursuance thereof; and all Treaties made, or which shall be made, under the Authority of the United States, shall be the supreme Law of the Land; and the Judges in every State shall be bound thereby, any Thing in the Constitution or Laws of any State to the Contrary notwithstanding.

The Senators and Representatives before mentioned, and the Members of the several State Legislatures, and all executive and judicial Officers, both of the United States and of the several States, shall be bound by Oath or Affirmation, to support this Constitution; but no religious Test shall ever be required as a Qualification to any Office or public Trust under the United States.

Article. VII.

The Ratification of the Conventions of nine States, shall be sufficient for the Establishment of this Constitution between the States so ratifying the Same.

The Word, "the," being interlined between the seventh and eighth Lines of the first Page, The Word "Thirty" being partly written on an Erazure in the fifteenth Line of the first Page, The Words "is tried" being interlined between the thirty second and thirty third Lines of the first Page and the Word "the" being interlined between the forty third and forty fourth Lines of the second Page.

Attest William Jackson Secretary

done in Convention by the Unanimous Consent of the States present the Seventeenth Day of September in the Year of our Lord one thousand seven hundred and Eighty seven and of the Independance of the United States of America the Twelfth In witness whereof We have hereunto subscribed our Names,

G°. Washington
Presidt and deputy from Virginia

Delaware	**North Carolina**	**New Hampshire**	**New Jersey**
Geo: Read	Wm. Blount	John Langdon	Wil: Livingston
Gunning Bedford jun	Richd Dobbs Spaight	Nicholas Gilman	David Brearley
John Dickinson	Hu Williamson		Wm. Paterson
Richard Bassett			Jona: Dayton
Jaco: Broom			

Maryland	**South Carolina**	**Massachusetts**	**Pennsylvania**
James McHenry	J. Rutledge	Nathaniel Gorham	B. Franklin
Dan of St Thos. Jenifer	Charles Cotesworth Pinckney		Thomas Mifflin
Danl. Carroll	Charles Pinckney	Rufus King	Robt. Morris
	Pierce Butler		Geo. Clymer

Virginia		Connecticut	Thos. FitzSimons
John Blair		Wm. Saml. Johnson	Jared Ingersoll
James Madison Jr.	**Georgia**	Roger Sherman	James Wilson
	William Few		Gouv Morris
	Abr Baldwin	**New York**	
		Alexander Hamilton	

The Bill of Rights: A Transcription

Note: The following text is a transcription of the enrolled original of the Joint Resolution of Congress proposing the Bill of Rights, which is on permanent display in the Rotunda at the National Archives Museum. The spelling and punctuation reflects the original.[2018]

On September 25, 1789, the First Congress of the United States proposed 12 amendments to the Constitution. The 1789 Joint Resolution of Congress proposing the amendments is on display in the Rotunda in the National Archives Museum. Ten of the proposed 12 amendments were ratified by three-fourths of the state legislatures on December 15, 1791. The ratified Articles (Articles 3–12) constitute the first 10 amendments of the Constitution, or the U.S. Bill of Rights. In 1992, 203 years after it was proposed, Article 2 was ratified as the 27th Amendment to the Constitution. Article 1 was never ratified.

Transcription of the 1789 Joint Resolution of Congress Proposing 12 Amendments to the U.S. Constitution

Congress of the United States begun and held at the City of New-York, on Wednesday the fourth of March, one thousand seven hundred and eighty nine.

THE Conventions of a number of the States, having at the time of their adopting the Constitution, expressed a desire, in order to prevent misconstruction or abuse of its powers, that further declaratory and restrictive clauses should be added: And as extending the ground of public confidence in the Government, will best ensure the beneficent ends of its institution.

RESOLVED by the Senate and House of Representatives of the United States of America, in Congress assembled, two thirds of both Houses concurring, that the following Articles be proposed to the Legislatures of the several States, as amendments to the Constitution of the United States, all, or any of which Articles, when ratified by three fourths of the said Legislatures, to be valid to all intents and purposes, as part of the said Constitution; viz.

ARTICLES in addition to, and Amendment of the Constitution of the United States of America, proposed by Congress, and ratified by the Legislatures of the several States, pursuant to the fifth Article of the original Constitution.

Article the first... After the first enumeration required by the first article of the Constitution, there shall be one Representative for every thirty thousand, until the number shall amount to one hundred, after which the proportion shall be so regulated by Congress, that there shall be not less than one hundred

Representatives, nor less than one Representative for every forty thousand persons, until the number of Representatives shall amount to two hundred; after which the proportion shall be so regulated by Congress, that there shall not be less than two hundred Representatives, nor more than one Representative for every fifty thousand persons.

Article the second... No law, varying the compensation for the services of the Senators and Representatives, shall take effect, until an election of Representatives shall have intervened.

Article the third... Congress shall make no law respecting an establishment of religion, or prohibiting the free exercise thereof; or abridging the freedom of speech, or of the press; or the right of the people peaceably to assemble, and to petition the Government for a redress of grievances.

Article the fourth... A well regulated Militia, being necessary to the security of a free State, the right of the people to keep and bear Arms, shall not be infringed.

Article the fifth... No Soldier shall, in time of peace be quartered in any house, without the consent of the Owner, nor in time of war, but in a manner to be prescribed by law.

Article the sixth... The right of the people to be secure in their persons, houses, papers, and effects, against unreasonable searches and seizures, shall not be violated, and no Warrants shall issue, but upon probable cause, supported by Oath or affirmation, and particularly describing the place to be searched, and the persons or things to be seized.

Article the seventh... No person shall be held to answer for a capital, or otherwise infamous crime, unless on a presentment or indictment of a Grand Jury, except in cases arising in the land or naval forces, or in the Militia, when in actual service in time of War or public danger; nor shall any person be subject for the same offence to be twice put in jeopardy of life or limb; nor shall be compelled in any criminal case to be a witness against himself, nor be deprived of life, liberty, or property, without due process of law; nor shall private property be taken for public use, without just compensation.

Article the eighth... In all criminal prosecutions, the accused shall enjoy the right to a speedy and public trial, by an impartial jury of the State and district wherein the crime shall have been committed, which district shall have been previously ascertained by law, and to be informed of the nature and cause of the accusation; to be confronted with the witnesses against him; to have compulsory process for obtaining witnesses in his favor, and to have the Assistance of Counsel for his defence.

Article the ninth... In suits at common law, where the value in controversy shall exceed twenty dollars, the right of trial by jury shall be preserved, and no fact tried by a jury, shall be otherwise re-examined in any Court of the United States, than according to the rules of the common law.

Article the tenth... Excessive bail shall not be required, nor excessive fines imposed, nor cruel and unusual punishments inflicted.

Article the eleventh... The enumeration in the Constitution, of certain rights, shall not be construed to deny or disparage others retained by the people.

Article the twelfth... The powers not delegated to the United States by the Constitution, nor prohibited by it to the States, are reserved to the States respectively, or to the people.

The U.S. Bill of Rights

The Preamble to The Bill of Rights

Congress of the United States
begun and held at the City of New-York, on
Wednesday the fourth of March, one thousand seven hundred and eighty nine.

THE Conventions of a number of the States, having at the time of their adopting the Constitution, expressed a desire, in order to prevent misconstruction or abuse of its powers, that further declaratory and restrictive clauses should be added: And as extending the ground of public confidence in the Government, will best ensure the beneficent ends of its institution.

RESOLVED by the Senate and House of Representatives of the United States of America, in Congress assembled, two thirds of both Houses concurring, that the following Articles be proposed to the Legislatures of the several States, as amendments to the Constitution of the United States, all, or any of which Articles, when ratified by three fourths of the said Legislatures, to be valid to all intents and purposes, as part of the said Constitution; viz.

ARTICLES in addition to, and Amendment of the Constitution of the United States of America, proposed by Congress, and ratified by the Legislatures of the several States, pursuant to the fifth Article of the original Constitution.

Note: The following text is a transcription of the first ten amendments to the Constitution in their original form. These amendments were ratified December 15, 1791, and form what is known as the "Bill of Rights."

Amendment I

Congress shall make no law respecting an establishment of religion, or prohibiting the free exercise thereof; or abridging the freedom of speech, or of the press; or the right of the people peaceably to assemble, and to petition the Government for a redress of grievances.

Amendment II

A well regulated Militia, being necessary to the security of a free State, the right of the people to keep and bear Arms, shall not be infringed.

Amendment III

No Soldier shall, in time of peace be quartered in any house, without the consent of the Owner, nor in time of war, but in a manner to be prescribed by law.

Amendment IV

The right of the people to be secure in their persons, houses, papers, and effects, against unreasonable searches and seizures, shall not be violated, and no Warrants shall issue, but upon probable cause, supported by Oath or affirmation, and particularly describing the place to be searched, and the persons or things to be seized.

Amendment V

No person shall be held to answer for a capital, or otherwise infamous crime, unless on a presentment or indictment of a Grand Jury, except in cases arising in the land or naval forces, or in the Militia, when in actual service in time of War or public danger; nor shall any person be subject for the same offence to be twice put in jeopardy of life or limb; nor shall be compelled in any criminal case to be a witness against himself, nor be deprived of life, liberty, or property, without due process of law; nor shall private property be taken for public use, without just compensation.

Amendment VI

In all criminal prosecutions, the accused shall enjoy the right to a speedy and public trial, by an impartial jury of the State and district wherein the crime shall have been committed, which district shall have been previously ascertained by law, and to be informed of the nature and cause of the accusation; to be confronted with the witnesses against him; to have compulsory process for obtaining witnesses in his favor, and to have the Assistance of Counsel for his defence.

Amendment VII

In Suits at common law, where the value in controversy shall exceed twenty dollars, the right of trial by jury shall be preserved, and no fact tried by a jury, shall be otherwise re-examined in any Court of the United States, than according to the rules of the common law.

Amendment VIII

Excessive bail shall not be required, nor excessive fines imposed, nor cruel and unusual punishments inflicted.

Amendment IX

The enumeration in the Constitution, of certain rights, shall not be construed to deny or disparage others retained by the people.

Amendment X

The powers not delegated to the United States by the Constitution, nor prohibited by it to the States, are reserved to the States respectively, or to the people.

The Constitution: Amendments 11-27

Constitutional Amendments 1-10 make up what is known as <u>The Bill of Rights</u>. Amendments 11-27 are listed below.[2019] Amendments through the original XIII belong to the de jure original Constitution of the United States. The non-original Amendment XIII through XXVII belong to the de facto Corporate UNITED STATES Constitution.

AMENDMENT XI

Passed by Congress March 4, 1794. Ratified February 7, 1795.

Note: Article III, section 2, of the Constitution was modified by amendment 11. The Judicial power of the United States shall not be construed to extend to any suit in law or equity, commenced or prosecuted against one of the United States by Citizens of another State, or by Citizens or Subjects of any Foreign State.

AMENDMENT XII

Passed by Congress December 9, 1803. Ratified June 15, 1804.

Note: A portion of Article II, section 1 of the Constitution was superseded by the 12th amendment. The Electors shall meet in their respective states and vote by ballot for President and Vice-President, one of whom, at least, shall not be an inhabitant of the same state with themselves; they shall name in their ballots the person voted for as President, and in distinct ballots the person voted for as Vice-President, and they shall make distinct lists of all persons voted for as President, and of all persons voted for as Vice-President, and of the number of votes for each, which lists they shall sign and certify, and transmit sealed to the seat of the government of the United States, directed to the President of the Senate; -- the President of the Senate shall, in the presence of the Senate and House of Representatives, open all the certificates and the votes shall then be counted; -- The person having the greatest number of votes for President, shall be the President, if such number be a majority of the whole number of Electors appointed; and if no person have such majority, then from the persons having the highest numbers not exceeding three on the list of those voted for as President, the House of Representatives shall choose immediately, by ballot, the President. But in choosing the President, the votes shall be taken by states, the representation from each state having one vote; a quorum for this purpose shall consist of a member or members from two-thirds of the states, and a majority of all the states shall be necessary to a choice. [And if the House of Representatives shall not choose a President whenever the right of choice shall devolve upon them, before the fourth day of March next following, then the Vice-President shall act as President, as in case of the death or other constitutional disability of the President. --]* The person having the greatest number of votes as Vice-President, shall be the Vice-President, if such number be a majority of the whole number of Electors appointed, and if no person have a majority, then from the two highest numbers on the list, the Senate shall choose the Vice-President; a quorum for the purpose shall consist of two-thirds of the whole number of Senators, and a majority of the whole number shall be necessary to a choice. But no person constitutionally ineligible to the office of President shall be eligible to that of Vice-President of the United States. *Superseded by section 3 of the 20th amendment.

AMENDMENT XVIII (**Original *de jure***)

Note: The original and lawful 13th Article of Amendment had been ratified on March 12, 1819 with the vote of the Virginia General Assembly and was published in the *Revised Code of the Laws of Virginia* with the original 13th Article of Amendment included in the *Constitution of the United States.* It was also published in the 1825 *Military Laws of the United States; to Which is Prefixed the Constitution of the United States Compiled and Published under Authority of the War Department* By Major Trueman Cross (Deputy Quarter-Master-General of the Army) [2020] This original 13th Article of Amendment was <u>replaced</u> by an unlawful amendment thereby displacing the "*titles of nobility*" clause.[2021]

If any citizen of the United States shall accept, claim, receive, or retain any title of nobility or honour, or shall without the consent of Congress accept and retain any present, pension, office, or emolument of any kind whatever, from any Emperor, King, Prince, or foreign Power, such person shall cease to be a citizen of the United States, and shall be incapable of holding any office of trust or profit under them, or either of them.

[**Amendments of the *de facto* Corporate UNITED STATES' Constitution**]

AMENDMENT XIII (**Non-original *de facto***)

Passed by Congress January 31, 1865. Ratified December 6, 1865.

Note: A portion of Article IV, section 2, of the Constitution was superseded by the 13th amendment.

Section 1.

Neither slavery nor involuntary servitude, except as a punishment for crime whereof the party shall have been duly convicted, shall exist within the United States, or any place subject to their jurisdiction.

Section 2.

Congress shall have power to enforce this article by appropriate legislation.

AMENDMENT XIV

Passed by Congress June 13, 1866. Ratified July 9, 1868.

Note: Article I, section 2, of the Constitution was modified by section 2 of the 14th amendment.

Section 1.

All persons born or naturalized in the United States, and subject to the jurisdiction thereof, are citizens of the United States and of the State wherein they reside. No State shall make or enforce any law which shall abridge the privileges or immunities of citizens of the United States; nor shall any State deprive any person of life, liberty, or property, without due process of law; nor deny to any person within its jurisdiction the equal protection of the laws.

Section 2.

Representatives shall be apportioned among the several States according to their respective numbers, counting the whole number of persons in each State, excluding Indians not taxed. But when the right to vote at any election for the choice of electors for President and Vice-President of the United States, Representatives in Congress, the Executive and Judicial officers of a State, or the members of the Legislature thereof, is denied to any of the male inhabitants of such State, being twenty-one years of age,* and citizens of the United States, or in any way abridged, except for participation in rebellion, or other crime, the basis of representation therein shall be reduced in the proportion which the number of such male citizens shall bear to the whole number of male citizens twenty-one years of age in such State.

Section 3.

No person shall be a Senator or Representative in Congress, or elector of President and Vice-President, or hold any office, civil or military, under the United States, or under any State, who, having previously taken an oath, as a member of Congress, or as an officer of the United States, or as a member of any State legislature, or as an executive or judicial officer of any State, to support the Constitution of the United States, shall have engaged in insurrection or rebellion against the same, or given aid or comfort to the enemies thereof. But Congress may by a vote of two-thirds of each House, remove such disability.

Section 4.

The validity of the public debt of the United States, authorized by law, including debts incurred for payment of pensions and bounties for services in suppressing insurrection or rebellion, shall not be questioned. But neither the United States nor any State shall assume or pay any debt or obligation incurred in aid of insurrection or rebellion against the United States, or any claim for the loss or emancipation of any slave; but all such debts, obligations and claims shall be held illegal and void.

Section 5.

The Congress shall have the power to enforce, by appropriate legislation, the provisions of this article.

*Changed by section 1 of the 26th amendment.

AMENDMENT XV

Passed by Congress February 26, 1869. Ratified February 3, 1870.

Section 1.

The right of citizens of the United States to vote shall not be denied or abridged by the United States or by any State on account of race, color, or previous condition of servitude--

Section 2.

The Congress shall have the power to enforce this article by appropriate legislation.

AMENDMENT XVI

Passed by Congress July 2, 1909. Ratified February 3, 1913.

Note: Article I, section 9, of the Constitution was modified by amendment 16.

The Congress shall have power to lay and collect taxes on incomes, from whatever source derived, without apportionment among the several States, and without regard to any census or enumeration.

AMENDMENT XVII

Passed by Congress May 13, 1912. Ratified April 8, 1913.

Note: Article I, section 3, of the Constitution was modified by the 17th amendment.

The Senate of the United States shall be composed of two Senators from each State, elected by the people thereof, for six years; and each Senator shall have one vote. The electors in each State shall have the qualifications requisite for electors of the most numerous branch of the State legislatures.

When vacancies happen in the representation of any State in the Senate, the executive authority of such State shall issue writs of election to fill such vacancies: Provided, That the legislature of any State may empower the executive thereof to make temporary appointments until the people fill the vacancies by election as the legislature may direct.

This amendment shall not be so construed as to affect the election or term of any Senator chosen before it becomes valid as part of the Constitution.

AMENDMENT XVIII

Passed by Congress December 18, 1917. Ratified January 16, 1919. Repealed by amendment 21.

Note: This (non-original) 13th Amendment (freeing the slaves) was enacted by Lincoln's executive government on December 18, 1865, eight months after President Lincoln was assassinated.

Section 1.

After one year from the ratification of this article the manufacture, sale, or transportation of intoxicating liquors within, the importation thereof into, or the exportation thereof from the United States and all territory subject to the jurisdiction thereof for beverage purposes is hereby prohibited.

Section 2.

The Congress and the several States shall have concurrent power to enforce this article by appropriate legislation.

Section 3.

This article shall be inoperative unless it shall have been ratified as an amendment to the Constitution by the legislatures of the several States, as provided in the Constitution, within seven years from the date of the submission hereof to the States by the Congress.

AMENDMENT XIX

Passed by Congress June 4, 1919. Ratified August 18, 1920.

The right of citizens of the United States to vote shall not be denied or abridged by the United States or by any State on account of sex.

Congress shall have power to enforce this article by appropriate legislation.

AMENDMENT XX

Passed by Congress March 2, 1932. Ratified January 23, 1933.

Note: Article I, section 4, of the Constitution was modified by section 2 of this amendment. In addition, a portion of the 12th amendment was superseded by section 3.

Section 1.

The terms of the President and the Vice President shall end at noon on the 20th day of January, and the terms of Senators and Representatives at noon on the 3d day of January, of the years in which such terms would have ended if this article had not been ratified; and the terms of their successors shall then begin.

Section 2.

The Congress shall assemble at least once in every year, and such meeting shall begin at noon on the 3d day of January, unless they shall by law appoint a different day.

Section 3.

If, at the time fixed for the beginning of the term of the President, the President elect shall have died, the Vice President elect shall become President. If a President shall not have been chosen before the time fixed for the beginning of his term, or if the President elect shall have failed to qualify, then the Vice President elect shall act as President until a President shall have qualified; and the Congress may by law provide for the case wherein neither a President elect nor a Vice President elect shall have qualified, declaring who shall then act as President, or the manner in which one who is to act shall be selected, and such person shall act accordingly until a President or Vice President shall have qualified.

Section 4.

The Congress may by law provide for the case of the death of any of the persons from whom the House of Representatives may choose a President whenever the right of choice shall have devolved upon them, and for the case of the death of any of the persons from whom the Senate may choose a Vice President whenever the right of choice shall have devolved upon them.

Section 5.

Sections 1 and 2 shall take effect on the 15th day of October following the ratification of this article.

Section 6.

This article shall be inoperative unless it shall have been ratified as an amendment to the Constitution by the legislatures of three-fourths of the several States within seven years from the date of its submission.

AMENDMENT XXI

Passed by Congress February 20, 1933. Ratified December 5, 1933.

Section 1.

The eighteenth article of amendment to the Constitution of the United States is hereby repealed.

Section 2.

The transportation or importation into any State, Territory, or possession of the United States for delivery or use therein of intoxicating liquors, in violation of the laws thereof, is hereby prohibited.

Section 3.

This article shall be inoperative unless it shall have been ratified as an amendment to the Constitution by conventions in the several States, as provided in the Constitution, within seven years from the date of the submission hereof to the States by the Congress.

AMENDMENT XXII

Passed by Congress March 21, 1947. Ratified February 27, 1951.

Section 1.

No person shall be elected to the office of the President more than twice, and no person who has held the office of President, or acted as President, for more than two years of a term to which some other person was elected President shall be elected to the office of the President more than once. But this Article shall not apply to any person holding the office of President when this Article was proposed by the Congress, and shall not prevent any person who may be holding the office of President, or acting as President, during the term within which this Article becomes operative from holding the office of President or acting as President during the remainder of such term.

Section 2.

This article shall be inoperative unless it shall have been ratified as an amendment to the Constitution by the legislatures of three-fourths of the several States within seven years from the date of its submission to the States by the Congress.

AMENDMENT XXIII

Passed by Congress June 16, 1960. Ratified March 29, 1961.

Section 1.

The District constituting the seat of Government of the United States shall appoint in such manner as the Congress may direct:

A number of electors of President and Vice President equal to the whole number of Senators and Representatives in Congress to which the District would be entitled if it were a State, but in no event more than the least populous State; they shall be in addition to those appointed by the States, but they shall be considered, for the purposes of the election of President and Vice President, to be electors appointed by a State; and they shall meet in the District and perform such duties as provided by the twelfth article of amendment.

Section 2.

The Congress shall have power to enforce this article by appropriate legislation.

AMENDMENT XXIV

Passed by Congress August 27, 1962. Ratified January 23, 1964.

Section 1.

The right of citizens of the United States to vote in any primary or other election for President or Vice President, for electors for President or Vice President, or for Senator or Representative in Congress, shall not be denied or abridged by the United States or any State by reason of failure to pay any poll tax or other tax.

Section 2.

The Congress shall have power to enforce this article by appropriate legislation.

AMENDMENT XXV

Passed by Congress July 6, 1965. Ratified February 10, 1967.

Note: Article II, section 1, of the Constitution was affected by the 25th amendment.

Section 1.

In case of the removal of the President from office or of his death or resignation, the Vice President shall become President.

Section 2.

Whenever there is a vacancy in the office of the Vice President, the President shall nominate a Vice President who shall take office upon confirmation by a majority vote of both Houses of Congress.

Section 3.

Whenever the President transmits to the President pro tempore of the Senate and the Speaker of the House of Representatives his written declaration that he is unable to discharge the powers and duties of his office, and until he transmits to them a written declaration to the contrary, such powers and duties shall be discharged by the Vice President as Acting President.

Section 4.

Whenever the Vice President and a majority of either the principal officers of the executive departments or of such other body as Congress may by law provide, transmit to the President pro tempore of the Senate and the Speaker of the House of Representatives their written declaration that the President is unable to discharge the powers and duties of his office, the Vice President shall immediately assume the powers and duties of the office as Acting President.

Thereafter, when the President transmits to the President pro tempore of the Senate and the Speaker of the House of Representatives his written declaration that no inability exists, he shall resume the powers and duties of his office unless the Vice President and a majority of either the principal officers of the executive department or of such other body as Congress may by law provide, transmit within four days to the President pro tempore of the Senate and the Speaker of the House of Representatives their written declaration that the President is unable to discharge the powers and duties of his office. Thereupon Congress shall decide the issue, assembling within forty-eight hours for that purpose if not in session. If the Congress, within twenty-one days after receipt of the latter written declaration, or, if Congress is not in session, within twenty-one days after Congress is required to assemble, determines by two-thirds vote of both Houses that the President is unable to discharge the powers and duties of his office, the Vice President shall continue to discharge the same as Acting President; otherwise, the President shall resume the powers and duties of his office.

AMENDMENT XXVI

Passed by Congress March 23, 1971. Ratified July 1, 1971.

Note: Amendment 14, section 2, of the Constitution was modified by section 1 of the 26th amendment.

Section 1.

The right of citizens of the United States, who are eighteen years of age or older, to vote shall not be denied or abridged by the United States or by any State on account of age.

Section 2.

The Congress shall have power to enforce this article by appropriate legislation.

AMENDMENT XXVII

Originally proposed Sept. 25, 1789. Ratified May 7, 1992.

No law, varying the compensation for the services of the Senators and Representatives, shall take effect, until an election of Representatives shall have intervened.

References Part I

1 Daniel J. Elazar, "Covenant and the American Founding," accessed on September 2, 2014, http://www.jcpa.org/dje/articles/cov-amer.htm

2 Frank Newport, "In U.S., 77% Identify as Christian," Gallup, Politics, December 24, 2012, http://www.gallup.com/poll/159548/identify-christian.aspx

3 Dr. Stephen Jones, *The Prophetic History of the United States,* (Fridley: God's Kingdom Ministries, 2006), 36

4 Dr. Jack L. Arnold, "The Cause and Results of the Reformation: Reformation Men and Theology, Lesson 2 of 11,"IIIM Magazine Online, Volume 1, Number 2, March 8 to March 14, 1999, http://www.thirdmill.org/files/english/html/ch/CH.Arnold.RMT.2.HTML

5 *Wikimedia Commons*, s.v. "Schaff P.jpg," https://commons.wikimedia.org/wiki/File:Schaff_P.jpg This work is in the public domain in its country of origin and other countries and areas where the copyright term is the author's life plus 70 years or less.

6 Philip Schaff, DD, LLD, *History of the Christian Church,* Vol. VII, *Modern Christianity. The German Reformation.*, 2d Ed., (Oak Harbor: Logos Research Systems Inc, 1997) ch. 1

7 History.com Staff, "Martin Luther and the 95 Theses," 2009, http://www.history.com/topics/martin-luther-and-the-95-theses

8 Ibid.

9 *Wikipedia*, s.v. "Martin Luther," last modified on September 2, 2014, http://en.wikipedia.org/wiki/Martin_Luther

10 Ibid.

11 Eric Jon Phelps, *Vatican Assassins*, (Eric Jon Phelps, PO Box 306, Newmanstown, PA 17073) (2001), 66

12 Ibid.

13 John 1:1, 14

14 *Wikimedia Commons* s.v., "Martin Luther," 1529, https://commons.wikimedia.org/wiki/File:Martin_Luther,_1529.jpg This is a faithful photographic reproduction of a two-dimensional, public domain work of art. The work of art itself is in the public domain for the following reason: This work is in the **public domain** in its country of origin and other countries and areas where the copyright term is the author's life plus 100 years or less. United States public domain tag

15 Phelps, *Vatican Assassins*, 66-67

16 2 Cor. 3:17

17 Thomas E. Watson, *Political and Economic Handbook*, (Thomson, Ga: The Jeffersonian Publishing Co., 1916), 4

18 *Wikimedia Commons*, s.v. "Emblem of the Papacy SE.svg," https://commons.wikimedia.org/wiki/File:Emblem_of_the_Papacy_SE.svg Author: https://commons.wikimedia.org/wiki/File:Emblem_of_the_Papacy_SE.svg Permission granted. I, the copyright holder of this work, release this work into the public domain. This applies worldwide.

19 *Wikipedia*, s.v. "Papal regalia and insignia," last modified December 9, 2016, https://en.wikipedia.org/wiki/Papal_regalia_and_insignia

20 Cailey Bennett,"Concessions that Changed the World," August 30, 2011, accessed November 27, 2015, http://amazingdiscoveries.org/S-deception-King-John_Pope_Crown

21 *Wikipedia,* s.v. "Magna Carta," last modified on November 24, 2015, https://en.wikipedia.org/wiki/Magna_Carta

22 Bennett, "Concessions that Changed the World"

23 History Channel, "Pope Declares Magna Carta Invalid," accessed December 23, 2016 as citing credit to National Archives and Records Administration, http://www.historychannel.com.au/this-day-in-history/pope-declares-magna-carta-invalid/

24 Wikimedia Commons s.v. "File:Joao sem terra assina carta Magna.jpg," Image from Cassell's History of England - Century Edition - published circa 1902, Scan by Tagishsimon, 23rd June 2004, https://commons.wikimedia.org/wiki/File:Joao_sem_terra_assina_carta_Magna.jpg This is a faithful photographic reproduction of a two-dimensional, public domain work of art. The work of art itself is in the public domain for the following reason: This work is in the public domain in its country of origin and other countries and areas where the copyright term is the author's life plus 70 years or less. United States public domain tag.

25 Bennett, "Concessions that Changed the World"

26 *Encyclopedia of the Nations,* s.v. "Vatican City - Politics, government, and taxation," accessed on November 30, 2015, http://www.nationsencyclopedia.com/economies/Europe/Vatican-City-POLITICS-GOVERNMENT-AND-TAXATION.html#ixzz3szQWAsjs

27 "Pilgrims," National Park Service, Cape Cod National Seashore, Massachusetts

28 Angie Mosteller, Why the Pilgrims Really Came to America," November 21, 2013, http://www.crosswalk.com/special-coverage/thanksgiving/why-the-pilgrims-really-came-to-america.html

[29] "Pilgrims," National Park Service, Cape Cod National Seashore, Massachusetts

[30] *Wikimedia Commons s.v.,* " St Ignatius of Loyola (1491-1556) Founder of the Jesuits," 1600s, https://commons.wikimedia.org/wiki/File:St_Ignatius_of_Loyola_(1491-1556)_Founder_of_the_Jesuits.jpg This is a faithful photographic reproduction of a two-dimensional, public domain work of art. The work of art itself is in the public domain for the following reason: This work is in the **public domain** in its country of origin and other countries and areas where the copyright term is the author's life plus 100 years or less.

[31] *Wikipedia,* s.v. "Society of Jesus, "last modified on August 5, 2014,http://en.wikipedia.org/wiki/Society_of_Jesus

[32] Richard Wigginton Thompson, *The Footprints of the Jesuits,* (Cincinnati: Cranston & Curts, 1894), 23

[33] Edward Hendrie, *Solving the Mystery of Babylon the Great: Tracking the Beast from the Synagogue to the Vatican,* (Garrisonville, Great Mountain Publishing, 2011), 52

[34] *Wikipedia,* s.v. "Counter-Reformation, "last modified on July 7, 2014, http://en.wikipedia.org/wiki/Counter-Reformation

[35] *Wikipedia,* s.v. "Council of Trent," last modified on August 28, 2014,http://en.wikipedia.org/wiki/Council_of_Trent

[36] *Wikipedia,* s.v. "Black Nobility," last modified on 23 November 2015,http://en.wikipedia.org/wiki/Black_Nobility

[37] "The Black Nobility," accessed June 27, 2014,http://www.biblebelievers.org.au/black.htm

[38] "Freemasonry and King Solomon's Temple," accessed September 2, 2014,http://www.nwotoday.com/the-new-world-orders-history/freemasonry-global-level-illumination/builders-of-king-solomons-temple

[39] *Wikipedia,* s.v. "Papal Infallibility," last modified on July 20, 2014,http://en.wikipedia.org/wiki/Papal_infallibility

[40] Phelps, *Vatican Assassins,* 67

[41] J. H. Merle D'Aubigne, *History of the Great Reformation,* quoted in Edward Beecher, *The Papal Conspiracy Exposed,*(New York: M. W. Dodd, 1855), 369.

[42] *Wikipedia,* s.v. "Pope Clement XIV," last modified on August 15, 2014, http://en.wikipedia.org/wiki/Pope_Clement_XIV

[43] Thompson, *Footprints Jesuits,* front matter page

[44] Catherine Hornby and Philip Pullella, "Pope Francis resisted revenge over 18th century Clement XIV," Ed. Mark Heinrich, *Reuters,* March 16, 2013, http://www.reuters.com/article/2013/03/16/us-pope-jesuits-idUSBRE92F09620130316

[45] *Wikimedia Commons,* s.v. "Clement XIV," https://commons.wikimedia.org/wiki/File:Clement_XIV.jpg#mw-jump-to-license This work is in the public domain in its country of origin and other countries and areas where the copyright term is the author's life plus 100 years or less.

[46] *Wikipedia,* s.v. "Suppression of the Society of Jesus," last modified on January 14, 2017, https://en.m.wikipedia.org/wiki/Suppression_of_the_Society_of_Jesus

[47] Phelps, *Vatican Assassins,* 270

[48] *Wikipedia,* s.v. "Giuseppe Nicolini," last modified March 27, 2014, http://en.wikipedia.org/wiki/Giuseppe_Nicolini_(writer)

[49] Dr. C. A. Yarbrough, *The Roman Catholic Church Challenged in the Discussion of Thirty-Two Questions with the Catholic Laymen's Association of Georgia,* (Macon: The Patriotic Societies of Macon, 1920), 229

[50] Brigadier General Thomas M. Harris, *Rome's Responsibility for the Assassination of Abraham Lincoln,*(Pittsburgh, Williams Publishing Company, 1897), 29

[51] Phelps, *Vatican Assassins,* 70

[52] Burke McCarty, *The Suppressed Truth About the Assassination of Abraham Lincoln,* as quoted, (Washington: 1922), 103-104

[53] Ibid., 257-258

[54] *Wikimedia Commons,* s.v. "JFK White House portrait looking up lighting corrected.jpg," https://commons.wikimedia.org/wiki/File:JFK_White_House_portrait_looking_up_lighting_corrected.jpg This work is in the public domain in the United States because it is a work prepared by an officer or employee of the United States Government as part of that person's official duties under the terms of Title 17, Chapter 1, Section 105 of the US Code.

[55] John F. Kennedy, "The President and the Press: Address before the American Newspaper Publishers Association, April 27, 1961," speech at the Waldorf-Astoria Hotel, New York City, accessed September 2, 2014, http://www.jfklibrary.org/Research/Research-Aids/JFK-Speeches/American-Newspaper-Publishers-Association_19610427.aspx

[56] *Encyclopedia of the Nations,* s.v. "Vatican City - Politics, government, and taxation," accessed October 24, 2014, http://www.nationsencyclopedia.com/economies/Europe/Vatican-City-POLITICS-GOVERNMENT-AND-TAXATION.html

[57]*Wikipedia, s.v.* "Baby boomers," last modified August 30, 2014,http://en.wikipedia.org/wiki/Baby_boomers

[58]*Wikipedia, s.v.* "Dave Hunt (Christian Apologist)," last modified on July 28, 2014, http://en.wikipedia.org/wiki/Dave_Hunt_(Christian_apologist)

[59] Dave Hunt, *A Woman Rides the Beast* (Eugene, Oregon: Harvest House Publishers, 1994), 403

[60] McCarty, *Suppressed Truth,* as quoted, (Washington: 1922), 42

[61] John 8:32

[62] Rev. 19:11

63 William J. Federer, *America's God and Country Encyclopedia of Quotations,* "Continental Congress July 2, 1776," (Coppell: FAME Publishing, Inc., 1994), 141

64Prov. 25:11;

65Abraham Lincoln, "Fragment on the Constitution and the Union, c. January, 1861," Collected Works of Abraham Lincoln. Vol. 4., 169, accessed on September 2, 2014, http://quod.lib.umich.edu/l/lincoln/lincoln4/1:264?rgn=div1;view=fulltext

66 Geoffrey Grider, "Heresy Preacher Priest Tony Palmer Dead After Urging Christians to Unite with Rome, July 21, 2014, http://www.nowtheendbegins.com/blog/?p=23566

67 "Pope Francis' Message to Kenneth Copeland Ministries, Calling for Unity in the Body of Christ," Youtube.com/Kenneth Copeland, Published on Feb 27, 2014, https://www.youtube.com/watch?v=eulTwytMWlQ#t=77

68 Deut.28:13

69 Isa. 10:5

70 Federer, *America's Quotations,* "July 3, 1776 letter of John Adams to his wife Abigail reflecting on what he had shared in Congress and with prophetic insight declaring the importance of that day,"9

71 Wendy Goubej, "Spring 2010: Amazing Discoveries and Conspiracy Theories," October 14, 2009, http://amazingdiscoveries.org/AD-newsletter-spring-2010-Editors_Corner

72 Isa. 60:1-2, Eph. 5:14-16, Rev. 18:4a

73 McCarty, *Suppressed Truth,* 257-258

74 Eph.5:11

75John Smith Dye, *The Adder's Den; or Secrets of the Great Conspiracy to Overthrow Liberty in America* (New York, John Smith Dye, 1864), 62

76 *Wikimedia Commons*, s.v. "Jacques-Louis David - The Emperor Napoleon in His Study at the Tuileries - Google Art Project.jpg," https://commons.wikimedia.org/wiki/File:Jacques-Louis_David_-_The_Emperor_Napoleon_in_His_Study_at_the_Tuileries_-_Google_Art_Project.jpg#mw-jump-to-license This work is in the public domain in its country of origin and other countries and areas where the copyright term is the author's life plus 100 years or less.

77 Quote by Napoleon Bonaparte in General Charles-Tristan Comte de Montholon in *Memorial of the Captivity of Napoleon at St. Helena,* vol. ii., 62 and cited in Rev. Charles Chiniquy, *Fifty Years in the "Church" of Rome*, (New York, Chicago, Ontario: Fleming H. Revell Company, 1886), 684

78 E. Boyd Barrett, *The Jesuit Enigma,* (New York: Boni and Liveright, 1927) p. 209

79 Etienne Pasquier, *The Jesuits Catechism, According to St. Ignatius Loyola, for the Instructing and Strengthening of All Those which are weak in that faith: wherein the impiety of their principles,* (1685), 4

80 *Wikimedia Commons*, s.v., "File:Samuel Morse 1840.jpg," https://commons.wikimedia.org/wiki/File:Samuel_Morse_1840.jpg This media file is in the public domain in the United States. This applies to U.S. works where the copyright has expired, often because its first publication occurred prior to January 1, 1923.

81 J. Wayne Laurens, *The Crisis: or, The Enemies of America Unmasked* (Philadelphia, G. D. Miller, 1855), 265-267

82 *Wikimedia Commons,* s.v. "James Parton - Schriftsteller.jpg," https://commons.wikimedia.org/wiki/File:James_Parton_-_Schriftsteller.jpg#mw-jump-to-license This media file is in the public domain in the United States. This applies to U.S. works where the copyright has expired, often because its first publication occurred prior to January 1, 1923.

83 *Wikipedia,* s.v. "James Parton," last modified August 24, 2014,http://en.wikipedia.org/wiki/James_Parton

84 James Parton, *The Life of Horace Greeley, Editor of The New York Tribune,* (Boston: Fields, Osgood and Company, 1869), 68

85 Phelps, *Vatican Assassins*, 68

86 Ibid.

87 Rev.17:6

88*Wikipedia,* s.v. "Temporal power (papal)," last modified June 2, 2014,http://en.wikipedia.org/wiki/Temporal_power_(papal)

89Pierre Claude François Daunou, *The Power of the Popes: An Historical Essay on Their Temporal Dominion, and the Abuse of Their Spiritual Authority,* Two Volumes in One, (1838), ch 1

90 2 Cor. 4:4

91*Wikipedia, s.v.* "Edward Beecher," last modified March 28, 2014, http://en.wikipedia.org/wiki/Edward_Beecher(accessed 11/9/2014)

92 Edward Beecher, D.D., *The Papal Conspiracy Exposed, and Protestantism Defended, in the Light of Reason, History, and Scripture,* (Boston: Stearns & Co., 1855), 137, 246, 382

[93] *Wikimedia,* s.v. "Edward Beecher.jpg," https://en.wikipedia.org/wiki/File:Edward_Beecher.jpg
This file is in the public domain because its copyright has expired in the United States and those countries with a copyright term of no more than the life of the author plus 100 years.

[94] Courtesy of the Ellen G. White Estate, Inc., E. G. White portrait, seated writing, c. 1864 (with cuffs, braids on left), https://photo.egwwritings.org/index.php?album=People&image=3.1.jpg

[95] "Ellen G. White A Brief Biography," The Ellen G. White Estate, Inc., accessed September 2, 2014, http://www.whiteestate.org/about/egwbio.asp

[96] Ellen G. White, *The Great Controversy Between Christ and Satan: The Conflict of the Ages in the Christian Dispensation,* (Pacific Press Publishing Assn., 1911),234-235

[97] Count Paul von Hoensbroech, *Fourteen Years a Jesuit: A Record of Personal Experience and a Criticism,* (London, New York, Toronto and Melbourne, Cassell and Company, Ltd., 1911), 430

[98] *Wikimedia Commons,* s.v. "Paul Graf of Hoensbroech.gif," https://de.wikipedia.org/wiki/Datei:Paul_Graf_von_Hoensbroech.gif This work is in the public domain because its copyright has expired protection period. This applies to the country of origin of the plant and those countries with a copyright term of 70 years or less after the death of the author.

[99] 1 John 5:4

[100] John 3:7

[101] Mark 3:29

[102] Mother of Buffalo Bob

[103] "Pilgrims," National Park Service, Cape Cod National Seashore, Massachusetts, last updated November 16, 2015,http://www.nps.gov/caco/learn/historyculture/pilgrims.htm

[104] *Wikimedia Commons,* s.v. "Williambradford bw.jpg," https://commons.wikimedia.org/wiki/File:Williambradford_bw.jpg#mw-jump-to-license This work is in the public domain in its country of origin and other countries and areas where the copyright term is the author's life plus 70 years or less.

[105] William Bradford, *Bradford's History of the Plymouth Settlement, 1608-1650,*rendered into modern English by Harold Paget, (E.P. Dutton & Company, 1920), 21

[106] Ibid.

[107] Matt. 28:16-20

[108] "Pilgrims, "National Park Service, Cape Cod National Seashore, Massachusetts,

[109] Elazar, "Covenant American"

[110] Gary DeMar, "The Restoration of the Republic," *God and Government* Vol. 3, (Atlanta: American Vision, Inc., 1990), 16

[111] "About the Pilgrims: The First Thanksgiving at Plymouth," Pilgrim Hall Museum, accessed September 2, 2014, http://www.pilgrimhallmuseum.org/ap_first_thanksgiving.htm

[112] William Bradford, *Bradford's History,* 89

[113] Ibid., 24

[114] *Wikimedia Commons,* s.v. "Squantoteaching.png," https://commons.wikimedia.org/wiki/File:Squantoteaching.png#mw-jump-to-license This media file is in the public domain in the United States. This applies to U.S. works where the copyright has expired, often because its first publication occurred prior to January 1, 1923. See this page for further explanation.

[115] Gary D. Schmidt, *William Bradford: Plymouth's Faithful Pilgrim*(Grand Rapids: Wm. B. Eerdmans Publishing Co. 1999), 94

[116] William Bradford, *Bradford's History,* 79

[117] Library of Congress, "The pilgrims signing the compact, on board the May Flower, Nov. 11th, 1620 / painted by T.H. Matteson ; engraved by Gauthier, Digital Id ppmsca 07842, http://www.loc.gov/item/2005684450/ No known restrictions on publication.

[118] PBS.org, *God in America, "*People & Ideas: the Puritans," accessed September 2, 2014, http://www.pbs.org/godinamerica/people/puritans.html

[119] C. Gregg Singe, *A Theological Interpretation of American History, (*Pelham: Solid Ground Christian Books,2009) as quoted at Truth in History, "No King but King Jesus," accessed November 30, 2015, http://truthinhistory.org/brochures/141.html?option=com_content&task=category&sectionid=1&id=1&Itemid=31&limit=5&limitstart=0

[120] "People & Ideas: the Puritans," PBS/God in America, accessed September 2, 2014, http://www.pbs.org/godinamerica/people/puritans.html

[121] Library of Congress, " In honor of the birthday of Governor John Winthrop, born June 12, 1587 / K. H. Burn del.," Illus. from: Gleasons Pictorial, 1854, v. 6, p. 353., Digital Id cph 3c20506, http://www.loc.gov/item/98505313/ No known restrictions on publication.

[122] Gary DeMar, *God and Government The Restoration of the Republic*, (Atlanta: American Vision, Inc., 1990), xi

[123] Pilgrim Hall Museum, "Beyond the Pilgrim Story," accessed September 2, 2014, http://www.pilgrimhallmuseum.org/mayflower_compact_text.htm

[124] Caleb Johnson's MayflowerHistory.com, "The Mayflower Compact**,"** accessed September 2, 2014, http://mayflowerhistory.com/mayflower-compact/

[125] John Winthrop, *A Modell of Christian Charity (1630)* Collections of the Massachusetts Historical Society (Boston, 1838, 3rd series 7:31-48.), accessed September 2, 2014, http://history.hanover.edu/texts/winthmod.html

[126] Peter Marshall and David Manuel, *The Light and the Glory* (Grand Rapids: Fleming H. Revell 1977), 155

[127] Gavin Finley, MD, "Puritan Belief and 'Manifest Destiny," http://endtimepilgrim.org/puritans03.htm

[128] Dr. Stephen E. Jones, *The Prophetic History of the United States*, (Fridley: God's Kingdom Ministries, 2006), 4

[129] Lev. 26

[130] Deut. 11:26-28

[131] Deut. 28:1-13

[132] Deut. 28:15-68

[133] Steven R. Pointer, "American Postmillennialism: Seeing the Glory," *Christian History Institute, Issue 61,* accessed October 24, 2014, https://www.christianhistoryinstitute.org/magazine/article/american-postmillennialism-seeing-the-glory/

[134] *Wikimedia Commons s.v.* "Johnathan Edwards," Uploaded to en: by en:User:Flex at June 13, 2005, This is a faithful photographic reproduction of a two-dimensional, public domain work of art. The work of art itself is in the public domain for the following reason: This work is in the public domain in its country of origin and other countries and areas where the copyright term is the author's life plus 70 years or less. United States public domain tag.

[135] Jonathan Edwards, "Some Thoughts Concerning the Present Revival of Religion in New England," The *Work of President Edwards, IV (New York: S. Converse, 1830),* 128-33 quoted in *God's New Israel Religious Interpretations of American Destiny,* ed. Conrad Cherry, (Chapel Hill and London: The University of North Carolina Press, 1998), 54-48

[136] Jones, *Prophetic History,* 9, 36

[137] Ibid., 9

[138] Marshall and Manuel, *Light and Glory*, 240

[139] Ibid., 246

[140] *Wikimedia Commons*, s.v. "James Edward Oglethorpe by Alfred Edmund Dyer.jpg," https://commons.wikimedia.org/wiki/File:James_Edward_Oglethorpe_by_Alfred_Edmund_Dyer.jpg#mw-jump-to-license This work is in the public domain in its country of origin and other countries and areas where the copyright term is the author's life plus 100 years or less.

[141] *Look and Learn Picture History Library*, s.v. "George Whitefield preaching in Moorfields, AD 1742 - in the exhibition of the Royal Academy," http://www.lookandlearn.com/history-images/XJ101786/George-Whitefield-preaching-in-Moorfields-AD-1742-in-the-exhibition-of-the-Royal-Academy Permission obtained

[142] Ibid. 251-252

[143] Federer, *America's Quotations,* "George Whitefield,"684

[144] Got Questions Ministries, *What is God's Relationship to Time?,* accessed September 2, 2014,http://www.gotquestions.org/God-time.html

[145] 2 Pet. 1:21, Dan. 12:4

[146] Federer, *America's Quotations,* "Jonathan Edwards," 223

[147] Thomas S. Kidd, *The Great Awakening: The Roots of Evangelical Christianity in Colonial America* (Yale University Press, 2009)

[148] Katherine Lee Bates, "America the Beautiful," Patriotic Song Lyrics, accessed September 2, 2014, http://www.patrioticon.org/patriotic-soundfiles-lyrics.htm

[149] Matt. 6:10

[150] Gen. 12:3

[151] Dr. Stephen E. Jones, *The Prophetic History of the United States*, (Fridley: God's Kingdom Ministries, 2006), 8

[152] First Parish Historical Committee, Much Preached At: The Early Ministers of First Parish Church in Beverly 1667-1958: Abiel Abbot 1803-1828. http://history.firstparishbeverly.org/archives/230

[153] *Wikipedia*, s.v. "Abiel Abbot, "http (accessed 10/24/2014)

[154] Reverend Abiel Abbot, "Thanksgiving Sermon, 1799," *God's New Israel Religious Interpretations of American Destiny,* ed. Conrad Cherry, (Chapel Hill and London: The University of North Carolina Press, 1998), front matter

[155] *Wikimedia Commons, s.v.* "King George III in coronation robes, " by artist Allan Ramsay, https://commons.wikimedia.org/wiki/File:Allan_Ramsay_-_King_George_III_in_coronation_robes_-_Google_Art_Project.jpg This is a faithful photographic reproduction of a two-dimensional, public domain work of art. The work of art itself is in the public domain for the following reason: The author died in 1784, so this work is in the public domain in its country of origin and other countries and areas where the copyright term is the author's life plus 100 years or less. This work is in the public domain in the United States because it was published (or registered with the U.S. Copyright Office) before January 1, 1923.

[156] *Wikipedia,* s.v. "George III of the United Kingdom," last modified November 16, 2015, https://en.wikipedia.org/wiki/George_III_of_the_United_Kingdom

[157] Phelps, *Vatican Assassins*, 270

[158] *Wikimedia Commons,* s.v. "The Rev. Jacob Duche (NYPL NYPG94-F149-419915).jpg," https://en.wikipedia.org/wiki/File:The_Rev._Jacob_Duche_(NYPL_NYPG94-F149-419915).jpg This work is in the public domain in its country of origin and other countries and areas where the copyright term is the author's life plus 70 years or less.

[159] Federer, *America's Quotations*, "Jacob Duche," 220-221

[160] *The Declaration of Independence,* A Transcription, National Archives and Records Administration, accessed September 2, 2014, http://dev.republicoftheunitedstates.org/wp-content/uploads/2014/03/NARA-The-Declaration-of-Independence-A-Transcription.pdf

[161] Elazar, "Covenant American"

[162] W. Cleon Skousen, The Majesty of God's Law, It's Coming to America, (Salt Lake City, Ensign Publishing, 1996), 4, 23

[163] *Wikipedia,* s.v. "Montesquieu," last modified October 11, 2014, http://en.wikipedia.org/wiki/Montesquieu

[164] *Wikipedia*, s.v. "William Blackstone," last modified October 21, 2014, http://en.wikipedia.org/wiki/William_Blackstone

[165] *Wikipedia*, s.v. "John Locke," last modified October 3, 2014, http://en.wikipedia.org/wiki/John_Locke

[166] *Wikipedia, s.v. "Edward Coke,"* last modified October 14, 2014, http://en.wikipedia.org/wiki/Edward_Coke

[167] *Wikipedia, s.v. "Cicero,"* last modified October 25, 2014, http://en.wikipedia.org/wiki/Cicero

[168] *Wikimedia*, s.v. "Montesquieu 1.png," https://commons.wikimedia.org/wiki/File:Montesquieu_1.png This work is in the public domain in its country of origin and other countries and areas where the copyright term is the author's life plus 100 years or less.

[169] *Wikimedia*, s.v. "SirWilliamBlackstone.jpg," https://commons.wikimedia.org/wiki/File:SirWilliamBlackstone.jpg This work is in the public domain in its country of origin and other countries and areas where the copyright term is the author's life plus 100 years or less.

[170] *Wikimedia*, s.v. "JohnLocke.png," https://commons.wikimedia.org/wiki/File:JohnLocke.png This work is in the public domain in its country of origin and other countries and areas where the copyright term is the author's life plus 100 years or less.

[171] *Wikimedia*, s.v. "Edward coke.jpg," https://commons.wikimedia.org/wiki/File:Edward_coke.jpg This work is in the public domain in its country of origin and other countries and areas where the copyright term is the author's life plus 100 years or less.

[172] *Wikimedia*, s.v. "Cicero - Musei Capitolini.JPG," https://commons.wikimedia.org/wiki/File:Cicero_-_Musei_Capitolini.JPG Permission granted by author Glauco92 . This file is licensed under the Creative Commons Attribution-Share Alike 3.0 Unported, 2.5 Generic, 2.0 Generic and 1.0 Generic license.

[173] W. Cleon Skousen, *Majesty of God's Law,* preface - 1

[174] Ibid., 5-6

[175] John Adams, "Thoughts on Government: Apr. 1776 Papers 4:86-93," Constitution Society, accessed October 25, 2014, http://www.constitution.org/jadams/thoughts.htm

[176] Correa Moylan Walsh, *The political science of John Adams, (*New York and London: G. P. Putnam's Sons, 1915), p. 1

[177] "II Awakenings and Enlightenments," *American Heritage A Reader*, ed. The Hillsdale College History Faculty, (Hillsdale: Hillsdale College Press, 2011) , 68-69

[178] "Beyond the Pilgrim Story," PilgrimHallMuseum.org, accessed October 25, 2014, http://www.pilgrimhallmuseum.org/plymouth_rock.htm

[179] Deut. 14:2

[180] Federer, *America's Quotations*, "An Oration Delivered Before the Inhabitants of the Town of Newburyport at Their Request on the Sixty-First Anniversary of the Declaration of Independence, July 4, 1837," 18

[181] Federer, *America's Quotations,* "The Boston Tea Party," 56

[182] Ibid., *Provincial Congress of Massachusetts,* 426-427

[183] Hezekiah Niles, *Principles and acts of the Revolution in America; or, An attempt to collect and preserve some of the speeches, orations, & proceedings, with sketches and remarks belonging to the men of the Revolutionary period in the United States,* (Baltimore: Printed and pub. for the editor, by W. O. Niles, 1822), 198

[184] Cushing Strout, *The New Heavens and the New Earth: Political Religion in America*, (New York: Harper & Row, 1973), 59

[185] Federer, *America's Quotations,* "Continental Congress,"144

[186] GreatSeal.com, "Benjamin Franklin's Great Seal Design," accessed on December 26, 2016, http://greatseal.com/committees/firstcomm/reverse.html

[187] *Wikimedia Commons, s.v.,* "BenFranklinDuplessis.jpg," by artist Joseph-Siffred Duplessis, https://commons.wikimedia.org/wiki/File:BenFranklinDuplessis.jpg

This is a faithful photographic reproduction of a two-dimensional, public domain work of art. The work of art itself is in the public domain for the following reason: This work is in the **public domain** in its country of origin and other countries and areas where the copyright term is the author's life plus 100 years or less. United States public domain tag

[188] GreatSeal.com, Benjamin Franklin's Great Seal Design," accessed January 2, 2016, http://www.greatseal.com/committees/firstcomm/reverse.html as scanned from Richard S. Patterson and Richardson Dougall, *The Eagle and the Shield: A History of the Great Seal of the United States*, published in 1976 by the Office of the Historian, Bureau of Public Affairs, Department of State, under the auspices of the American Revolution Bicentennial Administration, p. 21 This is a faithful photographic reproduction of a two-dimensional, public domain work of art. The work of art itself is in the public domain for the following reason: This work is in the public domain in its country of origin and other countries and areas where the copyright term is the author's life plus 70 years or less. United States public domain tag.

[189] GreatSeal.com, "First Great Seal Committee – July/August 1776: Thomas Jefferson," accessed on December 26, 2016, http://greatseal.com/committees/firstcomm/reverse.html

[190] Ibid.

[191] The Founders' Constitution, Volume 1, Chapter 14, Document 10, "The Papers of Thomas Jefferson. Edited by Julian P. Boyd et al.," The University of Chicago Press, (Princeton: Princeton University Press, 1950--). http://press-pubs.uchicago.edu/founders/documents/v1ch14s10.html

[192] Founders Online, "From Thomas Jefferson to Edmund Pendleton, 13 August 1776," http://founders.archives.gov/documents/Jefferson/01-01-02-0205

[193] Founders Online, "John Adams to Abigail Adams, 14 August 1776," http://founders.archives.gov/documents/Adams/04-02-02-0059

[194] *Wikimedia Commons, s.v.* "J S Copley - Samuel Adams.jpg," by artist John Singleton Copley, https://commons.wikimedia.org/wiki/File:J_S_Copley_-_Samuel_Adams.jpg

This is a faithful photographic reproduction of a two-dimensional, public domain work of art. The work of art itself is in the public domain for the following reason: This work is in the public domain in its country of origin and other countries and areas where the copyright term is the author's life plus 100 years or less. United States public domain tag

[195] Ibid., "Samuel Adams,"23

[196] "II Awakenings and Enlightenments," *American Heritage A Reader,* ed. The Hillsdale College History Faculty, (Hillsdale: Hillsdale College Press, 2011) , 69

[197] *Wikimedia Commons,* s.v. "Patrick henry.JPG," https://commons.wikimedia.org/wiki/File:Patrick_henry.JPG This work is in the public domain in the United States because it is a work prepared by an officer or employee of the United States Government as part of that person's official duties under the terms of Title 17, Chapter 1, Section 105 of the US Code.

[198] Federer, *America's Quotations,* "Patrick Henry,"288

[199] Charles T. Evans, *The Patriot Preachers of the Revolution,* (New York: Charles T. Evans, 1862) Preface

[200] John Wingate Thornton, A.M, *The Pulpit of the American Revolution, or, the Political Sermons of the Period of 1776,* (Boston: D. Lothrop and Company, 1876) v.

[201] *The Book of Abigail and John: Selected Letters of the Adams Family, 1762-1784*, (Cambridge: Harvard University Press, 1975), 142

[202] Skousen, *Majesty of God's Law,* 23

[203] Irving Wallace, et al., "Hebrew: National Language of the U.S.," *Parade Magazine,* (New York: Parade Publications, May 30, 1982), 16

[204] Jones, *Prophetic History,* 8

[205] "Articles of Confederation : March 1, 1781," as sourced from Documents Illustrative of the Formation of the Union of the American States, Government Printing Office, 1927, House Document No. 398, Selected, Arranged and Indexed by Charles C. Tansill, accessed at *The Avalon Project,* Lillian Goldman Law Library, Yale Law School, accessed September 2, 2014, http://avalon.law.yale.edu/18th_century/artconf.asp

[206] Ibid.

[207] "George Washington to John Jay, 1 Aug. 1786, Writings 28:502--3," *Deficiencies of the Confederation,* The Founders' Constitution, Vol.1, Ch. 5, Doc. 11,The University of Chicago Press, accessed September 2, 2014, http://press-pubs.uchicago.edu/founders/documents/v1ch5s11.html

[208] *Wikimedia Commons, s.v.,* "George Washington as CIC of the Continental Army bust.jpg," https://commons.wikimedia.org/wiki/File:George_Washington_as_CIC_of_the_Continental_Army_bust.jpg This image is in the public domain because it contains materials that originally came from the United States Army Center of Military History.

[209] *Wikimedia Commons,* s.v. "John Jay (Gilbert Stuart portrait).jpg," https://commons.wikimedia.org/wiki/File:John_Jay_(Gilbert_Stuart_portrait).jpg This work is in the public domain in its country of origin and other countries and areas where the copyright term is the author's life plus 100 years or less.

[210] Myron Magnet, "The Education of John Jay: America's indispensable diplomat," Winter, 2010, http://www.city-journal.org/2010/20_1_urb-john-jay.html

[211] *The Oxford Handbook of History of Nationalism*, ed. John Breuilly, (Oxford University Press, ed. 2013), 399

[212] *Wikimedia Commons,* s.v. "Alexander Hamilton portrait by John Trumbull 1806.jpg," https://commons.wikimedia.org/wiki/File:Alexander_Hamilton_portrait_by_John_Trumbull_1806.jpg This work is in the public domain in its country of origin and other countries and areas where the copyright term is the author's life plus 100 years or less. United States public domain tag

[213] Skousen, *Majesty of God's Law,* p. 1 as citing Donald S. Lutz, *The Relative Influence of European Writers on Late Eighteenth Century American Political Thought,* 78 American Political Science Review, p. 189; citied by John Eidsmoe in *Restoration of the Constitution,* H. Wayne House, ed. (Dallas: Probe Books, 1987), p.78

[214] 1 Kings 12:12-24

[215] 2 Kings 17:6

[216] Skousen, *Majesty of God's Law*, 14-15

[217] Skousen, *The Majesty of God's Law,* 18

[218] *Wikimedia Commons* s.v., "John Smibert - Bishop George Berkeley - Google Art Project.jpg," https://commons.wikimedia.org/wiki/File:John_Smibert_-_Bishop_George_Berkeley_-_Google_Art_Project.jpg#mw-jump-to-license The author died in 1751, so this work is in the public domain in its country of origin and other countries and areas where the copyright term is the author's life plus 100 years or less.

[219] *Wikipedia,* s.v. "George Berkeley," last modified October 23, 2014,http://en.wikipedia.org/wiki/George_Berkeley

[220] Dan. 2

[221] Isa. 18:2

[222] Skousen, *Majesty of God's Law,* 20-24

[223] *God's New Israel Religious Interpretations of American Destiny,* ed. Conrad Cherry, (Chapel Hill and London: The University of North Carolina Press, 1998)

[224] Frank Moore, *The Patriot Preachers of the American Revolution: with Biographical Sketches,* (New York: Charles T. Evans, 1862),

[225] *77 Bible Verses About Signs of the End Times*, ed. Stephen Smith., (OpenBible.info., Nov 30, 2015) http://www.openbible.info/topics/signs_of_the_end_times

[226] Skousen, *Majesty of God's Law,* 15

[227] Ezra Stiles, "The United States Elevated to Glory and Honor: A sermon preached before Governor Jonathan Trumbull and the General Assembly of the State of Connecticut, convened at Hartford at the Anniversary Election, May 8th, 1783," Second edition, (Worcester, Mass.: Isaiah Thomas, 1785), 5-9, 58-75, 88-92, 95-98, quoted in *God's New Israel Religious Interpretations of American Destiny,* ed. Conrad Cherry, (Chapel Hill and London: The University of North Carolina Press, 1998), 82-92

[228] A phrase from the parable in Jesus' Sermon on the Mount as in Matthew 5:14.

[229] *The Constitution of the United States*, A Transcription, National Archives and Records Administration, accessed September 2, 2014, http://dev.republicoftheunitedstates.org/wp-content/uploads/2014/03/NARA-The-Constitution-of-the-United-States-A-Transcription.pdf

[230] *Will The Great American Experiment Succeed?,* National Center for Constitutional Studies, accessed September 2, 2014, http://www.nccs.net/will-the-great-american-experiment-succeed.php

[231] *Wikimedia Commons,* s.v. "John Quincy Adams by GPA Healy, 1858.jpg," https://commons.wikimedia.org/wiki/File:John_Quincy_Adams_by_GPA_Healy,_1858.jpg This work is in the public domain in its country of origin and other countries and areas where the copyright term is the author's life plus 100 years or less.

[232] John Quincy Adams, *The Jubilee of the Constitution*, (New York: Published by Samuel Colman, 1839), 54, 119

[233] David Carroll Stephenson letter to David and Jean Hertler, September 15, 2014

[234] *Wikimedia Commons*, s.v. "Gilbert du Motier Marquis de Lafayette.jpg," https://commons.wikimedia.org/wiki/File:Gilbert_du_Motier_Marquis_de_Lafayette.jpg#mw-jump-to-license This work is in the public domain in its country of origin and other countries and areas where the copyright term is the author's life plus 100 years or less.

[235] Phelps, *Vatican Assassins*, 296

[236] Carole Bos, "John Adams" AwesomeStories.com. Oct 07, 2013, http://www.awesomestories.com/asset/view/John-Adams1 giving media credit to Image online, courtesy the abigailadams.org website, http://abigailadams.org/welcome_files/Page353.htm

[237] George Riemer, *The New Jesuits*, (Boston, Massachusetts: Little, Brown & Co., 1971), xiv.

[238] *Wikimedia Commons,* s.v. "Jefferson Portrait West Point by Thomas Sully.jpg," https://commons.wikimedia.org/wiki/File:Jefferson_Portrait_West_Point_by_Thomas_Sully.jpg#mw-jump-to-license https://commons.wikimedia.org/wiki/File:Jefferson_Portrait_West_Point_by_Thomas_Sully.jpg#mw-jump-to-license

[239] Emmett McLoughlin, *An Inquiry Into the Assassination of Abraham Lincoln*, (New York: Lyle Stuart, 1963), 4

[240] 2 Thess. 2:1-12

[241] John 8:32

[242] 1 Pet. 5:8

[243] Chris Price, *Puritan Education—The Old Deluder Satan Act of 1647,* February 4, 2012, http://americanchurchhistory.blogspot.com/2012/02/puritan-education-old-deluder-satan-act.html

[244] 1 Pet. 5:8

[245] "Letter of Oct. 7, 1801 from Danbury (CT) Baptist Assoc. to Thomas Jefferson," *Thomas Jefferson Papers,* Library of Congress, Manuscript Division

[246] Thomas Jefferson, *The Writings of Thomas Jefferson*, Vol. XVI, ed. Albert E. Bergh, (Washington, D. C.: The Thomas Jefferson Memorial Association of the United States, 1904), 281-282

[247] Federer, *America's Quotations,* "John Adams," 10

[248] Dr. Benjamin Rush, "Thoughts, Upon the Mode of Education Proper in a Republic," *A Plan for the Establishment of Public Schools and the Diffusion of Knowledge in Pennsylvania; to Which Are Added, Thoughts upon the Mode of Education Proper in a Republic*, (Philadelphia: Thomas Dobson, 1786). Reproduced in *Essays on Education in the Early Republic*, ed. Frederick Rudolph, (Cambridge, MA: The Belknap Press of Harvard University Press, 1965), 9-23, accessed September 2, 2014, http://www.schoolchoices.org/roo/rush.htm

[249] Noah Webster College, "About Noah Webster," accessed September 2, 2014, http://www.nwebstercollege.com/736949

[250] Jared Sparks, *The Life of Gouverneur Morris with Selections from His Correspondence and Miscellaneous Papers,* Vol I, p. 413; Vol III, p. 32, (Boston: Gray & Bowen, 1832)

[251] Fisher Ames, *Works of Fisher Ames* (Boston: T.B. Wait & Co., 1809), 134-135

[252] James H. Hutson, *The Founders on Religion: A Book of Quotations,* (Princeton, NJ, Princeton University Press, 2005), 52

[253] James Wilson, *The Works of James Wilson, associate justice of the Supreme Court of the United States and Professor of Law in the College of Philadelphia,* Vol. I, ed. James De Witt Andrews, (Chicago: Callaghan and Company, 1896), 93-95

[254] Federer, *America's Quotations,* "Noah Webster," 678

[255] Ibid., *Robert Charles Winthrop,* 702

[256] "Letter from George Washington to the Clergy of Different Denominations Residing In and Near the City of Philadelphia, Mar. 3, 1797," *The Writings of George Washington, 1745-1799,* Vol. 36, ed. John C. Fitzpatrick, (1931), 416

[257] "Letter to Messrs. The Abbes Chalut and Arnaud, Philadelphia, 17 April, 1787," *The Works of Benjamin Franklin*, Vol X, ed. Jared Sparks, (Boston: Charles Tappan, Publisher. Louisville, KY, Alston Mygatt, 1844), 297

[258] *Journals of the Continental Congress 1774-1789*, Volume XII, (Washington: Government Printing Office, 1908), 1001

[259] April Shenandoah, "History of America's Education, Universities, Textbooks and Our Founders," Last of Three Parts, *The American Partisan,* March 12, 2002, http://www.american-partisan.com/cols/2002/shenandoah/qtr1/0312.htm

[260] George Washington, "Washington's Farewell Address 1796," accessed November 30, 2015 at *The Avalon Project,* Lillian Goldman Law Library, Yale Law School, http://avalon.law.yale.edu/18th_century/washing.asp

[261] Eustace Mullins, *The Rape of Justice, America's Tribunals Exposed*, (Staunton: National Commission for Judicial Reform, First Ed., 1989), 55

[262] Library of Congress, "James Madison," https://www.loc.gov/item/2002725261/ This media file is in the public domain in the United States. This applies to U.S. works where the copyright has expired, often because its first publication occurred prior to January 1, 1923.

[263] Ibid., 54, 55

[264] *Wikimedia Commons*, s.v. "Martin Luther King, Jr..jpg," https://en.wikipedia.org/wiki/File:Martin_Luther_King,_Jr..jpg This Swedish photograph is in the public domain in Sweden because one of the following applies: The work is non-artistic (journalistic, …) and has been created before 1969. The photographer is not known, and cannot be traced, and the work has been created before 1944. If the photographer died before 1946, {{PD-old-70}} should be used instead of this tag.

[265] Mlkday.gov, "Rev. Dr. Martin Luther King, Jr. Quotes," accessed September 2, 2014, http://mlkday.gov/plan/library/communications/quotes.php

[266] John A. Logan, *The Great Conspiracy,*(New York, A. R. Hart & Co., Publishers, 1886), 1-2

[267] Jones, *Prophetic History,* 36

[268] Logan, *Great Conspiracy,* 1

[269] "Less well known is Thomas Jefferson's First Draft of the Declaration of Independence in which he denounced the slave trade as an "execrable Commerce" and slavery itself as a "cruel war against nature itself" (1776)," The Portable Library of Liberty, accessed September 2, 2014, http://files.libertyfund.org/pll/quotes/59.html

[270] Logan, *Great Conspiracy,* 1

[271] Jones, *Prophetic History,* 11

[272] "Rough Draft of the Declaration of Independence: Thomas Jefferson, 1776," TeachingAmericanHistory.org, sourced from Boyd, J.P. et al, editors, *The Papers of Thomas Jefferson.* Vol. I,(Princeton: Princeton University Press, 1950), 426,accessed September 2, 2014, http://teachingamericanhistory.org/library/document/rough-draft-of-the-declaration-of-independence/

[273] Carl Lotus Becker, *The Declaration of Independence: A Study on the History of Political Ideas* (New York: Harcourt, Brace and Co., 1922), accessed November 23, 2015, http://oll.libertyfund.org/titles/1177

[274] Library of Congress, "Declaration of Independence, July 4th, 1776," No known restrictions on publication. http://www.loc.gov/pictures/item/96521535/

[275] *Wikimedia Commons*, s.v. "United States 1789-03 to 1789-08 eastern.jpg," https://commons.m.wikimedia.org/wiki/File:United_States_1789-03_to_1789-08_eastern.jpg Author: Notuncurious, Permission is granted to copy, distribute and/or modify this document under the terms of the GNU Free Documentation License, Version 1.2 or any later version published by the Free Software Foundation; with no Invariant Sections, no Front-Cover Texts, and no Back-Cover Texts.

[276] *Wikimedia Commons, s.v.* "Thomas Jefferson 1786 by Mather Brown.JPG," https://commons.wikimedia.org/wiki/File:Thomas_Jefferson_1786_by_Mather_Brown.JPG This is a faithful photographic reproduction of a two-dimensional, public domain work of art. The work of art itself is in the public domain for the following reason: This work is in the **public domain** in its country of origin and other countries and areas where the copyright term is the author's life plus 100 years or less. United States public domain tag

[277] John A. Logan, *The Great Conspiracy,*(New York, A. R. Hart & Co., Publishers, 1886), 3-4

[278] Ibid., 4

[279] *Wikimedia Commons*, s.v. "Northwest-territory-usa-1787.png," https://commons.wikimedia.org/wiki/File:Northwest-territory-usa-1787.png Permission is granted to copy, distribute and/or modify this document under the terms of the GNU Free Documentation License, Version 1.2 or any later version published by the Free Software Foundation; with no Invariant Sections, no Front-Cover Texts, and no Back-Cover Texts. A copy of the license is included in the section entitled GNU Free Documentation License. Subject to disclaimers.

[280] John A. Logan, *The Great Conspiracy,* 3-5

[281] *Constitution of the United States of America,* Article I, Section 9

[282] *Wikimedia Commons*, s.v. "John Alexander Logan crop.jpg," https://commons.wikimedia.org/wiki/File:William_Tecumseh_Sherman_and_staff_-_Brady-Handy.jpg#mw-jump-to-license This work is in the public domain in its country of origin and other countries and areas where the copyright term is the author's life plus 100 years or less.

[283] Wayne Holstad, *Leviticus v. Leviathan,* (St. Paul: Alethos Press LLC, 2004), 98

[284] *Wikimedia Commons*, s.v. "Rufus King - National Portrait Gallery.JPG," https://commons.wikimedia.org/wiki/File:Rufus_King_-_National_Portrait_Gallery.JPG#mw-jump-to-license This work is in the public domain in its country of origin and other countries and areas where the copyright term is the author's life plus 100 years or less.

[285] *Wikimedia Commons*, s.v. "Gouverneur Morris.jpg," https://commons.wikimedia.org/wiki/File:Gouverneur_Morris.jpg#mw-jump-to-license This work is in the public domain in its country of origin and other countries and areas where the copyright term is the author's life plus 70 years or less.

[286] Ibid., 99

[287] Ibid.

[288] Library of Congress, "Eli Whitney, half-length portrait, facing slightly left] / painted by Mr. King ; Wm. Hoogland sculpt. N.Y.," https://www.loc.gov/resource/cph.3g12270/ No known restrictions on publication.

[289] Ibid.

[290] Ibid.

[291] *Wikimedia Commons*, s.v. "Cotton gin harpers.jpg," https://commons.wikimedia.org/wiki/File:Cotton_gin_harpers.jpg#mw-jump-to-license This image is available from the United States Library of Congress's Prints and Photographs division under the digital ID cph.3c03801. This image is available from the United States Library of Congress's Prints and Photographs division under the digital ID cph.3c03801

[292] Federer, *America's Quotations,* "Benjamin Franklin," 248-249

[293] Library of Congress, "Benjamin Franklin, 1706-1790," https://www.loc.gov/item/2004679607/ This work is in the public domain in its country of origin and other countries and areas where the copyright term is the author's life plus 100 years or less.

[294] Wallbuilders Staff, "Franklin's Appeal for Prayer at the Constitutional Convention, 1787, " accessed September 2, 2014, http://www.wallbuilders.com/libissuesarticles.asp?id=98

[295] Ibid.

[296] *Wikimedia Commons*, s.v. "Scene at the Signing of the Constitution of the United States.jpg,"

[297] *Who is W. Cleon Skousen?*, accessed October 25, 2014, http://wcleonskousen.com/ https://commons.wikimedia.org/wiki/File:Scene_at_the_Signing_of_the_Constitution_of_the_United_States.jpg#mw-jump-to-license This work is in the public domain in the United States because it is a work prepared by an officer or employee of the United States Government as part of that person's official duties under the terms of Title 17, Chapter 1, Section 105 of the US Code.

[298] *Wikimedia Commons*, s.v. "Augustinus 1.jpg," https://commons.wikimedia.org/wiki/File:Augustinus_1.jpg#mw-jump-to-license This work is in the public domain in its country of origin and other countries and areas where the copyright term is the author's life plus 70 years or less.

[299] Skousen, *Majesty of God's Law,* 272

[300] Ibid., 272-273

[301] "Autobiography Benjamin Franklin (1706-1790),"*American Heritage A Reader,* ed. The Hillsdale College History Faculty, (Hillsdale: Hillsdale College Press, 2011) , 104-105

[302] Skousen, *Majesty of God's Law,* 279-280

[303] Ibid., 6-7

[304] *Wikimedia Commons*, S.V. "T Jefferson by Charles Willson Peale 1791 2.jpg," https://commons.wikimedia.org/wiki/File:T_Jefferson_by_Charles_Willson_Peale_1791_2.jpg#mw-jump-to-license This work is in the public domain in its country of origin and other countries and areas where the copyright term is the author's life plus 100 years or less.

[305] Ibid., 8

[306] *The Complete Jefferson,* ed. Saul K. Padover, (New York: Tudor Publishing Company, 1943), 88-102

[307] Quoted by Norman Cousings, *In God We Trust,* New York: Harper Brothers, 1958, p. 167 as cited by W. Cleon Skousen, *The Majesty of God's Law, It's Coming to America,* (Salt Lake City: Ensign Publishing, 1996), 4

[308] Federer, *America's Quotations,* "John Adams," 5

[309] *Wikimedia Commons*, s.v. "John Adams (1766).jpg," https://commons.wikimedia.org/wiki/File:John_Adams_(1766).jpg This work is in the public domain in the United States because it was published (or registered with the U.S. Copyright Office) before January 1, 1923.

[310] WallBuilders Staff, "Franklin's Appeal for Prayer at the Constitutional Convention, 1787," accessed on September 2, 2014, http://www.wallbuilders.com/libissuesarticles.asp?id=98

[311] *Wikimedia Commons*, s.v. "U Penn Statue.jpg," https://commons.wikimedia.org/wiki/File:U_Penn_Statue.jpg#mw-jump-to-license Permission granted by author, "The Pancake of Heaven!" This file is licensed under the Creative Commons Attribution-Share Alike 4.0 International license

[312] Federer, *America's Quotations,* "George Whitefield," 684-685

[313] Ibid.

[314] Bartleby.com, "American Historical Documents, 1000–1904: The Harvard Classics. 1909–14: Treaty with France (Louisiana Purchase) (1803), accessed on January 7, 2017, http://www.bartleby.com/43/25.html

[315] Logan, *Great Conspiracy,* 9

[316] Thomas Jefferson, *Notes on the State of Virginia,* Query XVIII, 1781, 270, accessed December 2, 2015, http://www.pbs.org/jefferson/archives/documents/frame_ih198145.htm

[317] *George Washington's Farewell Address to the People of the United States,* September 17, 1796, Point 18, Archiving Early America as sourced from *The Independent Chronicle,* September 26, 1796, accessed November 1, 2014, http://www.earlyamerica.com/milestone-events/george-washingtons-farewell-address-full-text/

[318] *Wikipedia,* s.v. "Divine Right of Kings," last modified August 28, 2014, http://en.wikipedia.org/wiki/Divine_right_of_kings

[319] Bill Hughes, *The Secret Terrorists,* (Eustis: Truth Triumphant, 2002), 21

[320] McCarty, *Suppressed Truth,* 16

[321] Michael A. Shea, *In God We Trust: George Washington and the Spiritual Destiny of the United States of America,* (Derry: Liberty Quest, LLC, 2012), 115

[322] Jas. 3:17

[323] Jonathan Mott, Ph.D., "Why is George Washington considered the Father of this nation?," accessed December 2, 2015, http://www.thisnation.com/question/017.html

[324] George Washington, *George Washington: A Collection,* compiled and edited by W.B. Allen (Indianapolis: Liberty Fund, 1988), accessed December 2, 2015, http://oll.libertyfund.org/titles/848

[325] Edwin A. Sherman, 32°, *The Engineer Corps of Hell; or, Rome's Sapper's and Miners,* 1883, (Sold by Private Subscription only and under Stipulated Conditions.), 118-124

[326] Gen. 12:3

[327] Heb. 12:6

[328] Num. 24:14-24

[329] Num. 24:14-20, Exod. 17:14-16

[330] 2 Thess. 2

[331] Rev. 2:14

[332] Library of Congress, "An American Time Capsule: Three Centuries of Broadsides and Other Printed Ephemera," http://memory.loc.gov/cgi-bin/ampage?collId=rbpe&fileName=rbpe28/rbpe282/28204300/rbpe28204300.db&recNum=0

[333] *Wikimedia Commons,* s.v. "Congress of Vienna.PNG," https://en.wikipedia.org/wiki/File:Congress_of_Vienna.PNG Permission granted by author Jean Godefroy, numbers added by User:Mathiasrex Maciej Szczepańczyk, This file is licensed under the Creative Commons Attribution-Share Alike 3.0 Unported license.

[334] McCarty, *Suppressed Truth,* 7

[335] Thomas E. Watson, *Political and Economic Handbook,* (Thomson: Press of The Jeffersonian Publishing Co., 1916) p. 90-92

[336] *Wikimedia Commons,* s.v. "Congress of Verona," https://en.m.wikipedia.org/wiki/Congress_of_Verona This work is in the public domain in its country of origin and other countries and areas where the copyright term is the author's life plus 70 years or less.

[337] *Wikimedia Commons s.v.,* "Berlin .Gendarmenmarkt .Deutscher Dom 010.jpg," https://commons.wikimedia.org/wiki/File:Berlin_.Gendarmenmarkt_.Deutscher_Dom_010.jpg This work is in the public domain in its country of origin and other countries and areas where the copyright term is the author's life plus 70 years or less. United States public domain tag

[338] Library of Congress, "Thompson, Hon. R.W. of Ind.," http://www.loc.gov/pictures/item/brh2003001650/PP/ No known restrictions on publication.

[339] Thompson, *Footprints Jesuits,* 251

[340] Hughes, *Secret Terrorists,* 3

[341] William Cooper, *Behold a Pale Horse,* (Flagstaff: Light Technology Publishing, 1991), 106

[342] Thomas E. Watson, *Political and Economic Handbook,* (Thomson: Press of The Jeffersonian Publishing Co., 1916) p. 91-92

[343] Hector Macpherson, *The Jesuits in History,* (Ozark Book Publishers, 1997), appendix

[344] *Wikimedia Commons,* s.v. "George Canning by Richard Evans - detail.jpg," https://commons.wikimedia.org/wiki/File:George_Canning_by_Richard_Evans_-_detail.jpg#mw-jump-to-license This work is in the public domain in its country of origin and other countries and areas where the copyright term is the author's life plus 100 years or less.

[345] McCarty, *Suppressed Truth,* 10

[346] Thomas E. Watson, *Political and Economic Handbook,* (Thomson: Press of The Jeffersonian Publishing Co., 1916) p. 90-92

[347] *Thomas Jefferson on the Monroe Doctrine,* History-world.org, accessed September 2, 2014, http://history-world.org/thomas_jefferson_on_the_monroe_d.htm

[348] *Wikimedia Commons,* s.v. " James Monroe White House portrait 1819.gif," https://en.wikipedia.org/wiki/File:James_Monroe_White_House_portrait_1819.gif This work is in the public domain in its country of origin and other countries and areas where the copyright term is the author's life plus 100 years or less.

[349] *Wikimedia Commons*, s.v. "Jefferson Portrait West Point by Thomas Sully.jpg," https://commons.wikimedia.org/wiki/File:Jefferson_Portrait_West_Point_by_Thomas_Sully.jpg#mw-jump-to-license https://commons.wikimedia.org/wiki/File:Jefferson_Portrait_West_Point_by_Thomas_Sully.jpg#mw-jump-to-license

[350] Hughes, *Secret Terrorists,* 10

[351] "Leaders discuss the Monroe Doctrine, which declared the Western Hemisphere to be free of further European expansion or ideology." Hispanic American Almanac: A Reference Work on Hispanics in the United States. Ed. Sonia Benson. 3rd ed. Detroit: Gale, 2003. Student Resources in Context. Web. 2 Jan. 2016.," sourced from the Library of Congress, http://ic.galegroup.com/ic/suic/ImagesDetailsPage/ImagesDetailsWindow?zid=083f906799f9c9738381ac96051660bc&action=2&catId=&documentId=GALE%7CEJ2210061178&source=Bookmark&u=sain62671&jsid=f5576ff16c56f08adb186f1064bfb27c

[352] United States History, *Second Great Awakening*, accessed September 2, 2014, http://tdl.org/txlor-dspace/bitstream/handle/2249.3/632/02_second_gr_awake.htm?sequence=3

[353] *Religion and the Founding of the American Republic: Religion and the New Republic,* accessed September 2, 2014, http://www.loc.gov/exhibits/religion/rel07.html

[354] *Wikimedia Commons*, s.v. "Timothy Dwight IV by John Trumbull 1817.jpeg," https://commons.wikimedia.org/wiki/File:Timothy_Dwight_IV_by_John_Trumbull_1817.jpeg This work is in the public domain in its country of origin and other countries and areas where the copyright term is the author's life plus 100 years or less.

[355] *Merriam-Webster Dictionary*, s.v. "Predestination," accessed September 2, 2014,http://www.merriam-webster.com/dictionary/predestination

[356] *Wikipedia,* s.v. "Lyman Beecher," last modified on October 17, 2014, http://en.wikipedia.org/wiki/Lyman_Beecher This work is in the public domain in its country of origin and other countries and areas where the copyright term is the author's life plus 100 years or less. United States tag.

[357] Steven R. Pointer, *American Postmillennialism: Seeing the Glory*, Christian History Institute Magazine Issue 61, accessed October 25, 2014, https://www.christianhistoryinstitute.org/magazine/article/american-postmillennialism-seeing-the-glory/

[358] Ibid.

[359] *Wikimedia Commons*, s.v. "Lyman Beecher - Brady-Handy.jpg," https://commons.wikimedia.org/wiki/File:Lyman_Beecher_-_Brady-Handy.jpg

his is a faithful photographic reproduction of a two-dimensional, public domain work of art. The work of art itself is in the public domain for the following reason: This work is in the **public domain** in its country of origin and other countries and areas where the copyright term is the author's life plus 100 years or less. United States public domain tag

[360] United States History, *Second Great Awakening*, accessed September 2, 2014, http://tdl.org/txlor-dspace/bitstream/handle/2249.3/632/02_second_gr_awake.htm?sequence=3

[361] Christian History Staff, "Charles Grandison Finney & the Second Phase of the Second Great Awakening," July 1, 1989,*Christianity Today*, Issue 23, http://www.christianitytoday.com/ch/1989/issue23/2329.html?start=1

[362] Diane Severance, Ph.D., *The 2nd Great Awakening,* accessed September 2, 2014, http://www.christianity.com/church/church-history/timeline/1701-1800/the-2nd-great-awakening-11630336.html

[363] Christian History Staff, "Charles Grandison Finney & the Second Phase of the Second Great Awakening."

[364] *Wikimedia Commons,* s.v. "Charles g finney.jpg," https://commons.wikimedia.org/wiki/File:Charles_g_finney.jpg This is a faithful photographic reproduction of a two-dimensional, public domain work of art. The work of art itself is in the public domain for the following reason: This work is in the public domain in its country of origin and other countries and areas where the copyright term is the author's life plus 70 years or less.

[365] Federer, *America's Quotations*, "Charles Grandison Finney,"235

[366] Christian History Staff, "Charles Grandison Finney & the Second Phase of the Second Great Awakening."

[367] "People & Ideas: Charles Finney," PBS/God in America, accessed September 2, 2014, https://www.pbs.org/godinamerica/people/charles-finney.html

[368] *Wikipedia,* s.v. "Second Great Awakening," last modified on September 2, 2014, http://en.wikipedia.org/wiki/Second_Great_Awakening#cite_ref-Timothy_2-2

[369] PBS.org, *God in America, "People & Ideas: Charles Finney,"* accessed September 2, 2014, https://www.pbs.org/godinamerica/people/charles-finney.html

[370] "Religion and the Founding of the American Republic: Religion and the New Republic," The Library of Congress, accessed September 2, 2014, http://www.loc.gov/exhibits/religion/rel07.html

[371] Dye, *Adder's Den*, 10-11

[372] Ibid., 6

[373] Gen. 12:3

[374] Peter Marshall and David Manuel, *Sounding Forth*, 12

[375] 1 Kings 11:30-39

[376] 2 Kings 17:6, 2 Kings 24

[377] Matt. 22:36-40

[378] Jas. 1:8

[379] Matt. 6:24

[380] Phelps, *Vatican Assassins*, 242

[381] 1 John 4:8

[382] Heb. 12:5-8, Prov. 3:12, 1 Cor. 11:32, Rev. 3:19

[383] Deut. 30:15-16

[384] 2 Cor. 4:4

[385] Matt. 24:15, Mark 13:14

[386] Ps. 83:3, Dan. 8:25

[387] Rom. 1

[388] Num. 24:14-24

[389] Ps. 83:3, Dan. 8:25

[390] Rev. 14:8, 18:4

[391] Matt. 24:24

[392] 2 Cor. 4:4

[393] Rom. 1:21, 25, 28

[394] Rom. 1: 18-32

[395] Eccles. 1:9

[396] Num. 31:16

[397] *Wikipedia*, s.v. "Judas Goat," last modified January 25, 2014, http://en.wikipedia.org/wiki/Judas_goat

[398] Arlen L. Chitwood, *Judgment Seat of Christ*, (Norman: The Lamp Broadcast, Inc., 2011 3rd printing), 109-115

[399] Num. 24:14-24

[400] Rev. 2:12-17

[401] *Wikipedia*, s.v. "Papal Infallibility," last modified November 11, 2015, http://en.wikipedia.org/wiki/Papal_infallibility

[402] John 8:44, 1 John 3:10, Acts 13:10

[403] Delaware.gov, Department of State: Division of Corporations: Entity Details, "Entity Name: THE UNITED STATES OF AMERICA, INC," File Number 4525682, https://delecorp.delaware.gov/tin/controller

[404] Strout, *New Heavens*, 59

[405] Dr. Marilyn F. Cheatham, *A Case for Christian Education*, 35, 41, 48, accessed on September 2, 2014, http://devotionalnet.faithsite.com/uploads/147/102353.pdf

[406] Dan. 2:28

[407] Dan. 2:44

[408] 2 Cor. 3:14-16

[409] Rev. 14:8, 18:4

[410] Isa. 60:1-2, Eph. 5:14-16

[411] Library of Congress, "Keep off! The Monroe Doctrine must be respected," Digital Id cph 3b22758, http://www.loc.gov/item/2002697703/ No known restrictions on publication.

[412] 2 Cor. 3:14-16

[413] Ps 2:2; Rev. 17:2

[414] Des Griffin, *Descent Into Slavery?*, (South Pasadena: Emissary Publications, 1980) chapter 5

[415] Library of Congress, Mathew Carey, "Map of the World from the best authorities.," https://www.loc.gov/resource/g3200.ct000160/ This work is in the public domain in its country of origin and other countries and areas where the copyright term is the author's life plus 70 years or less.

[416] Phelps, *Vatican Assassins*, 68, 217, 225

[417] *Wikipedia*, s.v. "Rothschild family," last modified August 31, 2014, http://en.wikipedia.org/wiki/Rothschild_family

[418] Neturei Karta International Staff, Jews United Against Zionism, *"What is Zionism? Judaism Versus Zionism,"* accessed September 2, 2014, http://www.nkusa.org/aboutus/whatzionism.cfm

[419] Ibid., "Judaism and Zionism Are Not the Same Thing," accessed September 2, 2014, http://www.nkusa.org/AboutUs/Zionism/judaism_isnot_zionism.cfm

[420] Eric Jon Phelps, *Historical and Biblical Review: Six Different Kinds of Zionists; Which One are You?*, May 21, 2012, http://vaticanassassins.org/2012/05/21/historical-and-biblical-review-six-different-kinds-of-zionists-which-one-are-you/

[421] Jeremiah Project Staff, *The New World Order,* accessed September 2, 2014, http://www.jeremiahproject.com/newworldorder/

[422] 2 Thess. 2:3-4

[423] Joseph Jacobs, et al., "Rothschild," accessed September 2, 2014, http://www.jewishencyclopedia.com/articles/12909-rothschild

[424] F. Tupper Sassy, *Rulers of Evil*, (Reno, Ospray Bookmakers, 1999),160-161

[425] Louis Even, *In this age of plenty - A new conception of economics: Social Credit*, (Montreal, Pilgrims of St. Michael, White Berets, 1946), Quote taken from "Who Rules America" by C.K. Howe and reproduced in "Lincoln Money Martyred" by Dr. R. E. Search (1933) , accessed December 24, 2015, http://www.michaeljournal.org/plenty49.htm

[426] *Wikimedia Commons,* s.v. "Nicholas Biddle by William Inman crop.jpg," https://commons.wikimedia.org/wiki/File:Nicholas_Biddle_by_William_Inman.jpg This is a faithful photographic reproduction of a two-dimensional, public domain work of art. The work of art itself is in the public domain for the following reason: This work is in the public domain in its country of origin and other countries and areas where the copyright term is the author's life plus 70 years or less. United States public domain tag.

[427] Library of Congress, "Andrew Jackson" http://www.loc.gov/pictures/item/96521663/ No known restrictions on publication.

[428] Hughes, *Secret Terrorists,* 12 https://commons.wikimedia.org/wiki/File:Nicholas_Biddle_by_William_Inman_crop.jpg *Wikimedia Commons s.v.* "Johnathan Edwards," Uploaded to en: by en:User:Flex at June 13, 2005, This is a faithful photographic reproduction of a two-dimensional, public domain work of art. The work of art itself is in the public domain for the following reason: This work is in the public domain in its country of origin and other countries and areas where the copyright term is the author's life plus 70 years or less. United States public domain tag.

[429] Stan V. Henkels, *Andrew Jackson and the Bank of the United States,* (Philadelphis, 1928) 2-3

[430] Des Griffin, *Descent Into Slavery?,* chapter 5

[431] *Wikimedia Commons,* s.v. "John C. Calhoun.jpeg," https://commons.wikimedia.org/wiki/File:John_C._Calhoun.jpeg This is a faithful photographic reproduction of a two-dimensional, public domain work of art. The work of art itself is in the public domain for the following reason: This work is in the public domain in its country of origin and other countries and areas where the copyright term is the author's life plus 100 years or less. United States public domain tag

[432] Frederic Hudson, *Journalism in the United States, from 1690-1872,* (New York: Harper & Brothers, 1873), 235

[433] Hughes, *Secret Terrorists,* 12, 13

[434] Dye, *Adder's Den,* 18-22

[435] Warren Getler and Bob Brewer, *Rebel Gold: One Man's Quest to Crack the Code Behind the Secret Treasure of the Confederacy*, (New York: Simon & Schuster, 2005), 49

[436] Jay Longley and Colin Eby, *Knights of the Golden Circle,* KnightsoftheGoldenCircle.webs.com, accessed September 2, 2014, http://knightsofthegoldencircle.webs.com/

[437] *Wikimedia Commons,* s.v. "Knights of the Golden Circle History of Seccession book, 1862.jpg," https://commons.wikimedia.org/wiki/File:Knights_of_the_Golden_Circle_History_of_Seccession_book,_1862.jpg This media file is in the public domain in the United States. This applies to U.S. works where the copyright has expired, often because its first publication occurred prior to January 1, 1923. See this page for further explanation.

[438] *Wikimedia Commons,* s.v. "William wilberforce.jpg," https://commons.wikimedia.org/wiki/File:William_wilberforce.jpg#mw-jump-to-license This work is in the public domain in its country of origin and other countries and areas where the copyright term is the author's life plus 100 years or less.

[439] *Wikipedia,* s.v. "William Wilberforce," last modified September 2, 2014, http://en.wikipedia.org/wiki/William_Wilberforce

[440] Dye, *Adder's Den,* 22

[441] Ibid., cover page

[442] U.S. History Staff, The Age of Jackson: 24e. Jackson vs. Clay and Calhoun, *"American History: From Pre-Columbian to the New Millennium,"* accessed September 2, 2014,http://www.ushistory.org/us/24e.asp

[443] Matt. 10:16

[444] Dye, *Adder's Den,* 19

[445] Federer, *America's Quotations*, "Daniel Webster,"668

[446] Dye, *Adder's Den,* 25

[447] *Wikimedia Commons,* s.v. "DanielWebster.png," https://commons.wikimedia.org/wiki/File:DanielWebster.png This work is in the public domain in the United States because it was published (or registered with the U.S. Copyright Office) before January 1, 1923.

[448] Mark 3:25

[449] Dye, *Adder's Den,* 25

[450] *Wikimedia Common*, s.v. "Chiniquy Portrait.png," https://commons.wikimedia.org/wiki/File:Charles_Chiniquy_Portrait.png This work is in the public domain in the United States because it was published (or registered with the U.S. Copyright Office) before January 1, 1923.

[451] Charles Chiniquy, *Fifty Years in the Church of Rome,*(New York: Fleming H. Revell Company, 1886), 690-691

[452] Luther S. Kauffman, *Romanism as a World Power, (True American Publishing Company, 1921),* 27-28

[453] *Wikimedia Commons*, s.v. "Papal Tiara with silver gems pearls.jpg," https://commons.wikimedia.org/wiki/File:Papal_Tiara_with_silver_gems_pearls.jpg#mw-jump-to-license Author, MatthiasKabel, I, the copyright holder of this work, hereby publish it under the following licenses: Permission is granted to copy, distribute and/or modify this document under the terms of the GNU Free Documentation License, Version 1.2 or any later version published by the Free Software Foundation; with no Invariant Sections, no Front-Cover Texts, and no Back-Cover Texts. A copy of the license is included in the section entitled GNU Free Documentation License.

[454] Vatican.va, "Holy See Press Office: Tiara," last updated March 4, 2001, http://www.vatican.va/news_services/press/documentazione/documents/sp_ss_scv/insigne/triregno_en.html

[455] *Wikipedia*, s.v. "Papal tiara," last updated December 16, 2016, https://en.m.wikipedia.org/wiki/Papal_tiara

[456] Library of Congress, "Andrew Jackson," https://www.loc.gov/item/99404956/ This media file is in the public domain in the United States. This applies to U.S. works where the copyright has expired, often because its first publication occurred prior to January 1, 1923.

[457] Dye, *Adder's Den,* 25,

[458] Hughes, *Secret Terrorists,* 21-22

[459] *Wikimedia Commons*, s.v. "George Peter Alexander Healy - John C. Calhoun - Google Art Project.jpg," https://commons.wikimedia.org/wiki/File:George_Peter_Alexander_Healy_-_John_C._Calhoun_-_Google_Art_Project.jpg The author died in 1894, so this work is in the public domain in its country of origin and other countries and areas where the copyright term is the author's life plus 100 years or less. This work is in the public domain in the United States because it was published (or registered with the U.S. Copyright Office) before January 1, 1923.

[460] McCarty, *Suppressed Truth,* 22

[461] Robert Y. Haynes, William Harper, Robert J. Turnbull and George McDuffie, *The Report, Ordinance, and Addresses of the Convention of the People of South Carolina: Adopted, November 24, 1832, (*Columbia, South Carolina: A.S. Johnston, 1832), Title page

[462] Ibid.

[463] Ibid.

[464] *Wikimedia Commons,* s.v. "JohnCCalhoun.jpeg," https://en.wikipedia.org/wiki/File:JohnCCalhoun.jpeg This work is in the public domain in its country of origin and other countries and areas where the copyright term is the author's life plus 70 years or less.

[465] Frank Moore, *The Civil War in Song and Story*, (P.F. Collier, Publisher, 1889), 30-31

[466] Hughes, *Secret Terrorists,* 15

[467] *Wikimedia Commons*, s.v. "Robert Morris.jpg," https://commons.wikimedia.org/wiki/File:Robert_Morris.jpg#mw-jump-to-license Author/ Photographer: cliff1066, Permission granted This file is licensed under the Creative Commons Attribution 2.0 Generic license.

[468] G. Edward Griffin, *The Creature from Jeckyll Island, (American Media, 1994) , 331*

[469] *Wikimedia Commons*, s.v. "G. Edward Griffin.jpg," https://commons.wikimedia.org/wiki/File:G._Edward_Griffin.jpg#mw-jump-to-license Copyright holder releases image per OTRS; permission granted.

[470] Derek Wilson, *Rothschild: The Wealth and Power of A Dynasty, (*New York: Charles Scribner's Sons, 1988), 178

[471] *Wikimedia Commons*, s.v. "Myers-gustavus-1909.jpg, https://en.wikipedia.org/wiki/File:Myers-gustavus-1909.jpg#mw-jump-to-license This image is in the public domain in the United States. In most cases, this means that it was first published prior to January 1, 1923

[472] *Wikipedia,s.v.* "Gustavus Myers," last modified April 7, 2014, http://en.wikipedia.org/wiki/Gustavus_Myers

[473] Gustavus Myers, *History of the Great American Fortunes,*(Random House, 1911), 556

[474] Hughes, *Secret Terrorists,* 47

[475] A Washington Reporter, *Shooting at the President. The Remarkable Trial of Richard Lawrence, Self-Styled King of the United States, King of England and of Rome, &c. &c. for an Attempt to Assassinate the President of the United States: Containing, also, an Engraving of the Eastern Portico of the Capitol, Descriptive of What Took Place on That Memorable Occasion: with Several Particulars Connected with the Event, Not before Known to the Public 1835* (265 Bowerty: W. Mitchell, 1835) http://heinonline.org/HOL/LandingPage?handle=hein.trials/abpu0001&div=1

[476] Robert J. Donovan, *The Assassins*, (New York: Harper & Brothers, 1952), 83

[477] *Wikimedia Commons,* s.v. "William Henry Harrison daguerreotype edit.jpg," https://commons.wikimedia.org/wiki/File:William_Henry_Harrison_daguerreotype_edit.jpg This work is in the public domain in its country of origin and other countries and areas where the copyright term is the author's life plus 70 years or less. United States public domain tag

[478] Dye, *Adder's Den,* 36

[479] Ibid., 36-40

[480] McCarty, *Suppressed Truth,* 51

[481] 2 Cor. 11:14

[482] McCarty, *Suppressed Truth,* 52

[483] Eph. 6:12

[484] McCarty, *Suppressed Truth,* 52

[485] Ibid., 44-46

[486] Dye, *Adder's Den, 37*

[487] Senator Thomas Benton, *Thirty Years View,* Vol. II, p. 21. (quoted in John Smith Dye's book, The Adder's Den, page 36).

[488] *Wikimedia Commons,* s.v. "Thomas Hart Benton.jpg," https://commons.wikimedia.org/wiki/File:Thomas_Hart_Benton.jpg This work is in the public domain in its country of origin and other countries and areas where the copyright term is the author's life plus 100 years or less. United States domain tag.

[489] Hughes, *Secret Terrorists,* 15

[490] Federer, *America's Quotations, "Zachary Taylor," 580*

[491] McCarty, *Suppressed Truth,* 55

[492] *Wikimedia Commons,* s.v. "Zachary Taylor by Joseph Henry Bush, c1848.jpg," https://commons.wikimedia.org/wiki/File:Zachary_Taylor_by_Joseph_Henry_Bush,_c1848.jpg This media file is in the public domain in the United States. This applies to U.S. works where the copyright has expired, often because its first publication occurred prior to January 1, 1923.

[493] Library of Congress, "Tyler, Pres. John," https://www.loc.gov/resource/cwpbh.03576/

[494] Senator Thomas Benton, *Thirty Years View,* Vol. II, p. 763, (quoted in Burke McCarty, *The Suppressed Truth About the Assassination of Abraham Lincoln*page 56).

[495] McCarty, *Suppressed Truth,* as quoted, 55

[496] *Wikimedia Commons,* s.v. "General Jackson Slaying the Many Headed Monster crop," https://commons.wikimedia.org/wiki/File:General_Jackson_Slaying_the_Many_Headed_Monster_crop.jpg This media file is in the public domain in the United States. This applies to U.S. works where the copyright has expired, often because its first publication occurred prior to January 1, 1923.

[497] Dye, *Adder's Den, 43*

[498] *Wikimedia Commons,* s.v. "John Tyler I.png," https://commons.wikimedia.org/wiki/File:John_Tyler_I.png This media file is in the public domain in the United States. This applies to U.S. works where the copyright has expired, often because its first publication occurred prior to January 1, 1923.

[499] Senator Thomas Benton, *Thirty Years View,* p.562 (quoted in Burke McCarty, *The Suppressed Truth About the Assassination of Abraham Lincoln*page 56).

[500] *Wikimedia Commons,* s.v. "Abel P. Upshur SecNavy.jpg," https://commons.wikimedia.org/wiki/File:Abel_P._Upshur_SecNavy.jpg#mw-jump-to-license This work is in the public domain in its country of origin and other countries and areas where the copyright term is the author's life plus 70 years or less.

[501] *Wikipedia,*s.v. "USS Princeton Disaster of 1844," last modified May 29, 2014, http://en.wikipedia.org/wiki/USS_Princeton_disaster_of_1844

[502] Dye, *Adder's Den, 44*

[503] *Wikimedia Commons,* s.v. "Explosion aboard USS Princeton.jpg," https://commons.wikimedia.org/wiki/File:Explosion_aboard_USS_Princeton.jpg This work is in the public domain in the United States because it was published (or registered with the U.S. Copyright Office) before January 1, 1923.

[504] *Wikipedia,*s.v. "John C. Breckenridge," last modified August 23, 2014, http://en.wikipedia.org/wiki/John_C._Breckinridge

[505] *Wikimedia Commons,* s.v. "John C Breckinridge-04775-restored.jpg," https://en.wikipedia.org/wiki/File:John_C_Breckinridge-04775-restored.jpg This work is based on a work in the public domain. It has been digitally enhanced and/or modified. This derivative work has been (or is hereby) released into the public domain by its author, AJCham. This applies worldwide. Permission granted.

[506] *Wikimedia Commons,* s.v. "Dred Scott photograph (circa 1857).jpg," https://commons.wikimedia.org/wiki/File:Dred_Scott_photograph_(circa_1857).jpg This media file is in the public domain in

the <u>United States</u>. This applies to U.S. works where the copyright has expired, often because its first publication occurred prior to January 1, 1923.

[507] Library of Congress, Roger B. Taney - Brady-Handy.jpg," https://commons.wikimedia.org/wiki/File:Roger_B._Taney_-_Brady-Handy.jpg No known restrictions on publication.

[508] Dye, *Adder's Den, 89*

[509] Ibid., 114

[510] World Wide Words, s.v. "*Trimmer,*" Page created July 28, 2007, http://www.worldwidewords.org/qa/qa-tri3.htm (accessed 9/2/2014)

[511] McCarty, *Suppressed Truth,* 59

[512] Ibid., 56

[513] Library of Congress, " [View of Washington looking down Pennsylvania Ave. toward unfinished Capitol. National Hotel on left, no. 1], https://www.loc.gov/item/2004662333/

[514] Ibid., 55

[515] *Wikimedia Commons*, s.v. "BUCHANAN, James-President (BEP engraved portrait).jpg," https://commons.wikimedia.org/wiki/File:BUCHANAN,_James-President_(BEP_engraved_portrait).jpg "This work is in the public domain in the United States because it is a work prepared by an officer or employee of the United States Government as part of that person's official duties under the terms of Title 17, Chapter 1, Section 105 of the US Code.

[516] Ibid., 60-61

[517] Chiniquy, *Fifty Years,* 668-670

[518] *Wikimedia Commons,* s.v. "James Meacham.jpg," https://commons.wikimedia.org/wiki/File:James_Meacham.jpg#mw-jump-to-license This media file is in the public domain in the United States. This applies to U.S. works where the copyright has expired, often because its first publication occurred prior to January 1, 1923.

[519] Lorenzo D. Johnson, *Chaplains of the General Government, with Objections to Their Employment Considered,* (New York: Sheldon, Blakeman & Co., 1856) 9

[520] Federer, *America's God and Country Encyclopedia of Quotations,* "Congress of the United States of America," (Coppell: FAME Publishing, Inc, 1994), 169-170

[521] Ibid., "Congress of the United States of America," 170

[522] Christianity Today Publisher, "Spiritual Awakenings in North America," *Christianity Today,* Issue 23, July 1, 1989, p 1, https://www.christianhistoryinstitute.org/uploaded/50cf796bc8bdb7.30632672.pdf

[523] Ibid.

[524] Ibid., 3

[525] Ibid., 4

[526] Gilbert H. Barnes, *The Anti-Slavery Impulse, 1830-1844,* (New York: D. Appleton-Centry, 1933)

[527] Charles Grandison Finney, "Lectures on Revivals on Religion, Sermon delivered to the congregation of Chatham Chapel, New York City, 1835.," Ed. William G. McLoughlin, (Cambridge: The Belknap Press of Harvard University Press, 1960)

[528] *Wikimedia Commons,* s.v. "1839-meth.jpg," https://commons.wikimedia.org/wiki/File:1839-meth.jpg This work is in the <u>public domain</u> in its country of origin and other countries and areas where the copyright term is the author's life plus 70 years or less.

[529] Charles Finney, "The Prevailing Prayer-Meeting: A SERMON,. Delivered in Blackfriars' Street Congregational Chapel, Glasgow, on 4th September, 1859, " printed 2013) p. 9, accessed September 2, 2014 at CharlesFinney.com http://www.charlesfinney.com/pdf/REVIVALS.pdf

[530] Ibid.

[531] Ibid.

[532] Ibid.

[533] *New York Times,* March 20, 1858, p. 4

[534] J. Edwin Orr, *America's Great Revival,* (London: Marshall, Morgan and Scott, LTD, 2nd Printing, May 1957), 12

[535] *Wikimedia Commons,* s.v. "Henry Ward Beecher - Brady-Handy.jpg," https://commons.wikimedia.org/wiki/File:Henry_Ward_Beecher_-_Brady-Handy.jpg This work is in the <u>public domain</u> in its country of origin and other countries and areas where the <u>copyright term</u> is the author's life plus 100 years or less.

[536] Christianity Today Publisher, "*Spiritual Awakenings in North America*," *Christianity Today,* Issue 23, July 1, 1989, p.45, https://www.christianhistoryinstitute.org/uploaded/50cf796bc8bdb7.30632672.pdf

[537] Ibid.

[538] Ibid.

[539] Ibid.

[540] Ibid.

[541] *Wikimedia Commons*, s.v. "James Gordon Bennett Sr.jpg," https://commons.wikimedia.org/wiki/File:James_Gordon_Bennett_Sr.jpg#mw-jump-to-license This image is available from the United States Library of Congress's Prints and Photographs division under the digital ID cph.3g04150.

[542] *Wikimedia Commons,* s.v. "Horace-Greeley-Baker.jpeg," https://commons.wikimedia.org/wiki/File:Horace-Greeley-Baker.jpeg This media file is in the public domain in the United States. This applies to U.S. works where the copyright has expired, often because its first publication occurred prior to January 1, 1923.

[543] Ibid., 46

[544] *Wikipedia*, s.v. "Dwight L. Moody," http(accessed 9/2/2014)

[545] *Wikimedia Commons*, s.v. "Dwight Lyman Moody c.1900.jpg," https://commons.wikimedia.org/wiki/File:Dwight_Lyman_Moody_c.1900.jpg This media file is in the public domain in the United States. This applies to U.S. works where the copyright has expired, often because its first publication occurred prior to January 1, 1923.

[546] "Dwight L. Moody: Revivalist with a common touch," *Christianity Today,* August 8, 2008, http://www.christianitytoday.com/ch/131christians/evangelistsandapologists/moody.html

[547] *Wikipedia*, s.v. "J. Edwin Orr," http (accessed 9/2/2014)

[548] Christianity Today Publisher, "Spiritual Awakenings in North America," *Christianity Today*, p.46

[549] Ibid.

[550] Roy Fish, *When Heaven Touched Earth*, (Need of the Times Publishers,1996) p.205, as referenced on TheGreatAwakenings.org, accessed September 2, 2014, http://www.thegreatawakenings.org/timeline.htm

[551] Rev. 14:8, 18:4

[552] Rom. 8:19-22

[553] Andy Borowitz, "Obama Says He has Fulfilled Campaign's Vague Catchprases," *Huff Post, Borowitz Report,* November 3, 2009, http://www.huffingtonpost.com/andy-borowitz/obama-says-he-has-fulfill_b_344259.html

[554] "Obama on Executive Actions, 'I've Got A Pen and I've Got A Cellphone,'" Washington CBS Local, accessed September 2, 2014, http://washington.cbslocal.com/2014/01/14/obama-on-executive-actions-ive-got-a-pen-and-ive-got-a-phone/

[555] "Obama Channels King Joffrey In the 'Westeros Wing,'" *The Huffington Post,* May 3, 2014http://www.huffingtonpost.com/2014/05/03/obama-game-of-thrones_n_5261302.html

[556] "Game of Thrones Wiki: Joffrey Baratheon," accessed September 2, 2014, http://gameofthrones.wikia.com/wiki/Joffrey_Baratheon

[557] New World Order Today Staff, "The Federal Reserve Banking System," accessed September 2, 2014, http://www.nwotoday.com/today/the-world-financial-system/the-federal-reserve-system

[558] "The Bankruptcy of The United States," United States Congressional Record, March 17, 1993 Vol. 33, page H-1303, accessed September 2, 2014, http://www.afn.org/~govern/bankruptcy.html

[559] Ibid.

[560] Mullins, *The Rape of Justice,* 54

[561] *George Washington's Farewell Address to the People of the United States,* September 17, 1796, Point 10, Archiving Early America as sourced from *The Independent Chronicle,* September 26, 1796, accessed November 1, 2014, http://www.earlyamerica.com/milestone-events/george-washingtons-farewell-address-full-text/

[562] Dr. R. E. Search, "Lincoln: Money Martyred," (Seattle: Lincoln Publishing Company, 1935), 47-48

[563] Gustavus Myers, *History of the Great American Fortunes,* Vol. I, (Chicago, Charles H. Kerr & Company, 1911), 41

[564] Ashley Lutz, "These 6 Corporations Control 90% Of The Media In America," June 4, 2012, *Business Insider,* http://www.businessinsider.com/these-6-corporations-control-90-of-the-media-in-america-2012-6#ixzz2ymuqnM64 (accessed 9/2/2014)

[565] "Joseph Goebbels: On the 'Big Lie,'" JewishVirtualLibrary.org, accessed September 2, 2014, www.jewishvirtuallibrary.org/jsource/Holocaust/goebbelslie.html

[566] Rom. 11:5

[567] Isa. 10:20-22

[568] John 15:10

[569] Acts 3:19

[570] Jer. 33:3

[571] Ps. 103:20

[572] Isa. 55:11

[573] Jer. 1:12

[574] 1 John 2:1
[575] Phil. 3:20
[576] Rev. 14:8, 18:4

References Part II

577 *Wikimedia Commons*, s.v. "George Washington by Gilbert Stuart, 1795-96.png," https://commons.wikimedia.org/wiki/File:George_Washington_by_Gilbert_Stuart,_1795-96.png#mw-jump-to-license This work is in the public domain in its country of origin and other countries and areas where the copyright term is the author's life plus 100 years or less.

578 Library of Congress, Religion and the Founding of the American Republic, VI. Religion and the Federal Government, "The Farewell Address," http://www.loc.gov/exhibits/religion/rel06.html#obj156 This work is in the public domain in the United States because it is a work of the United States Federal Government under the terms of Title 17, Chapter 1, Section 105 of the US Code.

579 Library of Congress, Religion and the Founding of the American Republic, VI. Religion and the Federal Government, "Washington's Farewell Address, http://adam2.org/articles/lib_congress_exhibit/rel06.html

580 *George Washington's Farewell Address to the People of the United States,* September 17, 1796, Point 18, Archiving Early America as sourced from *The Independent Chronicle,* September 26, 1796, accessed November 1, 2014, http://www.earlyamerica.com/milestone-events/george-washingtons-farewell-address-full-text/

581 *Wikipedia,* s.v. "Abraham Lincoln," http://en.wikipedia.org/wiki/Abraham_Lincoln (accessed 9/3/2014)

582 *Wikipedia,* s.v. "Separate Baptists,"http://en.wikipedia.org/wiki/Separate_Baptists (accessed 9/3/2014)

583 Prov. 22:6

584 McCarty, *Suppressed Truth,* 42

585 Library of Congress, "Lincoln the rail splitter," http://www.loc.gov/pictures/item/93504457/ c1909, This work is in the public domain in the United States because it was published (or registered with the U.S. Copyright Office) before January 1, 1923.

585 Ibid., 626

586 McCarty, *Suppressed Truth,* 44

587"The Emancipation Proclamation," National Archives & Records Administration, accessed September 3, 2014, http://www.archives.gov/exhibits/featured_documents/emancipation_proclamation/

588 *Wikipedia,* s.v. "Whig Party," http://en.wikipedia.org/wiki/Whig_Party_(United_States) (accessed 9/3/2014)

589 *Wikimedia Commons,* s.v. "Abraham Lincoln by Nicholas Shepherd, 1846-crop.jpg," https://commons.wikimedia.org/wiki/File:Abraham_Lincoln_by_Nicholas_Shepherd,_1846-crop.jpg This work is in the public domain in its country of origin and other countries and areas where the copyright term is the author's life plus 70 years or less. United States tag

590*Wikipedia, s.v. "History of the United States Democratic Party,"* http://en.wikipedia.org/wiki/History_of_the_United_States_Democratic_Party(accessed 9/3/2014)

591*Wikipedia, s.v. "Stephen A. Douglas,"*http://en.wikipedia.org/wiki/Stephen_A._Douglas(accessed 9/3/2014)

592 McCarty, *Suppressed Truth,* 46

593 Gordon Leidner, "Abraham Lincoln's great laws of truth, integrity: A long career ruled by honesty," http://www.greatamericanhistory.net/honesty.htm(accessed 9/3/2014)

594 McCarty, *Suppressed Truth,* 46

595*Wikipedia, s.v. "Swing state,"* http://en.wikipedia.org/wiki/Swing_state (accessed 9/3/2014)

596*Wikipedia, s.v. "History of the United States Republican Party,"*http://en.wikipedia.org/wiki/History_of_the_Republican_Party_(United_States) (accessed 9/3/2014)

597 .Leidner, "Abraham Lincoln's great laws of truth.

598 *Wikimedia Commons,* s.v. "Stephen A Douglas - headshot.jpg," https://commons.wikimedia.org/wiki/File:Stephen_A_Douglas_-_headshot.jpg#mw-jump-to-license This work is in the public domain in its country of origin and other countries and areas where the copyright term is the author's life plus 100 years or less.

599 Federer, *America's Quotations,* "Charles Chinquy", 103

600 Charles Chiniquy, *The Finished Wonder,* reprint by Pensacola Christian College, PCC Update, Spring, 2005, *5, 6, 14,* http://www.pcci.edu/update/PDFs/2005/update05-1.pdf (accessed 9/3/2014)

601 Charles Chiniquy, *The Finished Wonder,* (Twentieth Century Edition), 15, http://www.lastdaysbible.org/Testimony-Booklet-Charles-Chiniquy-The-Finished-Wonder-.pdf (accessed 9/3/2014)

602Chiniquy, *Fifty Years,* 623

603 Ibid., 617-623

[604] Hughes, *Secret Terrorists,* 28

[605] *Wikimedia Commons,* s.v. "Abraham Lincoln by Nicholas Shepherd, 1846-crop.jpg," https://commons.wikimedia.org/wiki/File:Abraham_Lincoln_by_Nicholas_Shepherd,_1846-crop.jpg This work is in the public domain in its country of origin and other countries and areas where the copyright term is the author's life plus 70 years or less. Chiniquy, *Fifty Years,* 625

[606] *Wikimedia Commons,* s.v. "Charles Chiniquy Portrait.png," https://commons.wikimedia.org/wiki/File:Charles_Chiniquy_Portrait.png This work is in the public domain in the United States because it was published (or registered with the U.S. Copyright Office) before January 1, 1923.

[607] Ibid., 626

[608] Ibid., 626-627

[609] McCarty, *Suppressed Truth,* 49

[610] Ibid.

[611] Ibid., 46

[612] Ibid., 49

[613] Ibid.

[614] Chiniquy, *Fifty Years,* 664

[615] Ibid.

[616] Ibid., 691-692

[617] Dye, *Adder's Den,* 113

[618] McCarty, *Suppressed Truth,* 9, 244

[619] Ibid., title page

[620] Bradley R. Hoch, *The Lincoln Trail in Pennsylvania: A History and Guide,* (Penn State University Press, 2001), ch.1

[621] *Wikimedia Commons,* s.v. "Seward full face.jpg," https://commons.wikimedia.org/wiki/File:Seward_full_face.jpg This media file is in the public domain in the United States. This applies to U.S. works where the copyright has expired, often because its first publication occurred prior to January 1, 1923.

[622] *Wikimedia Commons,* s.v. "

[623] *Wikimedia Commons,* s.v. "FWSeward2.jpg," https://commons.wikimedia.org/wiki/File:FWSeward2.jpg#mw-jump-to-license This work is in the public domain in its country of origin and other countries and areas where the copyright term is the author's life plus 70 years or less.

[624] Dye, Adder's Den, 8 Winfield Scott, 1862," https://commons.wikimedia.org/wiki/File:Winfield_Scott_by_Fredricks,_1862.jpg#mw-jump-to-license This work is in the public domain in its country of origin and other countries and areas where the copyright term is the author's life plus 70 years or less.

[625] Abraham Lincoln, "Speech in Independence Hall, Philadelphia, Pennsylvania, February 22, 1861," *Collected Works of Abraham Lincoln,* Vol. 4, accessed December 2, 2015, http://quod.lib.umich.edu/l/lincoln/lincoln4/1:376?rgn=div1;view=fulltext

[626] McCarty, *Suppressed Truth,* as quoted, 77

[627] *Wikimedia Commons,* s.v. "John Wilkes Booth-portrait.jpg," https://commons.wikimedia.org/wiki/File:John_Wilkes_Booth-portrait.jpg This work is in the public domain in its country of origin and other countries and areas where the copyright term is the author's life plus 100 years or less.

[628] *Wikipedia,* s.v. "John Wilkes Booth," last modified August 27, 2014, http://en.wikipedia.org/wiki/John_Wilkes_Booth

[629] *Wikipedia,* s.v. "Charles Selby," last modified June 29, 2014, http://en.wikipedia.org/wiki/Charles_Selby

[630] McCarty, *Suppressed Truth,* as quoted, 144-145

[631] Ibid., 145

[632] 1 Thess. 4:16-17, Heb. 9:28, 2 Pet. 3:10, Rev 1:7, John 14:3, Matt. 24:36, Matt. 24:44, John 14:1-3, Acts 1:10-11, Acts 1:11, Jas. 5:7, Matt.16:27, Tit. 2:13, Matt. 24:42-44, Luke 21:27, 1 Thess. 5:2, 1 Thess. 4:13-18, 1 Thess. 5:23, Luke 9:26, Rev. 22:12, Matt. 24:27, Ps.96:13, 1 John 3:2-3, Matt. 25:31-32, Matt. 24:30-31, 2 Thess. 1:5-10, Mark 14:62, Matt. 24:1-51, 2 Thess.2:1-6, Matt.25:13, 2 Tim. 4:1, 1 Thess. 3:13, 1 Cor. 13:8-10, John 19:37, Matt. 26:64

[633] Library of Congress, "One of the people's saints for the calendar of liberty 1852," http://www.loc.gov/pictures/item/2008661536/ This media file is in the public domain in the United States. This applies to U.S. works where the copyright has expired, often because its first publication occurred prior to January 1, 1923.

[634] *Wikipedia,* s.v. "James Buchanan," last modified September 1, 2014, http://en.wikipedia.org/wiki/James_Buchanan

[635] Ibid.

[636] *Wikimedia Commons*, s.v. "James Buchanan.jpg," https://commons.wikimedia.org/wiki/File:James_Buchanan.jpg#mw-jump-to-license This work is in the public domain in its country of origin and other countries and areas where the copyright term is the author's life plus 70 years or less.

[637] Dye, *Adder's Den,* 89

[638] McCarty, *Suppressed Truth,* 61

[639] *Wikipedia,*s.v. "James Buchanan"

[640] McCarty, *Suppressed Truth,* as quoted, 62

[641] *Wikipedia*, s.v. "Isaac Toucey," last modified July 29, 2014,http://en.wikipedia.org/wiki/Isaac_Toucey

[642] Dye, Adder's Den, 110

[643] *Wikipedia,*s.v. "John B. Floyd," last modified August 25, 2014, http://en.wikipedia.org/wiki/John_B._Floyd

[644] Dye, *Adder's Den,* 110

[645] *Wikimedia Commons,* s.v. "Buchanan Cabinet.jpg," https://commons.wikimedia.org/wiki/File:Buchanan_Cabinet.jpg This media file is in the public domain in the United States. This applies to U.S. works where the copyright has expired, often because its first publication occurred prior to January 1, 1923.

[646] Ibid., 112

[647] Ibid.

[648] Ibid., 67

[649] Ibid., 112

[650] "Abraham Lincolns Election: The Election of Abraham into Office as the 16th President ," AbrahamLincolns.com, accessed September 3, 2014, http://abrahamlincolns.com/abraham-lincolns-election

[651] Jones, *Prophetic History,* 17

[652] *American Civil War History,* accessed September 3, 2014, http://www.charleston1865.com/1865history.asp

[653] Thomas P. Kittell, *The History of the Great Rebellion,* (Cincinnati: L. Stebbins, 1865), 18

[654] Marshall and Manuel, *Sounding Trumpet,* 11

[655] *Wikipedia*, s.v. "Jefferson Davis+," last modified November 27, 2014, http://en.wikipedia.org/wiki/Jefferson_Davis

[656] Getler and Brewer, *Rebel Gold,* 70

[657] *Wikimedia Commons,* s.v. "President-Jefferson-Davis.jpg," https://commons.wikimedia.org/wiki/File:President-Jefferson-Davis.jpg This work is in the public domain in its country of origin and other countries and areas where the copyright term is the author's life plus 100 years or less.

[658] *Wikipedia,* s.v. "James Murray Mason," last modified July 30, 2014, http://en.wikipedia.org/wiki/James_Murray_Mason

[659] John A. Logan, *The Great Conspiracy,*(New York, A. R. Hart & Co., Publishers, 1886), 34

[660] *Wikimedia Commons*, s.v. "JMMason.jpg," https://commons.wikimedia.org/wiki/File:JMMason.jpg#mw-jump-to-license This work is in the public domain in its country of origin and other countries and areas where the copyright term is the author's life plus 100 years or less.

[661] Kennedy, Cohen, Baily, *The American Pageant Volume I: To 1877,* (Boston, Wadsworth, 2010), 373

[662] Des Griffin, *Descent Into Slavery?,* chapter 5

[663] Dye, *Adder's Den,*56

[664] Ibid., 27

[665] *The Illustrated University History,*(1878), p. 504 as quoted in Des Griffin, *Descent Into Slavery,* "The Rothschild Dynasty," accessed September 3, 2014, http://www.biblebelievers.org.au/slavery.htm

[666] Chiniquy, *Fifty Years* 713-714

[667] *The Illustrated University History*, 1878, p. 504,

[668] Logan, *Great Conspiracy,* 117-118

[669] Library of Congress, "South Carolina's 'ultimatum,'" http://www.loc.gov/pictures/item/2003674566/ No known restrictions on publication.

[670] Journal of the Senate of The United States of America, "MONDAY, March 4, 1861," pp. 309-409, http://memory.loc.gov/cgi-bin/query/r?ammem/hlaw:@field(DOCID+@lit(sj05269)): (accessed 11/1/2014)

[671] "Assassination of President Lincoln," with cited references including: Chiniquy, Charles. *Fifty Years in the "church" of Rome,* Chick Pub., 1982; Davis, Varina. *Jefferson Davis a Memoir* (in 2 volumes), The Nautical & Aviation Pub. Co., Baltimore, Maryland, reprinted 1990; Harris, T. M. *A History of the Great Conspiracy,* Patriot Pub. Co., Boston, 1890; Manhattan, Avro. *Vatican Moscow Washington Alliance,* Chick Pub., Chino, CA, 1982; McLoughlin, Emmett (ex-priest) *An Inquiry into the Assassination of Lincoln,* Citadel Press, Secaucus, NJ, 1977; Tyrner-Tyrnaer, *A. R. Lincoln and the Emperors*, London, 1962.; Woldman, Albert A. *Lincoln and the Russians, World Pub., Cleveland & New York, 1952;* Reformation.org, http://www.reformation.org/lincoln.html (accessed 9/3/2014)

[672] "American Civil War History: Union and Confederate Army of Infantry, Cavalry, and Artillery," accessed September 3, 2014, http://thomaslegion.net/americancivilwar/civilwarmilitaryarmyunionconfederate.html

[673] *Wikimedia Commons*, s.v. "Gen. Pierre Gustave Toutant de Beauregard, C.S.A - NARA - 528596.jpg," https://commons.wikimedia.org/wiki/File:Gen._Pierre_Gustave_Toutant_de_Beauregard,_C.S.A_-_NARA_-_528596.jpg#mw-jump-to-license This work is in the public domain in the United States because it is a work prepared by an officer or employee of the United States Government as part of that person's official duties under the terms of Title 17, Chapter 1, Section 105 of the US Code.

[674] Getler and Brewer, *Rebel Gold,* 58

[675] McCarty, *Suppressed Truth,* 77

[676] Reid Mitchell, *The American Civil War 1861-1865,* (New York: Routledge, 2013), 41

[677] McCarty, *Suppressed Truth,* 84-85

[678] *Wikipedia,*s.v. "Pope Pius IX," last modified September 2, 2014,http://en.wikipedia.org/wiki/Pope_Pius_IX

[679] *Wikimedia Commons*, s.v. "Pio9pepeking.jpg," https://en.wikipedia.org/wiki/File:Pio9pepeking.jpg#mw-jump-to-license This file is in the public domain because its copyright has expired in the United States and those countries with a copyright term of no more than the life of the author plus 100 years.

[680] *Wikipedia*, s.v. "Pope Pius IX," last edited January 2, 2017, https://en.m.wikipedia.org/wiki/Pope_Pius_IX

[681] *Wikipedia,*s.v. "de facto," last modified July 9, 2014, http://en.wikipedia.org/wiki/De_facto

[682] Chinquy, *Fifty Years,* 700

[683] *Wikipedia*, s.v. "Papal Infallibility," last modified July 20, 2014,http://en.wikipedia.org/wiki/Papal_infallibility

[684] *Wikipedia*, s.v. "Pope Pius IX," last modified September 2, 2014, http://en.wikipedia.org/wiki/Pope_Pius_IX

[685] Presented by Linda Fluharty,"Brevet Major General Thomas Maley Harris," http://www.lindapages.com/cwar/gen-tmharris.htm as sourced from Theodore F. Lang *Loyal West Virginia, 1861-1865*, (Deutsch Publishing Co., 1895) 324-326. This media file is in the public domain in the United States. This applies to U.S. works where the copyright has expired, often because its first publication occurred prior to January 1, 1923.

[686] *Wikipedia*, s.v. "Thomas Maley Harris," last modified November 30, 2014,http://en.wikipedia.org/wiki/Thomas_Maley_Harris

[687] Jim Marrs, *Rule by Secrecy: The Hidden History that Connects the Trilateral Commission, the Freemasons and the Great Pyramids,* (Harper-Collins Publishers, 2000) 68

[688] James G. Blaine, *Political Discussions: Legislative, Diplomatic and Popular: 1856-1886*, (Norwich: The Henry Bill Publishing Co, 1887) 397-398

[689] Wharton Barker, "The Secret of Russia's Friendship," *The Independent, A Weekly Magazine,* Vol. 56, January to June, 1904, (New York), 648

[690] Webster Griffin Tarpley, Ph.D., "American Banker Wharton Barker's First-Person Account Confirms: Russian Tsar Alexander II Was Ready for War with Britain and France in 1862-1863 to Defend Lincoln and the Union – Americans "Will Understand," September 23, 2013, accessed September 3, 2014, http://tarpley.net/2013/09/23/american-banker-wharton-barkers-first-person-account-confirms-russian-tsar-alexander-ii-was-ready-for-war-with-britain-and-france-in-1862-1863-to-defend-lincoln-and-the-union-americans-will-und/

[691] *Wikimedia Commons,* s.v. "Alexander II of Russia photo.jpg," https://commons.wikimedia.org/wiki/File:Alexander_II_of_Russia_photo.jpg This work is in the public domain in its country of origin and other countries and areas where the copyright term is the author's life plus 70 years or less.

[692] *Wikimedia Commons*, s.v. "Wharton Barker cph.3b20311.jpg," https://commons.wikimedia.org/wiki/File:Wharton_Barker_cph.3b20311.jpg#mw-jump-to-license This work is in the public domain in the United States because it was published (or registered with the U.S. Copyright Office) before January 1, 1923.

[693] Darryl Eberhart, "Who Were Czars Alexander I and Alexander II of Russia?," *ETI & TTT Newsletters,* January 18, 2011, http://www.toughissues.org/whowereczars.htm

[694] Dye, *Adder's Den, 119*

[695] "The Emancipation Proclamation," National Archives & Records Administration, accessed September 3, 2014, http://www.archives.gov/exhibits/featured_documents/emancipation_proclamation/

[696] Library of Congress, "The first reading of the Emancipation Proclamation before the cabinet," http://www.loc.gov/pictures/item/96521764/ No known restrictions on publication.

[697] *Wikimedia Commons*, s.v. "Abraham Lincoln giving his second Inaugural Address (4 March 1865).jpg," https://commons.wikimedia.org/wiki/File:Abraham_Lincoln_giving_his_second_Inaugural_Address_(4_March_1865).jpg This

media file is in the <u>public domain</u> in the <u>United States.</u> This applies to U.S. works where the copyright has expired, often because its <u>first publication</u> occurred prior to January 1, 1923.

[698] Abraham Lincoln, *Second Inaugural Address of Abraham Lincoln,* accessed at *The Avalon Project,* Lillian Goldman Law Library, Yale Law School, accessed September 3, 2014, http://avalon.law.yale.edu/19th_century/lincoln2.asp

[699] Library of Congress, "The outbreak of the rebellion in the United States 1861," http://www.loc.gov/item/2004665366/#about-this-item No known restrictions on publication.

[700]*Wikipedia,*s.v. "Origins of the American Civil War," last modified September 3, 2014, http://en.wikipedia.org/wiki/Origins_of_the_American_Civil_War

[701]Dye, *Adder's Den,* 108

[702]*Wikipedia,*s.v. "Origins of the American Civil War," last modified September 3, 2014, http://en.wikipedia.org/wiki/Origins_of_the_American_Civil_War

[703] *Wikimedia Commons,* s.v. "Americana Civil War in America - Map 1.jpg," https://commons.wikimedia.org/wiki/File:Americana_Civil_War_in_America_-_Map_1.jpg This work is in the <u>public domain</u> in the United States because it was published (or registered with the U.S. Copyright Office) before January 1, 1923.

[704]Ibid.

[705] *Wikimedia Commons,* s.v. "A Slave Auction.jpg," Author Austa Malinda French (1810-1880), https://commons.wikimedia.org/wiki/File:A_Slave_Auction.jpg
This media file is in the <u>public domain</u> in the <u>United States</u>. This applies to U.S. works where the copyright has expired, often because its first <u>publication</u> occurred prior to January 1, 1923.

[706]Getler and Brewer, *Rebel Gold,* 66

[707] Kennedy, Cohen, and Baily, *American Pageant,* 373

[708] Logan, *Great Conspiracy,* 9-10

[709]"Letter to John Holmes," *The U.S. Constitution: A Reader,* .ed Hillsdale College Politics Faculty, accessed September 3, 2014, http://www.constitutionreader.com/searchresults.engz?uq=*&c=%5Btitle-taxonomy%5D%3D%22Roots%20of%20the%20Slavery%20Crisis%09Letter%20to%20John%20Holmes%22

[710] Dr. Paul Rahe, "Democracy: American Promise and its Dangers," *History 102: American Heritage—From Colonial Settlement to the Reagan Revolution*, accessed August 15, 2013, http://online.hillsdale.edu/page.aspx?pid=1785

[711]*Wikipedia,*s.v. "Second Party System*,"* last modified on July 24, 2014, http://en.wikipedia.org/wiki/Second_Party_System

[712]Wisconsin Historical Society, *Wisconsin and the Republican Party,* accessed September 3, 2014, http://www.wisconsinhistory.org/turningpoints/tp-022/?action=more_essay

[713] *Wikimedia Commons,* s.v. "Alexander Stephens.jpg," https://commons.wikimedia.org/wiki/File:Alexander_Stephens.jpg
This media file is in the <u>public domain</u> in the United States. This applies to U.S. works where the copyright has expired, often because its first publication occurred prior to January 1, 1923.

[714]*Wikipedia,*s.v. "Alexander H. Stephens," last modified August 13, 2014, http://en.wikipedia.org/wiki/Alexander_H._Stephens
This media file is in the public domain in the United States. This applies to U.S. works where the copyright has expired, often because its first publication occurred prior to January 1, 1923.

[715]Dye, Adder's Den, 122-123

[716] *Wikipedia,* s.v. "Howell Cobb," as photographed by Matthew Brady, This image is available from the United States Library of Congress's Prints and Photographs division under the digital ID cph.3c10081. https://en.wikipedia.org/wiki/Howell_Cobb#/media/File:Howell_Cobb-crop.jpg
This work is in the <u>public domain</u> in its country of origin and other countries and areas where the copyright term is the author's life plus 100 years or less. <u>United States domain tag.</u>
Library of Congress, [Howell Cobb, half-length portrait, facing front], http://www.loc.gov/item/2004663908/

[717] *Wikimedia Commons,* s.v. "Postbellum-Cobb.jpg," https://commons.wikimedia.org/wiki/File:Postbellum-Cobb.jpg#mw-jump-to-license This work is from the Brady-Handy collection at the Library of Congress. According to the library, there are no known copyright restrictions on the use of this work.
Mathew Brady died in 1896 and Levin C. Handy died in 1932. Photographs in this collection are in the public domain in the US as works published before 1923 or as unpublished works whose copyright term has expired (life of author + 70 years).

[718]*Wikipedia,*s.v. "Howell Cobb," last modified September 2, 2014, http://en.wikipedia.org/wiki/Howell_Cobb

[719]"Statutes of The Supreme Council of the Thirty-third Degree," *Ancient & Accepted Scottish Rite of Freemasonry, S.J., U.S.A.*, p. 126, August, 2011, http://scottishrite.org/wp-content/uploads/2011/12/statutes_2011.pdf

[720]*Albert Pike and the Scottish Rite,* accessed September 3, 2014,http://www.nwotoday.com/the-new-world-orders-history/freemasonry-global-level-illumination/albert-pike-and-the-scottish-rites

[721] Getler and Brewer, *Rebel Gold,*. 58

[722] Anton Chaitkin, *The Scottish Rite's KKK Project*, from the speech delivered by Mr. Chaitkin at the Labor Day weekend conference of the Schiller Institute in suburban Washington, D.C, accessed September 3, 2014, http://itwasjohnson.impiousdigest.com/kkkmas.htm

[723] Dye, *Adder's Den,* 123

[724] Wikipedia, *De Bow's Review,* last modified August 2, 2014, http://en.wikipedia.org/wiki/De_Bow's_Review (accessed 9/3/2014)

[725] Dye, *Adder's Den,* 125

[726] Ibid.

[727] *Wikimedia Commons*, s.v. "BenjaminMPalmerOld.jpg," https://commons.wikimedia.org/wiki/File:BenjaminMPalmerOld.jpg#mw-jump-to-license This media file is in the public domain in the United States. This applies to U.S. works where the copyright has expired, often because its first publication occurred prior to January 1, 1923.

[728] *Wikipedia,* s.v. "Benjamin M. Palmer," last modified August 21, 2014, http://en.wikipedia.org/wiki/Benjamin_M._Palmer

[729] Dye, *Adder's Den,* 122

[730] Bruce Gourley, "Baptists and the American Civil War: January 27, 1861,"Baptists and the American Civil War, In their Own Words, January 27, 2011, http://www.civilwarbaptists.com/thisdayinhistory/1861-january-27/

[731] Bruce Gourley, "Yes, It Was About Slavery…," Baptists and the American Civil War, In their Own Words, December 24, 2010, http://www.civilwarbaptists.com/featured/slavery/

[732] *Wikimedia Commons*, s.v. "Clay.png," https://commons.wikimedia.org/wiki/File:Clay.png This media file is in the public domain in the United States. This applies to U.S. works where the copyright has expired, often because its first publication occurred prior to January 1, 1923.

[733] Dr. Paul Rahe, "Democracy: American Promise and its Dangers," History 102: American Heritage—From Colonial Settlement to the Reagan Revolution, accessed August 15, 2013, http://online.hillsdale.edu/page.aspx?pid=1785

[734] *Wikimedia Commons,* s.v. "Gilbert Stuart - John Quincy Adams - Google Art Project.jpg," https://commons.wikimedia.org/wiki/File:Gilbert_Stuart_-_John_Quincy_Adams_-_Google_Art_Project.jpg The author died in 1828, so this work is in the public domain in its country of origin and other countries and areas where the copyright term is the author's life plus 100 years or less.

[735] Dr. Paul Rahe, "Democracy: American Promise and its Dangers," Supplementary Readings and Lecture Quotes, accessed August 15, 2013, http://online.hillsdale.edu/document.doc?id=454

[736] Tim Unsworth, "Catholics move to the center of the bench," National Catholic Reporter, January 24, 2013, http://www.natcath.org/NCR_Online/archives/012403/012403k.htm

[737] Ibid.

[738] Dye, *Adder's Den,* 89

[739] "Dred Scott case: the Supreme Court decision," PBS/Africans in America, accessed September 3, 2014, http://www.pbs.org/wgbh/aia/part4/4h2933.html

[740] Library of Congress, Roger B. Taney - Brady-Handy.jpg," https://commons.wikimedia.org/wiki/File:Roger_B._Taney_-_Brady-Handy.jpg No known restrictions on publication.

[741] *Wikimedia Commons,* s.v. "DredScott.jpg," https://commons.wikimedia.org/wiki/File:DredScott.jpg This work is in the public domain in the United States because it was published (or registered with the U.S. Copyright Office) before January 1, 1923.

[742] Ibid.

[743] Ibid.

[744] Wayne B. Holstad, J.D., *Leviticus v. Leviathan Choosing Our Sovereign,* (St. Paul: Alethos Press LLC, 2004), 102

[745] Abraham Lincoln, "Fragment on the Constitution and the Union, c. January, 1861," *Collected Works of Abraham Lincoln.* Vol. 4, accessed September 3, 2014, http://quod.lib.umich.edu/l/lincoln/lincoln4/1:264?rgn=div1;view=fulltext

[746] Prof. Kevin Portteus, "Abraham Lincoln and the Constitution," Constitution 101: The Meaning and History of the Constitution, accessed September 3, 2014, https://online.hillsdale.edu/document.doc?id=279

[747] *Wikimedia Commons*, s.v. "Gordon, scourged back, NPG, 1863.jpg," https://commons.wikimedia.org/wiki/File:Gordon,_scourged_back,_NPG,_1863.jpg#mw-jump-to-license This work is in the public domain in its country of origin and other countries and areas where the copyright term is the author's life plus 100 years or less.

[748] *Wikipedia,* s.v. "David W. Blight," last modified February 15, 2014, http://en.wikipedia.org/wiki/David_W._Blight

[749] "The Abolitionists," American Experience documentary [at 1:52:00] quote by Historian David W. Blight, accessed November 1, 2014, http://www.pbs.org/wgbh/americanexperience/films/abolitionists/player/

[750] Kennedy, Cohen, and Baily, *American Pageant*, 412

[751] "The Trial of John Brown: The Secret Six: Samuel G. Howe Testimony," accessed November 1, 2014, http://law2.umkc.edu/faculty/projects/ftrials/johnbrown/secretsixdetails.html

[752] *Wikipedia*,s.v. "The Secret Six," last modified June 7, 2014,http://en.wikipedia.org/wiki/Secret_Six (accessed 11/1/2014)

[753] *Wikimedia Commons,* s.v. "TWHigginson.jpg," https://commons.wikimedia.org/wiki/File:TWHigginson.jpg#mw-jump-to-license This work is in the public domain in its country of origin and other countries and areas where the copyright term is the author's life plus 70 years or less.

[754] *Wikimedia Commons*, s.v. "Samuel Gridley Howe.jpg," https://commons.wikimedia.org/wiki/File:Samuel_Gridley_Howe.jpg#mw-jump-to-license This work is in the public domain in its country of origin and other countries and areas where the copyright term is the author's life plus 70 years or less.

[755] *Wikimedia Commons*, s.v. "Theodore Parker BPL c1855-crop.jpg," https://commons.wikimedia.org/wiki/File:Theodore_Parker_BPL_c1855-crop.jpg#mw-jump-to-license This media file is in the public domain in the United States. This applies to U.S. works where the copyright has expired, often because its first publication occurred prior to January 1, 1923.

[756] *Wikimedia Commons*, s.v. "Franklin Benjamin Sanborn.jpg," https://commons.wikimedia.org/wiki/File:Franklin_Benjamin_Sanborn.jpg#mw-jump-to-license This work is in the public domain in its country of origin and other countries and areas where the copyright term is the author's life plus 70 years or less.

[757] Library of Congress, "Hon. Gerrit Smith of N.Y.," http://www.loc.gov/pictures/item/brh2003004625/PP/ No known restrictions on publication.

[758] *Wikimedia Commons*, s.v. "George Luther Stearns.jpg," https://commons.wikimedia.org/wiki/File:George_Luther_Stearns.jpg#mw-jump-to-license This work is in the public domain in its country of origin and other countries and areas where the copyright term is the author's life plus 70 years or less.

[759] *The American Experience,*" The Secret Six," accessed November 1, 2014, http://www.pbs.org/wgbh/amex/brown/peopleevents/pande06.html

[760] *Wikimedia Commons,* s.v. "

[761] "Facts about John Brown, an Abolitionist," History Net, accessed November 1, 2014, http://www.historynet.com/john-brown

[762] Ibid. John Brown by Southworth & Hawes, 1856.png," https://commons.wikimedia.org/wiki/File:John_Brown_by_Southworth_%26_Hawes,_1856.png This media file is in the public domain in the United States. This applies to U.S. works where the copyright has expired, often because its first publication occurred prior to January 1, 1923.

[763] "II Awakenings and Enlightenments," *American Heritage A Reader,* ed. The Hillsdale College History Faculty, (Hillsdale: Hillsdale College Press, 2011), 369

[764] "Facts about John Brown, an Abolitionist," History Net.

[765] *Wikimedia Commons*, s.v. "Southern Chivalry.jpg," https://commons.wikimedia.org/wiki/File:Southern_Chivalry.jpg This work is in the public domain in its country of origin and other countries and areas where the copyright term is the author's life plus 100 years or less.

[766] Dye, *Adder's Den,* 80

[767] Ibid., 67

[768] *Facts about John Brown, an Abolitionist,* accessed November 1, 2014, http://www.historynet.com/john-brown

[769] *Wikipedia*,s.v. "Harriet Tubman," last modified October 12, 2014,http://en.wikipedia.org/wiki/Harriet_Tubman

[770] *Wikipedia,* s.v. "Frederick Douglass," last modified October 28, 2014, http://en.wikipedia.org/wiki/Frederick_Douglass

[771] *Wikimedia Commons*, s.v. "Harriet Tubman by Squyer, NPG, c1885.jpg," https://commons.wikimedia.org/wiki/File:Harriet_Tubman_by_Squyer,_NPG,_c1885.jpg This media file is in the public domain in the United States. This applies to U.S. works where the copyright has expired, often because its first publication occurred prior to January 1, 1923.

[772] *Wikimedia Commons*, s.v. "Frederick Douglass by Samuel J Miller, 1847-52.png," https://commons.wikimedia.org/wiki/File:Frederick_Douglass_by_Samuel_J_Miller,_1847-52.png This media file is in the public domain in the United States. This applies to U.S. works where the copyright has expired, often because its first publication occurred prior to January 1, 1923.

[773] *Raid on Harper's Ferry,* accessed November 1, 2014, http://www.historynet.com/raid-on-harpers-ferry

[774] Ibid.

[775] R. J. Rushdoony, "The Coming of the Civil War," *American History to 1865,* accessed November 1, 2014, http://chalcedon.edu/research/audio/?query=RR144R31.mp3

[776] Sharon Eolis, *John Brown called her 'General Tubman,'* March 20, 2013, http://www.workers.org/articles/2013/03/20/john-brown-called-her-general-tubman/

[777] Jean M. Humez, *Harriet Tubman: The Life and the Life Stories,* (Madison: The University of Wisconsin Press, 2003), 40

[778] "Abraham Lincoln, Cooper Union Address, February 27, 1860," sourced from "The Address of the Hon. Abraham Lincoln...Delivered at Cooper Institute" (New York: George F. Nesbitt & Co., 1860), 21, 23, 24, 25, accessed November 1, 2014, http://www.digitalhistory.uh.edu/active_learning/explorations/brown/public_lincoln.cfm

[779] *Wikimedia Commons,* s.v. "John brown interior engine house.jpg," https://commons.wikimedia.org/wiki/File:John_brown_interior_engine_house.jpg This work is in the public domain in its country of origin and other countries and areas where the copyright term is the author's life plus 70 years or less.

[780] *Wikipedia,* s.v. "Abraham Lincoln," last modified September 2, 2014, http://en.wikipedia.org/wiki/Abraham_Lincoln

[781] David C. Keehn, *Knights of the Golden Circle: Secret Empire, Southern Secession, Civil War*, (Louisiana State University Press, 2013), 180

[782] McCarty, *Suppressed Truth,* 134

[783] *Wikimedia Commons,* s.v. "Lincolnassassination.jpg," https://commons.wikimedia.org/wiki/File:Lincolnassassination.jpg This media file is in the public domain in the United States. This applies to U.S. works where the copyright has expired, often because its first publication occurred prior to January 1, 1923.

[784] *Wikimedia Commons,* s.v. "Fords Theatre.jpg," https://commons.wikimedia.org/wiki/File:Fords_Theatre.jpg This work is in the public domain in its country of origin and other countries and areas where the copyright term is the author's life plus 100 years or less.

[785] "1861: William Seward is named secretary of state," Jan. 10 This Day in History, accessed September 2, 2014, http://www.history.com/this-day-in-history/william-seward-named-secretary-of-state

[786] McCarty, *Suppressed Truth,* as quoted, 134, 122

[787] Ibid., 136

[788] *An Authentic Exposition of the "K.G.C." "Knights of the Golden Circle;" or, A History of Secession 1834 to 1861, Illustrated. By a member of the Order,* (Indianapolis, Ind., C. O. Perrine, 1861) title page

[789] Ibid., 226-227

[790] Ibid., 210

[791] David O. Stewart, "The Family Plot to Kill Lincoln," *Smithsonian Magazine,* August 28, 2013, http://www.smithsonianmag.com/history/the-family-plot-to-kill-lincoln-2093807/?no-ist

[792] *Wikimedia Commons,* s.v. "John Surratt.jpg," https://commons.wikimedia.org/wiki/File:John_Surratt.jpg This work is in the public domain in its country of origin and other countries and areas where the copyright term is the author's life plus 70 years or less. United States public domain tag

[793] Darryl Eberhart, "The Jesuit Order – The Society of Jesus," *ETI & TTT Newsletters,* Issue #81, ToughIssues.org, December 18, 2009, accessed December 3, 2015, http://www.archive-org-2014.com/org/t/2014-06-03_4069549/

[794] David C. Keehn, *Knights of the Golden Circle: Secret Empire, Southern Secession, Civil War,* (Louisiana State University Press, 2013), 1-2

[795] *Journal of the House of Representatives of the United States, 1860-1861,* "SATURDAY, March 2, 1861," p 474, accessed September 2, 2014, http://memory.loc.gov/cgi-bin/query/r?ammem/hlaw:@field(DOCID+@lit(hj05765))

[796] *Journal of the Senate of the United States of America, 1789-1873,* "THURSDAY, March 28, 1861," pp 431-433, accessed September 2, 2014, http://memory.loc.gov/cgi-bin/query/r?ammem/hlaw:@field(DOCID+@lit(sj05289))

[797] James Buchanan: "Proclamation," February 11, 1861. Online by Gerhard Peters and John T. Woolley, The American Presidency Project., accessed October 15, 2015, http://www.presidency.ucsb.edu/ws/?pid=68458

[798] *American Heritage Dictionary,* "rump," https://ahdictionary.com/word/search.html?q=rump

[799] *Journal of the Senate of the United States of America, 1789-1873,* "THURSDAY, March 28, 1861," pp 431-433

[800] *Journal of the House of Representatives of the United States, 1860-1861,* "SATURDAY, March 2, 1861,"

[801] *Wikipedia,* s.v. "Adjournment sine die," last modified August 26, 2014, http://en.wikipedia.org/wiki/Adjournment_sine_die

[802] *TheFreeDictionary.com,* s.v. "sine die," accessed November 1, 2014, http://www.thefreedictionary.com/sine+die

[803] *Journal of the Senate of the United States of America,* "MONDAY, March 4, 1861," pp 399-409, accessed September 2, 2014, http://memory.loc.gov/cgi-bin/query/r?ammem/hlaw:@field(DOCID+@lit(sj05269)):

[804] Dye, *Adder's Den,* 108

[805] "Article 4, Section 4," The Founders Constitution, accessed November 1, 2014, http://press-pubs.uchicago.edu/founders/tocs/a4_4.html

[806] *Wikimedia Commons*, s.v. "George Peter Alexander Healy - James Buchanan - Google Art Project.jpg," https://commons.wikimedia.org/wiki/File:George_Peter_Alexander_Healy_-_James_Buchanan_-_Google_Art_Project.jpg The author died in 1894, so this work is in the public domain in its country of origin and other countries and areas where the copyright term is the author's life plus 100 years or less.

[807] *Wikimedia Commons*, s.v. "Abraham Lincoln O-55, 1861-crop.jpg," https://commons.wikimedia.org/wiki/File:Abraham_Lincoln_O-55,_1861-crop.jpg This work is in the public domain in its country of origin and other countries and areas where the copyright term is the author's life plus 70 years or less.

[808] Abraham Lincoln: "Proclamation 80 - Calling Forth the Militia and Convening an Extra Session of Congress," April 15, 1861. Online by Gerhard Peters and John T. Woolley, The American Presidency Project., accessed October 15, 2014, http://www.presidency.ucsb.edu/ws/?pid=70077

[809] "Article I, Section 8, Clause 11," The Founders Constitution, accessed November 1, 2014, http://press-pubs.uchicago.edu/founders/tocs/a1_8_11.html

[810] "Militia Act of 1792,"Constitution Society, accessed November 1, 2014, http://www.constitution.org/mil/mil_act_1792.htm

[811] *Act of Feb 28, 1795, 1 Stat 424*, accessed December 3, 2015, http://csa.systekproof.com/wp-content/uploads/2014/03/CHAP.-XXXVI.%E2%80%94An-Act-to-provide-for-calling-forth-the-Militia-to-execute-the-laws-of-the4.pdf

[812] Prof. Mackubin Owens, *The Heritage Guide to the Constitution*," Militia Clause," accessed September 2, 2014, http://www.heritage.org/constitution#!/articles/1/essays/55/militia-clause

[813] McCarty, *Suppressed Truth,* 62

[814] Bruce A. Ragsdale, *Ex parte Merryman and Debates on Civil Liberties During the Civil War,* (Federal Judicial Center, Federal Judicial History Office, 2007), 1 accessed December 19, 2014, online at http://www.fjc.gov/history/home.nsf/page/tu_merryman_background.html

[815] Abraham Lincoln: "Executive Order," April 25, 1861. Online by Gerhard Peters and John T. Woolley, The American Presidency Project. , accessed December 30, 2014, http://www.presidency.ucsb.edu/ws/?pid=70145

[816] Abraham Lincoln: "Executive Order," April 27, 1861. Online by Gerhard Peters and John T. Woolley, The American Presidency Project., accessed October 15, 2014, http://www.presidency.ucsb.edu/ws/?pid=69748

[817] "Presidential Proclamations," The American Presidency Project, accessed November 2, 2014, http://www.presidency.ucsb.edu/proclamations.php?year=1789&Submit=DISPLAY

[818] *The Free Dictionary,* s.v. "Habeas Corpus," accessed December 19, 2014, http://legal-dictionary.thefreedictionary.com/writ+of+habeas+corpus

[819] "FAQ: What is Habeas Corpus," Center for Constitutional Rights, last modified January 11, 2010, http://ccrjustice.org/learn-more/faqs/faqs%3A-what-habeas-corpus

[820] "Article 1, Section 9, Clause 2," The Founders' Constitution, accessed December 19, 2014, http://press-pubs.uchicago.edu/founders/tocs/a1_9_2.html

[821] *Wikimedia Commons*, S.V. "T Jefferson by Charles Willson Peale 1791 2.jpg," https://commons.wikimedia.org/wiki/File:T_Jefferson_by_Charles_Willson_Peale_1791_2.jpg#mw-jump-to-license This work is in the public domain in its country of origin and other countries and areas where the copyright term is the author's life plus 100 years or less.

[822] *Wikimedia Commons*, s.v., "James Madison, by Charles Willson Peale, 1783.png," https://commons.wikimedia.org/wiki/File:James_Madison,_by_Charles_Willson_Peale,_1783.png This media file is in the public domain in the United States. This applies to U.S. works where the copyright has expired, often because its first publication occurred prior to January 1, 1923.

[823] "Rights, Thomas Jefferson to James Madison, 31 July 1788, *Papers 13:442—43,*" The Founders' Constitution, accessed November 24, 2015, http://press-pubs.uchicago.edu/founders/documents/v1ch14s46.html

[824] *Wikipedia*, s.v. "Aaron Burr, last modified December18, 2014,http://en.wikipedia.org/wiki/Aaron_Burr

[825] *Wikimedia Commons*, s.v. "Vanderlyn Burr.jpg," https://commons.wikimedia.org/wiki/File:Vanderlyn_Burr.jpg This work is in the public domain in its country of origin and other countries and areas where the copyright term is the author's life plus 100 years or less. United States public domain tag

[826] *Wikimedia Commons,* s.v. "Alexander Hamilton portrait by John Trumbull 1806.jpg," https://commons.wikimedia.org/wiki/File:Alexander_Hamilton_portrait_by_John_Trumbull_1806.jpg This work is in the public domain in its country of origin and other countries and areas where the copyright term is the author's life plus 100 years or less. United States public domain tag

[827] *Wikipedia,*s.v. "Burr conspiracy," last modified October 20, 2014, http://en.wikipedia.org/wiki/Burr_conspiracy

[828] *Wikimedia Commons*, s.v. "Louisiana Purchase.png," https://commons.wikimedia.org/wiki/File:Louisiana_Purchase.png Permission granted, Author: William Morris

[829] Charles Warren, *The Supreme Court in United States History 1789-1821, Vol. I,* (Boston: Little, Brown, and Company, 1922), 301-302

[830] *Wikipedia,*s.v. "Burr conspiracy."

[831] *Wikimedia Commons*, s.v. "James Wilkinson.jpg," https://commons.wikimedia.org/wiki/File:James_Wilkinson.jpg This image is in the public domain because it contains materials that originally came from the United States Army Center of Military History, subject to the following qualification.

[832] *Wikipedia,*s.v. "James Wilkinson," last modified December 12, 2014, http://en.wikipedia.org/wiki/James_Wilkinson This work is in the public domain in its country of origin and other countries and areas where the copyright term is the author's life plus 100 years or less. United States public domain tag

[833] Ibid.

[834] Charles Warren, *The Supreme Court in United States History 1789-1821, Vol. I,* (Boston: Little, Brown, and Company, 1922), 302

[835] Ibid., 302-303

[836] Ibid., 303

[837] "Article 1, Section 9, Clause 2: House of Representatives, Suspension of the Habeas Corpus, 26 Jan. 1807Annals 16:402, 403--15, 422--24," The Founder's Constitution accessed December 19, 2014, http://press-pubs.uchicago.edu/founders/documents/a1_9_2s13.html (accessed 12/19/2014)

[838] *Wikipedia,*s.v. "Salus populi suprema lex esto," last modified June 3, 2015,http://en.wikipedia.org/wiki/Salus_populi_suprema_lex_esto

[839] *Wikimedia Commons*, s.v. "Official Presidential portrait of Thomas Jefferson (by Rembrandt Peale, 1800).jpg," https://commons.wikimedia.org/wiki/File:Official_Presidential_portrait_of_Thomas_Jefferson_(by_Rembrandt_Peale_1800).jpg *This work is in the public domain in the United States because it is a work prepared by an officer or employee of the United States Government as part of that person's official duties* under the terms of Title 17, Chapter 1, Section 105 of the US Code.

[840] *Wikimedia Commons*, s.v. "John Marshall by Henry Inman, 1832.jpg," https://commons.wikimedia.org/wiki/File:John_Marshall_by_Henry_Inman,_1832.jpg This work is in the public domain in its country of origin and other countries and areas where the copyright term is the author's life plus 100 years or less. United States public domain tag

[841] *Wikipedia,*s.v. "Aaron Burr."

[842] "James Wilkinson," PBS/The Duel, accessed December 28, 2014, http://www.pbs.org/wgbh/amex/duel/peopleevents/pande13.html

[843] Bruce A. Ragsdale, *Ex parte Merryman and Debates on Civil Liberties During the Civil War,* (Federal Judicial Center, Federal Judicial History Office, 2007), 1 http://www.fjc.gov/history/home.nsf/page/tu_merryman_background.html (accessed 12/19/2014)

[844] Abraham Lincoln: "Executive Order," April 25, 1861. Online by Gerhard Peters and John T. Woolley, The American Presidency Project., accessed December 19, 2014, http://www.presidency.ucsb.edu/ws/?pid=70145

[845] "May 25, 1861: President Lincoln suspends the writ of habeas corpus during the Civil War," May 25 This Day in History, accessed December 19, 2014, http://www.history.com/this-day-in-history/president-lincoln-suspends-the-writ-of-habeas-corpus-during-the-civil-war

[846] Maryland State Archives, "John Merryman (1824-1881)," Etching from Scharf, J. Thomas. History of Baltimore City and County. Baltimore, MD: Regional Publishing Company, 1971, p. 884. http://msa.maryland.gov/megafile/msa/speccol/sc3500/sc3520/001500/001543/html/1543images.html This information resource of the Maryland State Archives is presented here for fair use in the public domain. When this material is used, in whole or in part, proper citation and credit must be attributed to the Maryland State Archives.

[847] Bruce A. Ragsdale, *Ex parte Merryman and Debates on Civil Liberties During the Civil War,* (Federal Judicial Center, Federal Judicial History Office, 2007), p. 2 accessed December 19, 2014, http://www.fjc.gov/history/home.nsf/page/tu_merryman_background.html

[848] "May 25, 1861: President Lincoln suspends the writ of habeas corpus during the Civil War."

[849] Abraham Lincoln, "July 4th Message to Congress (July 4, 1861)," University of Virginia Miller Center accessed December 19, 2014, http://millercenter.org/president/speeches/speech-3508

[850] Abraham Lincoln: "Proclamation 93 - Declaring the Objectives of the War Including Emancipation of Slaves in Rebellious States on January 1, 1863," September 22, 1862. Online by Gerhard Peters and John T. Woolley, *The American Presidency Project.,* accessed November 1, 2014, http://www.presidency.ucsb.edu/ws/?pid=69782

[851] Abraham Lincoln: "Proclamation 94 - Suspending the Writ of Habeas Corpus," September 24, 1862. Online by Gerhard Peters and John T. Woolley, The American Presidency Project., accessed October 15, 2014, http://www.presidency.ucsb.edu/ws/?pid=69783

[852] Shmoop Editorial Team. "Article 4, Section 4" Shmoop University, Inc. 11 November 2008. http://www.shmoop.com/constitution/article-4-section-4.html

[853] Abraham Lincoln," *July 4th Message to Congress (July 4, 1861)."*

[854] Library of Congress, "Abraham Lincoln, seated and holding a book, with his son Tad (Thomas) leaning on a table," http://www.loc.gov/pictures/item/2007675781/ No known restrictions on publication.

[855] Dye, *Adder's Den,* 112

[856] Francis Lieber, LL.D., *Instruction for the Government of Armies of the United States in the Field,* Originally issued as General Orders No. 100, Adjutant General's Office (Washington: Government Printing 1863), accessed September2, 2014, http://www.loc.gov/rr/frd/Military_Law/Lieber_Collection/pdf/Instructions-gov-armies.pdf

[857] "General Orders No. 100 : The Lieber Code, INSTRUCTIONS FOR THE GOVERNMENT OF ARMIES OF THE UNITED STATES IN THE FIELD," Yale Law School, Lillian Goldman Law Library, accessed September 2, 2014, http://avalon.law.yale.edu/19th_century/lieber.asp

[858] *Wikimedia Commons,* s.v. "Abraham Lincoln November 1863.jpg," https://commons.wikimedia.org/wiki/File:Abraham_Lincoln_November_1863.jpg This work is in the public domain in its country of origin and other countries and areas where the copyright term is the author's life plus 100 years or less. United States public domain tag

[859] Todd Pierce, Judge Advocate General, U.S. Army (Retired), "The Dark Side of Lieber's Code (or, Cheneyite Jurisprudence)," April 7, 2014, http://original.antiwar.com/todd_pierce/2014/04/06/the-dark-side-of-liebers-code-or-cheneyite-jurisprudence/

[860] "Instructions for the Government of Armies of the United States in the Field (Lieber Code). 24 April 1863: Section I : Martial law -- Military jurisdiction -- Military necessity -- Retaliation - Art. 1.," International Committee of the Red Cross, accessed September 2, 2014, http://www.icrc.org/applic/ihl/ihl.nsf/Article.xsp?action=openDocument&documentId=4C9F845595A5618BC12563CD00514963

[861] "Instructions for the Government of Armies of the United States in the Field (Lieber Code). 24 April 1863: Section V : Safe-conduct -- Spies -- War-traitors -- Captured messengers -- Abuse of the flag of truce - Art. 90.," International Committee of the Red Cross, accessed September 2, 2014, http://www.icrc.org/applic/ihl/ihl.nsf/Article.xsp?action=openDocument&documentId=E1237344A5C69807C12563CD00514F00

[862] "Senate Report No. 93-549, Emergency Powers Statues: Provisions of Federal Law Now in Effect Delegating to the Executive Extraordinary Authority in Time of National Emergency: Report of the Special Committee on the Termination of the National Emergency United States Senate" accessed September 2, 2014, http://anticorruptionsociety.files.wordpress.com/2013/08/senate-report-93-549-copy-of-original.pdf

[863] Bruce Yandle, "Rahm's Rule of Crisis Management: A Footnote to the Theory of Regulation," Foundation for Economic Education, February 11, 2013,http://fee.org/freeman/detail/rahms-rule-of-crisis-management-a-footnote-to-the-theory-of-regulation#axzz2KizozPJ4

[864] "Rahm's Rule: 'Never Let a Serious Crisis Go to Waste,'" Property and Environment Research Center, accessed November 25, 2014, http://perc.org/blog/rahms-rule-never-let-serious-crisis-go-waste#sthash.J82OXOCA.dpuf

[865] Abraham Lincoln: "Proclamation 94 - Suspending the Writ of Habeas Corpus," September 24, 1862. Online by Gerhard Peters and John T. Woolley, The American Presidency Project., accessed October 15, 2014, http://www.presidency.ucsb.edu/ws/?pid=69783

[866] Abraham Lincoln: "Proclamation 113 - Declaring Martial Law and a Further Suspension of the Writ of Habeas Corpus in Kentucky," July 5, 1864. Online by Gerhard Peters and John T. Woolley, The American Presidency Project., accessed October 15, 2014, http://www.presidency.ucsb.edu/ws/?pid=69993

[867] Abraham Lincoln: "Proclamation 84 - Declaring Martial Law, and Suspending the Writ of Habeas Corpus in the Islands of Key West," May 10, 1861. Online by Gerhard Peters and John T. Woolley, The American Presidency Project., accessed October 15, 2014, http://www.presidency.ucsb.edu/ws/?pid=70134

[868] Abraham Lincoln: "Proclamation 104 - Suspending the Writ of Habeas Corpus Throughout the United States," September 15, 1863. Online by Gerhard Peters and John T. Woolley, The American Presidency Project., accessed October 15, 2014, http://www.presidency.ucsb.edu/ws/?pid=69898

[869] Abraham Lincoln: "Proclamation 113 - Declaring Martial Law and a Further Suspension of the Writ of Habeas Corpus in Kentucky," July 5, 1864. Online by Gerhard Peters and John T. Woolley, The American Presidency Project., accessed October 15, 2014, http://www.presidency.ucsb.edu/ws/?pid=69993

[870] Phelps, *Vatican Assassins*, 391, 418

[871] *Wikimedia Commons*, s.v. "President Andrew Johnson.jpg,"
https://commons.wikimedia.org/wiki/File:President_Andrew_Johnson.jpg This media file is in the public domain in the United States. This applies to U.S. works where the copyright has expired, often because its first publication occurred prior to January 1, 1923.

[872] Andrew Johnson: "Proclamation 148 - Revoking the Suspension of the Writ of Habeas Corpus, Except in Certain States and Territories," December 1, 1865. Online by Gerhard Peters and John T. Woolley, The American Presidency Project., accessed September 2, 2014, http://www.presidency.ucsb.edu/ws/?pid=72046

[873] Andrew Johnson: "Proclamation 153 - Declaring the Insurrection in Certain Southern States to be at an End," April 2, 1866. Online by Gerhard Peters and John T. Woolley, The American Presidency Project., accessed October 15, 2014, http://www.presidency.ucsb.edu/ws/?pid=71987

[874] Andrew Johnson: "Proclamation 157 - Declaring that Peace, Order, Tranquillity, and Civil Authority Now Exists in and Throughout the Whole of the United States of America," August 20, 1866. Online by Gerhard Peters and John T. Woolley, The American Presidency Project., accessed October 15, 2014,http://www.presidency.ucsb.edu/ws/?pid=71992

[875] Abraham Lincoln: "Proclamation 93 - Declaring the Objectives of the War Including Emancipation of Slaves in Rebellious States on January 1, 1863," September 22, 1862. Online by Gerhard Peters and John T. Woolley, The American Presidency Project., accessed October 15, 2014, http://www.presidency.ucsb.edu/ws/?pid=69782

[876] "V Sectionalism and Civil War," *American Heritage A Reader,* ed. The Hillsdale College History Faculty, (Hillsdale: Hillsdale College Press, 2011), 371

[877] *Wikimedia Commons,* s.v. "Hsl-River queen-neg.jpg," https://en.wikipedia.org/wiki/River_Queen_(steamboat) This image is in the public domain in the United States. In most cases, this means that it was first published prior to January 1, 1923

[878] *Wikimedia Commons*, s.v. "The Peacemakers 1868.jpg,"
https://commons.wikimedia.org/wiki/File:The_Peacemakers_1868.jpg This work is in the public domain in its country of origin and other countries and areas where the copyright term is the author's life plus 100 years or less. United States public domain tag

[879] Abraham Lincoln: "Proclamation 93 - Declaring the Objectives of the War Including Emancipation of Slaves in Rebellious States on January 1, 1863," September 22, 1862. Online by Gerhard Peters and John T. Woolley, The American Presidency Project., accessed November 1, 2014, http://www.presidency.ucsb.edu/ws/?pid=69782

[880] "The Emancipation Proclamation," National Archives & Records Administration,
http://www.archives.gov/exhibits/featured_documents/emancipation_proclamation/transcript.html (accessed 11/29/2014)

[881] *Wikimedia Commons*, s.v. "George Washington by Gilbert Stuart, 1795-96.png,"
https://commons.wikimedia.org/wiki/File:George_Washington_by_Gilbert_Stuart,_1795-96.png#mw-jump-to-license This work is in the public domain in its country of origin and other countries and areas where the copyright term is the author's life plus 100 years or less.

[882] *George Washington's Farewell Address to the People of the United States,* September 17, 1796, Point 18, Archiving Early America as sourced from *The Independent Chronicle,* September 26, 1796, accessed November 1, 2014, http://www.earlyamerica.com/milestone-events/george-washingtons-farewell-address-full-text/

[883] Delaware.gov, Department of State: Division of Corporations: Entity Details, "Entity Name: THE UNITED STATES OF AMERICA, INC," File Number 4525682, https://delecorp.delaware.gov/tin/controller

[884] "Statutes of The Supreme Council of the Thirty-third Degree," *Ancient & Accepted Scottish Rite of Freemasonry, S.J., U.S.A.*, p. 126, August, 2011, http://scottishrite.org/wp-content/uploads/2011/12/statutes_2011.pdf

[885] Dye, *Adder's Den,* 123

[886] Library of Congress, "Abraham Lincoln and his Emancipation Proclamation / The Strobridge Lith. Co., Cincinnati.,"
https://www.loc.gov/pictures/item/97507511/ This image is in the public domain in the United States. In most cases, this means that it was first published prior to January 1, 1923.

[887] Library of Congress, "Articles of confederation and perpetual union between the states,"
https://www.loc.gov/item/rbpe.17802600/ This image is in the public domain in the United States. In most cases, this means that it was first published prior to January 1, 1923.

[888] Yale Law School, Lillian Goldman Law Library, The Avalon Project, "Articles of Confederation : March 1, 1781," http://avalon.law.yale.edu/18th_century/artconf.asp

[889] Alexander Hamilton, "The Federalist Papers : No. 15; The Insufficiency of the Present Confederation to Preserve the Union

For the Independent Journal. HAMILTON," http://avalon.law.yale.edu/18th_century/fed15.asp and "The Federalist Papers : No. 23; The Necessity of a Government as Energetic as the One Proposed to the Preservation of the Union From the New York Packet. Tuesday, December 18, 1787. HAMILTON," http://avalon.law.yale.edu/18th_century/fed23.asp

[890] John S. Wise, *A Treatise on American Citizenship*, (Northport: Edward Thompson Co., 1906) 10-12

[891] Eric Jon Phelps, *Seven Transitions of American Citizenship*, "Interlude II: 1868" (ISBN 978-0-9793734-9-2, Dec 12, 2013) 13-14

[892] James G. Blaine, *Political Discussions: Legislative, Diplomatic and Popular: 1856-1886*, (Norwich: The Henry Bill Publishing Co, 1887) p 63

[893] John S. Wise, *A Treatise on American Citizenship*, (Northport: Edward Thompson Co., 1906) 24, 196-197

[894] Eric Jon Phelps, *Seven Transitions of American Citizenship*, "III. From New Status to Contract: 1906: Birth and Death records" (ISBN 978-0-9793734-9-2, Dec 12, 2013) 26-27

[895] *Wikipedia*, s.v. "Naturalization Act of 1790," Last modified March 17, 2017, https://en.wikipedia.org/wiki/Naturalization_Act_of_1790

[896] GenealogyToday, "When were African Americans granted citizenship?," (accessed March 19, 2017), http://www.genealogytoday.com/genealogy/answers/When_were_African_Americans_granted_citizenship.html

[897] *Wikipedia*, s.v. "Thirteenth Amendment to the United States Constitution," last modified March 16, 2017, https://en.m.wikipedia.org/wiki/Thirteenth_Amendment_to_the_United_States_Constitution

[898] *Wikipedia*, s.v. "Fourteenth Amendment," last modified December 22, 2014, http://en.wikipedia.org/wiki/Fourteenth_Amendment_to_the_United_States_Constitution

[899] "An Act Concerning American Citizens in foreign States," July 27, 1868, A Century of Lawmaking for a New Nation: U.S. Congressional Documents and Debates, 1774 – 1875, *Statutes at Large,* 40th Congress, 2nd Session, p. 223-224 accessed November 1, 2014, http://memory.loc.gov/cgi-bin/ampage?collId=llsl&fileName=015/llsl015.db&recNum=256

[900] "An Act Concerning American Citizens in foreign States," July 27, 1868, *Statutes at Large*, available for view on one page accessed September 2, 2014, http://home.earthlink.net/~walterk1/Patr/US/ExpatriationAct.html

[901] Fortieth Congress, Session II, Chapter 249, 250; 1868, "An Act Concerning American Citizens in foreign States," https://en.wikipedia.org/wiki/File:Ex_Pat_Act.jpg

[902] James G. Blaine, *Political Discussions: Legislative, Diplomatic and Popular: 1856-1886*, (Norwich: The Henry Bill Publishing Co, 1887) p 64

[903] *George Washington's Farewell Address to the People of the United States,* September 17, 1796, Archiving Early America as sourced from *The Independent Chronicle,* September 26, 1796, accessed November 1, 2014, http://www.earlyamerica.com/milestone-events/george-washingtons-farewell-address-full-text/

[904] Library of Congress, "Currier & Ives portrait of the Lincoln Family," https://www.loc.gov/resource/lprbscsm.scsm0404/ This image is in the public domain in the United States. In most cases, this means that it was first published prior to January 1, 1923.

[905] Library of Congress, "The end of the rebellion in the United States, 1865 / C. Kimmel," https://www.loc.gov/resource/cph.3a15123/ This work is in the public domain in its country of origin and other countries and areas where the copyright term is the author's life plus 70 years or less.

[906] Abraham Lincoln: "First Annual Message," December 3, 1861. Online by Gerhard Peters and John T. Woolley, The American Presidency Project. Accessed September 2, 2014, http://www.presidency.ucsb.edu/ws/?pid=29502

[907] *Wikimedia Commons,* s.v. "SPChase.jpg," https://commons.wikimedia.org/wiki/File:SPChase.jpg This work is in the public domain in its country of origin and other countries and areas where the copyright term is the author's life plus 70 years or less.

[908] Dr. R. E. Search, *Lincoln: Money Martyred*, (Seattle: Lincoln Publishing Company, 1935), 44-45

[909] *Wikimedia Commons,* s.v. "Edmunddicktaylor.jpg," by Joseph Scott Morris, https://commons.wikimedia.org/wiki/File:Edmunddicktaylor.jpg This file is licensed under the Creative Commons Attribution-Share Alike 3.0 Unported license. Author Josephscottmorris

[910] *Wikimedia Commons,* s.v. "US-$1-LT-1862-Fr-16c.jpg," https://commons.wikimedia.org/wiki/File:US-$1-LT-1862-Fr-16c.jpg This is a faithful photographic reproduction of an original two-dimensional work of art. The work of art itself is in the public domain. Wikimedia has received an e-mail confirming that the copyright holder has approved publication as courtesy of the National Numismatic Collection, National Museum of American History.. This correspondence has been reviewed by an OTRS member and stored in our permission archive. The correspondence is available to trusted volunteers as ticket #2013030510011547.

[911] Ellen Hodgson Brown, J.D., "Revive Lincoln's Monetary Policy: an Open Letter to President Obama," April 8, 2009, http://www.webofdebt.com/articles/lincoln_obama.php

[912] Search, *Money Martyred,* 46

[913] Abraham Lincoln, "Senate document no. 23, page 91, 1865" as cited from Michael Rowbotham, *The Grip of Death: A Study of Modern Money, Debt Servitude, and Destructive Economics* (Jon Carpenter Publishing, 1998), pages 220-221 accessed September 2, 2014, http://economics.arawakcity.org/node/179

[914] Mike Nickerson, *Life, Money and Illusion: Living on Earth as if we want to stay*, (New Society Publishers, 2009), 175

[915] *George Washington's Farewell Address to the People of the United States,* September 17, 1796, Archiving Early America as sourced from *The Independent Chronicle,* September 26, 1796, accessed November 1, 2014, http://www.earlyamerica.com/milestone-events/george-washingtons-farewell-address-full-text/

[916] Melissa Melton, "HOLY SH*T: U.S. National Debt Has Officially Hit $18 Trillion," December 8, 2014, http://www.dcclothesline.com/2014/12/08/holy-sht-u-s-national-debt-officially-hit-18-trillion/

[917] Robert Bridge, "US debt six times greater than declared – study," *RT News,* August 6, 2013 http://rt.com/usa/us-debt-study-hamilton-economy-103/

[918] "California economist says real US debt $70 trillion," August 15, 2013, *Fox News,* http://www.foxnews.com/politics/2013/08/15/california-economist-says-real-us-debt-70-trillion-not-16-trillion-government/

[919] Brown, "Revive Lincoln's Monetary Policy."

[920] "Funeral Procession of President Lincoln," Reformation.org, accessed September 2, 2014, *http://www.reformation.org/lincoln.html*

[921] Library of Congress, "President Lincoln's funeral procession in New York City," Photographed by Brady. From Harper's Weekly, May 13, 1865, https://memory.loc.gov/ammem/alhtml/alrb/stbdsd/00406600/001.html No known restrictions on publication.

[922] Ibid.

[923] McCarty, *Suppressed Truth,* 175

[924] Ibid., 190

[925] *Wikimedia Commons*, s.v. "Edwin McMasters Stanton Secretary of War.jpg," https://commons.wikimedia.org/wiki/File:Edwin_McMasters_Stanton_Secretary_of_War.jpg#mw-jump-to-license This work is in the public domain in its country of origin and other countries and areas where the copyright term is the author's life plus 70 years or less. This image is available from the United States Library of Congress's Prints and Photographs division under the digital ID cwpbh.00958.

[926] Getler and Brewer, *Rebel Gold,* 42

[927] *Wikipedia,* s.v. "Henry B. Carrington," last modified October 11, 2013, http://en.wikipedia.org/wiki/Henry_B._Carrington

[928] *Wikipedia,* s.v. "John P. Sanderson," last modified April 30, 2013, http://en.wikipedia.org/wiki/John_P._Sanderson

[929] Getler and Brewer, *Rebel Gold,* 42

[930] *Wikimedia Commons*, s.v. "Joseph Holt.jpg," https://commons.wikimedia.org/wiki/File:Joseph_Holt.jpg#mw-jump-to-license This work is in the public domain in its country of origin and other countries and areas where the copyright term is the author's life plus 70 years or less. This image is available from the United States Library of Congress's Prints and Photographs division under the digital ID cwpbh.00873.

[931] *Wikimedia Commons*, s.v. "Joseph Holt.jpg," https://commons.wikimedia.org/wiki/File:Joseph_Holt.jpg#mw-jump-to-license This work is in the public domain in its country of origin and other countries and areas where the copyright term is the author's life plus 70 years or less. This image is available from the United States Library of Congress's Prints and Photographs division under the digital ID cwpbh.00873.

[932] "Colonel John P. Sanderson (USA)," https://www.geni.com/people/Colonel-John-P-Sanderson-USA/6000000039151801226 This image is in the public domain in the United States. In most cases, this means that it was first published prior to January 1, 1923.

[933] Ibid., snapshot of cover

[934] J. Holt, Judge Advocate General, *Report of the Judge Advocate General on "The Order of American Knights," alias "The Sons of Liberty" : a western conspiracy in aid of the Southern Rebellion (*Washington, DC: Chronicle Print, 1864*),* accessed September 2, 2014, https://archive.org/details/reportofjudgeadv00unit

[935] Frank L. Klement, *Dark Lanterns: Secret Political Societies, Conspiracies, and Treason Trials in the Civil War,* (Louisiana State University Press, 1984), 145

[936] J. Holt, United States Army Judge Advocate General, *Report on "The Order of American Knights," alias "The Songs of Liberty." A western conspiracy in aid of the Southern Rebellion,* (Washington, DC, Chronicle Print, 1864), accessed September 2, 2014, https://archive.org/details/reportontheorder02unit

[937] Library of Congress, "Joseph Holt papers, 1797-1917, Scope and Content," accessed September 2, 2014, http://findingaids.loc.gov/db/search/xq/searchMfer02.xq?_id=loc.mss.eadmss.ms012038&_faSection=overview&_faSubsection=scopecontent&_dmdid=d3694e19

[938]*Wikipedia,*s.v. "Albert Pike," last modified August 28, 2014, http://en.wikipedia.org/wiki/Albert_Pike

[939]Jay Longley and Colin Eby, *Knights of the Golden Circle,* accessed September 2, 2014, http://knightsofthegoldencircle.webs.com/

[940] New World Order Today Staff, "Albert Pike and the Scottish Rite," accessed September 2, 2014, http://www.nwotoday.com/the-new-world-orders-history/freemasonry-global-level-illumination/albert-pike-and-the-scottish-rites

[941] YouTube/HowStuffWorks, "Stuff They Don't Want You to Know - Albert Pike," Published on Mar 7, 2012, https://www.youtube.com/watch?v=3NzNO_9-3Ko&sns=em

[942]Getler and Brewer, *Rebel Gold,* 59

[943] *Wikimedia Commons,* s.v. "Pierre-Jean De Smet - Brady-Handy.jpg," https://commons.wikimedia.org/wiki/File:Pierre-Jean_De_Smet_-_Brady-Handy.jpg#mw-jump-to-license This work is in the public domain in its country of origin and other countries and areas where the copyright term is the author's life plus 100 years or less. This image is available from the United States Library of Congress's Prints and Photographs division under the digital ID cwpbh.03561.

[944] Phelps, *Vatican Assassins*, 194

[945]Longley and Eby, *Knights of the Golden Circle.*

[946]S. W. Harman, *Hell on the Border: He Hanged Eighty-eight Men,* (Fort Smith, The Phoenix Publishing Company, 1898), 147-148

[947] *Wikimedia Commons,* s.v. "Cavalry and Indians.JPG," https://commons.wikimedia.org/wiki/File:Cavalry_and_Indians.JPG#mw-jump-to-license This media file is in the public domain in the United States. This applies to U.S. works where the copyright has expired, often because its first publication occurred prior to January 1, 1923.

[948]*Wikipedia,*s.v. "American Indian Wars," last modified December 1, 2015, http://en.wikipedia.org/wiki/American_Indian_Wars

[949]*Wikipedia,* s.v. "Indian removal," last modified November 28, 2015, *http://en.wikipedia.org/wiki/Indian_removal*

[950]"Palladism," Ancient and Primitive Right of Memphis Misraim, accessed December 31, 2014, https://sites.google.com/site/memphismizraimbg/palladism

[951]"Albert Pike, Freemasonry and the KGC," Knights-of-the-Golden-Circle.blogspot.com, December 10, 2011, http://knights-of-the-golden-circle.blogspot.com/2011/12/albert-pike-freemasonry-and-kgc.html

[952] Library of Congress, "The Union as it was The lost cause, worse than slavery / / Th. Nast.," https://www.loc.gov/item/2001696840/ This media file is in the public domain in the United States. This applies to U.S. works where the copyright has expired, often because its first publication occurred prior to January 1, 1923.

[953]"Albert Pike did not found the Ku Klux Klan," Grand Lodge of British Columbia and Yukon, last updated November 26, 2012,http://freemasonry.bcy.ca/anti-masonry/kkk.html#1

[954] YouTube/HowStuffWorks, "Stuff They Don't Want You to Know - Albert Pike," Published on Mar 7, 2012, https://www.youtube.com/watch?v=3NzNO_9-3Ko&sns=em

[955] YouTube/HowStuffWorks, "Stuff They Don't Want You to Know - Albert Pike," Published on Mar 7, 2012, https://www.youtube.com/watch?v=3NzNO_9-3Ko&sns=em

[956]"Palladism," Ancient and Primitive Right of Memphis Misraim.

[957]Edward Hendrie, *The Anti-Gospel: The Perversion of Christ's Grace Gospel,* (Great Mountain Publishing, 2005), Ch. 30

[958]"History of the Temple," The Scottish Rite of Freemasonry Supreme Council, 33° Southern Jurisdiction, U.S.A, accessed November 1, 2014, http://scottishrite.org/headquarters/history-of-the-temple/

[959]*Wikipedia,s.v.* "Supreme Council, Scottish Rite (Southern Jurisdiction, USA)," last modified May 28, 2014, http://en.wikipedia.org/wiki/Supreme_Council,_Scottish_Rite_(Southern_Jurisdiction,_USA)

[960] "History of the Rite: The Second American Supreme Council: New York, 1806,"The Scottish Rite of Freemasonry Supreme Council, 33° Southern Jurisdiction, U.S.A., accessed September 25, 2014, http://scottishrite.org/about/history/

[961] "Palladism," Ancient and Primitive Right of Memphis Misraim.

[962] Thomas P. Kittell, *The History of the Great Rebellion,* (Cincinnati: L. Stebbins, 1865), 18

[963]*Encyclopedia Britannica,* s.v. "Guiseppe Mazzini," last modified July 17, 2014, http://en.wikipedia.org/wiki/Giuseppe_Mazzini

[964] Ibid.

[965]"Who Was Albert Pike?,"ThreeWorldWars.com, last updated February 2, 2012, http://www.threeworldwars.com/albert-pike.htm

[966] "Morals and Dogma Exposed!," ThreeWorldWars.com, last updated February 2, 2012, http://www.threeworldwars.com/dogma.htm

[967] *Albert Pike, a 33° Freemason,* accessed September 2, 2014, http://amazingdiscoveries.org/albums/Freemasonry#Albert-Pike-Lucifer-light-bearer

[968] Albert Pike, *Morals and dogma of the ancient and accepted Scottish Rite of Freemasonry,* Entered according to the Act of Congress, in the year 1871, by Albert Pike, (Charleston), https://archive.org/details/moralsdogmaofanc00pikeiala

[969] William Guy Carr, R.D., *SATAN, Prince of this World, (*www.ThreeWorldWars.com – An Introduction to Conspiratorial History, compiled 1959), 11, 29, accessed September 2, 2014, https://archive.org/details/pdfy-CF3PRqb1CblGB8-3

[970] *Encylopaedia Brittanica,* s.v. "Giuseppe Mazzini."

[971] Library of Congress, "Albert Pike," Control Number brh2003002446/PP, http://www.loc.gov/item/brh2003002446/PP/ No known restrictions on publication.

[972] *Wikimedia Commons, s.v.* "Giuseppe Mazzini.jpg," https://commons.wikimedia.org/wiki/File:Giuseppe_Mazzini.jpg#mw-jump-to-license This work was published before January 1, 1923 and it is anonymous or pseudonymous due to unknown authorship. It is in the public domain in the United States as well as countries and areas where the copyright terms of anonymous or pseudonymous works are 94 years or less since publication.

[973] "Pillars of Charity," The Scottish Rite of Freemasonry Supreme Council, 33° Southern Jurisdiction, U.S.A., accessed September 25, 2014, http://scottishrite.org/headquarters/virtual-tour/pillars-of-charity/

[974] Roadside America Staff, "House of the Temple," RoadsideAmerica.com, accessed September 2, 2014, http://www.roadsideamerica.com/story/19865

[975] "Albert Pike Museum," The Scottish Rite of Freemasonry Supreme Council, 33° Southern Jurisdiction, U.S.A., accessed September 25, 2014, http://scottishrite.org/headquarters/virtual-tour/albert-pike-museum/

[976] Got Questions Staff, "Is Lucifer Satan? Does the fall of Lucifer describe Satan?," accessed September 2, 2014, *http:*//www.gotquestions.org/Lucifer-Satan.html

[977] "Lucifer is the god of Freemasonry," accessed September 2, 2014, http://amazingdiscoveries.org/S-deception-Freemason_Lucifer_Albert_Pike

[978] Robert Gates, Sr., *The Conspiracy That Will Not Die: How the Rothschild Cabal Is Driving America into One World Government*, (Oakland, Red Anvil Press, 2011), p. 114 as citing: A.C. De La Rive, *La Femme et l'enfant dans la Franc-Maconnerie Universelle*, p. 588; Lady Queenborough, *Occult Theocracy* pp. 220-221

[979] "Who Was Albert Pike?,"ThreeWorldWars.com.

[980] Masonicinfo.com, *Pike's Statue,* as citing Gary Scott, *MPS, "Attack on the Albert Pike Statue, Washington, DC,"* http://www.masonicinfo.com/pikestatue.htm(accessed 11/1/2014)

[981] Library of Congress, "Albert Pike statue," Created / Published between 1909 and 1919, Digital Id npcc 19486 http://www.loc.gov/pictures/item/npc2007019485/ No known restrictions on publication.

[982] The Scottish Rite of Freemasonry Supreme Council, 33° Southern Jurisdiction, U.S.A., *Grand Staircase,* http://scottishrite.org/headquarters/virtual-tour/grand-staircase/ (accessed 9/25/2014)

[983] Anton Chaitkin, *The Scottish Rite's KKK Project,* excerpt from the transcript of a speech as cited athttp://www.theforbiddenknowledge.com/hardtruth/scottishriteproject.htm (accessed 9/2/2014)

[984] The Revelation, *Washington D.C. and Masonic/Luciferic Symbology*, http://www.theforbiddenknowledge.com/chapter3/ (accessed 12/23/2014)

[985] Library of Congress, "Theodore Roosevelt, the master mason," Digital Id ppmsca 35829, http://www.loc.gov/item/2010645452/ No known restrictions on publication. No renewal in Copyright office.

[986] Phelps, *Vatican Assassins*, 388

[987] *Wikipedia,*s.v. "Lost Cause of the Confederacy," last modified July 28, 2014, http://en.wikipedia.org/wiki/Lost_Cause_of_the_Confederacy

[988] *Wikipedia,*s.v. "James Dunwoody Bulloch," last modified August 29, 2014, http://en.wikipedia.org/wiki/James_Dunwoody_Bulloch

[989] *Wikipedia,*s.v. "Spanish-American War," last modified August 16, 2014,http://en.wikipedia.org/wiki/Spanish%E2%80%93American_War

[990] Anton Chaitkin, *The Scottish Rite's KKK Project,* excerpt from the transcript of a speech as cited athttp://www.theforbiddenknowledge.com/hardtruth/scottishriteproject.htm(accessed 9/2/2014)

[991] *Wikimedia Commons*, s.v. "Mckinley.jpg," https://commons.wikimedia.org/wiki/File:Mckinley.jpg#mw-jump-to-license This media file is in the public domain in the United States. This applies to U.S. works where the copyright has expired, often because its first publication occurred prior to January 1, 1923.

[992] *Wikimedia Commons*, s.v. "Bulloch Brothers James & Irvine.gif," https://en.wikipedia.org/wiki/File:Bulloch_Brothers_James_%26_Irvine.gif#mw-jump-to-license This image is in the public domain because under the Copyright law of the United States, originality of expression is necessary for copyright protection,

and a mere photograph of an out-of-copyright two-dimensional work may not be protected under American copyright law. The official position of the Wikimedia Foundation is that all reproductions of public domain works should be considered to be in the public domain regardless of their country of origin (even in countries where mere labor is enough to make a reproduction eligible for protection). This image is in the public domain in the United States. In most cases, this means that it was first published prior to January 1, 1923 (see the template documentation for more cases). Other jurisdictions may have other rules, and this image might not be in the public domain outside the United States

993 *Wikipedia*, s.v. "James Dunwoody Bulloch," last modified November, 2016, https://en.m.wikipedia.org/wiki/James_Dunwoody_Bulloch

994 U.S. History Staff, *American History: From Pre-Columbian to the New Millennium,* "*The New England Colonies:* 3c. Massachusetts Bay — "The City Upon a Hill," accessed November 1, 2014, http://www.ushistory.org/us/3c.asp

995 NWOToday.com, *The Bavarian Illuminati 1776,* http://www.nwotoday.com/the-new-world-orders-history/freemasonry-global-level-illumination/the-bavarian-illuminati-1776-thru-2014 (accessed 11/1/2014)

996 "Adam Weishaupt," accessed December 17, 2015, http://www.bibliotecapleyades.net/sociopolitica/esp_sociopol_illuminati_0a.htm

997 *Wikimedia Commons*, s.v. "Johann Adam Weishaupt.jpg," https://commons.wikimedia.org/wiki/File:Johann_Adam_Weishaupt.jpg This work is in the public domain in its country of origin and other countries and areas where the copyright term is the author's life plus 100 years or less.

998 *Wikipedia,* s.v. "Temporal power (papal)," last modified September 4, 2014, http://en.wikipedia.org/wiki/Temporal_power_(papal)

999 Pierre Claude François Daunou, *THE POWER OF THE POPES AN HISTORICAL ESSAY ON THEIR TEMPORAL DOMINION, AND THE ABUSE OF THEIR SPIRITUAL AUTHORITY,* Two Volumes in One, (1838), http://www.gutenberg.org/files/39267/39267-h/39267-h.htm (accessed 11/1/2014)

1000 2 Cor. 4:4

1001 New World Order Today Staff, *An Improved System of Illuminati,* accessed November 1, 2014, http://www.nwotoday.com/the-new-world-orders-history/freemasonry-global-level-illumination/the-improved-system-of-illuminism

1002 Ibid.

1003 New World Order Today Staff, *Freemasonry and King Solomon's Temple, accessed November 1, 2014,* http://www.nwotoday.com/the-new-world-orders-history/freemasonry-global-level-illumination/builders-of-king-solomons-temple

1004 *Wikipedia,* s.v. "Papal Infallibility.,"

1005 II Thess. 2:3-12

1006 I John 2:18

1007 Rev. 13:4-18

1008 Dan. 8:23

1009 Matth.24:15 in referring to Dan. 9:27; 12:11

1010 Phelps, *Vatican Assassins*, 67

1011 The Scottish Rite of Freemasonry Supreme Council, 33° Southern Jurisdiction, U.S.A., *George Washington Banquet Hall,* http://scottishrite.org/headquarters/virtual-tour/george-washington-banquet-hall/ (accessed 9/25/2014)

1012 *Wikipedia,* s.v. "John Clark Ridpath," last modified July 19, 2014, http://en.wikipedia.org/wiki/John_Clark_Ridpath

1013 John Clark Ridpath, LL.D., *Universal History*, Vol. XIV, (Cincinnati: The Jones Brothers Publishing Co., 1894), 617

1014 Phelps, *Vatican Assassins*, 236

1015 Founders Online, National Archives, "To George Washington from G. W. Snyder, 22 August 1798," last modified December 6, 2016, http://founders.archives.gov/documents/Washington/06-02-02-0435 [Original source: The Papers of George Washington, Retirement Series, vol. 2, 2 January 1798–15 September 1798, ed. W. W. Abbot. Charlottesville: University Press of Virginia, 1998, pp. 554–557.]

1016 Charles G. Finney, *The Character, Claims and Practical Workings of Freemasonry*, (Boring, Oregon: CPA Book Publisher, no date; originally published in 1869) p. 222 as cited by Eric Jon Phelps, *Vatican Assassins*, (Eric Jon Phelps, PO Box 306, Newmanstown, PA 17073) (2001), p. 236; pdf version pp. 90- 91 at http://www.libraryoftheology.com/writings/cultsandheresies/Freemasonry_Finney.pdf (accessed 11/1/24014)

1017 Federer, *America's Quotations,* "Abraham Lincoln," 391

1018 Jones, *Prophetic History,* 37

1019 Barefoot Bob Hardison, *The Real Thirteenth Article of Amendment to the Constitution of the United States – Titles of Nobility and Honour,* "Amendment Article XIII" accessed September 2, 2014, http://www.barefootsworld.net/real13th.html

[1020] Barefoot Bob Hardison, Barefoot's World, "Additional Links to Data on The Original Thirteenth Amendment: Images of Documents with the Original 13th TONA in place," http://www.barefootsworld.net/13links.html

[1021] Library of Congress, *History of the Library, accessed September 2, 2014,* http://www.loc.gov/about/history-of-the-library/

[1022] Library of Congress, "Capture and burning of Washington by the British, in 1814," https://www.loc.gov/pictures/item/96519729/ This is a faithful photographic reproduction of a two-dimensional, public domain work of art. This work is in the public domain in its country of origin and other countries and areas where the copyright term is the author's life plus 100 years or less.

[1023] *Wikimedia Commons,* s.v. "Philip Reed portrait.png," https://commons.wikimedia.org/wiki/File:Philip_Reed_portrait.png This media file is in the **public domain** in the United States. This applies to U.S. works where the copyright has expired, often because its first publication occurred prior to January 1, 1923.

[1024] *Wikipedia,* s.v. "Democratic-Republican Party," last modified October 30, 2014, http://en.wikipedia.org/wiki/Democratic-Republican_Party

[1025] *Wikimedia Commons*, s.v. "Elisha Reynolds Potter 1764-1835.jpg," https://commons.wikimedia.org/wiki/File:Elisha_Reynolds_Potter_1764-1835.jpg This media file is in the public domain in the United States. This applies to U.S. works where the copyright has expired, often because its first publication occurred prior to January 1, 1923.

[1026] Amendment-13.org, *The Original Thirteenth Article of Amendment To The Constitution For The United States,* last updated March 29, 2006, http://www.amendment-13.org/index.html as linked from Barefootsworld.net, *Additional Links to Data on The Original Thirteenth Amendment,* accessed September 2, 2014, http://www.barefootsworld.net/13links.html

[1027] Trueman Cross, *Military Laws of the United States; to Which is Prefixed the Constitution of the United States Compiled and Published under Authority of the War Department* (Washington, Edward De Krafft Printers, 1825) as displayed at Amendment-13.org, *The Original Thirteenth Article of Amendment To The Constitution For The United States,* last updated September 9, 2002, http://www.amendment-13.org/publications.html
By Major Trueman Cross (Deputy Quarter-Master-General of the Army)

[1028] Amendment-13.org, "The TONA Research Committee," last updated October 15, 2002, http://www.amendment-13.org/trc.html

[1029] *Wikipedia,* s.v. "Reconstruction Era," last modified November 25, 2014, http://en.wikipedia.org/wiki/Reconstruction_Era

[1030] Hebrew for Christians, *The Letter Dalet*, accessed November 29, 2014, http://www.hebrew4christians.com/Grammar/Unit_One/Aleph-Bet/Dalet/dalet.html

[1031] Abraham Lincoln," Second Inaugural Address of Abraham Lincoln," accessed at *The Avalon Project,* Lillian Goldman Law Library, Yale Law School, accessed November 29, 2014, http://avalon.law.yale.edu/19th_century/lincoln2.asp

[1032] Num. 35:33

[1033] The Heritage Foundation, Colleen Sheehan, PhD, *James Madison: Father of the Constitution*, April 8, 2013, http://www.heritage.org/research/reports/2013/04/james-madison-father-of-the-constitution

[1034] Mullins, *The Rape of Justice,* 54-55

[1035] *Wikimedia Commons,* s.v. "James Madison.jpg," https://commons.wikimedia.org/wiki/File:James_Madison.jpg This work is in the public domain in its country of origin and other countries and areas where the copyright term is the author's life plus 100 years or less.

[1036] Abraham Lincoln, *Fragment on the Constitution and the Union,* c. January, 1861, accessed November 29, 2014, Collected Works of Abraham Lincoln. Volume 4, http://quod.lib.umich.edu/l/lincoln/lincoln4/1:264?rgn=div1;view=fulltext

[1037] Prof. Kevin Portteus, *Constitution 101: The Meaning and History of the Constitution,* "Abraham Lincoln and the Constitution," accessed November 29, 2014, https://online.hillsdale.edu/document.doc?id=279

[1038] MillerCenter.org, *July 4th Message to Congress (July 4, 1861), Abraham Lincoln,* accessed December 19, 2014, http://millercenter.org/president/speeches/speech-3508

[1039] *Wikimedia Commons*, s.v. "Postbellum-Cobb.jpg," https://commons.wikimedia.org/wiki/File:Postbellum-Cobb.jpg#mw-jump-to-license This work is from the Brady-Handy collection at the Library of Congress. According to the library, there are no known copyright restrictions on the use of this work.
Mathew Brady died in 1896 and Levin C. Handy died in 1932. Photographs in this collection are in the public domain in the US as works published before 1923 or as unpublished works whose copyright term has expired (life of author + 70 years).

[1040] New World Order Today Staff, *Albert Pike and the Scottish Rite,* accessed November 29, 2014, http://www.nwotoday.com/the-new-world-orders-history/freemasonry-global-level-illumination/albert-pike-and-the-scottish-rites

[1041] Getler and Brewer, *Rebel Gold,* 58

[1042] Anton Chaitkin, *The Scottish Rite's KKK Project*, from the speech delivered by Mr. Chaitkin at the Labor Day weekend conference of the Schiller Institute in suburban Washington, D.C, http://www.theforbiddenknowledge.com/hardtruth/scottishriteproject.htm (accessed 11/29/2014)

[1043] Dye, *Adder's Den,* 123

[1044] Myers, *Great American Fortunes,*41

[1045] *Wikipedia*,s.v. "Counter-Reformation," last modified November 24, 2014,http://en.wikipedia.org/wiki/Counter-Reformation

[1046] *Freemasonry and King Solomon's Temple,* accessed November 29, 2014, http://www.nwotoday.com/the-new-world-orders-history/freemasonry-global-level-illumination/builders-of-king-solomons-temple

[1047] Shmoop Editorial Team. *Reconstruction,* Shmoop University, Inc. 11 November 2008., http://www.shmoop.com/reconstruction/

[1048] Shmoop Editorial Team. *Reconstruction Summary & Analysis*, Shmoop University, Inc. 11 November 2008. http://www.shmoop.com/reconstruction/summary.html

[1049] President James Buchanan Geiger, *Republic for the United States of America,* 2014.

[1050] Shmoop Editorial Team. *Article 4, Section 4* Shmoop University, Inc. 11 November 2008. http://www.shmoop.com/constitution/article-4-section-4.html

[1051] *Marbury v. Madison, 1803*, "A law repugnant to the Constitution is void." With these words, Chief Justice John Marshall established the Supreme Court's role in the new government. Hereafter, the Court was recognized as having the power to review all acts of Congress where constitutionality was at issue, and judge whether they abide by the Constitution.

[1052] Abraham Lincoln: "Proclamation 93 - Declaring the Objectives of the War Including Emancipation of Slaves in Rebellious States on January 1, 1863," September 22, 1862. Online by Gerhard Peters and John T. Woolley, The American Presidency Project. Accessed November 1, 2014, http://www.presidency.ucsb.edu/ws/?pid=69782

[1053] "*The Emancipation Proclamation*," National Archives & Records Administration, accessed November 29, 2014, http://www.archives.gov/exhibits/featured_documents/emancipation_proclamation/transcript.html

[1054] Abraham Lincoln: "Proclamation 108 - Amnesty and Reconstruction," December 8, 1863. Online by Gerhard Peters and John T. Woolley, The American Presidency Project., accessed October 15, 2014,http://www.presidency.ucsb.edu/ws/?pid=69987

[1055] Abraham Lincoln: "Proclamation 93 - Declaring the Objectives of the War Including Emancipation of Slaves in Rebellious States on January 1, 1863," September 22, 1862. Online by Gerhard Peters and John T. Woolley, The American Presidency Project., accessed October 15, 2014, http://www.presidency.ucsb.edu/ws/?pid=69782

[1056] *American Heritage A Reader,* "V Sectionalism and Civil War," ed. The Hillsdale College History Faculty, (Hillsdale: Hillsdale College Press, 2011) , 371

[1057] Abraham Lincoln, *Senate document no. 23,* page 91, 1865 as cited from Michael Rowbotham, *The Grip of Death: A Study of Modern Money, Debt Servitude, and Destructive Economics* (Jon Carpenter Publishing, 1998), pages 220-221 accessed November 29, 2014, http://economics.arawakcity.org/node/179

[1058] Search, *Money Martyred,* 46

[1059] Ibid., 47-48

[1060] Andrew Johnson: "Proclamation 148 - Revoking the Suspension of the Writ of Habeas Corpus, Except in Certain States and Territories," December 1, 1865. Online by Gerhard Peters and John T. Woolley, The American Presidency Project., accessed October 15, 2014,http://www.presidency.ucsb.edu/ws/?pid=72046

[1061] Shmoop Editorial Team. "Reconstruction" Shmoop University, Inc. 11 November 2008. http://www.shmoop.com/reconstruction/

[1062] President James Buchanan Geiger, *Republic for the United States of America,* 2014

[1063] Kennedy, Cohen, Baily, *The American Pageant Volume I: To 1877,* (Boston, Wadsworth, 2010), 478

[1064] *Wikipedia,* s.v. "Reconstruction Era, Military governors installed," last modified November 25, 2014, http://en.wikipedia.org/wiki/Reconstruction_Era

[1065] *Wikipedia,* s.v. "Andrew Johnson," last modified November 21, 2014, http://en.wikipedia.org/wiki/Andrew_Johnson

[1066] *Wikimedia Commons,* s.v. "AndrewJohnson1860.png," https://commons.wikimedia.org/wiki/File:AndrewJohnson1860.png This media file is in the public domain in the United States. This applies to U.S. works where the copyright has expired, often because its first publication occurred prior to January 1, 1923.

[1067] *Wikipedia,* s.v. "Edward Stanly," last modified September 8, 2014, http://en.wikipedia.org/wiki/Edward_Stanly

[1068] *Wikimedia Commons,* s.v. "Edward Stanly by Brady.jpg," https://commons.wikimedia.org/wiki/File:Edward_Stanly_by_Brady.jpg This work is from the Brady-Handy collection at the Library of Congress. According to the library, there are no known copyright restrictions on the use of this work. Mathew Brady died in 1896 and Levin C. Handy died in 1932. Photographs in this collection are in the public domain as works published before 1923 or as unpublished works whose copyright term has expired (life of author + 70 years).

[1069] *Wikimedia Commons,* s.v. "George F Shepley.jpg," https://commons.wikimedia.org/wiki/File:George_F_Shepley.jpg This work is in the public domain in its country of origin and other countries and areas where the copyright term is the author's life plus 100 years or less. United States public domain tag

[1070] *Wikipedia,* s.v. *"George Foster Shepley (Maine and Louisiana),"* last modified November 17, 2014, http://en.wikipedia.org/wiki/George_Foster_Shepley_(Maine_and_Louisiana)

[1071] *Wikipedia,* s.v. *"Benjamin Flanders,"* last modified October 20, 2014, http://en.wikipedia.org/wiki/Benjamin_Flanders

[1072] *Wikipedia,* s.v. *"Michael Hahn,"* last modified November 9, 2014, http://en.wikipedia.org/wiki/Michael_Hahn

[1073] *Wikipedia,* s.v. *"John S. Phelps,"* last modified October 17, 2014, http://en.wikipedia.org/wiki/John_S._Phelps

[1074] *Wikimedia Commons,* s.v. "Benjamin Franklin Flanders.jpg," https://commons.wikimedia.org/wiki/File:Benjamin_Franklin_Flanders.jpg This media file is in the public domain in the United States. This applies to U.S. works where the copyright has expired, often because its first publication occurred prior to January 1, 1923.

[1075] *Wikimedia Commons,* s.v. "Michael Hahn.jpg," https://commons.wikimedia.org/wiki/File:Michael_Hahn.jpg This media file is in the public domain in the United States. This applies to U.S. works where the copyright has expired, often because its first publication occurred prior to January 1, 1923.

[1076] *Wikimedia Commons,* s.v. "John smith phelps.jpg," https://en.wikipedia.org/wiki/File:John_smith_phelps.jpg#mw-jump-to-license This image is in the public domain in the United States. In most cases, this means that it was first published prior to January 1, 1923

[1077] Shmoop Editorial Team. *Reconstruction,* Shmoop University, Inc. 11 November 2008. http://www.shmoop.com/reconstruction/

[1078] Abraham Lincoln: "Proclamation 108 - Amnesty and Reconstruction," December 8, 1863. Online by Gerhard Peters and John T. Woolley, The American Presidency Project., accessed October 15, 2014, http://www.presidency.ucsb.edu/ws/?pid=69987

[1079] Library of Congress, "Abraham Lincoln, three-quarter length portrait, seated, facing right; hair parted on Lincoln's right side," http://www.loc.gov/pictures/item/2009630693/ This media file is in the public domain in the United States. This applies to U.S. works where the copyright has expired, often because its first publication occurred prior to January 1, 1923..

[1080] Shmoop Editorial Team. *Reconstruction Statistics,* Shmoop University, Inc. 11 November 2008. http://www.shmoop.com/reconstruction/statistics.html

[1081] Kennedy, Cohen, and Baily, *American Pageant,* 479

[1082] *Wikipedia,* s.v. "Jefferson Davis."

[1083] Cornell University Law School, Legal Information Institute, *U.S. Constitution,* "Sixth Amendment," accessed November 29, 2014, http://www.law.cornell.edu/constitution/sixth_amendment

[1084] *Wikimedia Commons,* s.v. "Jefferson Davis by Vannerson, 1859.jpg," https://commons.wikimedia.org/wiki/File:Jefferson_Davis_by_Vannerson,_1859.jpg This media file is in the public domain in the United States. This applies to U.S. works where the copyright has expired, often because its first publication occurred prior to January 1, 1923..

[1085] *Wikipedia,* s.v. "Gerrit Smith," last modified November 22, 2014, http://en.wikipedia.org/wiki/Gerrit_Smith

[1086] *Wikipedia,* s.v. "The Secret Six." https://commons.wikimedia.org/wiki/File:Gerrit_Smith_-_Brady-Handy.jpg This work is in the public domain in its country of origin and other countries and areas where the copyright term is the author's life plus 100 years or less.

[1087] Library of Congress, "Hon. Gerrit Smith of N.Y.," http://www.loc.gov/pictures/item/brh2003004625/PP/ No known restrictions on publication.

[1088] Shmoop Editorial Team. "Reconstruction Summary & Analysis" Shmoop University, Inc. 11 November 2008. http://www.shmoop.com/reconstruction/summary.html

[1089] Kennedy, Cohen, Baily, *The American Pageant Volume I: To 1877,* (Boston, Wadsworth, 2010), 485

[1090] *Wikipedia,* s.v. "Charles Sumner," last modified November 13, 2014, http://en.wikipedia.org/wiki/Charles_Sumner

[1091] *Wikipedia,* s.v. "Benjamin Wade," last modified June 26, 2014, http://en.wikipedia.org/wiki/Benjamin_Wade

[1092] *Wikipedia,* s.v. "George Washington Julian," last modified November 17, 2014, http://en.wikipedia.org/wiki/George_Washington_Julian

[1093] *Wikipedia,* s.v. "Thaddeus Stevens," last modified November 6, 2014, http://en.wikipedia.org/wiki/Thaddeus_Stevens

[1094] *American Heritage A Reader,* "V Sectionalism and Civil War,"ed. The Hillsdale College History Faculty, (Hillsdale: Hillsdale College Press, 2011) , 371

[1095] American Experience, *Reconstruction The Second Civil War,* accessed November 29, 2014, http://www.pbs.org/wgbh/amex/reconstruction/filmmore/pt.html

[1096] *Wikimedia Commons,* s.v. "Charles Sumner steel engraving c1860.jpg," https://commons.wikimedia.org/wiki/File:Charles_Sumner_steel_engraving_c1860.jpg This media file is in the public domain in the United States. This applies to U.S. works where the copyright has expired, often because its first publication occurred prior to January 1, 1923.

[1097] Library of Congress, "Benjamin F Wade - Brady-Handy.jpg," https://commons.wikimedia.org/wiki/File:Benjamin_F_Wade_-_Brady-Handy.jpg No known restrictions on publication.

[1098] Library of Congress, "Hon. Geo. Washington of Indiana," http://www.loc.gov/pictures/item/brh2003001893/PP/ No known restrictions on publication.

[1099] Library of Congress, "Hon. Thaddeus Stevens of Penn.," http://www.loc.gov/pictures/item/brh2003001359/PP/ No known restrictions on publication.

[1100] *Wikipedia*, s.v. "Wade-Davis Bill," last modified November 11, 2014, http://en.wikipedia.org/wiki/Wade%E2%80%93Davis_Bill

[1101] *Wikipedia,*s.v. "Henry Winter Davis," last modified August 13, 2014, http://en.wikipedia.org/wiki/Henry_Winter_Davis

[1102] *Wikipedia,*s.v. "Ironclad oath," last modified June 27, 2014,http://en.wikipedia.org/wiki/Ironclad_oath

[1103] Library of Congress, " H. Winter Davis, Representative from Maryland, Thirty-fifth Congress, half-length portrait," http://www.loc.gov/pictures/item/2010649160/ No known restrictions on publication.

[1104] *Wikipedia,*s.v. "Pocket veto," last modified November 12, 2014,http://en.wikipedia.org/wiki/Pocket_veto

[1105] Abraham Lincoln: "Proclamation 115 - Concerning a Bill "To Guarantee to Certain States, Whose Governments Have Been Usurped or Overthrown, a Republican Form of Government," and Concerning Reconstruction," July 8, 1864. Online by Gerhard Peters and John T. Woolley, The American Presidency Project., accessed October 15, 2014, http://www.presidency.ucsb.edu/ws/?pid=69995

[1106] Kennedy, Cohen, and Baily, *American Pageant,* 486

[1107] Richard Wormser, Jim Crow Stories, *Reconstruction 1865-77,* accessed November 29, 2014, http://www.pbs.org/wnet/jimcrow/stories_events_reconstruct.html

[1108] Phelps, *Vatican Assassins*, (359, 391, 352, 418

[1109] *Wikimedia Commons*, s.v. "Johnson inauguration.jpg," https://commons.wikimedia.org/wiki/File:Johnson_inauguration.jpg Scanned by Library of Congress, originally published in Frank Leslie's Illustrated Newspaper This media file is in the public domain in the United States. This applies to U.S. works where the copyright has expired, often because its first publication occurred prior to January 1, 1923.

[1110] American Experience, *Reconstruction The Second Civil War,* accessed November 29, 2014, http://www.pbs.org/wgbh/amex/reconstruction/filmmore/pt.html

[1111] Ibid.

[1112] Ibid.

[1113] Shmoop Editorial Team. *Article 4, Section 4,* Shmoop University, Inc. 11 November 2008. http://www.shmoop.com/constitution/article-4-section-4.html

[1114] *Marbury v. Madison, 1803*, "A law repugnant to the Constitution is void." With these words, Chief Justice John Marshall established the Supreme Court's role in the new government. Hereafter, the Court was recognized as having the power to review all acts of Congress where constitutionality was at issue, and judge whether they abide by the Constitution.

[1115] Shmoop Editorial Team. *Reconstruction Summary & Analysis,* Shmoop University, Inc. 11 November 2008. http://www.shmoop.com/reconstruction/summary.html

[1116] H. Paul Jeffers, *Freemasons: A History and Exploration of the World's Oldest Secret Society,* (New York: Citadel Press Books Kensington Publishing Corp., 2005), 105

[1117] 37th Masonic District, The Grand Lodge of Free & Accepted Masons of Pennsylvania, *Andrew Johnson,* http://www.pagrandlodge.org/district37/D37_Presidents/D37-AJohnson.php (accessed November 17, 2014)

[1118] Photographer Carl Casper Giers (1828-1877), "President Andrew Johnson in Masonic Regalia, 1869," Shades of Gray and Blue, as sourced from Tennessee State Museum, http://www.civilwarshades.org/andrew-johnson-in-masonic-regalia/ No known restrictions on publication.

[1119] Loyal Publication Society, *The Conditions of Reconstruction; in a Letter from Robert Dale Owen to the Secretary of State,* August 27, 1863, (New York: Wm. C. Bryant & Co, Printers 1863), p. 3, accessed November 5, 2014, https://archive.org/details/conditionsofrec00owen

[1120] *Wikimedia Commons,* s.v. "George Peter Alexander Healy - William T. Sherman - Google Art Project.jpg," https://commons.wikimedia.org/wiki/File:George_Peter_Alexander_Healy_-_William_T._Sherman_-_Google_Art_Project.jpg
    The author died in 1894, so this work is in the public domain in its country of origin and other countries and areas where the copyright term is the author's life plus 100 years or less.

[1121] Library of Congress, "Glimpses at the Freedmen - The Freedmen's Union Industrial School, Richmond, Va. / from a sketch by Jas E. Taylor.," http://www.loc.gov/item/98501491/ No known restrictions on publication.

[1122] Library of Congress, "Glimpses at the Freedmen's Bureau. Issuing rations to the old and sick / from a sketch by our special artist, Jas. E. Taylor.," http://www.loc.gov/item/2009633700/ No known restrictions on publication.

[1123] Andrew Johnson: "Proclamation 134 - Granting Amnesty to Participants in the Rebellion, with Certain Exceptions," May 29, 1865. Online by Gerhard Peters and John T. Woolley, The American Presidency Project., accessed October 15, 2014, http://www.presidency.ucsb.edu/ws/?pid=72392

[1124] University of Virginia Miller Center, *Andrew Johnson,* accessed November 29, 2014, http://millercenter.org/president/johnson/essays/biography/print

[1125] *American Experience,* "Reconstruction The Second Civil War," accessed November 29, 2014, http://www.pbs.org/wgbh/amex/reconstruction/filmmore/pt.html

[1126] Shmoop Editorial Team. *"Reconstruction Summary & Analysis,"* Shmoop University, Inc. 11 November 2008. http://www.shmoop.com/reconstruction/summary.html

[1127] Kennedy, Cohen, and Baily, *American Pageant,* 488

[1128] *Wikimedia Commons,* s.v. "ConfederateCabinet.jpg," https://commons.wikimedia.org/wiki/File:ConfederateCabinet.jpg Public domain due to publication in U.S. prior to 1923. This image is available from the United States Library of Congress's Prints and Photographs division under the digital ID cph.3c32563.

[1129] *Wikipedia,*s.v. "Lost Cause of the Confederacy," last modified October 22, 2014, http://en.wikipedia.org/wiki/Lost_Cause_of_the_Confederacy

[1130] University of Chicago Press and the Liberty Fund, *The Founders Constitution,* "Article 1, Section 5, Clauses 1," accessed November 29, 2014, http://press-pubs.uchicago.edu/founders/tocs/a1_5.html

[1131] Shmoop University, Inc., "How to Cite Shmoop," http://www.shmoop.com/help/cite-shmoop/

[1132] Shmoop Editorial Team. "Article 1, Section 5," Shmoop University, Inc. 11 November 2008. http://www.shmoop.com/constitution/article-1-section-5.html

[1133] Richard Wormser, *Jim Crow Stories,* "Reconstruction 1865-77," accessed November 29, 2014, http://www.pbs.org/wnet/jimcrow/stories_events_reconstruct.html

[1134] Ibid.

[1135] "Who Was Albert Pike?,"ThreeWorldWars.com.

[1136] H. Paul Jeffers, *Freemasons: A History and Exploration of the World's Oldest Secret Society,* (New York: Citadel Press Books, Kensington Publishing Corp., 2005), 105

[1137] B.Huldah & Company, "The Lincoln File: Albert Pike," http://www.officialbhuldahcompany.com/thelincolnfile.htm No known restrictions on this publication.

[1138] Andrew Johnson: "Proclamation 148 - Revoking the Suspension of the Writ of Habeas Corpus, Except in Certain States and Territories," December 1, 1865. Online by Gerhard Peters and John T. Woolley, The American Presidency Project., accessed November 29, 2014,http://www.presidency.ucsb.edu/ws/?pid=72046

[1139] Abraham Lincoln: "Proclamation 94 - Suspending the Writ of Habeas Corpus," September 24, 1862. Online by Gerhard Peters and John T. Woolley, The American Presidency Project., accessed November 29, 2014, http://www.presidency.ucsb.edu/ws/?pid=69783

[1140] Kennedy, Cohen, and Baily, *American Pageant,* 488

[1141] Shmoop Editorial Team. "Reconstruction Timeline of Important Dates," Shmoop University, Inc. 11 November 2008. http://www.shmoop.com/reconstruction/timeline.html

[1142] Richard Wormser, "Reconstruction 1865-77," PBS/Jim Crow Stories, accessed November 29, 2014, http://www.pbs.org/wnet/jimcrow/stories_events_reconstruct.html

[1143] Steven Hager, "Is Simon Wolf a key to the Lincoln assassination?," September 23, 2014, http://stevenhager420.wordpress.com/2014/09/23/is-simon-wolf-a-key-to-the-lincoln-assassination/

[1144] Phelps, *Vatican Assassins*, 359, 391, 359

[1145] Ibid., 352

[1146] Library of Congress, Abraham Lincoln Papers, "U.S. War Dept. War department, Washington, April 20, 1865. 100,000 reward!," https://memory.loc.gov/ammem/alhtml/alrb/stbdsd/00003900/001.html No known restrictions on publication.

[1147] "Grand Staircase," The Scottish Rite of Freemasonry Supreme Council, 33° Southern Jurisdiction, U.S.A., accessed September 25, 2014, http://scottishrite.org/headquarters/virtual-tour/grand-staircase/

[1148] *Wikipedia,*s.v. "United States Congress Joint Committee on Reconstruction," last modified March 29, 2013, http://en.wikipedia.org/wiki/United_States_Congress_Joint_Committee_on_Reconstruction

[1149] "Report of the Joint Committee on Reconstruction," Constitutional Accountability Center, accessed November 29, 2014, http://theusconstitution.org/sites/default/files/briefs/Report_of_the_Joint_Committee_on_Reconstruction.pdf

[1150] *Wikipedia,* s.v. "Thirteenth Amendment to the United States Constitution," last modified November 11, 2014, http://en.wikipedia.org/wiki/Thirteenth_Amendment_to_the_United_States_Constitution

[1151] Shmoop Editorial Team. "Reconstruction Timeline of Important Dates," Shmoop University, Inc. 11 November 2008. http://www.shmoop.com/reconstruction/timeline.html

[1152] H. Paul Jeffers, *Freemasons: A History and Exploration of the World's Oldest Secret Society,* (New York: Citadel Press Books Kensington Publishing Corp., 2005), 106

[1153] "Report of the Joint Committee on Reconstruction," Constitutional Accountability Center.

[1154] "Black Legislators: Primary Sources: The 1866 Civil Rights Act," PBS/Reconstruction The Second Civil War American Experience, December 19, 2003,http://www.pbs.org/wgbh/amex/reconstruction/activism/ps_1866.html

[1155] Ibid.

[1156] *Wikimedia Commons,* s.v. "Black Americans attacked in Memphis Riot of 1866.jpg," https://commons.wikimedia.org/wiki/File:Black_Americans_attacked_in_Memphis_Riot_of_1866.jpg This media file is in the public domain in the United States. This applies to U.S. works where the copyright has expired, often because its first publication occurred prior to January 1, 1923.

[1157] "The Meaning of Freedom: Black and White Responses to the End of Slavery," Digital History/America's Reconstruction/People and Politics After the Civil War, accessed November 29, 2014,http://www.digitalhistory.uh.edu/exhibits/reconstruction/section2/section2_33.html

[1158] "Report of the Joint Committee on Reconstruction," Constitutional Accountability Center.

[1159] Kennedy, Cohen, Baily, *The American Pageant Volume I: To 1877,* (Boston, Wadsworth, 2010), 489

[1160] "New Orleans Massacre (1866)," BlackPast.org, accessed November 29, 2014http://www.blackpast.org/aah/new-orleans-massacre-1866

[1161] Ibid.

[1162] *Wikimedia Commons,* s.v. "RiotInNewOrleansMurderingNegros1866.jpeg," https://commons.wikimedia.org/wiki/File:RiotInNewOrleansMurderingNegros1866.jpeg This media file is in the **public domain** in the United States. This applies to U.S. works where the copyright has expired, often because its first publication occurred prior to January 1, 1923.

[1163] *Wikipedia,*s.v. "Freedmen's Bureau bills," last modified May 24, 2014, http://en.wikipedia.org/wiki/Freedmen's_Bureau_bills

[1164] Shmoop Editorial Team. "Reconstruction Timeline of Important Dates," Shmoop University, Inc. 11 November 2008, http://www.shmoop.com/reconstruction/timeline.html

[1165] Kennedy, Cohen, and Baily, *American Pageant,* 491-492

[1166] *Wikipedia,*s.v. "Anti-Masonic Party," last modified November 12, 2014, http://en.wikipedia.org/wiki/Anti-Masonic_Party

[1167] *Wikimedia Commons,* s.v. "Charles Sumner Brady-Handy.jpg," https://commons.wikimedia.org/wiki/File:Charles_Sumner_Brady-Handy.jpg This work is from the Brady-Handy collection at the Library of Congress. According to the library, there are no known copyright restrictions on the use of this work. Mathew Brady died in 1896 and Levin C. Handy died in 1932. Photographs in this collection are in the public domain as works published before 1923 or as unpublished works whose copyright term has expired (life of author + 70 years).

[1168] *Wikipedia, s.v. "Charles Sumner,"* last modified November 13, 2014, http://en.wikipedia.org/wiki/Charles_Sumner (accessed 11/29/2014)

[1169] Library of Congress, "Hon. Thaddeus Stevens of Penn.," http://www.loc.gov/pictures/item/brh2003001359/PP/ No known restrictions on publication.

[1170] *Wikipedia,s.v. "Thaddeus Stevens,"* last modified November 6, 2014, http://en.wikipedia.org/wiki/Thaddeus_Stevens

[1171] Strout, *New Heavens,* 59

[1172] Jer. 33:3

[1173] *The Phrase Finder* s.v. "The meaning and origin of the expression: Truth is stranger than fiction," *accessed November 29, 2014,* http://www.phrases.org.uk/meanings/truth-is-stranger-than-fiction.html

[1174] *Wikipedia,*s.v. "Anti-Masonic Party."

[1175] *Wikipedia,*s.v. "William Morgan (anti-Mason)," last modified November 5, 2014, http://en.wikipedia.org/wiki/William_Morgan_(anti-Mason)#Book_on_Freemasonry

[1176] Michael F. Holt, Ph.D., "The Antimasonic Party," accessed December 3, 2015,http://lincoln.lib.niu.edu/message/antimasonic

[1177] *Wikipedia,*s.v. "Anti-Masonic Party."

[1178] *Wikipedia,* s.v. "Radical Republican," last modified November 26, 2014, http://en.wikipedia.org/wiki/Radical_Republican

[1179] *Wikipedia,* s.v. "Benjamin Wade," last modified June 26, 2014, http://en.wikipedia.org/wiki/Benjamin_Wade

[1180] Library of Congress, "Benjamin F Wade - Brady-Handy.jpg," https://commons.wikimedia.org/wiki/File:Benjamin_F_Wade_-_Brady-Handy.jpg No known restrictions on publication.

[1181] *Wikipedia,* s.v. "George Washington Julian," last modified November 17, 2014, http://en.wikipedia.org/wiki/George_Washington_Julian

[1182] Library of Congress, "Hon. Geo. Washington of Indiana," http://www.loc.gov/pictures/item/brh2003001893/PP/ No known restrictions on publication.

[1183] *Wikipedia,* s.v. "John Bingham," last modified October 20, 2014, http://en.wikipedia.org/wiki/John_Bingham

[1184] *Wikipedia,* s.v. "Opposition Party (United States)," last modified January 6, 2014, http://en.wikipedia.org/wiki/Opposition_Party_(United_States)

[1185] *Wikimedia Commons,* s.v. "BinghamFacingForward.jpg," https://commons.wikimedia.org/wiki/File:BinghamFacingForward.jpg This work is in the public domain in the United States because it is a work prepared by an officer or employee of the United States Government as part of that person's official duties under the terms of Title 17, Chapter 1, Section 105 of the US Code.

[1186] *Wikipedia,* s.v. "Henry Winter Davis," last modified August 13, 2014, http://en.wikipedia.org/wiki/Henry_Winter_Davis

[1187] Library of Congress, ",Hon. Henry W. Davies, Md - NARA - 528664.jpg" https://commons.wikimedia.org/wiki/File:Hon._Henry_W._Davies,_Md_-_NARA_-_528664.jpg This media is available in the holdings of the National Archives and Records Administration, cataloged under the ARC Identifier (National Archives Identifier) 528664. This work is in the public domain in its country of origin and other countries and areas where the copyright term is the author's life plus 70 years or less.

[1188] "Wm. Morgan" as included in Elder David Bernard's 1829 book *Light on Masonry,* (Utica:William Williams, Printer, 1829) Front matter pages http://economictheology.com/Downloads/Special/Light_on_Masonry-by_David_Bernard.pdf "Works of unknown authors or where the author's death date is unknown are copyrighted until the shorter of 95 years since the first publication or 120 years since their creation"- See 17 USC 302

[1189] *Wikimedia Commons,* s.v. "Washington Lincoln Greatest of Men (national picture) 1865.jpg," https://commons.wikimedia.org/wiki/File:Washington_Lincoln_Greatest_of_Men_(national_picture)_1865.jpg This media file is in the public domain in the United States. This applies to U.S. works where the copyright has expired, often because its first publication occurred prior to January 1, 1923.

[1190] *Wikipedia, s.v. "Charles Grandison Finney,"* last modified December 24, 2014, http://en.wikipedia.org/wiki/Charles_Grandison_Finney

[1191] Rev. C. G. Finney, Late President of Oberlin College, Ohio, *The Character, Claims and Practical Workings of Freemasonry,* (1869) http://www.libraryoftheology.com/writings/cultsandheresies/Freemasonry_Finney.pdf

[1192] Charles G. Finney, *Memoirs of Rev. Charles G. Finney,* (New York: A. S. Barnes & Company, 1876) photo front matter page

[1193] Rev. C. G. Finney, Late President of Oberlin College, Ohio, *The Character, Claims and Practical Workings of Freemasonry,* (Cincinnati: Western Tract and Book Society, 1869) https://books.google.com/books?id=BdY1AQAAMAAJ&pg=PP11&lpg=PP11&dq=The+Character,+Claims+and+Practical+Workings+of+Freemasonry.%E2%80%9D&source=bl&ots=nvqKKTB0xt&sig=aBAJvA8jic5XptYoL3SAOIswS7Q&hl=en&sa=X&ved=0ahUKEwiTnNL8oZbKAhWPth4KHWhtArYQ6AEIUzAJ#v=onepage&q=The%20Character%2C%20Claims%20and%20Practical%20Workings%20of%20Freemasonry.%E2%80%9D&f=false

[1194] Ibid., 108

[1195] Ibid., 5

[1196] Ibid., 5-6

[1197] Ibid., 6-7

[1198] Ibid., 8

[1199] (Elder) John G. Stearns, *Letters on Freemasonry*, (Utica: T.W. Seward, 1860) http://tinyurl.com/Stearns-on-Freemasonry Note: Finney was referring to Stearn's first book, Stearns on Masonry, which was later re-written by Mr. Stearns and then re-published as "Letters on Masonry." The same confession mentioned by Mr. Finney above, however, is found on page 17 of this 1860 edition of Brother Stearns' second book.

[1200] (Elder) David Bernard, *Light on Masonry, (Utica: William Williams, 1829)* http://tinyurl.com/Bernard-on-Freemasonry

[1201] *Wikimedia Commons,* s.v. "William Morgan (anti-Mason).jpg," last modified May 17, 2015, https://commons.wikimedia.org/wiki/File:William_Morgan_%28anti-Mason%29.jpg "Works of unknown authors or where the author's death date is unknown are copyrighted until the shorter of 95 years since the first publication or 120 years since their creation"- See 17 USC 302

[1202] Avery Allyn, *A Ritual of Freemasonry*, (New York: William Gowans, 1853) http://tinyurl.com/Avery-Allyn-on-Freemasonry

[1203] Martin L. Wagner, *Freemasonry: An Interpretation,* (Chicago: Ezra A. Cook, 1912; reprinted Seminar Tapes and Books of Grosse Pointe, MI), accessed November 29, 2014,
http://www.mindserpent.com/American_History/organization/mason/freemasonry/freemasonry.html#p_163

[1204] Ibid., 164

[1205] *Wikimedia Commons,* s.v. "ADAMS, John Q-President (BEP engraved portrait).jpg,"
https://commons.wikimedia.org/wiki/File:ADAMS,_John_Q-President_(BEP_engraved_portrait).jpg This work is in the public domain in the United States because it is a work prepared by an officer or employee of the United States Government as part of that person's official duties under the terms of Title 17, Chapter 1, Section 105 of the US Code.

[1206] Jack Harris, *Freemasonry Invisible Cult,* (New Kensington, Whitaker House, 2001), pp. 9-10

[1207] *Wikipedia,*s.v. "Masonic Lodge Officers," last modified October 21, 2014,
http://en.wikipedia.org/wiki/Masonic_Lodge_Officers

[1208] Harris, *Freemasonry Invisible Cult,* 9-10

[1209] Ibid., 124-125

[1210] Ibid., 48

[1211] Ibid., 139

[1212] Ibid., 102

[1213] Ibid., 159-160

[1214] 1 Cor. 5:4, Matt.18:20

[1215] Harris, *Freemasonry Invisible Cult,* 103

[1216] John 11:25

[1217] Harris, *Freemasonry Invisible Cult,* 121

[1218] Ibid., 121-122

[1219] Harmon R. Taylor, "A Grand Chaplain Speaks Out," Providence Baptist Ministries, accessed November 24, 2014,
http://www.pbministries.org/Parachurch/free%20masonry/grand_chaplin.htm

[1220] Andrew Johnson: "Proclamation 137 - Removing Trade Restrictions on Confederate States Lying East of the Mississippi River," June 13, 1865. Online by Gerhard Peters and John T. Woolley, The American Presidency Project. Accessed October 15, 2014, http://www.presidency.ucsb.edu/ws/?pid=71925

[1221] Andrew Johnson: "Proclamation 153 - Declaring the Insurrection in Certain Southern States to be at an End," April 2, 1866. Online by Gerhard Peters and John T. Woolley, The American Presidency Project., accessed October 15, 2014, http://www.presidency.ucsb.edu/ws/?pid=71987

[1222] Andrew Johnson: "Proclamation 157 - Declaring that Peace, Order, Tranquillity, and Civil Authority Now Exists in and Throughout the Whole of the United States of America," August 20, 1866. Online by Gerhard Peters and John T. Woolley, The American Presidency Project., accessed October 15, 2014,http://www.presidency.ucsb.edu/ws/?pid=71992

[1223] Shmoop Editorial Team. *"Reconstruction Summary & Analysis,"* Shmoop University, Inc. 11 November 2008. http://www.shmoop.com/reconstruction/summary.html

[1224] *"(1867) Thaddeus Stevens, 'Reconstruction'"* speech at BlackPast.org, sourced from Beverly Wilson Palmer and Holly Byers Ochoa, eds., *The Selected Papers of Thaddeus Stevens,* Vol. 2 April 1865-August 1868 (Pittsburgh: University of Pittsburgh Press, 1998)., accessed http://www.blackpast.org/1867-thaddeus-stevens-reconstruction

[1225] *Wikimedia Commons, s.v.* "Thaddeus Stevens2.jpg," https://commons.wikimedia.org/wiki/File:Thaddeus_Stevens2.jpg This media file is in the public domain in the United States. This applies to U.S. works where the copyright has expired, often because its first publication occurred prior to January 1, 1923.

[1226] *Wikimedia Commons,* s.v. "Charles Sumner Brady-Handy.jpg,"
https://commons.wikimedia.org/wiki/File:Charles_Sumner_Brady-Handy.jpg This work is from the Brady-Handy collection at the Library of Congress. According to the library, there are no known copyright restrictions on the use of this work. Mathew Brady died in 1896 and Levin C. Handy died in 1932. Photographs in this collection are in the public domain as works published before 1923 or as unpublished works whose copyright term has expired (life of author + 70 years).

[1227] *Wikipedia,*s.v. "Habeas Corpus Act 1867," last modified May 3, 2013,
http://en.wikipedia.org/wiki/Habeas_Corpus_Act_1867

[1228] "TEXAS v. WHITE," The Oyez Project at IIT Chicago-Kent College of Law, accessed November 10, 2014,
http://www.oyez.org/cases/1851-1900/1868/1868_0/

[1229] Shmoop Editorial Team. "Reconstruction Summary & Analysis" Shmoop University, Inc. 11 November 2008.
http://www.shmoop.com/reconstruction/summary.html

[1230] NPS.gov, United States Department of the Interior National Park Service, *National Register of Historic Places Inventory – Nomination Form* as recorded, accessed October 18, 2014, http://pdfhost.focus.nps.gov/docs/NRHP/Text/74002164.pdf

[1231] Ibid.

[1232] Ibid.

[1233] *Wikipedia,*s.v. "Supreme Council, Scottish Rite (Southern Jurisdiction, USA)," last modified May 28, 2014, http://en.wikipedia.org/wiki/Supreme_Council,_Scottish_Rite_(Southern_Jurisdiction,_USA)

[1234] Bernard Shusman, "New York Revisits Plan to Build Muslim Center Near Ground Zero," *Voice of America News,* May 12, 2014, http://www.voanews.com/content/proposal-to-build-ground-zero-muslim-center-revisited/1913143.html

[1235] *Wikipedia,*s.v. "Supreme Council, Scottish Rite (Southern Jurisdiction, USA)."

[1236] Dr. Stephen E. Jones, *Wars of the Lord,* Chapter 39, "The Federal City, Washington D.C.," (Fridley: Gods Kingdom Ministries, 2009), http://gods-kingdom-ministries.net/teachings/books/wars-of-the-lord/chapter-39-the-federal-city-washington-d-c/

[1237] Dr. Stephen E. Jones, *Wars of the Lord,* Chapter 38, "2004: The Fifth Bowl,"(Fridley: Gods Kingdom Ministries, 2009), http://gods-kingdom-ministries.net/teachings/books/wars-of-the-lord/chapter-38-2004-the-fifth-bowl/

[1238] Frank Joseph, "America's Arcane Origins," March 15, 2014, http://thegipster.blogspot.com/2014/03/americas-arcane-origins-frank-joseph.html with graphic sourced from http://worldtruth.tv/wp-content/uploads/2014/03/star.jpg

[1239] *Wikimedia Commons, s.v.* " Baphomet.png," from Eliphas Levi's "Dogme et Rituel de la Haute Magie", 1854, https://commons.wikimedia.org/wiki/File:Baphomet.png This work is in the public domain in its country of origin and other countries and areas where the copyright term is the author's life plus 70 years or less.
This work is in the public domain in its country of origin and other countries and areas where the copyright term is the author's life plus 70 years or less. United States public domain tag

[1240] pumpkinhead90, "Baphomet," http://pumpkinhead90.deviantart.com/art/Baphomet-32136295 No known restriction on publication.

[1241] *Wikipedia,*s.v. "Tenure of Office Act (1867)," last modified November 19, 2015, http://en.wikipedia.org/wiki/Tenure_of_Office_Act_%281867%29

[1242] Shmoop Editorial Team. "Reconstruction Summary & Analysis" Shmoop University, Inc. 11 November 2008. http://www.shmoop.com/reconstruction/summary.html

[1243] "Impeaching a President," PBS/Freedom: A History of US, Webisode 7. Segment 4, accessed November 29, 2014, http://www.pbs.org/wnet/historyofus/web07/segment4_p.html

[1244] *Wikimedia Commons*, s.v. "Johnson Impeachment Committee.jpg," https://commons.wikimedia.org/wiki/File:Johnson_Impeachment_Committee.jpg This media file is in the public domain in the United States. This applies to U.S. works where the copyright has expired, often because its first publication occurred prior to January 1, 1923.

[1245] Peter Carlson, "Thaddeus Stevens," February 19, 2013, HistoryNet.com, http://www.historynet.com/thaddeus-stevens.htm

[1246] "Impeaching a President," PBS/Freedom: A History of US.

[1247] "Burial Site of Thaddeus Stevens," Shreiner-Concord Cemetery, accessed November 29, 2014, http://www.shreinercemetery.org/(

[1248] "Thaddeus Stevens Biography," Biography.com, accessed November 29, 2014, http://www.biography.com/people/thaddeus-stevens-21011351#synopsis

[1249] "(1867) The Reconstruction Acts," African American History: Primary Documents, BlackPast.org as sourced from The Library of Congress American Memory, U.S. Congressional Documents and Debates, 39 Cong. Ch. 153; 14 Stat. 428, 40 Cong. Ch. 6; 15 Stat. 2, 40 Cong. Ch. 30; 15 Stat. 14), Ch. 25, 15 Stat. 41., accessed December 4, 2015, http://www.blackpast.org/primary/1867-reconstruction-acts

[1250] *Wikipedia,* s.v. "Reconstruction Acts," last modified November 28, 2014, http://en.wikipedia.org/wiki/Reconstruction_Acts

[1251] Ibid.

[1252] Library of Congress, ""This is a white man's government" "We regard the Reconstruction Acts (so called) of Congress as usurpations, and unconstitutional, revolutionary, and void" - Democratic Platform / / Th. Nast.," https://www.loc.gov/item/98513794/ No known restrictions on publication.

[1253] John S. Wise, *A Treatise on American Citizenship*, (Northport: Edward Thompson Co., 1906) 24, 196-197

[1254] "History of the Oath," United States Senate, Senate History, Oath of Office, accessed November 29, 2014, https://www.senate.gov/artandhistory/history/common/briefing/Oath_Office.htm

[1255] *Wikipedia,*s.v. "Ironclad oath," last modified June 27, 2014, http://en.wikipedia.org/wiki/Ironclad_oath

[1256] "Lawmakers, Loyalty and the 'Ironclad Oath,'" "Senate Loyalty Oathbook," January 24, 1866," U.S. Capitol Visitor Center, accessed November 29, 2014, http://www.visitthecapitol.gov/exhibition-hall/timeline/photos/1373

[1257] President James Buchanan Geiger, "Executive Summary," Republic for the United States of America, accessed November 29, 2014, http://www.republicoftheunitedstates.org/executive-summary/

[1258] Christopher L. Tomlins, *The United States Supreme Court: The Pursuit of Justice,* (New York: Houghton Mifflin Company, 2005), 110

[1259] *Wikipedia,s.v.* "Freedmen's Bureau," last modified November 29, 2014,http://en.wikipedia.org/wiki/Freedmen's_Bureau

[1260] *Wikimedia Commons,* s.v. "Carpetbagger.jpg," https://commons.wikimedia.org/wiki/File:Carpetbagger.jpg This work is in the public domain in its country of origin and other countries and areas where the copyright term is the author's life plus 100 years or less.

[1261] Richard Wormser, "Reconstruction 1865-77," PBS/Jim Crow Stories, accessed November 29, 2014, http://www.pbs.org/wnet/jimcrow/stories_events_reconstruct.html

[1262] Shmoop Editorial Team. "Reconstruction Summary & Analysis" Shmoop University, Inc. 11 November 2008. http://www.shmoop.com/reconstruction/summary.html

[1263] Richard Wormser, "Reconstruction 1865-77."

[1264] Phelps, *Vatican Assassins*, 359, 391, 336

[1265] Shmoop Editorial Team. "Reconstruction Summary & Analysis."

[1266] Library of Congress, "Two members of the Ku-Klux Klan in their disguises," http://www.loc.gov/pictures/item/97516403/ No known restrictions on publication.

[1267] Phelps, *Vatican Assassins*, 359, 391, 336

[1268] "Will the Great American Experiment, Succeed?," National Center for Constitutional Studies citing W. David Stedman& La Vaughn G. Lewis, Editors *Our Ageless Constitution,* (Asheboro, NC, W. David Stedman Associates, 1987) Part VII, accessed November 29, 2014, http://www.nccs.net/will-the-great-american-experiment-succeed.php

[1269] *Wikipedia,s.v.* "Enforcement Acts," last modified September 13, 2014,http://en.wikipedia.org/wiki/Enforcement_Acts

[1270] Library of Congress, "Visit of the Ku-Klux," http://www.loc.gov/pictures/item/2001695506/ No known restrictions on publication.

[1271] Shmoop Editorial Team. "Reconstruction Summary & Analysis."

[1272] Ibid.

[1273] Ibid.

[1274] Ibid.

[1275] Library of Congress, Lee, Russell, 1903-1986, photographer, "Negro drinking at "Colored" water cooler in streetcar terminal, Oklahoma City, Oklahoma," http://www.loc.gov/pictures/item/fsa1997026728/PP/ No known restrictions.

[1276] Shmoop Editorial Team. "Reconstruction Summary & Analysis."

[1277] *Wikipedia*, s.v. "Gilded Age," last modified on April 7, 2017, https://en.wikipedia.org/wiki/Gilded_Age

[1278] Ibid.

[1279] Shmoop Editorial Team. *Article 4, Section 4,* Shmoop University, Inc. 11 November 2008. http://www.shmoop.com/constitution/article-4-section-4.html

[1280] Abraham Lincoln: "Proclamation 93 - Declaring the Objectives of the War Including Emancipation of Slaves in Rebellious States on January 1, 1863," September 22, 1862. Online by Gerhard Peters and John T. Woolley, The American Presidency Project., accessed October 15, 2014, http://www.presidency.ucsb.edu/ws/?pid=69782

[1281] "The Emancipation Proclamation," National Archives & Records Administration, http://www.archives.gov/exhibits/featured_documents/emancipation_proclamation/transcript.html (accessed 11/29/2014)

[1282] *Wikipedia,* s.v. "De facto."

[1283] Andrew Johnson: "Proclamation 179 - Granting Full Pardon and Amnesty for the Offense of Treason Against the United States During the Late Civil War," December 25, 1868. Online by Gerhard Peters and John T. Woolley, The American Presidency Project., accessed November 29, 2014, http://www.presidency.ucsb.edu/ws/?pid=72360

[1284] "An Act to provide a Government for the District of Columbia" *Statutes at Large,* Forty-First Congress, Sess. III, Vol. 16, Ch. 62, p. 419, February 21, 1871, accessed November 29, 2014, TeamLaw.org, http://www.teamlaw.org/DCOA-1871.pdf

[1285] New World Order Today Staff, "The Powers – Behind the Global Empire," accessed November 29, 2014,http://www.nwotoday.com/today/the-powers-behind-the-global-empire

[1286] *Wikimedia Commons*, "Map of the District of Columbia, 1835.jpg," https://commons.wikimedia.org/wiki/File:Map_of_the_District_of_Columbia,_1835.jpg This media file is in the public domain in the United States. This applies to U.S. works where the copyright has expired, often because its first publication occurred prior to January 1, 1923.

[1287] The United States Statutes at Large, Vol 2, 6th Congress (1799-1801), Sess. II, p 103-108, ch. 15, "An Act concerning the District of Columbia.(a), Feb 27, 1801 https://www.loc.gov/law/help/statutes-at-large/

[1288] The United States Statutes at Large, Vol 2, 7th Congress (1801-1803), Sess. I, p 193-195, ch. 52 "An Act additional to, and amendatory of, an act, intituled 'An act concerning the District of Columbia.'" May 3, 1802 https://www.loc.gov/law/help/statutes-at-large/

[1289] "Title 28, 'Judiciary and Judicial Procedure,'" United States Code, Clerk of the United States House of Representatives, accessed November 29, 2014, http://library.clerk.house.gov/reference-files/PPL_080_773_JudiciaryAndJudicialProcedure.pdf

[1290] "28 U.S. Code § 3002 – Definitions," Cornell University Law School, Legal Information Institute, accessed November 29, 2014, http://www.law.cornell.edu/uscode/text/28/3002

[1291] JJMcCullough.com, "The Constitution of the Confederate States of America: What was changed? And why?," accessed December 4, 2015, http://www.jjmccullough.com/CSA.htm

[1292] "Revised Statutes § 1992, 8 United States Code Annotated section 1," The American and English Encyclopaedia of Law, Vol. VI, ed. John Houston Merrill, (Long Island: Edward Thompson Company, Law Publishers, 1888), 265

[1293] John S. Wise, A Treatise on American Citizenship, (Northport, Long Island: Edward Thompson Company, 1906) p 199

[1294] Ibid., p 195

[1295] Ibid., p 196

[1296] Peter Carlson, "Thaddeus Stevens," February 19, 2013, HistoryNet.com, http://www.historynet.com/thaddeus-stevens.htm

[1297] State v. Phillips, Pacific Reporter, 2nd Series, Vol. 540, (1975), 941, 942

[1298] "Walter R. (Bud) Ellett: The Quintessential Lawyer," The Salt Lake Tribune, Sept 13, 1927 - Feb 15, 2012, http://www.legacy.com/obituaries/saltlaketribune/obituary.aspx?n=walter-r-ellett-bud&pid=155924768&

[1299] Chief Justice Harvey Pete Moake, Republic Information Call for the Governors (RICG) and Building the States, Wednesday, January 13, 2016; David Barton, Original Intent: The Courts, The Constitution, and Religion, 5th Ed., (Aledo: WallBuilder Press, 2013), pp 7-8

[1300] David Barton, "Republic v. Democracy," WallBuilders, January, 2001, http://www.wallbuilders.com/libissuesarticles.asp?id=111

[1301] NOTE: An example of this is demonstrated in the anecdote where, having concluded their work on the Constitution, Benjamin Franklin walked outside and seated himself on a public bench. A woman approached him and inquired, "Well, Dr. Franklin, what have you done for us?" Franklin quickly responded, "My dear lady, we have given to you a republic--if you can keep it." Taken from "America's Bill of Rights at 200 Years," by former Chief Justice Warren E. Burger, printed in Presidential Studies Quarterly, Vol. XXI, No. 3, Summer 1991, p. 457. This anecdote appears in numerous other works as well.

[1302] Alexander Hamilton, John Jay, James Madison, The Federalist on the New Constitution (Philadelphia: Benjamin Warner, 1818), p. 53, #10, James Madison.

[1303] John Adams, The Works of John Adams, Second President of the United States, Charles Francis Adams, editor (Boston: Charles C. Little and James Brown, 1850), Vol. VI, p. 484, to John Taylor on April 15, 1814.

[1304] Fisher Ames, Works of Fisher Ames (Boston: T. B. Wait & Co., 1809), p. 24, Speech on Biennial Elections, delivered January, 1788.

[1305] Ames, Works, p. 384, "The Dangers of American Liberty," February 1805.

[1306] Gouverneur Morris, An Oration Delivered on Wednesday, June 29, 1814, at the Request of a Number of Citizens of New-York, in Celebration of the Recent Deliverance of Europe from the Yoke of Military Despotism (New York: Van Winkle and Wiley, 1814), pp. 10, 22.

[1307] John Quincy Adams, The Jubilee of the Constitution. A Discourse Delivered at the Request of the New York Historical Society, in the City of New York on Tuesday, the 30th of April 1839; Being the Fiftieth Anniversary of the Inauguration of George Washington as President of the United States, on Thursday, the 30th of April, 1789, (New York: Samuel Colman, 1839), 53.

[1308] Benjamin Rush, The Letters of Benjamin Rush, L. H. Butterfield, editor (Princeton: Princeton University Press for the American Philosophical Society, 1951), Vol. I, p. 523, to John Adams on July 21, 1789.

[1309] Noah Webster, The American Spelling Book: Containing an Easy Standard of Pronunciation: Being the First Part of a Grammatical Institute of the English Language, To Which is Added, an Appendix, Containing a Moral Catechism and a Federal Catechism (Boston: Isaiah Thomas and Ebenezer T. Andrews, 1801), 103-104.

[1310] John Witherspoon, The Works of John Witherspoon (Edinburgh: J. Ogle, 1815), Vol. VII, p. 101, Lecture 12 on Civil Society.

[1311] Zephaniah Swift, A System of the Laws of the State of Connecticut (Windham: John Byrne, 1795), Vol. I, p. 19.

[1312] See, for example, Benjamin Rush, Letters, Vol. I, p. 498, to John Adams on January 22, 1789.

[1313] Noah Webster, History of the United States (New Haven: Durrie & Peck, 1832), 6.

[1314] George Bancroft, History of the United States from the Discovery of the American Continent (Boston: Little, Brown & Co., 1859), Vol. V, p. 24; see Baron Charles Secondat de Montesquieu, Spirit of the Laws (Philadelphia: Isaiah Thomas, 1802), Vol. I, pp. 17-23, and ad passim.

[1315] Rush, Letters, Vol. I, p. 454, to David Ramsay, March or April 1788.

[1316] William Blackstone, *Commentaries on the Laws of England* (Philadelphia: Robert Bell, 1771), Vol. I, pp. 42-43.

[1317] James Wilson, The Works of the Honorable James Wilson, Bird Wilson, editor (Philadelphia: Lorenzo Press, 1804), Vol. I, pp. 103-105, "Of the General Principles of Law and Obligation."

[1318] Alexander Hamilton, *The Papers of Alexander Hamilton,* Vol. I, .ed Harold C. Syrett, (New York: Columbia University Press, 1961), 87, February 23, 1775, quoting William Blackstone, *Commentaries on the Laws of England,* Vol. I, (Philadelphia: Robert Bell, 1771), 41

[1319] Rufus King, to C. Gore on February 17, 1820, *The Life and Correspondence of Rufus King,* Vol. VI, .ed Charles R. King, (New York: G. P. Putnam's Sons, 1900), 276,

[1320] John Adams, *The Papers of John Adams,* Vol. 1,.ed Robert J. Taylor, (Cambridge: Belknap Press, 1977), 83, from "An Essay on Man's Lust for Power, with the Author's Comment in 1807," written on August 29, 1763, but first published by John Adams in 1807.

[1321] Ps. 43:3

[1322] Exod. 3:6; Matt. 22:32; Acts 3:13, 7:32

[1323] Exod. 3:15

[1324] Nehemia Gordon, "The Pronunciation of the Name," accessed December 1, 2014, http://www.karaite-korner.org/yhwh_2.pdf

[1325] Rom. 1:18-32

[1326] Rev. 14:8, 18:4

[1327] Margaret Minnicks, "Satan's counterfeits," accessed December 1, 2014, http://www.examiner.com/article/satan-s-counterfeits

[1328] Ted Montgomery, "Realities vs. Counterfeits," *Creation…Counterfeits…and the 70th Week: A Comprehensive, Detailed Study of the Bible, (1989)* Ch. 9, accessed December 1, 2014, http://www.tedmontgomery.com/bblovrvw/C_9a.html

[1329] Rev. 20:10

[1330] 2 Cor. 4:4

[1331] Ibid.

[1332] Federal Dictionary Act of 1871, "An Act prescribing the Form of the enacting and resolving Clauses of Acts and Resolutions of Congress, and Rules for the Construction thereof.," Statutes at Large, Forty-First Congress, Sess. III, Vol. 16, Ch. P. 71, February 25, 1871, accessed June 28, 2013, http://www.scribd.com/doc/158698122/Federal-Dictionary-Act-of-1871#scribd

[1333] Gen.1:26

[1334] Chiniquy, *Fifty Years,* 621

[1335] Ibid., 617

[1336] Jas. 3:17

[1337] Rom. 3:19

[1338] John Quincy Adams, *Letters on the Masonic Institution*, (Boston: Press of T. R. Marvin, 1847) Title page https://archive.org/stream/lettersonmasoni00adamgoog#page/n8/mode/2up

[1339] John Quincy Adams, *Letters and Addresses on Freemasonry*, (Dayton: United Brethren Publishing House, 1875) Title page https://archive.org/details/Letters_And_Addresses_On_Freemasonry_-_J_Quincy_Adams

[1340] John Quincy Adams, *Letters and Addresses on Freemasonry: To a Reviewer of Sheppard's Defense of the Masonic Institution*, 22 August, 1831, (Boston: Press of T. R. Marvin, 1847) Title p. 49

[1341] Texe Marrs, "Nation's Sixth President Opposed Masonic Lodge: John Quincy Adams and Freemasonry," accessed January 30, 2017, *Exclusive Intelligence Examiner Report,* http://www.texemarrs.com/072001/john_quincy.htm

[1342] Library of Congress, "John Quincy Adams, President of the United States / painted by T. Sully ; eng. by A.B. Durand," https://www.loc.gov/resource/ppmsca.15717/ This media file is in the public domain in the United States. This applies to U.S. works where the copyright has expired, often because its first publication occurred prior to January 1, 1923

[1343] *Wikimedia Commons*, s.v. "69workmen.jpg," https://commons.wikimedia.org/wiki/File:69workmen.jpg This work is in the public domain in its country of origin and other countries and areas where the copyright term is the author's life plus 100 years or less. This work is in the public domain in the United States because it was published (or registered with the U.S. Copyright Office) before January 1, 1923.

[1344] *Wikipedia*, s.v. "Gilded Age," last modified on April 18, 2017, https://en.wikipedia.org/wiki/Gilded_Age

[1345] Jim Marrs, *Rule by Secrecy*, (New York: Harper-Collins Publishers, 2000) 83

[1346] *Wikipedia*, s.v. "Robber baron (industrialist)," last modified on April 4, 2017, https://en.wikipedia.org/wiki/Robber_baron_(industrialist)

[1347] Jim Marrs, *Rule by Secrecy*, (New York: Harper-Collins Publishers, 2000) 5-12

[1348] *Library of Congress*, "The great race for the Western stakes 1870," http://www.loc.gov/pictures/item/2003656591/ This work is in the public domain in its country of origin and other countries and areas where the copyright term is the author's life plus 100 years or less.

[1349] Kennedy, Cohen, Baily, *The American Pageant Volume I: To 1877,* (Boston, Wadsworth, 2010), 478

[1350] *Wikipedia*, s.v. "Plessy v. Ferguson," last modified on May 15, 2017, https://en.wikipedia.org/wiki/Plessy_v._Ferguson

[1351] U.S. Supreme Court Justice Hugo Black as quoted in Thom Hartmann, *Unequal Protection: The Rise of Corporate Dominance and the Theft of Human Rights*, (San Francisco: Berrett-Koehler Publishers, Inc, 2002) 126

[1352] *Wikimedia Commons*, s.v. "HugoLaFayetteBlack.jpg," https://commons.wikimedia.org/wiki/File:HugoLaFayetteBlack.jpg This image is available from the United States Library of Congress's Prints and Photographs division under the digital ID cph.3a34024. This work is from the Harris & Ewing collection at the Library of Congress. According to the library, there are no known copyright restrictions on the use of this work.

[1353] *Wikimedia Commons*, s.v. "The Bosses of the Senate, a cartoon by Joseph Keppler. First published in Puck 1889.," https://commons.wikimedia.org/wiki/File:The_Bosses_of_the_Senate_by_Joseph_Keppler.jpg This work is in the public domain in its country of origin and other countries and areas where the copyright term is the author's life plus 100 years or less. This work is in the public domain in its country of origin and other countries and areas where the copyright term is the author's life plus 100 years or less.

[1354] Thom Hartmann, *Unequal Protection: The Rise of Corporate Dominance and the Theft of Human Rights*, (San Francisco: Berrett-Koehler Publishers, Inc, 2002) 110, 96-119

[1355] *Wikipedia*, s.v. "Roscoe Conkling," last modified on February 23, 2017, https://en.wikipedia.org/wiki/Roscoe_Conkling

[1356] Thom Hartmann, *Unequal Protection: The Rise of Corporate Dominance and the Theft of Human Rights*, (San Francisco: Berrett-Koehler Publishers, Inc, 2002) 110

[1357] *Wikimedia Commons*, s.v. "RConkling," https://commons.wikimedia.org/wiki/File:RConkling.jpg This work is in the public domain in its country of origin and other countries and areas where the copyright term is the author's life plus 100 years or less.

[1358] Howard Jay Graham, *The Yale Law Journal*, "The 'Conspiracy Theory' of the Fourteenth Amendment," (Vol. 47, 1937) p 371

[1359] Thom Hartmann, *Unequal Protection: The Rise of Corporate Dominance and the Theft of Human Rights*, (San Francisco: Berrett-Koehler Publishers, Inc, 2002) 109

[1360] *Wikipedia,* s.v. "Crédit Mobilier of America scandal," last modified on April 9, 2017, https://en.wikipedia.org/wiki/Cr%C3%A9dit_Mobilier_of_America_scandal

[1361] *Wikipedia*, s.v. "Salary Grab Act," last modified on January 22, 2017, https://en.wikipedia.org/wiki/Salary_Grab_Act

[1362] Woodrow Wilson, "What is Progress?," 1912, cited at The Heritage Foundation, "Woodrow Wilson Asks "What Is Progress?," http://origin.heritage.org/initiatives/first-principles/primary-sources/woodrow-wilson-asks-what-is-progress

[1363] *Wikipedia*, "Salary Grab Act," last modified on January 22, 2017, https://en.wikipedia.org/wiki/Salary_Grab_Act

[1364] *The Free Dictionary,* s.v. "Statism," accessed November 24, 2015, http://www.thefreedictionary.com/statism

[1365] *Wikimedia Commons*, s.v. "President Theodore Roosevelt, 1904.jpg," https://commons.wikimedia.org/wiki/File:President_Theodore_Roosevelt,_1904.jpg#mw-jump-to-license This image is available from the United States Library of Congress's Prints and Photographs division under the digital ID cph.3a53299.

[1366] *Wikimedia Commons*, s.v. "William Howard Taft, Bain bw photo portrait, 1908.jpg," William Howard Taft, Bain bw photo portrait, 1908.jpg This media file is in the public domain in the United States. This applies to U.S. works where the copyright has expired, often because its first publication occurred prior to January 1, 1923.

[1367] *Wikimedia Commons*, s.v. "Thomas Woodrow Wilson, Harris & Ewing bw photo portrait, 1919.jpg, https://commons.wikimedia.org/wiki/File:Thomas_Woodrow_Wilson,_Harris_%26_Ewing_bw_photo_portrait,_1919.jpg#mw-jump-to-license This image is available from the United States Library of Congress's Prints and Photographs division under the digital ID cph.3f06247. This work is from the Harris & Ewing collection at the Library of Congress. According to the library, there are no known copyright restrictions on the use of this work.

[1368] *Wikipedia*, s.v. "Progressive Era," last modified January 20, 2017, https://en.m.wikipedia.org/wiki/Progressive_Era This media file is in the public domain in the United States. This applies to U.S. works where the copyright has expired, often because its first publication occurred prior to January 1, 1923

[1369] Jones, *Prophetic History*, 37

[1370] 2 Tim. 4:3-4

[1371] Jones, *Prophetic History*, 37

[1372] Prof. Paul Moreno, "Progressivism," *History 102: American Heritage—From Colonial Settlement to the Reagan Revolution*, accessed August 25, 2013, http://online.hillsdale.edu/page.aspx?pid=1919

[1373] *Wikimedia Commons*, s.v. "JusticeJamesWilson.jpg,"
https://commons.wikimedia.org/wiki/File:JusticeJamesWilson.jpg#mw-jump-to-license This work is in the public domain in the United States because it is a work prepared by an officer or employee of the United States Government as part of that person's official duties under the terms of Title 17, Chapter 1, Section 105 of the US Code.

[1374] James Wilson, *"The Works of James Wilson, associate justice of the Supreme Court of the United States and Professor of Law in the College of Philadelphia,"* Vol. I, ed. James De Witt Andrews, (Chicago: Callaghan and Company, 1896) , 93-95

[1375] Federer, *America's Quotations,* "David Josiah Brewer," 70

[1376] Library of Congress, "David Josiah Brewer, 1837-1910," http://www.loc.gov/pictures/item/2001704066/ No known restrictions on reproduction.

[1377] Ibid., 71

[1378] *Wikimedia Commonsl, s.v.* "JudgeJMHarlan.jpg," *https://commons.wikimedia.org/wiki/File:JudgeJMHarlan.jpg#mw-jump-to-license* This image is available from the United States Library of Congress's Prints and Photographs division under the digital ID cwpbh.04615. his work is from the Brady-Handy collection at the Library of Congress. According to the library, there are no known copyright restrictions on the use of this work.
Mathew Brady died in 1896 and Levin C. Handy died in 1932. Photographs in this collection are in the public domain in the US as works published before 1923 or as unpublished works whose copyright term has expired (life of author + 70 years).

[1379] Supreme Court Justice Marshall Harlan in his dissenting opinion Downes v. Bidwell, 182 U.S. 244 (1901), accessed on December 15, 2016, http://www.supremelaw.org/decs/downes/Justice.Harlan.dissent.htm

[1380] *Wikimedia Commons, s.v.* "Cover of McGuffey's First Eclectic Reader.jpeg," https://commons.wikimedia.org/wiki/File:Cover_of_McGuffey%27s_First_Eclectic_Reader.jpeg This work is in the public domain in its country of origin and other countries and areas where the copyright term is the author's life plus 100 years or less.

[1381] *The McGuffy Readers*, accessed December 1, 2014, http://www.mcguffeyreaders.com/1836_original.htm

[1382] "State of Tennessee v. Scopes," ACLU.org, accessed December 1, 2014, https://www.aclu.org/religion-belief/state-tennessee-v-scopes

[1383] Fritz Springmeier, *Bloodlines of the Illuminati,* (Spring Arbor Distributors, 1998)

[1384] Dean Henderson, "The Federal Reserve Cartel: the Eight Families," *Global Research,* December 1, 2011, http://www.globalresearch.ca/the-federal-reserve-cartel-the-eight-families/25080

[1385] The short title of the Act of December 23, 1913, ch. 6, 38 Stat. 251, shall be the "Federal Reserve Act," Cornell University Law School, Legal Information Institute, accessed December 4, 2015, https://www.law.cornell.edu/uscode/text/12/226

[1386] Alan Lamont, "The Jesuit Vatican New World Order: THIS IS WORLD HISTORY," April 6, 2012, http://vaticannewworldorder.blogspot.com/2012/04/fidel-castro-of-cuba-profile-of.html

[1387] Federal Reserve History, "Signing of the Federal Reserve Act, Courtesy of Woodrow Wilson Presidential Library; Painting by Wilbur G. Kurtz," http://www.federalreservehistory.org/Events/DetailView/10 This media file is in the public domain in the United States. This applies to U.S. works where the copyright has expired, often because its first publication occurred prior to January 1, 1923.

[1388] *Wikimedia Commons, s.v.* "Fed Reserve.JPG," https://commons.wikimedia.org/wiki/File:Fed_Reserve.JPG This media file is in the public domain in the United States. This applies to U.S. works where the copyright has expired, often because its first publication occurred prior to January 1, 1923.

[1389] Bill Still, "The Money Masters - How International Bankers Gained Control of America," Youtube/Канал корисника deja035, Uploaded on May 11, 2011, https://www.youtube.com/watch?v=TwqUr7PSRO8

[1390] TheMoneyMasters.com, "Famous Quotes on Banking: President Woodrow Wilson," accessed December 1, 2014, http://www.themoneymasters.com/the-money-masters/famous-quotations-on-banking/

[1391] Dean Henderson, "The Federal Reserve Cartel: the Eight Families."

[1392] Jones, *Prophetic History,* 21

[1393] "Governments Have Descended to the Level of Mere Private Corporations: Supreme Court Annotated Statute, Clearfield Trust Co. v. United States, 318 U.S. 363-371 (1942)," AntiCorruption Society, accessed December 4, 2015, https://anticorruptionsociety.files.wordpress.com/2014/05/clearfield-doctrine.pdf

[1394] Judge Dale, retired, *The Great American Adventure,* (CreateSpace Independent Publishing Platform, 2014), 4, 78, 80, accessed December 4, 2015, http://anticorruptionsociety.files.wordpress.com/2013/11/the-great-american-adventure-sm-book-format_pdf.pdf

[1395] Shmoop Editorial Team. "16th Amendment" *Shmoop* University, Inc. 11 November 2008. http://www.shmoop.com/constitution/16th-amendment.html

[1396] Phelps, *Vatican Assassins*, 354

[1397] Jones, *Prophetic History,* 22

[1398] "Article 1, Section 3," Cornell University Law School, Legal Information Institute, accessed December 10, 2014, http://www.law.cornell.edu/constitution/articlei

[1399] *Wikipedia,*s.v. "Seventeenth Amendment to the United States Constitution," last modified http://en.wikipedia.org/wiki/Seventeenth_Amendment_to_the_United_States_Constitution

[1400] Shmoop Editorial Team. "Article 1, Section 3" Shmoop University, Inc. 11 November 2008. http://www.shmoop.com/constitution/article-1-section-3.html

[1401] *Wikimedia Commons*, s.v. "Standard oil octopus loc color.jpg," https://commons.wikimedia.org/wiki/File:Standard_oil_octopus_loc_color.jpg This image is available from the United States Library of Congress's Prints and Photographs division under the digital ID ppmsca.25884. This media file is in the public domain in the United States. This applies to U.S. works where the copyright has expired, often because its first publication occurred prior to January 1, 1923.

[1402] Franklin D. Roosevelt: "Executive Order 6073 - Reopening Banks," March 10, 1933. Online by Gerhard Peters and John T. Woolley, The American Presidency Project. http://www.presidency.ucsb.edu/ws/?pid=14507

[1403] Franklin D. Roosevelt: "Executive Order 6102 - Requiring Gold Coin, Gold Bullion and Gold Certificates to Be Delivered to the Government," April 5, 1933. Online by Gerhard Peters and John T. Woolley, The American Presidency Project. http://www.presidency.ucsb.edu/ws/?pid=14611

[1404] Franklin D. Roosevelt: "Executive Order 6111 on Transactions in Foreign Exchange.," April 20, 1933. Online by Gerhard Peters and John T. Woolley, The American Presidency Project. http://www.presidency.ucsb.edu/ws/?pid=14621

[1405] Franklin D. Roosevelt: "Executive Order 6260 on Hoarding and Exporting Gold.," August 28, 1933. Online by Gerhard Peters and John T. Woolley, The American Presidency Project. http://www.presidency.ucsb.edu/ws/?pid=14509

[1406] John B. Nelson, "Declaration of Cause and Necessity to Abolish and Declaration of Separate and Equal Station," (referencing Senate Report 93-549, 93rd Congress, 1st Session, 1973, pp. 187, 594), February 21, 1992, accessed on December 4, 2015, http://home.absolute.net/xode/nwofraud/Bankruptcy_fraud/Bankfraud1.htm

[1407] "The Federal Reserve Bank Offer: As it was presented in 1913," TeamLaw.org, accessed December 1, 2014, http://www.teamlaw.org/FRB1913.htm

[1408] "The Federal Reserve Bank Offer: As it was compelled in 1933, " TeamLaw.org, accessed December 1, 2014, http://www.teamlaw.org/FRB1933.htm

[1409] "Roosevelt Orders 4-Day Bank Holiday, Puts Embargo on Gold, Calls Congress," *New York Times,* March 4, 1933, as posted on Martin Armstrong, "Happy New Year — Bail-In Passed for Europe's Banks," December 30, 2015, http://www.armstrongeconomics.com/archives/tag/roosevelt No known restrictions on publication.

[1410] New World Order Today Staff, "Franklin D. Roosevelt," accessed December 1, 2014, http://www.nwotoday.com/the-new-world-orders-history/the-socialist-review-american-politicians/franklin-d-roosevelt

[1411] Steven Sora, *Secret Societies of America's Elite: From the Knights Templar to Skull and Bones,* (Rochester, Destiny Books, 2003), 270

[1412] In Roosevelt History, Sharing the Franklin D. Roosevelt Presidential Library and Museum Collections and Programs, "Found in the Archives: FDR and the Masons," https://fdrlibrary.wordpress.com/tag/freemasons/ This work is in the public domain in its country of origin and other countries and areas where the copyright term is the author's life plus 70 years or less. United States public domain tag. No known restrictions.

[1413] Library of Congress, "Franklin Delano Roosevelt, head-and-shoulders portrait, facing slightly left," https://www.loc.gov/resource/cph.3c17121/ No known restrictions

[1414] New World Order Today Staff, "Franklin D. Roosevelt."

[1415] The American Presidency Project, Franklin D. Roosevelt, *34 - Executive Order 6102 - Requiring Gold Coin, Gold Bullion and Gold Certificates to Be Delivered to the Government.*

[1416] *Wikipedia*, s.v. "Executive Order 6102," last modified November 22, 2014, http://en.wikipedia.org/wiki/Executive_Order_6102 (accessed 12/1/2014)

[1417] New World Order Today Staff, "1933 - The Confiscation of Gold, accessed December 1, 2014," accessed December 1, 2014, http://www.nwotoday.com/today/the-world-financial-system/the-federal-reserve-system/1933-the-confiscation-of-gold-and-silver

[1418] "Inflation Calculator, The Changing Value of a Dollar," DollarTimes.com, accessed December 1, 2014, http://www.dollartimes.com/calculators/inflation.htm

[1419] *House Joint Resolution 192,* 73d Congress, Sess. I, Ch. 48, June 5, 1933 (Public Law No. 10); Approved, June 5, 1933, 4:40 p.m. 31 U.S.C.A. 462, 463

[1420] Federal Reserve Bank of Chicago, *Modern Money Mechanics, (Chicago: 1975), accessed April 14, 2014,* http://lisgi1.engr.ccny.cuny.edu/~makse/Modern_Money_Mechanics.pdf

[1421] "The Sheppard-Towner Maternity and Infancy Act," United States House of Representatives, History, Art & Archives, accessed December 1, 2014, http://history.house.gov/HistoricalHighlight/Detail/36084?ret=True

[1422] *USLegal.com Definitions,* s.v. "Sheppard-Towner Act Law & Legal Definition," accessed December 1, 2014, http://definitions.uslegal.com/s/sheppard-towner-act/

[1423] Mary Elizabeth: Croft, *How I Clobbered Every Bureaucratic Cash-Confiscatory Agency Known to Man,* (www.spiritualeconomicsnow.net, 2008), 21, accessed June 4, 2014, http://www.spiritualeconomicsnow.net/solutions/How_I_08.pdf

[1424] "Your Birth Certificate is a Stock on the NYSE!"YouTube.com/Gzus Cryst, Uploaded July 8, 2010, https://www.youtube.com/watch?v=R63AH_LneaQ

[1425] Alan Lamont, "The Jesuit Vatican New World Order: World War One" April 18, 2012, http://vaticannewworldorder.blogspot.com/2012/04/unseen-titanic-photos-from-jesuit.html

[1426] Robert Higgs, PhD, "Who Was Edward M. House?," August 13, 2008, http://www.independent.org/newsroom/article.asp?id=2294

[1427] Professor Ralph Raico, "FDR: The Man, the Leader, the Legacy," *Independent Institute,* April 1, 2001, http://www.independent.org/publications/article.asp?id=1468

[1428] G. Edward Griffin, *Creature from Jeckyll Island, 239*

[1429] The Public Ownership League of America, *Proceedings Public Ownership Conference, Bulletin No. 11,* (Chicago, 1919), 165-171

[1430] Library of Congress, "Edward Mandell House, 1858-1938," http://www.loc.gov/pictures/item/2003653873/ This work is in the public domain in the United States because it was published (or registered with the U.S. Copyright Office) before January 1, 1923.

[1431] New World Order Today Staff, *The United Nations is World Government,* accessed December 1, 2014, http://www.nwotoday.com/the-new-world-orders-agenda/the-united-nations-is-world-government

[1432] Hughes, *Secret Terrorists,* 48

[1433] *Wikipedia,* s.v. "Edward M. House," last modified October 7, 2014,http://en.wikipedia.org/wiki/Edward_M._House

[1434] Higgs, PhD, *Who Was Edward M. House?.*

[1435] Croft, *How I Clobbered,*21

[1436] Professor Ralph Raico, *FDR: The Man, the Leader, the Legacy.*

[1437] Croft, *How I Clobbered,* 22

[1438] Ibid., 37

[1439] Reality Blog, "Do You Own Your Children," accessed December 9, 2014, http://realitybloger.wordpress.com/2011/12/16/do-you-own-your-children/

[1440] Croft, *How I Clobbered,* 22

[1441] Ps.127:3

[1442] "Aug 14, 1935: FDR signs Social Security Act," Aug 14: This Day in History, accessed December 1, 2014, http://www.history.com/this-day-in-history/fdr-signs-social-security-act

[1443] "Corp. U.S. Mythology: Corp. U.S'. Myth 10:The Social Security card is: 'your Social Security card;' and/or, the Social Security Number is: 'your Social Security Number.'"TeamLaw.org, accessed December 1, 2014, http://teamlaw.net/Mythology-CorpUS.htm#SSn=You

[1444] *Wikimedia Commons,* s.v. "Signing Of The Social Security Act.jpg," https://commons.wikimedia.org/wiki/File:Signing_Of_The_Social_Security_Act.jpg This image is available from the United States Library of Congress's Prints and Photographs division under the digital ID cph.3c23278. This image is available from the United States Library of Congress's Prints and Photographs division under the digital ID cph.3c23278.

[1445] "Title 22 – Foreign Relations and Intercourse: Chapter 7 – International Bureaus, Congresses, etc.: Subchapter XV – International Monetary Fund and Bank for Reconstruction and Development: Code § 286 - Acceptance of membership by United States in International Monetary Fund," Cornell University Law School, Legal Information Institute, accessed November 2, 2014,http://www.law.cornell.edu/uscode/pdf/uscode22/lii_usc_TI_22_CH_7_SC_XV_SE_286.pdf

[1446] New Hampshire Historical Markers, Historical marker of the location of the Bretton Woods Monetary Conference, 1944, http://www.images-of-new-hampshire-history.com/New-Hampshire-Historical-Markers.php

[1447] *Wikimedia Commons,* s.v. "Senator Lyndon Johnson.jpg," https://commons.wikimedia.org/wiki/File:Senator_Lyndon_Johnson.jpg#mw-jump-to-license This United States Congress image is in the public domain. This may be because it is an official Congressional portrait, because it was taken by an employee of the Congress as part of that person's official duties, or because it has been released into the public domain and posted on the official websites of a member of Congress. As a work of the U.S. federal government, the image is in the public domain.

[1448] "Charities, Churches and Politics," Internal Revenue Service, Updated July 12, 2007 http://www.irs.gov/uac/Charities,-Churches-and-Politics

[1449] New World Order Today Staff, "Lyndon B. Johnson," accessed November 2, 2014, http://www.nwotoday.com/the-new-world-orders-history/the-socialist-review-american-politicians/lyndon-b-johnson

[1450] Ed. Gary Cass, *Gag Order,* (Fairfax: Xulon Press, 2005), 26

[1451] David Barton, "The Black Robed Regiment," August 30, 2011, WallBuilders.com, http://www.wallbuilders.com/libissuesarticles.asp?id=105213

[1452] *Wikimedia Commons*, "Official Presidential portrait of Thomas Jefferson (by Rembrandt Peale, 1800).jpg," https://commons.wikimedia.org/wiki/File:Official_Presidential_portrait_of_Thomas_Jefferson_(by_Rembrandt_Peale,_1800).jpg#mw-jump-to-license This work is in the public domain in the United States because it is a work prepared by an officer or employee of the United States Government as part of that person's official duties under the terms of Title 17, Chapter 1, Section 105 of the US Code.

[1453] *Wikimedia Commons*, s.v. "James Caldwell American Revolution.jpg," https://commons.wikimedia.org/wiki/File:James_Caldwell_American_Revolution.jpg#mw-jump-to-license This work is in the public domain in its country of origin and other countries and areas where the copyright term is the author's life plus 70 years or less.

[1454] "Churches & Religious Organizations: Filing Requirements," Internal Revenue Service, page last updated November 18, 2015, http://www.irs.gov/Charities-&-Non-Profits/Churches-&-Religious-Organizations/Filing-Requirements

[1455] Boundaries for Effective Ministry, "Ministry and the 501c3 Application Gag," http://www.boundaries-for-effective-ministry.org/501c3-application.html

[1456] "Article 1, Section 10, Clause 1," The Founders' Constitution, accessed November 2, 2014, http://press-pubs.uchicago.edu/founders/tocs/a1_10_1.html

[1457] "Commercial Law Research Guide," Georgetown Law Library, last updated December 4, 2015, http://www.law.georgetown.edu/library/research/guides/commerciallaw.cfm

[1458] *Northwest Ordinance; July 13, 1787,* "Article 5," accessed at The Avalon Project, Lillian Goldman Law Library, Yale Law School, accessed November 2, 2014, http://avalon.law.yale.edu/18th_century/nworder.asp

[1459] Daniel L. Dreisbach, "The Mythical 'Wall of Separation': How a Misused Metaphor Changed Church-State Law, Policy and Discourse," (The Heritage Foundation, First Principles Series Report #6, June 23, 2006) http://www.heritage.org/research/reports/2006/06/the-mythical-wall-of-separation-how-a-misused-metaphor-changed-church-state-law-policy-and-discourse (accessed 11/2/2014)

[1460] WallBuilders.com, "Letters Between the Danbury Baptists and Thomas Jefferson," accessed November 2, 2014, http://www.wallbuilders.com/libissuesarticles.asp?id=65

[1461] Federer, *America's Quotations*, "Thomas Jefferson," 324-325

[1462] *Wikimedia Commons,* S.V. "T Jefferson by Charles Willson Peale 1791 2.jpg," https://commons.wikimedia.org/wiki/File:T_Jefferson_by_Charles_Willson_Peale_1791_2.jpg#mw-jump-to-license This work is in the public domain in its country of origin and other countries and areas where the copyright term is the author's life plus 100 years or less.

[1463] Ibid.

[1464] Library of Congress, Religion and the Founding of the American Republic: VI. Religion and the Federal Government, "The Old House of Representatives," http://adam2.org/articles/lib_congress_exhibit/rel06-2.html This media file is in the public domain in the United States. This applies to U.S. works where the copyright has expired, often because its first publication occurred prior to January 1, 1923.

[1465] WallBuilders, David Barton, "Church in the U.S. Capitol," accessed November 2, 2014, http://www.wallbuilders.com/libissuesarticles.asp?id=90

[1466] Library of Congress, "School opens with prayer. This is the private school in the Farm Bureau building. Pie Town, New Mexico," https://www.loc.gov/item/fsa2000017906/PP/ No known restrictions.

[1467] Engel v. Vitale, 370 U.S. 421 (1962)

[1468] *Wikimedia Commons,* s.v. "Editorial cartoon depicting Charles Darwin as an ape (1871).jpg," https://commons.wikimedia.org/wiki/File:Editorial_cartoon_depicting_Charles_Darwin_as_an_ape_(1871).jpg This work is in the public domain in the United States because it was published (or registered with the U.S. Copyright Office) before January 1, 1923.

[1469] The Forerunner Editorial Staff, "What Happened When the Praying Stopped," The Forerunner, April 6, 2008, http://www.forerunner.com/forerunner/X0124_When_America_stopped.html

[1470] Linda Clements, What You Know Might Not Be So, graphs as sourced from David Barton, "America to Pray or not to Pray" http://www.whatyouknowmightnotbeso.com/graphs.html

[1471] David Barton, "America, To Pray Or Not To Pray?: A Statistical Look at What Happened When Religious Principles Were Separated From Public Affairs," (Aledo: WallBuilders Press, 1991)

[1472] Sham Gad, "Private Prisons Have Future Growth All Locked Up," October 17, 2009, http://www.investopedia.com/stock-analysis/2009/private-prisons-have-future-growth-all-locked-up-cxw-geo-crn1020.aspx

[1473] Mark Rice, "Archive for the 'education' Category," January 25, 2013, https://rankingamerica.wordpress.com/category/education/

[1474] Pearson Staff, "United States," accessed November 2, 2014,http://thelearningcurve.pearson.com/country-profiles/united-states

[1475] Huff Post Staff, "Education, Best Education In The World: Finland, South Korea Top Country Rankings, U.S. Rated Average," Huff Post: Education, November 27, 2012, http://www.huffingtonpost.com/2012/11/27/best-education-in-the-wor_n_2199795.html

[1476] Michael Brendan Dougherty, "If America Spends More Than Most Countries Per Student, Then Why Are Its Schools So Bad?," Business Insider, January 7, 2012, http://www.businessinsider.com/us-education-spending-compared-to-the-rest-of-the-developed-world-2012-1

[1477] Jeff Faux, "NAFTA's Impact on U.S Workers," Economic Policy Institute, December 9, 2013 http://www.epi.org/blog/naftas-impact-workers/

[1478] Michael Kling, "US Unemployment Rate Is Really 14.3 Percent," Newsmax: Finance, July 31, 2013, http://www.moneynews.com/Economy/unemployment-rate-U-6-jobs/2013/07/31/id/517936/

[1479] Wikimedia Commons, s.v. "Noah Webster The Schoolmaster of the Republic.jpg," https://commons.wikimedia.org/wiki/File:Noah_Webster_The_Schoolmaster_of_the_Republic.jpg print by Root & Tinker. Courtesy of the Library of Congress, Division of Prints and Photographs Online,

[1480] Federer, America's Quotations, "Noah Webster," 675-676 This media file is in the public domain in the United States. This applies to U.S. works where the copyright has expired, often because its first publication occurred prior to January 1, 1923.

[1481] Noah Webster. "Our Christian Heritage," Letter from Plymouth Rock (Marlborough, NY: The Plymouth Rock Foundation), 5

[1482] Ibid.

[1483] Verna M. Hall and Rosalie J. Slater, The Bible and the Constitution of the United States (San Francisco: Foundation for American Christian Education, 1983), 27; Tim LaHaye, Faith of Our Founding Fathers (Brentwood, TN: Wolgemuth & Hyatt, Publishers, Inc., 1987), 76-78

[1484] Wikimedia Commons, s.v. "Noah Webster pre-1843 IMG 4412 Cropped.JPG," This work is in the public domain in its country of origin and other countries and areas where the copyright term is the author's life plus 100 years or less.

[1485] Wikimedia Commons, s.v. ""New-England Primer Enlarged printed and sold by Benjamin Franklin.jpg," https://commons.wikimedia.org/wiki/File:New-England_Primer_Enlarged_printed_and_sold_by_Benjamin_Franklin.jpg This work is in the public domain in its country of origin and other countries and areas where the copyright term is the author's life plus 100 years or less.

[1486] Abington School District v. Schempp, 374 U.S. 203 (1963),

[1487] Stone v. Graham 449 U.S. 39

[1488] Federer, America's Quotations, "William Hubbs Rehnquist," 531-532

[1489] One Hundred Third Congress of the United States of America At the Second Session, "H.R. 1804, Goals 2000: Educate America Act," accessed December 4, 2014, http://www2.ed.gov/legislation/GOALS2000/TheAct/index.html

[1490] One Hundred Third Congress of the United States of America, "School-to-Work Opportunities Act of 1994," Public Law 103-239, 108 Stat 568, May 4, 1994, accessed December 2, 2014, http://www.fessler.com/SBE/act.htm

[1491] Michael M. Heise, Goals 2000: Educate America Act: The Federalization and Legalization of Educational Policy, 63 Fordham L. Rev. 345 (1994), accessed December 4, 2014, http://ir.lawnet.fordham.edu/flr/vol63/iss2/2

[1492] "The History of Goals 2000," National Center for Home Education, Special Report September, 2002, http://www.hslda.org/docs/nche/000010/200209010.asp

[1493] David C. Hertler, Jean M. Hertler, Letter to the Editor, "Objections to Goals 2000 given," Keystone Reporter, March 1, 1997

[1494] Phyllis Schlafly, "Big Brother Education, 1994:Out-based Education Nonsense," The Phyllis Schlafly Report, May, 1994,http://www.eagleforum.org/psr/1994/may94/psrmay94.html

[1495] Cathy Duffy and K. L. Billingsley, "Government Nannies: The Cradle to Grave Agenda of Goals 2000 and Outcome Based Education: Do Our Children Belong to the State?" The Freeman, October 1, 1995, http://fee.org/the_freeman/detail/government-nannies-the-cradle-to-grave-agenda-of-goals-2000-and-outcome-based-education

[1496] Schlafly, "Big Brother Education."

[1497] Jeff Lindsay, "Public Education: Views of a Concerned Parent: Introduction," last updated October 12, 2012, http://www.jefflindsay.com/Education.shtml

[1498] Vicky Pelaez, "The Prison Industry in the United States: Big Business or a New Form of Slavery?," *Global Research,* March 31, 2014, http://www.globalresearch.ca/the-prison-industry-in-the-united-states-big-business-or-a-new-form-of-slavery/8289

[1499] Richard Branson, "War on drugs a trillion-dollar failure," *CNN,* December 7, 2012, http://www.cnn.com/2012/12/06/opinion/branson-end-war-on-drugs/

[1500] Dave Hodges, "The U.S. Criminal Justice System Has Created Debtors Prisons and Slave Labor Camps (Part One)," *The Common Sense Show*, January 4, 2015, http://www.thecommonsenseshow.com/2015/01/04/u-s-criminal-justice-system-created-debtors-prisons-slave-labor-camps-part-one/

[1501] Ibid.

[1502] Branson, "War on drugs."

[1503] "The War is About So Much More: The CIA Drug connection under Reagan," last updated October 20, 2007, http://www.rationalrevolution.net/war/cia_drug_connection_under_reagan.htm

[1504] Corrections Corporation of America, "About CCA: Learn About Us and Our Role in Corrections," accessed January 5, 2015, http://www.cca.com/about-cca

[1505] "G4S USA: Who We Are, accessed January 5, 2015, http://www.g4s.us/en-US/Who%20we%20are/

[1506] Branson, "War on drugs."

[1507] Pelaez, "The Prison Industry in the United States."

[1508] Ibid.

[1509] Ibid.

[1510] Pelaez, "The Prison Industry in the United States."

[1511] Michael Rivero, "What Really Happened: All Wars Are Bankers Wars!," accessed December 4, 2014, http://whatreallyhappened.com/WRHARTICLES/allwarsarebankerwars.php#axzz3Nt54gSJb

[1512] Ibid.

[1513] Pelaez, "The Prison Industry in the United States."

[1514] Eric Stirgus, "Unemployment rate comparable to Great Depression, congressman says," *Politifact Georgia,* September 14th, 2012, http://www.politifact.com/georgia/statements/2012/sep/14/phil-gingrey/unemployment-rate-comparable-great-depression-cong/

[1515] Washington's Blog, "Great Depression-Level Unemployment in America," June 3, 2011, http://www.globalresearch.ca/great-depression-level-unemployment-in-america/25098

[1516] Pelaez, "The Prison Industry in the United States."

[1517] The GEO Group, Inc.: Welcome to The GEO Group, Inc.," accessed January 5, 2015, http://www.geogroup.com/

[1518] Dave Hodges, "Children Increasingly Comprise the Rapidly Growing Prison Slave Labor Force," *The Common Sense Show,* January 5, 2015, http://www.thecommonsenseshow.com/2015/01/05/children-increasingly-comprise-rapidly-growing-prison-slave-labor-force/

[1519] *State of Wisconsin Blue Book 2013-2014,* Chapter 6, Executive Branch, "Department of Corrections," p. 395, accessed December 5, 2014, http://legis.wisconsin.gov/lrb/bb/13bb/Executive.pdf

[1520] Ibid., Chapter 8, "Statistics: State and Local Finance," accessed December 5, 2014, http://legis.wisconsin.gov/lrb/bb/13bb/Stats_SocialServices.pdf

[1521] Hodges, *Children Increasingly Comprise."*

[1522] *State of Wisconsin Blue Book 2013-2014,* Ch. 8, "Statistics: State and Local Finance"

[1523] Branson, "War on drugs."

[1524] Michael Suede, "Victimless Crime Constitutes 86% of The Federal Prison Population," *Libertarian News,* September 29, 2011, https://www.libertariannews.org/2011/09/29/victimless-crime-constitutes-86-of-the-american-prison-population/

[1525] Pelaez, "The Prison Industry in the United States."

[1526] Human Rights Watch Staff, "Profiting from Probation: America's "Offender-Funded" Probation Industry," *Human Rights Watch,* February 5, 2014, http://www.hrw.org/reports/2014/02/05/profiting-probation-0

[1527] Ibid.

[1528] Tom Fitton, "About Judicial Watch," accessed January 5, 2015, http://www.judicialwatch.org/about/

[1529] Hodges, "The U.S. Criminal Justice System Has Created Debtors Prisons"

[1530]Shmoop Editorial Team. "Society in Reconstruction" Shmoop University, Inc. 11 November 2008. http://www.shmoop.com/reconstruction/society.html

[1531]*Wikipedia,*s.v. "Black Codes (United States)," http://en.wikipedia.org/wiki/Black_Codes_%28United_States%29 http://www.u-s-history.com/pages/h411.html This work is in the public domain in its country of origin and other countries and areas where the copyright term is the author's life plus 100 years or less.

[1532] U.S. History.com, "The Black Codes: Convicts who had violated the Black Codes," http://www.u-s-history.com/pages/h411.html

[1533]*Wikipedia,*s.v. "Howell Cobb," http://en.wikipedia.org/wiki/Howell_Cobb (accessed 9/3/2014)

[1534]Dye, *Adder's Den,* 123

[1535]Pelaez, "The Prison Industry in the United States."

[1536] *Wikimedia Commons,* s.v. "Postbellum-Cobb.jpg," http://www.loc.gov/pictures/item/brh2003001166/PP/ No known restrictions on publication.

[1537] "Common Core State Standards Initiative: Preparing America's students for success.," accessed December 4, 2014, http://www.corestandards.org/

[1538]"Common Core Issues: What is the Common Core?," *Homeschool Legal Defense Association,* accessed December 4, 2014, http://www.hslda.org/commoncore/

[1539]Dr. James Milgram, Emmett McGroarty, "Do the math -- Common Core = a massive, risky experiment on your kids," *Fox News,* July 30, 2013, http://www.foxnews.com/opinion/2013/07/30/do-math-common-core-massive-risky-experiment-on-your-kids/

[1540] Ibid.

[1541]"Common Core Issues: What is the Common Core?," *Homeschool Legal Defense Association.*

[1542]"Dr. Marlene McMillan Speaks on the Dialectic & How to Recognize It," *Operation Jericho Project Radio,* accessed December 4, 2014, http://www.blogtalkradio.com/operationjerichoprojectradio/2014/08/21/our-guest-dr-marlene-mcmillan-speaks-on-the-dialectic-how-to-recognize-it

[1543] Homeschool Legal Defense Association, "Common Core Issues: What is the Common Core?."

[1544] Dr. Marlene McMillan, "About," accessed December 4, 2014, http://www.drmarlenemcmillan.com/about.php

[1545] Dr. Marlene McMillian, "Does Liberty Really Matter?," accessed December 4, 2014, http://www.whylibertymatters.com/index.php

[1546]Tiffany Gabbay, "What Is Agenda 21? After Watching This, You May Not Want to Know," *The Blaze,* Nov. 19, 2012, http://www.theblaze.com/stories/2012/11/19/what-is-agenda-21-after-watching-this-you-may-not-want-to-know/

[1547] "Sustainable Development: Knowledge Platform: Agenda 21," United Nations, http://sustainabledevelopment.un.org/index.php?page=view&nr=23&type=400 (accessed 12/4/2014)

[1548] Dr. Marlene McMillan, "Why Liberty Matters: Common Core is unBiblical," accessed December 4, 2014,http://www.whylibertymatters.com/blog.php

[1549] Alex Newman, "Common Core and UN Agenda 21: Mass Producing Green Global Serfs," *The New American,* March 27, 2014, http://www.thenewamerican.com/culture/education/item/17930-common-core-and-un-agenda-21-mass-producing-green-global-serfs

[1550] Christian Financial Concepts hosting Dr. Marlene McMillan, "Common Core Part 1: Centralized Control," October 13, 2014, http://christianfinancialconcepts.com/article.php?id=4272

[1551] Republic News Network, hosting Dr Marlene McMillan, "The Nation's Expert on the Principles of Liberty," October 23, 2014, http://www.republicoftheunitedstates.org/rnn-recording/

[1552] Christian Financial Concepts hosting Dr. Marlene McMillan, "Common Core Part 1: Centralized Control."

[1553] Ze'ev Wurman, "'Common Cores' Validation: A Weak Foundation for a Crooked House," *Pioneer Institute Public Policy Research*, April 2014, http://pioneerinstitute.org/download/common-cores-validation-a-weak-foundation-for-a-crooked-house/

[1554]*Wikipedia,*s.v. "Southern Poverty Law Center," http://en.wikipedia.org/wiki/Southern_Poverty_Law_Center (accessed 3/4/2015)

[1555] Family Research Council, "February 10, 2014 letter to Attorney General Eric H. Holder, Jr. and FBI Director James B. Comey," http://www.republicoftheunitedstates.org/dev/wp-content/uploads/2014/09/Boykin%20letter%20to%20Holder%20and%20Comey%2002102014.pdf

[1556]President James Buchanan Geiger, "Retired General says FBI association w/Southern Poverty Law Center is Unacceptable," *Republic for the United States of America,* April 5, 2014, http://www.republicoftheunitedstates.org/tag/general-boykin-fbi-association-with-southern-poverty-law-center-is-unacceptable/

[1557] Southern Poverty Law Center, "Public Schools in the Crosshairs: Far-Right Propaganda and the Common Core State Standards," May, 2014, http://www.splcenter.org/sites/default/files/downloads/publication/public_schools_in_the_crosshairs.pdf

[1558] Southern Poverty Law Center, *Public Schools in the Crosshairs."*

[1559] Ibid., 30

[1560] "Northwest Ordinance; July 13, 1787,"accessed at *The Avalon Project,* Lillian Goldman Law Library, Yale Law School, accessed November 2, 2014,http://avalon.law.yale.edu/18th_century/nworder.asp

[1561] Southern Poverty Law Center, "Antigovernment Movement," accessed January 19, 2016, https://www.splcenter.org/fighting-hate/extremist-files/ideology/antigovernment

[1562] Federer, *America's Quotations,* "Thomas Jefferson," 324

[1563] Worship Tools for those who serve the church, "Isaac Watts: The Hymn Writer: The title page of Watt's first hymnal published in 1707," http://yourworshiptools.com/isaac-watts-hymn-writer/

[1564] *Wikimedia Commons,* s.v. "JFK White House portrait looking up lighting corrected.jpg," https://commons.wikimedia.org/wiki/File:JFK_White_House_portrait_looking_up_lighting_corrected.jpg This work is in the public domain in the United States because it is a work prepared by an officer or employee of the United States Government as part of that person's official duties under the terms of Title 17, Chapter 1, Section 105 of the US Code.

[1565] Justice Network, "President John F. Kennedy issued Executive Order 11110," http://www.nosue.org/banking/united-states-note-vs-federal-reserve-note/ Fair use under United States copyright law

[1566] Martin Armstrong, "Executive Order 11110 – End of Silver Coinage: 1957 Silver Certificate," Armstrong Economics, http://www.armstrongeconomics.com/research/a-brief-history-of-paper-money/executive-order-11110-end-of-silver-coinage

[1567] New World Order Today Staff, "Lyndon B. Johnson," accessed November 2, 2014, http://www.nwotoday.com/the-new-world-orders-history/the-socialist-review-american-politicians/lyndon-b-johnson

[1568] New World Order Today Staff, "Richard Milhous Nixon," accessed November 2, 2014,http://www.nwotoday.com/the-new-world-orders-history/the-socialist-review-american-politicians/richard-nixon

[1569] New World Order Today Staff, "Gerald Ford," accessed November 2, 2014, , http://www.nwotoday.com/the-new-world-orders-history/the-socialist-review-american-politicians/gerald-ford

[1570] New World Order Today Staff, "Jimmy Carter," accessed November 2, 2014,http://www.nwotoday.com/the-new-world-orders-history/the-socialist-review-american-politicians/jimmy-carter

[1571] New World Order Today Staff, "Ronald Reagan," accessed November 2, 2014,http://www.nwotoday.com/the-new-world-orders-history/the-socialist-review-american-politicians/ronald-reagan

[1572] *Wikimedia Commons,* s.v. "Official Portrait of President Reagan 1981.jpg," https://commons.wikimedia.org/wiki/File:Official_Portrait_of_President_Reagan_1981.jpg This image is a work of an employee of the Executive Office of the President of the United States, taken or made as part of that person's official duties. As a work of the U.S. federal government, the image is in the public domain.

[1573] *Wikipedia,*s.v. "Executive Order 12608,"http://en.wikipedia.org/wiki/Executive_Order_12608 (accessed 11/2/2014)

[1574] Wikipedia, s.v. "Executive Order 11110,"http://en.wikipedia.org/wiki/Executive_Order_11110(accessed 1/5/2015)

[1575] Matt. 21:12-13

[1576] Cedric X, "President Kennedy, The Fed and Executive Order 11110," *Rense.com,* November 20, 2003,http://www.rense.com/general44/exec.htm

[1577] *Wikimedia Commons,* s.v. "Aldrich-plan-1912.png," https://commons.wikimedia.org/wiki/File:Aldrich-plan-1912.png This media file is in the public domain in the United States. This applies to U.S. works where the copyright has expired, often because its first publication occurred prior to January 1, 1923.

[1578] Alfred Owen Crozier, *U.S. Money Vs Corporation Currency, "Aldrich Plan"* cartoon included: "'White Man's Burden' – Bank Incubus on U.S," (Cincinnati: The Magnet Company, 1912), p 328 This media file is in the public domain in the United States. This applies to U.S. works where the copyright has expired, often because its first publication occurred prior to January 1, 1923.

[1579] *Wikimedia Commons,* s.v. "Nathan Rothschild.jpg," https://commons.wikimedia.org/wiki/File:Nathan_Rothschild.jpg#mw-jump-to-license This work is in the public domain in its country of origin and other countries and areas where the copyright term is the author's life plus 70 years or less.

[1580] *Wikimedia Commons,* s.v. "Lionel Nathan de Rothschild.jpg," https://en.wikipedia.org/wiki/File:Lionel_Nathan_de_Rothschild.jpg#mw-jump-to-license This image is in the public domain in the United States. In most cases, this means that it was first published prior to January 1, 1923

[1581] *Wikimedia Commons,* s.v. "Anthony Nathan de Rothschild.jpg," https://commons.wikimedia.org/wiki/File:Anthony_Nathan_de_Rothschild.jpg#mw-jump-to-license

[1582] *Wikimedia Commons*, s.v. "Nathaniel de Rothschild.PNG,"
https://commons.wikimedia.org/wiki/File:Nathaniel_de_Rothschild.PNG#mw-jump-to-license This work is in the public domain in its country of origin and other countries and areas where the copyright term is the author's life plus 100 years or less.

[1583] *Wikimedia Commons,* s.v. "Mayer Amschel Rothschild.jpg," This work is in the public domain in its country of origin and other countries and areas where the copyright term is the author's life plus 100 years or less.
https://commons.wikimedia.org/wiki/File:Mayer_Amschel_Rothschild.jpg#mw-jump-to-license This media file is in the public domain in the United States. This applies to U.S. works where the copyright has expired, often because its first publication occurred prior to January 1, 1923.

[1584] *Wikimedia Commons*, s.v. "Barry Goldwater photo1962.jpg,"
https://commons.wikimedia.org/wiki/File:Barry_Goldwater_photo1962.jpg#mw-jump-to-license This work is from the U.S. News & World Report collection at the Library of Congress. According to the library, there are no known copyright restrictions on the use of this work. This photograph is a work for hire created between 1952 and 1986 by one of the following staff photographers at U.S. News & World Report: Warren K. Leffler (WKL) Thomas J. O'Halloran (TOH) Marion S. Trikosko (MST) John Bledsoe (JTB) Chick Harrity (CWH) It is part of a collection donated to the Library of Congress. Per the deed of gift, U.S. News & World Report dedicated to the public all rights it held for the photographs in this collection upon its donation to the Library.

[1585] Library of Congress, "Lindbergh, Charles A., Sr. Honorable," http://www.loc.gov/pictures/item/hec2009003041/ No known restrictions on publication.

[1586] *Wikimedia Commons*, s.v. "John William Wright Patman.jpg,"
https://commons.wikimedia.org/wiki/File:John_William_Wright_Patman.jpg#mw-jump-to-license This United States Congress image is in the public domain. This may be because it is an official Congressional portrait, because it was taken by an employee of the Congress as part of that person's official duties, or because it has been released into the public domain and posted on the official websites of a member of Congress. As a work of the U.S. federal government, the image is in the public domain.

[1587] Library of Congress, "Louis T. McFadden, 1876-1936," http://www.loc.gov/pictures/item/2004672302/ This work is from the Library of Congress. According to the library, there are no known copyright restrictions on the use of this work.
Images submitted for copyright by Underwood & Underwood are in the public domain due to expiration or lack of renewal.

[1588] *Wikimedia Commons,* s.v. "John danforth.JPG," https://commons.wikimedia.org/wiki/File:John_danforth.JPG#mw-jump-to-license This United States Congress image is in the public domain. This may be because it is an official Congressional portrait, because it was taken by an employee of the Congress as part of that person's official duties, or because it has been released into the public domain and posted on the official websites of a member of Congress. As a work of the U.S. federal government, the image is in the public domain.

[1589] Biblioteca Pleyades Staff, "Addendum," accessed January 7, 2016,
http://www.bibliotecapleyades.net/sociopolitica/esp_sociopol_fed06h.htm

[1590] *Wikimedia Commons*, s.v. "Henry Cabot Lodge cph.3a38855.jpg,
https://commons.wikimedia.org/wiki/File:Henry_Cabot_Lodge_cph.3a38855.jpg#mw-jump-to-license This image is available from the United States Library of Congress's Prints and Photographs division under the digital ID cph.3a38855. This image is available from the United States Library of Congress's Prints and Photographs division under the digital ID cph.3a38855.

[1591] Library of Congress, "Pres. James Garfield," http://www.loc.gov/pictures/item/brh2003000342/PP/ No known restrictions on publication.

[1592] *Wikimedia Commons*, s.v. "Thomas Woodrow Wilson, Harris & Ewing bw photo portrait, 1919.jpg,
https://commons.wikimedia.org/wiki/File:Thomas_Woodrow_Wilson,_Harris_%26_Ewing_bw_photo_portrait,_1919.jpg#mw-jump-to-license This image is available from the United States Library of Congress's Prints and Photographs division under the digital ID cph.3f06247. This work is from the Harris & Ewing collection at the Library of Congress. According to the library, there are no known copyright restrictions on the use of this work.

[1593] *Wikimedia Commons*, s.v. "Official Presidential portrait of Thomas Jefferson (by Rembrandt Peale, 1800).jpg,"
https://commons.wikimedia.org/wiki/File:Official_Presidential_portrait_of_Thomas_Jefferson_(by_Rembrandt_Peale,_1800).jpg *This work is in the public domain in the United States because it is a work prepared by an officer or employee of the United States Government as part of that person's official duties under the terms of* Title 17, Chapter 1, Section 105 of the US Code.

[1594]Library of Congress, "Andrew Jackson," http://www.loc.gov/pictures/item/99404956/ No known restrictions on publication.

[1595] Library of Congress, "James Madison," https://www.loc.gov/item/2002725261/ This media file is in the public domain in the United States. This applies to U.S. works where the copyright has expired, often because its first publication occurred prior to January 1, 1923.

[1596] *Wikimedia Commons,* s.v. "Henry ford 1919.jpg," https://commons.wikimedia.org/wiki/File:Henry_ford_1919.jpg This media file is in the public domain in the United States. This applies to U.S. works where the copyright has expired, often because its first publication occurred prior to January 1, 1923.

[1597] Whale.to Staff, "Eustace Mullins (1923-2010)," http://www.whale.to/b/mullins_h.html fair use under United States copyright law

[1598] *Wikimedia Commons,* s.v. "Horace-Greeley-Baker.jpeg," https://commons.wikimedia.org/wiki/File:Horace-Greeley-Baker.jpeg This media file is in the public domain in the United States. This applies to U.S. works where the copyright has expired, often because its first publication occurred prior to January 1, 1923.

[1599] *Wikimedia Commons,* s.v. "WhiteandKeynes.jpg," https://commons.wikimedia.org/wiki/File:WhiteandKeynes.jpg This file from http://www.imf.org/ is in the public domain and can be used for any purpose, including commercial use, because it has the following byline: These photographs are in the public domain. They are free to use for publication purposes.

[1600] *Wikimedia Commons,* s.v. "Thomas Edison2.jpg," https://commons.wikimedia.org/wiki/File:Thomas_Edison2.jpg This media file is in the public domain in the United States. This applies to U.S. works where the copyright has expired, often because its first publication occurred prior to January 1, 1923.

[1601] *Wikimedia Commons,* s.v. "Lang Labor 1935.jpg," https://commons.wikimedia.org/wiki/File:Lang_Labor_1935.jpg This image is of Australian origin and is now in the public domain because its term of copyright has expired. According to the Australian Copyright Council (ACC), ACC Information Sheet G023v17 (Duration of copyright) (August 2014).l

[1602] *Wikimedia Commons,* s.v. "37 Lyndon Johnson 3x4.jpg," https://commons.wikimedia.org/wiki/File:37_Lyndon_Johnson_3x4.jpg This image is a work of an employee of the Executive Office of the President of the United States, taken or made as part of that person's official duties. As a work of the U.S. federal government, the image is in the public domain.

[1603] New World Order Today Staff, "Lyndon B. Johnson," accessed November 2, 2014, http://www.nwotoday.com/the-new-world-orders-history/the-socialist-review-american-politicians/lyndon-b-johnson

[1604] William T. Still, "New World Order The Ancient Plan of Secret Societies," (Lafayette, Huntington House Publishers, 1990), 21

[1605] "United States Presidents and The Illuminati / Masonic Power Structure. Pt.3," *The Forbidden Knowledge,* accessed November 2, 2014, http://www.theforbiddenknowledge.com/hardtruth/uspresidentasmasonspt3.htm

[1606] The American Presidency Project, Lyndon B. Johnson, XXXVI President of the United States:1963-1969, *380* –"Remarks at the Signing of the Coinage Act, July 23, 1965," accessed November 2, 2014, http://www.presidency.ucsb.edu/ws/?pid=27108

[1607] Vern Bullough, "When Did the Gay Rights Movement Begin?," *History News Network,* April 17, 2005, http://hnn.us/article/11316#sthash.DEB3onrp.dpuf

[1608] "50th Anniversary Celebration of the LGBT Civil Rights Movement at Independence Hall, July 4, 2015," *Reuters,* November 6, 2014, http://www.reuters.com/article/2014/11/06/pa-visit-philly-lgbt-idUSnPn67B1n5+88+PRN20141106

[1609] *"Advancing LGBT Civil Rights,* 'Historic Marker,'" accessed January 29, 2015, *Equality Forum,* http://www.equalityforum.com/other-initiatives

[1610] "50th Anniversary Celebration of the LGBT Civil Rights Movement," *Reuters.*

[1611] Library of Congress, "George Washington," http://www.loc.gov/item/98501986/ This work is in the public domain in its country of origin and other countries and areas where the copyright term is the author's life plus 100 years or less.

[1612] Ibid.

[1613] David Barton, "Homosexuals in the Military," 2001, *WallBuilders,* http://www.wallbuilders.com/LIBissuesArticles.asp?id=101

[1614] *Wikimedia Commons,* s.v. "Thomas Jefferson by John Trumbull 1788.jpg," https://commons.m.wikimedia.org/wiki/File:Thomas_Jefferson_by_John_Trumbull_1788.jpg This work is in the public domain in its country of origin and other countries and areas where the copyright term is the author's life plus 100 years or less.

[1615] 1 Cor. 6:9-10, 18; 1 Tim. 1:10; 2 Tim. 3:1-7; 2 Pet. 2:6; Jude 1:7;

[1616] Lev. 18:22, 20:13

[1617] "Major corporations funding 'gay' indoctrination in elementary schools across America," *Mass Resistance,* December 28, 2014, http://www.massresistance.org/docs/gen2/14d/hrc-banquet/welcoming-schools.html

[1618] Julie Pace, "Obama Pushes African Leaders On Gay Rights, Rebuked by Senegalese President Macky Sall," Huff Post: Politics, June 27, 2013, http://www.huffingtonpost.com/2013/06/27/obama-africa-gay-rights_n_3512530.html

[1619] "Russian lawmakers ask President Obama to impose sanctions on them all," *RT News,* March 18, 2014, http://rt.com/politics/russian-duma-sanctions-crimea-594/

[1620] YouTube.com/DivineSolja, "Russian president Putin defends Christian culture, Western values, condemns political correctness," September 19, 2013, https://www.youtube.com/watch?v=HSX2ALtIejw

[1621] "50th Anniversary Celebration of the LGBT Civil Rights Movement," *Reuters.*

[1622] Adam Liptak, "Supreme Court Bolsters Gay Marriage With Two Major Rulings," *New York Times,* June 26, 2013, http://www.nytimes.com/2013/06/27/us/politics/supreme-court-gay-marriage.html?pagewanted=all&_r=0

[1623] Gen. 2:21-24, Matt. 19:4-6

[1624] Lev. 18:22; Rom.1:26-27

[1625] *Wikipedia,*s.v. "President's Commission on Obscenity and Pornography," http://en.wikipedia.org/wiki/President's_Commission_on_Obscenity_and_Pornography (accessed 11/2/2014)

[1626] "Letter from George Washington to the Clergy of Different Denominations Residing In and Near the City of Philadelphia (Mar. 3, 1797)" in 36 *The Writings of George Washington*, 1745-1799, (John C. Fitzpatrick ed. 1931), 416

[1627] Focus on the Family Issue Analysts, "Cause for Concern (Pornography), Whether legally classified as obscene or indecent, all pornography is harmful," 2008, http://www.focusonthefamily.com/socialissues/social-issues/pornography/cause-for-concern.aspx

[1628] "Ted Bundy, Serial Killer and Rapist, Wanted to Tell the World about Pornography,"EndAllDisease.com, accessed November 2, 2014, http://www.endalldisease.com/ted-bundy-serial-killer-and-rapist-wanted-to-tell-the-world-about-pornography/

[1629] Russ Warner, "What Serial Killers and Murderers Think about Pornography,"*NetNanny.com,* July 2, 2013, https://www.netnanny.com/blog/what-serial-killers-and-murderers-think-about-pornography/

[1630] Understanding the Compulsive Internet Pornography User," RealFamiliesRealAnswers.org, accessed January 12, 2005, "http://realfamiliesrealanswers.org/?page_id=84

[1631] Ibid.

[1632] Hope & Freedom Counseling Services, from research conducted by Dr. Patrick Carnes, "what is acting out?," accessed January 13, 2015, http://www.hopeandfreedom.com/sex-addiction/what-is-acting-out

[1633] "Understanding the Compulsive Internet Pornography User,"RealFamiliesRealAnswers.org.

[1634] Candace Kim, *Child Sexual Exploitation Program Update*, Candice Kim, "From Fantasy to Reality: The Link Between Viewing Child Pornography and Molesting Children," *American Prosecutors Research Institute,* Vol. I No. 3, 2004, http://www.ndaa.org/pdf/Update_gr_vol1_no3.pdf

[1635] *Wikipedia* s.v. "Victor Cline," last updated October 13, 2014, http://en.wikipedia.org/wiki/Victor_Cline

[1636] "Understanding the Compulsive Internet Pornography User,"RealFamiliesRealAnswers.org.

[1637] *Wikipedia,*s.v. "Pedophilia," last updated November 2, 2015, http://en.wikipedia.org/wiki/Pedophilia

[1638] National Center for Missing & Exploited Children, "Statistics," as citing Janis Wolak, Kimberly J. Mitchell, and David Finkelhor, *Online Victimization of Youth: Five Years Later*, (Alexandria, Virginia: National Center for Missing & Exploited Children, 2006, respectively pages 8 and 33), accessed January 12, 2015, http://www.missingkids.com/en_US/archive/documents/Statistics.pdf

[1639] Joyce Meyer Ministries: Missions, "Hand of Hope: Human Trafficking Rescue," accessed January 13, 2015, http://www.joycemeyer.org/HandOfHope/WhatWeAreDoing/HumanTrafficking.aspx

[1640] North American Mission Board, "Love Neglected Neighbors: Human Trafficking," accessed January 13, 2015, http://www.namb.net/Human_Trafficking/

[1641] Vineyard Church of Anaheim, "Human Trafficking Ministry," accessed January 13, 2015, http://www.vcfanaheim.com/contentpages.aspx?viewcontentpageguid=9596afcb-aacc-4484-8dfa-b7c223ced224&parentnavigationid=24602

[1642] CBN Ministries, "Stop Human Trafficking," accessed January 13, 2015, http://www.cbn.com/partners/about/our-ministries/project-humanTrafficking.aspx

[1643] SheHasAName.com, "Who We Are," accessed December 15, 2015, http://www.shehasaname.org/about-us

[1644] Irving Bible Church, "Global Missions: Our Mission Statement," accessed December 15, 2015,http://legacy.irvingbible.org/missions/global-missions/

[1645] Linda A. Smith, Samantha Healy Vardaman, Melissa A. Snow, "The National Report on Domestic Minor Sex Trafficking, America's Prostituted Children," May, 2009, http://sharedhope.org/wp-content/uploads/2012/09/SHI_National_Report_on_DMST_2009.pdf

[1646] Julie Taylor Shematz, "BFA Founder,"BeautyFromAshes.org, accessed January 13, 2015, http://beautyfromashes.org/contentpages.aspx?parentnavigationid=9781&viewcontentpageguid=e963a45b-299c-449c-a822-45867fedaf35

[1647] BeautyFromAshes.org, "Human Trafficking Quick Facts," accessed January 13, 2015, http://beautyfromashes.org/contentpages.aspx?parentnavigationid=10029&viewcontentpageguid=48690df5-c4ad-43bb-bc53-9be36c266181

[1648] Matt Barger, "'Gay' DNC Bundler, Founder of HRC Charged with Raping Boy," November 23, 2014, http://townhall.com/columnists/mattbarber/2014/11/23/gay-dnc-bundler-founder-of-hrc-charged-with-raping-boy-n1922701/page/full

[1649] Alexandra Jaffe, "Obama backer, Democratic fundraiser Terry Bean charged in sexual abuse case," *CNN*, November 23, 2014 http://www.cnn.com/2014/11/23/politics/terry-bean-sex-abuse-charges/

[1650] "Billionaire Sex Offender's Phone Book Contained E-Mail Addresses, 21 Phone Numbers For Bill Clinton," TheSmokingGun.com, January 5, 2015, http://www.thesmokinggun.com/buster/bill-clinton/bill-clinton-and-jeffrey-epstein-908671

[1651] Daily Mail Reporter, "Bill Clinton identified in lawsuit against his former friend and pedophile Jeffrey Epstein who had 'regular' orgies at his Caribbean compound that the former president visited multiple times," DailyMail.com, March 19, 2014, http://www.dailymail.co.uk/news/article-2584309/Bill-Clinton-identified-lawsuit-against-former-friend-pedophile-Jeffrey-Epstein-regular-orgies-Caribbean-compound-former-president-visited-multiple-times.html#ixzz3OST39dnH

[1652] Shepard Ambellas, "St. James Island exposed: The elites best kept secret, until now," January 5, 2015, https://www.intellihub.com/st-james-island-exposed-elites-best-kept-secret-now/

[1653] Dave Hodges, "Prince Charles, Queen Elizabeth and Pappy Bush Are Leaders in Child Trafficking,"DCClothesline.com, May 19, 2014, http://www.dcclothesline.com/2014/05/19/prince-charles-queen-elizabeth-pappy-bush-leaders-child-trafficking/

[1654] Hayden Fox, "Sandusky Part of Illuminati Pedophile Network,"HenryMakow.com, November 13, 2011, http://www.henrymakow.com/penn_state_scandal_is_bigger_t.html#sthash.hGkwZoEi.dpuf

[1655] Paul M. Rodriguez and George Archibald, "Homosexual Prostitution Inquiry Ensnares VIPs with Reagan, Bush," *The Washington Times,* June 29, 1989, http://endthelie.com/wp-content/uploads/2011/05/washington-times-call-boys-at-white-house.gif#?1#?1#WebrootPlugIn#?1#?1#PhreshPhish#?1#?1#agtpwd

[1656] Senator John W. DeCamp, "Drugs and The Monarch Project: The Franklin Cover-Up, Child Abuse, Satanism, and Murder in Nebraska," Chapter 21, May, 1992, http://educate-yourself.org/cn/franklincoverupexcerpt.shtml

[1657] Dave Hodges, "Your Child Is Not Safe from the Global Elite's Child Sex Trafficking Rings," DCClothesline.com, May 18, 2014, http://www.dcclothesline.com/2014/05/18/child-safe-global-elites-child-sex-trafficking-rings/

[1658] Dr. Eowyn, "Ex-CIA agent says Obama had Andrew Breitbart and Tom Clancy assassinated," DCClothesline.com, October 11, 2013, http://www.dcclothesline.com/2013/10/11/ex-cia-agent-says-obama-andrew-breitbart-tom-clancy-assassinated/

[1659] Tim Brown, "Video & 911 Calls Released Of Michael Hastings' Mysterious Accident," DCClothesline.com, August 7, 2013, http://www.dcclothesline.com/2013/08/07/video-911-calls-released-of-michael-hastings-mysterious-accident/

[1660] Eowyn, "Ex-CIA agent says Obama."

[1661] Dave Hodges, "Prince Charles, Queen Elizabeth and Pappy Bush Are Leaders in Child Trafficking."

[1662] Brian Shilhavy, "Child Sex Trafficking through Child "Protection" Services Exposed – Kidnapping Children for Sex," HealthImpactNews.com, July 22, 2015, http://healthimpactnews.com/2015/child-sex-trafficking-through-child-protection-services-exposed-kidnapping-children-for-sex/#sthash.bhmuAb4u.dpuf

[1663] "CPS WARRIOR NANCY SCHAEFER GUNNED DOWN,"Infowars.com from the Associated Press, March 29, 2010, http://www.infowars.com/cps-warrior-nancy-schaefer-gunned-down/

[1664] Garland Favorito, "Oddities in the Nancy Schaefer 'Suicide' Case," Infowars.*com,* March 30, 2010, http://www.infowars.com/oddities-in-the-nancy-schaefer-suicide-case/

[1665] Hodges, "Your Child Is Not Safe."

[1666] "The Common Sense Show with Dave Hodges," RepublicBroadcasting.org, accessed January 5, 2015, http://republicbroadcasting.org/the-common-sense-show-with-dave-hodges/

[1667] "Dave Hodges: Who Am I and What Do I Do?,"Dvdave.blogspot.com, May 26, 2008, http://dvdave.blogspot.com/2008/05/dave-hodges-who-am-i-and-what-do-i-do.html

[1668] Dave Hodges, "Congress Knows About Government Sponsored Child Sex Trafficking and Its Relationship to the Present Immigration Crisis,"*BeforeItsNews.com,* July 9, 2014, http://beforeitsnews.com/conspiracy-theories/2014/07/congress-knows-about-government-sponsored-child-sex-trafficking-its-relationship-to-the-present-immigration-crisis-2464000.html

[1669] Dave Hodges, "The Obama Youth Movement & the Seizing of American Children," *The Common Sense Show,* April 29, 2014, http://www.thecommonsenseshow.com/2014/04/29/the-obama-youth-movement-the-seizing-of-american-children/

[1670] "Missing Children Milk Carton Program," NationalChildSafetyCouncil.org, accessed January 12, 2015, "http://www.nationalchildsafetycouncil.org/index.php?option=com_content&view=article&id=159:missing-children-milk-carton-program&catid=185

[1671] Judy Byington, "High Court Justice, Pope Francis co-defendants in child abuse, trafficking," *ChildAbuseRecovery.com,* March 13, 2014, http://childabuserecovery.com/high-court-justice-pope-francis-co-defendants-in-child-abuse-trafficking/#.VLQd6ytzQ9Y

[1672] Dave Hodges, "If Ambassador Stevens Had Lived, the Benghazi Child Trafficking Practices Would've Been Revealed," DCClothesline.com, May 23, 2014, http://www.dcclothesline.com/2014/05/23/ambassador-stevens-lived-benghazi-child-trafficking-practices-wouldve-revealed/#?1#?1#WebrootPlugIn#?1#?1#PhreshPhish#?1#?1#agtpwd

[1673] Tim Brown, "Obama Administration Negligent On Human Trafficking," FreedomOutpost.com, July 31, 2012, http://freedomoutpost.com/2012/07/obama-administration-negligent-on-human-trafficking/

[1674] Dean Garrison, "Child Protective Services Stealing & Sex Trafficking Children Stories Could Get You Killed – But They Must Be Exposed," FreedomOutpost.com, May 31, 2014, http://freedomoutpost.com/2014/05/child-protective-services-stealing-sex-trafficking-children-stories-get-killed-must-exposed/#6IBiQj6yiAgEzprd.99

[1675] Steve Watson, "UN Child Sex Slave Scandals Continue,"InfoWars.net, January 3, 2007, http://www.infowars.net/articles/january2007/030107UN_Sex.htm

[1676] *Roe v. Wade*, 410 U.S. 113, 93 S. Ct. 705, 35 L. Ed. 2d 147 (1973)

[1677] Richard McDonald, "Abortion, Homosexuality, and the 14th Amendment," SupremeLaw.org, Dec. 1989, http://www.supremelaw.org/authors/mcdonald/vol1-2.htm

[1678] Ps. 106:37-38, Num. 35:33-34,

[1679] John 8:44, 1 John 3:10, Acts 13:10

[1680] Branson, "War on drugs."

[1681] "The War is About So Much More: The CIA Drug connection under Reagan," last updated October 20, 2007, http://www.rationalrevolution.net/war/cia_drug_connection_under_reagan.htm

[1682] *Wikipedia,* s.v. "Contras," http://en.wikipedia.org/wiki/Contras (accessed 12/9/2014)

[1683] The War is About So Much More: The CIA Drug connection under Reagan.

[1684] Lutz, "These 6 Corporations Control 90% Of The Media In America."

[1685] The War is About So Much More: The CIA Drug connection under Reagan.

[1686] *Wikimedia Commons*, s.v. "44 Bill Clinton 3x4.jpg," https://commons.wikimedia.org/wiki/File:44_Bill_Clinton_3x4.jpg#mw-jump-to-license

[1687] Derry Brownfield, "OThis image is a work of an employee of the Executive Office of the President of the United States, taken or made as part of that person's official duties. As a work of the U.S. federal government, the image is in the public domain.ur Land – Collateral for the National Debt," *NewsWithViews.com,* August 17, 2007, http://www.newswithviews.com/brownfield/brownfield59.htm

[1688] Ben S. Bernanke, Chairman, Board of Governors of the Federal Reserve System, "January 4, 2012 letter to The Honorable Spencer Bachus, Chairman, Committee on Financial Services, House of Representatives and The Honorable Barney Frank, Ranking Member, Committee on Financial Services, House of Representatives,"

[1689] Federal Supply Service: Authorized Federal Supply List, "The U.S. Housing Market: Current Conditions and Policy Considerations," Pricelist Supplement 02, Period cover by Contract: June 15, 2008 to June 14, 2013

[1690] Westby Co-op Credit Union vs. David C Hertler and Jean M Hertler, Richland County, Wisconsin Case Number 2011CV000198

[1691] John Perkins, *Confessions of an Economic Hit Man,* (New York, Plume, Penguin Group 2006), accessed January 17, 2015, http://library.uniteddiversity.coop/Money_and_Economics/confessions_of_an_economic_hitman.pdf

[1692] Gen.12:3

[1693] Manta.com, "The Army United States Department Of, A privately held company in Washington, DC.," accessed January 5, 2013, http://www.manta.com/c/mryywxp/the-army-united-states-department-of?utm_expid=82789632-30.8Ue3RXoXRoWAwC0cgSs_wg.0&utm_referrer=http%3A%2F%2Fwww.manta.com%2Fsearch%3Fsearch_source%3Dnav%26pt%3D38.8749%252C-77.0325%26search_location%3DWashington%2BDC%26search%3Dunited%2Bstates%2Barmy

[1694] Manta.com, "The Navy United States Department Of, A privately held company in Arlington, VA," accessed January 6, 2015, http://www.manta.com/c/mr4jrhr/the-navy-united-states-department-of?utm_expid=82789632-30.8Ue3RXoXRoWAwC0cgSs_wg.0&utm_referrer=http%3A%2F%2Fwww.manta.com%2Fsearch%3Fsearch_source%3Dnav%26pt%3D38.8749%252C-77.0325%26search_location%3DWashington%2BDC%26search%3Dunited%2Bstates%2Bnavy

[1695] Manta.com, "Marine Corps United States, A privately held company in Washington, DC," accessed January 6, 2015, http://www.manta.com/c/mb05sq4/marine-corps-united-states?utm_expid=82789632-30.8Ue3RXoXRoWAwC0cgSs_wg.0&utm_referrer=http%3A%2F%2Fwww.manta.com%2Fsearch%3Fsearch_source%3Dnav%26pt%3D38.8749%252C-77.0325%26search_location%3DWashington%2BDC%26search%3Dunited%2Bstates%2Bmarines

[1696] Manta.com, "United States Department of The Air Force, A privately held company in Denver, CO," accessed January 6, 2015, http://www.manta.com/c/mmjmfcn/united-states-department-of-the-air-force?utm_expid=82789632-30.8Ue3RXoXRoWAwC0cgSs_wg.0&utm_referrer=https%3A%2F%2Fwww.google.com%2F

[1697] Manta.com, "Department of Army, A privately held company in Washington, DC," accessed January 6, 2015, http://www.manta.com/c/mtrtvp1/department-of-army?utm_expid=82789632-30.8Ue3RXoXRoWAwC0cgSs_wg.0&utm_referrer=https%3A%2F%2Fwww.google.com%2F

[1698] John 8:44, 1 John 3:10, Acts 13:10

[1699] *Wikimedia Commons*, s.v. "George H.W. Bush as President in 1989," https://commons.wikimedia.org/wiki/File:George_H._W._Bush,_President_of_the_United_States,_1989_official_portrait.jpg This image is a work of an employee of the Executive Office of the President of the United States, taken or made as part of that person's official duties. As a work of the U.S. federal government, the image is in the public domain.

[1700] New World Order Today Staff, "George H. W. Bush," accessed November 2, 2014, http://www.nwotoday.com/the-new-world-orders-history/the-socialist-review-american-politicians/george-herbert-walker-bush

[1701] Dean Garrison, "Inside the Bohemian Grove: Where Conservative 'Christian' Leaders Go to Dabble in the Occult," Posted on February 20, 2014, http://www.dcclothesline.com/2014/02/20/inside-bohemian-grove-conservative-christian-leaders-go-dabble-occult/

[1702] Kris Millegan, "Yale's Skull & Bones Secret Society: The Order of Skull and Bones: Everything You Ever Wanted to Know, But Were Afraid to Ask" from Shepherd College Website, accessed January 14, 2015, http://www.bibliotecapleyades.net/sociopolitica/esp_sociopol_skullbones04.htm

[1703] By W.E.B., "The Council on Foreign Relations (CFR) and The New World Order," December 31, 1995, http://www.conspiracyarchive.com/2013/12/21/the-council-on-foreign-relations-cfr-and-the-new-world-order/

[1704] Gene Berkman, "The Trilateral Commission and the New World Order,"AntiWar.com, 1993, http://www.antiwar.com/berkman/trilat.html

[1705] New World Order Today Staff, "George H. W. Bush."

[1706] New World Order Today Staff, "The Socialist Review of Politicians: A Little Peak Behind the Curtain of the New World Order," accessed November 2, 2014, http://www.nwotoday.com/the-new-world-orders-history/the-socialist-review-american-politicians/

[1707] "President George Bush Announcing War Against Iraq," The History Place Great Speeches Collection, accessed November 2, 2014, http://www.historyplace.com/speeches/bush-war.htm

[1708] "Satanic Link to number 11 and 11:11," March 8, 2013, Unifiedserenity.com,http://unifiedserenity.wordpress.com/2013/03/08/satanic-link-to-number-11-and-1111/

[1709] United Nations Conference on Environment & Development, Rio de Janerio, Brazil, 3 to 14 June 1992: AGENDA 21,United Nations Sustainable Development," accessed November 2, 2014, http://sustainabledevelopment.un.org/content/documents/Agenda21.pdf

[1710] "The United Nations *Agenda 21*: Agenda 21 - In one easy lesson," accessed November 2, 2014, http://whatisagenda21.net/agenda21.htm

[1711] Devvy Kidd, "President Bush Supporting Global Communist Domination," *WND*, January 7, 2005, http://www.wnd.com/2005/01/28360/

[1712] Youtube.com/liberalbias100, "Agenda 21 For Dummies," uploaded January 23, 2009, https://www.youtube.com/watch?v=TzEEgtOFFlM#t=15

[1713] Ibid.

[1714] New World Order Today Staff, "Bill Clinton born - William Jefferson Blythe III," accessed November 2, 2014, http://www.nwotoday.com/the-new-world-orders-history/the-socialist-review-american-politicians/bill-clinton

[1715] The American Presidency Project, William J. Clinton, Executive Order 12852 - Presidents Council on Sustainable Development, June 29, 1993, accessed November 2, 2014, http://www.presidency.ucsb.edu/ws/index.php?pid=61547

[1716] "Overview: President's Council on Sustainable Government," accessed November 2, 2014, http://clinton2.nara.gov/PCSD/Overview/index.html

[1717] The American Presidency Project, William J. Clinton, *Executive Order 13053 - Adding Members to and Extending the President's Council on Sustainable Development,* June 30, 1997, accessed November 2, 2014, http://www.presidency.ucsb.edu/ws/index.php?pid=54346

[1718] The American Presidency Project, William J. Clinton, *Executive Order 13114 - Further Amendment to Executive Order 12852, as Amended, Extending the President's Council on Sustainable Development,* February 25, 1999, accessed November 2, 2014, http://www.presidency.ucsb.edu/ws/index.php?pid=57165

[1719] New World Order Today Staff, "George W. Bush," accessed November 2, 2014, http://www.nwotoday.com/the-new-world-orders-history/the-socialist-review-american-politicians/george-w-bush

[1720] *Wikimedia Commons*, s.v. "George-W-Bush.jpeg," https://commons.wikimedia.org/wiki/File:George-W-Bush.jpeg This image is a work of an employee of the Executive Office of the President of the United States, taken or made as part of that person's official duties. As a work of the U.S. federal government, the image is in the public domain.

[1721] Paul Craig Roberts, "9/11 After 13 years," September 10, 2014, http://www.paulcraigroberts.org/2014/09/10/911-13-years-paul-craig-roberts/

[1722] Jeffrey Berwick, "The Walls Are Crumbling Down Around the 'Official 9/11 Story' – Why?," *Global Research,* January 4, 2015, http://www.globalresearch.ca/the-walls-are-crumbling-down-around-the-official-911-story-why/5394984

[1723] New World Order Today Staff, "George W. Bush."

[1724] New World Order Today Staff, "Barack Hussein Obama," accessed November 2, 2014, http://www.nwotoday.com/the-new-world-orders-history/the-socialist-review-american-politicians/barack-hussain-obama

[1725] *Wikimedia Commons*, s.v. "President Barack Obama, 2012 portrait crop," https://commons.wikimedia.org/wiki/File:George-W-Bush.jpeg This image is a work of an employee of the Executive Office of the President of the United States, taken or made as part of that person's official duties. As a work of the U.S. federal government, the image is in the public domain.

[1726] Webster Tarpley, "Confirmed - Obama Is Zbigniew Brzezinski Puppet*,"Rense.com,* March 21, 2008, http://www.rense.com/general81/abig.htm

[1727] Leon Puissegur, "George Soros – Obama's Puppet Master,"*FreedomOutpost.com,* April 7, 2014, http://freedomoutpost.com/2014/04/george-soros-obamas-puppet-master/#46Ez7qAJYCciUuSl.99

[1728]*Wikipedia,*s.v. "Black Nobility," http://en.wikipedia.org/wiki/Black_Nobility (accessed 11/2/2014)

[1729]"The Black Nobility,"BibleBelievers.org, accessed November 2, 2014, http://www.biblebelievers.org.au/black.htm

[1730]New World Order Today Staff, "The Bavarian Illuminati 1776," accessed November 2, 2014,http://www.nwotoday.com/the-new-world-orders-history/freemasonry-global-level-illumination/the-bavarian-illuminati-1776-thru-2014

[1731] New World Order Today Staff, "Freemasonry and King Solomon's Temple," accessed November 2, 2014, http://www.nwotoday.com/the-new-world-orders-history/freemasonry-global-level-illumination/builders-of-king-solomons-temple

[1732]*Wikipedia,*s.v. "Papal Infallibility."

[1733] II Thess. 2:3-12

[1734] I John 2:18

[1735] Rev. 13:4-18

[1736]Dan. 8:23

[1737]Matt. 24:15 in referring to Dan. 9:27; 12:11

[1738] Phelps, *Vatican Assassins*, 67

[1739] ed. Wikipedians, *Sustainability,* (PediaPress), 409

[1740] "Joe the Plumber: A Transcript," *Tampa Bay Times,* October 18, 2008, http://www.tampabay.com/news/perspective/joe-the-plumber-a-transcript/858299

[1741]"Obama on Executive Actions, 'I've Got A Pen and I've Got A Cellphone,'" *Washington CBS,* January 14, 2014, http://washington.cbslocal.com/2014/01/14/obama-on-executive-actions-ive-got-a-pen-and-ive-got-a-phone/

[1742]New World Order Today Staff, "Barack Hussein Obama."

[1743]*Wikipedia,*s.v. "Kangaroo court," last modified January 11, 2015, http://en.wikipedia.org/wiki/Kangaroo_court

[1744]"Direct Home Owner Solutions: The Bank's Big Secret," DirectHomeOwnerSolution.weebly.com, accessed November 2, 2014, http://directhomeownersolutions.weebly.com/the-banks-secret.html

[1745] John W. Whitehead, "Cliven Bundy and the American Police State," *Huff Post: Politics,* April 21, 2014,http://www.huffingtonpost.com/john-w-whitehead/the-bundy-paradigm-will-y_b_5185606.html

[1746] "False Flag: Summary of False Flag Operations and False Flag Terrorism," WantToKnow.info, accessed November 2, 2014, http://www.wanttoknow.info/falseflag

[1747] Paul Joseph Watson, "Seal Veteran: Military Leaders Being Asked if They Will Disarm Americans," InfoWars.com*,* October 23, 2013,http://www.infowars.com/ex-navy-seal-military-leaders-being-asked-if-they-will-disarm-americans/

[1748]Dave Gibson, "Shock claim: Obama only wants military leaders who 'will fire on U.S. citizens'," Planet.Infowars.com as citing Examiner.com article, January 21, 2013, http://planet.infowars.com/worldnews/usnews/shock-claim-obama-only-wants-military-leaders-who-will-fire-on-u-s-citizens-2

[1749] Scott Bennett, "Full Disclosure: A Letter to Military Families," ArmyPsyop.wix.com, July 5, 2014, http://armypsyop.wix.com/scottbennett#!"FULL-DISCLOSURE-A-LETTER-TO-MILITARY-FAMILIES"-/c1lxb/1

[1750] Paul Joseph Watson, "Fort Hood Soldiers Told that Christians, Tea Partiers A Radical Terror Threat,"*Infowars.com,* October 24, 2013, http://www.infowars.com/fort-hood-soldiers-told-christians-tea-partiers-a-radical-terror-threat/

[1751] Judicial Watch Staff, "Judicial Watch: Defense Department Teaching Documents Suggest Mainstream Conservative Views 'Extremist,'" JudicialWatch.org, August 22, 2013, http://www.judicialwatch.org/press-room/press-releases/judicial-watch-defense-department-teaching-documents-suggest-mainstream-conservative-views-extremist/

[1752] AFSS 0910 EQUAL OPPORTUNITY AND TREATMENT INCIDENTS (EOTI), LESSON PLAN, PART I, SYNOPSIS, July 7, 2011, http://www.judicialwatch.org/wp-content/uploads/2013/08/2161-docs.pdf

[1753] Adan Salazar, "DOD Training Manual: 'Extremist' Founding Fathers 'Would Not Be Welcome in Today's Military,'" Infowars.com, August 24, 2013, http://www.infowars.com/dod-training-manual-suggests-extremist-founding-fathers-would-not-be-welcome-in-todays-military/

[1754] Robert Bridge, "DoD training manual suggests Founding Fathers followed 'extremist ideology,'" RT News, August 25, 2013, http://rt.com/usa/us-military-extremism-terrorism-right-963/

[1755] Paul Joseph Watson, "Homeland Security Report Lists 'Liberty Lovers' as Terrorists," Infowars.com, July 4, 2012, http://www.infowars.com/homeland-security-report-lists-liberty-lovers-as-terrorists/

[1756] National Consortium for the Study of Terrorism and Responses to Terrorism, A Department of Homeland Security Science and Technology Center of Excellence, Based at the University of Maryland, Hot Spots of Terrorism and Other Crimes in the United States, 1970 to 2008, Final Report to Human Factors/Behavioral Sciences Division, Science and Technology Directorate, U.S. Department of Homeland Security, January 31, 2012, http://www.start.umd.edu/sites/default/files/files/publications/research_briefs/LaFree_Bersani_HotSpotsOfUSTerrorism.pdf

[1757] National Consortium for the Study of Terrorism and Responses to Terrorism, A Center of Excellence of the U.S. Department of Homeland Security Based at the University of Maryland, PROFILES OF PERPETRATORS OF TERRORISM- UNITED STATES (PPT-US),Last Update: January 30, 2012, https://info.publicintelligence.net/START-US-TerrorismProfiles.pdf

[1758] Brandon Turbeville, "DHS Funded Report: Sovereign Citizens Greatest Threat To U.S.," ActivistPost.com, August 5, 2014, http://www.activistpost.com/2014/08/dhs-funded-report-sovereign-citizens.html

[1759] National Consortium for the Study of Terrorism and Responses to Terrorism, A Department of Homeland Security Science and Technology Center of Excellence.

[1760] National Consortium for the Study of Terrorism and Responses to Terrorism, A Center of Excellence of the U.S. Department of Homeland Security Based at the University of Maryland, PROFILES OF PERPETRATORS OF TERRORISM- UNITED STATES (PPT-US),Last Update: January 30, 2012, p. 18, https://info.publicintelligence.net/START-US-TerrorismProfiles.pdf

[1761] Southern Poverty Law Center, "Who We Are," accessed 3/10/2015, http://www.splcenter.org/who-we-are ; Southern Poverty Law Center, "About Us," accessed January 19, 2016, https://www.splcenter.org/about

[1762] Southern Poverty Law Center, 2013 Form 990, Part 1, Page 1, Line 18, http://www.splcenter.org/sites/default/files/downloads/resource/990_103114.pdf

[1763] Southern Poverty Law Center, 2013 Form 990, Schedule D, Part V, Page 2, Line 1g, http://www.splcenter.org/sites/default/files/downloads/resource/990_103114.pdf

[1764] "Southern Poverty Law Center Inc.: Company Profile," Zoominfo.com, accessed March 6, 2015, http://www.zoominfo.com/s/#!search/profile/company?companyId=69271990&targetid=profile

[1765] Youtube.com/The Alex Jones Channel, "Stewart Rhodes: It's Official, Southern Poverty Law Center Is Now Part of DHS! Alex Jones TV," October 8, 2010, https://www.youtube.com/watch?v=K-1lGFS3zFc

[1766] "Countering Violent Extremism (CVE) Working Group, Homeland Security Advisory Council, Spring 2010," pp. 27, 30, Department of Homeland Security, https://www.dhs.gov/xlibrary/assets/hsac_cve_working_group_recommendations.pdf

[1767] "The Federal Bureau of Investigation: Civil Rights: 'Hate Crime-Overview,'" accessed March 11, 2015,http://www.fbi.gov/about-us/investigate/civilrights/hate_crimes/overview

[1768] "The Federal Bureau of Investigation: About Us: Frequently Asked Questions: Overview," accessed March 11, 2015, http://www.fbi.gov/about-us/faqs

[1769] Southern Poverty Law Center, "Active U.S. Hate Groups," accessed March 9, 2015, http://www.splcenter.org/get-informed/hate-map

[1770] Southern Poverty Law Center, "What We Do: Hate and Extremism," accessed March 10, 2015,http://www.splcenter.org/what-we-do/hate-and-extremism

[1771] For example, the SPLC boasts, "We've crippled some of the country's most notorious hate groups by suing them for murders and other violent acts committed by their members. Accessed March 10, 2015, http://www.splcenter.org/what-we-do/hate-and-extremism

[1772] Southern Poverty Law Center, "Get Informed: Hate Map:"Active U.S. Hate Groups," accessed March 11, 2015, http://www.splcenter.org/hate-map-2014

[1773] Family Research Council, "The Southern Poverty Law Center (SPLC) and Its So-Called 'Hate Groups,'" September, 2012, http://downloads.frc.org/EF/EF12I53.pdf

438

[1774] Jerry Kammer, "Immigration and the SPLC: How the Southern Poverty Law Center Invented a Smear, Served La Raza, Manipulated the Press, and Duped its Donors," Center for Immigration Studies, March 2010, http://www.cis.org/immigration-splc

[1775] Ibid.

[1776] Southern Poverty Law Center, "Extremist Files," accessed March 10, 2015, http://www.splcenter.org/get-informed/intelligence-files

[1777] Southern Poverty Law Center, "Extremist Files: Groups," accessed March 10, 2015, http://www.splcenter.org/get-informed/intelligence-files/groups

[1778] Southern Poverty Law Center, "Extremist Files: [Individual] Profiles," accessed March 10, 2015, http://www.splcenter.org/get-informed/intelligence-files/profiles

[1779] Southern Poverty Law Center, "Extremist Files: Ideology," accessed March 20, 2015, http://www.splcenter.org/get-informed/intelligence-files/ideology

[1780] Southern Poverty Law Center, "Extremist Files: Ideology: Sovereign Citizen Movement," accessed March 29, 2014 and March 4, 2015, http://www.splcenter.org/get-informed/intelligence-files/ideology/sovereign-citizens-movement

[1781] Southern Poverty Law Center, *Intelligence Report,* Summer 2012, Issue Number: 146, "30 New Activists Heading Up the Radical Right," May 26, 2012, http://www.splcenter.org/get-informed/intelligence-report/browse-all-issues/2012/summer/30-to-watch

[1782] Southern Poverty Law Center, "Extremist Files: Ideology: Patriot Movement," accessed March 10, 2015, http://www.splcenter.org/get-informed/intelligence-files/ideology/patriot-movement

[1783] "A Guide to the Political Left: SOUTHERN POVERTY LAW CENTER (SPLC)," DiscovertheNetworks.org, accessed March 11, 2015, http://www.discoverthenetworks.org/groupProfile.asp?grpid=6989

[1784] Internet Archive Wayback Machine, accessed January 19, 2016, https://web-beta.archive.org/

[1785] Internet Archive Wayback Machine, report with snapshot photos of redirecting links for http://web-beta.archive.org/web/20150701000000*/http://www.splcenter.org/get-informed/intelligence-files/ideology/sovereign-citizens-movement

[1786] Internet Archive Wayback Machine, report showing 9/6/2015 as creation saved date for new SPLC Sovereign Citizen webpage http://web-beta.archive.org/web/20150701000000*/https://www.splcenter.org/fighting-hate/extremist-files/ideology/sovereign-citizens-movement

[1787] Southern Poverty Law Center, "Antigovernment Movement," accessed January 19, 2016, https://www.splcenter.org/fighting-hate/extremist-files/ideology/antigovernment

[1788] Southern Poverty Law Center, "Extremist Files:[Individual] Profiles," accessed March 10, 2015, http://www.splcenter.org/get-informed/intelligence-files/profiles

[1789] Family Research Council, "February 10, 2014 letter to Attorney General Eric H. Holder, Jr. and FBI Director James B. Comey," http://www.republicoftheunitedstates.org/dev/wp-content/uploads/2014/09/Boykin%20letter%20to%20Holder%20and%20Comey%2002102014.pdf

[1790] Southern Poverty Law Center, *Hate and Extremism,* "Law Enforcement Training," accessed March 11, 2015, http://www.splcenter.org/what-we-do/hate-and-extremism/law-enforcement/law-enforcement-training accessed January 19, 2016, https://www.splcenter.org/fighting-hate/law-enforcement-resources

[1791] Bureau of Justice Statistics, Brian A. Reaves, "Census Of State And Local Law Enforcement Agencies, 2008" July 26, 2011, http://www.bjs.gov/index.cfm?ty=pbdetail&iid=2216

[1792] Southern Poverty Law Center, *Get Informed*, "Intelligence Reports," accessed March 11, 2015, http://www.splcenter.org/get-informed/intelligence-report/browse-all-issues/2010/fall

[1793] Southern Poverty Law Center, *Extremism*, "Law Enforcement Resources," accessed March 11, 2015, http://www.splcenter.org/what-we-do/hate-and-extremism/law-enforcement accessed January 19, 2016, https://www.splcenter.org/fighting-hate/law-enforcement-resources

[1794] Ibid.

[1795] "Teaching Tolerance: A Project of the Southern Poverty Law Center,"Tolerance.org, accessed March 11, 2015, http://www.tolerance.org/

[1796] Family Research Council Staff, "Southern Poverty Law Center's 'Teaching Tolerance' Project," March 2014, http://frc.org/SPLCTeachingTolerance

[1797] DiscovertheNetworks.org: A Guide to the Political Left, "THE IRS SCANDAL: TIMELINE," accessed March 11, 2015, http://www.discoverthenetworks.org/viewSubCategory.asp?id=1935

[1798] Chairman Paul Ryan, Brendan Buck, United States House or Representatives Committee on Ways and Means, "Timeline of the IRS's Abuse of Conservatives," June 24, 2014, http://waysandmeans.house.gov/news/documentsingle.aspx?DocumentID=385679

[1799] Robert Wilde, "IRS Targets Tea Party and Conservative Non-Profits for Audit," *Breitbart,* Feb 12, 2014, http://www.breitbart.com/big-government/2014/02/12/irs-targets-tea-party-and-conservative-non-profits-for-audit/

[1800] Jim Hoft, "BREAKING... Audit CONFIRMS IRS Targeted 292 Conservative Groups – Just 6 Liberal Groups," *TheGatewayPundit.com,* June 27, 2013, http://www.thegatewaypundit.com/2013/06/breaking-audit-confirms-irs-targeted-292-conservative-groups-just-6-liberal-groups/

[1801] Youtube.com/MidNightRider2001,"Letters to Governors Contain No Threats Sparks FBI's Fears Anyway," Uploaded April 2, 2013, https://www.youtube.com/watch?v=zQCq014SCMo

[1802] Robert W. Wood, "In 'Lost' Trove Of IRS Emails, 2,500 May Link White House To Confidential Taxpayer Data," *Forbes,* November 27, 2014, http://www.forbes.com/sites/robertwood/2014/11/27/in-lost-trove-of-irs-emails-2500-may-link-white-house-to-confidential-taxpayer-data/

[1803] "Learn, What is the Administration's FOIA Policy?," United States Department of Justice, FOIA.gov, accessed March 19, 2015, http://www.foia.gov/about.html

[1804] Stephan Dinan, "White House that promised transparency refuses to cooperate with IRS probe," *Washington Times,* February 22, 2015, http://www.washingtontimes.com/news/2015/feb/22/irs-taxpayer-information-sharing-probe-stiff-armed/#ixzz3UaKwlNkP

[1805] Gregory Korte, "White House office to delete its FOIA regulations," *USA Today,* March 16, 2015, http://www.usatoday.com/story/news/politics/2015/03/16/white-house-foia-regulations-deleted/24844253/

[1806] Tyler Durden, "The Lies End Now: 'Most Transparent Administration Ever' Is No More: White House To Delete Its FOIA Regulations,"*Zerohedge.com,* March 16, 2015, http://www.zerohedge.com/news/2015-03-16/lies-end-now-most-transparent-administration-ever-no-more-white-house-delete-its-foi

[1807] David Partenheimer, Media Relations Manager, "Postal Service Statement on Cyber Intrusion Incident," November 10, 2014, USPS.com, https://about.usps.com/news/fact-sheets/scenario/media-statement-final.pdf

[1808]"Cyber threat-sharing bill clears House committee, would give immunity to companies," *RT News,* March 27, 2015,http://rt.com/usa/244449-house-approves-cybersecurity-bill/

[1809] Southern Poverty Law Center, *Intelligence Report,* Summer 2010, Issue Number: 138, "Meet the 'Patriots,'" http://www.splcenter.org/get-informed/intelligence-report/browse-all-issues/2010/summer/meet-the-patriots?page=0,0

[1810] Southern Poverty Law Center, *Intelligence Report,* Summer 2010, Issue Number: 138, "The Enablers," http://www.splcenter.org/get-informed/intelligence-report/browse-all-issues/2010/summer/meet-the-patriots/the-enablers

[1811]*Wikipedia,*s.v. "List of organizations designated by the Southern Poverty Law Center as anti-LGBT hate groups," last modified November 28, 2015, http://en.wikipedia.org/wiki/List_of_organizations_designated_by_the_Southern_Poverty_Law_Center_as_anti-LGBT_hate_groups

[1812] Southern Poverty Law Center, By Mark Potok, *Intelligence Report,* Spring 2011, Issue Number: 141, "The Year in Hate & Extremism, 2010,"http://www.splcenter.org/get-informed/intelligence-report/browse-all-issues/2011/spring/the-year-in-hate-extremism-2010

[1813] Internet Archive Wayback Machine, accessed January 19, 2016, https://web-beta.archive.org/

[1814] Internet Archive Wayback Machine, report with 5 snapshot photos for http://web-beta.archive.org/web/20150806185920*/https://www.splcenter.org/fighting-hate/extremist-files/ideology/antigovernment

[1815] Internet Archive Wayback Machine, report with 19 snapshot photos for http://web-beta.archive.org/web/20150514074516*/http://www.splcenter.org/get-informed/intelligence-files/ideology/patriot-movement

[1816] Homeland Security, *Intelligence Assessment, (U//FOUO) Sovereign Citizen Extremist Ideology Will Drive Violence at Home, During Travel, and at Government facilities*, 5 Feb 2015, p.1, http://cloudfront-assets.reason.com/media/pdf/Sovereign_Citizen_Extremist_Ideology_2-5-15.pdf

[1817]Evan Perez and Wes Bruer, "DHS intelligence report warns of domestic right-wing terror threat," p.1*CNN,*February 20, 2015, p. 1, http://www.cnn.com/2015/02/19/politics/terror-threat-homeland-security/

[1818] Jesse Walker, "Exclusive: Here is the New Homeland Security Report on 'Sovereign Citizen Extremist' Violence," *Reason.com,* Feb.25, 2015, http://reason.com/blog/2015/02/25/homeland-security-sovereign-citizens

[1819] Brandon Turbeville, "DHS Funded Report: Sovereign Citizens Greatest Threat To U.S.," *ActivistPost.com,* August 5, 2014, http://www.activistpost.com/2014/08/dhs-funded-report-sovereign-citizens.html

[1820] Jesse Walker, "What Exactly Is In Homeland Security's Report on Sovereign Citizens?," *Reason.com,* February 24, 2015, http://reason.com/blog/2015/02/24/what-exactly-is-in-homeland-securitys-re

[1821] Brandon Turbeville, "DHS Funded Report: Sovereign Citizens Greatest Threat To U.S."

[1822] National Consortium for the Study of Terrorism and Responses to Terrorism (START), Understanding Law Enforcement Intelligence Processes , Report to the Office of University Programs, Science and Technology Direcorate, U.S. Department of Homeland Security, July 2014, https://www.start.umd.edu/pubs/START_UnderstandingLawEnforcementIntelligenceProcesses_July2014.pdf

[1823] Paul Joseph Watson, "Church Document Encourages Congregation to Obey Government," *Infowars.com,* March 4, 2009, http://www.infowars.com/church-document-encourages-congregation-to-obey-government/

[1824] Paul Joseph Watson, "Feds Train Clergy To "Quell Dissent" During Martial Law," *Infowars.com,* http://www.prisonplanet.com/articles/august2007/160807_quell_dissent.htm (accessed 11/2/2014)

[1825] Chuck Baldwin, "Romans 13: Setting It Straight," July 28, 2011, http://chuckbaldwinlive.com/Articles/tabid/109/ID/320/Romans-13-Setting-It-Straight.aspx

[1826] Federer, *America's Quotations*, "Charles Grandison Finney," 235

[1827] Jonathan Smith, "Here's the First Look at the New Satanic Monument Being Built for Oklahoma's Statehouse, May 1, 2014, http://www.vice.com/read/heres-the-first-look-at-the-new-satanic-monument-being-built-for-oklahomas-statehouse

[1828] Brownie Marie, "Satanic Baphomet statue nearly finished, may be placed next to Ten Commandments monument," May 6, 2014, http://www.christiantoday.com/article/satanic.baphomet.statue.next.to.ten.commandments.monument.in.oklahoma.capitol/37211.htm

[1829] Billy Hallowell, "Take a Look Inside Satanists' Kids Activity Book That Might Soon Be Handed Out to Public School Students," *The Blaze,* September 18, 2014, http://www.theblaze.com/stories/2014/09/18/satanists-reveal-plan-to-join-atheists-in-battling-bibles-at-public-schools-and-take-a-look-inside-their-controversial-satanic-coloring-book/

[1830] Dr. Eowyn, "Calif. high school students taught sex toys & porn by Planned Parenthood," Posted on January 16, 2015, http://www.dcclothesline.com/2015/01/16/calif-high-school-students-taught-sex-toys-porn-planned-parenthood/

[1831] Sarah Pulliam Bailey, "Houston subpoenas pastors' sermons in gay rights ordinance case," *Religion News Service,* October 14, 2014, http://www.religionnews.com/2014/10/14/houston-subpoenas-pastors-sermons-equal-rights-ordinance-case-prompting-outcry/

[1832] Raquel Okyay, "The Terry Trussell Story," *PatriotsForAmerica.ning.com,* March 16, 2015, http://patriotsforamerica.ning.com/forum/topics/the-terry-trussell-story?xg_source=activity

[1833] 2 Cor. 4:4

[1834] Rev. 17, 18

[1835] 2 Tim. 4:3-4

[1836] Jonathan Cahn, *The Harbinger*, (Lake Mary, FrontLine, Charisma Media, 2011)

[1837] 1599 Geneva Bible, Patriot's Edition, Isa. 27:7 footnote, (Powder Springs: Tolle Lege Press & White Hall Press, 2010), 704

[1838] Mal. 3:6

[1839] Num. 23:19; Tit. 1:2

[1840] *Wikimedia Commons*, s.v. "Government-Vedder-Highsmith-detail-2.jpeg," https://commons.wikimedia.org/wiki/File:Government-Vedder-Highsmith-detail-2.jpeg This media file is in the public domain in the United States. This applies to U.S. works where the copyright has expired, often because its first publication occurred prior to January 1, 1923.

[1841] *Wikimedia Commons*, s.v. "Gilbert Stuart Williamstown Portrait of George Washington.jpg," https://commons.wikimedia.org/wiki/File:Gilbert_Stuart_Williamstown_Portrait_of_George_Washington.jpg   This work is in the public domain in its country of origin and other countries and areas where the copyright term is the author's life plus 100 years or less.

[1842] "George Washington's First Inaugural Address, April 30, 1789,"National Archives, The Center for Legislative Archives, accessed November 2, 2014, http://www.archives.gov/legislative/features/gw-inauguration/

[1843] *Wikimedia Commons*, s.v. "WilliamMaclay.jpg," https://commons.wikimedia.org/wiki/File:WilliamMaclay.jpg#mw-jump-to-license, This United States Congress image is in the public domain. This may be because it is an official Congressional portrait, because it was taken by an employee of the Congress as part of that person's official duties, or because it has been released into the public domain and posted on the official websites of a member of Congress. As a work of the U.S. federal government, the image is in the public domain.

[1844] "Rediscovering George Washington: Introduction," *PBS,* accessed November 2, 2014, http://www.pbs.org/georgewashington/father/

[1845] "Washington's Inaugural Address of 1789, A Transcription," National Archives and Records Administration, http://www.archives.gov/exhibits/american_originals/inaugtxt.html (accessed 11/2/2014)

[1846] "President George Washington's First Inaugural Speech (1789),"Although not required by the Constitution, George Washington presented the first Presidential inaugural address on April 30, 1789, OurDocuments.gov, accessed November 2, 2014, http://www.ourdocuments.gov/doc.php?flash=true&doc=11

[1847] *Wikimedia Commons,* s.v. "New York by sunlight and gaslight - a work descriptive of the great American metropolis; its high and low life; its splendors and miseries; its virtu (1882) (14593309848).jpg," This image was taken from Flickr's The Commons. The uploading organization may have various reasons for determining that no known copyright restrictions exist, such as: The copyright is in the public domain because it has expired; The copyright was injected into the public domain for other reasons, such as failure to adhere to required formalities or conditions; The institution owns the copyright but is not interested in exercising control; or The institution has legal rights sufficient to authorize others to use the work without restrictions. Source book page: https://archive.org/stream/newyorkbysunligh00mcca_1/newyorkbysunligh00mcca_1#page/n134/mode/1up

[1848] *Wikimedia Commons*, s.v. "St Paul's Chapel sunny jeh.JPG," https://commons.wikimedia.org/wiki/File:St_Paul%27s_Chapel_sunny_jeh.JPG Copyright holder of this work has released this work into the public domain.

[1849] Eph. 6:17

[1850] Gen. 12:3

[1851] Deut. 28:15-68

[1852] Ps. 105:25; Isa. 9:11, 13; 10:5-6

[1853] Deut. 28:1-14

[1854] Num. 31:16

[1855] U.S. History Staff, *American History: From Pre-Columbian to the New Millennium*, "The New England Colonies: 3c. Massachusetts Bay — 'The City Upon a Hill,' " accessed November 2, 2014,http://www.ushistory.org/us/3c.asp

[1856] Melissa Steffan, "The Surprising Countries Most Missionaries Are Sent From and Go To," *Christianity Today,* July 25, 2013, http://www.christianitytoday.com/gleanings/2013/july/missionaries-countries-sent-received-csgc-gordon-conwell.html?paging=off

[1857] Isa. 9:16

[1858] Isa. 9:13

[1859] Deut. 28:22, 24, 45, 48, 51, 61

[1860] Matt. 13:16

[1861] Jer. 5:21

[1862] Isa. 9:9-10

[1863] "The United Nations Agenda 21: Agenda 21 - In one easy lesson," accessed November 2, 2014, http://whatisagenda21.net/agenda21.htm (accessed 11/2/2014)

[1864] "United Nations Sustainable Development: United Nations Conference on Environment & Development, Rio de Janerio, Brazil, 3 to 14 June 1992, "AGENDA 21," United Nations, accessed November 2, 2014, http://sustainabledevelopment.un.org/content/documents/Agenda21.pdf

[1865] Youtube.com/liberalbias100, "Agenda 21 For Dummies."

[1866] 1 John 4:16

[1867] John 3:16

[1868] Rom. 5:8

[1869] Ps. 103:8

[1870] Isa. 6:3, Rev. 4:8

[1871] 1 Pet. 1:16

[1872] Rom. 1:18

[1873] Ps. 69:24; 78:49; Isa. 30:27, 30; 34:2; Jer. 10:10; Ezek. 21:31; 22:31; Nah. 1:6; Mal. 1:4; Mic. 7:9; Hab. 3:12; Zeph. 3:8; Zech. 1:12; Rom. 2:8; Heb. 10:27; Rev. 14:10

[1874] 1 John 4:8, 4:10, 4:16; John 3:16; Rom. 5:8, 8:39; Eph. 2:4; Gal. 2:20;

[1875] Deut. 4:31; 2 Sam. 24:14; Ps.86:5; Ps.145:9; Luke 6:36; Eph. 2:4; Tit. 3:5; 1 Pet. 1:3

[1876] Num. 14:18; Ps.86:15; Nah. 1:3; Rom. 2:3-4; 2 Pet. 3:9

[1877] Ps. 36:7; Ps. 117:2; Eph. 4:32

[1878] Rom. 11:22

[1879] Prov. 3:12; Heb. 12:6

[1880] Rom. 5:10; Col. 1:20

[1881] Prov. 9:10

[1882] 1599 Geneva Bible, Patriot's Edition, Isa. 27:7 footnote, (Powder Springs: Tolle Lege Press & White Hall Press, 2010), p. 704

[1883] Mal. 3:6

[1884] Num. 23:19; Tit. 1:2

[1885] "Signs of the End Times," OpenBible.info, accessed November 2, 2014, http://www.openbible.info/topics/signs_of_the_end_times

[1886] "Hebrew Names of God," Hebrew4Christians.com, accessed November 24, 2015, http://www.hebrew4christians.com/Names_of_G-d/Yeshua/yeshua.html

[1887] John 5:29; Matt. 25:46; 2 Pet. 3:7; 2 Thess. 1:9; Matt. 13:42-43, 49-50; Mark 9:44,48

[1888] Rom. 11:5; Isa. 1:9; Rom. 9:27

[1889] Deut. 28

[1890] Isa. 1:18

[1891] *Wikipedia,*s.v. "David Wilkerson," last modified October 26, 2014, http://en.wikipedia.org/wiki/David_Wilkerson

[1892] David Wilkerson History, "History and ministry of David Wilkerson," WorldChallenge.org, accessed November 2, 2014, https://www.worldchallenge.org/david-wilkerson

[1893] *Wikimedia Commons,* s.v. "St. Paul's Chapel in New York City, America's first Capital," https://commons.wikimedia.org/wiki/File:Wilkerson_Conference.JPG The copyright holder of this work has released this work into the public domain.

[1894] "39 Bible Verses about Watchman," OpenBible.info, accessed November 2, 2014, http://www.openbible.info/topics/watchman

[1895] Mal.3:6

[1896] Heb. 13:8

[1897] David Wilkerson, "The Towers Have Fallen, but We Missed the Message," SermonIndex.net, accessed November 2, 2014, http://ia600602.us.archive.org/25/items/SERMONINDEX_SID4014/SID4014.mp3

[1898] David Wilkerson, "*The Towers Have Fallen-Part1-David Wilkerson,*Youtube.com/Lisa Schultz," Sept 16 2001, https://www.youtube.com/watch?v=I2OpxjwwrIA

[1899] David Wilkerson, "The Towers Have Fallen But We Missed the Message."

[1900] Ps. 94:11

[1901] Ps. 139:2

[1902] 1 Cor. 15:27

[1903] Rom. 11:33

[1904] Isa. 65:12

[1905] Isa. 9:13

[1906] 2 Kings 17:14

[1907] 2 Kings 17:13-14

[1908] Isa. 9:1

[1909] Isa. 9:8

[1910] Amos 3:7

[1911] Ezek. 3:17

[1912] Isa. 9:11, 13

[1913] Isa. 10:5-6

[1914] Isa.9:10

[1915] Isa. 9:9

[1916] Isa. 9:10

[1917] Isa. 29:13

[1918] 2 Chron. 7

[1919] Ps.56:8

[1920] John 3:16

[1921] 2 Kings 22

[1922] Jer. 18:5-10

[1923] "About Jonathan Cahn," BethIsraelWorshipCenter.org, accessed November 2, 2014,
http://www.bethisraelworshipcenter.org/aboutjonathan.htm

[1924] Jonathan Cahn, "The Mystery of the Shemitah," (Lake Mary: Charisma Media/Charisma House Book Group, 2014), 8

[1925] The 700 Club Staff, "Jonathan Cahn: The Harbinger,", Cbn.com, accessed November 2, 2014,
http://www.cbn.com/700club/guests/bios/jonathan_Cahn_010312.aspx

[1926] *Wikimedia Commons*, s.v. "National Park Service 9-11 Statue of Liberty and WTC fire.jpg,"
https://commons.wikimedia.org/wiki/File:National_Park_Service_9-11_Statue_of_Liberty_and_WTC_fire.jpg This image or
media file contains material based on a work of a National Park Service employee, created as part of that person's official
duties. As a work of the U.S. federal government, such work is in the public domain in the United States.

[1927] *Wikimedia Commons*, s.v. "Tree at Trinity Church.JPG,"
https://commons.wikimedia.org/wiki/File:Tree_at_Trinity_Church.JPG This work has been released into the public domain by
its author, Navendu shirali at English Wikipedia. This applies worldwide. In some countries this may not be legally possible; if
so: Navendu shirali grants anyone the right to use this work for any purpose, without any conditions, unless such conditions
are required by law.

[1928] "Jonathan Cahn: The Harbinger," *CBN,* accessed November 2, 2014, http://www.cbn.com/tv/1471942971001

[1929] "'Harbinger' Author Says Loss of 'Tree of Hope' A Warning, Cites reports it won't be replaced because of book's impact,"
WND, August 9, 2014,
http://www.wnd.com/2014/08/harbinger-author-says-loss-of-tree-of-hope-a-warning/

[1930] "The Presidential Inaugural Prayer Breakfast Guest Speaker Rabbi Jonathan Cahn..." Youtube.com/airsoftmaster417, Jan 21,
2013, https://www.youtube.com/watch?v=1mhRBOKb_6I

[1931] "'Harbinger' Author's Speech To Inaugural Prayer Breakfast, Jonathan Cahn explains why America is being warned by God to
repent," *WND,* February 5, 20;13, http://www.wnd.com/2013/02/see-harbinger-authors-speech-to-inaugural-prayer-
breakfast/

[1932] "Mark This Date For Potential Disaster, Isaiah 9:10 Code suggests watchful eye on specific day,"
WND, May 14, 2012, http://www.wnd.com/2012/05/mark-this-date-for-potential-disaster/

[1933] "Washington's Inaugural Address of 1789, A Transcription," National Archives and Records Administration, accessed
November 2, 2014, http://www.archives.gov/exhibits/american_originals/inaugtxt.html

[1934] Nehemia's Wall: Uncovering Ancient Hebrew Sources of Faith: About Nehemia Gordon," accessed November 2, 2014,
http://www.nehemiaswall.com/about

[1935] "In the Last Days TV Programme 24 – Nehemia Gordon," Youtube/In The Last Days TV Programme , Published August 2,
2012, https://www.youtube.com/watch?v=uiNbvp6MYhs

[1936] *Wikimedia Commons*, s.v. "Psalms Scroll.jpg," https://commons.m.wikimedia.org/wiki/File:Psalms_Scroll.jpg#mw-jump-to-
license This work is in the public domain in its country of origin and other countries and areas where the copyright term is the
author's life plus 70 years or less.

[1937] Library of Congress, "Scrolls from the Dead Sea: The Ancient Library of Qumran and Modern Scholarshipk"
http://www.loc.gov/exhibits/scrolls/scr1.html as per Reference: Sanders, J. A. The Psalms Scroll of Qumran Cave 11
(11QPs[superscript]a). Discoveries in the Judaean Desert, IV. Oxford, 1965.

[1938] *Wikimedia Commons,* s.v. "NYC - St Paul Chapel - Interior 1.JPG," https://commons.wikimedia.org/wiki/File:NYC_-
_St_Paul_Chapel_-_Interior_1.JPG The copyright holder, Jean-Christophe BENOIST, of this work publishes it under the license:
w:en:Creative Commons attribution. This file is licensed under the Creative Commons Attribution 3.0 Unported license.

[1939] Deut.19:15

[1940] *Wikimedia Commons,* s.v. " Kirk Cameron by Gage Skidmore.jpg,"
https://commons.wikimedia.org/wiki/File:Kirk_Cameron_by_Gage_Skidmore.jpg#mw-jump-to-license This file is licensed
under the Creative Commons Attribution-Share Alike 3.0 Unported license. Attribution: Gage Skidmore

[1941] "Who Is Kirk,"KirkCameron.com, accessed November 2, 2014, http://kirkcameron.com/about/

[1942] "Dr. Marshall Foster,"WorldHistoryInstitute.com, accessed November 2, 2014,
http://www.worldhistoryinstitute.com/about/dr-marshall-foster/

[1943] Andrew Thompson, "Kirk Cameron's 'Monumental' Issues," March 26, 2012,
http://www.christianitytoday.com/ct/2012/marchweb-only/monumentalissues.html

[1944] Ibid.

[1945] "National Monument to the Forefathers, Plymouth, Massachusetts," Youtube.com/Dave Pelland, March 24, 2012,
https://www.youtube.com/watch?v=UiyTjjnMef4

[1946] T.S. Custadio, aka ToddC4176, Wikimedia Commons s.v. "File:Monument to the Forefathers 1.jpg," last modified January
11, 2015, https://commons.wikimedia.org/wiki/File:Monument_to_the_Forefathers_1.jpg

[1947] *Wikipedia,* s.v. "National Monument to the Forefathers," last modified October 7, 2014, http://en.wikipedia.org/wiki/National_Monument_to_the_Forefathers

[1948] Patrick Browne, "Forefathers Monument in Plymouth, an Overlooked Colossus," HistoricalDigression.com, January 31, 2012, http://historicaldigression.com/2012/01/31/forefathers-monument-in-plymouth-an-overlooked-colossus/

[1949] Ibid.

[1950] Stephen McDowell, "The Forefathers Monument: A Matrix of Liberty," ProvidenceFoundation.com, accessed November 2, 2014, http://providencefoundation.com/?page_id=3250

[1951] Patrick Browne, "Forefathers Monument in Plymouth, an Overlooked Colossus."

[1952] "Monumental - National Monument to the Forefathers: Liberty and Faith," Youtube.com/John Truong, Published July 21, 2012, https://www.youtube.com/watch?v=liUtyo2l9ds

[1953] Luke 21:25; Matt. 24:29

[1954] Paul Grevas, Statistician, "Blood Moons Coming," Bloodmoonscoming.com, accessed November 2, 2014, http://bloodmoonscoming.com/

[1955] "Blood Moons and Daniel's 70 Weeks Prophecy," JeussOnMyMind.com, accessed November 2, 2014, http://www.jesusonmymind.com/services

[1956] Paul Grevas, Statistician, "Blood Moons Coming."

[1957] "'BLOOD MOONS' REVELATIONS ROCK TV AUDIENCE, 'These signs are potentially closing this chapter of human history,'" *WND,* September 15, 2014, http://www.wnd.com/2014/09/blood-m oons-revelations-rock-tv-audience/

[1958] Paul Grevas, Statistician, "Blood Moons Coming."

[1959] Paul Grevas, Statistician, "Lord's Perfect Sign Epic Closure Charts," Bloodmoonscoming.com, accessed December 24, 2015, http://bloodmoonscoming.com/?page_id=593

[1960] Library of Congress, "United States Capitol, Washington, D.C.," 1857-1872, http://tpsnva.sonjara.com/primary_sources/item.php?item=12307 This media file is in the public domain in the United States. This applies to U.S. works where the copyright has expired, often because its first publication occurred prior to January 1, 1923.

[1961] *Wikipedia,* s.v. last modified September 24, 2015, "National Intelligencer," https://en.wikipedia.org/wiki/National_Intelligencer

[1962] F. E. Pitts, *A Defence of Amageddon, or Our Great Country Foretold in the Holy Scriptures,* (Baltimore: J.W. Bull, 1859) , v-vi

[1963] Ibid., iiv

[1964] Ibid., title page

[1965] Isa. 28:16; 1 Pet. 2:6

[1966] 1 Pet. 2:5

[1967] 1 Pet. 1:23

[1968] John 1:1, 14

[1969] Jer. 31:10

[1970] Heb. 13:8

[1971] Mal. 3:6

[1972] John Winthrop, *A Modell of Christian Charity (1630)* Collections of the Massachusetts Historical Society (Boston, 1838, 3rd series 7:31-48.), accessed November 2, 2014, http://history.hanover.edu/texts/winthmod.html

[1973] Hab. 2:1-2

[1974] 2 Cor. 3:16

[1975] Rom. 11:5

[1976] Deut. 30:19, 20

[1977] Joel 3:14

[1978] WikiTree, "Nathaniel Whittaker (abt. 1708 - 1795)" https://www.wikitree.com/wiki/Whittaker-99 This work is in the **public domain** in its country of origin and other countries and areas where the copyright term is the author's life plus 100 years or less.

[1979] Frank Moore, *The Patriot Preachers of the American Revolution: with Biographical Sketches,* (New York: Charles T. Evans, 1862), 186-231

[1980] I John 4:8

[1981] John 3:16

[1982] John 1:12

[1983] Federer, *America's of Quotations,* "John Adams," 5

[1984] *Wikimedia Commons,* s.v. "John Adams (1766).jpg," https://commons.wikimedia.org/wiki/File:John_Adams_(1766).jpg This work is in the public domain in the United States because it was published (or registered with the U.S. Copyright Office) before January 1, 1923.

[1985] *Wikimedia Commons,* s.v. "Abraham Lincoln November 1863.jpg," https://commons.wikimedia.org/wiki/File:Abraham_Lincoln_November_1863.jpg This work is in the public domain in its country of origin and other countries and areas where the copyright term is the author's life plus 100 years or less. United States public domain tag

[1986] Federer, *America's Quotations,* "James Madison," 391

[1987] Ibid.," 409

[1988] *Wikimedia Commons,* s.v. "James Madison.jpg," https://commons.wikimedia.org/wiki/File:James_Madison.jpg This work is in the public domain in its country of origin and other countries and areas where the copyright term is the author's life plus 100 years or less.

[1989] *The Federalist No. 51,* "The Structure of the Government Must Furnish the Proper Checks and Balances Between the Different Departments," *Independent Journal,* Wednesday, February 6, 1788, [James Madison], accessed December 1, 2014, http://www.constitution.org/fed/federa51.htm

[1990] Federer, *America's Quotations,* "James Madison," 411

[1991] *Wikipedia,* s.v. "John Adams, Thoughts on Government," last modified October 28, 2014, http://en.wikipedia.org/wiki/John_Adams

[1992] *Wikimedia Commons*, s.v. "GustaveDoreParadiseLostSatanProfile.jpg," https://commons.wikimedia.org/wiki/File:GustaveDoreParadiseLostSatanProfile.jpg#mw-jump-to-license This work is in the public domain in its country of origin and other countries and areas where the copyright term is the author's life plus 100 years or less.

[1993] Moore, *Patriot Preachers,* 188-189

[1994] Matt. 5:39

[1995] Mal. 3:6

[1996] Judg.5:23

[1997] Deut. 8:18-19

[1998] Library of Congress, "Moses receiving the law," https://www.loc.gov/item/2007684725/ This work is in the public domain in its country of origin and other countries and areas where the copyright term is the author's life plus 100 years or less.

[1999] *Wikimedia Commons*, s.v. "United States Declaration of Independence.jpg," https://commons.wikimedia.org/wiki/File:United_States_Declaration_of_Independence.jpg This image is in the public domain because it is a mere mechanical scan or photocopy of a public domain original, or – from the available evidence – is so similar to such a scan or photocopy that no copyright protection can be expected to arise. The original itself is in public domain for the following reason: This work is in the public domain in its country of origin and other countries and areas where the copyright term is the author's life plus 100 years or less.

[2000] Judg. 4:1-3

[2001] Moore, *Patriot Preachers,* 191-192

[2002] Ibid., 192

[2003] Ibid., 193

[2004] Ibid., 194

[2005] *Wikimedia*, s.v. "JohnLocke.png," https://commons.wikimedia.org/wiki/File:JohnLocke.png This work is in the public domain in its country of origin and other countries and areas where the copyright term is the author's life plus 100 years or less.

[2006] Federer, *America's Quotations,* "Men of Marlborough Massachusetts," 56

[2007] Library of Congress, "The 'minute-men' of the revolution," https://www.loc.gov/item/2002710565/ This work is in the public domain in its country of origin and other countries and areas where the copyright term is the author's life plus 100 years or less.

[2008] Ibid., "Provincial Congress of Massachusetts,"426-427

[2009] Ibid., "Congress of Massachusetts, Provincial," 135

[2010] Ibid., "Continental Congress July 2, 1776,"436

2011 *Wikimedia Commons*, s.v. "Jonathan Mayhew, engraving published 1885.jpg," https://commons.wikimedia.org/wiki/File:Jonathan_Mayhew,_engraving_published_1885.jpg#mw-jump-to-license This media file is in the public domain in the United States. This applies to U.S. works where the copyright has expired, often because its first publication occurred prior to January 1, 1923.

2012 Chuck Baldwin, "The Pulpit Is Responsible For It," ChuckBaldwinLive.com, April 11, 2013, http://chuckbaldwinlive.com/Articles/tabid/109/ID/78/The-Pulpit-Is-Responsible-For-It.aspx

2013 Federer, *America's Quotations,* "Charles Grandison Finney," 235

2014 *Britannica* s.v. "Finney, 1850, Courtesy of Oberlin College, Ohio" https://www.britannica.com/biography/Charles-Grandison-Finney This media file is in the public domain in the United States. This applies to U.S. works where the copyright has expired, often because its first publication occurred prior to January 1, 1923.

2015 Library of Congress, "The cradle of Liberty," https://www.loc.gov/item/91722980/ This media file is in the public domain in the United States. This applies to U.S. works where the copyright has expired, often because its first publication occurred prior to January 1, 1923.

2016 National Archives, America's Founding Documents, "Declaration of Independence: A Transcription," https://www.archives.gov/founding-docs/declaration-transcript

2017 National Archives, America's Founding Documents, "The Constitution of the United States: A Transcription," https://www.archives.gov/founding-docs/constitution-transcript

2018 National Archives, America's Founding Documents, "The Bill of Rights: A Transcription," https://www.archives.gov/founding-docs/bill-of-rights-transcript

2019 National Archives, America's Founding Documents, "The Constitution: Amendments 11-27," https://www.archives.gov/founding-docs/amendments-11-27

2020 Trueman Cross, *Military Laws of the United States; to Which is Prefixed the Constitution of the United States Compiled and Published under Authority of the War Department* (Washington, Edward De Krafft Printers, 1825) as displayed at Amendment-13.org, *The Original Thirteenth Article of Amendment To The Constitution For The United States,* last updated September 9, 2002, http://www.amendment-13.org/publications.html
By Major Trueman Cross (Deputy Quarter-Master-General of the Army)

2021 Barefoot Bob Hardison, *The Real Thirteenth Article of Amendment to the Constitution of the United States – Titles of Nobility and Honour,* "Amendment Article XIII" accessed September 2, 2014, http://www.barefootsworld.net/real13th.html

It was December, 2010, when Jean Hallahan Hertler learned of the lawful re-inhabitation of the American Republic and immediately offered her executive skills in the restoration process. Ms. Hertler multitasked in various functions while assisting in the foundation of the interim government of her home State, Wisconsin. Once the basic structure was achieved for the interim government, Jean began in-depth studies of the founding and operating documents of the American Republic.

Ms. Hertler has also participated in historical research of various sectors of government, including finance and money. Jean pinpointed fraud while learning to verify and validate constitutional law, and worked with passion toward a constitutionally guaranteed republican form of governance (National and State). Jean has also completed classwork in land patents and allodial title.

In 2013 Jean contributed her writing gifts to the American Republic in having authored *The Hertler Report,* "Weekly Coverage and Reporting of Current Events, Issues, and Trends of the Republic for the United States of America."

Together with her husband David, supported and guided by national leaders of the American Republic, Jean has authored the two-volume series, *Re-inhabited: Republic for the United States of America.* The result of the *Re-inhabited* series contributed to the inspiration of penning *James Timothy Turner, An American President, Political Prisoner: A Legal Brief in Appeal to the Courts of Heaven.*

Jean has 40 years of business experience, primarily in executive management with organizations and corporations throughout the United States. Previous to her work in the American Republic, her last employment was a 10-year venture as the Executive Assistant to the President of a Wisconsin corporation who was also an entrepreneur of many ventures including a renewable energy project which successfully completed commercial phase. Jean assisted in management of all of her employer's business ventures which included writing and filing grant applications, both State and Federal, successfully achieving three financial awards. Through the years Jean has also had rapport with various *de facto* Federal and State legislators with face-to-face meetings at the State Capitol building.

Jean Hallahan Hertler has many achievements, some of which include valedictorian of her high school class, receiving a lifetime National Honor Student award. She achieved a perfect grade point average in college work, however, has not completed a degree other than to say that she has a doctorate in "The School of Hard Knocks" and continues to work on her masters in "The School of the Holy Spirit." Claiming that "life is about learning," Ms. Hertler loves to read and study. She continues her education through Hillsdale College in southern Michigan of which she has received a certificate of award of completion in American History while she continues her studies of the Constitution.

A daughter to first-generation Americans, (Ireland, Italy/England), Jean is a post-World War II Baby Boomer raised with five sisters and two brothers in the southwest Chicago suburbs back when there were still forests, cornfields, and unpaved roads. Jean and her husband David have five grown children. Their posterity includes 14 grandsons.

Since 2011, David Carl Hertler has faithfully served in the restoration process of the re-inhabited *Republic for the United States of America*. Throughout the first session of Republic Congress, he served in the capacity of dual roles in the House of Representatives as well as the Wisconsin free State legislative Assembly. Mr. Hertler continues as an Assemblyman with his home State legislature as he also assists the Speaker of the House by leading education related to the American Republic's founding and operating documents, as well as teaching America's rich heritage as preserved in the writings of the founding fathers.

Together with his wife, Jean, supported and guided by national leaders of the American Republic, David has co-authored the two-volume series, *Re-inhabited: Republic for the United States of America*.

Born at David City, Nebraska in the mid-1940s, Mr. Hertler lived the first ten years of his life in the small town of Naper, where his father pastored a church. The Hertler family then moved to David's mother's home state of Wisconsin where he graduated from Reedsburg High School.

In the early 1960s, David honorably served our country as a weatherman in the United States Navy. His awareness of life was expanded in that time as he traveled our beautiful country for various schools, as well as in experiencing the Atlantic and Pacific Oceans while serving aboard ship. Upon honorable discharge, Mr. Hertler worked as a cost control accountant at IBM in Colorado and then in control data. Preferring the outdoors, he began working in construction in southern Wisconsin for a decade before briefly venturing into real estate sales. David began a U.S. Postal Service career in 1982 working as a rural mail carrier in south-central Wisconsin until his retirement 30 years later.

Bird hunting has been a love for David as well as raising bird dogs. Having owned and updated a "hobby farm" over the last 20 years, his passion for animal husbandry and belief in the family farm as the backbone of America includes a desire to see the family farm restored. Mr. Hertler has also served as a youth pastor and has led Bible studies throughout his adult life.

In addition to being selected as jury foreman while serving in jury duty, Mr. Hertler has also represented himself in business in a *de facto* courtroom. Being told by a *de facto* judge that our original *Constitution of the United States of America* was "ancient" and "no good any longer," as well as threatened with jail for stating the *Bill of Rights*, David holds a conviction to restore our country to the Founding Fathers' original intent with a true representative form government.

While studying the lives of our Founding Fathers and early statesmen, David has memorized countless speeches and quotes in the last 4 years. He has made presentation in early American attire before audiences. He views the Black Robe Regiment as heroes. Mr. Hertler has intently researched and studied pre-1860 legislative and Congressional Journals as well as Statutes at Large while acquainting himself with State and National law. David has engaged in-depth studies on finance and money, as well as completed classwork in land patents and allodial title. He has received various certificates of award of completion in American History as well as constitutional studies in education through Hillsdale College in southern Michigan. David has studied constitutional law under lovers of Liberty such as Richard Church, Michael Badnarik, and Carl Miller. David and his wife Jean have five grown children. Their posterity includes 14 grandsons. Mr. Hertler has one sibling, a sister.

1 - 3 - 7 - 11 - 13
& any multiple of these #'s

Printed in the USA
CPSIA information can be obtained
at www.ICGtesting.com
LVHW080603030824
787112LV00008B/1306

9 780997 276602